THE CHARTER OF
RIGHTS AND FREEDOMS

SIXTH EDITION

Other Books in the *Essentials of Canadian Law* Series

ESSENTIALS OF
CANADIAN LAW

THE CHARTER OF RIGHTS AND FREEDOMS

SIXTH EDITION

HON. ROBERT J. SHARPE
Court of Appeal for Ontario

KENT ROACH
Faculty of Law, University of Toronto

Published in 2017 by

Irwin Law Inc.
14 Duncan Street
Suite 206
Toronto, ON
M5H 3G8

www.irwinlaw.com

ISBN: 978-1-55221-446-6
e-book ISBN: 978-1-55221-447-3

Library and Archives Canada Cataloguing in Publication

Sharpe, Robert J., author
    The Charter of Rights and Freedoms / Hon. Robert J. Sharpe (Court of Appeal for Ontario), Kent Roach (Faculty of Law, University of Toronto).

(Essentials of Canadian law)
Includes bibliographical references and index.
Issued in print and electronic formats.
ISBN 978-1-55221-446-6 (softcover).—ISBN 978-1-55221-447-3 (PDF)

    1. Canada. Canadian Charter of Rights and Freedoms. 2. Civil rights—Canada. I. Roach, Kent, 1961–, author II. Title. III. Series: Essentials of Canadian law

KE4381.5 S54 2017   342.7108'5   C2016-907897-3
KF4483 C519 S54 2017   C2016-907898-1

Ontario Media Development
Corporation
Société de développement
de l'industrie des médias
de l'Ontario

Printed and bound in Canada.

1 2 3 4 5   21 20 19 18 17

SUMMARY
TABLE OF CONTENTS

DETAILED
TABLE OF CONTENTS

PREFACE
To the Sixth Edition

There have been many significant developments in *Charter* jurisprudence since the publication of this book's fifth edition in 2013. The book continues to attempt to provide comprehensive-yet-succinct coverage of all major *Charter* issues. This edition highlights new developments under section 7 of the *Charter*, including discussion of the landmark *Bedford* and *Carter* decisions and Parliament's replies to those decisions. It also features developments under section 1, including increased emphasis on the final balancing stage of the proportionality test in the 2016 case of *R v KRJ*. We also consider the development in freedom of association jurisprudence to embrace not only rights of collective bargaining, but also the right to strike. As always, many *Charter* decisions relate to the criminal process and they appear in this edition, including the new approach to trial in a reasonable time in *Jordan*, and a range of cases relating to mandatory sentences and retroactive punishment.

We thank Scarlett Smith for her excellent research assistance, and Sooin Kim and others at the Bora Laskin Law Library. We also thank our publisher, Jeff Miller; Lesley Steeve and Alisa Posesorski for their careful editing; and the staff at Irwin Law for all their help in the production of this edition.

INTRODUCTION

The amendment of the Canadian constitution in 1982 to include the *Charter of Rights and Freedoms* brought about a fundamental change in Canadian law and politics.[1] The *Charter* significantly increased the law-making power of Canadian courts. Decisions on many important public issues, formerly within the exclusive authority of Parliament and the provincial legislatures, are now subject to judicial review. *Charter* litigation has become an important tool used by interest groups to advance their political ends. Canadian courts now play a central role in deciding how the law should deal with such intractable issues as assisted dying,[2] abortion,[3] mandatory retirement,[4] the legitimacy of laws restricting pornography[5] and hate propaganda,[6] laws concerning prostitution,[7] and the treatment accorded minorities such as gays and lesbians.[8]

---

1   *Canadian Charter of Rights and Freedoms*, Part I of the *Constitution Act, 1982*, being Schedule B to the *Canada Act 1982* (UK), 1982, c 11 [*Charter*].
2   *Carter v Canada (Attorney General)*, [2015] 1 SCR 331.
3   *R v Morgentaler*, [1988] 1 SCR 30, 44 DLR (4th) 385.
4   *McKinney v University of Guelph*, [1990] 3 SCR 229, 76 DLR (4th) 545; *Stoffman v Vancouver General Hospital*, [1990] 3 SCR 483, 76 DLR (4th) 700.
5   *R v Butler*, [1992] 1 SCR 452, 70 CCC (3d) 129; *R v Sharpe*, [2001] 1 SCR 45, 194 DLR (4th) 1.
6   *R v Keegstra*, [1990] 3 SCR 697, 61 CCC (3d) 1.
7   *Canada (Attorney General) v Bedford*, [2013] 3 SCR 1101.
8   *Vriend v Alberta*, [1998] 1 SCR 493, 156 DLR (4th) 385; *M v H*, [1999] 2 SCR 3, 177 DLR (4th) 577; *Little Sisters Book and Art Emporium v Canada (Minister of Justice)*, [2000] 2 SCR 1120, 193 DLR (4th) 193; *Halpern v Canada (Attorney*

The *Charter* has unquestionably had a profound impact upon the role of the judiciary. The courts are now empowered to deal with issues that range far beyond what was seen as appropriate to the judicial function before 1982. In the pre-1982 era, to most Canadians the Supreme Court of Canada was a remote institution that had little, if any, real impact upon their lives. Since entrenchment, however, the Supreme Court has been recognized by the Canadian public as a seat of great power and influence. It has become the institution to which citizens may turn for protection of their fundamental rights and freedoms.

Media attention to legal issues has increased significantly, which is undoubtedly attributable in large part to the *Charter*. Decisions of the courts are routinely front-page news. The Supreme Court of Canada has developed a media-relations policy to ensure that its judgments are adequately reported, and the Canadian Judicial Council has suggested that provincial superior and appellate courts do the same.[9] Some judges have taken the view that they should become more visible and vocal. Interviews and profiles of judges in the daily news media are not uncommon as reporters try to demystify the judicial process and explain it in terms the ordinary citizen can understand. Judges contribute to scholarly journals, discussing their changed role under the *Charter*.[10]

This book attempts to provide an accessible account of the *Charter of Rights and Freedoms* for law students and lawyers as well as non-specialist readers interested in acquiring a basic understanding of the Canadian legal system and the Canadian constitution. We will survey the manner in which the Canadian courts have come to terms with a constitutionally entrenched bill of rights, focusing on the decisions of the Supreme Court of Canada. The purpose is to explain the *Charter*, its interpretation by the courts, and its practical application, rather than to present anything approaching a theoretical or philosophical account of *Charter* rights. It is, however, almost impossible to discuss the *Char-*

General) (2003), 65 OR (3d) 161 (CA); *Reference Re Same-Sex Marriage*, [2004] 3 SCR 698, 246 DLR (4th) 193.

9   See RJ Sharpe, "The Role of a Media Spokesperson for the Courts — The Supreme Court of Canada Experience" (1991) 1 Media & Comm L Rev 271.

10   Chief Justice Beverley McLachlin, a former academic, has been particularly active in this regard. See the following by BM McLachlin: "The Role of the Court in the Post-*Charter* Era: Policy-Maker or Adjudicator?" (1990) 39 UNBLJ 43; "The *Charter of Rights and Freedoms*: A Judicial Perspective" (1989) 23 UBC L Rev 579; "The *Charter*: A New Role for the Judiciary" (1991) 29 Alta L Rev 540; "The Canadian *Charter* and the Democratic Process" (1991) 18 Melb U L Rev 350; "Equality: The Most Difficult Right" (2001) 14 Sup Ct L Rev (2d) 17; "The Supreme Court and the Public Interest" (2001) 64 Sask L Rev. 309; "*Charter* Myths" (1999) 33 UBC L Rev 23.

ter without a theoretical framework. As will become apparent, we are believers in the *Charter* and in the important role it confers upon the courts. In our view, the courts are properly charged with the task of defining and protecting fundamental rights and freedoms in a modern liberal democracy. Furthermore, the Canadian experience to date suggests that an entrenched bill of rights enhances rather than detracts from fundamental democratic values.[11]

---

11   Further discussion is found in K Roach, *The Supreme Court on Trial: Judicial Activism or Democratic Dialogue*, rev ed (Toronto: Irwin Law, 2016).

CHAPTER 1

HISTORICAL CONTEXT

A. THE PRE-1982 CANADIAN CONSTITUTION

The *Charter of Rights and Freedoms* should be seen as one element in Canada's evolving constitution. While the *Charter* now occupies centre stage and has become the focus of public attention, its enactment in 1982 did not mark the beginning of rights protection in Canadian law. This introductory chapter will focus on placing the *Charter* in its proper constitutional context and will provide a brief survey of the protection of fundamental rights and freedoms in Canadian law before 1982.

Canada's primary constitutional document, the *British North America Act, 1867* (renamed the *Constitution Act, 1867* in 1982) contained two major features: a parliamentary system of government and federalism.

1) Parliamentary Supremacy

The first feature of our pre-1982 constitution was a parliamentary system of government modelled upon the principles of British parliamentary democracy. The preamble to the *Constitution Act, 1867* states that Canada is to have "a Constitution similar in Principle to that of the United Kingdom." Apart from this very general reference, the basic principles of British constitutionalism are not spelled out in the written constitution. They are to be found in conventions, traditions, and practices that evolved over time and that continue to govern the structure of Canadian government.

The central concept of the British constitution is the supremacy of Parliament. The elected representatives of the people, assembled in Parliament, have unlimited power to make the law. The role of the courts is limited to deciding cases by interpreting the law as laid down by Parliament or as defined by the common law. In particular, judges do not have the authority to invalidate laws that have been duly enacted through the democratic process of Parliament. The one thing — perhaps the only thing — Parliament cannot do is to bind its successors. Whatever one Parliament has laid down as the law can be changed by the next.

The fundamental rights and freedoms of a liberal democracy (that is, freedom of expression, religion, association, and assembly) as well as basic legal rights (fair trial, freedom from arbitrary arrest, the presumption of innocence, and right to a jury trial) are, however, very much a part of our British parliamentary heritage. That tradition clearly recognizes and respects the importance of fundamental rights and freedoms but holds that Parliament is the proper institution to decide upon their meaning and scope. Courts are entitled to take fundamental rights into account when deciding cases and interpreting statutes, particularly where there is any ambiguity in the law. Nevertheless, the primary and final responsibility for achieving an appropriate balance between the rights of the individual and the general public interest remains with the elected representatives of the people sitting in Parliament.

Until 1982, the Canadian approach to the protection of fundamental rights and freedoms was strongly influenced by the principle of the supremacy of Parliament. As will be seen shortly, Canadian courts did exercise the power of judicial review in some cases to protect fundamental rights, but these cases were really exceptions rather than the rule. Canada's written constitution offered relatively little by way of rights protection until 1982.

2) Federalism

The second fundamental element of the Canadian constitution is federalism, that is, the division of legislative powers between the Parliament of Canada and the ten provincial legislatures. This division of powers is contained in Canada's original constitution, the *Constitution Act, 1867*. Canada is geographically, culturally, and linguistically diverse. The division of legislative power between a central national Parliament and ten provincial legislatures, defining the areas in which each level of government is entitled to act, represents an effort to accommodate that diversity.

The federal structure itself contains a form of rights protection. When an ethnic or religious minority is concentrated in a geographical area, the grant of state or provincial status ensures a measure of self-government for that minority, especially if it constitutes a majority within that unit. Self-government allows the group to adopt laws that are informed by its distinctive culture or language. One of the reasons for adopting a federal state in Canada was to provide a measure of self-government for French Canadians who were and continue to be a majority in the province of Quebec.

While Canada's pre-1982 written constitution was silent on the power of judicial review, from the early years of Confederation, Canadian courts routinely acted as the referee in deciding whether legislative matters fell within federal or provincial jurisdiction, and they have invalidated those laws enacted without a proper constitutional basis. In this respect, the Canadian constitution has, almost from the very beginning, departed in one respect from the fundamental principle of parliamentary supremacy. Canadian judges have exercised the power of judicial review for well over one hundred years, striking down a significant number of statutes, both federal and provincial, on the ground that the law fell outside the authority assigned to the enacting body by the constitution.

The division of powers between the federal Parliament and the provincial legislatures and the role played by the courts in resolving jurisdictional conflicts is a complex subject that is dealt with in another volume in this series.[1] It is, however, appropriate here briefly to consider the manner in which the pre-*Charter* constitution protected certain fundamental rights.

B. RIGHTS PROTECTION THROUGH COMMON LAW AND STATUTORY INTERPRETATION

The legal protection of fundamental rights and freedoms does not rest entirely upon the explicit provisions of the constitution nor upon the *Charter of Rights and Freedoms*. Concern for civil liberties has always been an important feature of Canadian law. Throughout our history, judicial decisions have played an important role in the protection of

---

1   P Monahan, B Shaw, & P Ryan, *Constitutional Law*, 5th ed (Toronto: Irwin Law, 2017).

fundamental rights,[2] and while Parliament may be supreme, our political culture has demanded that it pay heed to the basic rights of all citizens.

Most of our most important civil rights, such as *habeas corpus*, trial by jury, and the presumption of innocence, were creations of the common law. These rights are founded upon judicial decisions extending far back in the Anglo-American legal tradition. They are judge-made rights, often supplemented or bolstered by statutes, which formed an essential aspect of our legal system long before 1982 and the *Charter*.

Another important part of our legal tradition has been judicial review of administrative action. Judicial commitment to the rule of law has resulted in the nullification of decisions by officials or administrative tribunals when they have acted without jurisdiction, while the rules of natural justice have ensured fairness in administrative procedures. One of the most famous pre-*Charter* cases held that the Premier of Quebec could not arbitrarily revoke a person's liquor licence for reasons unrelated to the purpose of the legislation.[3]

In addition, in the interest of protecting liberal values, courts have imported certain presumptions when interpreting statutes.[4] For example, it is presumed that the state would not expropriate property without compensation. If property is taken, compensation must be given absent a clear signal from a legislature that it does not intend to provide it. Similarly, the courts presumed that criminal laws would only punish people who were at fault in the absence of a clear signal from the legislature. These presumptions played a role both in protecting fundamental values and requiring democratic debate and accountability for departures from those values.

Other rights and freedoms now enshrined in the *Charter* never crystallized as specific rights in the common law but did have force as basic principles that underlay the whole structure of the law, informing both political debate in Parliament and legal decision making in the courts. As the Supreme Court of Canada has said, rights and freedoms did not spring from a vacuum in 1982.[5] Freedom of expression and religion, for

---

2   See B Laskin, "An Inquiry into the Diefenbaker *Bill of Rights*" (1959) 37 Can Bar Rev 77 [Laskin].

3   *Roncarelli v Duplessis* (1958), [1959] SCR 121, 16 DLR (2d) 689.

4   See J Willis, "Statutory Interpretation in a Nutshell" (1938) 16 Can Bar Rev 1; K Roach, "Common Law Bills of Rights as Dialogue between Courts and Legislatures" (2005) 55 UTLJ 733.

5   See, for example, *R v Big M Drug Mart Ltd*, [1985] 1 SCR 295, 18 DLR (4th) 321; *Reference Re Provincial Electoral Boundaries (Saskatchewan)*, [1991] 2 SCR 158, 81 DLR (4th) 16.

example, were well-known and well-respected principles of the Canadian constitution. These values were sometimes embodied in statutes to extend protection in specified circumstances.[6] They were vitally important principles that the courts drew upon when interpreting and applying statutes or developing the common law. A leading example is the decision of the 1951 Supreme Court of Canada in *Boucher v R*,[7] where a Jehovah's Witness was charged with seditious libel because of a pamphlet that he distributed. The Supreme Court of Canada ordered a new trial because the trial judge had virtually ignored a defence of speaking in good faith.

C. THE *CONSTITUTION ACT, 1867* AND THE PROTECTION OF FUNDAMENTAL RIGHTS

While the scope for judicial review under the 1867 constitution was essentially limited to questions of legislative jurisdiction as between the provinces and the federal Parliament, the courts did establish an element of rights protection through judicial review.

First, the *Constitution Act, 1867* contains certain specific minority rights enforceable through the courts. The right to use English and French in Parliament, in the legislature of Quebec, and in the courts established by the federal Parliament (that is, the Supreme Court of Canada, the Federal Court, and the Tax Court) and by the province of Quebec is guaranteed by section 133.[8] Minority-religion education rights were secured for the Roman Catholic minority in Ontario and the Protestant minority in Quebec by section 93, and similar rights were accorded by the terms admitting some new provinces after 1867. Provisions relating to the appointment and tenure of judges (sections 96–100) have been interpreted to guarantee an independent judiciary and to secure the role of the courts as overseers of the legality of administrative and executive action. Although probably not judicially enforceable, the 1867 constitution also secures certain democratic rights relating to the length (section 50) and regularity (section 20) of sessions of Parliament.[9] As noted above, federalism itself may be seen as a

---

6   *Freedom of Worship Act*, (1850–51), 14 & 15 Vict, c 175; *Constitution Act, 1867*, s 93.

7   [1951] SCR 265, [1951] 2 DLR 369.

8   Similar rights with respect to the legislature and courts of Manitoba were specified in the *Manitoba Act, 1870*, and language rights have been expanded under the *Charter*: See Chapter 16.

9   Section 20 was repealed by the *Charter* in 1982. For further discussion of democratic rights, see Chapters 8 and 11.

form of minority-rights protection, particularly in the case of Quebec and the preservation of French language and culture and the civil law tradition.

Second, despite the limited nature of explicit rights protection under the 1867 constitution, civil liberties were protected in a number of cases through federalism review. The Supreme Court of Canada found that certain laws that limited fundamental rights could be attacked in the courts on the ground that authority to enact the law fell outside the scope of the powers accorded the enacting provincial legislature by the *Constitution Act, 1867*.

Perhaps the most notable example was the 1938 decision, *Reference Re Alberta Legislation*,[10] striking down Alberta legislation that interfered with the right of newspapers to report freely on the economic policies of the government. The law at issue was part of the package of measures put forth by the newly elected Social Credit government, which asserted that its economic and monetary policies would be effective only if media coverage was "accurate." While provinces normally have extensive authority to regulate businesses operating within the province, the Supreme Court of Canada held that the Alberta legislature lacked the legislative authority to enact a law that struck at the very foundation of our parliamentary democracy. Although freedom of expression and freedom of the press were not specifically protected by the constitution, the Court found that the right of every citizen to criticize government was a necessary and inherent element of Canada's constitution, and beyond the reach of a provincial legislature. Justice Cannon reasoned as follows:

> Freedom of discussion is essential to enlighten public opinion in a democratic State; it cannot be curtailed without affecting the right of the people to be informed through sources independent of the Government concerning matters of public interest. There must be an untrammelled publication of the news and political opinions of the political parties contending for ascendancy. As stated in the preamble of the *British North America Act* [now the *Constitution Act, 1867*], our constitution is and will remain, unless radically changed, "similar in principle to that of the United Kingdom." At the time of Confederation, the United Kingdom was a democracy. Democracy cannot be maintained without its foundation: free public opinion and free discussion throughout the nation of all matters affecting the State within the limits set by the Criminal Code and the common law.[11]

10   [1938] SCR 100, [1938] 2 DLR 81 [*Alberta Press*].
11   *Ibid* at 145–46 (SCR).

Fifteen years later, in *Saumur v Quebec (City)*,[12] the Supreme Court
of Canada returned to the theme of the inherent rights of citizenship in a democracy, striking down a municipal bylaw that forbade
the distribution of pamphlets without the permission of the chief of
police. The action challenging the validity of the bylaw was brought
by a member of the Jehovah's Witnesses. By a majority, the Court held
that the bylaw was invalid. While the judges offered various reasons,
Rand J, one of the majority of the Court that found in Saumur's favour,
held that the effect of this measure was to confer on the police an unacceptably open-ended discretion amounting to a power of censorship.
Like Cannon J in the *Alberta Press* case, Rand J drew upon the rights of
citizenship inherent in democratic government to determine that the
action was beyond the power of the provinces or the municipalities. He
stated:

> [F]reedom of speech, religion and the inviolability of the person, are
> original freedoms which are at once the necessary attributes and
> modes of self-expression of human beings and the primary condi-
> tions of their community life within a legal order . . . . The Confed-
> eration Act recites the desire of the three Provinces to be federally
> united in one Dominion "with a constitution similar in principle to
> that of the United Kingdom." Under that constitution, Government is
> by parliamentary institutions, including popular assemblies elected
> by the people at large in both Provinces and Dominion: Government
> resting ultimately on public opinion reached by discussion and the
> interplay of ideas. If that discussion is placed under licence, its basic
> condition is destroyed: the Government, as licensor, becomes dis-
> joined from the citizenry.[13]

Four years later, in *Switzman v Elbling*,[14] another case from Quebec,
the Supreme Court again adverted to the inherent rights of the citizen
and the necessary conditions fundamental to democracy. At issue was
the provincial "Padlock Act," which made it illegal for anyone to make
use of a house for the propagation of communism or bolshevism. Justice
Rand again made an eloquent appeal to the fundamental rights of citizens in a democracy in finding the law to be beyond the powers of the
provincial legislature:

> Parliamentary Government postulates a capacity in men, acting free-
> ly and under self-restraints, to govern themselves; and that advance

---

12   [1953] 2 SCR 299, [1953] 4 DLR 641.
13   *Ibid* at 329–30 (SCR).
14   [1957] SCR 285, 7 DLR (2d) 337 [*Switzman*].

is best served in the degree achieved of individual liberation from subjective as well as objective shackles. Under that Government, the freedom of discussion in Canada, as a subject-matter of legislation, has a unity of interest and significance extending equally to every part of the Dominion . . . . This constitutional fact is the political expression of the primary condition of social life, thought and its communication by language. Liberty in this is little less vital to man's mind and spirit than breathing is to his physical existence. As such an inherence in the individual is embodied in his status of citizenship.[15]

These judicial pronouncements are significant. They identify a rationale for judicial review grounded in the principles of democracy so powerful that it can be exercised in the absence of an explicit bill of rights. Thus, even before the *Charter*, the courts were able to justify interference with legislative choices that were inimical to the principles of democratic government. It has to be recognized, however, that the success of pre-*Charter* rights protection was limited. As noted, the cases and individual opinions referred to stand out as exceptions to the norm. More often, judges were unwilling to challenge the traditional conception of a strictly limited judicial role. Moreover, the cases cited all dealt with challenges to provincial authority, and the suggestion that there was an "unwritten bill of rights" in the 1867 constitution protecting fundamental freedoms from both levels of government garnered little support.[16] Constitutional protection of rights and freedoms based upon the division of powers between the federal and provincial governments, while significant in certain specific instances, was necessarily limited and subordinate to the basic rule of the pre-1982 approach to the protection of rights, namely, parliamentary supremacy. While the courts were prepared to protect fundamental democratic rights from provincial invasion, the general rule was that if the elected representatives of the people decided that the public interest required a law curtailing an individual right, there was little the courts could do.

---

15   *Ibid* at 358 (DLR).

16   See the opinion of Abbott J in *Switzman*, above note 14 at 371 (DLR). For a post-*Charter* affirmation of this principle, see *OPSEU v Ontario (AG)*, [1987] 2 SCR 2, 41 DLR (4th) 1, Beetz J; *Reference Re Public Sector Pay Reduction Act (PEI), s 10* (1997), 150 DLR (4th) 577 at 623–28 (SCC).

D. THE *CONSTITUTION ACT, 1867* AND PROTECTION AGAINST DISCRIMINATION

Another significant limitation of pre-*Charter* rights protection was the failure of the courts (and indeed, until the advent of human rights codes, discussed below, of the entire legal system) to protect minorities from discrimination. A series of cases coming before the Supreme Court and the Judicial Committee of the Privy Council (then Canada's court of last resort) dealt with challenges to overtly racist legislation.[17] It was argued that the federal power with respect to "naturalization and aliens" in section 91(25) of the *Constitution Act, 1867* and Parliament's residual power to ensure "peace, order and good government" under section 91 included authority to ensure the enjoyment of ordinary legal rights without discrimination on the basis of race and national origin. These challenges proved unsuccessful.

Union Colliery Co. of British Columbia Ltd v Bryden,[18] the first case to raise these issues at the highest level, involved a challenge to British Columbia legislation forbidding the employment of "Chinamen" below ground in a coal mine. The prohibition was but one of a shockingly long list of legislative measures introduced in British Columbia attempting to prevent or restrict the settlement of Chinese immigrants in the province. The province asserted that the law was designed to ensure safety in the mines. The Privy Council rejected this characterization of the law and found that the law was unconstitutional: "[T]he whole pith and substance of the enactments . . . consists in establishing a statutory prohibition which affects aliens or naturalized subjects, and therefore trench upon the exclusive authority of the Parliament of Canada."[19] Although written in a formalistic style, with virtually no explicit appeal to the concept of equality, the Privy Council's opinion in *Bryden* gave some hope that, despite the absence of any explicit anti-discrimination provision in the constitution, the courts might be prepared to protect racial minorities on the basis of the division of powers. The opinion

---

17   The discussion that follows is an abbreviated version of the first part of RJ Sharpe, "Citizenship, the *Constitution Act, 1867*, and the *Charter*" in W Kaplan, ed., *Belonging: The Meaning and Future of Canadian Citizenship* (Montreal: McGill-Queen's University Press, 1993) at 221. For further discussion, see B Ryder, "Racism and the Constitution: The Constitutional Fate of British Columbia Anti-Asian Legislation, 1884–1909" (1991) 29 Osgoode Hall LJ 619; J St-G Walker, *Race, Rights and the Law of the Supreme Court of Canada* (Waterloo, ON: Wilfrid Laurier University Press, 1997).

18   [1899] AC 580, 68 LJPC 118, 81 LT 277 (PC) [*Bryden*].

19   *Ibid* at 587 (AC).

provided a possible ground for the elaboration of an important branch of federal legislative power to ensure the rights and privileges attached to Canadian citizenship.

That hope proved short-lived. Shortly after *Bryden*, a naturalized Japanese resident of British Columbia challenged the constitutional validity of the province's electoral law, which denied the vote to all those of Japanese descent, whether naturalized or not. The plaintiff, Tomey Homma, relied upon the expansive definition of the Dominion's power over naturalization in *Bryden* and upon the specific terms of the *Naturalization Act* of Canada, which provided that a naturalized alien was entitled to all political and other rights, powers, and privileges to which a natural-born British subject is entitled in Canada.[20] The province contended that section 92(1) of the *Constitution Act, 1867*, granting the power to legislate with respect to the constitution of the province, authorized it to decide which British subjects residing in the province should enjoy the franchise. The franchise was considered a privilege conferred by legislation rather than a right. Many subjects — women, those under the voting age, and certain office holders — did not have the vote. Tomey Homma succeeded in the British Columbia courts, but the case was appealed to the Privy Council.[21] There, *Bryden* was abandoned and in its place was adopted an analysis that emphasized, to the exclusion of other values, the protection of provincial legislative authority. The franchise was seen as a privilege the province was entitled to grant or withhold as it saw fit. The constitution's grant of federal power was said to be too narrow to preclude discrimination on racial grounds. Race, like gender, was simply a category the province was entitled to adopt in determining who should have the "privilege" of the franchise.

For a time, the courts continued to follow *Bryden* with respect to legislative barriers to employment on racial lines. But even this suffered a setback with the decision of the Supreme Court of Canada in *Quong-Wing v R* in 1914.[22] At issue was the constitutional validity of a Saskatchewan law that created the following offence:

> No person shall employ in any capacity any white woman or girl or permit any white woman or girl to reside or lodge in or to work in or, save as a *bona fide* customer in a public apartment thereof only, to frequent any restaurant, laundry or other place of business or amusement owned, kept or managed by any Chinaman.

---

20 RSC 1886, c 113, s 15, Fitzpatrick CJ.
21 *Cunningham v Tomey Homma*, [1903] AC 151.
22 (1914), 49 SCR 440.

Quong-Wing, described in the decision of the Supreme Court of Canada as "a Chinaman and a naturalized Canadian citizen,"[23] was convicted of employing a white woman. He challenged the law, relying on *Bryden*. However, a majority of the Supreme Court of Canada saw the legislation as a valid exercise of the provincial legislative capacity to establish proper conditions of employment for women and thought that "[t]he difference between the restrictions imposed on all Canadians by such legislation and those resulting from the Act in question is one of degree, not of kind."[24]

The overt racism of the legislation challenged in these cases is shocking to the modern reader. Equally disturbing is the implicit acceptance of the racist assumptions underlying the legislation by many of the judges. Yet the failure of the courts to develop an expansive conception of basic rights of citizenship as implicit in the federal power with respect to "naturalization and aliens" is perhaps not surprising. The language of the constitution hardly led inexorably to that conclusion. It would have taken an exercise of judicial creativity and imagination of considerable magnitude to articulate a conception of citizenship that would embody at the federal level the authority to define and protect the essential attributes of citizenship, while at the same time respecting the legitimate claims of provincial power.

E. INTERNATIONAL HUMAN RIGHTS CHARTERS

The failure of the Canadian legal system to respond to the issue of racial and other forms of discrimination was not an isolated phenomenon. In the period immediately following the Second World War, there was an international trend towards the elaboration of human rights charters of various kinds. The horrors of war, the Holocaust, and the rise of totalitarianism created a climate in which it was increasingly felt that human rights values deserved enhanced recognition and protection. No nation was blameless — the fears of war had prompted Canada to perpetuate shameful discrimination against Japanese Canadians. There was an awakening to the evils of racism, and a widespread feeling that new laws and legal techniques were required.

The adoption of formal charters proclaiming fundamental rights and freedoms occurred at both the national and international levels.

---

23   *Ibid* at 443.
24   *Ibid* at 445.

The United Nations adopted the *Universal Declaration of Human Rights* in 1948. A large number of European states signed the European *Convention for the Protection of Human Rights and Fundamental Freedoms* in 1950. Other instruments, to which Canada was a signatory, came into being over the next two decades. The *International Covenant on Civil and Political Rights*, adopted in 1966, is one of them. Some of the rights in these modern bills of rights could be subject to limits prescribed by law, limits that are necessary in a democratic society, and some of the rights could be subject to formal derogation in times of officially proclaimed emergencies. These and other features of international human rights charters influenced the drafting of the *Charter*.

As colonialism collapsed, the constitutions of newly independent states almost invariably contained entrenched charters of rights and freedoms. Even in nations with established constitutional regimes, the protection of human rights and the struggle against discrimination and racism attracted unprecedented attention. The decision of the Supreme Court of the United States in its 1954 ruling, *Brown v Board of Education*,[25] was a watershed. The Court found that racially segregated schools violated the guarantee of equal protection of the laws, and it overruled a late-nineteenth-century precedent that had implicitly sanctioned racial segregation by allowing states to establish "separate but equal" facilities.[26] In *Brown*, the Supreme Court proclaimed that separate schools were inherently unequal and thereby created an impetus for the dismantling of racial segregation in all areas. The focus of rights protection in American constitutional law shifted from property and traditional democratic rights to the struggle for equality, and the courts assumed an overtly activist role.

Both the *Canadian Bill of Rights*, enacted in 1960, and the Canadian *Charter* of 1982 were certainly influenced by these international developments and may be seen as a product of the same general trend. Canada's international human rights commitments also continue to play an important role in the interpretation of the *Charter*, something that will be examined in Chapter 3. As will be discussed in Chapter 6, breach of Canada's international commitments when Canadian officials act outside of Canada can also trigger the extraterritorial application of the *Charter*.

---

25   347 US 483 (1954) [*Brown*].

26   *Plessy v Ferguson*, 163 US 537 (1895).

F. HUMAN RIGHTS CODES

In domestic Canadian law, human rights codes emerged in the post-war period as important tools in the legal protection of the basic right to be free from discrimination. These codes, first enacted at the provincial level, initially provided protection against racial and religious discrimination. As awareness of other forms of discrimination has grown, so too has the list of forbidden grounds of discrimination. Age and gender followed race and religion, and eventually disability was added. Other grounds found in different codes and applying to various activities include place of origin, marital status, receipt of public assistance, record of offence, and, most recently, sexual orientation. Some human rights codes regulate hate speech as a form of discrimination, and some of these provisions have been challenged — so far, without success — as infringing freedom of expression under the *Charter*.[27]

A significant feature of human rights legislation is that, with some exceptions, anti-discrimination protection is achieved through an administrative process rather than through judges and courts. Typically, legislation creates a commission that is mandated to deal with individual complaints and to take appropriate educative and related remedial measures. Individual complaints are investigated by the commission at no cost to the complainant, and an attempt is made to resolve the matter by agreement or through mediation. Cases that cannot be resolved informally are referred to a judicial-style board of inquiry, which decides disputed questions of fact and law and which exercises broad remedial powers. In Ontario, human rights complaints are now made to a new human rights tribunal.

Human rights codes played an important role in the struggle against racism, sexism, and other forms of discrimination before the *Charter* and will continue to do so in light of the *Charter*'s limited application to private action.[28] Moreover, when interpreting and applying the equality guarantee of the *Charter*, the courts have paid close heed to the provisions of human rights codes and to the jurisprudence developed by human rights commissions.

---

27   *Canada (Human Rights Commission) v Taylor*, [1990] 3 SCR 892. Note that this provision was, however, repealed in SC 2013, c 37. See also *Saskatchewan (Human Rights Commission) v Whatcott*, 2013 SCC 11, discussed in Chapter 9.

28   See Chapter 5. For further discussion of human rights codes, see WS Tarnopolsky & WF Pentney, *Discrimination and the Law* (Toronto: DeBoo, 1990).

G. THE *CANADIAN BILL OF RIGHTS, 1960*

While human rights legislation has been a success, another post-war, pre-*Charter* experiment in the statutory protection of fundamental freedoms was a disappointment. The 1960 *Canadian Bill of Rights*, an ordinary Act of Parliament, declared a list of important civil rights to be fundamental and provided that all laws should "be so construed and applied so as not to abrogate, abridge or infringe" any of the rights or freedoms so declared.[29] The list of rights and freedoms protected is similar, although not identical, to that found in the *Charter*. Although the *Bill of Rights* has been superseded in importance, it remains on the books and, as will be explained, should not be ignored, for it contains certain guarantees not found in the *Charter*.

The *Bill of Rights* suffered from two fundamental defects.

First, it applied only to federal laws and thus did not reach the laws of the provinces. This limitation meant that the actions of provincial legislatures and those acting under provincial authority were immune from its application. This feature of the *Bill of Rights* was seen by future chief justice of Canada Bora Laskin, then a law professor, as an inexcusable abdication of federal authority.[30]

Second, as the *Bill of Rights* was an ordinary Act of Parliament and did not form part of the constitution, the mandate it conferred upon the courts was suspect. Judges were reluctant to find that Parliament had, with one stroke of the legislative pen, authorized them to invalidate other duly enacted laws. The very notion seemed to run counter to the basic precepts of parliamentary supremacy.

Although the *Bill of Rights* acquired "*quasi*-constitutional" status in the view of Laskin CJC,[31] with the notable exception of *R v Drybones*,[32] the courts did not consider that this enactment of the Parliament of Canada conferred upon the judiciary the authority to invalidate duly enacted laws. *Drybones* involved a provision of the federal *Indian Act* that made it an offence for an Indian to be intoxicated off a reserve, a harsher regime than that applied to others in the Northwest Territories, who were guilty of an offence only if found intoxicated in a public place. The Supreme Court of Canada struck down the offence on the ground that it violated the *Bill*'s guarantee of "equality before the law and the protection of the law." The ruling in *Drybones* suggested that the Court

---

29 RSC 1985, App III, s 2.
30 Laskin, above note 2.
31 *Hogan v R*, [1975] 2 SCR 574 at 597, 48 DLR (3d) 427.
32 (1969), [1970] SCR 282, 9 DLR (3d) 473 [*Drybones*].

was prepared to give some weight to the *Bill of Rights*, but that promise proved short-lived. Instead, the Supreme Court made a hasty retreat. Although *Drybones* was never repudiated or overruled, its motivating spirit was abandoned. The rights and freedoms the *Bill* declared were almost invariably interpreted in a disappointingly formal and narrow fashion. In *Canada (Attorney General) v Lavell*,[33] the Court refused to apply *Drybones* in the suit of an Aboriginal woman who lost her *Indian Act* status upon marrying a non-Aboriginal man. The same result did not apply where a man with *Indian Act* status married a non-status woman. Thus, the law created what seems to be an obvious form of sex discrimination. The Court adopted a purely formal definition of equality and dismissed the challenge on the ground that the law was applied equally to all women in Lavell's situation. This is but one of a long list of cases in which the courts adopted a narrow and restrictive interpretation of the *Bill of Rights*, thereby rendering much of its authority nugatory.

Despite its limited success, in the *Bill of Rights* there are two sections that have to be kept in mind since they have no counterpart in the *Charter*. The right of property is protected by section 1(a), and section 2(e) guarantees everyone "the right to a fair hearing in accordance with the principles of fundamental justice for the determination of his rights and obligations." The *Charter* does not protect property rights, and its guarantee of a fair hearing is arguably narrower, applying only in the criminal process under section 11(d) or, under section 7, where one's "life, liberty and security of the person" are implicated. Both of the above provisions were relied upon by war veterans to challenge legislation that limited the federal government's liability for mismanagement of their pensions. The Supreme Court rejected this challenge in *Authorson v Canada (Attorney General)*[34] on the basis that the *Bill of Rights* does not protect against expropriation of property without compensation by the passage of unambiguous legislation or require Parliament to give property holders notice and a hearing before their property is expropriated. Although the Court acknowledged that federal legislation that is inconsistent with the *Bill of Rights* will be inoperative unless the legislation expressly declares that it operates notwithstanding the *Bill of Rights*, the Supreme Court also stressed that the *Bill of Rights* only protects rights as they existed in 1960 prior to its passage.[35] This

---

33   [1974] SCR 1349, 38 DLR (3d) 481.
34   [2003] 2 SCR 40, 227 DLR (4th) 385.
35   *Ibid* at para 33.

decision may well dissuade litigants from relying on the *Bill of Rights* as a means to protect property rights from legislative encroachment.

The *Bill of Rights* experience was very much in the minds of the political actors who enacted the *Charter*. The courts were given a deliberate push away from the cautious and highly deferential posture they exhibited in the *Bill of Rights* caselaw. As the Supreme Court of Canada has observed,[36] the judges of Canada did not seek a mandate for judicial review: that choice was consciously and deliberately made by the political leaders of the day.

H. THE DRAFTING OF THE *CHARTER*

The drafting of the *Charter* was a difficult affair involving initial opposition by most provinces to the very idea of a charter; challenges by the provinces to the constitutionality of asking the British Parliament to amend the constitution without unanimous provincial consent; and the eventual refusal of one province, Quebec, to agree to the enactment of the *Charter*. What is most significant in terms of understanding the *Charter* are a number of changes made between October 1980 and the eventual agreement that was reached in November 1981 among all governments except Quebec to enact the *Charter*, as well as a domestic amending formula to govern future changes to the constitution. During this time, a Joint Committee of Parliament heard from many witnesses representing civil liberties and women's groups, defence lawyers and prosecutors, the police, and others. Many of these groups were critical of the October 1980 version of the *Charter*. That draft had been weakened in an unsuccessful attempt to win provincial consent. The critics feared that the October 1980 version of the *Charter* would produce weak protection of rights and freedoms, as had the *Canadian Bill of Rights*. The federal government accepted many of these criticisms and introduced some fundamental changes to strengthen the *Charter*.

Section 1 of the *Charter* is perhaps its most important provision. In October 1980, it provided that the rights and freedoms would be "subject only to such reasonable limits as are generally acceptable in a free and democratic society with a parliamentary system of government." Some critics coined this the "Mack Truck clause" on the basis that the traditions of parliamentary supremacy, examined above, would allow governments to drive a truck through guaranteed rights and free-

---

36 *Reference Re s 94(2) of the Motor Vehicle Act (BC)*, [1985] 2 SCR 486 at 497, 24 DLR (4th) 536.

doms.[37] The federal government accepted this argument, and section 1 was changed to provide new requirements that any reasonable limit on *Charter* rights be "prescribed by law" and be "demonstrably justified in a free and democratic society."

Many of the legal rights of the *Charter* were also strengthened. For example, the October 1980 draft provided that "everyone has the right not to be subjected to search or seizure except on grounds, and in accordance with procedures, established by law." This guarantee that searches and seizures would be conducted in accordance with laws was changed to the more substantive guarantee now found in section 8 of the *Charter* of "the right to be secure against unreasonable search or seizure." Section 9 of the *Charter* was similarly changed from the right "not to be detained or imprisoned except on grounds, and in accordance with procedures, established by law" to the present right "not to be arbitrarily detained or imprisoned," as was section 11(e), which now provides a right "not to be denied reasonable bail without just cause," as opposed to the more limited right not to be denied reasonable bail "except on grounds and in accordance with procedures, established by law." The effects of these changes were to limit parliamentary supremacy in defining the rules to govern search and seizure and detention. Section 10(b) was changed to provide not only the right to retain and instruct counsel without delay, but also the right to be informed of that right. Legal rights were also strengthened by replacing a provision of the October 1980 draft, which preserved legislative supremacy over the laws of evidence, with section 24(2) of the *Charter*, which requires the exclusion of unconstitutionally obtained evidence "if it is established that, having regard to all the circumstances, the admission of it would bring the administration of justice into disrepute."[38]

The *Canadian Bill of Rights* had been criticized for its lack of effective remedies, but the October 1980 draft provided no specific provision for remedies. The general remedial provision in what is now section 24(1) was added at the suggestion of civil liberties groups. It allows anyone whose rights and freedoms have been infringed to apply to a court of competent jurisdiction "to obtain such remedy as the court considers appropriate and just in the circumstances."

In addition to some strengthening of voting rights in section 3 of the *Charter* and minority-language education rights in section 23, equality rights also were strengthened in part to avoid the restrictive

---

37   See L Weinrib, "Canada's *Charter of Rights*: Paradigm Lost?" (2002) 6 Rev Const Stud 119 at 132–46.

38   See K Roach, *Due Process and Victims' Rights: The New Law and Politics of Criminal Justice* (Toronto: University of Toronto Press, 1999) at 42–50.

interpretation that equality rights had received under the *Canadian Bill of Rights*. According to the October 1980 draft, "[e]veryone has the right to equality before the law and to the equal protection of the law without discrimination because of race, national or ethnic origin, colour, religion, age or sex." This was changed to the more open-ended and expansive provision contained now in section 15(1) of the *Charter*: "Every individual is equal before and under the law and has the right to the equal protection and equal benefit of the law without discrimination and, in particular, without discrimination based on race, national or ethnic origin, colour, religion, sex, age, or mental or physical disability." Section 28 was subsequently added to underline the importance of gender equality by providing "Notwithstanding anything in this *Charter*, the rights and freedoms referred to in it are guaranteed equally to male and female persons." Section 27 was also added, providing that the *Charter* "shall be interpreted in a manner consistent with the preservation and enhancement of the multicultural heritage of Canada."

Not all the changes made in the drafting of the *Charter* expanded its rights and freedoms. Section 29, which provides that nothing in the *Charter* takes away from denominational school rights, was added. Section 33 was added, as a result of the agreement between the federal government and all provinces except Quebec in November 1981, allowing provincial and federal legislatures to enact legislation notwithstanding the fundamental freedoms, legal rights, or equality rights for renewable five-year periods.

I. THE *SECESSION REFERENCE* AND THE UNWRITTEN STRUCTURAL PRINCIPLES OF THE CONSTITUTION

In 1998, the Supreme Court of Canada was asked to decide whether Quebec had the right to secede from Canada unilaterally.[39] The Court's answer to this difficult and politically loaded question represents a significant statement of the basic principles underlying the Canadian constitution. The Court ruled that a constitutional amendment would be required in order for a province to legally secede from Confederation. However, the Court also stated that considerable weight would have to be given to a clear expression of the will of the people of Quebec to secede. The other provinces and the federal government would

---

39   *Reference Re Secession of Quebec*, [1998] 2 SCR 217, 161 DLR (4th) 385 [*Quebec Secession Reference*].

have to respect that democratically expressed choice and enter into negotiations with Quebec. In those negotiations, "four fundamental and organizing principles of the Constitution"[40] would have to be respected. These principles are "not expressly dealt with by the text of the Constitution,"[41] but they nonetheless have normative force as operative instruments of our constitutional order. The four principles are federalism, constitutionalism and the rule of law, respect for minorities, and democracy. The Court stated that these principles "inform and sustain the constitutional text: they are the vital unstated assumptions upon which the text is based."[42] The unwritten principles represent the "major elements of the architecture of the Constitution itself and are as such its lifeblood." They "infuse our Constitution and breathe life into it."[43]

The first unwritten principle — federalism — has already been discussed. In the *Quebec Secession Reference*, the Court explained that federalism is "a legal response to the underlying political and cultural realities that existed at Confederation and continue to exist today."[44] Federalism is what the Court described as "the political mechanism by which diversity could be reconciled with unity."[45]

The second unwritten principle — constitutionalism and the rule of law — reflects the values of an orderly and civil society in which the constitution is the supreme source of law and authority. The Court identified three essential elements of the rule of law. First, "[t]here is . . . one law for all"[46] and the law is supreme over both public officials and private actors. Second, the normative basis for civil society is the creation and maintenance of a positive legal order. Third, the law governs the relationship between the state and the individual, and the exercise of public power must be based on law.

Closely related to the rule of law is constitutionalism, the idea that all government action must comply with the constitution as Canada's supreme source of law. Constitutionalism constrains power, even the power of the elected representatives of the majority. Constitutionally entrenched individual and minority rights are protected against the will of the majority. The constitution may, the Court explained, "seek to ensure that vulnerable minority groups are endowed with the institutions

---

40   *Ibid* at 240 (SCR).
41   *Ibid*.
42   *Ibid* at 247.
43   *Ibid* at 248.
44   *Ibid* at 244.
45   *Ibid* at 245.
46   *Ibid* at 258.

and rights necessary to maintain and promote their identities against the assimilative pressures of the majority."[47]

The third unwritten or structural principle is "respect for minorities" or "protection of minorities." As the Supreme Court explained, "[t]here are linguistic and cultural minorities, including aboriginal peoples, unevenly distributed across the country who look to the Constitution of Canada for the protection of their rights."[48] The protection of minority rights has always been a feature of Canada's constitution and was significantly enhanced by the *Charter* and other 1982 amendments. The guarantee of equality rights in section 15, the enhancement of minority language rights, and the provisions requiring respect for and protection of Aboriginal rights are particularly notable. As the Supreme Court of Canada explained, respect for and protection of minorities transcend the specific guarantees and "[a] superficial reading of selected provisions of the written constitutional enactment, without more, may be misleading."[49]

The fourth unwritten structural principle is democracy, "a fundamental value in our constitutional law and political culture"[50] and a "baseline against which the framers of our Constitution, and subsequently, our elected representatives under it, have always operated."[51] Although democracy is not mentioned in the text of the *Constitution Act, 1867*, it has always been a fundamental feature of our constitutional structure.

Aspects of the democratic principle have already been discussed above. Democracy was the foundation for the principle of parliamentary supremacy. As will be discussed in Chapter 2, many argue that the *Charter* is anti-democratic as it allows unelected judges to strike down the laws Parliament and the legislatures have enacted. In this regard, there may appear to be a tension between democracy and the other three unwritten principles, each of which posits significant power in the courts to ensure that those elected by the majority respect the constitutionally imposed limits on their power. However, as the Supreme Court pointed out, the principle of democracy may be reconciled with the other three principles. Democracy can operate only under the rule of law and within a constitutional and legal framework upon which democratic institutions depend for their legitimacy. Through federalism, Canada's constitution recognizes that there can be "different and equally legitimate majorities in different provinces and territories and

47 *Ibid* at 259.
48 *Ibid* at 269.
49 *Ibid* at 292.
50 *Ibid* at 252.
51 *Ibid* at 253.

at the federal level." Federalism offers a richer form of democracy by enabling citizens "to participate concurrently in different collectivities and to pursue goals at both a federal and provincial level."[52] A properly functioning democracy "requires a continuous process of discussion"[53] and the opportunity for full participation by all. By limiting the power of the majority to infringe upon the rights of individuals and by allowing vulnerable minorities to fully participate in Canadian society, the constitution reinforces rather than weakens the democratic principle.

J. USE OF UNWRITTEN CONSTITUTIONAL PRINCIPLES IN SUBSEQUENT LITIGATION

As discussed above, the rule of law was recognized in the *Quebec Secession Reference*[54] as one of four unwritten constitutional principles that are fundamental to the Canadian constitutional order. The rule of law is also mentioned in the preamble of the *Charter* and is promoted by the requirement under section 1 of the *Charter* that all limits on *Charter* rights must be "prescribed by law." The rule of law requires that the law apply to governmental officials as well as private citizens; that there be a positive legal order and that the relationship between the state and the individual be regulated by law.[55] This understanding of the rule of law has been said by the Court to focus on the existence and application of the law and not on its content. "So understood, it is difficult to conceive of how the rule of law could be used as a basis for invalidating legislation . . . based on its content."[56]

In *Reference Re Senate Reform*, the Court insisted that "the Constitution should not be viewed as a mere collection of discrete textual provisions" and that the interpretation of the amendment provisions must take account of the Constitution's "architecture" and "basic structure."[57] The Court has made reference to the unwritten principle of the rule of law in a number of cases. In a series of references involving the setting of judicial salaries, the Court has cited the unwritten principle of the rule of law in support of its conclusion that a commission independent of the judiciary and the state should be able to make recommenda-

---

52   *Ibid* at 255–56.
53   *Ibid* at 256.
54   *Ibid*.
55   *British Columbia v Imperial Tobacco Canada Ltd*, [2005] 2 SCR 473 at para 58; *British Columbia (Attorney General) v Christie*, [2007] 1 SCR 873 at para 20.
56   *British Columbia v Imperial Tobacco Canada Ltd*, above note 55 at para 59.
57   *Reference re Senate Reform*, 2014 SCC 32 at para 27.

tions to the legislature about judicial salaries.[58] This decision resulted in strong criticism by some including La Forest J who argued in dissent that the Court should not resort to unwritten constitutional principles.[59]

The Court rejected a claim made by tobacco companies that provincial legislation that allowed the government to bring actions against them related to health-care costs infringed the rule of law because it retroactively targeted them. The Court concluded that the appeals to unwritten principles of the rule of law relating to the desirability of general and prospective legislation "fail to recognize that in a constitutional democracy such as ours, protection from legislation that some might view as unjust or unfair properly lies not in the amorphous underlying principles of our Constitution, but in its text and the ballot box."[60] The Court has also held that "general access to legal services is not a currently recognized aspect of the rule of law" and as such could not be a basis for invalidating a tax on legal services.[61] The Court in that judgment paid attention to the text of the *Charter* in noting that the right to counsel under section 10(b) did not include a general right to legal assistance and that section 7 of the *Charter* had been interpreted to require legal assistance only in specific situations.[62] The Court has also held that the absence of any appeal rights from a finding that a security certificate issued under immigration law was reasonable or a requirement of automatic detention once the executive had issued a certificate also did not offend unwritten principles of the rule of law.[63] However, the Court relied on the rule of law when striking down court filing fees that unduly interfered with a litigant's right of access to justice.[64]

The recognition of federalism, constitutionalism and the rule of law, respect for minorities and democracy as fundamental unwritten principles of the Canadian constitution is an important recognition of the basic values that pervade and influence the constitution, including the *Charter*. In most respects, the values are mutually reinforcing. For example, respect for the rule of law can support democracy by requiring the legislature to make clear statements that authorize limits on rights and freedoms. At the same time, these foundational principles can be in tension, for example, when rulings about federalism, the rule of law,

---

58 *Reference re Remuneration of Judges of the Provincial Court of PEI*, [1997] 3 SCR 3.
59 *Ibid* at paras 296–325.
60 *British Columbia v Imperial Tobacco Canada Ltd*, above note 55 at para 66.
61 *British Columbia (Attorney General) v Christie*, above note 55 at para 21.
62 *Ibid* at paras 24–26.
63 *Charkaoui v Canada*, [2007] 1 SCR 350 at paras 133–37.
64 *Trial Lawyers Association of British Columbia v British Columbia (Attorney General)*, 2014 SCC 59 at para 38.

or the rights of minorities overturn legislation that has been enacted by elected governments.

All four principles and especially those relating to the rule of law, the rights of minorities, and democracy will play a role in the interpretation of various sections of the *Charter*. At the same time, the Supreme Court has in recent years demonstrated more caution about relying on unwritten constitutional principles as a direct source of authority, and these principles are at their strongest when they can be supported by the text of the constitution.

FURTHER READINGS

BEHIELS, ML, "Canada's Supreme Court, Constitutional Principles, Federalism, and the 1998 Quebec Secession Reference Case: Toxic Wine in a Very Old Bottle?" (2013) 31 NJCL 129

DAWOOD, Y, "The Senate Reference: Constitutional Change and Democracy" (2015) 60 McGill LJ 737

ELLIOT, R, "References, Structural Argumentation and the Organizing Principles of Canada's Constitution" (2001) 80 Can Bar Rev 67

LYSYK, KM, "The *Canadian Charter of Rights and Freedoms*: General Principles" (1994) 16 Advocates' Q 1

MCLACHLIN, BM, "The *Charter*: A New Role for the Judiciary" (1991) 29 Alta L Rev 540

MCMURTRY, RR, "The Creation of an Entrenched *Charter of Rights and Freedoms*" (2006) 31 Queens LJ 456

NEWMAN, D, & L BINNION, "The Exclusion of Property Rights from the Charter: Correcting the Historical Record" (2015) 52 Alta L Rev 543

ROACH, K, "Common Law Bills of Rights as Dialogue between Courts and Legislatures" (2005) 55 UTLJ 733

ROMANOW, R, J WHYTE, & H LEESON, *Canada . . . Notwithstanding: The Making of the Constitution 1976–1982*, 25th anniversary ed (Toronto: Carswell, 2007)

RUSSELL, PH, "The Political Purposes of the *Canadian Charter of Rights and Freedoms*" (1983) 61 Can Bar Rev 30

TARNOPOLSKY, WS, *The Canadian Bill of Rights*, 2d rev ed (Toronto: McClelland and Stewart, 1975)

CHAPTER 2

THE LEGITIMACY OF JUDICIAL REVIEW

There has been a lively debate in Canada, particularly since the enactment of the *Charter of Rights and Freedoms* in 1982, regarding the legitimacy of judicial review. Although judicial review on federalism grounds has been a feature of the Canadian constitution since the early days of Confederation, the tradition of parliamentary supremacy remained strong until the advent of the *Charter*. In that tradition, there are no constraints upon what Parliament can do, and it is thought that Parliament is the best place to achieve an appropriate balance between individual rights and freedoms and the broader public interest. This principle had always been qualified in Canada by the practice of judicial review on federalism grounds, but the *Charter of Rights and Freedoms* added significantly to the judiciary's power.

Under the *Charter*, the questions put to judges involve issues of value and moral choice, which are not only more open-ended and apparently less constrained by strict legal principles, but also of greater significance to the average citizen than those relating to federalism. For example, does the right to life, liberty, and security of the person in section 7 include a woman's right to choose whether to have an abortion? Does the right to freedom of expression include the right to spread hatred against particular racial or religious groups? Can the government deny benefits or marital status to couples who are of the same sex?

The result of a *Charter* decision can also be more significant than one made on federalism grounds. Because the Canadian constitution exhaustively grants legislative power to either the federal Parliament or the provincial legislatures, the result of a decision holding that, say, a province cannot enact a certain law will almost inevitably be that the federal government can. On the other hand, the result of a *Charter* decision striking down a law is that, unless resort is had to the "override" clause or if a new law can be justified under section 1, neither level of government can enact exactly the same law. Hence, a *Charter* decision can have a much more telling impact upon the scope for legislative choice.

The debate over the legitimacy of judicial review is fuelled by the fact that the Canadian judicial system in general, and the adjudication of constitutional cases in particular, are premised on the assumption that questions coming before the courts are legal rather than political and as such are to be decided strictly upon legal grounds. As will be noted later in Chapter 7, the procedure for a constitutional case is more or less the same as that used for a property or contracts dispute between two private parties. The same judges decide the constitutional issue as decide the private dispute, and in theory, they decide the constitutional issue on grounds similar to those that apply to the private dispute. It has become increasingly obvious, however, that many, if not most, *Charter* issues involve matters of value and public policy quite different in nature from the questions formerly posed to the courts. It is not surprising to find many observers asking whether it is legitimate to give unelected and unaccountable judges a definitive say on these vitally important and highly controversial matters. In particular, some have questioned the qualifications of the lawyers who sit on the bench to decide political, moral, and philosophical controversies.

From a formal perspective, there is a clear answer. As the Supreme Court itself has pointed out, the judges did not ask for the *Charter of Rights and Freedoms* nor for the powers that the *Charter* confers upon them.[1] The enactment of the *Charter* and the decision to confer a broader mandate upon the courts was the conscious choice of the elected

---

1   In *Reference Re s 94(2) of the Motor Vehicle Act (BC)*, [1985] 2 SCR 486, 24 DLR (4th) 536, Lamer J states at 497 (SCR):

> It ought not to be forgotten that the historic decision to entrench the *Charter* in our Constitution was taken not by the courts but by the elected representatives of the people of Canada. It was those representatives who extended the scope of constitutional adjudication and entrusted the courts with this new and onerous responsibility. Adjudication under the *Charter* must be approached free of any lingering doubts as to its legitimacy.

See also *Vriend v Alberta*, [1998] 1 SCR 493, 156 DLR (4th) 385 at paras 131–32, Iacobucci J [*Vriend*].

representatives of the people. In 1982 the constitution was amended to include an explicit supremacy clause that provides that the constitution, including the *Charter*, "is the supreme law of Canada, and any law that is inconsistent is, to the extent of the inconsistency, of no force and effect."[2] Individuals were also expressly given the right, under section 24(1) of the *Charter*, "to obtain such remedy as the court considers appropriate and just in the circumstances." Accordingly, the text of the constitution reflects the conscious political choice to grant judges extensive power to interfere with decisions of the democratically elected representatives of the people.[3] At the same time, the framers of the *Charter* did not necessarily grant courts the last word on matters affected by the *Charter*. Legislatures can enact laws and justify them to the courts under section 1 of the *Charter* as "reasonable limits prescribed by law as can be demonstrably justified in a free and democratic society." Legislatures also retain the ability under section 33 of the *Charter* to enact laws notwithstanding the *Charter's* fundamental freedoms, legal rights, and equality rights for a renewable five-year period. Sometimes, as discussed in Chapter 17, courts suspend declarations of invalidity in order to give legislatures an opportunity to enact a new law that is consistent with the *Charter*.

While it is clear that the power of judicial review is legally legitimate, one may still ask whether this power is legitimate in a more fundamental sense. Is it consistent with the most fundamental values of the constitution — the principles of democracy and the right of the citizens of Canada to elect and remove those who exercise political power?

A. JUSTIFICATION FOR JUDICIAL REVIEW — FEDERALISM

The legitimacy of judicial review on federalism grounds has been challenged, but this practice is perhaps more readily justified than is judicial review under the *Charter*. A federal system needs a referee to resolve

---

2   Section 52(1) of the *Constitution Act, 1982*.

3   As Wilson J has written: "we should keep in mind that by a widely accepted constitutional process Canadians decided to charge the courts with the onerous responsibility of reviewing legislative and executive action for compliance with the constitution, and they did so with full knowledge of the American experience and the criticism of the role of the courts in that society by some of its most eminent judges." Hon B Wilson, "We Didn't Volunteer" in P Howe & P Russell, eds, *Judicial Power and Canadian Democracy* (Montreal: McGill-Queen's University Press, 2001) at 75.

jurisdictional disputes that cannot be sorted out through the ordinary political process. The federal structure of government represents a conscious decision to allocate functions between national and regional governments and to divide responsibility for certain legislative subject matters accordingly. Situations where the political actors will not be able to resolve their differences about jurisdiction are bound to arise — hence the need for some specified body to settle the matter according to the principles established by the constitution. Canadian courts have not hesitated to wield the power of judicial review on federalism grounds, striking down many laws, both federal and provincial. While some scholars have argued that the resolution of jurisdictional disputes could be the responsibility of a non-judicial political authority,[4] their arguments have been unpersuasive.[5]

Nevertheless, controversy has, at times, surrounded particular decisions of the courts on the division of powers between the federal and provincial authorities. For example, judicial invalidation of federal attempts to implement a "New Deal" to regulate the economy during the Great Depression of the 1930s produced widespread criticism. Unlike the *Charter*, the division of powers is not subject to legislative override, and the eventual response to judicial decisions holding that the federal government could not implement the New Deal was a constitutional amendment to give it jurisdiction to legislate in relation to unemployment insurance, as well as the commencement of a process that abolished appeals to the highest court at the time — the Judicial Committee of the Privy Council. In the 1980s, there was also controversy over natural resources, which again resulted in constitutional amendments. Despite these controversies, the appropriateness of the courts exercising the power of judicial review is generally well accepted.[6]

An important factor contributing to the acceptance of judicial review in the area of federalism has been the development of interpretative doctrines designed to minimize intrusion into legislative decision making. The emphasis upon purpose over effects limits judicial review significantly, avoiding a situation where the courts would be called upon to review the impact of all manner of legislation. It reflects the modern judicial tolerance for overlapping powers, and this deferential

---

4   P Weiler, *In the Last Resort: A Critical Study of the Supreme Court of Canada* (Toronto: Carswell Methuen, 1974).

5   KE Swinton, *The Supreme Court and Canadian Federalism: The Laskin-Dickson Years* (Toronto: Carswell, 1990) ch 2, refutes the arguments made by Weiler, above note 4.

6   Compare, however, H Brun & G Tremblay, *Droit constitutionnel*, 2d ed (Montreal: Yvon Blais, 1990) at 453–54 and 490–92.

judicial stance has produced many areas where both levels of government act concurrently. The courts have not insisted upon excessively
sharp distinctions being drawn or upon jurisdictional categories being
viewed as watertight compartments.

Another element of judicial deference has been the adoption of a
traditionally narrow view of paramountcy. While the rule is that, in the
event of conflict, federal law prevails, the courts have, in the past, defined conflict narrowly, as being a situation where one law requires one
thing and the other law requires precisely the opposite.[7] Recent cases
suggest the acceptance of a broader test in some circumstances, which
leads to a finding of paramountcy when the provincial law seriously
interferes with the underlying policy objectives of the federal legislation.[8] At the same time, the Court continues to allow federal criminal
laws to operate even though they affect health matters under provincial
jurisdiction.[9] In other words, there are still many policy areas in which
federal and provincial laws overlap and in which federal paramountcy
does not lead to dismantling of the provincial scheme in the absence of
conflict in the strict sense. These techniques of functional concurrency
are important because once a court has held that a particular type of
law is clearly beyond the jurisdictional capacity of one level of government, the options for that government are extremely limited. As will be
seen, a government faced with an adverse *Charter* decision frequently
has less drastic options than changing the constitution or the court's
mind.

B. CONCERNS ABOUT JUDICIAL POWER UNDER THE *CHARTER*

More controversial is judicial review under the *Charter*, which clearly
puts the courts in the position of overruling the democratically elected
representatives of the people on value-laden questions of public policy.
Many critics argue that an entrenched bill of rights undermines democratic debate and decision making. In Peter Russell's words, "[t]he prin-
cipal impact of a charter on the process of government can be neatly

---

7   *Multiple Access Ltd v McCutcheon*, [1982] 2 SCR 161, 138 DLR (3d) 1.

8   *Bank of Montreal v Hall*, [1990] 1 SCR 121, 65 DLR (4th) 361; *Husky Oil Opera-
     tions Ltd v MNR*, [1995] 3 SCR 453, 128 DLR (4th) 1.

9   *Canada (Attorney General) v PHS Community Services Society*, [2011] 3 SCR 134;
     Carter v Canada (Attorney General), [2015] 1 SCR 331.

summarized as a tendency to judicialize politics and politicize the judiciary."[10] He goes on to say:

> The danger here is not so much that non-elected judges will impose their will on a democratic majority, but that questions of social and political justice will be transformed into technical legal questions and the great bulk of the citizenry who are not judges and lawyers will abdicate their responsibility for working out reasonable and mutually acceptable resolutions of the issues which divide them.[11]

The fear is that litigation in the courts will replace open public debate on important issues of public policy.

Other critics add a concern about the lack of judicial expertise in many of the areas litigated. In view of the relative resources and expertise of judges vis-à-vis legislatures and bureaucracies in making decisions on complex issues, these critics denounce the use of *Charter* litigation to make determinations affecting important policy matters involving difficult trade-offs between competing interests.

Still other critics point to the vagueness and indeterminacy of constitutional language as a reason for concern about judicial review. Words such as "liberty," "equality," and "reasonable limits" are so open-ended, it is argued, that judges cannot help but infuse the constitution with their own values. Critics express concerns that judges will use the open-ended nature of the *Charter* to increase their own power and impose their own views.[12] Why, it is asked, should we trust nine Supreme Court judges with the task of delineating the meaning of those phrases for a diverse society, rather than leave such issues to be resolved through open legislative debate? Some of these critics suggest that legislatures should be able to act on their own interpretations of the *Charter* even when they differ from that of the courts.[13]

This criticism of judicial review is shared by those from the left, who worry that judicial decisions will tend to favour liberal values hostile to an interventionist state, especially where the state intervenes to promote greater equality among groups and classes. For example, Andrew Petter has written:

---

10   P Russell, "The Political Purposes of the *Canadian Charter of Rights and Freedoms*" (1983) 61 Can Bar Rev 30 at 51–52.

11   *Ibid* at 52.

12   C Manfredi, *Judicial Power and the* Charter: *Canada and the Paradox of Liberal Constitutionalism*, 2d ed (Toronto: Oxford University Press, 2001) at 33–35.

13   *Ibid*. See also D Baker, *Not Quite Supreme* (Montreal: McGill-Queens Press, 2010).

First, we must bear in mind what has just been said about a charter of rights: it gives to citizens only insofar as it takes from government. For example, the guarantee of equality rights in the *Charter* does not give people a guarantee of social equality; it does not even commit the government to guaranteeing social equality. Its role is much more limited. What it does is inhibit government from implementing measures that would bring about or perpetuate inequality.[14]

In effect, the fear is that the individual-rights focus of the *Charter* will undermine a more communitarian spirit expressed through legislative action. Inevitably, those on the left invoke the ghost of the *Lochner* case from the turn-of-the-century United States, where the Supreme Court struck down protective labour legislation limiting the hours of bakery workers to ten in a day and sixty in a week as an unjustifiable limitation on liberty.[15] These critics fear that powerful forces will be able to use the *Charter*'s framework of individual rights to protect their own self-interest at the expense of the less advantaged. Even if the *Charter* does not always harm progressive state activity, many critics fear that it provides only limited and "blunt tools for redressing social injustice."[16]

The legitimacy of judicial review under the *Charter* has also been challenged by critics on the political right.[17] They are concerned that courts have too much freedom to impose their own views under the *Charter* and that they have decided issues that could have been avoided and left to legislators and administrators. These scholars argue that unelected judges have assumed an unacceptable law-making role under the *Charter* and that a "Court Party" made up of interest groups such as women's and civil liberties groups has been able to exploit this new-found judicial power to achieve policies that would not otherwise attract majority support.[18] Abortion, equality rights for minorities, especially

---

14   AJ Petter, "The Politics of the *Charter*" (1986) 8 Sup Ct L Rev 473 at 476. Another critic from this perspective, who examines the Supreme Court's performance in some detail, is M Mandel, *The* Charter of Rights *and the Legalization of Politics in Canada*, 2d ed (Toronto: Thompson, 1994).

15   *Lochner v New York*, 198 US 45 (1905) [*Lochner*].

16   J Bakan, *Just Words: Constitutional Rights and Social Wrongs* (Toronto: University of Toronto Press, 1997) at 152; A Petter, *The Politics of the Charter* (Toronto: University of Toronto Press, 2010).

17   See R Knopff & FL Morton, Charter *Politics* (Scarborough, ON: Nelson Canada, 1992); and FL Morton & R Knopff, *The* Charter *Revolution and the Court Party* (Peterborough, ON: Broadview Press, 2000) [Morton & Knopff, *The* Charter *Revolution*].

18   Robert Bork endorses the "Court Party" thesis, arguing that "the courts are enacting the agenda of the cultural left" and that "the same liberal intelligentsia

gays and lesbians, and rights for those accused of crime have attracted particular attention. FL Morton and Rainer Knopff have argued:

> Our primary objection to the *Charter* Revolution is that it is deeply and fundamentally undemocratic, not just in the simple and obvious sense of being anti-majoritarian, but also in the more serious sense of eroding the habits and temperament of representative democracy . . . . The kind of courtroom politics promoted by the Court Party, in short, is authoritarian, not just in process but, more dangerously, in spirit.[19]

Although their politics differ, critics of judicial power on both the left and the right share some common concerns. They are both concerned that judges will have discretion to read their own personal preferences into the vague words of the *Charter*. They are concerned that the *Charter* will give some groups too much power in our democracy. The left is troubled about corporations and other advantaged interests using the *Charter*, while the right is troubled about minorities and accused persons using the *Charter*.[20]

Critics are also uneasy with the rights guaranteed in the *Charter*. The left believes that these rights are too individualistic and negative, while the right is concerned about group, positive, and inflated rights. Critics of judicial activism on both the left and the right also share the view that elected legislatures are the best vehicle to promote democracy. They both worry that unelected courts under the *Charter* will frequently have the last word over elected legislatures.

C. JUSTIFICATIONS FOR JUDICIAL REVIEW — *CHARTER OF RIGHTS AND FREEDOMS*

There are a variety of defences of judicial review. These include the ideas that judicial review is necessary to protect the fundamental principles of democracy; that judicial review is necessary to protect rights; and that judicial review can be justified on the basis of the intent of the

---

dominates the jurisprudence" of Canada and the United States. R Bork, *Coercing Virtue: The Worldwide Rule of Judges* (Toronto: Vintage, 2002) at 3, 58, and 68.

19   Morton & Knopff, *The Charter Revolution*, above note 17 at 149.

20   This paragraph is adapted from K Roach, *The Supreme Court on Trial: Judicial Activism or Democratic Dialogue*, rev ed (Toronto: Irwin Law, 2016), ch 5 [Roach, *The Supreme Court on Trial*].

democratically enacted framers of the constitution. Finally, there has been support for the idea that judicial review is part of a democratic dialogue that involves not only the courts but also legislatures and society.

1) Judicial Review to Protect Democracy

One of the best defences of judicial review is the argument that the entrenchment of constitutional rights is consistent with the fundamental principles of democracy. There is a strong argument that democracy cannot be explained simply in terms of majority rule and that adherence to certain fundamental values and principles is necessary for democracy to flourish.[21] An obvious example would be judicial review to protect the right to vote, a right that "underpins the legitimacy of Canadian democracy and Parliament's claim to power." The right to vote has been robustly defended by the courts "unaffected by the shifting winds of public opinion and electoral interests" against legislative curtailment.[22] Should majorities be entitled to deny that right to certain members of society, without having to justify the decision other than by the force of their numbers? The power of judicial review, requiring demonstrable justification for decisions to limit rights, enhances, rather than detracts from, democratic values. Similarly, free and open debate of public issues is essential to democracy, and the exercise of the power of judicial review to protect the fundamental freedoms of expression, opinion, and the press can be seen as enhancing and reinforcing democracy. Majorities of the day have a tendency to try to suppress the expression of unpopular views that threaten the status quo. Judicial review serves to bolster democratic values by requiring reasoned justification for laws that limit the rights of those who hold views diverging from the prevailing wisdom of the day. As noted in Chapter 1, even before the introduction of the *Charter*, the Supreme Court, at times, protected freedom of expression on the basis that it was necessary for democracy.

Other fundamental freedoms, less directly implicated in the democratic process, are nonetheless essential if democracy is to flourish. The values of individual dignity, autonomy, and freedom of choice, reflected in the freedom of religion and equality and in the protection of life,

---

21 JH Ely is a strong proponent of this view in *Democracy and Distrust: A Theory of Judicial Review* (Cambridge: Harvard University Press, 1980). Patrick Monahan echoes this view, with his own refinements, in *Politics and the Constitution: The Charter, Federalism and the Supreme Court of Canada* (Toronto: Carswell, 1987).

22 *Sauvé v Canada (Chief Electoral Officer)*, [2002] 3 SCR 519 at paras 34 and 13 [*Sauvé*]. See further discussion in Chapter 11.

liberty, and security of the person, are preconditions to individuals being capable of making independent, intelligent, and informed decisions. Judicial intervention to protect these values against incursions by majoritarian actors may be seen as enhancing and protecting democracy rather than undermining it. Chief Justice Dickson made this point when striking down a law that infringed on freedom of religion: "The ability of each citizen to make free and informed decisions is the absolute prerequisite for the legitimacy, acceptability, and efficacy of our system of self-government."[23]

In a similar vein, decisions of the courts protecting minorities or other vulnerable groups may be defended on the basis of democratic principle.[24] Judicial review, from this perspective, is justified to protect those whose voices are not adequately heard in political debate because they are too few or too unpopular. It is argued that judicial review strengthens democracy by ensuring that the rights and interests of all citizens are protected. The Supreme Court of Canada has been particularly active in defending the legal rights of those accused of crimes, as well as the equality rights of minorities under section 15 of the *Charter*. This aspect of judicial review is also reflected in the manner in which the Court has interpreted existing Aboriginal and treaty rights, which are guaranteed in section 35 of the *Constitution Act, 1982*.[25] The minority-language education rights in the *Charter* have also been interpreted liberally by the Court.[26]

Perhaps even more significant was the Court's initial interpretation of the equality guarantee, section 15 of the *Charter*. It stressed that the focus for equality review must be upon historic patterns of discrimination and disadvantage, an interpretation that included explicit reference to the need to protect those vulnerable groups who lack an effective voice in majoritarian politics. In the leading decision, the Court held that a law prohibiting non-citizens from being admitted to the legal profession was contrary to the guarantee of equality and justified interfering with the majoritarian decision to exclude non-citizens by an appeal to basic democratic principles:

> Non-citizens, to take only the most obvious example, do not have the right to vote. Their vulnerability to becoming a disadvantaged group in our society is captured by John Stuart Mill's observation in Book III of *On Liberty and Considerations of Representative Government* that

---

23 *R v Big M Drug Mart Ltd*, [1985] 1 SCR 295, 18 DLR (4th) 321 at 361.
24 *Vriend*, above note 1.
25 *R v Sparrow*, [1990] 1 SCR 1075, 70 DLR (4th) 385.
26 *Mahé v Alberta*, [1990] 1 SCR 342, 68 DLR (4th) 69.

"in the absence of its natural defenders, the interests of the excluded is always in danger of being overlooked . . ."[27]

The Court reiterated this theme in a 1998 decision holding that Alberta's human rights legislation, which failed to protect gays and lesbians, violated the guarantee of equality:

> Democratic values and principles under the *Charter* demand that legislators and the executive take these [democratic attributes] into account; and if they fail to do so, courts should stand ready to intervene to protect these democratic values as appropriate. As others have so forcefully stated, judges are not acting undemocratically by intervening when there are indications that a legislative or executive decision was not reached in accordance with the democratic principles mandated by the *Charter*.[28]

The above justification for judicial review is sometimes called a "process-based" approach, since the main function of the *Charter* is seen to be the checking of malfunctions in the operation of the democratic process. The underlying assumption is that Parliament and the legislatures should be left with considerable scope to make determinations about the shape of public policy, but that the *Charter* allows the courts to intervene where the political process is deficient in some way.[29]

2) Judicial Review and Rights Protection

Another justification offered for judicial enforcement of a charter of rights emphasizes the central importance of rights protection to individual self-development. As with the process model, this theory is based on a perception that majoritarian politics may have deficiencies that require correction. But this model can take the courts much further in curtailing government action and, in the abstract, is based upon an unwavering and unqualified commitment to the protection of individual autonomy. This justification for judicial review is sometimes based on the idea of rights as trumps over the policy preferences of governments.[30] Consider, for example, the following quotation from

---

27 *Andrews v Law Society (British Columbia)*, [1989] 1 SCR 143 at 152, 56 DLR (4th) 1, Wilson J. This approach is further described in Chapter 15.

28 *Vriend*, above note 1 at para 142, Iacobucci J.

29 Ely, above note 21. For a similar defence of the role of the *Charter*, from the perspective of the left, see R Penner, "The Canadian Experience with the *Charter of Rights*: Are There Lessons for the United Kingdom?" [1996] Pub L 104 at 113.

30 Ronald Dworkin is a strong proponent of this view. See, for example, R Dworkin, *Taking Rights Seriously* (Cambridge: Harvard University Press, 1977).

Lorraine Weinrib advocating a "constitutional rights" model of judicial review:

> This model welcomes judicial protection of individual rights and their value structure to continuously correct for the perceived inadequacies of majoritarian politics. Underlying this model is respect for the dignity, equality and autonomy of each member of the community. The individual must be able to espouse, and follow, and modify his or her own conception of the good. Whatever the sources and trajectories of these commitments, the aim of collective political life is to create and preserve a structure in which each of us, to an equal extent, may pursue and act upon these commitments, either alone or in a given or chosen community.[31]

An exclusive focus on rights protection may be in conflict with the ability of legislatures to justify limitations on rights under section 1 of the *Charter*. Another robust approach to judicial review is that advocated by David Beatty, who argues that courts should not impose definitional limits on rights and only accept limits on rights under section 1 if "there is no other, less drastic policy available that would interfere less with people's rights and freedoms."[32] As will be seen, however, the courts have resisted a mechanical approach to the justification of reasonable limits under section 1, which would invalidate legislation simply because a less drastic alternative could be imagined. They have stressed that a contextual approach is required under section 1 with attention to the competing policies at stake in many *Charter* cases.

3) Judicial Review and Framers' Intent

Another theory of judicial review that has had little influence under the *Charter* is the idea that courts act legitimately only to the extent that they implement the intent of the framers of the constitution. This theory assumes that following the framers' intent is more democratic than relying on a judge's interpretation of the text of the constitution and that judges should constrain democratically elected legislatures only if they have a clear mandate in the constitution to do so. Robert Bork, for example, has argued that because both the *Charter* and the American *Bill of Rights* "are silent" on the issue of abortion, "the Supreme Court should have stated that neither provision was enacted with abortion in

---

31   L Weinrib, "Limitations on Rights in a Constitutional Democracy" (1996) 6 Caribbean L Rev 428 at 439.

32   D Beatty, *Constitutional Law in Theory and Practice* (Toronto: University of Toronto Press, 1995) at 70.

mind, and that the *Charter*, having deliberately avoided the issue, had nothing to say and so the issue must remain with the legislature."[33]

There are many problems with the framers' intent approach. One problem is that the *Charter*, like other bills of rights, is generally framed in terms that are "vague and open" and whose meaning "cannot be determined by recourse to a dictionary, nor for that matter, by reference to the rules of statutory interpretation."[34] Another problem is the difficulty of determining the intent of the framers: the Supreme Court has rejected being bound by the expectations of senior civil servants who helped draft the *Charter*, in part, on the basis that "the intention of the legislative bodies which adopted the *Charter*" is a "fact which is nearly impossible of proof."[35]

The *Charter* is also a part of the constitution that can be amended only with the consent of the federal government and all provinces. This requirement makes amending the *Charter* very difficult. If the *Charter* is to remain relevant to the needs of a rapidly evolving society, it must be interpreted in a manner that allows for growth over the years. The Supreme Court has held that limiting its interpretation of the Charter on the basis of the drafters' expectations would create a danger of *Charter* rights becoming

> frozen in time to the moment of adoption with little or no possibility of growth, development and adjustment to changing societal needs . . . If the newly planted "living tree" which is the *Charter* is to have the possibility of growth and adjustment over time, care must be taken to ensure that historical materials . . . do not stunt its growth.[36]

The issue of the intent of the framers is also not very helpful in resolving whether the government has justified reasonable limits on *Charter* rights under section 1 of the *Charter* in a particular case. As we shall see in Chapter 4, the reasonable limits clause gives both Parliament and the courts considerable scope to adapt the *Charter* to changing social needs. Finally, the existence of the section 33 override suggests that the framers of the *Charter* recognized that courts might interpret the *Charter* in unexpected ways.

---

33   Bork, above note 18 at 87.
34   *Hunter v Southam*, [1984] 2 SCR 145, 11 DLR (4th) 641 at 649.
35   *Reference Re s 94(2) of the Motor Vehicle Act (BC)*, above note 1 at para 51.
36   *Ibid* at para 52.

4) Judicial Review as Part of a Democratic Dialogue

Another approach to the justification of judicial review is to situate judicial review in the context of an ongoing dialogue between courts and legislatures in which there is neither legislative nor judicial supremacy.[37] A judicial decision invalidating a law or an administrative action under the *Charter* need not be the final word as legislatures can reformulate laws and authorize administrative actions. Such reply legislation can be defended under section 1 of the *Charter* as a reasonable limit on *Charter* rights as interpreted by the courts. In exceptional cases, the legislature can override a *Charter* decision with legislation that is enacted notwithstanding the fundamental freedoms, legal rights, and equality rights of the *Charter*.

One of the strengths of dialogue theory is its ability to account for the power of legislatures under the *Charter* to place explicit limits and overrides on rights as interpreted by the courts. Another strength of dialogue theory is its ability to account for the frequent interplay between courts and legislatures on matters affected by the *Charter*. Legislatures frequently enact new legislation after the courts have invalidated legislation under the *Charter*, though there is dispute about whether all legislative replies constitute genuine dialogue.[38] For example, Parliament has enacted new laws in response to some of the Supreme Court's more unpopular criminal law judgments concerning the right of the accused to introduce and have access to evidence affecting the privacy of complainants in sexual assault cases, rights against unreasonable

---

37   Alexander Bickel argued for a form of dialogue in which "the Court placed itself in position to engage in a continual colloquy with the political institutions, leaving it to them to tell the Court what expedients of accommodation and compromise they deemed necessary. The Court would reply in the negative . . . only when a suggested expedient amounted to the abandonment of principle." A Bickel, *The Least Dangerous Branch: The Supreme Court at the Bar of Politics*, 2d ed (New Haven: Yale University Press, 1986) at 254.

38   Peter Hogg and his co-authors argue that there have been legislative replies in about two-thirds of cases. See P Hogg & A Bushell, "The *Charter* Dialogue between Courts and Legislatures (Or Perhaps the *Charter of Rights* Isn't Such a Bad Thing After All)" (1997) 35 Osgoode Hall LJ 75 and P Hogg, A Bushell Thornton, & W Wright, "*Charter* Dialogue Revisited" (2007) 45 Osgoode Hall LJ 1. Others who would restrict genuine dialogue to cases where legislatures act on a different interpretation of the *Charter* than the courts conclude that there is only dialogue in about 20 percent to a third of all cases in which legislation is struck down. C Manfredi & J Kelly, "Six Degrees of Dialogue: A Response to Hogg and Bushell" (1999) 37 Osgoode Hall LJ 513, and E Macfarlane, "Dialogue or Compliance? Measuring Legislatures Policy Responses to Court Rulings on Rights" (2013) 34 International Political Science Rev 39.

search and seizures, and the defence of extreme intoxication. Parliament has also responded legislatively to judgments dealing with the voting rights of prisoners, the right of tobacco companies to advertise their product, assisted dying, prostitution, and supervised injection sites. In some of these cases, legislative replies have been facilitated by the court suspending its declaration of invalidity to provide Parliament with an opportunity to enact new legislation.[39]

The Supreme Court appears to accept the idea that judicial review under the *Charter* is part of a dialogue between courts and legislatures. In its 1998 decision, holding that protection for gays and lesbians against discrimination should be read into Alberta's human rights legislation, the Court observed that "the work of the legislature is reviewed by the courts and the work of the court in its decisions can be reacted to by the legislature in the passing of new legislation (or even overarching laws under section 33 of the *Charter*). This dialogue between and accountability of each of the branches have the effect of enhancing the democratic process, not denying it."[40] Alberta decided not to respond to the Court's decision in that case, but it did later enact legislation using the section 33 override that reserved marriage to opposite-sex couples. The override expired after five years and was not renewed by the Alberta legislature. It may well be that courts could adopt a more vigorous approach to judicial review knowing that their decisions will not necessarily be the last word.

The implications of dialogue theory are less clear when the courts are reviewing legislation that has been enacted in response to a court's decision under the *Charter*. In *R v Mills*, the Supreme Court upheld legislation passed in response to an earlier decision by the Court, concerning the accused's right of access to the private records of complainants in sexual assault cases. Noting that dialogue between courts and legislatures occurs under the common law as well as the *Charter*, the Court observed that "if the common law were to be taken as establishing the only possible constitutional regime, then we could not speak of a dialogue with the legislature. Such a situation could only undermine rather than enhance democracy." In upholding Parliament's reply legislation, which not only emphasized the privacy rights of complainants and the equality rights of women and children, but also took into account the accused's right to full answer and defence, the Court observed that "courts do not hold a monopoly on the protection and promotion

---

39   These legislative replies are examined in Roach, *The Supreme Court on Trial*, above note 20, chs 10, 14 and 16, and J Hiebert, Charter *Conflicts: What Is Parliament's Role?* (Montreal: McGill-Queen's University Press, 2002).

40   *Vriend*, above note 1 at para 139.

of rights and freedoms."[41] However, the majority's decision to uphold a limitation on the right to bail when needed to maintain public confidence enacted in response to a decision striking down a very similar law provoked a sharp dissent from Iacobucci J, who complained that upholding the law "transformed dialogue into abdication."[42] *Sauvé v Canada (Chief Electoral Officer)*[43] represents a strong reassertion of the Court's determination to subject responsive legislation to careful *Charter* scrutiny. In *Sauvé*, the Supreme Court struck down legislation denying the vote to prisoners serving sentences longer than two years, a law that had been enacted in response to the Court's earlier decision striking down a blanket prohibition on inmate voting.[44] Chief Justice McLachlin rejected any suggestion that "the fact that the challenged denial of the right to vote followed judicial rejection of an even more comprehensive denial" means "that the Court should defer to Parliament as part of a 'dialogue.'" She insisted that conformity to the demands of the constitution must be ensured "at whatever stage of the process" and that "[t]he healthy and important promotion of a dialogue between the legislature and the courts should not be debased to a rule of 'if at first you don't succeed, try, try again.'"[45] In a 2007 decision,[46] the Court upheld Parliament's reply to its controversial 1995 decision striking down an absolute ban on tobacco advertising,[47] but also agreed that "[t]he mere fact that the legislation represents Parliament's response to a decision of this Court does not militate for or against deference." This suggests that the Court will decide such a "second look" on the basis of the evidence and arguments in the particular case. Dialogue is an approach to judicial review that focuses on institutional interaction and does not tell judges how to decide hard cases.

The metaphor of judicial review as dialogue is likely to continue to evolve. It remains to be seen in what direction. Courts and legislatures could play distinct and complementary roles with dialogue being conducted under section 1 of the *Charter* about the objectives of the legislation and the alternatives that the legislature has considered. Another possibility is that both institutions will see fit to act on their own interpretations of the constitution, though this may result in con-

---

41   *R v Mills*, [1999] 3 SCR 668, 180 DLR (4th) 1 at paras 56–58.
42   *R v Hall*, [2002] 3 SCR 309 at para 127.
43   *Sauvé*, above note 22.
44   *Sauvé v Canada (Attorney General)*, [1993] 2 SCR 438.
45   *Sauvé*, above note 22 at para 17.
46   *Canada (Attorney General) v JTI-Macdonald Corp*, [2007] 2 SCR 610 at para 11.
47   *RJR-MacDonald Inc v Canada (Attorney General)*, [1995] 3 SCR 199. These cases are discussed in greater detail in Chapter 9.

flict between the two institutions and even undermine respect for the Court's decisions. Yet another is that both institutions will hold each other accountable.[48] Whatever precise direction is taken, the metaphor of dialogue and the recognition it accords to the distinct but related roles played by courts and legislatures reflects a fundamental aspect of the Canadian approach to judicial review under the *Charter*.

D. THE ROLE OF THE COURTS UNDER THE *CHARTER*

Assessing the relative merits of the arguments for and against judicial review requires looking at what the courts do not do, as well as what they do. While the critics on the left assert that the courts will import conservative values, it is important to put in perspective the outcomes of some of the so-called "bad cases" that they decry. In some of these cases, the failure to adopt the view of the left does not automatically translate into a victory for the right. For example, when the Supreme Court of Canada refused to find that collective bargaining was a constitutional right under the guarantee of freedom of association, that did not mean an end to collective bargaining; rather, it pushed the debate about the nature and scope of labour powers into the political arena. In addition, the Supreme Court revisited the matter to hold the *Charter* protects some of the basics of collective bargaining.[49] The Court has more recently protected the rights of unions in a more robust way, but at the same time the legislature, in a sign of continued dialogue, has also placed and justified limits on the rights as interpreted by the Court.[50]

Similarly, when the courts refuse to recognize positive rights — for example, to welfare as an element of security of the person — that does not prevent political debate and action with respect to welfare policy; instead, it leaves the difficult policy choices to the political process. There will be a danger to continued democracy only if the legislature confuses

---

48   K Roach, "Constitutional and Common Law Dialogues between the Supreme Court and Canadian Legislatures" (2001) 80 Can Bar Rev 481.

49   *Reference Re Public Service Employee Relations Act (Alberta)*, [1987] 1 SCR 313, 38 DLR (4th) 161; *Dunmore v Ontario (Attorney General)*, [2001] 3 SCR 1016, 2001 SCC 94, discussed in Chapter 10.

50   Roach, *The Supreme Court on Trial*, above note 20 at 349–52.

the court's decision that some measure is consistent with the *Charter* with the separate question of whether it is wise and necessary policy.[51]

Finally, in other areas, while the result in a given case may provide a victory to a powerful economic interest, the decision often has implications throughout the legal system in ways that may also benefit the less advantaged. For instance, when a powerful corporation wins protection against unreasonable searches and seizures in the criminal process, it will not be the only beneficiary. As discussed above, many *Charter* decisions on controversial topics, such as the rights of tobacco companies to advertise, have not proven to be the final word on the subject. Legislatures still retain the right to enact new legislation that can be justified under section 1 of the *Charter* or subject to the section 33 override.

In the chapters that follow, we will see that Canadian courts have demonstrated a marked deference in certain areas which, it may be argued, results from their recognition of the limits of the judicial function. The Canadian Supreme Court has been unsympathetic to claims of pure economic rights and has refused to become embroiled in most distributional issues.[52] This has been manifested by the Court's refusal to imply a right of property in the constitution and its rejection of overtures to protect rights of contract. This cautious and deferential stance contrasts sharply with the Court's willingness to engage its power to protect freedom of expression and the rights of criminally accused. While the Court has expressed a commitment to vigilance in the protection of minorities from prejudice and stereotypes, it has also insisted that governments be given some leeway in making difficult social-policy decisions — for example, with respect to mandatory retirement and the criminalization of marijuana.

The Court's refusal to intervene in the areas of property and contract reflects its view that economic and social-policy questions are best left to the legislative arenas.[53] Similarly, the Court has respected and

---

51   Some theorists have expressed a concern that legislatures will "fall into a habit of assuming that whatever they could constitutionally do they may do" so that the people "lose the political experience, and the moral education and stimulus that comes from fighting the question out in the ordinary way, and correcting their own errors." Bickel, above note 37 at 21–22, quoting James Bradley Thayer.

52   See, for example, *Irwin Toy Ltd v Quebec (AG)*, [1989] 1 SCR 927, 58 DLR (4th) 577, holding that commercial expression is protected by s 2(b) of the *Charter*, but making it clear that purely economic rights are not protected. In *Gosselin v Quebec (Attorney General)*, [2002] 4 SCR 429, a majority of the Court rejected welfare rights while not closing the door on future acceptance of rights in that context.

53   Peter Russell has observed that "[t]here is not much empirical evidence to support" the concerns of the left or the right about judicial activism because "none

upheld legislative initiatives to protect vulnerable groups when these initiatives have been challenged as violating the fundamental freedoms of more powerful interests in society.[54] The Court recognizes that Parliament and the legislatures have an important role in enhancing and protecting these very same values that inform judicial review, wisely refusing to claim the exclusive authority to determine when those rights should be protected.

In sum, it can be argued that the purpose of constitutionalizing rights is to facilitate, not frustrate, democracy. The *Charter* protects the values of individual dignity, autonomy, and respect, which are essential for free and open democratic debate, and it gives a voice to many in our society who are effectively excluded from the political process. A true democracy is surely one in which the exercise of power by the many is conditional on respect for the rights of the few. Majorities may fail to respect individual dignity and conscience, and may be inclined to shut out annoying and unpopular views. Constitutionalizing rights empowers the courts to check these unworthy inclinations by requiring those who exercise power to justify their actions through evidence and reasoned argument when the bedrock values of our democratic tradition are impinged. The Canadian experience to date indicates that the judiciary is capable of exercising the powers of judicial review to protect such fundamental rights as freedom of religion and expression and the right to equality without unduly inhibiting the capacity of the elected representatives to develop social policy.

E. CONCLUSION

Overall, we suggest that the *Charter* has had a beneficial impact upon democratic life in Canada. Fundamental human rights are now properly

---

of the key economic and social policy interests of government — monetary and fiscal policy, international trade, resource development, social welfare, education, labour relations, environmental protection — have been significantly encroached by judicial enforcement of the *Charter*." P Russell, "Canadian Constraints on Judicialization from Without" (1994) 15 International Political Science Rev 165 at 168, 169.

54 See *Edwards Books & Art Ltd v R*, [1986] 2 SCR 713, 35 DLR (4th) 1 at 49, where Dickson CJC stated that care had to be taken so that the *Charter* "does not simply become an instrument of better situated individuals to roll back legislation that has as its object the improvement of the condition of less advantaged persons." See also *R v Kapp*, [2008] 2 SCR 483 and *Alberta (Aboriginal Affairs and Northern Development) v Cunningham*, [2011] 2 SCR 670, upholding affirmative action programs under s 15(2) of the *Charter*.

at the forefront of public debate, and the claims of those often drowned out in the cut and thrust of day-to-day politics can no longer be ignored. Indeed, the *Charter* has made an important contribution to Canadian political life by creating what Roland Penner calls a "culture of liberty."[55] Legislators cannot enact laws without consideration of their impact on individual rights, and government legal officers play an important role in encouraging their political masters to justify any limitations on *Charter* rights.

The *Charter* has the potential to strengthen the Canadian democratic tradition and commitment to toleration and equal respect for all, and judges have an appropriate part to play in protecting those values. As interpreted by the courts to date, the *Charter* neither precludes nor entrenches particular socio-economic outcomes but rather enriches the democratic process.

FURTHER READINGS

BAKAN, J, *Just Words: Constitutional Rights and Social Wrongs* (Toronto: University of Toronto Press, 1997)

BAKER, D, *Not Quite Supreme: The Courts and Coordinate Constitutional Interpretation* (Montreal: McGill-Queen's University Press, 2010)

BEATTY, DM, *Constitutional Law in Theory and Practice* (Toronto: University of Toronto Press, 1995)

————, *The Ultimate Rule of Law* (Oxford: Oxford University Press, 2004)

BOGART, WA, *Courts and Country: The Limits of Litigation and the Social and Political Life of Canada* (Toronto: Oxford University Press, 1994)

DICKSON, B, ed, *Judicial Activism in Common Law Supreme Courts* (Oxford: Oxford University Press, 2007)

ELY, JH, *Democracy and Distrust: A Theory of Judicial Review* (Cambridge: Harvard University Press, 1980)

GARDBAUM, S, *The New Commonwealth Model of Constitutionalism* (Cambridge: Cambridge University Press, 2013)

HARDING, M, & R KNOPFF, "'*Charter* Values' vs *Charter* Dialogue" (2013) 31 NJCL 161

---

55   Penner, above note 29 at 114–15.

HIEBERT, J, Charter *Conflicts? What Is Parliament's Role?* (Montreal: McGill-Queen's University Press, 2002)

HOGG, P, & A THORNTON, "The *Charter* Dialogue between Courts and Legislatures" (1997) 35 Osgoode Hall LJ 75

HUTCHINSON, AC, *Waiting for CORAF: A Critique of Law and Rights* (Toronto: University of Toronto Press, 1995)

KAVANAGH, A, "The Lure and the Limits of Dialogue" (2016) 66 UTLJ 83

KELLY, J, & C MANFREDI, eds, *Contested Constitutionalisms: Reflections on the* Canadian Charter of Rights and Freedoms (Vancouver: UBC Press, 2009)

KNOPFF, R, & FL MORTON, Charter *Politics* (Scarborough, ON: Nelson Canada, 1992)

MANDEL, M, *The* Charter of Rights *and the Legalization of Politics in Canada*, 2d ed (Toronto: Thompson, 1994)

MANFREDI, C, *Judicial Power and the* Charter: *Canada and the Paradox of Liberal Constitutionalism*, 2d ed (Toronto: Oxford University Press, 2001)

MCLACHLAN, B, "The *Charter* 25 Years Later: The Good, the Bad, and the Challenges" (2007) 45 Osgoode Hall LJ 365.

MONAHAN, P, *Politics and the Constitution: The* Charter, *Federalism and the Supreme Court of Canada* (Toronto: Carswell, 1987)

MORTON, FL, & R KNOPFF, *The* Charter *Revolution and the Court Party* (Peterborough, ON: Broadview Press, 2000)

PENNER, R, "The Canadian Experience with the *Charter of Rights*: Are There Lessons for the United Kingdom?" [1996] Pub. L. 104

ROACH, K, *The Supreme Court on Trial: Judicial Activism or Democratic Dialogue*, rev ed (Toronto: Irwin Law, 2016)

SLATTERY, B, "A Theory of the *Charter*" (1987) 25 Osgoode Hall LJ 701

SYMPOSIUM, "*Charter* Dialogue: Ten Years Later" (2007) 45 Osgoode Hall LJ 1–202

WALDRON, J, "The Core of the Case against Judicial Review" (2006) 115 Yale LJ 1346

WEBBER, G, *The Negotiable Constitution on the Limitation of Rights* (Cambridge: Cambridge University Press, 2009)

CHAPTER 3

INTERPRETATION OF THE *CHARTER OF RIGHTS AND FREEDOMS*

Entrenching rights in the constitution does not end the debate about the legitimacy of judicial review. Rather, the debate takes on a different form, revolving around the justification for various approaches to constitutional interpretation. Some argue for a strict reading of the constitutional text, often maintaining that the words of the document should be understood in light of their meaning at the time of drafting. Others argue for a more "progressive" approach that will allow the content to adapt to new societal needs and values. Those who take this latter position turn to moral philosophy, international human rights norms, or evolving community values for help in the interpretive process.

In this chapter, we outline the structure of the *Canadian Charter of Rights and Freedoms* and then canvass some of the debates about its interpretation.

A. THE NATURE OF *CHARTER* RIGHTS

The Canadian *Charter* identifies and enshrines six broad categories of rights:

- the "fundamental freedoms" of conscience, religion, thought, belief, opinion, expression, assembly, and association;[1]

---

1   Section 2.

- democratic rights, including the right to vote, the guarantee of regular elections, and annual parliamentary sessions;[2]
- mobility rights to enter and leave the country and the right to reside in and gain a livelihood in any province;[3]
- legal rights, particularly those pertaining to the criminal process, such as the rights to counsel, protection against unreasonable search and seizure, *habeas corpus*, trial within a reasonable time, and the presumption of innocence until proven guilty, as well as a more general right to life, liberty, and security of the person, and the right not to be deprived thereof except in accordance with principles of fundamental justice;[4]
- the right to equality before and under the law and to the equal protection and equal benefit of the law;[5] and
- language rights.[6]

These rights are both guaranteed and made subject to limitations in section 1 of the *Charter*, which states that the *Charter* "guarantees the rights and freedoms set out in it subject to such reasonable limits prescribed by law as can be demonstrably justified in a free and democratic society." Thus, the Canadian *Charter* follows the model of international human rights documents rather than the American constitution. While the American document sets out the rights as if they are absolute, international documents, such as the *International Covenant on Civil and Political Rights*, expressly acknowledge that rights can be limited to protect other individual rights or broader community interests.

The *Charter* also includes a number of distinctive interpretive provisions, including a clause ensuring that there will be no derogation from Aboriginal rights by the *Charter* in section 25,[7] a commitment to preserve and enhance our multicultural heritage in section 27, and a further guarantee of gender equality in section 28. Also significant to interpretive issues is the specific remedial clause in section 24, discussed in Chapter 17, as well as a mechanism to override certain *Charter* rights, found in section 33, which is discussed in Chapter 5.

The rights included in a constitutional document reflect the concerns prevalent at the time of drafting. To the extent that the goal of the constitution is to curtail majority tyranny and government excesses,

---

2   Sections 3–5.
3   Section 6.
4   Sections 7–14.
5   Section 15.
6   Sections 16–23.
7   Aboriginal rights are recognized and affirmed in s 35 of the *Constitution Act, 1982*, which does not form part of the *Charter*.

the rights protected will tend to lie in those areas where there has been evidence of problems — for example, government measures against unpopular expression or the practices of some religions. Similarly, to the extent that the constitution expresses an aspiration to greater equality in society, the listed grounds of discrimination may reflect historical or contemporary bases for unfair treatment against individuals and groups. The Canadian *Charter*, for example, was one of the world's first to include disability, while South Africa's new constitution, in force since December 1996, goes further to include sexual orientation in its equality guarantee.[8]

The emphasis in many countries has been on a liberal approach that protects the individual *from* certain state actions. There is, however, pressure in many countries today for the inclusion of positive rights — that is, rights to make governments act in order to provide greater equality or human dignity. While the Canadian *Charter* does include the positive right to minority-language schools in section 23, it does not contain the range of positive rights found, for example, in the new South African constitution, which includes the right to a healthy environment, the right to have access to adequate housing, health-care services, sufficient food and water, and social security, and the right to a basic education.[9] Efforts were made to add a "social charter" to the Canadian constitution during the constitutional-reform discussions occurring between 1990 and 1992, but serious opposition from a wide range of opinion undermined the project.[10]

In sum, the Canadian catalogue of rights and freedoms in the *Charter* looks essentially liberal in nature, in the sense that its language of rights and freedoms seems to define a zone of autonomy for the individual within which the state may not intrude. This feature of the *Charter* has been a cause for concern on the part of those who fear that its emphasis upon traditional liberal values will have an Americanizing influence on a Canadian legal and political culture, which emphasizes the communitarian values of "peace, order, and good government" rather

---

8   *Constitution of the Republic of South Africa, 1996*, No 108 of 1996, s 9.

9   *Ibid*, ss 24, 26, 27, 29. These rights often contain qualifications — for example, the right to access to adequate housing states in s 26(2) that "[t]he state must take reasonable legislative and other measures, within its available resources, to achieve the progressive realisation of this right."

10   Some of the arguments pro and con are found in W Kymlicka & WJ Norman, "The Social *Charter* Debate: Should Social Justice Be Constitutionalized?" (Ottawa: Network on the Constitution, 1992); J. Bakan & D Schneiderman, *Social Justice and the Constitution: Perspectives on the Social Union for Canada* (Ottawa: Carleton University Press, 1992).

than the American ideal of the "right to life, liberty, and the pursuit of happiness." Instead of seeing government as a positive force because of its capacity to create greater equality or help the vulnerable, the *Charter* may foster the view that the state is the enemy of individual freedom.[11]

In looking at the experience under the *Charter*, one would have to conclude that the Canadian legal system has moved closer to the American model. However, this conclusion should be tempered by a realization that both the text and the interpretation of the *Charter* reflect an attitude more receptive to affirmative state measures designed to advance certain collective interests than that found in American constitutional law. For instance, "affirmative action" measures that have as their object the amelioration of conditions of disadvantaged individuals or groups are explicitly protected from claims of "reverse discrimination" and, thus, denials of equality.[12] The promise of equality itself has been found to require affirmative measures by the state.[13] The Supreme Court has rejected the view that collective rights are inconsistent with individual rights and pointed out that there is a group or collective element to many *Charter* rights, including the freedoms of association, assembly, religion, and the right to vote.[14] Also significant is the Supreme Court's pronouncement that even rights that are cast in negative terms may impose positive obligations in some situations.[15] Unless the *Charter* right is cast in positive terms, ordinarily a claimant cannot assert the *Charter* right against the government to insist upon statutory protection.[16] Likewise, an existing statutorily created platform, such as collective bargaining legislation, that relates to a *Charter* right will not by itself ground a claim advanced by individuals excluded from the statutory regime. However, where the claimant can demonstrate that exclusion from a statutory regime permits a substantial interference with a *Charter* right, and the state is thereby accountable for the

---

11   This passage echoes the criticisms of Andrew Petter, among others, discussed in Chapter 2.

12   Section 15(2). In addition, s 6(4) protects discriminatory labour practices against out-of-province workers in provinces with unemployment rates above the national average.

13   *Eldridge v British Columbia (AG)*, [1997] 3 SCR 624, 151 DLR (4th) 577; *Vriend v Alberta*, [1998] 1 SCR 493, 156 DLR (4th) 385 [*Vriend*].

14   *Mounted Police Association of Ontario v Canada (Attorney General)*, [2015] 1 SCR 3 at paras 63–65.

15   *Dunmore v Ontario (Attorney General)*, [2001] 3 SCR 1016, 207 DLR (4th) 193 [*Dunmore*]; *Baier v Alberta*, [2007] 2 SCR 673 at paras 21–30.

16   *Haig v Canada (Chief Electoral Officer)*, [1993] 2 SCR 995, 105 DLR (4th) 577 at 607; *Native Women's Association of Canada v Canada* (1994), 119 DLR (4th) 224 at 245 (SCC); *Vriend*, above note 13 at para 64.

claimant's inability to exercise a protected right or freedom, the *Charter* requires that affirmative measures be taken. While there are few cases where the Court has been prepared to interpret one of the negative rights against government interference as giving rise to positive obligations, a notable example is the decision requiring a provincial legislature to enact legislation to protect the right of vulnerable agricultural workers to engage in associational activities necessary to protect their interests as employees.[17]

Most important, section 1 of the *Charter*, the "reasonable limits" clause discussed in Chapter 4, has been interpreted to permit legislative measures designed to enhance the values underlying the fundamental rights and freedoms and to acknowledge that the liberty of the individual is sometimes justifiably limited in the interests of broader community interests and values.

Especially in the early years, American jurisprudence was frequently cited in *Charter* litigation and treated as relevant and sometimes persuasive. But American approaches have also been flatly rejected in some areas and American jurisprudence is certainly not determinative, as the Supreme Court of Canada has frequently stated, given the differences in Canadian and American political and legal traditions.[18]

B. INTERPRETATION OF *CHARTER* RIGHTS

The Canadian courts have adopted a two-step process of interpretation and justification to give the general language of the *Charter* concrete meaning. First, the courts interpret the meaning of the right or freedom at issue to determine whether the matter complained of constitutes an infringement. Often, at this first stage, the courts have avoided narrow definitional limitations on rights that take into account the general social interest. It has been held, for example, that commercial advertising,[19] hate propaganda,[20] and pornography[21] are, subject to

---

17   *Dunmore*, above note 15.

18   See J Cameron, "The *Motor Vehicle Reference* and the Relevance of American Doctrine in *Charter* Adjudication" in RJ Sharpe, ed, Charter *Litigation* (Toronto: Butterworths, 1987) c 4. Indeed, the Canadian Court has embarked on jurisprudence that is quite distinctive from the American in areas such as hate propaganda and pornography, equality rights, and the drawing of electoral boundaries.

19   *Irwin Toy Ltd v Quebec (AG)*, [1989] 1 SCR 927, 58 DLR (4th) 577.

20   *R v Keegstra*, [1990] 3 SCR 697, 61 CCC (3d) 1 [*Keegstra*].

21   *R v Butler*, [1992] 1 SCR 452, 70 CCC (3d) 129.

limitations justifiable under section 1, forms of expression protected by section 2(b). Only violence has been held to be excluded from the definition of expression.

With respect to some other rights, however, the courts have taken a more restrictive approach and defined certain limits to their scope. In interpreting the right to vote in section 3, for example, the courts have held that this provision gives a right to effective representation, not a guarantee of "one person, one vote."[22] Freedom of association was initially limited by excluding some group activities, such as the right to strike.[23] Section 15, the equality guarantee, can be invoked only by those discriminated against on the basis of the enumerated grounds (for example, race, sex, or disability) or analogous grounds.[24] Certain rights are defined in a contextual manner. For example, the section 8 right to be protected against unreasonable search and seizure requires the courts to take into account the context in which the right is claimed when defining what searches and seizures are "unreasonable."[25]

A claimant can demonstrate that a right has been infringed either by looking at the government's purpose or at the effects of the government's actions. In some cases, the legislature's purpose will directly interfere with the exercise of the right — for example, a state-imposed compulsory religion for all would violate freedom of religion in section 2(a). In most cases, while the underlying objective of state action is not to interfere with a protected freedom, the legislation being challenged has that effect. For example, when a government prohibits individuals from fastening anything to telephone poles, the objective may be to prevent unsightly displays or even obstructions that may interfere with traffic safety. However, the effect of such a rule is to prevent the putting up of posters, which can be seen as an interference with freedom of expression.[26]

Once a right is infringed, the case is not over. The *Charter* recognizes that rights are not absolute; there are many situations when the interests of society at large or the rights of other individuals will require that the claimant's rights be limited. The consideration of whether these limits are justified under section 1 of the *Charter*, as reasonable limits prescribed by law in a free and democratic society, is left to the second step of a rights case — justification pursuant to section 1. The

---

22 See Chapter 11.
23 See Chapter 10.
24 See Chapter 15.
25 See Chapter 14.
26 *Peterborough (City) v Ramsden*, [1993] 2 SCR 1084, 106 DLR (4th) 233.

balance of this chapter discusses the initial interpretive stage, leaving the limitation of rights to Chapter 4.

1) The Purposive Method

From the earliest *Charter* cases, the Supreme Court of Canada clearly recognized that *Charter* adjudication should be different from the traditional work of the courts. In *Law Society of Upper Canada v Skapinker*,[27] the first *Charter* case to reach the Court, the judges indicated that they were prepared to assume responsibility for interpreting this "new yardstick of reconciliation between the individual and the community and their respective rights." Mindful that the "*Charter* is designed and adopted to guide and serve the Canadian community for a long time," Estey J added that "narrow and technical interpretation" that could "stunt the growth of the law and hence the community it serves"[28] would be avoided.

In another early case, *Hunter v Southam*,[29] the Supreme Court distinguished the method of statutory construction from that of constitutional interpretation. Insisting that the *Charter* must "be capable of growth and development over time to meet new social, political, and historical realities often unimagined by its framers," Dickson CJC repeated Professor Paul Freund's plea that courts should not "read the provisions of the Constitution like a last will and testament lest it become one."[30] A similar note was struck by Beetz J in *Manitoba (Attorney General) v Metropolitan Stores (MTS) Ltd*[31] when he dismissed the contention that the "presumption of constitutionality" should be weighed in the scales of *Charter* adjudication: "[T]he innovative and evolutive character of the Canadian *Charter of Rights and Freedoms* conflicts with the idea that a legislative provision can be presumed to be consistent with the *Charter*."[32] The rights and freedoms set out were not "frozen" in content and had to "remain susceptible to evolve in the future."[33]

These passages harken back to earlier decisions of the Privy Council and the Supreme Court of Canada interpreting the *Constitution Act, 1867*, in which the judges advocated an "organic" or "progressive" theory of interpretation with respect to the constitution. The judges rejected

---

27   [1984] 1 SCR 357, 9 DLR (4th) 161.
28   *Ibid* at 366 (SCR).
29   [1984] 2 SCR 145, 11 DLR (4th) 641.
30   *Ibid* at 649 (DLR).
31   [1987] 1 SCR 110, 38 DLR (4th) 321.
32   *Ibid* at 122 (SCR).
33   *Ibid* at 124.

an approach advocated by some American scholars and judges, which emphasizes the original intent of the framers of the constitution and interprets the document in light of the meaning of its terms at the time it was created. The "original intent" approach was soundly rejected by the Privy Council as being inconsistent with the idea of an enduring constitution that, if it is to last, must be capable of growth and expansion. In the *Edwards* case, the Privy Council determined that, in the twentieth century, women were qualified "persons" for the purposes of eligibility for Senate appointments, even though in 1867, at the time the constitution was adopted, women were not eligible to hold public office. Viscount Sankey's words from that case have been frequently quoted:

> The *B.N.A. Act* planted in Canada a living tree capable of growth and expansion within its natural limits. The object of the Act was to grant a Constitution to Canada . . . .
>
> Their Lordships do not conceive it to be the duty of this Board — it is certainly not their desire — to cut down the provisions of the Act by a narrow and technical construction, but rather to give it a large and liberal interpretation . . . .[34]

The Supreme Court reaffirmed the vitality of the "living tree" approach to constitutional interpretation in *Reference Re Same-Sex Marriage*[35] when it unanimously rejected the idea that Parliament's jurisdiction over marriage under section 91(26) of the *Constitution Act, 1867* was limited to marriages as understood at the time of Confederation.

The Supreme Court of Canada has specifically held that the supposed "original intent" of those who drafted the *Charter* will not be conclusive in its interpretation for two reasons.[36] First, statements of the intent of particular individuals are an unreliable guide to discerning the intent of many others who took an active role in the creation of the *Charter*. Furthermore, it is doubtful that there was a single or identifiable intent shared by all, given the number of federal and provincial politicians and bureaucrats involved. Second, adoption of a strict interpretivist approach would freeze the meaning of the *Charter* at a particular time "with little or no possibility of growth, development and adjustment to changing societal needs."[37] Even if there were concrete evidence to help in determining the original understanding of the right, it would be wrong to fasten on to that meaning without question,

---

34 *Edwards v R*, [1930] AC 124 at 136–37 [*Edwards*].
35 [2004] 3 SCR 698 at paras 22–30.
36 *Reference Re s 94(2) of the Motor Vehicle Act (BC)*, [1985] 2 SCR 486 at 508–9, 24 DLR (4th) 536.
37 *Ibid* at 554 (DLR), Lamer J.

for the original drafters themselves in all likelihood considered this to be an inappropriate method of interpretation. Constitutions are deliberately phrased in general, open-ended terms in order to let them adapt to changing circumstances and needs over the years. In the words of the late Ronald Dworkin, constitutions are meant to set out concepts, not conceptions, and thus, their content necessarily varies over time and place.[38]

Given the rejection of "original intent" to guide interpretation, how should a court proceed? In *Hunter v Southam*, the Supreme Court of Canada first enunciated and applied the "purposive" method that has served as the standard approach in the elaboration of *Charter* rights and freedoms. This is a complex, value-laden exercise that draws upon a range of sources in the innovative spirit that the *Charter* demands. It calls upon the judge to reflect upon the purpose of and rationale for the *Charter* right at issue in the light of the overall structure of the *Charter*, our legal and political traditions, our history, and the changing needs and demands of modern society.

Perhaps the most often cited passage describing the nature of this exercise of purposive interpretation is from the judgment of Dickson J in *R v Big M Drug Mart Ltd*:

> In my view, this analysis is to be undertaken, and the purpose of the right or freedom in question is to be sought by reference to the character and the larger objects of the *Charter* itself, to the language chosen to articulate the specific right or freedom, to the historical origins of the concepts enshrined, and where applicable, to the meaning and purpose of the other specific rights and freedoms with which it is associated within the text of the *Charter*. The interpretation should be, as the judgment in *Southam* emphasizes, a generous rather than a legalistic one, aimed at fulfilling the purpose of the guarantee and securing for individuals the full benefit of the *Charter*'s protection. At the same time it is important not to overshoot the actual purpose of the right or freedom in question, but to recall that the *Charter* was not enacted in a vacuum, and must therefore, as this Court's decision in *Law Society of Upper Canada v Skapinker* illustrates, be placed in its proper linguistic, philosophic and historical contexts.[39]

The purposive method of interpretation is indicative of the most significant effect of the *Charter* upon the role of the judiciary. *Charter*

---

38   R Dworkin, *Taking Rights Seriously* (Cambridge: Harvard University Press, 1977) at 134.

39   [1985] 1 SCR 295 at 344, 18 DLR (4th) 321 [*Big M Drug Mart*].

adjudication is anything but the mechanical application of pre-established rules. The judges are called upon to delve deeply into the very foundations of our legal system and political culture to answer questions of the most fundamental nature, and many of these questions cannot be answered adequately by reference only to traditional legal sources.

2) The Contextual Method

Although the purposive approach to interpretation remains the dominant approach to the interpretation of the *Charter*, a growing number of cases emphasize the need to take a contextual approach to the interpretation of *Charter* rights. A contextual approach will most often be used to impose some definitional limits on *Charter* rights and when the court assesses whether a limit on a *Charter* right is reasonable under section 1 of the *Charter*.

One example of a contextual approach to the interpretation of a *Charter* right is the emphasis given to the context of Canadian democracy when interpreting section 3 of the *Charter* to require effective representation as opposed to a strict "one person, one vote" standard for electoral districts. The Supreme Court's interpretation of the right to vote was influenced by contextual factors such as Canadian history and geography.[40] A contextual approach is also often taken when the courts interpret section 7 of the *Charter* which provides that "everyone has the right to life, liberty and security of the person and the right not to be deprived thereof except in accordance with the principles of fundamental justice."[41] When interpreting section 7 of the *Charter*, the Court has drawn a distinction between matters of public policy or philosophy and matters that fall "squarely within 'the inherent domain of the judiciary as a guardian of the justice system.'"[42] Thus the Court ruled that extradition of a fugitive without assurances that the death penalty would not be imposed would generally violate section 7 not because of any conclusion about the morality or efficacy of the death penalty, but because of the contextual factors of Canadian and foreign experience of wrongful convictions and a growing international movement towards abolition of the death penalty and Canada's participation in that movement. The Court has also rejected concepts such as that

---

40 *Reference Re Provincial Electoral Boundaries (Saskatchewan)*, [1991] 2 SCR 158, 81 DLR (4th) 16. For further discussion, see Chapter 11.

41 Discussed in Chapter 13.

42 *United States of America v Burns*, [2001] 1 SCR 283, 195 DLR (4th) 1 at para 38.

the criminal law should be used only to protect others from harm[43] or that criminal law should reflect the best interests of the child,[44] on the basis that there was not a sufficient societal consensus that such principles were essential to the administration of justice. The Court has also taken a contextual approach in determining the extent of *Charter* rights in the regulatory or criminal context. The accused will generally have diminished *Charter* rights when operating in a regulated or licensed field, but will have access to full *Charter* rights when the predominant purpose of the state is to determine penal liability.[45]

Contextual factors also play a crucial role in the interpretation of equality rights.[46] From the start, the Supreme Court has rejected the idea that every inequality in the law will violate the *Charter* and has called for an examination of whether a particular inequality will result in discrimination when viewed in a larger political and social context.[47] A feature of the test for determining when equality rights in section 15 of the *Charter* are violated is an open-ended list of "contextual factors" that includes whether there is pre-existing disadvantage and whether the government is attempting to ameliorate disadvantage. The current test also endorses a contextual approach to interpretation by suggesting that the relevant point of view for determining whether an inequality in the law results in substantive discrimination "is that of a reasonable person, in circumstances similar to those of the claimant."[48]

A contextual approach that judges the *Charter* claim in a larger social context is also very important for determining whether a limitation on a *Charter* right is justified and reasonable under section 1 of the *Charter*. In an early *Charter* case holding that Sunday closing laws enacted for the secular purpose of providing a common day of rest were a reasonable limit on religious freedom, Dickson CJC observed that the courts should be cautious about allowing the *Charter* to "become an instrument of better situated individuals to roll back legislation that has as its object the improvement of the conditions of less advantaged persons."[49] As discussed in Chapter 4, the Supreme Court

---

43   R v *Malmo-Levine, R v Caine*, [2003] 3 SCR 571 at para 103. For further discussion, see Chapter 13.

44   *Canadian Foundation for Children, Youth and the Law v Canada (Attorney General)*, [2004] 1 SCR 76 at para 8. For further discussion, see Chapter 13.

45   R v *Jarvis*, [2002] 3 SCR 757 at paras 63–65. For further discussion, see Chapter 14.

46   Discussed in Chapter 15.

47   *Andrews v Law Society (British Columbia)*, [1989] 1 SCR 143, 56 DLR (4th) 1 [*Andrews*].

48   *Law v Canada*, [1999] 1 SCR 497 at para 88. For further discussion, see Chapter 15.

49   *Edwards Books & Art Ltd v R*, [1986] 2 SCR 713, 35 DLR (4th) 1 at 49 [*Edwards Books*], discussed in Chapter 4.

has also taken into account the context of social and economic policy and legislative attempts to mediate between competing groups when determining whether particular limits on rights are reasonable. Indeed, the Court has even viewed the context of a severe financial crisis in a province as an important factor in determining whether legislation that deferred and extinguished part of a pay equity scheme for female health-care workers was justified under section 1 of the *Charter*.[50] Both in determining the ambit of some *Charter* rights and the justification for limiting *Charter* rights, the courts pay attention to the wider social and political context of the *Charter* claim.

Social science evidence can be decisive in certain cases. Evidence of this kind relates to what are called "social or legislative facts," as distinct from questions of "adjudicative fact." The former deals with the operation and effect of legislation, while the latter deals with the actual conduct and events at issue in the case. In *Canada (Attorney General) v Bedford*,[51] the successful challenge to the *Criminal Code* provisions banning certain activities associated with prostitution rested on social science evidence that the effect of the laws was not to protect vulnerable sex-trade workers, but rather to put them at risk of physical harm.

3) The Reconciliation of Competing Rights

One of the most difficult dilemmas for courts in interpreting *Charter* rights is how to deal with claims of competing and potentially conflicting rights. For example, what should be done when a person's right to freedom of expression in the context of hate speech or pornography could affect the right of a disadvantaged group to enjoy the equal protection of the law? What should happen when the accused's right to full answer and defence and disclosure of the state's case could conflict with a complainant's right to privacy and equality with respect to confidential documents? What should happen when freedom of religion competes with equality rights on issues such as same-sex marriage?

The Supreme Court has rejected a hierarchical approach to rights that places some *Charter* rights above others. For example, it has rejected pre-*Charter* common law that placed the accused's right to a fair trial before freedom of expression and has urged courts to balance and reconcile fair trial and free expression rights. Thus courts should restrict expression by ordering publication bans only when necessary to prevent a real and substantial risk to the accused's right to a fair trial

---

50 *Newfoundland (Treasury Board) v NAPE*, [2004] 3 SCR 381.
51 [2013] 3 SCR 1101, discussed in Chapter 13.

and only after considering the adequacy of reasonable alternatives that are more respectful of freedom of expression. In the final analysis, the court must determine that the benefits of any proposed publication ban outweigh its harms after considering all of the relevant rights, including the accused's right to a fair trial and the public's right to freedom of expression.[52]

The Supreme Court has indicated that courts must try to reconcile equality rights with religious freedom as much as possible. For example, religious freedom should protect a Christian college from being refused certification as a teachers college even though the college teaches that homosexuality is a sin, but it may not protect individual teachers who act on such beliefs.[53] In most cases, freedom of religion would protect religious officials from being required to perform same-sex marriages, but freedom of religion would not prevent the recognition of same-sex marriage as a matter of secular law.[54]

In a case dealing with the controversial issue of whether courts and judges should have access to the private therapeutic documents of complainants in sexual assault cases, the Supreme Court has indicated that the accused's right to full answer and defence should be defined in a manner that reconciles that right with the competing privacy and equality rights of the complainant in sexual assault cases. This reconciliation of rights takes place outside of the section 1 justification process under which the state bears the burden of demonstrating that limits on *Charter* rights are demonstrably justifiable.[55] At the same time, however, the internal reconciliation process draws on factors such as reasonable alternatives that are quite important under section 1 of the *Charter*.

Another manifestation of the Supreme Court's commitment to reconciling competing rights is its refusal to allow one *Charter* right to nullify another constitutional right. For example, the Court has rejected arguments that denominational schools that were constitutionally protected before the enactment of the *Charter*[56] or specific minority language rights[57] are inconsistent with equality rights because they

---

52   R v Mentuck, [2001] 3 SCR 442; *Dagenais v Canadian Broadcasting Corp*, [1994] 3 SCR 835. For further discussion, see Chapter 9.
53   *Trinity Western University v British Columbia College of Teachers*, [2001] 1 SCR 772.
54   *Reference Re Same-Sex Marriage*, above note 35; *EGALE Canada Inc. v Canada (Attorney General)* (2003), 225 DLR (4th) 472 (BCCA); *Halpern v Canada (Attorney General)* (2003), 65 OR (3d) 161 (CA).
55   R v Mills, [1999] 3 SCR 668 at para 66.
56   *Reference Re Bill 30, An Act to Amend the Education Act (Ontario)*, [1987] 1 SCR 1148; *Adler v Ontario*, [1996] 3 SCR 609.
57   *Gosselin (Tutor of) v Quebec (Attorney General)*, 2005 SCC 15.

single out particular minorities for preferential treatment. One constitutional right should not be allowed to nullify another.

The courts also confront the problems of competing rights under section 1 of the *Charter*. This issue has frequently arisen in the context of freedom of expression claims. The courts have interpreted the right to freedom of expression in a broad and purposive manner to include speech such as hate speech and pornography that may cause harms to others. At the same time, however, the courts have recognized that competing rights, such as equality rights, are at stake and constitute governmental objectives that are important enough to justify restrictions on freedom of expression.[58]

4) Interpretive Sources

The task of *Charter* interpretation has structure and discipline. The first source is obvious — the language of the *Charter* itself. For example, the recognition of Aboriginal rights, commitment to multiculturalism, and protection of affirmative action in section 15(2) all helped the Supreme Court to determine that the meaning of equality in section 15(1) did not require that all must be treated in the same way and that equality sometimes requires different treatment for different individuals and groups.[59]

Although the Supreme Court has avoided an overtly philosophical approach, many of its opinions are sprinkled with references to philosophical writings. In *Dolphin Delivery*, the first case to interpret the meaning of freedom of expression, reference was made to the writings of John Stuart Mill and John Milton in elaborating the meaning of freedom of expression.[60] In fact, Mill has been cited with some frequency in a range of cases,[61] as has Ronald Dworkin.[62] Justice Wilson was probably the most frequent user of philosophical materials in her years on

---

58   *Keegstra*, above note 20.
59   *Andrews*, above note 47.
60   *RWDSU, Local 580 v Dolphin Delivery Ltd*, [1986] 2 SCR 573 at 583, 33 DLR (4th) 174 [*Dolphin Delivery*].
61   *Reference Re Public Service Employee Relations Act (Alberta)*, [1987] 1 SCR 313 at 365, 38 DLR (4th) 161, Dickson CJC; *Jones v R*, [1986] 2 SCR 284 at 318, 31 DLR (4th) 569 [*Jones*], Wilson J.
62   *Edwards Books*, above note 49 at 809 (SCR), Wilson J; *Operation Dismantle Inc v R*, [1985] 1 SCR 441 at 481, 18 DLR (4th) 481, Wilson J; *R v Therens*, [1985] 1 SCR 613 at 638, 18 DLR (4th) 655, LeDain J.

the bench as she strove to give meaning to the rights and freedoms in the early days of *Charter* interpretation.[63]

While the Supreme Court rejected appeals to original intent, the judges have nevertheless looked to historical material and traditions to inform the meaning of the rights. In *Big M Drug Mart*, the first major case on freedom of religion, Dickson J looked back in history to determine the rationale for protecting individuals' choice of religion, noting the many excesses of governments in the past to suppress religions with which they did not agree.[64] Justice McLachlin, in the first case on electoral boundaries under section 3, looked closer to home to determine the meaning of the right to vote within Canadian history. In rejecting an interpretation that guaranteed "one person, one vote," as in the United States, she drew on Canada's history (and geography) to explain why the right in Canada should aspire towards equality of voters in various electoral constituencies while at the same time emphasizing a right to effective representation. With quotations from our first prime minister, Sir John A Macdonald, and other references to tradition, she concluded:

> [T]he history of our right to vote and the context in which it existed at the time the *Charter* was adopted support the conclusion that the purpose of the guarantee of the right to vote is not to effect perfect voter equality, in so far as that can be done, but the broader goal of guaranteeing effective representation . . . . [D]emocracy in Canada is rooted in a different history than in the United States . . . .[65]

Justice McLachlin made it clear that she did not accept history or tradition as definitive. However, she did insist that the *Charter* should be seen as a Canadian document rooted in certain cultural and historical traditions that courts should take into consideration.[66]

---

63   For example, in an opinion in a case dealing with language rights under s 133 of the *Constitution Act, 1867*, she includes an extensive discussion of the views of various legal philosophers — Hohfeld, Austin, Hart, Stone, and Salmond — on the meaning of rights: *MacDonald v Montreal (City)*, [1986] 1 SCR 460 at 515–18, 27 DLR (4th) 321. She also cites the writings of various philosophers when elaborating the meaning of "liberty" in s 7: *R v Morgentaler*, [1988] 1 SCR 30 at 178–79, 44 DLR (4th) 385; *Jones*, above note 61 at 318–19 (SCR); *Reference Re ss 193 and 195.1(1)(c) of the Criminal Code (Canada)*, [1990] 1 SCR 1123, 56 CCC (3d) 65 at 135.

64   *Big M Drug Mart*, above note 39.

65   *Reference Re Provincial Electoral Boundaries (Saskatchewan)*, above note 40 at 184 (SCR).

66   *Ibid*. For example, she stated at 187 (SCR): This is not to suggest, however, that inequities in our voting system are to be accepted merely because they have

The Supreme Court has also been asked to look outside Canada's borders to assist in the interpretation of rights. In some cases, the meaning of a right in other countries is discussed. Often but not always, American sources are used. Increasingly, reference is made to norms of international law, such as Canada's commitments under the *International Covenant on Economic, Social and Cultural Rights*, the *International Covenant on Civil and Political Rights*, conventions of the International Labour Organization, and the *Convention on the Elimination of Racial Discrimination*. The Court has said that "the *Charter* should be presumed to provide at least as great a level of protection as is found in the international human rights documents that Canada has ratified."[67]

The use of international norms is a reflection of the fact that the rights and freedoms guaranteed by the *Charter* are specific emanations of internationally recognized human rights. While international treaties are not directly enforceable in Canadian courts, the Supreme Court does see international commitments as a valid consideration, concluding that the *Charter* should be interpreted, where possible, in a manner consistent with Canada's international obligations.[68] In a recent case concerning section 7, the Court stated: "[O]ur concern is not with Canada's international obligations *qua* obligations; rather our concern is with the principles of fundamental justice. We look to international law as evidence of these principles and not as controlling in itself."[69] Similarly, in cases involving collective bargaining rights, the Court has held that "Canada's current international law commitments and the current state of international thought on human rights provide a persuasive source for interpreting the scope of the *Charter*."[70] As noted in Chapter 13, the decision in *Canada (Justice) v Khadr*[71] reflects the importance of Canada's international human rights obligations in the in-

---

historical precedent. History is important in so far as it suggests that the philosophy underlying the development of the right to vote in this country is the broad goal of effective representation. It has nothing to do with the specious argument that historical anomalies and abuses can be used to justify continued anomalies and abuses, or to suggest that the right to vote should not be interpreted broadly and remedially as befits *Charter* rights.

67 *Health Services and Support — Facilities Subsector Bargaining Assn v British Columbia*, [2007] 2 SCR 391 at para 70 [*Health Services*].

68 For example, see the reasons of Dickson CJC in *Slaight Communications Inc v Davidson*, [1989] 1 SCR 1038 at 1056–57, 59 DLR (4th) 416.

69 *Suresh v Minister of Citizenship and Immigration and Attorney General of Canada*, 2002 SCC 1, 208 DLR (4th) 1 at 32.

70 *Health Services*, above note 67 at para 78; *Saskatchewan Federation of Labour v Saskatchewan*, [2015] 1 SCR 245.

71 2008 SCC 28.

terpretation of section 7 rights. That decision suggests that a violation of Canada's international human rights obligations may also constitute a violation of the principles of fundamental justice in section 7 that requires application of the *Charter* to activities of Canadian officials outside of Canada. These cases reflect a shift from the traditional "dualist" tradition according to which Canada's international commitment had to be specifically incorporated into domestic law and towards a position where international obligations have more immediate impact.

C. CONCLUSION

Judges are subject to significant restraints when interpreting the *Charter*. They must pay heed to its language, to past decisions under the doctrine of precedent, and to the respective institutional roles of the courts and the legislatures, albeit redefined by the *Charter*. Yet it is apparent that judicial interpretation of the rights and freedoms guaranteed by the *Charter* has proved to be a complex and controversial task that, at times, involves the difficult burden of reconciling competing rights. Our legal regime does not provide judges with precise rules to guide them in this exercise. Indeed, our constitutional tradition directs the courts to resist the argument that the language of the constitution has a rigid and fixed meaning. The constitution is seen as an organic document that must grow with the times and remain capable of responding to the demands of a changing society. The debate about the *Charter*'s meaning is legal in structure, but the purposive and contextual approaches adopted by the Supreme Court to *Charter* interpretation require the judges to consider a rich array of historical, philosophical, and comparative sources.

FURTHER READINGS

ARBOUR, L, & F LAFONTAINE, "Beyond Self-Congratulation: The *Charter* at 25 in an International Perspective" (2007) 45 Osgoode Hall LJ 239

BAKAN, J, *Just Words: Constitutional Rights and Social Wrongs* (Toronto: University of Toronto Press, 1997)

BASTARACHE, M, "The *Canadian Charter of Rights and Freedoms*: Domestic Application of Universal Values" (2003) 19 Sup. Ct. L. Rev. (2d) 371

BEATTY, DM, *Talking Heads and the Supremes: The Canadian Production of Constitutional Review* (Toronto: Carswell, 1990)

GOLDSWORTHY, J, *Interpreting Constitutions: A Comparative Study* (Oxford: Oxford University Press, 2007)

HOGG, PW, "The *Charter of Rights* and American Theories of Interpretation" (1987) 15 Osgoode Hall LJ 87

———, "Interpreting the *Charter of Rights*: Generosity and Justification" (1990) 28 Osgoode Hall LJ 817

HUSCROFT, G, "A Constitutional 'Work in Progress': The *Charter* and the Limits of Progressive Interpretation" (2004) 25 Sup Ct L Rev 241

———, & B MILLER, eds, *The Challenge of Originalism* (Cambridge: Cambridge University Press, 2011)

LEBEL, L, "The Rise of International Law in Canadian Constitutional Litigation: Fugue or Fusion?" (2002) 16 Sup Ct L Rev (2d) 23

ROACH, K, "Dialogic Judicial Review and Its Critics" (2004) 23 Sup Ct L Rev (2d) 49

ROTHSTEIN, THE HONOURABLE JUSTICE M, "Checks and Balances in Constitutional Interpretation" (2016) 79 Sask L Rev 1

SCHABAS, W, & S BEAULAC, *International Human Rights and Canadian Law: Legal Commitment, Implementation and the* Charter, 3d ed (Toronto: Thomson, 2007)

TRAKMAN, LE, *Reasoning with the* Charter (Toronto: Butterworths, 1991)

WEINRIB, L, "Canada's *Charter of Rights*: Paradigm Lost?" (2002) 6 Rev Const Stud 119

———, "A Primer on International Law and the *Charter*" (2007) 21 NJCL 313

CHAPTER 4

LIMITATION OF
CHARTER RIGHTS

A central task in the interpretation of any instrument guaranteeing fundamental rights and freedoms is to reconcile the rights of the individual with the interests of the community at large. The effect of the *Charter* is to shift an important share of responsibility for this task from the elected representatives of the people to the judiciary. In light of the Supreme Court's generous definition of most enumerated rights through the purposive method of interpretation described in Chapter 3, it is not surprising to find that the Court places heavy reliance on the second stage of *Charter* adjudication, defining the limitation of rights. This is mandated by section 1, which provides that the rights and freedoms guaranteed are "subject only to such reasonable limits prescribed by law as can be demonstrably justified in a free and democratic society." The Supreme Court has interpreted that provision as encompassing both a formal and a substantive element — the formal element is caught by the words "prescribed by law" and the substantive element is contained in an examination of the state's justification for limiting the right and its chosen means for doing so. At the same time, the imposition of definitional limits on some *Charter* rights — most notably, sections 7, 8, and 12 of the *Charter*, suggests that it may be more difficult for the government to justify limits on rights after laws have been found to violate such rights. This is particularly the case if the Court has determined that some substantive aspects of proportionality have been violated in the course of finding a rights violation. In other words, the Court's approach to section 1 will inevitably be influenced by how narrowly or broadly the Court defines the underlying right.

A. LIMITS PRESCRIBED BY LAW

The first requirement for a justifiable limit is that it be, in the words of section 1, "prescribed by law." Initially, the courts refused to uphold laws that conferred an open-ended or vaguely defined discretion to limit protected freedoms. Thus, for example, the courts struck down as too ill-defined a customs regulation that allowed officials to restrict entry into Canada of materials that they considered to be "immoral."[1] Similarly, a provincial scheme conferring the power of censorship on a film board without setting out the criteria by which such powers were to be exercised was struck down as a violation of freedom of expression that was not prescribed by law.[2]

In the words of LeDain J, "the requirement that the limit be prescribed by law is chiefly concerned with the distinction between a limit imposed by law and one that is arbitrary."[3] In that case, a *Charter* violation could not be justified under section 1 because the legislation authorizing the police to require a driver to provide a breath sample did not clearly authorize a denial or limitation of the detainee's right to counsel. Following this approach, section 1 does not play a role in many *Charter* challenges to the exercise of police powers, where the police officer's actions in limiting the *Charter* right are not specifically authorized or prescribed by law. This was reaffirmed in *Little Sisters*, where the Supreme Court stated: "Violative conduct by government officials that is not authorized by statute is not 'prescribed by law' and cannot therefore be justified under section 1." In such cases, courts must "therefore proceed directly to the remedy phase of the analysis."[4]

There are important justifications for a rigorous approach to the "prescribed by law" requirement under section 1 of the *Charter*. Government actions that infringe *Charter* rights should be accompanied by notice to citizens of the conduct that is permitted and prohibited so that they can regulate their activities accordingly. Similarly, the law should

---

1   *Luscher v Deputy Minister of National Revenue (Customs & Excise)*, [1985] 1 FC 85, 17 DLR (4th) 503.

2   *Re Ontario Film & Video Appreciation Society and Ontario Board of Censors* (1984), 5 DLR (4th) 766 (Ont CA).

3   *R v Therens*, [1985] 1 SCR 613, 18 DLR (4th) 655 at 680 [*Therens*].

4   *Little Sisters Book and Art Emporium v Canada (Minister of Justice)*, [2000] 2 SCR 1120, 193 DLR (4th) 193 at para 141 [*Little Sisters*].

set adequate limits on officials who exercise discretion in applying and enforcing the law, and limits on *Charter* rights should be clearly stated to encourage democratic debate and accountability about such limitations.

Despite these concerns, the courts have more often tended to apply a relatively relaxed standard under the "prescribed by law" require-ment. A common law rule or a regulation, in addition to legislation, can constitute a limit "prescribed by law."[5] As an example, a public transit authority's policy, adopted pursuant to a statutory power, on what ad-vertising it would accept for display on the sides of buses, was held to be a form of "law" that satisfies the "prescribed by law" requirement,[6] as was a ministerial directive limiting the activities of journalists with-in courthouses.[7] A limitation on freedom of expression was held to be "prescribed by law" even though the labour relations adjudicator made the restriction in the exercise of a general remedial discretion that did not specifically contemplate remedial orders that would restrict *Charter* rights.[8] A more recent case holds that, where a discretionary decision is challenged on *Charter* grounds, section 1 does not apply and the case is to be decided on the administrative law reasonableness standard that centres on proportionality. Decisions that disproportionately interfere with a *Charter* right will invariably be struck down as unreasonable.[9]

It has also been held that limitations can be implicitly "prescribed by law." For example, a *Criminal Code* provision providing for a road-side breathalyzer test implicitly authorizes a limitation on the right to counsel by requiring that the sample be provided "forthwith" without access to counsel.[10] Although the Court held in *Therens* that a viola-tion of the right to counsel was not prescribed by law with respect to the application of an evidential breathalyzer, twenty years later it held that roadside sobriety tests were authorized by the combined ef-fect of provincial and federal laws governing roadside stops and despite a strong dissent that limits on the *Charter* right to counsel should be

---

5   *Irwin Toy Ltd v Quebec*, [1989] 1 SCR 927 (regulation); *R v Swain*, [1991] 1 SCR 933 (common law rule). At the same time, administrative guidelines cannot constitute a limit that is prescribed by law or a source of law that can be directly challenged under the *Charter* because "it is simply not feasible for the courts to review for *Charter* compliance the vast array of manuals and guides prepared by the public service for the internal guidance of officials." *Little Sisters*, above note 4 at para 85.

6   *Greater Vancouver Transportation Authority v Canadian Federation of Students* — *British Columbia Component*, [2009] 2 SCR 295 [*Greater Vancouver*].

7   *Canadian Broadcasting Corp v Canada (Attorney General)*, [2011] 1 SCR 19 [*CBC*].

8   *Slaight Communications Inc v Davidson*, [1989] 1 SCR 1038, 59 DLR (4th) 416.

9   *Doré v Barreau du Québec*, [2012] 1 SCR 395.

10   *R v Thomsen*, [1988] 1 SCR 640.

more clearly prescribed by law.[11] The Supreme Court has also accepted that an open-ended legislative provision allowing police to stop drivers is a "prescribed by law" limit on the right against arbitrary detention in section 9 of the *Charter*.[12] Finally, a majority of the Court in *Little Sisters* upheld customs legislation despite evidence that custom officials had frequently erred in applying the standard of detaining obscene material. The Court stated: "While there is evidence of actual abuse here, there is the potential for abuse in many areas, and a rule requiring Parliament to enact in each case special procedures for the protection of *Charter* rights would be unnecessarily rigid."[13]

The issue of whether a limit on a *Charter* right is "prescribed by law" is also connected with the issue of vagueness. Excessively vague laws that do not define powers in a precise manner do not provide effective limitations on the exercise of those powers. Here again, the trend is towards a more relaxed approach that leaves the legislature room to limit *Charter* rights by the use of vague terms. The Supreme Court has stated that merely because a law is subject to various shadings of interpretation does not render it unacceptably vague.[14] In some instances, laws that appear more than unusually vague and uncertain have been upheld.[15] The cases that have considered the vagueness point in most detail have arisen under the fundamental-justice guarantee in section 7 and are discussed in Chapter 13. As will be seen there, the Supreme Court has said that, since laws define standards of general application, there is an inherent element of uncertainty in all laws. While there must be some limit to open-ended and ill-defined standards, the vagueness argument is not one that has found favour with the Supreme Court in recent years.

---

11   *R v Orbanski; R v Elias*, [2005] 2 SCR 3 at para 52.

12   *R v Hufsky*, [1999] 1 SCR 621; *R v Ladouceur*, [1990] 1 SCR 1257. Note, however, that a stop that is not conducted for valid reasons related to traffic safety will not constitute a reasonable limit on the right against arbitrary detention, and the *Charter* analysis will proceed directly from the rights violation to the remedy phase: *R v Mellenthin*, [1992] 3 SCR 615.

13   *Little Sisters*, above note 4 at para 137.

14   *R v Lucas*, [1998] 1 SCR 439, 157 DLR (4th) 423 [*Lucas*].

15   *Suresh v Canada*, [2002] 1 SCR 3, 208 DLR (4th) 1 [*Suresh*] (undefined reference to "terrorism" and "national security" in immigration legislation not unconstitutionally vague); *Little Sisters*, above note 4 at para 145 (undefined reference to the prohibition of "obscene" material not unconstitutionally vague and satisfying "prescribed by law" requirement for a limitation on freedom of expression); *Greater Vancouver*, above note 6 at para 54: "[u]nless the impugned law 'is so obscure as to be incapable of interpretation with any degree of precision using the ordinary tools,' it will be deemed to have met the 'prescribed by law' requirement."

B. PROPORTIONALITY

The text of the *Charter* says little about how limitations on rights are to be justified, but the Supreme Court of Canada, employing the purposive approach, established the basic framework for analysis in *R v Oakes*.[16] It is at the justification stage that a court must consider the interest in limiting a right or freedom and weigh collective interests or the competing rights of other individuals against the right of the claimant. The reconciliation of the competing interests against individual rights is achieved by focusing on the legitimacy of the government's objective and the "proportionality" between the means chosen to achieve that objective and the burden on the rights claimant.

In addition to the "prescribed by law" requirement discussed above, there are four steps to the section 1 analysis:

1) The objective of the measure must be important enough to warrant overriding a *Charter* right.
2) There must be a rational connection between the limit on the *Charter* right and the legislative objective.
3) The limit should impair the *Charter* right as little as possible.
4) There should be an overall balance or proportionality between the benefits of the limit and its deleterious effects.

1) Sufficiently Important Objective

First, it must be established that there is an objective "of sufficient importance to warrant overriding a constitutionally protected right or freedom."[17] In *Oakes*, the Supreme Court of Canada said that the objective must "relate to concerns which are pressing and substantial in a free and democratic society." The courts have been relatively deferential to legislative judgment of the importance of the objective. However, the government has failed on a number of occasions to satisfy this requirement. In one case, the Supreme Court held that Quebec legislation limiting the rights of English-speaking parents to have their children attend English-language schools unless the parents had been

---

16   [1986] 1 SCR 103, 26 DLR (4th) 200 [*Oakes*]. For a good discussion of the evolution of s 1, see PW Hogg, "Section 1 Revisited" (1991) 1 NJCL 1; E Mendes, "Section 1 of the *Charter* after 30 Years: The Soul or the Dagger at its Heart?" in E Mendes & S Beaulac, eds, *The* Canadian Charter of Rights and Freedoms, 5th ed (Markham, ON: LexisNexis, 2013).

17   *R v Big M Drug Mart Ltd*, [1985] 1 SCR 295 at 352, 18 DLR (4th) 321 [*Big M Drug Mart*], Dickson CJC.

educated in English in Quebec constituted a direct attack on the very right enshrined in section 23 of the *Charter*, and hence the law was not motivated by a proper objective.[18] In another early *Charter* case, the Supreme Court indicated that compelling the observance of the Christian Sabbath was not a satisfactory objective for limiting the rights of non-Christians by requiring stores to close on Sundays. This objective was not satisfactory because "it would justify the law upon the very basis upon which it is attacked for violating s 2(a)," namely, the protection of freedom of all religions and not just the religion of Christians.[19] Similarly, in an Ontario case, the Court of Appeal held that legislation requiring the recital of the Lord's Prayer in non-denominational public schools constituted an attempt to impose a form of religious observance and that such an objective was not permitted by the guarantee of freedom of religion.[20] In all these cases, the stated objective denied rather than limited or qualified the right. As McLachlin CJC put it in a right-to-vote case, "a simple majoritarian political preference for abolishing a right altogether would not be a constitutionally valid objective."[21] In another case, the Supreme Court dealt with a challenge to a vague law prohibiting the spreading of "false news."[22] Given the ancient origin of the law, it was unclear what its objective was at the time it was enacted. While the law was now used to deal with hate propaganda, it had not been designed for that purpose, and the majority of the Court held that it was not acceptable for the government to advance a new objective or shifting purpose not in the mind of Parliament when the law was enacted.

---

18 *Quebec (Attorney General) v Quebec Association of Protestant School Boards*, [1984] 2 SCR 66, 10 DLR (4th) 321. *Nguyen v Quebec (Education, Recreation and Sports)*, [2009] 3 SCR 208, makes it clear that s 1 can apply to language rights.

19 *Big M Drug Mart*, above note 17. The Court indicated that a secular justification for a common day of rest was acceptable, but not available in this case because the impugned *Lord's Day Act* had been enacted by Parliament as a criminal law for religious reasons, and legislation in relation to a common day of rest for workers could be enacted only by the provinces. The Court subsequently accepted the secular justification for provincial Sunday closing laws and found them to be a justified restriction on freedom of religion. See *Edwards Books & Art Ltd v R*, [1986] 2 SCR 713, 35 DLR (4th) 1 [*Edwards Books*]. See Chapter 8, Section A, for further discussion.

20 *Zylberberg v Sudbury Board of Education (Director)* (1988), 52 DLR (4th) 577 (Ont CA).

21 *Sauvé v Canada (Chief Electoral Officer)*, [2002] 3 SCR 519 at para 20 [*Sauvé*] (denying federal inmates the right to vote).

22 *R v Zundel*, [1992] 2 SCR 731, 95 DLR (4th) 202.

In *Vriend v Alberta*,[23] the Supreme Court found that Alberta had failed to articulate any objective or purpose that would be achieved by denying the protection of its human rights law to gays and lesbians. As Iacobucci J stated, to sustain a limit on a protected freedom, a government must offer more than an explanation why it chose to deny the right — it must be pursuing some objective: "An 'objective,' being a goal or an 'explanation' which makes plain that which is not immediately obvious."[24] The Court also hinted that the "legislative omission is on its face the very antithesis of the principles involved in the legislation as a whole" which, like the *Charter*, was concerned with preventing discrimination and protecting the equal dignity of all persons.

On the other hand, the state has not been held to a strict standard of proof of the harm at which challenged legislation is aimed.[25] Indeed, in most cases, the Court has accepted the objective once asserted without the need for evidence.[26] Cases in which the government fails to satisfy this first branch of the section 1 test are the exception rather than the rule. One study has concluded that, in 97 percent of cases, the state is readily able to satisfy the court that the law being challenged is motivated by a permissible objective of sufficient weight.[27]

Although courts will accept most articulated and non-discriminatory legislative objectives as sufficiently important to limit *Charter* rights, this first step in proportionality analysis can have a crucial effect on subsequent stages of the analysis. As the Court observed in *Toronto Star Newspapers Ltd v Canada*,[28] "all steps of the *Oakes* test are premised on a proper identification of the objective of the impugned measure."

If the court defines the legislative objective broadly, it may be more difficult for the government to demonstrate that there has been minimal impairment of the right and that there is no less restrictive means to advance the legislative objective. On the other hand, if the objective is defined more narrowly, it may be easier to justify the limitation as

---

23   [1998] 1 SCR 493, 156 DLR (4th) 385.

24   *Ibid* at para 114. See also *Canada (Attorney General) v Hislop*, [2007] 1 SCR 429 (no pressing and substantial objective to justify denial of spousal benefits to gay couple); *Canada (Attorney General) v PHS Community Services Society*, [2011] 3 SCR 134 at para 137 [*PHS Community Services*] (minister's refusal of exemption from drug laws for safe injection site bearing no relation to law's health and safety objectives).

25   *Harper v Canada (Attorney General)*, [2004] 1 SCR 827 at para 90 [*Harper*]. See also discussion in Section B(2), below in this chapter.

26   *R v Bryan*, [2007] 1 SCR 527 at paras 32–34.

27   L Trakman *et al*, "*R v Oakes* 1986–1987: Back to the Drawing Board" (1998) 36 Osgoode Hall LJ 83 at 95.

28   [2010] 1 SCR 721 at para 20.

a proportionate means of advancing the particular objective. Indeed, if the objective is defined too narrowly, there is a danger that the rest of the proportionality analysis may become "no more than a pair of tautologies"[29] that are self-fulfilling. The Supreme Court has indicated that under section 1 of the *Charter*, "it is desirable to state the purpose of the limiting provision as precisely and specifically as possible so as to provide a clear framework for evaluating its importance, and the precision with which the means have been crafted to fulfil that objective."[30] "Vague and symbolic objectives" render proportionality analysis hollow and "almost guarantee a positive answer."[31] One exception to this general preference for a fairly narrow definition of the objective is in the case of under-inclusive legislation, in which case the courts will examine not only the purposes of the unconstitutional omission, but also of the legislation as a whole.[32]

2) Rational Connection between Limit and Objective

The next phase in proportionality review is to consider whether there is a rational, non-arbitrary, non-capricious connection between the legislative objective and the law that is challenged.

At this second stage, the courts again have been deferential, and it is rare to find that there is no rational connection between the legislative objective and the law that is subject to scrutiny. As Iacobucci J remarked in a freedom of expression case, "[t]his test is not particularly onerous."[33] In the *Oakes* case, however, the Supreme Court held that there was no rational connection between the objective of curbing traffic in drugs and a law that reversed the usual onus of proof in criminal cases and required anyone found in possession of any amount of drugs to prove that he or she did not have the intent to traffic. In the Court's view, there was a lack of internal rationality in the legislation, because the reverse-onus provision assumed that an individual in possession of even a very small amount of a drug would be likely to traffic. In the words of Dickson CJC:

> [P]ossession of a small or negligible quantity of narcotics does not support the inference of trafficking. In other words, it would be ir-

---

29   PW Hogg, *Constitutional Law of Canada*, 5th ed (Toronto: Carswell, 2007) at 35.9(a).

30   *Thomson Newspapers Co v Canada (Attorney General)*, [1998] 1 SCR 877 at para 98 [*Thomson Newspapers*].

31   *Sauvé*, above note 21 at para 22.

32   *M v H*, [1999] 2 SCR 3, 171 DLR (4th) 577.

33   *Little Sisters*, above note 4 at para 228.

rational to infer that a person had an intent to traffic on the basis of his or her possession of a very small quantity of narcotics. The presumption required under s 8 of the *Narcotic Control Act* is over-inclusive and could lead to results in certain cases which would defy both rationality and fairness.[34]

Most commentators suggest that the Court might more readily have justified striking down the law under the minimal impairment test, discussed below. Some have argued that there is a rational connection between the objective of suppressing drug trafficking and making convictions easier for the state by a reverse-onus clause.[35] However, the Court in *Oakes* not only looked at the rationality of the means to meet the objective from the state's point of view, but also considered the arbitrariness of the law with respect to the rights claimant, a consideration now more likely to be addressed under the minimal impairment and overall balance components.[36] Indeed in a subsequent case, the Court held that a requirement of internal rationality between the proven and presumed fact as required under the *Oakes* approach to rational connection was no longer required.[37] In other words, all that has to be established is that there is a rational connection between the limitation and the legislative objective of facilitating the detection and conviction of crime.

The rational connection test can be used to prevent the justification of laws based on arbitrary or discriminatory assumptions and a choice of discriminatory means to implement a standard will be vulnerable under the rational connection requirement. For example, the Supreme Court has indicated that requiring a security check for those born of Canadian mothers, but not of Canadian fathers, was not rationally connected to the legitimate objective of screening citizenship applicants.[38] Similarly, the exclusion of same-sex couples from support provisions was held not to be rationally connected to the objective of assisting women to deal with the financial hardships of the

---

34   *Oakes*, above note 16 at 142 (SCR).
35   See, for example, PJ Monahan & AJ Petter, "Developments in Constitutional Law (The 1986–87 Term)" (1988) 10 Sup Ct L Rev 61.
36   The way in which Dickson CJC phrased this stage of inquiry in *Oakes* is as follows: "[The measures] must not be arbitrary, unfair or based on irrational considerations. In short, they must be rationally connected to the objective." *Oakes*, above note 16 at 227 (DLR).
37   *R v Laba*, [1994] 3 SCR 965, 94 CCC (3d) 385 at 417.
38   *Benner v Canada (Secretary of State)*, [1997] 1 SCR 358 at para 95, 143 DLR (4th) 577.

breakdown of marriages and common law partnerships.[39] The Court has also found a lack of rational connection to the objective of ensuring a safe and welcoming public transit system by allowing commercial — but not political — advertisements on public transit vehicles.[40] A provision that only allowed for the use of dried medical marijuana as opposed to other forms was both arbitrary under section 7 and because of the "same disconnect" with the health and safety objectives also not rationally connected to those objectives.[41] Prohibiting the RCMP from engaging in any collective bargaining was held not to be rationally connected to the objective of ensuring a stable and neutral police force, given evidence that all other police forces were allowed to engage in collective bargaining.[42] These cases affirm that the rational connection test can be decisive,[43] but generally only with respect to laws that have irrational features.

Cases that reject the government's justification at the rational connection stage remain the exception rather than the rule. In *Chaoulli v Quebec (Attorney General)*,[44] McLachlin CJC and Major J (Bastarache J concurring) took a much more demanding approach to the rational connection requirement. They concluded that Quebec had failed to demonstrate that its prohibition on private health insurance was rationally connected to the objective of preserving the integrity of the health system because of "the absence of evidence that the prohibition on the purchase and sale of private health insurance protects the health care system." They also questioned "whether an arbitrary provision, which by reason of its arbitrariness cannot further its stated objective, will ever meet the rational connection test under *R v Oakes*."[45] This latter statement may suggest that three judges are willing to reconsider the post-*Oakes* jurisprudence that suggests that lack of internal rationality within a law that produces a violation of a *Charter* right is not necessarily fatal to a section 1 justification. Justices Binnie and LeBel (Fish J concurring) in dissent concluded that there was a rational connection between the prohibition of private medical insurance and the protection of the public health system on the basis of royal commission reports and

---

39   *M v H*, above note 32 at para 108.
40   *Greater Vancouver Transportation Authority v Canadian Federation of Students —
     British Columbia Component*, [2009] 2 SCR 295 at para 76.
41   *R v Smith*, [2015] 2 SCR 602 at para 29.
42   *Mounted Police Association of Ontario v Canada (Attorney General)*, 2015 SCC 1 at
     para 145 [*Mounted Police*].
43   See *Figueroa v Canada (Attorney General)*, [2003] 1 SCR 912 [*Figueroa*].
44   [2005] 1 SCR 791 [*Chaoulli*].
45   *Ibid* at para 155.

other policy statements.[46] They also rejected the argument that Quebec's prohibition on private insurance violated section 7 of the *Charter* because it was arbitrary. More recently, however, the Court has stated that to establish a rational connection, it is not necessary to demonstrate that the limit on a right "will *inevitably* achieve the government's objective. A reasonable inference that the means adopted by the government will help bring about the objective suffices."[47]

Rational connection between the limit on the *Charter* right and the legislative objective does not require scientific proof.[48] The Supreme Court has recognized that "[w]hile some matters can be proved with empirical or mathematical precision, others, involving philosophical, political and social considerations, cannot."[49] For example, the Court has held that there was a rational connection between prohibiting obscene materials and the objective of protecting women and children from violence, even though the social science data about causal connections between pornography and violence were far from conclusive.[50] Similarly, the Court has found a rational connection between limiting freedom of expression by restricting tobacco advertising and the legislative objective of curbing the use of tobacco, even though, again, the evidence was inconclusive.[51] Courts should be cautious about demanding an unrealistically high level of proof or requiring that the government demonstrate success or effectiveness in pursuing its objective at this stage of section 1 analysis. The effectiveness of the government's measure can be evaluated at a later stage in section 1 analysis when the court assesses the overall balance of the harms and benefits of the impugned measure.

3) Minimal Impairment

The core element of proportionality review is the minimal impairment test. While *Oakes* described this as the principle of "least intrusive means," later cases, discussed below, seemed to relax the test, asking whether there was some other reasonable way for the legislature to satisfy the objective that would not impair the right or freedom at issue, or that would have less impact on the right or freedom than does

---

46   *Ibid* at para 276.
47   *Mounted Police*, above note 42 at para 143 [emphasis in original].
48   *Harper*, above note 25 at para 104.
49   *Sauvé*, above note 21 at para 18.
50   *R v Butler*, [1992] 1 SCR 452, 89 DLR (4th) 449 [*Butler*].
51   *RJR–MacDonald v Canada*, [1995] 3 SCR 199, 127 DLR (4th) 1 [*RJR*].

the law under review.[52] In one of the most notable cases to be decided by the Supreme Court in this area, it was held that a Quebec law prohibiting the display of commercial signs in English could not survive scrutiny under the minimal impairment test.[53] The Court was prepared to find that the preservation and enhancement of the French language was a sufficiently important objective in the province of Quebec to justify limiting the guarantee of freedom of expression and that a law that required such signs to be in French and forbade signs in English was rationally connected to this objective. However, the Court found that the law went too far in prohibiting English altogether. The province could, in the Court's view, have satisfied the legitimate objective of preserving and enhancing French by requiring that commercial signs display a marked predominance of French. Such a law would achieve the goal of enhancing the aim of a *visage linguistique* appropriate to a predominantly French society but at the same time would respect, to the extent possible consistent with the attainment of that goal, the right of non-francophones to use their language. The Court was not persuaded that a total ban on English was necessary, and the law therefore failed, since it was not the least intrusive means of satisfying the legislative objective.

A violation that is characterized as a total denial of the right in question will often be struck down on the basis that it does not minimally impair the right in question. Thus the complete denial of the right of Indian Band members, not residing on their Band's reserve, to vote in their Band's elections[54] has been held not to be justified, as has a total ban on all forms of secondary picketing, including peaceful leafleting,[55] and the failure to provide for any association of farm workers.[56]

Evidence of the use of less restrictive means in other Canadian jurisdictions and in other countries may be relevant,[57] but will rarely be

---

52 Specifically, in *Edwards Books*, above note 19, Dickson CJC reformulated the test to ask whether the right was impaired "as little as reasonably possible," which suggested that the limitation need not be the least intrusive, but the least intrusive given the legislature's objective and other competing interests — that is, the test more openly balanced the interests of the state and the rights claimant.

53 *Ford v Quebec (Attorney General)*, [1988] 2 SCR 712, 54 DLR (4th) 577. The case was decided under the Quebec *Charter of Human Rights and Freedoms*, but the Supreme Court made it clear that the same principles applied as under the Canadian *Charter*.

54 *Corbiere v Canada (Minister of Indian and Northern Affairs)*, [1999] 2 SCR 202, 172 DLR (4th) 1.

55 *UFCW v KMart*, [1999] 2 SCR 1083, 176 DLR (4th) 607.

56 *Dunmore v Ontario (Attorney General)*, [2001] 3 SCR 1016, 207 DLR (4th) 193.

57 See, for example, *CBC*, above note 7 at paras 95–96.

determinative given the value placed on federalism[58] and the particular context of Canada.[59] If there is evidence of a less restrictive alternative, however, the government would be well advised to demonstrate why that alternative would not be as effective in advancing the government's objective as the impugned legislation.

The minimal-impairment test remains the core of the section 1 proportionality analysis, but there has been a trend away from a rigorous or mechanical approach to the question of minimal impairment towards a more contextual approach. The reasons for this trend will be examined in Section C, below.

4) Overall Balance

The final step in proportionality review, in the words of *Oakes*, requires that there "be a proportionality between the *effects* of the measure which are responsible for limiting the *Charter* right or freedom, and the objective which has been identified as of 'sufficient importance.'"[60] This final step applies when all the other aspects of proportionality have been satisfied. It engages the court in a balancing exercise, weighing the significance of the infringement of the right against the importance of attaining the objective of the legislation. In a later case, Lamer CJC refined this test by saying that this step requires "both that the underlying *objective* of a measure and the *salutary effects* that actually result from its implementation be proportional to the deleterious effects the measure has on fundamental rights and freedoms."[61]

What matters in the overall balance is not simply the objective of the legislation but its effectiveness in achieving that objective. In *Alberta v Hutterian Brethren of Wilson Colony*,[62] McLachlin CJC pointed out that this final step in the *Oakes* analysis does not merely recapitulate the earlier stages, which are anchored in the law's purpose. Endorsing the observation of Aharon Barack,[63] a leading exponent of this aspect of the test as the core consideration in proportionality analysis, McLachlin CJC pointed out that only the fourth stage takes full account

---

58   *R v Advance Cutting and Coring Ltd*, [2001] 3 SCR 209, 205 DLR (4th) 385 [*Advance Cutting*].

59   *Thomson Newspapers*, above note 30 at para 121. See the different views of McLachlin CJC and Abella J on this point in *Quebec (Attorney General) v A*, 2013 SCC 5 at paras 370–71 and 440.

60   *Oakes*, above note 16 at 139 (SCR).

61   *Dagenais v Canadian Broadcasting Corp*, [1994] 3 SCR 835 at 887, 120 DLR (4th) 12.

62   [2009] 2 SCR 567 at para 76 [*Hutterian Brethren*].

63   "Proportional Effect: The Israeli Experience" (2007) 57 UTLJ 369 at 374.

of the severity of the deleterious effects of the impugned measure upon the protected human right. At the same time, she upheld a law in that case that had severe effects on a religious minority by requiring them, in an act that was contrary to their beliefs, to have their photos on their licences in an effort to respond to the dangers of identity fraud. Justice Abella wrote in dissent that the salutary effects of the law in countering identity fraud were slight, and there was evidence that the law would have a harmful effect on the minority.[64] In a more recent case, the Court noted that the beneficial effect to public safety of extending sentences and exposure to rehabilitation for all offenders was not "trivial," but was nevertheless outweighed because the "law's overbreadth means that offenders who have neither committed violent offences nor present a risk to public safety will be unnecessarily deprived of liberty."[65]

Until recently, this final balancing step has not been decisive and was thought by many to be redundant. It appeared unlikely that the Supreme Court would ever find that the objective was of sufficient importance to justify overriding a protected freedom, and that the least intrusive means had been employed, but nevertheless conclude that on balance the effects on the right were disproportionate. In cases such as *Keegstra* (upholding the federal hate-propaganda offence in the *Criminal Code*) and *McKinney* (upholding mandatory retirement), the Court fairly quickly concluded that the respective legislation passed the balancing test, having found that each was justified under the minimal impairment stage.[66] More recently, however, this final stage has taken on more importance and it could be decisive in cases where the legislation is relatively well-tailored but imposes very severe effects on those whose rights are infringed that are disproportionate to their importance of the government's objective and/or the ability of the restriction on the right to achieve the government objective. In *Thomson Newspapers v Canada*, the Court struck down a ban on the publication of opinion polls within seventy-two hours of an election as an unjustified violation of freedom of expression. Although the Court accepted the objective of preventing inaccurate polls from influencing the last days of an election campaign as pressing and substantial under the first part of the test, it held that under the fourth part of the test, the benefits of pursuing this objective were "marginal" because "the postulated harm

---

64   *Hutterian Brethren*, above note 62 at paras 155–70. See also LeBel J in dissent at paras 200–1.

65   *R v Safarzadeh-Markhali*, 2016 SCC 14 at para 65.

66   *R v Keegstra*, [1990] 3 SCR 697, 61 CCC (3d) 1 [*Keegstra*]; *McKinney v University of Guelph*, [1990] 3 SCR 229, 76 DLR (4th) 545 [*McKinney*].

will seldom occur." On the other hand, the deleterious effects of the ban were "substantial" because the ban interfered with press reporting of an election and deprived voters of information about the election.[67] Similarly, the Court was prepared to take a closer look at the effectiveness of a *Charter* violation in achieving the government's objective, when it refused to find that a denial of legal aid in violation of section 7 of the *Charter* was justified under section 1, on the basis that the budgetary savings achieved by the violation were minimal, especially when compared to the harmful effects of an unfair hearing.[68]

The Court described the overall balance component in 2016 as "the essence of the proportionality enquiry" and one that "allows courts to stand back to determine on a normative basis whether a rights infringement is justified in a free and democratic society."[69] The case dealt with a section 11(i) violation when Parliament enacted new restrictions on those convicted of sexual offences against children that could be imposed retroactively to offences committed before the law was amended. The Court held that the provisions were rationally connected to the important objective of protecting children from sexual violence and also that they constituted the least rights-invasive means to achieve the objective. The overall balance stage was decisive. The majority of the Court held that the state had justified the retroactive imposition of a complete ban on Internet use given its importance in preventing the luring of children through new social media technology. At the same time, the Court held that the state had failed to justify the retroactive imposition of a complete ban on unsupervised contact with those under sixteen years of age. It stressed the severe effects that such a provision would have on the offender. It noted that Parliament had not acted on new evidence about the risk of offending against children and concluded that the benefits of retroactive imposition were both "marginal and speculative."[70] The Court's acknowledgment that the overall balance stage involves "difficult value judgments"[71] was underlined by one dissent that would have held that both retroactive provisions were justified under section 1 and another dissent that stated that neither was justified.

If the fourth part of the proportionality review continues to assume increasing importance, governments will bear a greater obligation to

---

67   *Thomson Newspapers*, above note 30 at para 129.
68   *New Brunswick (Minister of Health and Community Services) v G(J)*, [1999] 3 SCR 46, 177 DLR (4th) 124 at para 100 [*New Brunswick v G(J)*].
69   *R v KRJ*, 2016 SCC 31 at para 79.
70   *Ibid* at para 92.
71   *Ibid* at para 79.

demonstrate that impugned legislation is not only rationally connected to its objectives, but also effective in achieving the objectives. This stage will further require the courts to balance the effectiveness of the violation in achieving the government's objective against the harms of denying the *Charter* right. In cases in which the harms of the *Charter* violations are great and the benefits are slight, the courts may strike down a law under this last stage of the section 1 test, even though there is not an obviously less restrictive means to pursue the government's objective.

C. THE *OAKES* TEST: STRICT RULES OR GUIDING PRINCIPLES?

The key issue is really how strictly the *Oakes* test is applied. The decided cases indicate that the stringency of review and particularly the application of the minimal impairment tests are both controversial and variable. Indeed, some judges quarrel with the term the *Oakes* "test." For example, La Forest J rejected the term, stating that *Oakes* did no more than establish some principles or guidelines to help in making a decision and insisted that these principles should be applied "flexibly, having regard to the specific factual and social context of each case."[72] However, the majority view is that the *Oakes* approach remains helpful, provided it is applied flexibly, with sensitivity to the context of the particular law at issue.[73]

The central element in the application of section 1 is the principle of least intrusive means. This aspect of the *Oakes* test is the focus of most litigation under the *Charter*. The least-intrusive-means principle is significant in assessing the impact the *Charter* has upon the role of the judiciary. Proportionality review, especially the minimal impairment test, requires judges to weigh and assess the choices made by the legislature and the other policy options available. This is not an exercise considered to fall within the realm of judicial competence in non-constitutional cases, yet it is often the central question in *Charter* litigation. It is now clear that the Supreme Court will not apply the minimal impairment test mechanically or literally to strike down a law simply because it is possible to conceive of another measure that might be less intrusive on a protected freedom. As Gonthier J put it, "it is not

---

72   *RJR*, above note 51 at 46 (DLR) (dissenting judgment).
73   *Ibid* at 88–90 (DLR), McLachlin J; *Libman v Quebec (AG)*, [1997] 3 SCR 569, 151 DLR (4th) 385 at 407 [*Libman*].

sufficient that a judge, freed from all such constraints, could imagine a less restrictive alternative."[74] Even Justice Wilson, a staunch defender of the minimal impairment test, held that only where there are measures "clearly superior to the measures currently in use" would a law fail on this ground.[75] A unanimous judgment of the Court adopted the following formulation of the test by McLachlin J:

> The impairment must be "minimal," that is, the law must be carefully tailored so that the rights are impaired no more than necessary. The tailoring process seldom admits of perfection and the courts must accord some leeway to the legislator. If the law falls within a range of reasonable alternatives, the courts will not find it overbroad merely because they can conceive of an alternative which might better tailor objective to infringement . . . .[76]

Although the Supreme Court has rejected the idea that "there is one category of cases in which a low standard of justification under section 1 is applied, and another category in which a higher standard is applied,"[77] it would seem that the standard of review is influenced by several factors.[78]

1) Broad Issues of Social and Economic Policy

The Supreme Court has demonstrated a marked tendency to defer to legislative judgment and apply a relatively deferential standard of review in cases involving broad issues of social and economic policy, especially where the problem is complex and the implications of various

---

74   *Nova Scotia (Workers' Compensation Board) v Martin; Nova Scotia (Workers' Compensation Board) v Laseur*, [2003] 2 SCR 504 at para 112 [*Martin*].

75   *Lavigne v Ontario Public Service Employees Union*, [1991] 2 SCR 211 at 296, 81 DLR (4th) 545.

76   *Libman*, above note 73 at 415 (DLR), adopting McLachlin J's statement from *RJR*, above note 51. See also *CBC*, above note 7 at para 77; *Montreal (City) v 2952-1366 Québec Inc*, [2005] 3 SCR 141 at para 94 [*City of Montreal*]: "The Court will not interfere simply because it can think of a better, less intrusive way to manage the problem. What is required is that the [government concerned] establish that it has tailored the limit to the exigencies of the problem in a reasonable way."

77   *Thomson Newspapers*, above note 30 at para 88.

78   The American Supreme Court has developed different standards of review depending on the particular right at issue or, in the case of the equal-protection clause, the basis for differential treatment. For example, differential treatment on the basis of race triggers "strict scrutiny," while differential treatment on the basis of a characteristic such as veteran's status leads to a much more deferential "rationality" review.

solutions are not fully understood. Courts are experts in the matter of liberty, but not in the realm of social policy:

> Where a complex regulatory response to a social problem is challenged, courts will generally take a more deferential posture throughout the s 1 analysis than they will when the impugned measure is a penal statute directly threatening the liberty of the accused.[79]

The Supreme Court has stated that "the role of the legislature demands deference from the courts to those types of policy decisions that the legislature is best placed to make."[80] The Court has recognized that the making of social policy "is a role properly assigned to the elected representatives of the people, who have at their disposal the necessary institutional resources to enable them to compile and assess social science evidence, to mediate between competing social interests and to reach out to protect vulnerable groups."[81] The Court has also indicated that deference to the legislature will usually be warranted on matters such as labour relations policy that involve complex issues of social and economic policy[82] and in relation to "environmental issues, where views and interests often conflict and precision is elusive."[83]

One of the most striking examples of a relaxed standard of section 1 review is the case dealing with mandatory retirement.[84] The Supreme Court found that mandatory retirement at age sixty-five violated the right conferred by section 15 not to be discriminated against on grounds of age, but it held that the legislation permitting this form of discrimination should be upheld under section 1. In the view of the majority of the Court, the issue was "whether the government had a reasonable basis, on the evidence tendered, for concluding that the legislation interferes as little as possible with a guaranteed right, given the government's pressing and substantial objectives."[85] This is plainly a much more relaxed standard of review than that applied in cases dealing with those rights or freedoms that do not pose complex social-policy questions.

---

79   *Hutterian Brethren*, above note 62 at para 37; *R v St-Onge Lamoureux*, 2012 SCC 57 at para 39.

80   *M v H*, above note 32 at para 78; *Newfoundland (Treasury Board) v NAPE*, [2004] 3 SCR 381 at paras 83–84 [*Newfoundland*].

81   *Libman*, above note 73 at 416 (DLR), adopting a passage from the dissenting judgment of La Forest J in *RJR*, above note 51.

82   *Advance Cutting*, above note 58 at paras 256–57 and 267.

83   *City of Montreal*, above note 76 at para 94.

84   *McKinney*, above note 66.

85   *Ibid* at 666 (DLR), La Forest J.

Chaoulli marked a dramatic break from the Supreme Court's previous deferential approach to broad issues of social and economic policy. The case involved a challenge to Quebec's prohibition of private medical insurance for procedures covered by the public health-care system. All seven judges[86] who heard the case agreed that the government's objective was to preserve the integrity of the public health system and that this objective was pressing and substantial.[87] A majority of four judges took a strict approach to proportionality and stressed the government's obligation under section 1 to justify any limitation on the basis of evidence. "The fact that the matter is complex, contentious or laden with social values does not mean that the courts can abdicate the responsibility vested in them by our Constitution to review legislation for *Charter* compliance when citizens challenge it."[88] The majority found that the prohibition on private health care was disproportionate in all respects. Chief Justice McLachlin and Major J (Bastarache J concurring) concluded that there was no rational connection between the prohibition and the protection of the public health-care system. In addition, the "denial of access to timely and effective medical care to those who need it is not proportionate to the beneficial effects of the prohibition on private insurance to the health system as a whole."[89] Finally, they also concluded that "the physical and psychological suffering and risk of death that may result outweigh whatever benefit (and none has been demonstrated to us here) there may be to the system as a whole."[90]

In their dissent, Binnie and LeBel JJ (Fish J concurring) stated that "the decision boils down to an application of the minimal impairment test. In respect of questions of social and economic policy, this test leaves a substantial margin of appreciation to the Quebec legislature."[91] In their view, difficult choices in the rationing of scarce medical resources and attempts to ensure equal access to medical care to all should be left to the legislature. They also warned that

---

86 Justice Deschamps dealt with the question under s 9.1 of the Quebec *Charter of Rights and Freedoms* which she concluded should be interpreted in accordance with the *Oakes* test. *Chaoulli*, above note 44 at para 48.

87 *Ibid* at para 55, Deschamps J; at para 155, McLachlin CJC and Major J; at para 239, Binnie and LeBel JJ.

88 *Ibid* at para 107, McLachlin CJC and Major J (Bastarache J concurring). Justice Deschamps similarly concluded that although legislatures create social policies, "when such social policies infringe rights that are protected by charters, the courts cannot shy away from considering them." (*Ibid* at para 89, Deschamps J.)

89 *Ibid* at para 156.

90 *Ibid* at para 157.

91 *Ibid* at para 276.

those who seek private health insurance are those who can afford it and can qualify for it. They are differentiated from the general population, not by their health problems, which are found in every group in society, but by their income status. We share the view of Dickson CJ that the *Charter* should not become an instrument to be used by the wealthy to 'roll back' the benefits of a legislative scheme that helps protect the poorer members of society.[92]

It remains to be seen whether this 4:3 decision signals a permanent willingness of the Court to enter into complex, distributional, and multi-faceted aspects of public policy, such as the design of the health-care system.

2) Reconciling Competing Claims and Protecting Vulnerable Groups

The Supreme Court has explicitly stated that a more relaxed standard of scrutiny is called for where the legislation challenged represents an attempt by the legislature to reconcile competing claims or protect vulnerable groups. In these cases, the majority judges in *Irwin Toy* indicated:

> If the legislature has made a reasonable assessment as to where the line is most properly drawn, especially if that assessment involves weighing conflicting scientific evidence and allocating scarce resources on this basis, it is not for the court to second guess. That would only be to substitute one estimate for another.[93]

In a case dealing with a Sunday closing law,[94] the Court noted that the legislature had been motivated by a secular purpose, namely, to provide workers with a common day of rest. The legislation did attempt to accommodate non-Sunday observers, but those exemptions were drafted with a view to protecting retail-sales workers, a particularly vulnerable group, from being forced to work. The exemptions were less than perfect from the perspective of non-Sunday observers. However, the majority held that, in such circumstances, the legislature had to be given a certain latitude to ensure that the *Charter* "does not simply become an instrument of better situated individuals to roll back legislation that has as its object the improvement of the condition of less advantaged persons."[95]

---

92 *Ibid* at para 274, citing *Edwards Books*, above note 19, discussed below.
93 *Irwin Toy Ltd v Quebec (AG)*, [1989] 1 SCR 927, 58 DLR (4th) 577 at 623 [*Irwin Toy*].
94 *Edwards Books*, above note 19.
95 *Ibid* at 49 (DLR), Dickson CJC.

This line of analysis was later expanded when the Court indicated that a distinction should be drawn between cases where "the government is best characterized as the singular antagonist of the individual whose right has been infringed" and those where the government is "mediating between the claims of competing groups" and attempting to strike a balance that will protect the vulnerable, while impinging as little as possible upon protected freedoms "without the benefit of absolute certainty concerning how that balance is best struck."[96] In the former case, a rigorous standard of review should be applied under section 1, while in the latter, the legislature will not be held to such a strict test. In practical terms, the line between these two types of laws cannot be sharply drawn, for many laws affecting the criminal process, while placing the state in opposition to the individual, also implicate the interests of other groups. The Court has held, for example, that hate-crimes laws, obscenity and child pornography laws, provisions limiting access to the medical records of sexual assault victims, or rules about the prior sexual conduct of a sexual assault victim all raise equality issues and affect the interests of competing groups.[97] The fact that a law is designed to protect the vulnerable, however, does not render it a reasonable limit. This is especially the case when the Court finds that a violation is overbroad to the legitimate aim of protecting the vulnerable,[98] or perhaps in cases where its harmful effects are much greater than its salutary effects.

The Court has also distinguished between defining competing rights in a non-hierarchical manner that minimizes conflict, and considering competing rights and interests as part of the section 1 process. As will be discussed below, the government only bears the onus with respect to the latter process of justifying a limit on a *Charter* right under section 1.[99]

3) Definitional Elements and Fundamental Freedoms

Definitional elements may affect proportionality review. As noted above, the Supreme Court has often minimized definitional limitations and given *Charter* rights a liberal and generous meaning. For example, both commercial expression and hate propaganda have been found to fall within the definition of "expression" and accordingly are *prima facie*

---

96   *Irwin Toy*, above note 93 at 993 & 994 (SCR).
97   See, for example, *R v Seaboyer*, [1991] 2 SCR 577, 83 DLR (4th) 193 (rape-shield case).
98   *Carter v Canada*, [2015] 1 SCR 331 at paras 115–21 [*Carter*].
99   *R v Mills*, [1999] 3 SCR 668, 180 DLR (4th) 1.

protected by section 2(b).[100] Any limits imposed upon those forms of expression must be justified under section 1 to survive *Charter* scrutiny. However, definitional considerations seem to affect the strictness of review under section 1, especially with respect to expression cases. The Court has spoken of a "core" meaning of freedom of expression, leading to a strict application of section 1 when a form of expression lies at or near that "core" — for example, political speech.[101] But when the form of expression at issue is peripheral to the core, legislation imposing limitations is much more likely to survive.

While neither commercial speech nor hate propaganda is excluded at the stage of defining *Charter* rights, it is equally the case that neither lies at or near the "core" meaning of freedom of expression and, as a result, a relatively relaxed level of *Charter* scrutiny is applied.

Again, the motivation is to avoid an unduly burdensome standard of *Charter* review when the legislature is acting to protect vulnerable groups. In the children's advertising case, *Irwin Toy*,[102] the law at issue was designed to protect children from exploitative commercial messages, and the Supreme Court felt that the government had struck a reasonable balance in limiting advertising directed at children under thirteen years of age. In upholding the hate-propaganda law designed to protect ethnic minorities[103] and obscenity laws aimed at protecting women from degrading portrayals and children from child pornography, the Court noted that the expression at issue was far from the core.[104] In upholding offences of defamatory libel, the Court also noted that intentional defamations were far from the core value of freedom of expression.[105] The Court makes distinctions based on the value of expression under section 1 of the *Charter* that it does not make in determining whether expression is protected under section 2(b).

The distinction between different forms of expression under section 1 does not mean, however, that speech further from the core is without *Charter* protection. For example, challenges to legislation in some commercial-speech cases have succeeded because the bans — advertising dentists' services and tobacco products — did not pass the minimal-impairment test.[106] At the same time, however, the Supreme

---

100 *Irwin Toy*, above note 93; *Keegstra*, above note 66.
101 *Thomson Newspapers*, above note 30 at para 91.
102 *Irwin Toy*, above note 93.
103 *Keegstra*, above note 66.
104 *Butler*, above note 50; *R v Sharpe*, [2001] 1 SCR 45, 194 DLR (4th) 1.
105 *Lucas*, above note 14.
106 *Rocket v Royal College of Dental Surgeons of Ontario*, [1990] 2 SCR 232, 71 DLR (4th) 68; *RJR*, above note 51.

Court's generous approach to defining freedom of expression to include matters such as obscenity, child pornography, hate speech, and even deliberate lies has influenced the section 1 analysis and led to many cases in which violations of section 2(b) have been held to be justified under section 1 of the *Charter*.

At the same time, the Supreme Court has been more reluctant to find that violations of freedom of association have been justified under section 1. In one case, the Court held that giving the government the unilateral power to designate essential services (thereby prohibiting strikes) without providing access to arbitration constituted a disproportionate manner for the government to pursue its important objective of ensuring that the public received essential services.[107] Privacy protections were also not justified under section 1 because they disproportionately infringed a union's right to freedom of expression in recording and posting identifying information about workers who crossed picket lines.[108] The Court also found that denying members of the RCMP access to collective bargaining was not even rationally connected to the government's objective of maintaining an independent and objective police force.[109]

4) Definitional Elements and Sections 7, 8, and 12

The strict definitional limitations imposed in determining violations of section 7 of the *Charter* also influences section 1 analysis. In *Reference Re s 94(2) of the Motor Vehicle Act (BC)*, the Court stated:

> Section 1 may, for reasons of administrative expediency, successfully come to the rescue of an otherwise violation of s 7, but only in cases arising out of exceptional conditions, such as natural disasters, the outbreak of war, epidemics, and the like.[110]

The Supreme Court has reaffirmed this dictum noting that "the rights protected by section 7 — life, liberty, and security of the person — are very significant and cannot ordinarily be overridden by competing social interests. Second, rarely will a violation of the principles of fundamental justice, specifically the right to a fair hearing, be upheld as a reasonable limit demonstrably justified in a free and democratic

---

107 *Saskatchewan Federation of Labour v Saskatchewan*, [2015] 1 SCR 245.

108 *Alberta (Information and Privacy Commissioner) v United Food and Commercial Workers, Local 401*, 2013 SCC 62.

109 *Mounted Police*, above note 42.

110 [1985] 2 SCR 486 at 518, 24 DLR (4th) 536.

society."[111] Section 1 justifications for violations of section 7 will be "rare," albeit possible.[112] In more than one case the Court had held that "[o]verbroad legislation which infringes s 7 of the *Charter* would appear to be incapable of passing the minimal impairment branch of the s 1 analysis."[113]

In *Carter* (the assisted dying case), that court noted that it could be possible to justify a violation of section 7 under section 1 in part because considerations of the "public good" should not be considered under section 7, and because sometimes competing interests may themselves be protected under the *Charter*.[114] That said, the Court, not surprisingly, found that an unconstitutionally overbroad assisted suicide offence was not justified under section 1. Even though the absolute offence was rationally connected to the important goal of protecting the vulnerable, it could not be justified compared to a more tailored offence that would allow competent adults subject to intolerable suffering from an irremediable illness to obtain assistance from a doctor in ending their life. The Court similarly found that an overbroad offence preventing all people from living off the avails of prostitution could not be justified under section 1 because of the possibility of a better-tailored offence limited to those in an exploitive relationship. The Court's section 1 analysis in this case was brief, and reflected much of the analysis in determining that the impugned legislation violated section 7 of the *Charter*.[115]

The Court has also been reluctant to hold the violations of the right against unreasonable search and seizure in section 8[116] of the *Charter* or the right against cruel and unusual punishment in section 12 of the *Charter* are justified under section 1, in part because of the definitional limits placed on those rights. The Court has found a variety of mandatory minimum penalties to be unconstitutional in large part because

---

111 *New Brunswick v G(J)*, above note 68 at para 99; *Suresh*, above note 15 at para 78 (SCR); *Charkaoui v Canada (Citizenship and Immigration)*, [2007] 1 SCR 350.

112 *United States of America v Burns*, [2001] 1 SCR 283, 195 DLR (4th) 1 at para 133.

113 *R v Heywood*, [1994] 3 SCR 761 at 802–3 [*Heywood*]; *R v Demers*, [2004] 2 SCR 489 at para 46. This approach would also apply to legislation that violates s 7 of the *Charter* because of gross disproportionality. See *PHS Community Services*, above note 24 at para 137.

114 *Carter*, above note 98 at para 95.

115 *Canada (Attorney General) v Bedford*, [2013] 3 SCR 1101 at para 162.

116 *Heywood*, above note 113; *Lavallee, Rackel & Heintz v Canada (Attorney General)*; *White, Ottenheimer & Baker v Canada (Attorney General)*; *R v Fink*, [2002] 3 SCR 209; *Goodwin v British Columbia (Superintendent of Motor Vehicles)*, [2015] 3 SCR 250; *Canada (Attorney General) v Federation of Law Societies of Canada*, 2015 SCC 7; *R v Appulonappa*, 2015 SCC 59.

they would be grossly disproportionate as applied to offenders at the low end of the blameworthiness system. Governments have consistently failed to justify these violations under section 1, with the Court indicating that a more proportionate alternative would be either to allow judges to depart from such sentences in exceptional cases or defining the offence in a more restrictive manner to achieve proportionality.[117]

5) Definitional Elements and Section 15

Even though the Court has imposed definitional limits in determining when equality rights in section 15 of the *Charter* are violated, it has been more receptive to section 1 justifications for section 15 violations than for violations of sections 7, 8, or 12 of the *Charter*. In other words, the Court has held limits on equality rights to be justified under section 1 despite the definitional limitations on what constitutes a violation of equality rights. Justice Bastarache (Gonthier, Iacobucci, and Major JJ concurring) stated that he rejects the suggestion

> that section 15(1) rights are all but absolute, in that their violation should only be justifiable in rare circumstances. This Court has often applied section 1 to breaches of section 15(1) . . . This is not indicative of undue deference, but of the need for a flexible approach to section 1 justification and, more broadly, the recognition that any balancing between individual rights and societal needs occurs in section 1, not section 15(1).[118]

A number of judges at different times have expressed concerns that an overly generous approach to finding violations of the section 15 equality rights will place unhealthy pressures to dilute the requirement that the state establish that limits on the right are reasonable and demonstrably justified under section 1 of the *Charter*.[119] This confirms the connection between section 1 and how rights are defined.

6) Relationship to Section 33

The Supreme Court has stated that an attempt to justify limits on rights not subject to the section 33 override will be subjected to "careful examination" rather than "deference."[120] The case dealt with the right to vote,

---

117 *R v Nur*, [2015] 1 SCR 773; *R v Lloyd*, 2016 SCC 13.
118 *Lavoie v Canada*, [2002] 1 SCR 769, 210 DLR (4th) 193 at para 49 [*Lavoie*].
119 *Andrews v Law Society of British Columbia*, [1989] 1 SCR 143, 56 DLR (4th) 1, Wilson J; *Lavoie*, above note 118, Arbour J (in dissent).
120 *Figueroa*, above note 43 at para 60.

said by the Court to be "fundamental to our system of democracy." It followed that "great care must be exercised in determining whether or not the government has justified a violation of s 3"[121] and, in the result, the Court rejected the government's argument that denying the vote to inmates of federal penitentiaries could be justified as a reasonable limit on the right to vote.

7) Cost

Should the government be able to justify limitations on *Charter* rights because the cost of compliance is too high? Rights are often expensive to implement. Respecting *Charter* rights represents a drain on the public purse and thereby limits the capacity of the state to carry out other worthy objectives. On the other hand, the very notion of a right is that it must be given priority over other claims and not made subject to utilitarian concerns such as cost and administrative inconvenience.

In several cases, the Supreme Court appeared to exclude the possibility that protecting the public purse could ever justify limiting a *Charter* right.[122] However, the decision in *Newfoundland (Treasury Board) v NAPE* holds that while cost arguments should be viewed with "strong scepticism,"[123] there is no absolute rule barring section 1 justification on grounds of cost. The Newfoundland government enacted legislation to avoid implementation of a pay equity scheme for female health-care workers. The legislation violated section 15 of the *Charter*, but the Supreme Court accepted the province's argument that a "severe" financial crisis justified denying the equality rights of this vulnerable group of workers. Writing for the Court, Binnie J stated that, in a case of financial crisis, "elected governments must be accorded significant scope to take remedial measures, even if the measures taken have an adverse effect on a *Charter* right, subject, of course, to the measures being proportional both to the fiscal crisis and to their impact on the affected *Charter* interests."[124]

121 *Ibid*; *Sauvé v Canada (Chief Electoral Officer)*, [2002] 3 SCR 519 at 537.
122 *Schachter v Canada*, [1992] 2 SCR 679 at 709: "budgetary considerations cannot be used to justify a violation under s 1"; *Egan v Canada*, [1995] 2 SCR 513 at para 99; *Reference Re Remuneration of Judges of the Provincial Court of Prince Edward Island*, [1997] 3 SCR 3 at para 281; *Martin*, above note 74 at para 109.
123 *Newfoundland*, above note 80 at para 72.
124 *Ibid* at para 64.

8) Consultation

While legislators are not required to consult with affected parties be-fore acting,[125] the Supreme Court has held that in some cases, it may be useful to consider "whether the government considered other options or engaged in consultations with the affected parties, in choosing to adopt its preferred approach."[126] That statement was made in a case involving drastic changes to collective bargaining rights, an environ-ment characterized by consultation, negotiation, and give-and-take bargaining. The government's failure to consult obviously influenced the Court's decision that it had failed to adopt a law that minimally impaired the employees' collective bargaining rights.

D. BURDEN OF PROOF AND SECTION 1 EVIDENCE

The initial burden of proving a violation of rights rests with the indi-vidual asserting a *Charter* violation. In light of the generous definition accorded *Charter* rights such as freedom of expression, this burden can, in some cases, be relatively easy to discharge. In other cases, it will be more difficult to establish a violation. Once a *prima facie* viola-tion is proved, the burden shifts to the party attempting to justify the infringement as a reasonable limit. The burden has been described as one based on "the preponderance of probabilities,"[127] the same standard used in civil trials and that applicants must satisfy in establishing the violation of their *Charter* rights. This means that the government has the burden of proof of establishing that limits on *Charter* rights are reasonable. Support for giving the government such a burden is found in the reference to limits that are "demonstrably justified" as well as the superior ability and resources of governments in establishing the need for limiting *Charter* rights. The standard of proof is the standard used in civil trial: proof on a balance of probabilities or preponderance of evidence.

The Supreme Court in *Oakes* indicated that governments seeking to justify limitations on rights will generally be required to present evidence

---

125 Compare the situation of Aboriginal rights where the Court has found the right to include a duty to consult: see, for example, *Haida Nation v British Columbia (Minister of Forests)*, [2004] 3 SCR 511.

126 *Health Services and Support — Facilities Subsector Bargaining Assn v British Co-lumbia*, [2007] 2 SCR 391 at para 157 [*Health Services*].

127 *RJR*, above note 51 at paras 137–38; *Mounted Police*, above note 42 at para 139.

in support of their argument. The result has been a significant expansion in the kinds of materials coming before the courts. Historical, philosophical, and economic data, as well as government reports (both domestic and international), are presented, sometimes through expert witnesses, sometimes by way of judicial notice.[128] Occasionally, however, the Court seems demanding with respect to evidence — for example, in the tobacco advertising case, the majority judges commented on the failure of the federal government to show why an alternative to a total ban on advertising would undermine the government's objective. Not only had the government failed to show that it was necessary to have a complete ban, it had also refused to disclose a study of alternatives to a total ban, despite the request by the party challenging the law to have the information.[129] In other cases, the Court seems to have taken a relaxed approach to the evidence. In an earlier case, for example, the Court relied on government data justifying Sunday closing legislation that was imprecise and over fifteen years old.[130]

E. CONCLUSION

Much of the debate about the Supreme Court's treatment of section 1 of the *Charter* revolves around the issue of deference. When should the courts intervene to protect rights and when should they leave decisions about rights and limits to the legislatures? There is no easy answer. Too much deference can easily undermine the purpose of the *Charter* — to protect individual rights against the majority. Yet a court that demands an extensive factual record and the least intrusive means for rights impairment in all cases could unduly constrain the legislature's efforts to govern in the broad public interest. In the end, while the *Oakes* test provides the basic framework for analysis, the courts have not adhered to a single test that serves in all cases to determine where to draw the line between protection of rights and respect for the legislative role and competing rights and claims. As the Supreme Court has made clear,[131] the context of a particular case is of fundamental importance in the application of section 1 of the *Charter*.

---

128 *Health Services*, above note 126 at paras 56–57.
129 *RJR*, above note 51 at 101 and 108 (DLR).
130 *Edwards Books*, above note 19.
131 *Edmonton Journal v Alberta (AG)*, [1989] 2 SCR 1326, 64 DLR (4th) 577.

FURTHER READINGS

ALON-SHENKER, P, & G DAVIDOV, "Applying the Principle of Proportionality in Employment and Labour Law Contexts" (2013) 59 McGill LJ 375

BARAK, A, *Proportionality: Constitutional Rights and Their Limitations* (Cambridge: Cambridge University Press, 2012)

BEATTY, D, *The Ultimate Rule of Law* (Oxford: Oxford University Press, 2004) c 5

BREDT, C, & A DODEK, "The Increasing Irrelevance of Section One" (2001) 14 Sup Ct L Rev (2d) 175

———, & H PESSIONE, "The Death of *Oakes*: Time for a Rights Specific Approach" (2013) 63 Sup Ct L Rev (2d) 485

CHOUDHRY, S, "So What Is the Real Legacy of *Oakes*? Two Decades of Proportionality Analysis under the Canadian *Charter*'s Section 1" (2006) 34 Sup Ct L Rev (2d) 501

HIEBERT, J, *Limiting Rights: The Dilemmas of Judicial Review* (Montréal: McGill-Queen's University Press, 1996)

HOGG, PW, "Section 1 Revisited" (1991) 1 NJCL 1

JACKMAN, M, "Protecting Rights and Promoting Democracy: Judicial Review under Section 1 of the *Charter*" (1996) 34 Osgoode Hall LJ 661

LECKEY, R, "Prescribed by Law" (2007) 45 Osgoode Hall LJ 571

MATHEN, C, "Rational Connections: *Oakes*, Section 1 and the *Charter*'s Legal Rights" (2012–2013) 43:3 Ottawa L Rev 491

MENDES, E, "Section 1 of the *Charter* after 30 Years: The Soul or the Dagger at its Heart" (2013) 61 Sup Ct L Rev (2d) 293

NEWMAN, D, "Canadian Proportionality Analysis: 5 ½ Myths" (2016) 73 Sup Ct L Rev (2d) 93

TRAKMAN, L, *et al*, "*R v Oakes* 1986–1997: Back to the Drawing Board" (1998) 36 Osgoode Hall LJ 83

WEBBER, G, *The Negotiable Constitution on the Limitations of Rights* (Cambridge: Cambridge University Press, 2009)

THE LEGISLATIVE OVERRIDE

There is a significant qualification in the Canadian constitution on the power of judicial review under the *Charter of Rights and Freedoms*, namely, the legislative override or notwithstanding clause found in section 33. This provision represents an important compromise reached at the time of the entrenchment of the *Charter* to meet concerns about the enhanced power of judicial review. It reflects the judgment that, while a strong element of judicial review is justifiable in a democracy, judicial power also needs to be constrained. Although the override has been rarely used, it is a fundamental structural feature of the *Charter* that shapes the respective responsibilities of the courts on the one hand and Parliament and the legislatures on the other.

Section 33 of the *Charter* permits Parliament or a provincial legislature to declare that a law shall operate "notwithstanding a provision included in section 2 or sections 7 to 15" of the *Charter*. In other words, a law containing a simple declaration from Parliament or a legislature that it is to have effect "notwithstanding" one of these sections will be protected from judicial review, and the law will remain in effect despite violating a *Charter*-guaranteed right or freedom. This means that the fundamental freedoms (expression, religion, association, and assembly) are subject to being overridden by legislative decision, as are the legal rights and, subject to section 28, the right to equality. The reach of the legislative override does not extend to democratic rights (the right to vote and the requirement of regular sessions of Parliament and the legislatures), mobility rights (the right of citizens to enter, leave, and move about the country), minority rights, or language rights. It also does not apply to the constitutional division of powers.

Override declarations can be in effect for a maximum period of five years, which is roughly tied to the life of a Parliament. As a result, the decision to renew an override will come before a newly elected Parliament or legislature and will have to be debated again by another group of elected legislators.

There is, as might be expected, enormous controversy concerning the wisdom of including the override clause in the constitution, but it was a fundamental compromise without which Canada probably would have no *Charter*. The notwithstanding clause was modelled on similar clauses in human rights codes and a provision in the *Canadian Bill of Rights*.[1] Other countries, notably the United Kingdom, have included an override clause in human rights instruments drafted after the *Charter*.[2]

The Supreme Court of Canada has clearly stated that it will not engage in reviewing the legitimacy of a legislative decision to invoke the override clause.[3] The Court made this pronouncement in a case involving the Quebec government's decision to enact an omnibus override clause shortly after the enactment of the *Charter*. Through one stroke of the legislative pen, all Quebec statutes were exempted from the *Charter* by a blanket repeal and then re-enacted with the inclusion of a standard override clause. In addition, all new Quebec statutes were enacted with an override clause. The result was to protect all Quebec statutes from judicial review under the *Charter*. The decision to enact the override was taken by the separatist Parti Québécois government, which had opposed the 1982 amendments to the constitution, including the *Charter*. Maintaining that the government of Quebec should have a veto over any such fundamental constitutional changes, the Quebec National Assembly refused to recognize the legitimacy of the *Charter*.

These override measures were challenged. The Quebec Court of Appeal held that such a sweeping and general declaration of override was invalid and that a much more specific approach was called for.[4] The Supreme Court of Canada disagreed, holding that, so long as the form of section 33 was observed, the courts had no business second-guessing or reviewing the exercise of the override power by a legislature. According to the Supreme Court, section 33 requires only a formal dec-

---

1   See, for example, Ontario *Human Rights Code*, RSO 1990, c H.19, s 47(2); *Canadian Bill of Rights*, SC 1960, c 44, s 2.
2   *Human Rights Act 1998*, (UK), s 14.
3   *Ford v Quebec (Attorney General)*, [1988] 2 SCR 712, 54 DLR (4th) 577 [*Ford*].
4   *Alliance des professeurs de Montréal v Quebec (AG)* (1985), 21 DLR (4th) 354 (Que CA).

laration expressly referring to the sections of the *Charter* being over-ridden. The Court did, however, impose one significant limitation — a declaration under the override power could not have retroactive effect.

The override clause has been resorted to infrequently, and the feder-al government under prime ministers Mulroney and Chrétien stated that it would never use the clause. The most dramatic invocation of the over-ride clause, apart from the general declaration exempting Quebec from the reach of the *Charter*, was the decision to override the Supreme Court of Canada's decision that the Quebec "signs law" was contrary to free-dom of expression.[5] As noted in Chapter 4, the Court recognized Que-bec's right to act to preserve and enhance the French language, but held that it had failed to justify the virtual total prohibition of the use of Eng-lish and other languages on such signs. The Quebec National Assembly immediately resorted to the override clause in enacting a new signs law (the general override enactment having expired after five years), thereby provoking an enormously negative reaction in the rest of Canada that significantly eroded support for the package of constitutional amend-ments known as the Meech Lake Accord.[6] Anglophone merchants who were adversely affected by the override also brought successful inter-national claims about the use of the override, adding an international di-mension to the issue.[7] Quebec did not renew its use of the override when it expired in 1993, and the language law now generally allows the use of languages other than French in commercial signs so long as French remains the predominant language. Alberta used the override in 2000 to declare that the limitation of marriage to opposite-sex partners would operate notwithstanding the *Charter* and particularly section 15 of the *Charter*. In addition, there have been other uses of the override that have attracted no attention from the media and the public.[8]

There are many who argue that the override clause represents a sig-nificant defect in the Canadian constitution, since fundamental rights should never have to yield to majoritarian decisions regarding the

---

5   *Ford*, above note 3.

6   While the Accord was much favoured in Quebec, it did not generate enough support in the rest of Canada to be enacted within the three-year time frame necessary under the amendment process. As a result, it died in June 1990.

7   *Ballantyne, Davidson, McIntyre v Canada, Communication No. 385/1989* (5 May 1993), Canada, CCPR/C/47/D/385/1989 (UN Human Rights Committee).

8   One study has concluded that there have been sixteen uses of the override since 1982. T Kahana, "The Notwithstanding Mechanism and Public Discussion: Lessons from the Ignored Practice of Section 33 of the *Charter*" (2001) 44 Can Public Admin 255 [Kahana, "The Notwithstanding Mechanism"].

general welfare.[9] It is argued that the courts should have the exclusive and final say in matters of fundamental rights and that the majority must forever comply with their interpretations of the *Charter*.

Another school of thought is more accepting of the override clause.[10] The override is seen as a useful safety valve, which can be invoked to escape significant errors or departures by the courts in the interpretation of constitutional guarantees. But for the override clause, nothing short of a subsequent case reversing the earlier decision or a constitutional amendment will correct the error.

Defenders of section 33 also argue that the override is deeply rooted in the Canadian political and constitutional tradition, which accepts that Parliament has an important role in the protection of rights.[11] Rather than seeing Parliament and the legislatures as being inevitably at odds with the courts in this sphere, the override clause recognizes the legitimate role of legislators in defining an appropriate balance between the rights of individuals and the interests of society at large.

Finally, the override clause may be seen as creating a check on the power of both legislatures and the courts. On the one hand, the *Charter* confers a broad mandate upon the judiciary to act to protect fundamental rights and freedoms, thereby significantly curtailing legislative power. On the other hand, the override clause ensures that the courts' power is not unlimited. Taken as a whole, section 33 ensures that no one has the last word. Even if the clause is invoked to overcome judicial review, the five-year limitation period on any use of the override ensures that the issue will have to be revisited after another election in which the people can hold accountable their democratically elected representatives. The net effect of the section is to achieve a subtle and effective check on both legislative and judicial power.[12]

It is impossible to know whether the override clause has had an impact on the Supreme Court of Canada's interpretation of the *Charter*. Some commentators have speculated that the availability of the override has made the judges more willing to engage in a rigorous protection

---

9   See especially JD Whyte, "On Not Standing for Notwithstanding" (1990) 28 Alta L Rev 347.

10   See especially PH Russell, "Standing Up for Notwithstanding" (1991) 29 Alta L Rev 293.

11   See B Slattery, "A Theory of the *Charter*" (1987) 25 Osgoode Hall LJ 701.

12   The theme of dialogue between the courts and the legislature is developed by Slattery, *ibid*, and by PW Hogg & AA Bushell, "The *Charter* Dialogue between Courts and Legislatures" (1997) 35 Osgoode Hall LJ 75. It is also discussed by Iacobucci J in *Vriend v Alberta*, [1998] 1 SCR 493, 156 DLR (4th) 385 at para 138 [*Vriend*], and in Chapter 2, Section C(4).

of rights[13] or assertion of judicial power.[14] At the same time, the Court has accepted legislative replies to a number of its decisions, replies that some commentators have argued should have been accompanied by the override because the legislation essentially reversed the Court's earlier *Charter* decision.[15] In the course of upholding Parliament's reply to its controversial 1995 decision striking down some restrictions on tobacco advertising, the Court has made clear that the fact that the legislature is replying to an earlier judgment merits no special deference.[16] A judicial invalidation of a legislative reply to an earlier *Charter* rule might create some of the conditions for the use of the override.

Saskatchewan invoked the override in an effort to protect back-to-work legislation introduced during a labour dispute. Its concern was with a Court of Appeal decision that had not been appealed to the Supreme Court. The Supreme Court of Canada subsequently upheld the constitutionality of the legislation, thereby removing any need for the override. Some observers have argued that the override should be used only in response to a Supreme Court decision,[17] but the override can and has been used to pre-empt *Charter* challenges. The premier of Saskatchewan also speculated that the override might be necessary to respond to a 2015 Court decision that struck down a law that limited freedom of association in order to preserve essential services, but the legislature enacted a new law governing the provision of essential services by government workers without the override before the one-year suspended declaration of invalidity expired.[18]

The suggestion by the Alberta government in 1998 that it intended to use the override to protect legislation limiting compensation for victims of forced sterilization provoked an outcry. Shortly thereafter, the same government refused to employ the override to reverse the decision of the Supreme Court extending the protection of the human-rights legislation to gays and lesbians.[19] Premier Klein suggested that the override should not be used unless authorized by the public in a

---

13 Russell, above note 10, and K Roach, *The Supreme Court on Trial*, rev ed (Toronto: Irwin Law, 2016), cc 12 and 15 [Roach, *Supreme Court*].

14 C Manfredi, *Judicial Power and the* Charter, 2d ed (Don Mills, ON: Oxford University Press, 2001).

15 *R v Mills*, [1999] 3 SCR 668, as discussed in K Roach, "Constitutional and Common Law Dialogues between the Supreme Court and Canadian Legislatures" (2001) 80 Can Bar Rev 481 at 528–30.

16 *Canada (Attorney General) v JTI-Macdonald Corp*, [2007] 2 SCR 610 at para 11.

17 Manfredi, above note 14 at 192; T Kahana, "Understanding the Notwithstanding Mechanism" (2002) 52 UTLJ 221.

18 As described in Roach, *Supreme Court*, above note 13, c 16.

19 *Vriend*, above note 12.

referendum.[20] In 2000, however, a private member's bill invoking the override to prevent *Charter* challenges to restrictions on marriage to opposite-sex couples was passed by the Alberta legislature. There was little public discussion of this use of the override, and there was no referendum authorizing its use. Some commentators have suggested that Alberta's use of the override would be vulnerable to challenge on the basis of the division of powers because Parliament, not the provincial legislature, has the exclusive jurisdiction to legislate in relation to marriage.[21] In any event, Alberta's use of the override lapsed when it was not renewed after five years.

The override gives the majority a legal mechanism to have its way, but it may well be that the people will rarely, if ever, assume the moral and political burden of overriding protected rights and freedoms. At the same time, a vigilant democracy is essential to ensure that the public closely examines and re-examines a legislature's decision to enact legislation notwithstanding the fundamental freedoms, legal rights, and equality rights of the *Charter*.

FURTHER READINGS

ALBERT, R, "The Theory and Doctrine of Unconstitutional Constitutional Amendment in Canada" (2015) 41 Queen's LJ 143

CAMERON, J, "The *Charter*'s Legislative Override: Feat or Figment of the Constitutional Imagination?" (2004) 23 Sup Ct L Rev (2d) 135

DODEK, A, "The Canadian Override: Constitutional Model or Bête Noire of Constitutional Politics?"(2016) 49 Israel LR 45

GARDBAUM, S, *The New Commonwealth Model of Judicial Review* (Cambridge: Cambridge University Press, 2013)

GRESCHNER, D, & K NORMAN, "The Courts and Section 33" (1987) 12 Queen's LJ 155

HIEBERT, J, "Is It Too Late to Rehabilitate Canada's Notwithstanding Clause?" (2004) 23 Sup Ct L Rev (2d) 169

---

20 See also S Reid, "Penumbras for the People: Placing Judicial Supremacy under Popular Control" in A Peacock, ed, *Rethinking the Constitution: Perspectives on Canadian Constitutional Reform* (Toronto: Oxford University Press, 1996).

21 T Kahana, "The Notwithstanding Mechanism," above note 8 at 268–69.

KAHANA, T, "The Notwithstanding Mechanism and Public Discussion: Lessons from the Ignored Practice of Section 33" (2001) 43 Can Public Admin 255

KAHANA, T, "Understanding the Notwithstanding Mechanism" (2002) 52 UTLJ 221

LECKEY, R, *Bills of Rights in the Common Law* (Cambridge: Cambridge University Press, 2015)

LESSON, H, "Section 33, The Notwithstanding Clause: A Paper Tiger?" in P Howe & PH Russell, eds, *Judicial Power and Canadian Democracy* (Montréal: McGill-Queen's University Press, 2001)

MANFREDI, C, *Judicial Power and the* Charter, 2d ed (Toronto: Oxford University Press, 2001) c 7

REID, S, "Penumbras for the People: Placing Judicial Supremacy under Popular Control" in A Peacock, ed, *Rethinking the Constitution: Perspectives on Canadian Constitutional Reform* (Toronto: Oxford University Press, 1996)

ROACH, K, "When Should the Section 33 Override Be Used?" (1999) 42 Crim LQ 1

RUSSELL, PH, "Standing Up for Notwithstanding" (1991) 29 Alta L Rev 293

SLATTERY, B, "A Theory of the *Charter*" (1987) 25 Osgoode Hall LJ 701

WEILER, P, "Rights and Judge in a Democracy: A New Canadian Version" (1984) U Mich JL Ref 51

WEINRIB, LE, "Learning to Live with the Override" (1990) 35 McGill LJ 541

WHYTE, JD, "On Not Standing for Notwithstanding" (1990) 28 Alta L Rev 347

CHAPTER 6

APPLICATION

Section 32 of the *Canadian Charter of Rights and Freedoms* states that the *Charter* applies to "the Parliament and government of Canada in respect of all matters within the authority of Parliament" and "to the legislature and government of each province in respect of all matters within the authority of the legislature of each province." In the early years of the *Charter*, there was considerable debate and uncertainty as to the appropriate interpretation of this section. It was not clear whether all legal relationships were subject to *Charter* scrutiny. In all provinces except Quebec, the residual source of law is the common law, which does not depend upon any explicit legislative enactment. Common law rules of contract, property, and tort govern an enormous range of social and economic activity. Does the *Charter* apply to the common law? Another aspect of the common law tradition is the concept that individuals are free to do as they please in the absence of some specific legal measure restraining their freedom. Does the *Charter* reach areas of human activity that are not subject to any specific legislation?

Despite the importance of these issues, the text of the *Charter* was ambiguous. Some commentators thought that the purpose of section 32 was to limit the application of the *Charter* to government action. They argued that it would be wrong to subject the entire legal regime to *Charter* review and that the essence of a constitutional charter of rights was to deal with the relationship between the individual and the state, not all relationships between individuals. Others argued that the supremacy clause in section 52 of the *Constitution Act, 1982*, made the

Charter applicable to all action, public and private, and that section 32 was included simply as a precautionary measure to ensure that all levels of governments were bound.

A. *DOLPHIN DELIVERY*— LIMITING THE APPLICATION OF THE *CHARTER*

This debate was largely put to rest in *Dolphin Delivery*, a case involving unlawful secondary picketing by a union.[1] The employer sought an injunction to prevent the picketing. While most provincial labour codes regulate secondary picketing, this dispute was governed by the *Canada Labour Code*, which was silent on the issue. The employer argued that the union's activity was unlawful on the basis that it amounted to a tort, or civil wrong, recognized by the common law. The union argued that an injunction would violate the guarantee of freedom of expression under section 2(b) of the *Charter*, and the issue arose as to whether the *Charter* had any application to the activities of non-governmental private actors and to the judge-made common law in areas such as tort, contract, and property.

The Supreme Court of Canada concluded that the *Charter* applies only to government. The Court determined that "government" includes the legislative, executive, and administrative branches. Therefore, all laws and regulations are subject to *Charter* scrutiny, as are the actions of the police or other governmental officials in their treatment of individuals. The Court also concluded that the *Charter* must apply to the common law, but only to the extent that the government relies upon it. For example, had the picketers been protesting some public matter and faced a suit by the government, the *Charter* would apply to any common law rules relied upon by the government.[2] As we explain below, the Court significantly qualified the impact of this restrictive approach. It added that the common law should always be interpreted and developed in a manner consistent with the values of the *Charter*, a move that has, as a practical matter, allowed the courts to extend the *Charter*'s reach over the common law in many cases.

Some commentators have argued that the judicial branch and the judge-made common law should be included within the definition of "government." Justice McIntyre, writing for the majority, rejected the argu-

---

1   *RWDSU, Local 580 v Dolphin Delivery Ltd*, [1986] 2 SCR 573, 33 DLR (4th) 174 [*Dolphin Delivery*].
2   *Ibid* at 194–95 (DLR).

ment that a court order constitutes government action.[3] In McIntyre J's words:

> The courts are, of course, bound by the *Charter* as they are bound by all law. It is their duty to apply the law, but in so doing they act as neutral arbiters, not as contending parties in a dispute. To regard a court order as an element of governmental intervention necessary to invoke the *Charter* would, it seems to me, widen the scope of *Charter* application to virtually all private litigation.[4]

The Supreme Court's decision in *Dolphin Delivery* generated much criticism. Many argued that the *Charter* should apply to the common law, since it is an important source of law in Canada.[5] Others were critical of the public/private distinction drawn, which would subject the government — but not other actors — to the *Charter*. In the view of some critics, the Court's decision ignored the fact that private power, often exercised by corporate entities, could just as easily undermine individual liberty and equality as could government action.[6]

Yet there are countervailing arguments to an expansive application of the *Charter*. Was the *Charter* really meant to govern all aspects of individual relationships? For example, should parents' constraints on children's expression or the refusal of a women's bridge group to include male members be subject to *Charter* review?[7] To invite the courts to scrutinize all private as well as public action would greatly extend the reach of the *Charter*, the scope of *Charter* litigation, and the power of the courts. Ironically, many of those who criticize *Dolphin Delivery* for restricting the reach of the *Charter* also contend that the *Charter* represents an unjustifiable expansion of judicial power.

Despite the academic invitation to rethink its approach, the Supreme Court of Canada affirmed its holding in *Dolphin Delivery* in later

---

3   This had been the holding in the leading American case on the point, *Shelley v Kraemer*, 334 US 1 (1948).

4   *Dolphin Delivery*, above note 1 at 196 (DLR).

5   B Slattery, "The *Charter*'s Relevance to Private Litigation: Does *Dolphin* Deliver?" (1987) 32 McGill LJ 905; DM Beatty, "Constitutional Conceits: The Coercive Authority of Courts" (1987) 37 UTLJ 183. Slattery, for example, pointed out the irrationality of having the *Charter* apply to the *Civil Code* in Quebec, which is found in statute, but not to common law.

6   AC Hutchinson & AJ Petter, "Private Wrongs/Public Wrongs: The Liberal Lie of the *Charter*" (1988) 38 UTLJ 278.

7   See, for example, J Whyte, "Is the Private Sector Affected by the *Charter*?" in L Smith *et al*, eds, *Righting the Balance: Canada's New Equality Rights* (Saskatoon: Canadian Human Rights Reporter, 1986) at 145; R Elliot & R Grant, "The *Charter*'s Application in Private Litigation" (1989) 23 UBC L Rev 459.

cases. The explanation for the Court's conclusion lies in its particular vision of the role of the *Charter*. Justice La Forest developed this conception in the mandatory-retirement case. He wrote: "[T]he *Charter* is essentially an instrument for checking the powers of government over the individual . . . . To open up all private and public action to judicial review could strangle the operation of society and . . . could seriously interfere with freedom of contract."[8] In other words, the Supreme Court of Canada sees the exclusive focus of the *Charter* as a judicially enforceable check on government, necessary to protect fundamental rights from the unreasonable actions of politicians and public officials. Absent the Court's intervention, the excesses of government could be curbed only by political action. As noted in Chapter 2, the philosophy underlying the constitutional guarantee of rights is that ordinary politics may not always be adequate to protect individuals and minorities from abuse by majorities. With respect to non-governmental action, this argument for the need for judicial oversight has no application. The legislature has the power to decide the appropriate scope of individual liberty or the balance between equality and liberty, as well as the power to intervene where necessary to check abuses of private authority that undermine individual rights.[9] To say that the *Charter* does not apply to private actors is not to ignore the potential for abuse of private power. Rather, it is to say that the locus of authority for legal controls is best left with the legislature and that it would be inappropriate for the courts to assume responsibility for all issues of social justice for all elements of society.[10]

B. WHAT IS GOVERNMENT?

In the cases following *Dolphin Delivery*, the task for the courts has been to determine what constitutes governmental action for the purposes of the *Charter*. The Supreme Court has held that the *Charter* applies to Cabinet decisions[11] but not to actions of legislative assemblies protect-

8   *McKinney v University of Guelph*, [1990] 3 SCR 229, 76 DLR (4th) 545 at 633–44 [*McKinney*].
9   In *Dolphin Delivery*, above note 1, McIntyre J noted that there are instruments such as human rights codes available to check private abuses.
10 Compare J Bakan, *Just Words: Constitutional Rights and Social Wrongs* (Toronto: University of Toronto Press, 1997).
11 *Operation Dismantle Inc v R*, [1985] 1 SCR 441, 18 DLR (4th) 481, a case involving a Cabinet decision to allow missile testing.

ed by parliamentary privilege.[12] The Court has found that professional bodies exercising regulatory power delegated by the government, such as law societies, are subject to the *Charter*.[13] An adjudicator, appointed under the federal labour code to determine whether an employee was unjustly dismissed, was held to have issued a remedial order contrary to the *Charter* when he ordered the former employer to issue a specific letter of reference. The fact that the statute was the source of the authority for the order made the exercise of the adjudicator's discretion subject to *Charter* principles.[14] Similarly, a provincial human rights commission derives its powers from statute and is subject to the *Charter*, despite the fact that it is not subject to direct government control but exercises independent judicial powers when dealing with particular cases.[15]

Cases have also considered, with varying results, the application of the *Charter* to a number of institutions in the broader public sector. In *McKinney* and *Harrison*, the Supreme Court of Canada held that the *Charter* does not apply to universities, even though they receive government funding, are created by statute, and may have government appointees on their governing bodies.[16] Despite these close links to government, the Court focused on the independence of universities from government control in their day-to-day operations and academic decision making, and it concluded that the *Charter* did not apply to the mandatory-retirement policies of these institutions. Similarly, in *Stoffman*, a hospital was held not to be subject to the *Charter*, despite government funding and some degree of oversight, since here, as well, there was a sufficient element of day-to-day independence.[17]

In contrast, school boards[18] and community colleges[19] have been held to be part of government for purposes of the *Charter*. In a British Columbia case involving a community college, the Supreme Court

12   *New Brunswick Broadcasting Co. v Nova Scotia (Speaker of the House of Assembly)*, [1993] 1 SCR 319, 100 DLR (4th) 212, which refused to subject to *Charter* scrutiny a decision to ban television proceedings in the legislative assembly.

13   *Black v Law Society of Alberta*, [1989] 1 SCR 591, 58 DLR (4th) 317; *Rocket v Royal College of Dental Surgeons of Ontario*, [1990] 2 SCR 232, 71 DLR (4th) 68.

14   *Slaight Communications Inc. v Davidson*, [1989] 1 SCR 1038, 59 DLR (4th) 416.

15   *Blencoe v British Columbia (Human Rights Commission)*, [2000] 2 SCR 307.

16   *McKinney*, above note 8; *Harrison v University of British Columbia* (1990), [1990] 3 SCR 451, [1991] 77 DLR (4th) 55 [*Harrison*].

17   *Stoffman v Vancouver General Hospital*, [1990] 3 SCR 483, 76 DLR (4th) 700 [*Stoffman*].

18   *Chamberlain v Surrey School District No 36*, [2002] 4 SCR 710.

19   *Douglas/Kwantlen Faculty Assn v Douglas College*, [1990] 3 SCR 570; *Lavigne v Ontario Public Service Employees Union*, [1991] 2 SCR 211.

found that the college was an agent of the Crown. In both cases it was noted that there was greater control of college operations and programs by governmental officials than with universities. The result in an Ontario case was to find not only that the college was part of government, but also that the collective agreement signed with a union was subject to the *Charter*. The Court concluded that government, through the college, was bound by the *Charter* not only with respect to its legislative function, but also when making a contract or engaging in commercial activity. As a result, public-sector employment rules are subject to *Charter* scrutiny.

Institutions such as hospitals, regarded as private for certain purposes, may still be subject to the *Charter* where they act on behalf of the government or in furtherance of some specific governmental policy or program. In *Eldridge v British Columbia (AG)*,[20] a hospital's failure to provide an interpreter for hearing-impaired patients was found to be contrary to section 15 of the *Charter*. Although a hospital is not a "government" for *Charter* purposes, its decisions regarding the provision of medically necessary services carried out the specific government objectives of the provincial *Hospital Insurance Act*. The government cannot, in effect, shield such decisions from *Charter* scrutiny by delegating a discretionary power to a private entity. As governments increasingly "contract out" the provision of public services, the issue of *Charter* application to private actors is likely to arise. The Supreme Court has held that, absent specific direction from the police, the actions of private security officers will not be subject to the *Charter*, but warned: "It may be that if the state were to abandon in whole or in part an essential public function to the private sector, even without an express delegation, the private activity could be assimilated to that of a state actor for *Charter* purposes."[21] In *Greater Vancouver Transportation Authority v Canadian Federation of Students — British Columbia Component*,[22] the Supreme Court held that a public transit authority designated by statute to be an "agent of the government" and that was subject to substantial control in its day-to-day activities by means of regulations, was "government" for the purposes of section 32 and therefore subject to the *Charter*.

In sum, the test for determining whether entities such as hospitals, public broadcasters, or the post office are "government" for purposes of the *Charter* turns on the degree to which there is significant control by government ministers or their officials in their day-to-day operations

---

20   [1997] 3 SCR 624, 151 DLR (4th) 577.
21   *R v Buhay*, [2003] 1 SCR 631 at para 31.
22   [2009] 2 SCR 295.

and on the extent to which the entity acts on the government's behalf or furthers some specific governmental policy or program.[23]

C. INDIRECT APPLICATION OF THE *CHARTER*

The *Charter* may also apply to non-governmental actors indirectly, where the courts find that a law fails to go far enough in protecting *Charter* rights. In *Vriend v Alberta*,[24] the issue was whether a private school could refuse to hire teachers because of their sexual orientation. The school was not subject to the *Charter* but did have to comply with Alberta's *Individual's Rights Protection Act*, a statute created to combat discrimination in the private sector. The *Individual's Rights Protection Act* dealt with various forms of discrimination but did not prohibit discrimination on grounds of sexual orientation. The Supreme Court held that the Act violated the gay teacher's *Charter* right to equality by failing to protect him from discrimination. The Court added sexual orientation as a prohibited ground of discrimination under the Act. The practical effect of this ruling was to extend the application of the *Charter*'s equality guarantee to the private sector. Similarly, in *Dunmore v Ontario (Attorney General)*,[25] the Court held that the freedom of association right of agricultural workers was denied by a law that excluded them from the reach of provincial labour laws. The law did nothing to prohibit agricultural workers from forming an association, but without the protection of the law, agricultural workers were impeded from organizing by the economic power of their private-sector employers. The Supreme Court held that this failure to protect *Charter* rights against private power amounted to a *Charter* violation and that the province was required to take the necessary steps to afford agricultural workers the protections enjoyed by other workers. Again, the practical effect of the ruling is indirectly to apply the *Charter* to private action.

---

23   Just as the Canadian test for what is government is developed on a case-by-case basis, so, too, do the American courts struggle with what constitutes "state action." See, for example, the discussion in KE Swinton, "Application of the *Canadian Charter of Rights and Freedoms*" in WS Tarnopolsky & GA Beaudoin, eds, *The* Canadian Charter of Rights and Freedoms: *Commentary* (Toronto: Carswell, 1982) at 41.
24   [1998] 1 SCR 493, 156 DLR (4th) 385 (also discussed in Chapter 17).
25   [2001] 3 SCR 1016, 207 DLR (4th) 193.

D. *CHARTER* VALUES AND THE COMMON LAW

In *Dolphin Delivery*, the Supreme Court concluded that the *Charter* did not apply to the common law unless government relied on it. Nevertheless, the Court went on to say that, although the *Charter* did not apply to disputes between private parties, this was "a distinct issue from the question whether the judiciary ought to apply and develop the principles of the common law in a manner consistent with the fundamental values enshrined in the constitution. The answer to this question must be in the affirmative."[26] Accordingly, the courts are to consider *Charter* principles when developing the common law. This is potentially a significant exception to the otherwise restrictive view of the *Charter*'s application reflected by the *Dolphin Delivery* decision.

In a decision rendered shortly after *Dolphin Delivery*, the Supreme Court of Canada held that the *Charter* applied in a proceeding involving an *ex parte* injunction.[27] The injunction was issued to restrain picketing of a courthouse during a lawful strike, on the basis that this constituted criminal contempt of court. The rules about contempt of court were found in the common law, but the Supreme Court held that the *Charter* nevertheless applied because the judge, in issuing the injunction, acted in a public capacity and invoked criminal law powers: "The criminal law is being applied to vindicate the rule of law and the fundamental freedoms protected by the *Charter*. At the same time, however, this branch of the criminal law, like any other, must comply with the fundamental standards established by the *Charter*."[28]

The *Charter* was similarly invoked in proceedings challenging a judge's order restraining the broadcast of a docudrama while a criminal trial on similar issues was ongoing or about to start.[29] The accused feared that the program might influence jurors and thereby affect the fairness of their criminal trials. On that basis, they obtained an order from a superior court judge prohibiting the broadcast until the completion of the criminal trials. The media then challenged the publication ban under section 2(b) of the *Charter*. Chief Justice Lamer stated that the discretion at common law to order a publication ban in criminal proceedings must be exercised so as to conform to the *Charter*. In his view, the pre-*Charter* common law rule emphasized the right to a fair

---

26 *Dolphin Delivery*, above note 1 at 198 (DLR).
27 *BCGEU v British Columbia (AG)*, [1988] 2 SCR 214, 53 DLR (4th) 1, also discussed in Chapter 9.
28 *Ibid* at 244 (SCR).
29 *Dagenais v Canadian Broadcasting Corp*, [1994] 3 SCR 835, 120 DLR (4th) 12, also discussed in Chapter 9.

trial over the right to freedom of expression. The enhanced protection accorded by the *Charter* to freedom of expression called for a reformulation of the common law rule.[30] Applying the new rule to the facts in the case, Lamer CJC concluded that the initial ban was not justified, since there were alternative measures to safeguard the trial process.[31]

In both these cases, the application of the common law arose in the context of the administration of the criminal law by the courts. In *Hill v Church of Scientology*,[32] the Supreme Court considered the interaction of the *Charter* and the common law in a purely private context. Hill, then a Crown prosecutor, sued the Church of Scientology and its counsel for libel because of various statements made about his conduct. The defendants challenged the validity of the common law of libel, claiming that it violated their right to freedom of expression. Speaking for the Court, Cory J explained why it was necessary to interpret the common law in a manner consistent with *Charter* principles:

> Historically, the common law evolved as a result of the courts making those incremental changes which were necessary in order to make the law comply with current societal values. The *Charter* represents a restatement of the fundamental values which guide and shape our democratic society and our legal system. It follows that it is appropriate for the courts to make such incremental revisions to the common law as may be necessary to have it comply with the values enunciated in the *Charter*.[33]

Justice Cory was careful to insist that the *Charter* does not apply directly to private activity and that it cannot be applied in the same manner as when government action is involved. Judicial law-making is constrained.

---

30 *Ibid* at 38 (DLR):

> A publication ban should only be ordered when:
> (a) Such a ban is *necessary* in order to prevent a real and substantial risk to the fairness of the trial, because reasonably available alternative measures will not prevent the risk; and
> (b) The salutary effects of the publication ban outweigh the deleterious effects to the free expression of those affected by the ban. [emphasis added]

31 *Ibid* at 40 (DLR). The *Charter* was also used to modify the common law rules allowing the Crown prosecutor to introduce evidence of an accused's insanity in *R v Swain*, [1991] 1 SCR 933, 63 CCC (3d) 481.

32 *Hill v Church of Scientology of Toronto*, [1995] 2 SCR 1130, 126 DLR (4th) 129, also discussed in Chapter 9. The Court rejected the argument that there was government action here because Hill was a government employee, concluding that the defamation had been made against him personally, not against the government.

33 *Ibid* at 1169 (SCR).

The courts will effect only incremental changes to the common law; more far-reaching change should be left to the legislature. The limitations clause in section 1 and the *Oakes* test do not apply to the modification of the common law in private litigation. Rather, said Cory J, a more flexible balancing of interests is required, with *Charter* values weighed against the principles underlying the common law. While the Court refused to make significant changes to the common law of libel, the Court did alter the common law rule relating to the reporting of court proceedings as being inconsistent with the *Charter* value of freedom of expression.

More recently, the Supreme Court was prepared to take an aggressive approach to rewriting the law of defamation to comport with the *Charter* value of freedom of expression.[34] In *WIC Radio Ltd v Simpson*,[35] Binnie J, for the majority, signalled that the tort of defamation "may require modification to provide broader accommodation to the value of freedom of expression" and that rules that chill "debate on matters of legitimate public interest" ought to be re-examined[36] and "will necessarily evolve in ways that are consistent with *Charter* values."[37] While those values include "the worth and dignity of each individual, including reputation,"[38] the direction is clearly to accommodate freedom of expression and to move away from common law rules that strongly favoured the protection of reputation. In *WIC Radio*, the Court found the common law defence of fair comment to be unduly restrictive and adopted the approach taken by Dickson J in a pre-*Charter* dissenting opinion. The defence is made out, held the Court, where the comment was on a matter of public interest, is based on fact but is recognizable as comment, and satisfies the following objective test: could any person honestly express that opinion on the proven facts?

An even more significant change came in *Grant v Torstar Corp.*[39] There, the Court held that the traditional common law of defamation gave inadequate weight to freedom of expression and that greater latitude had to be given to the media when reporting on matters of public interest. The common law rule required the defendant to prove the truth of what was said to avoid liability — this rule inhibited debate on matters of public importance. It was replaced by a new defence of responsible communication on matters of public interest. The defendant must show that the matter was of public interest and that he or she had

---

34 These developments are discussed in greater detail in Chapter 9.
35 [2008] 2 SCR 420 [*WIC Radio*].
36 *Ibid* at para 15.
37 *Ibid* at para 24.
38 *Ibid* at para 2.
39 [2009] 3 SCR 640.

acted responsibly and had been diligent in trying to verify the information that was alleged to be defamatory.

In *Retail, Wholesale and Department Store Union, Local 558 v Pepsi-Cola Canada Beverages (West) Ltd,*[40] the Supreme Court returned to the issue of secondary picketing, the same issue raised in *Dolphin Delivery.* While the Court did not depart from its earlier ruling on *Charter* application, it overruled the result in *Dolphin Delivery* by changing the common law rule on secondary picketing. The Court stressed the importance of freedom of expression in the labour context and the need to modify common law rules that impinge upon *Charter* values. The Court found that the common law rule that secondary picketing was in and of itself unlawful conflicted with the fundamental rights of striking workers. The Court ruled that the common law should be modified to allow secondary picketing unless it involved tortious or criminal conduct.

The *Charter* values approach has also been adopted with reference to statutory interpretation, including interpretation of the *Criminal Code.* It has played an important role in interpreting overbroad criminal laws that unduly restrict fundamental freedoms, in particular, freedom of expression.[41] However, *Charter* values may not be used "to create ambiguity when none exists"[42] and have no role to play as an interpretive tool when a statute is unambiguous.[43]

The Court's recognition of the application of *Charter* values to the common law in a private context is significant. By expanding the powers of the courts to modify common law rules, the Supreme Court has greatly lessened the impact of the strict public/private distinction drawn in *Dolphin Delivery* so much so that the same legal point that was decided in *Dolphin Delivery* was determined differently in *Retail, Wholesale and Department Store Union.*

E. EXTRATERRITORIAL APPLICATION

The *Charter* does not, as a general rule, apply to control the conduct of foreign officials acting outside Canada. Ordinarily, the laws of one

40   [2002] 1 SCR 156, 208 DLR (4th) 385 [*Retail, Wholesale and Department Store Union*].
41   *R v Sharpe,* [2001] 1 SCR 45 at para 33; *Application under s 83.28 of the Criminal Code (Re),* [2004] 2 SCR 248 at para 35; *R v Mabior,* 2012 SCC 47 at para 44; *R v Khawaja,* 2012 SCC 69 at para 53.
42   *R v Clarke,* [2014] 1 SCR 612 at para 1.
43   *Wilson v British Columbia (Superintendent of Motor Vehicles),* [2015] 3 SCR 300 at para 25.

state do not have extraterritorial effect nor do they interfere with the sovereignty of another state, and foreign states are not mentioned in section 32. In extradition matters, the Canadian courts have no authority to limit or control the manner in which criminal proceedings are conducted elsewhere.[44] However, where it would "shock the conscience" of Canadians to send an accused person to face treatment that would amount to a violation of fundamental human rights, extradition may be refused on the grounds that the individual's section 7 rights would be violated.[45] In addition, where the requesting state relies upon evidence gathered in Canada, the accused person can challenge the admissibility of such evidence on *Charter* grounds in the Canadian extradition proceedings.[46]

A person facing charges in Canada cannot complain that foreign police gathered evidence in a way that would not be permitted under the *Charter* if the investigation had taken place in Canada.[47] The situation is more complicated where Canadian government officials, such as police, exercise their authority extraterritorially. In *R v Cook*,[48] the appellant, suspected in a murder that had taken place in Vancouver, was arrested in New Orleans by a US marshal pursuant to a Canadian extradition request. Two days after the arrest, two Canadian police officers interviewed the appellant in custody in New Orleans. The officers did not properly advise the appellant of his section 10(b) rights, and the appellant proceeded to make a statement to the officers. At trial, the appellant sought to have the statement excluded from the evidence and argued that it was taken in violation of his *Charter* rights. The Crown argued that the *Charter* did not apply to the officers' actions in New Orleans. The Supreme Court of Canada held that the *Charter* applied to the officers while they were interviewing the appellant and excluded the evidence. The majority recognized that the extraterritorial application of the *Charter* could possibly infringe on the sovereignty of the United States, but found that this did not totally preclude the *Charter* from applying. They held that the *Charter* would apply outside of Canada only when two factors were met: (1) the impugned act fell within section 32(1) of the *Charter* and (2) the application of the

---

44   *Canada v Schmidt*, [1987] 1 SCR 500, 39 DLR (4th) 18.
45   *United States of America v Burns*, [2001] 1 SCR 283, 195 DLR (4th) 1.
46   *United States of America v Anekwu*, [2009] 3 SCR 3.
47   *R v Harrer*, [1995] 3 SCR 562, 128 DLR (4th) 98; *R v Terry*, [1996] 2 SCR 207, 135 DLR (4th) 214.
48   [1998] 2 SCR 597, 164 DLR (4th) 1.

Charter would not generate "an objectionable extraterritorial effect" by interfering with the sovereign authority of the foreign state.[49]

This Court took a more restrictive approach in *R v Hape*.[50] The RCMP suspected that the appellant, a Canadian citizen, was using his investment company, based in Turks and Caicos, to launder money. The RCMP received permission from the detective superintendent of the Turks and Caicos Police Force to conduct an investigation in Turks and Caicos, subject to the condition that the RCMP would work under the detective superintendent's authority. On several occasions, the detective superintendent and the RCMP surreptitiously searched the company's premises and seized a large number of documents. The appellant was subsequently charged in Canada for money laundering, and he claimed that the searches and seizures violated his rights under section 8 of the *Charter*. A majority of the Supreme Court found that the international legal norm of the sovereign equality of states prevents Canada from enforcing its laws within the territory of other nations. Application of section 8 of the *Charter* in favour of the appellant would involve enforcing the *Charter* in the foreign country and thus was held to be prohibited by the norms of public international law.

However, application of the *Charter* is not excluded where the norm of sovereign equality of states does not apply. The Court identified two situations where this may occur. The first is where the foreign state consents to Canada enforcing its laws within the foreign state, a situation which, the Court conceded, "may be rare."[51] The second is where Canada's actions in the foreign state have involved it in activities that violate international law. In such a situation, the principle of comity does not require that Canada respect the sovereign equality of the foreign state to breach international law, and thus there is no obstacle to the *Charter*'s application. It was on this basis that the Supreme Court held, in *Canada (Justice) v Khadr*,[52] that a prisoner at Guantanamo Bay was entitled to disclosure of interviews conducted by Canadian authorities there because the process of indefinite detention subject to possible trial as unlawful combatants by military commission at Guantanamo Bay had been found by the Supreme Court of the United States to violate international norms, namely, the Geneva Conventions. Omar Khadr's right to disclosure, however, did not follow domestic standards accorded to those in Canada. Khadr was only entitled to disclosure

---

49   *Ibid* at para 25.
50   [2007] 2 SCR 292 [*Hape*].
51   *Ibid* at para 106.
52   [2008] 2 SCR 125 [*Khadr*]. See also *Canada (Prime Minister) v Khadr*, [2010] 1 SCR 44.

of material that was directly related to Canadian participation in the violation of international human rights. The Court did not specify the exact nature of the *Charter* violation in this case, but it indicated that Canadian conduct that violates Canada's international human rights obligations will violate section 7 of the *Charter*.[53] In addition, the Court in *Khadr* made reference to Omar Khadr's Canadian citizenship, and lower courts have rejected similar claims for disclosure of material collected by Canadian officials about non-citizens held at Guantanamo Bay.[54] *Khadr* has also been distinguished by the Federal Court of Appeal in holding that the *Charter* does not apply with respect to the Canadian detention of captives in Afghanistan in large part because the captives were not Canadian citizens.[55] The relevance of Canadian citizenship should be clarified in this context given that section 7 rights are extended to "everyone," not only Canadian citizens.

Even in cases where the *Charter* is found to be inapplicable to extraterritorial activities of the Canadian authorities, claimants may not be without a remedy. In situations where an accused being tried in Canada claims that evidence was gathered in a foreign jurisdiction in breach of *Charter* rights but the *Charter* does not apply, the accused may still seek to have the evidence excluded pursuant to sections 7 or 11(d) of the *Charter* where admitting the evidence would render the trial unfair.[56] Application of the *Charter* in this manner to protect fair trial rights in Canada does not violate the international legal norm as it does not involve the enforcement of Canadian law in a foreign state.

F. CLAIMING *CHARTER* RIGHTS

To this point, the focus has been on whether the *Charter* applies to particular actions or entities, but another important application issue should also be mentioned: namely, who can invoke *Charter* rights? Some of the rights are framed as "everyone has the right" (for example, the fundamental freedoms of expression and religion in section 2 and the right to life, liberty, and security of the person in section 7). Others are available to "any person," as in the legal rights in section 11, or to an "individual," as in the equality rights in section 15. Some are available to citizens or permanent residents (for example, mobility rights in

---

53   See discussion below in Chapter 13.
54   *Slahi and Zemiri v Canada (Minister of Justice)*, 2009 FCA 259.
55   *Amnesty International v Canada*, 2008 FCA 401.
56   *Hape*, above note 50 at paras 107–9.

section 6 and minority-language education rights in section 23). The *Charter* applies to foreign nationals seeking entry into Canada.[57]

Some *Charter* rights have been held to be unavailable to corporations. For example, the equality rights in section 15 and the right to life, liberty, and security of the person in section 7 have been deemed to be rights that can be exercised only by human beings.[58] Corporations can, however, invoke certain rights that have been seen as appropriate for a corporate entity — for example, freedom of expression.[59]

Even if a corporation cannot directly claim that its rights have been violated, it may have standing to raise a *Charter* issue in criminal or regulatory proceedings, where a law under which it is being prosecuted is alleged to be in violation of others' *Charter* rights. For example, if a corporation is prosecuted under a law prohibiting Sunday shopping, it can challenge the law as a denial of freedom of religion even though section 2(a), the guarantee of freedom of religion, does not apply directly to a corporation.[60] The reason for this lies in the concept of the rule of law: that no one should be subject to prosecution under an unconstitutional law.[61]

G. CONCLUSION

Dolphin Delivery determined that the basic principle of *Charter* application is that the purpose of the constitution is to check the power of government over the individual. There is no question but that this represents a significant constraint on the reach of the *Charter*, especially in an age of shrinking government. The sharp distinction between the public and private domains and the immunity of powerful private interests from *Charter* scrutiny is thought by many to be unduly restrictive. On the other hand, the courts have also been criticized for assuming too much power under the *Charter* and, indeed, the reach of the *Charter* would be unlimited were it not for *Dolphin Delivery*. In the end, the question is an institutional one: which body is best able to deal with the power of private interests — the courts or the legislatures? The Supreme Court has determined that it is not prepared to assume responsibility for all issues of social justice and that it should focus its

---

57   *Singh v Canada (Minister of Employment and Immigration)*, [1985] 1 SCR 177; *R v Appulonappa*, [2015] 3 SCR 754.

58   *Irwin Toy v Quebec (Attorney General)*, [1989] 1 SCR 927 at 1001–3.

59   *Ibid.*

60   *R v Big M Drug Mart Ltd*, [1985] 1 SCR 295, 18 DLR (4th) 321.

61   Further discussion of constitutional litigation is found in Chapter 7.

efforts under the *Charter* to resolving conflicts between the individual and the state. On the other hand, *Dolphin Delivery* leaves considerable scope for extending the *Charter*'s reach into the common law. While not directly subject to the *Charter*, the common law is a form of judge-made law, and the courts are directed to pay heed to *Charter* values in its development. This has produced some significant changes and represents an important gloss on the principle that limits the *Charter*'s application to government action.

FURTHER READINGS

BEATTY, DM, "Constitutional Conceits: The Coercive Authority of Courts" (1987) 37 UTLJ 183

BERGER, B, "The Reach of the Security State" (2008) 56 CR (6th) 268

DE MESTRAL, A, & E FOX-DECENT, "Rethinking the Relationship between International and Domestic Law" (2008) 53 McGill LJ 573

ELLIOT, R, & R GRANT, "The *Charter*'s Application in Private Litigation" (1989) 23 UBC L Rev 459

FAIRLEY, HS, "International Law Comes of Age: *R v Hape*" (2008) 87 Can Bar Rev 229

HARDING, M, & R KNOPFF, "Constitutionalizing Everything: The Role of '*Charter* Values'" (2013) 18 Rev Const Stud 141

MARIN, M, "Should the *Charter* Apply to Universities?" (2015) 35 Nat'l J Const L 29

REICHMAN, A, "A *Charter*-Free Domain: In Defence of *Dolphin Delivery*" (2002) 35 UBC L Rev 329

ROACH, K, "The Supreme Court at the Bar of Politics: The Afghan Detainee and Omar Khadr Cases" (2011) 28 NJCL 115

SLATTERY, B, "The *Charter*'s Relevance to Private Litigation: Does *Dolphin* Deliver?" (1987) 32 McGill LJ 905

SWINTON, KE, "Application of the *Canadian Charter of Rights and Freedoms*" in WS Tarnopolsky & GA Beaudoin, eds, *The* Canadian Charter of Rights and Freedoms: *Commentary* (Toronto: Carswell, 1982)

WALDMAN, L, "The *Charter* in an International Context" (2007) 23 NJCL 85

WHYTE, J, "Is the Private Sector Affected by the *Charter?*" in L Smith *et al*, eds, *Righting the Balance: Canada's New Equality Rights* (Saskatoon: Canadian Human Rights Reporter, 1986)

CHAPTER 7

CHARTER LITIGATION

Charter issues are decided in the ordinary course of litigation.[1] Any citizen whose rights are affected is entitled to raise a constitutional issue in a civil proceeding or by way of defence to a criminal prosecution. Canadian law follows the Anglo-American legal tradition and does not assign particular responsibility to a specialized court for the adjudication of constitutional disputes. The court that has jurisdiction over the dispute has, by virtue of that jurisdiction, authority to decide the constitutional issue.

This method of dealing with constitutional cases has important implications for the manner in which constitutional issues are decided. It means that *Charter* issues will almost always arise in a fact-specific context and be decided in the course of a concrete dispute between two parties. The primary task of the court is to decide the case before it, not to pronounce at large upon the constitution or its meaning. It is an established practice in Canadian law that, if a judge can decide a case without dealing with a constitutional issue, he or she should do so. Moreover, because proceedings in Canadian courts are strictly adversarial, a judge will not ordinarily comment upon a constitutional issue unless one is raised by the parties. Even if there is believed to be a constitutional issue that may arise on the facts, it would be unusual

---

1   Both this chapter and Chapter 17 draw freely on a contribution to a collection on Canadian constitutional law published in Italian: RJ Sharpe, "Ordinamento giudiziario e giustizia costituzionale" in *L'ordinamento costituzionale del Canada* (Torino: G Giappichelli Editore, 1997).

for a judge to deal with the issue if the parties do not raise it. It is for the parties to the dispute to define the issues before the court. Similarly, the parties control the presentation of evidence and argument.

A. INTERVENTION BY THE ATTORNEY GENERAL AND PUBLIC-INTEREST GROUPS

While constitutional cases generally follow the same procedural path as other cases, there are some important exceptions and special procedural rules to reflect the wide range of interests implicated and the importance of any decision for the future. The first concerns the representation of the public and other interests. A party who challenges the constitutional validity of a statute is required to give notice to the attorney general — provincial, federal, or both, as appropriate.[2] The attorney general has the right to intervene in the proceeding and to present whatever evidence or argument he or she deems necessary to defend the constitutionality of the law. This may seem to depart from the adversarial system by allowing for non-party participation, but, in fact, interventions by the attorney general reflect the underlying values of the adversarial system. A constitutional case implicates the public interest, and it is a basic tenet of the adversarial system that rights should not be affected without affording the right-holder a hearing. The intervention of the attorney general ensures that the public interest will be represented before the courts when the constitutionality of a statute is attacked and that any evidence required to satisfy section 1 to justify a *prima facie Charter* violation will be brought before the court.[3]

A second important development in constitutional litigation, particularly at the level of the Supreme Court of Canada, is the generous allowance for public-interest groups to appear as intervenors.[4] While the courts were initially cautious in this area,[5] the discretion to permit public-interest groups to intervene has been frequently exercised. Once again, this is a reflection of the fact that the decision of the court on a constitutional matter will have broad public ramifications. Those

---

2   See BL Strayer, *The Canadian Constitution and the Courts: The Function and Scope of Judicial Review*, 3d ed (Toronto: Butterworths, 1988) at 73–86.

3   *Guindon v Canada,* [2015] 3 SCR 3 at para 113.

4   PR Muldoon, *Law of Intervention: Status and Practice* (Aurora, ON: Canada Law Book, 1989).

5   K Swan, "Intervention and *Amicus Curiae* Status in *Charter* Litigation" in RJ Sharpe, ed, Charter *Litigation* (Toronto: Butterworths, 1987).

who have particular interests that are affected and who can assist the court should be heard.

Certain public-interest groups have appeared regularly before the Supreme Court of Canada in *Charter* litigation and they have had a significant influence. Notable are the interventions of the Canadian Civil Liberties Association, a body that exists to defend the interests of civil liberties, and the Women's Legal Education and Action Fund, or LEAF, a feminist group concerned with equality rights. There can be little question but that the reasoning of certain Supreme Court judgments has been influenced by, or even based upon, arguments presented by these groups. At the same time, it should be noted that these two groups have opposed each other on issues such as hate propaganda and obscenity and that attorneys general remain the most frequent intervenors in *Charter* cases. To be accepted as an intervenor, a group must apply to the court before the case is heard and demonstrate both that it has a serious interest in the issues to be litigated and that it has a distinctive perspective to bring to bear upon those issues. If given intervenor status, the group will have the opportunity to file written argument and will often be permitted to make brief oral submissions. Intervenors are bound by the evidence heard at trial, but they can call the attention of the court to published articles and reports.

B. REFERENCES

There is one significant exception to the general rule that constitutional disputes are decided in the course of ordinary litigation. The *Supreme Court Act* provides that the federal government may refer directly to the Court questions of law or fact concerning the interpretation of the constitution or the constitutionality or interpretation of any federal or provincial legislation.[6] There is similar legislation in each province permitting provincial governments to refer questions to the provincial Court of Appeal.[7] References have become a familiar and distinctive feature of Canadian constitutional law.[8] Most countries that follow the common law tradition do not permit references, and the device has been rejected as unconstitutional in both the United States[9] and Australia[10]

---

6   RSC 1985, c S-26, s 53.

7   See, for example, *Courts of Justice Act*, RSO 1990, c C.43, s 8.

8   See Strayer, above note 2 at 315–18.

9   L Tribe, *American Constitutional Law*, 2d ed (Mineola: Foundation Press, 1988) at 73–77.

10 *Re Judiciary and Navigation Acts* (1921), 29 CLR 257.

and exists only in a very different and modified form in England.[11] Technically, a reference asks the court for an advisory opinion and, accordingly, the answer given by the court lacks the formal quality of a judgment for purposes of the doctrine of precedent. However, in practice, opinions rendered on references are almost invariably followed in subsequent litigation and treated in the same way as a judgment given in an ordinary case.[12]

References have often been used when a government considers it to be in the public interest to have an immediate resolution by the appellate court of a constitutional issue. The procedure circumvents the normal process of trial, appeal, and further appeal to the Supreme Court of Canada and allows the government to obtain a relatively quick answer to a constitutional issue. It is also possible for one government to direct a reference as to the constitutionality of another government's law or proposed course of action. There are important examples of this being done by the federal government,[13] and the technique has also been used by provincial governments.

The most notable instance of a provincial reference with regard to a proposed federal course of action arose in connection with the patriation of the constitution in 1981.[14] The federal government had indicated that it would proceed to request the United Kingdom Parliament to amend the Canadian constitution, although it had the consent of only two of the ten provinces. Three provincial governments referred the question to their courts of appeal, and those cases were then appealed to the Supreme Court of Canada, which ruled that constitutional convention precluded the federal government from proceeding in the manner proposed. The result was that all governments were sent back to the bargaining table for a further round of talks and negotiation, and significant changes were made to the constitutional amendments that were eventually enacted.[15]

The most notable instance of a federal reference in relation to possible provincial action was the 1998 reference on the constitutionality of unilateral separation of a province. The reference, known as the

---

11   See J Jaconelli, "Hypothetical Disputes, Moot Points of Law, and Advisory Opinions" (1985) 101 Law Q Rev 587.

12   *Canada (Attorney General) v Bedford*, [2013] 3 SCR 1101 at para 40.

13   *Reference Re Alberta Legislation*, [1938] SCR 100, [1938] 2 DLR 81.

14   *Reference Re Amendment to the Constitution of Canada*, [1981] 1 SCR 753, 125 DLR (3d) 1 [*Patriation Reference*].

15   For an account of the process and negotiations, see RJ Romanow, J Whyte, & HA Leeson, *Canada . . . Notwithstanding: The Making of the Constitution, 1976–1982* (Toronto: Carswell Methuen, 1984).

Quebec Secession Reference,[16] posed a hypothetical question because the province was not proposing to separate from Canada. The Quebec government refused to participate in the reference, and the Court appointed an *amicus curiae* or friend of the court to argue that Quebec had a right under domestic and international law to unilateral separation from Canada. The Court concluded that there was no right to unilateral separation. It indicated, however, that there would be an obligation for Canada to negotiate separation should a province receive a sufficient popular mandate, on a sufficiently clear question, to separate from Canada. The Court, however, refused to decide what would be a sufficiently clear question or mandate. As with the earlier *Patriation Reference*, the ultimate effect of this reference may be to send the parties to the bargaining table should a province ever decide to vote to separate from Canada.

One shortcoming of the reference procedure is that the court lacks the usual factual foundation because it is presented with an abstract question. Canadian judges are often troubled by this, since it is out of keeping with the fact-specific manner in which constitutional issues are ordinarily presented. On occasion, the Supreme Court has complained of being asked to answer a constitutional question without a specific factual context.[17] The Court has even said that it is not obliged to answer a reference if there is an insufficient basis for adjudication,[18] but the right to decline has been exercised infrequently. The most significant case in which the Supreme Court has refused to answer a reference question was *Reference Re Same-Sex Marriage*.[19] In that high-profile reference, the Court exercised its discretion to refuse to answer one of four questions placed before it by the federal government. The question, which had been added by the government after the reference was originally posed, was whether restricting marriages to unions of men with women was consistent with the *Charter*. Courts in five provinces and one territory had already decided that the opposite-sex requirement violated equality rights under section 15 of the *Charter* and could not be justified under section 1. The Supreme Court concluded that an answer to this question was not advisable given that a ruling might undermine the government's stated goal of legislating

---

16 *Reference Re Secession of Quebec*, [1998] 2 SCR 217, 161 DLR (4th) 385, also discussed in Chapter 1.

17 *Manitoba (AG) v Manitoba Egg and Poultry Association*, [1971] SCR 689 at 704–5, 19 DLR (3d) 169.

18 *Reference Re Legislative Authority of Parliament to Alter or Replace the Senate*, [1980] 1 SCR 54, 102 DLR (3d) 1.

19 [2004] 3 SCR 698, 246 DLR (4th) 193.

to recognize same-sex marriages and achieving uniformity in the law. The Court also noted that perhaps thousands of same-sex couples had relied on the finality of the lower court judgments and that their vested rights outweighed the benefits of answering the question. At the same time, the Court answered three other questions relating to Parliament's exclusive legislative authority to legislate in relation to marriage, the consistency of proposed legislation extending the right to marry to same-sex couples with the *Charter*, and the protection that freedom of religion provided religious officials from being compelled to perform a same-sex marriage.

References have been used to resolve pressing *Charter* issues. In Ontario, the provincial government employed the reference procedure when it decided to extend full funding to Roman Catholic separate schools. A variety of interests, including private and religious schools, which did not enjoy like support, attacked this measure as being contrary to the section 15 guarantee of equality. Prolonged litigation could have disrupted the administration of Ontario schools for years and the government decided that it would be in the public interest to have the matter resolved quickly. A reference was directed to the Ontario Court of Appeal,[20] and an appeal was then taken to the Supreme Court of Canada.[21] Both courts upheld the constitutionality of the scheme. With a few exceptions, however, there has been little use of the reference procedure to decide *Charter* issues and almost all *Charter* cases have been decided through ordinary litigation between parties in adversarial disputes, most frequently in cases in which the state prosecuted an individual.

C. DECLARATORY PROCEEDINGS, STANDING, ADVANCE COSTS, AND MOOTNESS

A private citizen is not entitled to direct a reference but may, in certain specific situations, bring what is known as a declaratory action in which no relief or remedy is sought other than an order of a court that a statute is contrary to the constitution. Canadian courts, like other common law courts, are wary of declaratory proceedings and have established certain rules of standing that must be met. Rules of standing

---

20 *Reference Re Bill 30, An Act to Amend the Education Act (Ontario)* (1986), 53 OR (2d) 513 (CA).

21 *Reference Re Bill 30, An Act to Amend the Education Act (Ontario)*, [1987] 1 SCR 1148, 40 DLR (4th) 18.

are thought to be necessary to avoid a flood of litigation, to conserve judicial resources and limit judicial power, and to ensure that constitutional disputes arise in the usual adversarial setting where only interested parties motivated to present strong arguments are represented.

Ordinarily, a citizen must indicate a specific legal interest or right that is threatened by the statute challenged; however, the Canadian courts have also carved out generous exceptions to the rules of standing and have said that the courts have a discretion to permit a declaratory suit to proceed even where the plaintiff does not present the usual specific legal right or interest.[22] According generous standing facilitates the legality principle "that state action should conform to the Constitution and statutory authority and that there must be practical and effective ways to challenge the legality of state action."[23]

There are three factors to consider. First, the citizen must demonstrate that the case raises a serious legal issue. Second, it must be shown that the citizen has some genuine interest in bringing the proceeding. Third, there must be no other reasonable or effective way to bring the issue before the court. Certain statutes do not specify penalties or other sanctions, or, if they do, it is unlikely that those who are subjected to such penalties or sanctions would challenge the statute. In these situations, a private citizen who lacks the usual special interest will be permitted to bring a declaratory proceeding. The underlying rationale to this exception to the standing rules is that no statute should be immune from judicial review.

Despite this relaxed approach, the Supreme Court denied public-interest standing to an interest group seeking to challenge the constitutionality of refugee procedures on the basis that individual refugee applicants were in a better position to bring challenges in individual cases.[24] However, a more receptive approach was taken in *Canada (Attorney General) v Downtown Eastside Sex Workers United Against Violence Society*,[25] where the Court upheld the standing of an association of sex-trade workers to challenge the constitutional validity of *Criminal*

22 *Thorson v Canada (AG)*, [1975] 1 SCR 138, 43 DLR (3d) 1; *Nova Scotia Board of Censors v McNeil*, [1976] 2 SCR 265, 55 DLR (3d) 632; *Borowski v Canada (Minister of Justice)*, [1981] 2 SCR 575, 130 DLR (3d) 588; *Canadian Council of Churches v Canada*, [1992] 1 SCR 236, 88 DLR (4th) 193 [*Canadian Council of Churches*]; *Hy and Zel's Inc v Ontario (Attorney General)*, [1993] 3 SCR 675, 107 DLR (4th) 634. For a general account of standing in Canadian law, see TA Cromwell, *Locus Standi* (Toronto: Carswell, 1986).

23 *Canada (Attorney General) v Downtown Eastside Sex Workers United Against Violence Society*, [2012] 2 SCR 524.

24 *Canadian Council of Churches*, above note 22.

25 Above note 23.

Code provisions dealing with prostitution. Justice Cromwell, writing for the Court, reformulated the third factor as "whether the proposed suit is, in all the circumstances . . . a reasonable and effective means to bring the challenge to the court."[26] Matters that bear upon this factor include the capacity, expertise, and resources of the plaintiff to bring the suit in an appropriate factual setting and the interest of providing access to justice to the disadvantaged. In assessing realistic alternatives, the courts should take a practical rather than a theoretical approach and look, as well, to the impact that granting standing could have upon those with a more direct interest. Justice Cromwell emphasized that the three factors, especially the final one, "should not be treated as hard and fast requirements or free-standing, independently operating tests" but rather as factors to "be assessed and weighed cumulatively, in light of the underlying purposes of limiting standing and applied in a flexible and generous manner that best serves those underlying purposes."[27] The Court, in this case, granted public-interest standing to a group to bring a coordinated *Charter* challenge to a variety of prostitution laws even though somewhat similar challenges had been brought in other provinces and those accused of committing such offences could also challenge their constitutionality.

In the *Chaoulli* case, the Supreme Court held that an opponent of medical waiting lists, who had received operations in the public system, and a doctor who wanted to open a private hospital, had public-interest standing to challenge a Quebec restriction on private health insurance. It was not reasonable to expect a person who was denied treatment because of a waiting list to bring the case because "the material, physical and emotional resources of individuals who are ill, and quite possibly dying, are likely to be focused on their own circumstances."[28]

Section 24(1) of the *Charter* has its own test for standing, which requires that "anyone whose rights or freedoms guaranteed by this *Charter*, have been infringed or denied" may apply for an appropriate and just remedy. The Supreme Court has interpreted this section to apply to apprehended violations of the *Charter* so that a person does not have to wait until his or her rights have been violated before obtaining a remedy.[29] At the same time, however, the Court has required that the

---

26 *Ibid* at para 44.
27 *Ibid* at para 20.
28 *Chaoulli v Quebec (Attorney General)*, [2005] 1 SCR 791 at para 189 [*Chaoulli*], Binnie and LeBel JJ, in dissent but not on this point. See also para 35, Deschamps J.
29 *New Brunswick (Minister of Health and Community Services) v G(J)*, [1999] 3 SCR 46, 177 DLR (4th) 124 at para 51; *United States of America v Kwok* (2001), 197 DLR (4th) 1 at para 66.

person's own rights be at stake and have not granted an accused standing under section 24(1) to argue that police seizure of evidence violated the rights of a third party.[30]

A more generous test for standing applies where the validity of a law is challenged under section 52 of the *Charter*. Individuals are entitled to challenge constitutionality of the law under which they are charged even if the alleged constitutional infirmity is not directed at them. In *R v Big M Drug Mart Ltd*,[31] a corporation was allowed to challenge Canada's Sunday closing law as an infringement of freedom of religion even though a corporation cannot have a religion. In the words of Dickson J, "no one can be convicted of an offence under an unconstitutional law."[32] The same principle allowed a person charged with unlawful possession of cannabis to challenge the validity of the medical marijuana exemptions even though he did not possess the drug for medical purposes.[33]

Even if a person has been granted public-interest standing or standing under section 24(1) of the *Charter*, *Charter* litigation is expensive. The majority of *Charter* cases that are decided by the Supreme Court arise in criminal cases. In such cases, the accused has every incentive to litigate a *Charter* issue and can generally obtain legal aid funding if he or she cannot afford to defend serious criminal charges and faces the risk of imprisonment. It may be more difficult to finance civil litigation, and a litigant who commences an action against the government also faces the downside risk of being liable for a portion of the successful party's costs should the litigant not prevail. The courts, however, have a discretion not to require an unsuccessful *Charter* litigant to pay the government's costs. The courts also have a discretion to award advance costs but have restricted this discretion to rare and exceptional cases where the party cannot afford to pay for litigation, where the claim is meritorious, and when the issues transcend the individual interests of the litigants and are of public importance.[34] Even when those conditions are satisfied, advance costs are ordered only as a "last resort"[35] and are

---

30   *R v Edwards*, [1996] 1 SCR 128, 132 DLR (4th) 31; *Benner v Canada (Secretary of State)* (1997), 143 DLR (4th) 577 at 604.

31   [1985] 1 SCR 295.

32   *Ibid* at 313.

33   *R v Smith*, [2015] 2 SCR 602.

34   *British Columbia (Minister of Forests) v Okanagan Indian Band*, [2003] 3 SCR 371; *Little Sisters Book and Art Emporium v Canada (Commissioner of Customs and Revenue)*, [2007] 1 SCR 38 at para 37 [*Little Sisters*]; *R v Caron*, [2011] 1 SCR 78, 2011 SCC 5.

35   *Little Sisters*, above note 34 at paras 73 and 105.

not intended "to create a parallel system of legal-aid."[36] The courts also have a discretion to award a successful public interest litigant "special costs" to provide full indemnification for the costs of bringing the suit if the case meets the same test as that for advanced costs.[37]

Another issue that arises with some frequency in *Charter* litigation is whether the courts should decide a *Charter* issue that is "moot" because there is no longer a concrete dispute between the parties. The courts have a discretion to decide moot cases, and the exercise of that discretion is influenced by factors similar to those used to decide whether to grant public-interest standing. These factors include the question of whether the case has been presented in an adversarial manner, judicial economy, relations with the executive and legislature, and the dangers of immunizing actions from review.[38] The last factor especially has been held to justify deciding a *Charter* issue that is moot, but that is "evasive of review" because the same issue is unlikely to come before the courts in a concrete form.[39]

D. THE SYSTEM OF COURTS AND JURISDICTION IN *CHARTER* CASES

As noted above, the general rule is that *Charter* issues are resolved in the ordinary course of litigation. The Supreme Court of Canada has rejected the proposition that the *Charter* itself confers jurisdiction to decide cases under either section 24(1) of the *Charter*, which contemplates courts awarding appropriate and just remedies, or section 52(1) of the *Constitution Act, 1982*, which provides that laws inconsistent with the *Charter* are of no force and effect. Accordingly, authority to decide a *Charter* issue turns on the pre-1982 court structure. In order to award a remedy under section 24(1) of the *Charter*, the court or administrative tribunal must have jurisdiction independent of the *Charter* over

---

36   *Ibid* at para 5. A superior court had inherent jurisdiction to order interim costs to a litigant involved in a regulatory prosecution in a provincial court that raises a significant *Charter* issue — here, language rights: *R v Caron*, above note 34.

37   *Carter v Canada (Attorney General)*, [2015] 1 SCR 331; *Association des parents de l'école Rose-des-vents v British Columbia (Education)*, [2015] 2 SCR 139.

38   *Borowski v Canada (Attorney General)*, [1989] 1 SCR 342, 57 DLR (4th) 231.

39   *New Brunswick (Minister of Health and Community Services) v G(J)*, above note 29 at para 45; *Doucet-Boudreau v Nova Scotia (Minister of Education)*, [2003] 3 SCR 3 at para 20.

the parties, the subject matter, and the remedy.[40] In order to apply the *Charter*, an administrative body must generally have the power to decide questions of law. More recently, the Court presumes that tribunals have *Charter* jurisdiction, but the presumption can still be rebutted by clear legislation.[41]

1) Administrative Tribunals

At both the federal and provincial levels, there are a significant number of specialized boards and tribunals with adjudicative powers. These boards and tribunals play a vital role in resolving disputes that arise as to the administration of a wide variety of legislative schemes that advance governmental policies. The Supreme Court has taken a generous approach to the ability of these administrative boards and tribunals to apply the *Charter*. A board or tribunal with the explicit or implicit authority to decide questions of law has the authority to apply the *Charter* in its decisions and to decide whether its enabling legislation is consistent with the *Charter*.[42] In *R v Conway*,[43] the Supreme Court held that if a specialized tribunal has the power to decide questions of law, the tribunal will also have jurisdiction to decide *Charter* issues and to grant *Charter* remedies arising in the course of carrying out its statutory mandate unless *Charter* jurisdiction is excluded by statute. The authority of an administrative tribunal to make a binding declaration of invalidity will be limited by the scope of the tribunal's authority to decide questions of law.

The decisions of administrative tribunals are ordinarily subject to review by the superior courts, either by way of a statutory appeal or by judicial review. The Supreme Court of Canada has modified its view that all *Charter* decisions made by administrative bodies are reviewed

---

40   *R v Mills*, [1986] 1 SCR 863, 29 DLR (4th) 161 [*Mills*]; *R v 974649 Ontario Inc*, [2001] 3 SCR 575, 206 DLR (4th) 444 [*974649 Ontario Inc*].

41   *R v Conway*, [2010] 1 SCR 765, 2010 SCC 22. For decisions holding that various administrative bodies could not apply the *Charter*, see *Canada (Employment and Immigration Commission) v Tétreault-Gadoury*, [1991] 2 SCR 22, 81 DLR (4th) 121 [*Tétreault-Gadoury*]. For a general account of jurisdiction under s 24(1) of the *Charter* and s 52(1) of the *Constitution Act, 1982*, see K Roach, *Constitutional Remedies in Canada*, 2d ed (Toronto: Canada Law Book, 2013) c 6.

42   *Douglas/Kwantlen Faculty Assn v Douglas College*, [1990] 3 SCR 570; *Cuddy Chicks Ltd v Ontario (Labour Relations Board)*, [1991] 2 SCR 5; *Tétreault-Gadoury*, above note 41.

43   Above note 41.

by the superior courts on a correctness standard.[44] Where a decision by an administrative body is challenged as being contrary to the *Charter*, the decision will be reviewed on the administrative law reasonableness standard. The strict section 1 *Oakes* proportionality test does not apply, and the question becomes whether the administrative decision-maker has reasonably balanced the *Charter* rights or values at issue with the statutory objective.[45]

2) Provincial Courts

Each of the ten provinces has its own judicial system with trial courts and a Court of Appeal. At the trial level, provincial courts deal with minor criminal offences and also have jurisdiction over more serious offences with the consent of the accused. In addition, provincial courts deal with small civil claims and some family matters. The judges of these courts are appointed by the provincial governments. As many *Charter* issues arise in criminal cases, the provincial courts are often the court of first instance for a *Charter* challenge. When conducting trials, provincial court judges have full jurisdiction to apply the *Charter*. They can rule on the constitutionality of the legislation under which charges are laid and make all necessary *Charter* procedural and evidentiary rulings.[46] However, because these courts are statutory and exercise only the jurisdiction that is specifically assigned to them, there are limits upon their authority to resolve *Charter* issues. For example, provincial court judges hearing preliminary inquiries, as opposed to trials, do not have jurisdiction to exclude unconstitutionally obtained evidence.[47] Provincial court judges in criminal courts also do not have jurisdiction to award damages as a section 24(1) *Charter* remedy, but they have been held to have jurisdiction to award costs as such a remedy.[48]

3) Superior Courts

The superior courts of each province exercise general and "inherent," or residual, jurisdiction over civil and criminal matters and play a special

---

44   *Nova Scotia (Workers' Compensation Board) v Martin*, [2003] 2 SCR 504; *Okwuobi v Lester Pearson School Board*, [2005] 1 SCR 257; *Multani v Commission scolaire Marguerite-Bourgeoys*, [2006] 1 SCR 256.

45   *Doré v Barreau du Québec*, [2012] 1 SCR 395; *Loyola High School v Quebec (Attorney General)*, [2015] 1 SCR 613.

46   *R v Lloyd*, 2016 SCC 13 at paras 14–20.

47   *Mills*, above note 40; *R v Hynes*, [2001] 3 SCR 623.

48   *974649 Ontario Inc*, above note 40.

and constitutionally guaranteed role under the Canadian constitution. The judges of these courts are appointed by the federal government. Superior courts also possess the authority of judicial review with respect to administrative agencies and have some appellate jurisdiction over the provincial courts. The provincial superior courts have authority to apply both federal and provincial laws. They have "constant, complete and concurrent jurisdiction"[49] to hear requests for *Charter* remedies under section 24(1) of the *Charter*, as well as to hear challenges to the constitutional validity of all laws. Thus, it follows that the provincial superior courts have the broadest possible authority to decide *Charter* issues in the first instance.

4) Federal Court

The Federal Court of Canada has specific jurisdiction over certain matters that fall within federal legislative competence as enumerated by the division of powers. Yet it does not have inherent jurisdiction and there are strict limits on its jurisdiction.[50] The Federal Court has authority over federal administrative law as well as certain special subjects such as admiralty, intellectual property, and suits against the federal government. Given its jurisdiction over federal administrative law and suits against the federal government, many *Charter* issues are decided by the Federal Court. However, the provincial superior courts also have full jurisdiction with respect to the constitutionality of federal laws, including declaratory suits brought against the federal Crown.[51] Hence, the provincial superior courts retain a much broader jurisdiction than the Federal Court and play a more important role in the adjudication of *Charter* issues.

5) The Supreme Court of Canada

Appeals from judgments from the provincial courts and the provincial superior courts are taken to the provincial Court of Appeal, and from there to the Supreme Court of Canada. Appeals from the Federal Court,

---

49   *R v Rahey*, [1987] 1 SCR 588, 39 DLR (4th) 481 at 491.
50   PW Hogg, "Comment" (1977) 55 Can Bar Rev 550; PW Hogg, "Federalism and the Jurisdiction of Canadian Courts" (1981) 30 UNBLJ 9; JM Evans, "Comment" (1981) 59 Can Bar Rev 124; B Laskin & RJ Sharpe, "Constricting Federal Court Jurisdiction" (1980) 30 UTLJ 283.
51   *Jabour v Law Society of British Columbia*, [1982] 2 SCR 307, 137 DLR (3d) 1; *Kourtessis v MNR*, [1993] 2 SCR 53, 102 DLR (4th) 456 at 496.

Trial Division, are taken to the Federal Court of Appeal, and then to the Supreme Court of Canada.

The Supreme Court of Canada, sitting at the top of the judicial hierarchy, is Canada's most important court. The common law doctrine of precedent or *stare decisis* makes its decisions binding upon all other courts. Accordingly, the Supreme Court exercises a considerable lawmaking role both in constitutional and in non-constitutional matters. The Supreme Court is seen, not only by lawyers and judges but also by the public at large, as one of our most important national institutions.

The high public profile of the Supreme Court is, however, a relatively recent phenomenon. The Court is not mentioned in the original 1867 constitution; indeed, despite an obscure and confusing reference to the Court in the amending formula enacted in 1982,[52] the Court lacks formal status in the written constitution to this day. The Court was created by an Act of Parliament in 1875 pursuant to the power conferred upon Parliament by section 101 of the *Constitution Act, 1867*, to establish a general court of appeal for Canada.[53] At the time of the Court's establishment, many thought it unnecessary since there already existed a supreme appellate authority for constitutional as well as non-constitutional issues, namely, the Judicial Committee of the Privy Council in England.[54] This body, consisting essentially of members of the English House of Lords, heard appeals from the colonial courts and, after the creation of the Dominion of Canada in 1867, entertained cases directly from the provincial courts of appeal. In the early years of Canada's history, it was thought that the establishment of the Supreme Court of Canada would merely add another costly and unnecessary level of appeal.

---

52   The *Constitution Act, 1982*, s 41(d), provides that amendments to the constitution in relation to "the composition of the Supreme Court of Canada" require the unanimous consent of the federal Parliament and the provincial legislatures, while s 42(1)(d) provides that other amendments in relation to the Court fall under the usual formula (federal Parliament and at least seven provinces having at least 50 percent of the population of all the provinces). For varying views as to the effect of these provisions, see PW Hogg, *Canada Act 1982 Annotated* (Toronto: Carswell, 1982) at 92–94; Strayer, above note 2 at 30–31; RI Cheffins, "The *Constitution Act, 1982* and the Amending Formula: Political and Legal Implications" (1982) 4 Sup Ct L Rev 43 at 53; WR Lederman, "Constitutional Procedure and Reform of the Supreme Court of Canada" (1985) 26 C de D 195.

53   For the history of the Supreme Court, see JG Snell & F Vaughan, *The Supreme Court of Canada: History of the Institution* (Toronto: University of Toronto Press, 1985).

54   See G Bale, *Chief Justice William Johnstone Ritchie: Responsible Government and Judicial Review* (Ottawa: Carleton University Press, 1990).

For a long time, the Supreme Court of Canada was supreme in name only: the Judicial Committee of the Privy Council functioned as Canada's highest appellate court until 1949 when appeals to the Privy Council were abolished. This body of English judges had an important influence upon the evolution of the Canadian constitution, and its judgments remain significant today.[55] The Privy Council established the principles of interpretation of Canada's federal structure and, throughout Canadian history, many have argued that its judgments unduly favoured provincial interests to the detriment of a strong and effective central government.[56]

An important step in the evolution of the Supreme Court of Canada to its present status occurred in 1975 when an amendment to the *Supreme Court Act* gave the Court control over the cases it hears. Most appeals as of right to the Court were abolished, and a leave-to-appeal procedure was introduced whereby the Court is able to screen cases and permit only those cases with national importance to proceed. This change has permitted the Court to focus its efforts on those cases that have the most legal and public significance. It has altered the role of the Supreme Court from that of error correction to one of law making.[57]

The final significant step in the evolution of the Supreme Court of Canada occurred in 1982 with the enactment of the *Charter of Rights and Freedoms*. As noted in Chapter 1, the *Charter* significantly increased the scope for judicial review and brought the Supreme Court of Canada into public prominence.

a) Composition of the Court and Appointment of Judges

The composition of the Supreme Court is fixed by the *Supreme Court Act*. The Court consists of nine judges. The *Supreme Court Act*, section 6, requires that three of the nine judges be appointed from the judges or bar of the province of Quebec. This provision is designed to ensure civil law expertise and the representation of Quebec's distinctive legal traditions and social values on the Court as well as to enhance the confidence of Quebec in the Court.[58] Although the Supreme Court is not

---

55   See J Saywell, *The Lawmakers: Judicial Power and the Shaping of Canadian Federalism* (Toronto: University of Toronto Press and the Osgoode Society, 2002).

56   See, for example, B Laskin, "Peace, Order and Good Government Re-examined" (1947) 25 Can Bar Rev 1054. Compare, however, AC Cairns, "The Judicial Committee and Its Critics" (1971) 4 Can J Pol Sci 301.

57   See RJ Sharpe & K Roach, *Brian Dickson: A Judge's Journey* (Toronto: University of Toronto Press, 2003) cc 7 & 8.

58   *Reference re Supreme Court Act, ss 5 and 6*, [2014] 1 SCR 433, 2014 SCC 21, holding that a judge of the Federal Court of Appeal does not qualify for appointment

specifically mentioned in the constitution other than in the amending formula, any change to the composition or other essential feature of the Court requires a constitutional amendment.[59]

By practice or convention, there are ordinarily three judges from Ontario, as it is Canada's most populous province, one judge from the eastern provinces, and two judges from the western provinces. A quorum of the Court is five judges, but it is usual for the Court to have all nine judges sit on important cases.

The office of chief justice usually, but not invariably, alternates between an English- and French-speaking judge. The chief justice has important public and administrative responsibilities, including the assignment of judges to each case. However, in terms of the Court's decisions, the chief justice has no special authority and exercises the usual functions of a justice of the Court, sitting on cases and voting as any other judge.

The qualifications for appointment to the Court are specified in section 5 of the *Supreme Court Act*. One must be a judge of a superior court or a barrister of ten years' standing. The same qualification is specified by the *Judges Act* for appointment to the superior and provincial appellate courts.[60] Most Supreme Court judges have had prior judicial experience. It is not unusual, however, for one or more of the judges to have been appointed directly from the bar and to have no prior judicial experience. In recent years, academics have frequently been appointed to the Court. The *Supreme Court Act* also provides (section 9) that judges of the Court hold office until reaching the age of seventy-five.

Judges of the Supreme Court of Canada and of the superior courts are appointed by the federal cabinet on the advice of the minister of justice. In the case of Supreme Court appointments, it has become the practice for the prime minister to make the appointments. Most observers recognize that the quality of individuals appointed to the Court has been high, but the secretive nature of Supreme Court appointments has come under increasing criticism.[61] It is felt by many critics that the public should have some prior knowledge of the background and abilities of the candidates. Provincial governments have long complained that it is unfair for the federal government to have the exclusive decision with respect to appointments since the Supreme Court acts as the referee in disputes between the federal government and the provinces.

to fill one of the Quebec positions on the Court [*Reference re Supreme Court Act*].

59   *Ibid.*

60   *Judges Act*, RSC 1985, c J-1, s 3.

61   See DM Beatty, *Talking Heads and the Supremes: The Canadian Production of Constitutional Review* (Toronto: Carswell, 1990).

Had constitutional amendments proposed in the Meech Lake and Charlottetown packages been enacted, the federal government would have been obliged to select Supreme Court justices from lists supplied by the provinces.

While it is unlikely that Canada would ever adopt the American practice of confirmation hearings whereby nominees to the Court are subjected to lengthy partisan questioning, it seems inevitable that demands for a less secretive and more open process will grow.[62] The federal government has also come under increasing pressure to appoint more women and members of cultural and ethnic minorities to the bench, an experience shared by provincial governments in their sphere of judicial appointments. Though this pressure stems partly from changing demographics and social attitudes, it is undoubtedly tied, as well, to the enhanced power of the courts in the *Charter* era. Since the *Charter* requires the courts to decide important public-policy issues, it is thought in many quarters that a diversity of backgrounds among judges is necessary to ensure that judicial decisions reflect a wide range of values.

In 2004, the minister of justice appeared before an *ad hoc* committee of members of Parliament, one representative of the Canadian Judicial Council, and one representative of the relevant provincial law society to discuss the qualifications of two appointments to the Supreme Court. He subsequently proposed a four-stage process for appointments to the Supreme Court. First, the minister of justice would compile an initial list of candidates after consulting with the relevant provincial attorney general, chief justices, and law societies. Next, an advisory committee with members of Parliament from various parties, a retired judge, a provincial representative, a representative of the relevant law society, and two lay members would prepare an unranked short list of three candidates. The advisory committee would consult widely, but not interview the candidates. Third, the prime minister would make a selection that would, in all but exceptional circumstances, come from the short list. Finally, the minister of justice would appear before the

---

62 For an interesting proposal, see ML Friedland, *A Place Apart: Judicial Independence and Accountability in Canada* (Ottawa: Canadian Judicial Council, 1995) at 256–57. Appointments to the provincial superior courts are now made after candidates have been privately reviewed by committees of senior judges, lawyers, and lay people. In some provinces, appointments to the provincial bench are made after a similar process that involves lay participation. For discussion, see Ontario Law Reform Commission, *Appointing Judges: Philosophy, Politics and Practice* (Toronto, 1991).

parliamentary justice committee to explain the process and qualifications of the appointee.[63]

In 2006, the government accepted a three-person short list prepared by a committee initiated under the previous government. The prime minister selected Rothstein J from that list and Rothstein J was subject to a public three-hour interview by an *ad hoc* committee chaired by the minister of justice and including members of Parliament from all major parties. The hearing was generally viewed as successful with parliamentarians understanding that it would not be appropriate to ask Rothstein J how he would decide particular cases. A few days after this process in which Rothstein J was asked about sixty questions, the prime minister appointed him to join the Court.[64]

A different process was used with respect to the appointment of the next justice. The government proposed to submit an initial list of candidates to a five-person selection panel composed of two government members of Parliament and three from each of the opposition parties. This process was, however, halted because of opposition objections to the composition of the selection panel. The government announced that Cromwell J would be the nominee. It was proposed that Cromwell J, like Rothstein J, would answer questions from an *ad hoc* all-party committee of members of the House of Commons before his official appointment. This public hearing was not held, however, because of the prorogation of Parliament. Justice Cromwell was appointed by the prime minister to the Court in January 2009, six months after the retirement of Bastarache J.[65]

A similar process was followed in 2011 with the appointments of Moldaver and Karakatsanis JJ from Ontario and in 2012, with the appointment of Wagner J from Quebec. The minister of justice submitted a list of potential candidates to an all-party parliamentary committee. That committee reviewed the proposed nominees and their dossiers but did not interview them and submitted to the prime minister a short list of three names for each position. The prime minister then publicly announced his intention to appoint the individual or individuals he chose from among the names on the short list. Within a few days, the nominees appeared before the parliamentary committee. They made

---

63 Minister of Justice, *Proposal to Reform the Supreme Court of Canada Appointments Process* (Ottawa: Department of Justice Canada, April 2005).
64 P Hogg, "Appointment of Justice Rothstein to the Supreme Court of Canada" (2006) 44 Osgoode Hall LJ 527.
65 P Hogg, "The Appointment of Justice Cromwell to the Supreme Court of Canada" (2009) 47 Sup Ct L Rev (2d) 413.

opening statements and answered questions from committee members. The prime minister confirmed their appointments shortly thereafter.

This process was abandoned following the failed attempt to appoint Nadon J to the Supreme Court in 2013.[66] For the following two appointments, the government reverted to a process where the prime minister simply announced the appointments with no visible input from the public, the judiciary, or the legal profession.[67]

A new process implemented in 2016 led to the appointment of Justice Malcom Rowe. A detailed list of qualifications and assessment criteria was announced.[68] The government emphasized the need to diversify the judiciary and indicated that only judges who were functionally bilingual would be considered. Applications for the position were invited from across the country although convention required the appointment to come from Atlantic Canada. The seven-member Independent Advisory Board reviewed the applications, interviewed a short list of candidates and provided a non-binding merits based list of three to five names to the minister of justice. The minister of justice consulted widely on the shortlist of candidates with the chief justice of Canada and others and then made a recommendation to the prime minister who then chose the nominee. The minister and the chair of the advisory board appeared before the House of Commons Standing Committee on Justice and Human Rights to explain how the chosen nominee met the statutory requirements and criteria established by the government, following which Justice Rowe appeared before the committee to answer questions. Shortly thereafter, the prime minister formalized the appointment.

The appointment process remains in a state of flux, and it remains to be seen whether the appropriate balance has been struck among parliamentary input, provincial input, transparency, merit, diversity, nonpartisanship, and judicial independence in selecting members of the Supreme Court.

b)   The Hearing of Appeals

The Supreme Court of Canada hears about seventy appeals each year.[69] In addition, it receives about 600 applications for leave to appeal. Approximately 35 percent of the cases heard by the Court are criminal,

---

66   *Reference re Supreme Court Act*, above note 58.

67   A Dodek, "Reforming the Supreme Court Appointment Process, 2004–2014: A 10-Year Democratic Audit" (2014) 67 Sup Ct L Rev (2d) 111.

68   See online: www.fja-cmf.gc.ca/scc-csc/qualifications-eng.html.

69   Statistics on the work of the Court are published regularly in the Supreme Court *Bulletin*.

while the remaining 65 percent are civil. The Court exercises important jurisdiction in private law, but it has become predominantly a public law court with *Charter* and constitutional cases constituting a significant portion of the civil or private law appeals.

The Supreme Court receives the full record of the proceedings in the lower courts, including all of the evidence led at trial and all judgments rendered in the case. The parties present written argument, ordinarily limited to forty pages, and they are afforded one hour each for oral argument. The procedure is adversarial, in keeping with the common law tradition.

After the presentation of oral arguments, all deliberations of the Court are confidential until the judgment is released. Following the oral argument, the Court retires to a conference of all the judges sitting on the case. Each judge presents his or her view of the case, until recently, commencing with the most junior judge. The chief justice assigns the task of preparing the first opinion to one of the judges who is in the majority. The first opinion is circulated among the judges sitting on the case, and each judge either agrees with the opinion as drafted or prepares concurring or dissenting reasons. It has become increasingly apparent that law clerks, recent law school graduates who serve for a period of one year with the justices, play an important role in doing background research and assisting in the preparation of the final opinions. The Court publishes all opinions, including dissents, and dissenting opinions not infrequently provide the foundation for future developments in the jurisprudence. When all judges sitting on the case have signed an opinion, the judgment of the Court is released to the parties and to the public in both English and French.

E. CONCLUSION

Charter cases are essentially dealt with in the same manner as any other litigation. It is apparent, however, that *Charter* issues pose special challenges for our courts. Special procedural rules relating to standing and intervention by attorneys general and interested groups reflect the public significance of *Charter* rulings.

The role of judges in dealing with complex social issues under the *Charter* has altered the mandate of our courts and resulted in increased public scrutiny of the judicial process. The method of appointing judges has come under particular criticism. Many observers have asked whether the traditional approach is adequate, especially for the selection of those who sit on our highest court. Though rarely, if ever, is exception taken to particular appointments, it may be expected that there will be continuing pressure to have a more open appointments process.

FURTHER READINGS

BAILEY, J, "Reopening Law's Gate: Public Interest Standing and Access to Justice" (2011) 44 UBC L Rev 255

BREDT, C, & H PESSIONE, "Advance Costs Awards: A Critical Analysis" (2015) 34 NJCL 31

CRANDALL, E, "Defeat and Ambiguity: The Pursuit of Judicial Selection Reform for the Supreme Court of Canada" (2015) 41 Queen's LJ 73

DES ROSIERS, N, "An Evaluation Model for Non-Governmental Organizations Engaged in Advocacy" (2014) 51 Osgoode Hall LJ 889

DODEK, A, "Reforming the Supreme Court Appointment Process, 2004–2014: A 10 Year Democratic Audit" (2014) 67 Sup Ct L Rev (2d) 111

MOREY, C, "A Matter of Integrity: Rule of Law, the Remuneration Reference, and Access to Justice" (2016) 49 UBC L Rev 275

MULLAN, D, "Administrative Tribunals and Judicial Review of *Charter* Issues after *Multani*" (2006–2007) 21 NJCL 127–49

PILKINGTON, M, "Enforcing the *Charter*: The Supervisory Role of Superior Courts and the Responsibility of Legislatures for Remedial Systems" (2004) 25 Sup Ct L Rev (2d) 77

ROACH, K, *Constitutional Remedies in Canada*, 2d ed (Aurora, ON: Canada Law Book, 2013)

SHARPE, RJ, ed, Charter *Litigation* (Toronto: Butterworths, 1986)

————, "Access to *Charter* Justice" (2013) 63 Sup Ct L Rev (2d) 3

STRAYER, BL, *The Canadian Constitution and the Courts: The Function and Scope of Judicial Review*, 3d ed (Toronto: Butterworths, 1988)

FREEDOM OF CONSCIENCE AND RELIGION

Freedom of religion was recognized by the courts as an important value of Canadian society long before the enactment of the *Charter of Rights and Freedoms*, but it could be protected only indirectly through the interpretation of statutes and the enforcement of the division of powers. In particular, the inability of provinces to enact criminal laws led to the striking down of some laws that had discriminatory effects against religious minorities.[1] The Supreme Court has recognized that "an important feature of our constitutional democracy is respect for minorities, which includes, of course, religious minorities. Indeed respect for and tolerance of the rights and practices of religious minorities is one of the hallmarks of an enlightened democracy."[2]

Section 2(a) of the *Charter* now provides that "freedom of conscience and religion" is a fundamental right of all Canadians. Although the *Charter* respects every individual's freedom of conscience and religion as a necessary element of personal dignity, autonomy, and self-development, this does not mean that it offers protection to all actions dictated by religious belief. Can the state prevent religious practices, such as female circumcision, which are regarded by the majority as harmful? Does the state have a positive duty to provide funding for religious schools or to make special allowances for the construction of places of worship? Does section 2(a) protect only the right to hold beliefs,

---

1   *Saumur v Quebec*, [1953] 2 SCR 299, [1953] 4 DLR 641, discussed in Chapter 1.
2   *Syndicat Northcrest v Amselem*, [2004] 2 SCR 551 at para 1 [*Syndicat Northcrest*].

or does it include the right to express those beliefs, free from state interference? Must the state be neutral to all religions? What should be done when religious beliefs clash with other *Charter* values, for example, equality and freedom from discrimination on issues such as same-sex marriage? As with the other *Charter* rights, the courts have had to determine the scope of the right to freedom of conscience and religion guaranteed by section 2(a), the proper approach to reconciling freedom of conscience and religion with other *Charter* rights, and the range of acceptable limitations under section 1.

Freedom of religion protects individual autonomy, freedom, and dignity. The Supreme Court has articulated the purpose of freedom of religion as related to the ability of every individual to "be free to hold and to manifest whatever beliefs and opinions his or her conscience dictates, provided *inter alia* only that such manifestations do not injure his or her neighbours or their parallel rights to hold and manifest beliefs and opinions of their own."[3] It has elaborated that "the purpose of section 2(a) is to ensure that society does not interfere with profoundly personal beliefs that govern one's perception of oneself, humankind, nature, and in some cases, a higher or different order of being. These beliefs, in turn, govern one's conduct and practices."[4]

When exactly is the section 2(a) right engaged? The Supreme Court has endorsed "a personal or subjective conception of freedom of religion, one that is integrally linked with an individual's self-definition and fulfillment and is a function of personal autonomy and choice, elements which undergird the right."[5] The subjective approach to freedom of religion means that the emphasis is on the sincerity of a person's subjective claim of belief and not whether a particular practice objectively fits into an official religion. In other words,

> Freedom of religion consists of the freedom to undertake practices and harbour beliefs, having a nexus with religion, in which an individual demonstrates that he or she sincerely believes or is sincerely undertaking in order to connect with the divine or as a function of his or her spiritual faith, irrespective of whether a particular practice or belief is required by official religious dogma or is in conformity with the position of religious officials.[6]

---

3   *R v Big M Drug Mart Ltd*, [1985] 1 SCR 295, 18 DLR (4th) 321 at 346 [*Big M Drug Mart*].
4   *Edwards Books & Art Ltd v R*, [1986] 2 SCR 713, 35 DLR (4th) 1 at 759 [*Edwards Books*].
5   *Syndicat Northcrest*, above note 2 at para 42.
6   *Ibid* at para 46.

At the same time, freedom of religion also applies to "the right to manifest religious belief by worship, teaching, dissemination and religious practice . . . . The practice of religious rites is a fundamental aspect of religious practice."[7]

As an initial matter, the *Charter* applicant must establish a sincere practice or belief that, for the applicant, is subjectively connected with the divine or with spiritual faith and establish that the impugned action interferes with the ability to act in accordance with his or her religious beliefs in a manner that is more than trivial or insubstantial.[8] Once such a violation is established, the onus is on the state under section 1 of the *Charter* to prove that the limitation on freedom of religion is reasonable and demonstrably justifiable. The Court has added that "no right, including freedom of religion is absolute . . . . This is so because we live in a society of individuals in which we must always take the rights of others into account."[9]

A. SUNDAY CLOSING LAWS AND RELIGIOUS NEUTRALITY

Sunday closing laws may be characterized as having a religious purpose. Their origins lie, at least in part, in the desire to protect against the profanation of the Christian Sabbath and to maintain Sunday as a holy day. Over time, however, Sunday closing laws have also taken on a secular purpose: that of providing workers with a day of rest or a "pause day." From this perspective, Sunday was chosen not because of its religious significance but because it historically has been a day without work. On the other hand, even if there is a secular purpose behind Sunday closing laws, they do impose burdens on those who observe another day of rest for religious reasons.

R v Big M Drug Mart,[10] a case dealing with the constitutionality of the federal *Lord's Day Act* prohibition of Sunday shopping, was the Supreme Court's first decision on the *Charter* guarantee of freedom of religion. As a corporate entity, the drug store could not claim a right to

---

7   *Reference Re Same-Sex Marriage*, [2004] 3 SCR 698 at para 57.
8   *Mouvement laïque québécois v Saguenay (City)*, [2015] 2 SCR 3 at para 86 [*Saguenay*]; *Alberta v Hutterian Brethren of Wilson Colony*, [2009] 2 SCR 567 at para 32; *Bruker v Marcovitz*, [2007] 3 SCR 607 at para 67; *Multani v Commission scolaire Marguerite-Bourgeoys*, [2006] 1 SCR 256 at para 34; *Syndicat Northcrest*, above note 2 at paras 56–59.
9   *Syndicat Northcrest*, *ibid* at para 61.
10   *Big M Drug Mart*, above note 3.

freedom of religion for itself, but, since it had been prosecuted, it was allowed to challenge the constitutionality of the *Lord's Day Act* on the theory that no one should be prosecuted under an unconstitutional law.

The distribution of powers between federal and provincial governments in the Canadian federal system allows the federal Parliament to enact laws designed to protect religion and to prevent profanation of the Sabbath. The *Lord's Day Act* was enacted pursuant to this authority to legislate with respect to the criminal law under section 91(27) of the *Constitution Act, 1867*. The federal Parliament does not, however, have jurisdiction to enact Sunday closing laws with a secular purpose. Legislation of that kind falls within the general provincial jurisdiction under section 92(13) over "property and civil rights," which includes labour relations and regulation of business within the province. Accordingly, any attempt to justify the *Lord's Day Act* as having a secular "day of rest" purpose would make it vulnerable to a finding of invalidity on federalism grounds. As a result, the federal *Lord's Day Act* was held to have the purpose of promoting observance of the Christian Sabbath.

Writing for the majority, Dickson J took the opportunity to interpret the guarantee broadly, as protecting not only the right to hold religious beliefs but also the right to express beliefs through observance, teaching, and practice. The state would violate an individual's freedom if it coerced religious observance and the section 2(a) guarantee extended to "expressions and manifestations of religious non-belief and refusals to participate in religious practice."[11] In his words,

> [F]reedom means that, subject to such limitations as are necessary to protect public safety, order, health, or morals or the fundamental rights and freedoms of others, no one is to be forced to act in a way contrary to his beliefs or his conscience.[12]

Justice Dickson concluded that the *Lord's Day Act* was coercive because its purpose was to compel universal observance of the Christian Sabbath:

> Non-Christians are prohibited for religious reasons from carrying out activities which are otherwise lawful, moral and normal. The arm of the State requires all to remember the Lord's day of the Christians and to keep it holy. The protection of one religion and the concomitant non-protection of others imports disparate impact destructive of the religious freedom of the collectivity.[13]

---

11 *Ibid* at 346–47 (SCR).
12 *Ibid* at 337.
13 *Ibid*.

In reaching this conclusion, Dickson J referred to section 27 of the *Charter*, which requires that the document be interpreted in a manner "consistent with the preservation and enhancement of the multicultural heritage of Canadians." The preferred position of the Christian religion under the *Lord's Day Act* was seen as undermining respect for the religions of other groups in Canadian society. He also stated:

> What may appear good and true to a majoritarian religious group, or to the state acting at their behest, may not, for religious reasons, be imposed upon citizens who take a contrary view. The *Charter* safeguards religious minorities from the threat of "the tyranny of the majority."[14]

The government's attempt to defend the legislation as a reasonable limit under section 1 of the *Charter* was unsuccessful. Given that the law was enacted under the federal power over the criminal law in order to enforce the Christian Sabbath, it was impossible for the federal government to establish a valid legislative objective. The result was a dilemma fatal to the law. Its purpose for the division-of-powers analysis, the protection of the majority's religion, was repugnant to the *Charter*'s protection of religious freedom for the minority. The law could not be defended as a worker-protection law, since that purpose would render it invalid on federalism grounds.

In light of the religious foundation of the law, *Big M Drug Mart* was not a particularly difficult case. More troublesome for the Supreme Court was the next Sunday closing case, *Edwards Books*.[15] This case involved Ontario legislation, secular in purpose, which was enacted to give retail workers a day of rest. The law made a concession to those who, for religious reasons, observed a different day of rest. It contained an exemption from the requirement that retail businesses close on Sundays if a store had closed the previous Saturday, had seven or fewer employees, and was smaller than 5,000 square feet.

On its face, the legislation did not require religious observance. However, in *Big M Drug Mart*, the Supreme Court had stated that rights could be infringed under the *Charter* not only by legislation whose purpose was to infringe the right but also by laws that had the effect of interfering with the right. Not every burden on the practice of religion will constitute a *Charter* violation. The Court had said that a *Charter* breach will be made out only where the burden is more than

---

14   *Ibid.*
15   *Edwards Books*, above note 4.

trivial and insubstantial.[16] However, many apparently "neutral" laws — that is, laws enacted for a perfectly proper reason unrelated to religion — may run afoul of the *Charter* guarantee because of their impact on religious practice.

In *Edwards Books*, five judges concluded that the effect of the closing law interfered with freedom of religion. For Dickson CJC and the majority of the Supreme Court, the problem was the impact of Sunday closing on those whose day of worship was Saturday (for example, those of the Jewish or Seventh Day Adventist faiths). Retailers whose holy day was Sunday were able to close their establishments and observe that day without any financial disadvantage. Saturday observers were faced with a dilemma: they could close Saturday, as required by their religion, but they would suffer a financial loss as a result. Alternatively, faced with the burden imposed by the law requiring them to close on Sunday, they might feel pressured to open on their holy day. Chief Justice Dickson found that the Sunday closing law was not neutral in its effect. It put Saturday observers at a disadvantage compared to Sunday observers who enjoyed statutory protection for their holy day. This financial burden was found to violate freedom of religion.

In dissent, Beetz J concluded that there was no interference with freedom of religion. In his view, when an individual closed a store on Saturdays to observe his or her faith, the cause of the closure was the individual's religious beliefs, not any action by the state. The fact that Sunday observers might get a financial advantage from the Sunday closing law did not affect the *Charter* claim. For Beetz J, it was telling that, if the Sunday closing law was repealed, the Saturday observers (as well as the Sunday observers) would still be at a business disadvantage in relation to the non-observant retailer who could open any day, while religious individuals would choose not to work. This, he thought, proved that religious belief caused the decision to close and the consequent loss of income on Saturday, and that the Sunday closing law did not interfere with freedom of religion.

While the majority concluded that the section 2(a) guarantee of freedom of religion was violated, the law was upheld under section 1 of the *Charter*, Wilson J dissenting.[17] The judges were split as to why the law was justified. In Dickson CJC's view (supported by two other judges), the exemption given to small retailers who observed Saturday was necessary to sustain the validity of the Act under section 1. He found that the state was justified in trying to protect a pause day for vulner-

---

16   *Jones v R*, [1986] 2 SCR 284, 31 DLR (4th) 569 [*Jones*], discussed below.
17   The importance of the *Edwards Books*, s 1 analysis is considered in Chapter 4.

able workers in the retail industry. Further, he found that it was not necessary, under the *Oakes* minimal-impairment test, to require that all retailers close. Small retailers could be allowed to open, without undue interference with their employees' interests or the general nature of the pause day. Justice La Forest held that no exemption was needed, since any effort to provide an exemption would create problems in enforcing the legislation and could undermine the protection of employees. He concluded that the courts should defer to the legislatures of the various provinces and allow them to determine whether they wanted to provide an exemption or not, and, if so, how to structure it.

Justice Wilson dissented on the basis that the exemption for only some Saturday observers and not others was an unprincipled decision that did not satisfy the *Oakes* test. If religious freedom was important and deserving of *Charter* protection for some members of a religious group, there was no reason, in her view, that it should not be provided for all members of that group.

The debate in *Edwards Books* may seem dated today, given the current widespread adoption of Sunday shopping in Canada. However, the issues remain significant for challenges to statutory holidays such as Christmas Day, Good Friday, and Easter Sunday. The requirement of retail closure on such days seems rooted in Christian tradition, although the argument will be made that these holidays now have a largely secular basis in the minds of many.

The Court's rejection of forced closing for a religious purpose in *Big M Drug Mart* also raised an important issue concerning the state's duty to be neutral and not to favour or enforce the tenets of one religion or belief system over another. In *Mouvement laïque Québécois,* the Court held that state neutrality towards religion and other belief systems was supported by the values of equality, multiculturalism, and democracy, as well as liberty. It concluded that:

> By expressing no preference, the state ensures that it preserves a neutral public space that is free of discrimination and in which true freedom to believe or not to believe is enjoyed by everyone equally, given that everyone is valued equally.[18]

The Court added a duty of state neutrality was derived from a generous interpretation of freedom of religion and conscience but did not mean that individuals had to be neutral on such matters. It also did

---

18   *Saguenay*, above note 8 at para 74. The case was decided under the Quebec *Charter of Rights* but the Court noted at para 68 the similarity with section 2(a) of the *Charter* and relied on *Big M Drug Mart*, above note 3.

not mean that the state was endorsing a position against neutrality and the Court indicated that starting council meetings with a statement denying a God would also violate section 2(a).[19] The Court noted the importance of "a neutral public space free from coercion, pressure and judgment on the part of public authorities in matters of spirituality is intended to protect every person's freedom and dignity."[20] The duty of the state was to "neither favour nor hinder any particular belief."[21] In upholding a complaint against a Christian prayer held before municipal council meetings by an atheist who regularly attended such meetings, the Court also concluded that reference to the supremacy of God in the preamble of the *Charter* does not mean that the state can "consciously profess a theistic faith."[22] This case affirms that the Court will interpret the guarantee of freedom of religion and conscience in section 2(a) in a broad manner to require that "[t]he state neither favour nor hinder any religion, and that it abstain from taking any position on this subject."[23]

B. ACCOMMODATION OF RELIGION

In *Syndicat Northcrest v Amselem*,[24] the Supreme Court dealt with whether Orthodox Jews could construct a succah, a temporary structure on their balconies, in order to observe the nine-day festival of Succot even though they had signed a contract prohibiting constructions on their balconies and they were offered an alternative of a communal succah. They relied on freedom of religion under the Quebec *Charter of Human Rights and Freedoms*,[25] which, unlike the Canadian *Charter*, applies to private conduct. The Supreme Court nevertheless indicated that its analysis of freedom of religion would also apply to the Canadian *Charter*.

The Court divided 5:4 on whether freedom of religion had been violated by the prohibition on balcony constructions and on whether any violation was justified. Justice Iacobucci held for the majority that, assuming that freedom of religion could be waived, there had not been a voluntary or clear and express waiver of rights when the applicants signed the co-ownership agreement prohibiting constructions on balconies. He also concluded that there was a violation of freedom of reli-

---

19   *Saguenay*, above note 8 at para 133.
20   *Ibid* at para 74.
21   *Ibid* at para 72.
22   *Ibid* at para 147.
23   *Ibid* at para 137.
24   Above note 2.
25   CQLR c C-12.

gion and that it had not been justified. He held that a trial judge who had granted a permanent injunction against the construction of the suc-cahs had erred in finding no violation of freedom of religion on the basis of the testimony of one rabbi over another rabbi about the objective and mandatory requirements of the Jewish religion. Justice Iacobucci warned that the proper focus was on the subjective, personal, and sin-cere beliefs of the applicants and that courts should not adjudicate questions of religious doctrine or obligations. He also indicated that "beliefs and observances evolve and change over time" for individuals and that their subjective distress at having to use a communal succah should be considered as it made the violation of freedom of religion more than trivial or insubstantial.[26]

The Court then found that the limitation on freedom of religion in order to protect the property interests of other residents in the balcon-ies was not justified, especially given that the succahs were constructed for only nine days each year. It recognized that "security concerns, if soundly established would require appropriate recognition in ascer-taining any limit on the exercise of the appellants' religious freedom."[27] The majority indicated that, in this case, the succahs could and should be constructed not to block any doors or fire lanes. The majority's deci-sion in this case indicates that the courts will take a broad and gener-ous approach to the protection of religious freedom that focuses on the subjective beliefs of adherents and that the state will have to satisfy a demanding and rigorous test for justifying limits on religion freedom.

Four judges dissented from the majority's finding of an unjustified violation of freedom of religion. Justice Bastarache, with the concur-rence of LeBel and Deschamps JJ, concluded that there was no viola-tion of freedom of religion. He did not accept that the appellants had a sincere belief, one based on religious precepts, that they were required to erect their own succahs and found that "it is their practice of eat-ing or celebrating Succot that is protected by the guarantee of freedom of religion . . . . The declaration of co-ownership does not hinder this practice, as it does not bar the appellants from celebrating Succot in a succah, whether at the homes of friends or family or even in a com-munal succah, as proposed by the respondent."[28] Even if one of the ap-pellants did sincerely believe that he was required to construct his own succah, Bastarache J held that the compromise of a communal succah was reasonable given the need to respect the property and safety rights

---

26   *Syndicat Northcrest*, above note 2 at para 71.
27   *Ibid* at para 88.
28   *Ibid* at para 162.

of others. Justice Binnie also dissented, but on the more limited basis that the appellants had contractually committed themselves to a neutral restriction on all changes to the exterior of the units and that there was "a vast difference . . . between using freedom of religion as a shield against interference with religious freedom by the State and as a sword against co-contractors in a private building."[29]

In *Congrégation des témoins de Jéhovah de St-Jérôme-Lafontaine v Lafontaine (Village)*,[30] the Supreme Court dealt with a municipality's repeated refusal to amend zoning bylaws to allow the Jehovah's Witnesses to construct a place of worship. The majority of the Court decided the case in the favour of the Jehovah's Witnesses on non-*Charter* grounds by ruling that the municipality had acted unfairly by providing no reasons for its refusal to amend the zoning bylaw. Justice LeBel, with the concurrence of Major, Bastarache, and Deschamps JJ, dissented and would have upheld the municipality's decision. The dissent raises, but does not resolve, the issue of whether and when the state has a positive obligation under the *Charter* to accommodate the exercise of religion. Justice LeBel concluded that there was no infringement of freedom of religion because the bylaws allowed at least one lot for the construction of a place of worship in the municipality, and freedom of religion did not include an absolute freedom to select the location for a place of worship. Moreover, a zoning bylaw amendment to allow the Jehovah's Witnesses to construct a place of worship might have been incompatible with the municipality's duty "to be neutral in matters of religion."[31] Justice LeBel added, "for the sake of discussion only,"[32] that freedom of religion would have been violated had no lots whatsoever been available in the municipality for the construction of a Kingdom Hall by the Jehovah's Witnesses. In such a hypothetical case, it would have been impossible for the Jehovah's Witnesses to practise their religion, and the zoning bylaws would have directly interfered with freedom of religion, requiring the municipality to take positive action by amending its zoning bylaws.

In *Alberta v Hutterian Brethren of Wilson Colony*,[33] the Supreme Court indicated that there are clear limits on the extent to which laws will be struck down for imposing indirect costs or burdens on religious beliefs. At issue was an Alberta regulation requiring all holders of a driver's licence to be digitally photographed. It was conceded that

---

29 *Ibid* at para 185.
30 [2004] 2 SCR 650.
31 *Ibid* at para 71.
32 *Ibid* at para 72.
33 [2009] 2 SCR 567.

the photo requirement interfered with the Hutterian religious belief against being photographed. The Supreme Court held, however, that the regulation was justified under section 1.

The Court accepted that the purpose of the photo requirement — to protect the integrity of the licensing scheme and to guard against identity theft — was an objective of sufficient importance to warrant overriding a *Charter* right. The Court also agreed that the government had demonstrated that the regulation was rationally connected to that objective. The claimants argued that given their small numbers, the government should have exempted them from the scheme and that not doing so failed the minimal impairment test. Writing for the majority, McLachlin CJC rejected that contention on the ground that allowing for exemptions would destroy the one-to-one correspondence between issued licences and photos in the data bank and that this would significantly undermine the government's objective of guarding against the use of drivers' licences as a tool for identity theft. Where the validity of a law is at stake and accommodating a religious belief would significantly compromise the government's objective, the majority held that accommodation is not required. The crucial phase of the proportionality test was the third stage, weighing the proportionality of effects: were the overall effects of the law on the claimants' rights disproportionate to the government's objective? The impugned law did not force Hutterites to be photographed or compel any religious practice or observance, but rather indirectly imposed a cost or burden on the claimants who had to choose between following the dictates of their religion and holding a driver's licence. Chief Justice McLachlin held that while the *Charter* guarantees freedom of religion, it "does not indemnify practitioners against all costs incident to the practice of religion."[34] In a multicultural, multi-religious society, "the duty of state authorities to legislate for the general good inevitably produces conflicts with individual beliefs"[35] and the resulting cost or burden on those who chose to follow the dictates of their religion will not always outweigh the salutary effect of the impugned law. Here, those who refused to be photographed for religious reasons could arrange alternative means of transportation and, as the salutary effect of the law would be significantly undermined by granting exemptions, the majority found that Alberta had satisfied the third stage of proportionality review. There were, however, strong dissents insisting that under the final stage of the section 1 test, the harmful effects on the Hutterites were severe and outweighed the problem

---

34   *Ibid* at para 95.
35   *Ibid* at para 90.

of identity threat as it was addressed by the requirement of photos on licences.

C. PARENTAL RIGHTS

Freedom of religion has been an issue in a number of cases involving the family and parental rights. For example, in *B(R) v Children's Aid Society of Metropolitan Toronto*,[36] parents of the Jehovah's Witness religion refused to allow their infant child to undergo a blood transfusion thought by doctors to be required to save the child's life. When the Children's Aid Society brought an application to take the child into care to ensure that she could be given necessary treatment, the parents argued that this application violated their freedom of religion. The Supreme Court of Canada upheld the order placing the child under the protection of the Society. Five of the judges agreed that the parents' right to freedom of religion was violated, concluding that the guarantee protected religious beliefs even if those beliefs could harm another. However, the limitation on the parents' rights was justified under section 1 in order to protect the child. In contrast, four judges argued that the guarantee of freedom of religion should not extend to conduct endangering the life or seriously endangering the health of the child.

Similarly, in *AC v Manitoba (Director of Child and Family Services)*,[37] the Court upheld legislation authorizing a court to order treatment of a child under sixteen years old where the treatment was in the young person's best interests. Properly interpreted, the "best interests" standard reflected the adolescent's maturity and developing autonomy interest and, where the court is satisfied that the adolescent is capable of making a mature and independent decision, greater weight must be given to the adolescent's views when deciding whether or not to order treatment.

This case followed an earlier pair of decisions dealing with restrictions on parents' rights to discuss religion with their children as a condition of access to their children following marriage breakdown. In *Young v Young*,[38] the trial judge had given custody of the children to the mother and permitted access to the father. However, the order had

36   [1995] 1 SCR 315, 122 DLR (4th) 1.
37   [2009] 2 SCR 181, also discussed in Chapter 13.
38   [1993] 4 SCR 3, 108 DLR (4th) 193. In *P(D) v S(C)*, [1993] 4 SCR 141, 108 DLR (4th) 287, the majority upheld a condition of access forbidding the father to indoctrinate the child in the Jehovah's Witness religion, although he was allowed to teach her about religion.

forbidden the father, a Jehovah's Witness, from taking his children to religious services or on his proselytizing activities or from commenting unfavourably on the mother's religion. This restriction was overturned by the British Columbia Court of Appeal as violating section 2(a). The Supreme Court of Canada, by a narrow majority, agreed that the father should not be forbidden from discussing his religion with his children. By this time, he had promised not to take them to services or to involve them in proselytizing. The majority reasoning noted that custody and access decisions are made on the basis of the "best interests of the child." Where a parent's religious beliefs are harmful to a child, the best-interests test will apply to protect the child from those beliefs. In the Court's view, there would be no *Charter* violation associated with such a determination, since the right to freedom of religion does not permit one to harm another. In light of the father's promises with respect to services and proselytizing, it was found that the children would not be harmed by discussions about his religious beliefs.

D. RELIGION AND EDUCATION

Another area of controversy under section 2(a) has been with respect to religion and education. A number of issues arise: the extent to which there is room for religious instruction and practice in the public school system, the right of parents to withdraw their children from public schools for religious reasons, the extent of the state's obligation to fund independent religious schools, and the reconciliation of freedom of religion with other *Charter* rights and freedoms.

1) School Prayer and Religious Instruction

The Supreme Court of Canada has not dealt directly with the issue of the role of religion in the public school system. However, two important decisions of the Ontario Court of Appeal struck down provincial laws and regulations requiring school prayer and religious education in public schools.

In *Zylberberg*,[39] the court dealt with a requirement that public schools open with religious exercises consisting of the reading of scripture or other suitable works and the repeating of the Lord's Prayer or other suitable prayers. The regulations provided that a student could be excused

---

39 *Zylberberg v Sudbury Board of Education (Director)* (1988), 52 DLR (4th) 577 (Ont CA).

from participating if a parent requested this. The province defended the legislation on the basis that there was no denial of freedom of religion, given the right to claim an exemption. The majority of the Court of Appeal disagreed. It found that the requirement of prayers and scripture reading violated the rights of both Christians and non-Christians by compelling religious observance. The right to claim an exemption did not negate the coercive quality of the regime, for the reality was that members of minority religions or those opposed to the practices felt pressured to conform. Indeed, the exemption provisions were described as imposing a penalty on religious minorities, "stigmatizing them as non-conforming."[40]

A similar result was reached in a subsequent case involving religious education.[41] Ontario legislation and regulations required two one-half-hour periods of religious instruction in each week in public schools, although, again, children could be exempted. While the regulations provided that issues of a controversial or sectarian nature were to be avoided, the curriculum in Elgin County was delivered by members of a local Bible club and clergy, with the result that the instruction had a strong evangelical Christian tone. Again, the Ontario Court of Appeal concluded that the curriculum was a form of religious indoctrination, which placed a burden on both religious minorities and non-observers. The court held that, while teaching children about religious perspectives is permissible under section 2(a), indoctrination is not.

There are limits, however, to the duty to accommodate. The Supreme Court subsequently held that a Minister of Education had acted disproportionately by requiring a private Catholic high school to teach those aspects of a mandated religion and ethics course dealing with Catholicism from a neutral perspective. Four judges held that the appropriate balance was to require the school to teach about other religions and value systems from a neutral perspective, but not to require a Catholic school to be neutral about Catholicism. Three judges would have struck the balance somewhat differently by allowing the school to teach about other religions in a respectful manner but one that pointed out Catholic beliefs.[42]

---

40 *Ibid* at 592. See also at 591: "The peer pressure and the class-room norms to which children are acutely sensitive, in our opinion, are real and pervasive and operate to compel members of religious minorities to conform with majority religious practices."

41 *Canadian Civil Liberties Assn v Ontario (Minister of Education)* (1990), 65 DLR (4th) 1 (Ont CA).

42 *Loyola High School v Quebec (Attorney General)*, [2015] 1 SCR 613.

In *SL v Commission scolaire des Chênes*,[43] the Supreme Court held that Roman Catholic parents were not entitled to insist that their children be exempted from attending a non-sectarian course on ethics and religious culture. The Court cited with apparent approval the Ontario school prayer and religious instruction cases discussed above. Nevertheless, the Court distinguished those cases on the ground that here, the parents had failed to establish that the ethics and religious culture course, which exposed children to a range of different religions, infringed their religious freedom.

It might be noted that the result of these cases does not necessarily draw a strict line between church and state. Unlike the language of the First Amendment to the American constitution, which guarantees the free exercise of religion and prohibits the establishment of religion, section 2(a) of the *Charter* does not prohibit government support for religion.

2) School Safety and Religious Requirements

When school policy conflicts with the freedom of religion, it is not always because the school has introduced religious elements into its curriculum. Instead, school policies may prevent students from freely practising their religion while at school. In *Multani v Commission scolaire Marguerite-Bourgeoys*,[44] the Supreme Court dealt with a Sikh student who had been prohibited from bringing his kirpan to school. A kirpan is a religious object which resembles a dagger and is made of metal. The prohibition on the kirpan was imposed after the school's governing board refused to ratify an agreement reached with the student and the school board, which would have allowed the student to bring the kirpan to school provided that it was kept in its sheath, sewn securely into a sturdy cloth envelope, and worn under his clothes. The student and his father challenged the prohibition, arguing that the student believed that his religion required him to keep the kirpan on his person at all times, even while sleeping.

A majority of the Court found that the prohibition violated the student's freedom of religion.[45] Writing for the majority, Charron J held that, in determining whether the ban violated the student's freedom of

---

43   [2012] 1 SCR 235.
44   [2006] 1 SCR 256.
45   In a concurring judgment, Deschamps and Abella JJ found that the matter was more appropriately resolved on principles of administrative law, rather than the *Charter*. They held that the board's decision was unreasonable, as it had failed to consider the student's freedom to practise his religion. In a further, brief concurring judgment, LeBel J dealt with both administrative law principles and

religion, it was inappropriate to view the kirpan as a weapon since the student held a genuine belief that he was required to wear the kirpan to comply with the demands of his religion. The fact that the kirpan is a bladed weapon that could be used to seriously injure another person was relevant to the section 1 inquiry but irrelevant for the purposes of determining whether the student's religious freedoms had been breached. Justice Charron further held that the fact that other Sikhs had been willing to accept compromises, such as substituting the metal kirpan with a plastic or wooden one, was not relevant to the section 2(a) analysis. Instead, concerns such as the dangerousness of the kirpan and possible compromises to the dispute were left for the section 1 analysis.

In conducting her section 1 analysis, Charron J held that the prohibition on the kirpan could not be justified, as it failed to minimally impair the rights of the student. She stated that in cases such as this, the minimal impairment prong of the *Oakes* test was analogous to the concept of reasonable accommodation. If there was a reasonable accommodation that the school board could make so as to allow the student to safely bring the kirpan to school, the prohibition could not be minimally impairing. Noting that the student in question had never exhibited any behavioural problems at school, and that the evidence suggested that there had not been a single incident in Canada of kirpan-related violence in school, Charron J found that the original compromise reached between the student and the school board, in which the kirpan would be sewn into its sheath and kept under the his clothes, was such a reasonable accommodation. Accordingly, the prohibition was deemed unconstitutional.

3) Sectarian Schools

Because of the secular nature of public schools, some parents refuse to send their children to the public system for religious reasons. Section 2(a) clearly affords parents the right to provide their children with alternative schooling if their religious beliefs require them to do so. However, the state may validly require that the child be provided with an education that meets minimum standards. Thus, in *Jones*,[46] the Supreme Court of Canada found no violation of section 2(a) because a father, educating his children and others at a church school, had to obtain an exemption from the school board on the basis that he was

---

Charter jurisprudence; he found that the board's decision violated s 2(a) and could not be saved under s 1.

46 *Jones*, above note 16.

providing "efficient instruction." In Wilson J's view, Jones had failed to show "any substantial impact of this legislation on his belief that God and not the State is the true source of authority over the education of his children."[47] Again, as in *Edwards Books*, the Court indicated that burdens on the practice of religion are not always in violation of the *Charter*.

While the *Jones* case indicated that members of religious groups could avoid public school attendance, the case did not deal with the question whether the state was required to fund independent religious schools. In a number of provinces, constitutional guarantees ensure funding for certain denominational schools.[48] Schools operated by other religious groups argue that they, too, should be included — either on the basis of the equality guarantee in section 15 of the *Charter* (which includes protection against discrimination on the ground of religion) or on the basis of section 2(a). Under section 2(a), the argument is that the secular program of the public school system may be considered inappropriate by adherents of certain religions. Though such parents have the right to send their children to religious schools, the cost of private education may be burdensome. Many may be unable to afford the tuition at independent religious schools. Such individuals, who still pay taxes to support the public system, argue that their religious beliefs are burdened and that the state should fund their religious schools, to ensure that those whose religion requires distinctive teaching may effectively enjoy their rights.

The specific guarantees for religious schools found in the earlier constitutional documents have to be taken into account in relation to these claims. The *Constitution Act, 1867*, section 93, guaranteed that the rights of certain religious denominations to schools possessed by law at the time of Confederation will be maintained. This provision gave constitutional protection to the Roman Catholic schools in Ontario and both the Catholic and Protestant schools in Quebec. Some of the other provinces were made subject to similar guarantees when they joined Confederation. Recently, constitutional amendments have altered these rights in Newfoundland and Labrador and Quebec.

Supporters of non-Catholic religious schools in Ontario contend that they, too, should be given public financial support for their schools. This argument was first raised in the *Bill 30 Reference*, a case arising when Ontario extended funding for the Roman Catholic school system

---

47   *Ibid* at 315 (SCR). However, Wilson J, in dissent, did find a violation of s 7.
48   *Constitution Act, 1867*, s 93.

to Grade 13.[49] Until that time, funding had stopped at Grade 10. The Supreme Court of Canada interpreted section 93 to require full funding to Grade 13 but dismissed the argument that sections 2(a) and 15 of the *Charter* required equal funding for other religious schools. The government had relied on section 29 of the *Charter* to defend its decision not to fund other religious schools:

> Nothing in this *Charter* abrogates or derogates from any rights or privileges guaranteed by or under the Constitution of Canada in respect of denominational, separate or dissentient schools.

The Court held that, even without this "non-derogation" clause, the rights enjoyed by Roman Catholic school supporters in Ontario were specially protected. The denominational school guarantees in section 93 of the *Constitution Act, 1867* were described as a "fundamental part of the Confederation compromise" immune from review under the *Charter*. The Court held that the general right to freedom of religion conferred by the *Charter* could not be used to qualify the specific rights conferred on religious minorities by the 1867 constitution.

Despite this ruling, adherents of independent religious schools tried again in the *Adler* case to seek public funding. As they were precluded by the *Bill 30 Reference* decision from basing their claim on the rights of the Roman Catholic schools in Ontario, they focused on the effect of a secular school education on their freedom of religion and equality rights. They argued that the compulsion to support a secular public school system, coupled with mandatory schooling, imposed a financial burden on those who believe in religion as part of education. This burden both interfered with their freedom of religion and meant that they were being treated unequally.

The Supreme Court of Canada again rejected these arguments.[50] Writing for the majority, Iacobucci J held that section 93 of the *Constitution Act, 1867*, was conclusive. Like Wilson J in the *Bill 30 Reference*, he emphasized that section 93 was part of a historical compromise leading to Confederation. Not only did it guarantee funding for Roman Catholic schools in Ontario, it also implicitly contemplated public, secular schools. The constitution entrenched a power in the provincial legislature to legislate with respect to non-denominational schools. The province had the power to fund other denominational schools, but its decision not to do so was protected from *Charter* review.

49   *Reference Re Bill 30, An Act to Amend the Education Act (Ontario)*, [1987] 1 SCR 1148, 40 DLR (4th) 18 [*Bill 30 Reference*].
50   *Adler v Ontario*, [1996] 3 SCR 609, 140 DLR (4th) 385 [*Adler*].

While other judges found that section 93 was not conclusive, none found a violation of the section 2(a) guarantee of freedom of religion.[51] Four members of the Court held that the legislative decision not to fund independent religious schools was subject to *Charter* review. However, there was, in their view, no violation of section 2(a). According to Sopinka J, although parents have the constitutional right to educate their children in the religion of their choice, there was no state obligation to fund religious schools. In his view, the state's failure to act in order to facilitate the practice of an individual's religion did not constitute state interference with freedom of religion. Any disadvantage flowing from a decision to send a child to a religious school rather than a public school flowed from the tenets of the religion, not state action.

The result is that in certain provinces, including Ontario, there is an apparently anomalous situation in which Roman Catholic schools are guaranteed public funding but other religious schools get none. Implicit in the decision of the Supreme Court in *Adler* is a belief that secular education is important to Canadian society. Indeed, McLachlin J, dissenting on other grounds, would have upheld the decision not to fund independent religious schools under section 1, even though she found it to be a violation of the equality guarantee. In her view, the preservation of an education system designed to encourage tolerance and harmony in a multicultural society was an important objective, reasonably achieved by funding only the public system.

While the issue of religious school funding seems to have been resolved under the *Charter*, this is not likely to be the end of the issue. Advocates of religious school funding are now turning to the arena of international law. They claim that the failure to fund their schools, especially in light of the funding for the Roman Catholic schools, is a violation of the right against religious discrimination in the *International Covenant on Civil and Political Rights*. The United Nations Human Rights Committee has found that Canada has breached that right by deciding to fund some religious schools, but not others. The Committee indicated that the fact that the religious distinction was enshrined in the *Constitution Act, 1867* did not make it reasonable or objective.[52]

---

51   In the case, all nine judges found no violation of s 2(a); McLachlin J found a violation of s 15 that was justified under s 1, although she dissented on the issue of funding for school health services: the failure to provide them to independent religious schools violated s 15 in her view. Justice L'Heureux-Dubé dissented on both the broad funding issue and the health services issue, arguing that both decisions were unjustified violations of s 15.

52   *Waldman v Canada*, Canada Communication No. #694/1996, United Nations Document CCPR/C/67/D/694/1996 at 10.5–10.6.

E. RECONCILING FREEDOM OF RELIGION WITH OTHER VALUES

A number of cases have raised the issue of reconciling freedom of religion with other *Charter* rights and freedoms, particularly the right to equality. In *Ross v New Brunswick School District No. 15*,[53] the Supreme Court of Canada held that the decision of a provincial human rights tribunal, ordering a school board to remove from the classroom a teacher who had expressed anti-Semitic views about Jews, violated the teacher's freedom of religion, as well as his freedom of expression. The Court stressed the need to interpret freedom of religion broadly to include all sincere religious belief and to leave the justifications for restricting freedom of religion to section 1 of the *Charter*. The Court then held that the removal order was justified under section 1 because

> any religious belief that denigrates and defames the religious beliefs of others erodes the very basis of the guarantee in s 2(*a*) — a basis that guarantees that every individual is free to hold and to manifest the beliefs dictated by one's conscience.[54]

Trinity Western University v British Columbia College of Teachers[55] involved the reconciliation of freedom of religion and equality rights. A private institution in British Columbia offered baccalaureate degrees in education and applied to the British Columbia College of Teachers (the College) for permission to assume full responsibility for its program. One of the institution's reasons for applying was its desire to have the full program reflect its Christian worldview. The College denied the application because it was concerned that the institution appeared to follow discriminatory practices against homosexuals; in particular, it was concerned that members were asked to sign a document agreeing to refrain from engaging in "sexual sins" including "homosexual behaviour." The majority of the Supreme Court held that the College had erred in not considering the freedom of religion of the institution's members and in not reconciling that freedom with British Columbia public school students' freedom from discrimination on the basis of sexual orientation. The majority held that neither freedom is absolute and that the appropriate place to draw the line is generally between belief and conduct. The freedom to hold beliefs is broader than the freedom to act on those beliefs. There was no evidence that training

---

53 [1996] 1 SCR 825.
54 *Ibid* at para 94.
55 [2001] 1 SCR 772, 199 DLR (4th) 1.

teachers at the institution fostered discrimination in British Columbia's public schools. Therefore, the freedom of members to hold certain religious beliefs while at the institution should be respected.

In dissent, L'Heureux-Dubé J held that the College was not required to reconcile freedom of religion with equality rights in considering the institution's application to assume full responsibility for its program. In her view, that was not the statutory mandate of the College, and the balancing and interpretation of human rights values was beyond the College's expertise. The College's decision engaged only one *Charter* right — equality — and did so only in the limited context of assessing the impact of the institution's proposal on the province's classrooms. Accordingly, the College was not required to consider other *Charter* rights, including freedom of religion.

A second round of litigation about the College is occurring. It relates to decisions by the Law Society of Upper Canada and two other legal regulators whether to accredit Trinity Western's proposed law school. The Ontario Court of Appeal distinguished that the Supreme Court's 2001 decision on the basis that the Law Society had considered freedom of religion and its decision not to accredit the proposed law school to be based on the idea that its policies discriminated against gay law students and not on the idea that Trinity Western graduates would discriminate against others after graduation.[56] The issue seems destined to eventually be decided by the Supreme Court in an elaboration of the appropriate reconciliation of freedom of religion and equality rights.

In *Chamberlain v Surrey School District No 36*,[57] the Supreme Court considered a decision by a school board not to approve books about same-sex families for use in kindergarten and grade one. The trial judge found that the school board had not approved the books in large part because of a concern about controversy involving some parents' religious objections to same-sex relationships. The majority of the Court overturned the board's decision on the basis that it conflicted with a statutory obligation that public schools in British Columbia be conducted "on strictly secular and non-sectarian principles."[58] The Court

---

56 *Trinity Western University v Law Society of Upper Canada*, 2016 ONCA 518 at paras 58 and 122. Other courts have, however, overturned the decision of other law societies not to accredit the law school. See *Trinity Western University v Law Society of British Columbia*, 2016 BCCA 423, and *Trinity Western University v Nova Scotia Barristers' Society*, 2016 NSCA 59.

57 [2002] 4 SCR 710 [*Chamberlain*].

58 *School Act*, RSBC 1996, c 412, s 76.

decided the case on statutory grounds and not under the *Charter*, but it did note that the statutory policy

> reflects the fact that Canada is a diverse and multicultural society, bound together by the values of accommodation, tolerance and respect for diversity. These values are reflected in our Constitution's commitments to equality rights and minority rights.[59]

Justice Gonthier dissented (Bastarache J concurring) and would have upheld the school board's decision not to allow use of books about same-sex families. He stressed the need to reconcile and balance freedom of religion, including some religious beliefs about the immorality of same-sex relationships, with equality rights. He concluded that the board's decision struck a reasonable balance given that same-sex relationships would be discussed in the higher grades.

The proper reconciliation between freedom of religion and equality rights was also considered in a number of cases dealing with same-sex marriage. The Supreme Court rejected arguments that a draft bill recognizing same-sex marriage would violate freedom of religion or the equality rights of those who believed on religious grounds that same-sex marriages were immoral. The Court stated:

> The mere recognition of the equality rights of one group cannot, in itself, constitute a violation of the rights of another. The promotion of *Charter* rights and values enriches our society as a whole and the furtherance of those rights cannot undermine the very principles that the *Charter* was meant to foster.[60]

The Court indicated that any conflict between the right to same-sex marriage and freedom of religion would be resolved within the *Charter* through an interpretation of the scope of the respective rights. It also stated that it

> seems clear that state compulsion on religious officials to perform same-sex marriages contrary to their religious beliefs would violate the guarantee of freedom of religion under s 2(a) of the *Charter*. It also seems apparent that, absent exceptional circumstances which we cannot at present foresee, such a violation could not be justified under s 1 of the *Charter*.[61]

---

59 *Chamberlain*, above note 57 at para 21.
60 *Reference Re Same-Sex Marriage*, above note 7 at para 46.
61 *Ibid* at para 58.

In *R v NS*,[62] the Supreme Court considered the clash between the religious freedom of a sexual assault complainant who, for religious reasons, wore a niqab to cover her face, and the fair trial rights of the accused. Two judges (LeBel and Rothstein JJ) held that the right of fair trial and the openness of court proceedings should always prevail and that all complainants should be required to expose their faces when testifying. One judge (Abella J) held that religious freedom should prevail and that complainants should always be permitted to testify with the niqab. However, the majority opted for a middle-ground solution that sought to reconcile and balance the conflicting *Charter* rights. The complainant should be permitted to testify while wearing the niqab unless doing so would interfere with the fair trial rights of the accused. As McLachlin CJC explained, an absolute rule favouring one right over another would be inconsistent with the fundamental *Charter* premise that rights should be limited only to the extent that the limits are shown to be justifiable and the deeply entrenched Canadian constitutional principle that religious beliefs should be balanced and accommodated against other values and interests.

Chief Justice McLachlin applied a modified version of the four-part *Dagenais/Mentuck* framework used to deal with publication bans.[63] This framework involves posing four questions:

1) Would requiring the witness to remove the niqab while testifying interfere with her religious freedom?
2) Would permitting the witness to wear the niqab while testifying create a serious risk to trial fairness?
3) Is there a way to accommodate both rights and avoid the conflict between them?
4) If no accommodation is possible, do the salutary effects of requiring the witness to remove the niqab outweigh the deleterious effects of doing so?[64]

The first question is answered by looking to the sincerity, not the strength, of the complainant's religious belief. The second question considers in a contextual manner the nature of the evidence and the extent to which the fair trial rights of the accused require the witness to expose her face, for example, to establish identity, to facilitate cross-examination, to observe demeanour, or to assess credibility. If the answer to the first two questions is yes, the court proceeds to the third

---

62   2012 SCC 72.
63   See Chapter 9.
64   Above note 62 at para 9.

question, which looks for ways to avoid the conflict between religious freedom and fair trial rights: for example, if fair trial requires the complainant to expose her face, could the interference with her religious freedom be minimized by allowing her to testify behind a screen or on closed circuit television? The fourth question is asked where there is an unavoidable conflict that cannot be accommodated. As with the final stage of the *Oakes* proportionality analysis,[65] the court assesses "the competing harms" and determines "whether the salutary effects of requiring the witness to remove the niqab (for example, reducing the risk of a wrongful conviction) outweigh the deleterious effects of doing so (for example, the harm from interfering with the witness's sincerely held religious belief)."[66]

F. CONCLUSION

Freedom of religion and conscience lies at the heart of a free and democratic society. While the principle of religious freedom is taken for granted, difficult issues arise when deeply held religious views and practices collide with other important state interests. The courts have been asked to pronounce on a number of controversial issues involving religious freedom. A dominant theme is the judicial tendency to protect vulnerable minorities in this area. Sunday closing laws imposing the religious values of the majority have been found to offend the *Charter* guarantee, as have policies involving school prayer, religious instruction and the prohibition of wearing religious objects. As with other *Charter* guarantees, however, difficult questions arise when the state is asked to take positive measures to ensure the better enjoyment of a protected freedom. For certain religious groups, religious education is fundamental. While there seems to be little question that the *Charter* protects the right of religious minorities to educate their children as they see fit, the courts have been unsympathetic to the claims that religious freedom requires state support for religious schools in the absence of a specific constitutional right to denominational schooling.

---

65   See Chapter 4.
66   Above note 62 at para 8.

FURTHER READINGS

BERGER, B, "Law's Religion: Rendering Culture" (2007) 45 Osgoode Hall LJ 277

————, *Law's Religion: Religious Difference and the Claims of Constitutionalism* (Toronto: University of Toronto Press, 2015)

————, & R MOON, eds, *Religion and the Exercise of Public Authority* (Oxford: Hart Publishing, 2016)

BHABHA, F, "From *Saumur* to *L(S)*: Tracing the Theory and Concept of Religious Freedom under Canadian Law" (2012) 58 Sup Ct L Rev (2d) 109.

BROWN, DM, "Freedom from or Freedom For? Religion as a Case Study in Defining the Content of *Charter* Rights" (2000) 33 UBC L Rev 551

————, "Where Can I Pray? Sacred Space in a Secular Land" (2004) 14 NJCL 121

BUCKINGHAM, JE, *Fighting Over God: A Legal and Political History of Religious Freedom in Canada* (Montreal: McGill-Queen's University Press, 2014)

————, "The Fundamentals of Religious Freedoms: The Case for Recognizing the Collective Aspects of Religion" (2007) 36 Sup Ct L Rev. (2d) 251

CHOUDHRY, S, "Rights Adjudication in a Plurinational State: The Supreme Court of Canada, Freedom of Religion, and the Politics of Reasonable Accommodation" (2013) 50 Osgoode Hall LJ 575

ELBERG, B, & M POWER, "Freedom of Conscience and Religion" in GA Beaudoin & E Mendes, eds, *The* Canadian Charter of Rights and Freedoms, 4th ed (Markham, ON: LexisNexis Butterworths, 2005)

EVANS, C, "Adjudicating Contested Values: Freedom of Religion and the *Oakes* Test" (2013) 10 JL & Equality 5

HORWITZ, P, "The Sources and Limits of Freedom of Religion in a Liberal Democracy: Section 2(a) and Beyond" (1996) 54 UT Fac L Rev. 1

KISLOWICZ, H, "Sacred Laws in Earthly Courts: Legal Pluralism in Canadian Religious Freedom Litigation" (2013) 39 Queen's LJ 175

MACKLEM, T., "Faith as a Secular Value" (2000) 45 McGill LJ 1

MATHEN, C., "What Religious Freedom Jurisprudence Reveals about Equality" (2008) 6 JL & Equality 163

MOON, R, ed, *Law and Religious Pluralism in Canada* (Vancouver: University of British Columbia Press, 2008)

————, "Freedom of Conscience and Religion" (2013) 61 Sup Ct L Rev (2d) 339

WOEHRLING, J, "L'obligation d'accommodement raisonnable et l'adaptation de la société à la diversité religieuse" (1998) 43 McGill LJ 325

CHAPTER 9

FREEDOM OF EXPRESSION

Even before the *Charter of Rights and Freedoms*, freedom of expression was recognized by the Supreme Court of Canada as inherent in our system of government.[1] Democracy rests on the premise that public issues be freely and openly debated. Indeed, the freedom to criticize those who exercise power in our society is the very lifeblood of our democratic tradition. Political debate is often heated and intemperate. Criticism of public institutions and officials will not always be respectful and measured: those who challenge established authority often have to resort to strong language and exaggeration in order to gain attention. "If these exchanges are stifled, democratic government itself is threatened."[2]

Freedom of expression is also vital in other areas of human activity outside the realm of politics. Artists and writers often push the limits of conventional values. Scholars question "sacred cows" and accepted wisdom. Freedom of expression represents society's commitment to tolerate the annoyance of being confronted by unacceptable views. As stated by the Ontario Court of Appeal in an early *Charter* case:[3] "[T]he constitutional guarantee extends not only to that which is pleasing, but also to that which to many may be aesthetically distasteful or morally offensive: it is indeed often true that 'one man's vulgarity is another's lyric.'" More recently, the Supreme Court of Canada emphasized that

---

1   *Reference Re Alberta Legislation*, [1938] SCR 100, [1938] 2 DLR 81.
2   *R v Kopyto* (1987), 62 OR (2d) 449 at 462, 47 DLR (4th) 213 (CA) [*Kopyto*], Cory JA.
3   *Re Information Retailers Association and Metropolitan Toronto* (1985), 22 DLR (4th) 161 at 180 (Ont CA), Robins JA.

freedom of expression must include the "right to express outrageous and ridiculous opinions" and that as "[p]ublic controversy can be a rough trade . . . the law needs to accommodate its requirements."[4]

There are two rationales for extending the guarantee this widely.

The first is instrumental in nature and is reflected by the metaphor of the "marketplace in ideas." The great American judge Oliver Wendell Holmes, echoing the thoughts of John Milton and John Stuart Mill, said that "the best test of truth is the power of the thought to get itself accepted in the competition of the market."[5] Suppression of ideas in the name of truth is notoriously dangerous. The rationale of the marketplace of ideas posits that the free flow of ideas is the best way to get at the truth.

The second important rationale values expression less for the results it produces than for its intrinsic worth to the individual. Expression is seen as a vital element of individual autonomy, personal growth, and self-realization. The ability to say what one thinks and to follow whatever lines of inquiry that occur to one's imagination is an essential attribute of a free society.

In a 2002 decision,[6] the Supreme Court of Canada summarized the values protected by freedom of expression in these terms:

> The core values which free expression promotes include self-fulfilment, participation in social and political decision-making, and the communal exchange of ideas. Free speech protects human dignity and the right to think and reflect freely on one's circumstances and condition. It allows a person to speak not only for the sake of expression itself, but also to advocate change, attempting to persuade others in the hope of improving one's life and perhaps the wider social, political, and economic environment.[7]

A. RECONCILING FREEDOM OF EXPRESSION WITH OTHER VALUES

Does freedom of expression preclude any law limiting what individuals can say or publish? The answer is surely no. To take a familiar example,

---

4   *WIC Radio Ltd v Simpson*, [2008] 2 SCR 420 at paras 4 and 15 [*WIC*].
5   *Abrams v United States*, 250 US 616 at 630 (1919).
6   *Retail, Wholesale and Department Store Union, Local 558 v Pepsi-Cola Canada Beverages (West) Ltd*, [2002] 1 SCR 156, 208 DLR (4th) 385 [*Retail, Wholesale and Department Store Union*].
7   *Ibid* at 399 (DLR).

freedom of expression does not protect the right, falsely, to shout "Fire!" in a crowded theatre.[8] As with the other rights and freedoms guaranteed by the *Charter*, freedom of expression is not absolute. There are situations in which the freedom of one individual must be curtailed so that other important social values may be respected and protected.

How should these competing claims be reconciled? The American approach has been to accord near-absolute respect to expression deemed worthy of the constitutional guarantee; however, the American courts define freedom of expression narrowly so as not to include forms of speech that do not qualify for protection. The Supreme Court of Canada has adopted a different method to reconcile respect for this vital freedom with competing claims. Our Court has said that the structure of the *Charter*, and in particular section 1, requires that freedom of expression be given a broad definition with virtually no limitations and that any curtailment of expression be justified under section 1 as a limit that is reasonable in a free and democratic society.

In 1988 the Supreme Court heard two cases from Quebec in which it charted the course to be followed. *Ford v Quebec (Attorney General)*[9] involved a challenge to the Quebec "signs law," which prohibited, with virtually no exception, the display of commercial signs not written in French. *Ford* was argued at the same time as *Irwin Toy Ltd v Quebec (AG)*,[10] which involved a challenge to a Quebec statute that limited the right to broadcast advertising aimed at children. In both cases, the Attorney General of Quebec argued that the law did not limit freedom of expression. In *Ford*, Quebec contended that the "signs law" did not limit in any way the message that could be conveyed. The language of the speaker was merely the medium for expression. It was contended in both cases that commercial expression is not worthy of constitutional protection and that the Court should adhere to a core definition of freedom of expression, limiting the right to the most vital areas of political speech and artistic expression. The Supreme Court rejected these arguments, holding that freedom of expression should be given a wide and generous definition admitting few exceptions. Yet at the same time, the Court recognized that expression may be curtailed if the standard of section 1 is met.

In *Ford* the Court stated that language was an essential component of expression:

---

8   *Schenk v United States*, 249 US 47 at 52 (1919), Holmes J.

9   [1988] 2 SCR 712, 54 DLR (4th) 577 [*Ford*].

10   [1989] 1 SCR 927, 58 DLR (4th) 577 [*Irwin Toy*].

> Language is so intimately related to the form and content of expression that there cannot be true freedom of expression by means of language if one is prohibited from using the language of one's choice. Language is not merely a means or medium of expression; it colours the content and meaning of expression.[11]

The Court was also unsympathetic to the argument that expression should be limited to political speech, thereby excluding advertising. The Court found that the purpose of protecting freedom of expression was not limited to political speech and the enhancement of democratic self-government. Other values were also involved. The Court accepted as a valid rationale for protecting expression the concept of a "marketplace of ideas." It also recognized the important element of individual autonomy and self-development inherent in expression. Informed by these purposes, the Court found that freedom of expression embraced expressive conduct extending to most areas of human activity, including commerce and the arts.

The Supreme Court has recognized that freedom of expression should be defined generously in other ways, as well. Although we usually regard the right as that of the speaker, meaningful expression assumes an audience. The purposes underlying the guarantee contemplate a recipient of the message, and the Court has said that the right extends to the listener as well as to the speaker.[12] Cases of freedom of expression typically involve a restraint on speech. The Court has acknowledged, however, that the freedom also protects the individual from being required to express one particular view.[13]

In *Irwin Toy*, the Supreme Court described in a formal manner the framework for interpretative analysis to be followed in a freedom of expression case. The first stage is definitional. Here, the Court said, a broad approach is called for. Expression includes any activity that conveys or attempts to convey a meaning. The use of the word "activity" is significant as the Court recognized that, in some situations, actions without words may have expressive content. For example, parking a car ordinarily has no expressive feature, but, as the Supreme Court explained, if an unmarried person, as a protest, were to park in a space reserved for spouses, that action would have expressive content. The only restriction the Court placed on conduct of an expressive nature was

---

11 *Ford*, above note 9 at 748 (SCR).

12 *Rocket v Royal College of Dental Surgeons of Ontario*, [1990] 2 SCR 232, 71 DLR (4th) 68 [*Rocket*].

13 *RJR-MacDonald Inc v Canada (Attorney General)*, [1995] 3 SCR 199, 127 DLR (4th) 1 [*RJR*].

for acts of violence. Violence is often used by terrorists as a means to convey a message, but laws against terrorism do not infringe freedom of expression. In *R v Khawaja*, the Court affirmed that neither violence nor threats of violence were protected forms of expression. The *Criminal Code* definition of terrorist activities, which includes politically or religiously motivated property damage and disruption of essential services such that life, health, or safety is endangered, did not violate section 2(b) of the *Charter*.[14] In *Montréal (City) v 2952-1366 Québec Inc*,[15] the Court added another definitional filter, namely, that there are some otherwise public places that must remain outside the protected sphere of section 2(b). The historical or actual function of the place may require a degree of privacy that would be undermined if anyone could intrude to offer an opinion. Likewise, where allowing free expression in a place would undermine the very values the guarantee is designed to promote, the constitutional right is excluded. Certain government functions — cabinet meetings, for example — can be conducted effectively only if accorded a level of privacy. Other highly public and political activities — such as sittings of Parliament — require a level of order and decorum that is incompatible with according any member of the public the right to intrude with an expression of views.

The second stage of the analysis is to determine whether there has been a violation. Here, the Supreme Court distinguished content-based restraints from those that merely have the effect of limiting expression. The former category includes laws or practices that have as their purpose the restriction of the actual type of speech as well as restraints on a form of expression tied to content. Content-based restraints are the most familiar: examples include the law of defamation, the prohibition of pornography, and restrictions on advertising. An example of a restraint on a form of expression tied to content is a law that prohibits the handing out of pamphlets. While such a law is indifferent to the content of the pamphlet, it inevitably bans whatever content the pamphlet has and thus necessarily constitutes a restraint on expression. An effects-based restraint is one that is aimed at some other aspect of the activity but that may nevertheless have an impact on expression. A prohibition against littering has a valid purpose and is not aimed at expression. Yet it may have the effect of limiting expression depending upon the circumstances. If enforced against someone handing out pamphlets, it would have that effect, but if applied to someone carelessly discarding a candy wrapper, it would not. In the case of an effects-based restraint,

---

14   *R v Khawaja*, 2012 SCC 69 [*Khawaja*].
15   [2005] 3 SCR 141 [*City of Montréal*].

the Supreme Court held, the party claiming the protection of the *Charter* must be able to show that the activity in question promotes one of the three principles underlying freedom of expression: political debate, the marketplace of ideas, or autonomy and self-fulfilment.

Given the generous scope of this definition of expression, most claims for *Charter* protection will survive these first two stages. The Supreme Court has found, for example, that in addition to commercial expression, pornography,[16] hate speech,[17] and even deliberate falsehoods[18] qualify as expression. The purpose of these activities is to convey a message, however unpleasant, and the purpose of the *Criminal Code* provisions criminalizing pornography and hate speech is to restrict the very content of the messages being conveyed.

There remains, however, the third stage of analysis under section 1 of the *Charter*. Here, as seen in Chapter 4, the burden is on the state to justify the limit it seeks to impose as being reasonable in a free and democratic society. In virtually all of the freedom of expression cases to reach the Supreme Court of Canada, the crucial analysis has been under section 1. The most significant decisions are discussed in the pages that follow.

B. COMMERCIAL EXPRESSION

The Supreme Court has decided a number of cases involving restraints on commercial speech, with mixed results. In *Ford*,[19] the case involving the Quebec "signs law," the issues extended well beyond what constitutes the permissible regulation of advertising. The Court struck down the "signs law" on the ground that Quebec had failed to justify it as a reasonable limit. While the Supreme Court was prepared to accept as a legitimate purpose the protection and enhancement of the French language in Quebec, it held that the virtual total ban on public signs in any other language went too far. Quebec had failed to introduce evidence to show that such an extreme measure was necessary, and the Court held that the law failed to meet the minimal-impairment test. In making the minimal-impairment assessment, the Court considered alternative measures that might satisfy the goal of protecting and enhancing the

---

16   *R v Butler*, [1992] 1 SCR 452, 70 CCC (3d) 129 [*Butler*].

17   *R v Keegstra*, [1990] 3 SCR 697, 61 CCC (3d) 1 [*Keegstra*].

18   *R v Zundel*, [1992] 2 SCR 731, 95 DLR (4th) 202 [*Zundel*]; *R v Lucas*, [1998] 1 SCR 439, 157 DLR (4th) 425 [*Lucas*].

19   *Ford*, above note 9.

French language. It suggested that a law that required the use of French in commercial signs but that did not ban other languages might be acceptable, even if such a measure called for a marked predominance of French. A law along these lines would meet the aim of protecting and enhancing the French language while, at the same time, respecting the rights of non-French speakers.

In the companion case, *Irwin Toy*,[20] the Supreme Court was faced with a more typical case of commercial speech. At issue was the right of a toy manufacturer to advertise its products for commercial purposes. Quebec legislation prohibited commercial advertising directed at persons under thirteen years of age. The statute established certain criteria to determine whether the advertising was directed at children. A majority of the Court found that the Quebec law could be justified as a reasonable limit on the right of freedom of expression. As noted in Chapter 4, the decision in *Irwin Toy* represents a significant statement by the Court on the application of section 1 where a law has been enacted to protect a vulnerable group. In the Court's view, the legislature had acted reasonably in protecting children who it deemed less than fully capable of making informed judgments on the basis of advertising. As in *Ford*, the law imposed a total ban, but in *Irwin Toy* there was some evidence that such a measure was required. The evidence, it must be said, fell well short of proving with certainty that the law enacted by Quebec was the only or even the least drastic way to achieve the goal of protecting children from advertising. However, the Supreme Court accepted that the evidence was sufficient to support Quebec's claim. The Court recognized that, in this area, the facts were not susceptible of clear proof and that the legislature had to be given some latitude:

> If the legislature has made a reasonable assessment as to where the line is most properly drawn, especially if that assessment involves weighing conflicting scientific evidence and allocating scarce resources on this basis, it is not for the court to second guess. That would only be to substitute one estimate for another.[21]

There is much to be said for the view that, while commercial expression does qualify for constitutional protection, Parliament and the legislatures are entitled to some latitude when enacting protective measures in the public interest. Commercial expression has only tenuous connection to the underlying values of democratic self-government and individual autonomy and self-development. There is an obvious

---

20   *Irwin Toy*, above note 10.
21   *Ibid* at 990 (SCR).

connection with the rationale of the marketplace of ideas, although here the search for the truth is surely less elusive than in other areas of human activity such as politics or the arts. Regulation to ensure "truth in advertising" is familiar, yet it would surely be unthinkable to impose comparable measures in the areas of political or artistic expression.

The pattern revealed by *Ford*, striking down a total ban, and by *Irwin Toy*, reflecting a significant judicial tolerance for more specific laws restricting commercial expression, has been repeated by later decisions of the Court. The Court has upheld as a reasonable limit under section 1 of the *Charter* a *Criminal Code* provision making it illegal to solicit in a public place for the purpose of prostitution.[22] Chief Justice Dickson stated that, when considering the reasonable-limits test, the Court should have in mind the nature of the expression at issue. Solicitation had an overt "economic purpose" and it could "hardly be said that communications regarding an economic transaction of sex for money lie at, or even near, the core of the guarantee of freedom of expression."[23]

However, where the law imposes a total ban on commercial speech rather than targeting the mischief with a more limited and specific measure, the Court has taken a tougher line. In *Rocket v Royal College of Dental Surgeons*,[24] a dentist challenged regulations imposing a ban on professional advertising. The Supreme Court accepted that a professional body was entitled to regulate advertising by its members to protect the public and that "restrictions on expression of this kind might be easier to justify than other infringements."[25] Yet the Court struck down the regulations on the grounds that they went well beyond what was necessary to protect the public interest and that they prevented dentists from giving straightforward and useful information such as hours of operation and languages spoken. Similarly, in *RJR*,[26] by a majority of 5:4, the Supreme Court found that a law imposing a complete ban on advertising of tobacco products could not survive section 1 scrutiny as a minimal infringement of freedom of expression. While the majority accepted that Parliament could limit the right to advertise tobacco with a view to promoting the health of Canadians, the total ban was not shown to be necessary nor had the government

---

22 *Reference Re ss 193 and 195.1(1)(c) of the Criminal Code (Canada)*, [1990] 1 SCR 1123, 56 CCC (3d) 65 [*Reference re ss 193 and 195*]. This issue was not revisited when the Court subsequently struck down the soliciting offence under s 7 in *Canada (Attorney General) v Bedford*, [2013] 2 SCR 1101 at para 47.

23 *Reference re ss 193 and 195*, above note 22 at 1136 (SCR).

24 *Rocket*, above note 12.

25 *Ibid* at 247 (SCR), McLachlin J.

26 *RJR*, above note 13.

shown that more limited alternatives would be ineffective. Parliament enacted a more nuanced piece of legislation in response to the *RJR* decision, prohibiting only certain forms of tobacco advertising — lifestyle advertising, advertisements appealing to young persons, and false or misleading advertising — and required manufacturers to include health warning labels of a certain size on their products' packaging. The Supreme Court found these restrictions "represented a genuine attempt by Parliament to craft controls on advertising and promotion that would meet its objectives as well as the concerns expressed by the majority of this Court in *RJR*" and upheld them as a justifiable limitation of the tobacco manufacturers' freedom of expression under section 1.[27]

The right of a consumer to engage in "counter-advertising" was recognized in *R v Guignard*.[28] A disgruntled customer used a billboard to make known to the public his dissatisfaction with an insurance company. He was convicted under a municipal bylaw prohibiting billboards in residential areas that mention the name of commercial entities. The Supreme Court struck down the bylaw as an infringement of freedom of expression. "Consumers may express their frustration or disappointment with a product or service. Consumers may share their concerns, worries or even anger with other consumers and try to warn them against the practices of a business."[29] While the Court agreed that municipalities could control and regulate the visual pollution created by public signs, this bylaw did not survive scrutiny as a reasonable limit under section 1. As only signs mentioning commercial entities were prohibited, there was no rational connection to the stated objective of preventing visual pollution. Nor did the bylaw satisfy the minimal-impairment test since it severely curtailed the consumer's right to express his dissatisfaction publicly. In a subsequent case, the Court indicated that a municipal bylaw limiting the size of billboards violated freedom of expression, but was justified under section 1 of the *Charter*.[30] In the same case, the Ontario Court of Appeal unanimously invalidated a bylaw prohibiting all advertising for third parties.[31] These cases fit into the pattern, observed above, of the courts striking down total bans on particular types of advertising while often accepting less drastic restrictions on commercial expression as reasonable.

---

27   *Canada (Attorney General) v JTI-Macdonald Corp*, [2007] 2 SCR 610 at para 7.
28   [2002] 1 SCR 472, 209 DLR (4th) 549.
29   *Ibid* at para 23.
30   *Vann Niagara Ltd v Oakville (Town)*, [2003] 3 SCR 158.
31   *Vann Niagara Ltd v Oakville (Town)* (2002), 60 OR (3d) 1 (CA). There was no appeal to the Supreme Court from this aspect of the decision of the Ontario Court of Appeal.

Expression that appears to be motivated by economic or commercial interests may involve other values protected by the *Charter.* The Supreme Court has accorded significant protection to picketing[32] and leafleting[33] in labour disputes as a form of freedom of expression. The Court has stated that the interests of striking workers often go beyond purely economic issues. "Working conditions, like the duration and location of work, parental leave, health benefits, severance and retirement schemes, may impact on the personal lives of workers even outside their working hours."[34] The Court has recognized the importance of picketing as a means of redressing the imbalance of power between powerful commercial interests and vulnerable workers and has modified the common law rules related to secondary picketing.[35] The Court has held that privacy legislation that made no exception for unions collecting and displaying identifying information about workers who crossed picket lines was a disproportionate infringement of the union's freedom of expression.[36]

C. POLITICAL EXPRESSION

As already noted, freedom of expression about political issues lies at the heart of our democratic tradition. But does this mean that Parliament is incapable of intervening in all situations? Expression in the real world of politics is closely tied to economic resources. Those who have money have the means to convey their message to the public; those who lack resources are at a disadvantage and to them the promise of freedom of expression may be ineffectual. Is Parliament entitled to alleviate economic inequalities by regulating election expenses? Such laws are designed to improve debate by ensuring that some voices do not drown out others. Does this laudable goal justify imposing restraints on the political expression of those who have more substantial resources?

In an early *Charter* case, a federal law prohibiting anyone other than a registered party or candidate from spending money during an

---

32 *Retail, Wholesale and Department Store Union,* above note 6.

33 *United Food and Commercial Workers, Local 1518 (UFCW) v KMart Canada Ltd,* [1999] 2 SCR 1083, 176 DLR (4th) 607; *Allsco Building Products Ltd v United Food and Commercial Workers, Local 1288P (UFCW),* [1999] 2 SCR 1136, 176 DLR (4th) 647.

34 *Retail, Wholesale and Department Store Union,* above note 6 at 400 (DLR).

35 See Chapter 6.

36 *Alberta (Information and Privacy Commissioner) v United Food and Commercial Workers, Local 401,* 2013 SCC 62 [*United Food and Commercial Workers*].

election campaign to promote a cause or a candidate was struck down.[37]
The federal government contended that limiting the right of individuals to participate in campaigns was necessary to ensure the integrity
of other provisions controlling expenditures by candidates. An Alberta
judge held that the government had failed to prove its case. Given the
importance of freedom of political expression, he was not satisfied
that this significant constraint on the participation of individuals and
groups who were not candidates was justifiable.

In 1996 the Alberta Court of Appeal came to a similar conclusion
with respect to a federal law prohibiting any advertising between the
date an election is called and the twenty-ninth day before voting day,
as well as the day before and the day of the election.[38] The law also
prohibited third parties from spending more than $1000 for advertis-
ing, promoting, or opposing a particular candidate. These measures
followed the recommendations of a royal commission on elections. The
"blackout" provision was intended to control escalating campaign costs
and to limit the advantage of an incumbent. The third party spending
provision was intended to prevent circumvention of spending limits
imposed on candidates and to enhance public confidence in the electoral process by avoiding the risk of patronage in return for such spending. The Alberta courts were not persuaded by the evidence adduced
by the Attorney General that these measures were justified as limits on
freedom of expression under section 1. In the Court of Appeal, Conrad
JA found that the government's case failed to establish a sufficiently
important objective to justify overriding a *Charter* right. In her view,
the harm feared from unconstrained advertising and spending was essentially speculative. She also expressed the view that such restrictions,
especially those effectively precluding participation by non-candidates,
were fundamentally at odds with basic *Charter* values:

> An important justification for the *Charter* guarantees of free expres-
> sion and association, and an informed vote, is the need in a democ-
> racy for citizens to participate in and affect an election. It follows that
> there can be no pressing and substantial need to suppress that input
> merely because it might have an impact.[39]

In a case dealing with Quebec's referendum law, the Supreme Court
of Canada reached a conclusion similar to that of the Alberta Court of
Appeal even while revealing a different perspective.[40] The Court struck

37   *National Citizens' Coalition v Canada (AG)* (1984), 11 DLR (4th) 481 (Alta QB).
38   *Somerville v Canada (AG)* (1996), 136 DLR (4th) 205 (Alta CA).
39   *Ibid* at 232, Conrad JA.
40   *Libman v Quebec (AG)*, [1997] 3 SCR 569, 151 DLR (4th) 385.

down a law imposing spending restrictions but expressly stated that third party spending limits of the kind at issue in the Alberta case could be justifiable. The Quebec referendum law limited expenditures and required that all expenses be paid from the funds of committees specifically authorized to represent one side or the other. The Court was entirely sympathetic to the view that limiting election expenses could be justified in order to ensure fairness in a campaign and to prevent the most affluent members of society from exercising a disproportionate influence, but it found that the Quebec law went too far. Individuals or groups not willing or able to affiliate with one of the authorized committees were precluded from even producing leaflets or posters to express their opinion. While limiting the rights of third parties to spend money during a campaign might be necessary to ensure the integrity of spending limits justifiably imposed on candidates or authorized committees, the Quebec law failed the minimal-impairment test by prohibiting all third party expenditures and thereby effectively precluding any third party expression of view.

The Supreme Court of Canada considered limits on third party spending under the *Canada Elections Act* in *Harper v Canada (Attorney General)*. The Act restricted third parties from spending more than $3,000 per riding or $150,000 nationally. Stephen Harper, then leader of the National Citizens Coalition, challenged these restrictions as a limitation on freedom of expression, as well as on freedom of association and the right to vote. In 2000, the Supreme Court set aside an interlocutory injunction restraining the enforcement of the spending limits.[41] In 2004, the Supreme Court decided the case on the merits. It held in a 6:3 decision that the spending restrictions violated freedom of expression but were justified under section 1 of the *Charter.*[42]

The majority judgment of Bastarache J recognized that political expression warrants a high degree of constitutional protection, but also indicated that third party advertising could be less deserving of constitutional protection because of the danger of wealthy third parties manipulating political discourse to their advantage, causing electoral unfairness. He concluded that "on balance, the contextual factors favour a deferential approach to Parliament in determining whether the third party advertising limits are demonstrably justified in a free and democratic society."[43] The restrictions on third party advertising during elections were justified as rationally connected to the objectives of ensuring

---

41 *Harper v Canada (Attorney General)*, [2000] 2 SCR 764 [*Harper* I]. For further discussion, see Chapters 11 and 17.

42 *Harper v Canada (Attorney General)*, [2004] 1 SCR 827 [*Harper* II].

43 *Ibid* at para 88.

fair elections by promoting equality in political discourse, protecting the integrity of spending restrictions on political parties and candidates, and ensuring that voters have confidence in the electoral process. The restrictions were proportionate because they applied only to third party advertising that was associated with a political party or candidate, and the beneficial effects of the restrictions in promoting electoral fairness outweighed their harms to free expression. Three judges in dissent accepted that promoting electoral fairness, preventing the wealthy from dominating political discourse, and preserving confidence in the electoral system were pressing and substantial objectives that could limit freedom of expression. Nevertheless, they held that the actual restrictions were disproportionate because they effectively prevented third parties from using effective radio and television ads and resulted in a virtual ban on political expression during elections except through registered political parties and candidates. The entire Court, however, was unanimous that a total ban on third party election advertising on polling day was a reasonable limit on freedom of expression, given the difficulty of responding to any misleading advertising during this time.

Another decision in this area, however, indicates that the Supreme Court will impose a high standard of justification for absolute prohibitions on expression in connection with elections.[44] At issue was a federal law banning the publication of opinion polls in the three days prior to a federal election. The majority found that the law could not be justified under section 1. The contention that it was desirable to provide voters with a period of rest and reflection, free from opinion polls, was rejected as a pressing and substantial objective. Writing for the majority, Bastarache J stated that "Canadian voters must be presumed to have a certain degree of maturity and intelligence" and that it was an insult to assume that "an individual would be so enthralled by a particular poll result as to allow his or her electoral judgment to be ruled by it."[45] While the Court accepted that measures to ensure an opportunity to assess the accuracy of opinion polls was a valid objective, it found that the law failed to meet the minimal-impairment test. Other measures would meet that objective in a manner less intrusive of freedom of expression, requiring the publication of the methodology used being one. Moreover, wrote Bastarache J, by imposing a complete ban on the publication of opinion polls within the three-day period, the law constituted such a serious infringement of freedom of expression that

---

44   *Thomson Newspapers Co v Canada (AG)* (1998), 159 DLR (4th) 385 (SCC).
45   *Ibid* at 437.

even if it satisfied the minimal-impairment test, its deleterious effects would have outweighed the benefit it sought to achieve.

Issues surrounding restrictions on third party spending during elections are now relatively settled in Canada, with the Supreme Court adopting a deferential approach to restrictions designed to achieve electoral fairness and preventing the wealthy from dominating political discourse. One remaining issue is the regulation of spending during elections by parties and candidates. *MacKay v Manitoba*[46] dealt with public subsidies for the campaign expenses of candidates. The plaintiff challenged Manitoba legislation that gave candidates the right to be reimbursed from public funds for a portion of their campaign expenses, provided they secured a specified percentage of the vote. The Court found that there were serious deficiencies in the evidence and that it was being asked to rule in the abstract rather than in response to a specific factual situation. A somewhat similar issue arose almost fifteen years later in *Figueroa v Canada (Attorney General)*[47] where the leader of the Communist Party of Canada successfully challenged, under section 3 of the *Charter*, the denial of state benefits to parties that ran fewer than fifty candidates in national elections. An egalitarian as opposed to a libertarian approach to elections may, as in *Harper v Canada*,[48] defer to state limits on spending during elections but, as in *Figueroa*, may be much less deferential to state benefit schemes that have the effect of excluding small or marginal parties or candidates. In other words, the object in the egalitarian model of elections is on promoting equality and fairness for all.

The Supreme Court's focus on the egalitarian model is further reflected in *R v Bryan*.[49] During the 2002 federal election, the accused posted the election results from thirty-two ridings in Eastern Canada onto a website while polls were still open in other parts of the country. He was charged under the *Canada Elections Act* with the offence of disseminating election results from one electoral district to another where the polls were still open. He argued that the prohibition on transmitting election results was a violation of his freedom of expression. A 5:4 majority rejected his argument, finding that the prohibition was justified under section 1. The majority held that no evidence was required to show that informational equality between voters in an election was a pressing and substantial objective. Adopting an explicitly deferential approach, the Court found that the restriction met the section 1 proportionality test. The four dissenting judges found the evidence offered to

46   [1989] 2 SCR 357, 61 DLR (4th) 385.
47   [2003] 1 SCR 912 [*Figueroa*], also discussed in Chapter 11.
48   *Harper* II, above note 42. See discussion above.
49   [2007] 1 SCR 527.

justify the ban to be "speculative, inconclusive and largely unsubstantiated" and that as the "harm or suppressing core political speech" is "profound" any benefits of the legislation were outweighed by its deleterious effects.[50]

Given the close connection between political expression and the exercise of democratic rights, it is not surprising that the Supreme Court has held that the act of voting is protected as freedom of expression under section 2(b).[51] What is perhaps surprising is the Court's conclusion that the entitlement to vote in a referendum or a municipal plebiscite is a matter to be left to the legislature.[52] The Court, however, has left the door open to challenges to discriminatory restrictions on the availability of the right to vote, something that is again consistent with an egalitarian model of elections. However, the Court has held that denying a vote in a referendum to those who have recently moved to a province or to those who live in a municipality that has already held its own plebiscite did not result in discrimination in extending the vote.[53] The Court has also ruled that a provincial statutory regime which precluded school employees from being elected as school trustees to any school board in the province, even if they were employed by a different school board, did not violate the employees' freedom of expression.[54] There, the Court found that the employees' freedom of expression was not violated as their claim was grounded in access to a particular statutory regime rather than in the fundamental freedom of expression.[55]

The Supreme Court has rejected an argument that a requirement for proof of political or religious motive for terrorism offences in the *Criminal Code* violates section 2(b) by chilling political or religious expression. There was no evidence that the law, as opposed to "the post 9/11 climate of suspicion," would chill such expression. In addition, any chill to expression resulting from patently incorrect interpretations of the law or investigative misconduct, such as religious profiling by the state, could not be attributable to the law. Indeed, the law specifically allows the non-violent expression of political and religious views.[56]

---

50   *Ibid* at para 107.
51   *Haig v Canada (Chief Electoral Officer)*, [1993] 2 SCR 995.
52   *Ibid*; *Siemens v Manitoba (Attorney General)*, [2003] 1 SCR 6.
53   *Ibid*.
54   *Baier v Alberta*, [2007] 2 SCR 673.
55   See further discussion of this point above in Chapter 3.
56   *Khawaja*, above note 14 at paras 81–84.

D. HATE SPEECH

The *Criminal Code* prohibits the communication of statements, other than in private conversation, that wilfully promote hatred against an identifiable group.[57] The purpose behind this prohibition is readily understood. In view of Canada's multicultural and multiracial social fabric, Parliament considered it appropriate to take steps to ensure that the values of tolerance, equality, and non-discrimination are respected. But anti-hate speech laws are opposed by many advocates of free speech. While it is impossible to see any redeeming value in the utterances of the hatemonger, it is argued that such laws pose an unjustifiable risk to the competing value of freedom of expression. Race, religion, and cultural difference are important issues of public concern and often give rise to heated public debate. The issues are exceedingly sensitive, and some may take offence at what others regard as fair comment. Is it possible to identify with sufficient clarity and precision that which is truly unworthy and reprehensible without posing a significant risk to honest and vigorous debate?

In *Keegstra*,[58] a majority of the Supreme Court of Canada answered yes. All members of the Court agreed that, despite its message, hate speech does convey a meaning and therefore constitutes expression within the ambit of the *Charter*. Following the course it had laid out in *Irwin Toy*, the Court refused to exclude hate speech from the protection of the *Charter* on definitional grounds. It held that, if this form of expression was to be limited, the law had to satisfy the reasonable-limits test of section 1. All members of the Court also accepted the argument that the objective of the anti-hate speech law was sufficiently compelling to justify limiting a *Charter* right. Such a law is intended to avoid tangible harm in the form of feelings of humiliation and degradation felt by those targeted. Furthermore, it is designed to enhance a social climate of mutual respect and tolerance. Anti-hate laws, said the Court, were not only consistent with certain international obligations assumed by Canada but also enhanced other important and competing *Charter* values of equality and multiculturalism.

The judges of the Supreme Court divided, however, on the question of minimal impairment. A purposive analysis led the majority to conclude that the minimal-impairment test was to be applied less rigorously than in other contexts. While hate speech qualified as expres-

---

57   Section 319. See also the related provisions prohibiting the wilful promotion of genocide (s 318).
58   Above note 17.

sion, in the majority's view, it had to be recognized that hate speech was inimical to the values underlying freedom of expression. It was clearly false, thereby not attracting support from the rationale of the marketplace of ideas. And, while democracy depends upon free and open debate, hate speech denies equal dignity and respect, a precondition for genuine debate. Hate speech also attacks the autonomy rights of those who are its targets. From this perspective, the majority concluded that the anti-hate law could be justified as a minimal impairment of freedom of expression. The law was, in the Court's view, drawn with sufficient precision to avoid posing a threat to honest or worthy expression. It does not prohibit private communications, and the prosecution has to prove as an essential ingredient of the offence that the speech represents the wilful promotion of hatred on behalf of the accused. The accused is also afforded a number of defences, including truth; the good-faith expression of opinion on a religious subject; the reasonable belief in the truth of statements relevant to the public interest, the discussion of which is for the public benefit; and the conviction that the statement was intended in good faith to remove feelings of hatred. The majority found that Parliament had carefully tailored the law to its legitimate objective and that the law should be upheld on the ground that it minimally impaired freedom of expression.

The dissenting judges saw the effect of the anti-hate law quite differently. While not disputing Parliament's laudable goals, the minority did not agree that the law had a rational connection to those goals. The effect of an anti-hate-law prosecution is to afford the hatemonger an otherwise unattainable platform and level of publicity. Attempts at suppression might only serve to create martyrs. Historical evidence of vigorous anti-hate-law prosecution in pre-Nazi Germany was offered to suggest that such laws were at best ineffective and at worst counterproductive. The dissenting judges also disagreed that the law was sufficiently precise, pointing to instances where prosecutions had been brought or threatened against forms of expression plainly tolerable in a free society. Though such prosecutions might not succeed, the very threat of prosecution could well stifle expression on controversial matters.[59]

In a companion case to *Keegstra*, the Supreme Court, in *Canada (Human Rights Commission) v Taylor*, upheld the *Canadian Human Rights Act* provisions curtailing hate speech.[60] It also upheld a decision of a

---

59   The American courts have tended to strike down restrictions on racist speech: see *Collin v Smith*, 578 F2d 1197 (1978); *RAV v City of St. Paul*, 112 S Ct 2538 (1992).
60   [1990] 3 SCR 892, 75 DLR (4th) 577 [*Taylor*].

provincial human rights tribunal ordering a school board to remove from the classroom a teacher who had expressed racist views.[61]

In 2013, the Court, in *Saskatchewan (Human Rights Commission) v Whatcott*,[62] held that a provision of the *Saskatchewan Human Rights Code* that prohibited publications that "exposes, ridicules, belittles or otherwise affronts the dignity of any person or class of persons on the basis of a prohibited ground" violated freedom of expression (and religion), but that it was a reasonable limit under section 1. The Court, however, imposed some limits on the provision as enacted by the legislature. First, the Court stressed that the provision should be interpreted to apply only to extreme speech that would in the eyes of a reasonable person expose persons to detestation and vilification on a prohibited ground of discrimination.[63] Second, the Court held that the provision could be justified as a reasonable limit only to the extent that it exposes people to hatred. In addition, the phrase "ridicules, belittles or otherwise affronts the dignity of" was not rationally connected to the legislation's anti-hatred objectives was overbroad, and could not be justified under section 1.[64] Hence, this phrase was struck down and severed from the Act. The unanimous Court stressed that hate speech shuts down free debate and contributes little to the values of freedom of expression. The fact that the Saskatchewan provision did not require proof of an intent to promote hatred or allow a defence of truth as did the *Criminal Code*'s hate speech provisions upheld in *Keegstra* was not fatal in this case given the different purposes and consequences of proceedings against discriminatory acts under human rights codes. In the result, the Court upheld damages awards and prohibition orders with respect to fliers that stated, in part, "Keep homosexuality out of Saskatoon's public schools" and "Sodomites in our public schools" because they called for discriminatory treatment of gay men. The Court also found that handbills did not amount to prohibited calls for discrimination even though they contained offensive comments about personal ads placed in a gay magazine.

In another case,[65] however, the Supreme Court struck down the "false news" provision of the *Criminal Code*, which had been used in an effort to silence a well-known purveyor of anti-Semitic and Holocaust-denial literature. The law in question prohibited the publication of statements, known by the speaker to be false, that cause or are likely

---

61 *Ross v New Brunswick School District No 15*, [1996] 1 SCR 825, 133 DLR (4th) 1.
62 2013 SCC 11.
63 *Ibid* at paras 55–60.
64 *Ibid* at paras 93–94 and 111.
65 *Zundel*, above note 18.

to cause injury or mischief to a public interest. All members of the Court agreed that, although the law was aimed at deliberate lies, freedom of expression was involved. Even lies convey a meaning, and if that meaning was to be suppressed, the Court held that the law had to satisfy the section 1 reasonable-limits test. However, as in the *Keegstra* hate-speech case, the Court was sharply divided on the application of the minimal-impairment test. This time the majority ruled that the law could not be justified. While the "false news" law was being used to combat a modern problem, its objective was shrouded in the mists of time. Its origins could be traced to a thirteenth-century law designed to protect the reputations of the great men of the realm. In the view of the majority, it was impossible to say what objective Parliament had in mind in retaining this ancient provision in the modern *Criminal Code*. The law lacked a clear objective or purpose, and the majority held that the objective of a law cannot shift to meet the demands of the reasonable-limits test. Even if the law could be said to relate to the pressing and substantial concern of promoting racial harmony, the majority found that it could not satisfy the minimal-impairment test. Unlike the hate speech provisions of the *Criminal Code*, the "false news" provision was far too broad. Falsity was difficult to determine, and, combined with the virtually unlimited reach of the phrase "injury to a public interest," the provision created an offence that posed a serious threat to freedom of expression. Writing for the majority, McLachlin J made reference to the significant "chilling effect" this provision could have on protected speech:

> To permit the imprisonment of people, or even the threat of imprisonment, on the ground that they have made a statement which 12 of their co-citizens deem to be false and mischievous to some undefined public interest, is to stifle a whole range of speech, some of which has long been regarded as legitimate and even beneficial to our society. I do not assert that Parliament cannot criminalize the dissemination of racial slurs and hate propaganda. I do assert, however, that such provisions must be drafted with sufficient particularity to offer assurance that they cannot be abused so as to stifle a broad range of legitimate and valuable speech.[66]

Justice McLachlin was not persuaded by the argument that the authorities could be trusted to use the law only when appropriate:

> The whole purpose of enshrining rights in the *Charter* is to afford the individual protection against even the well-intentioned majority. To

---

66   *Ibid* at 743 (SCR).

justify an invasion of a constitutional right on the ground that public authorities can be trusted not to violate it unduly is to undermine the very premise upon which the *Charter* is predicated.[67]

Issues of hate speech can also arise with respect to the civil law of defamation, which will be examined in greater detail below. The Supreme Court has not rejected the idea that individuals may be defamed by statements made about a group of which they are a part and has even recognized that "the fact that a group has historically been stigmatized may mean that insults and offensive comments made about the group will stick more easily to its members. The vulnerability of the members of the group thus makes them targets more susceptible to personal defamation."[68] At the same time, however, the Court held that no injury to individual reputation had been established in a class action launched after a Montréal radio host had made "scornful and racist"[69] comments about taxi drivers in that city whose mother tongue was Arabic or Creole. The subjective hurt felt by the taxi drivers was not enough to establish that an ordinary person would have applied the offensive accusations to each driver personally, especially given the large size and heterogeneity of the taxi driver group. Justice Abella dissented and would have found injury given that the "highly stigmatizing" and "blatantly racist" comments were directed at Arab and Haitian taxi drivers.[70]

E. PORNOGRAPHY

Pornography poses a problem similar to that of hate speech. Pornography is a form of expression in that it does convey a meaning; however, pornography is degrading, dehumanizing, and inimical to other *Charter* values, especially the equality of women. Defining what constitutes pornography with sufficient precision to avoid threatening legitimate artistic or scientific treatment of eroticism and sexuality is notoriously difficult. Is it possible to criminalize that which is of no redeeming value without posing an unjustifiable risk to the freedom to explore the important human issues of sexuality and eroticism?

---

67 *Ibid* at 773.
68 *Bou Malhab v Diffusion Métromédia CMR Inc*, 2011 SCC 9, [2011] 1 SCR 214 at para 68.
69 *Ibid* at para 82.
70 *Ibid* at para 107.

The Supreme Court of Canada was confronted with these issues in *R v Butler*.[71] The *Criminal Code* makes it an offence to make, publish, or circulate "obscene" materials. An obscene publication has as its "dominant characteristic" "the undue exploitation of sex, or of sex and any one or more of . . . crime, horror, cruelty, and violence."[72] This definition is vague and prosecutions for the offence are susceptible to misuse. The offence was enacted in an era when the use of criminal prosecutions to enforce standards of sexual propriety and decency was readily accepted. Prosecutions against sexually explicit works of literary or artistic merit are certainly not unheard of. On the other hand, the reach of the provision has been to some degree restricted in recent years by judicial decisions that viewed the law as aimed at a different harm, namely, the legitimization or encouragement of sexual violence and victimization of women. These decisions interpreted the law as a means to protect the values of equality, specifically with respect to women, and emphasized the harm of sexual violence, degradation, and dehumanization.

In *Butler*, faced with a challenge to the law on the ground that it infringed freedom of expression, the Supreme Court built upon this interpretive framework for the obscenity offence. The judgment of Sopinka J first developed a test for determining whether representations of sex in any given case could be described as obscene. That test requires the courts to determine "what the community would tolerate others being exposed to on the basis of the degree of harm that may flow from such exposure."[73] Justice Sopinka then went on to describe three categories of pornography: first, explicit sex with violence, which would almost always be punishable; second, explicit sex without violence but that is degrading and dehumanizing, which would be punishable if the risk of harm is substantial; and, third, explicit sex without violence and that is not dehumanizing or degrading, which would not be punishable unless children are employed in its production.[74] In effect, the Court found that it was possible to interpret an offence originally intended to protect a certain view of sexual morality as having evolved to the point where it now protects against sexual violence and the denial of equality for women. The Court reinterpreted the obscenity offence so that it became an anti-pornography provision.

---

71   *Butler*, above note 16.
72   Section 163.
73   *Butler*, above note 16 at 485.
74   Two members of the Court, Gonthier and L'Heureux-Dubé JJ, disagreed and said that the depiction of explicit sex could be punished if displayed in certain public settings.

The Court was unanimous in finding that the offence, interpreted in this way, could withstand *Charter* scrutiny. As with hate speech, the Court had little hesitation in holding that, however reprehensible, pornography is a form of expression since it is intended to convey a meaning. This meant that the law had to be subjected to section 1 analysis. The Court held that the enforcement of decency and sexual propriety is not an objective sufficient to override a *Charter* right because such an objective would be inimical to individual freedom of choice. However, the Court was satisfied that, with the refined definition it accorded to the offence, the law was aimed at values essential to a free and democratic society, namely, the dignity and autonomy of women and the avoidance of degradation and dehumanization. In the Supreme Court's view, this did not conflict with the "false news" case,[75] where the Court had refused to accept that the purpose of the law could shift to meet a modern problem.

On the issue of proportionality, pornography, like hate speech, was found to lie outside the core values underlying freedom of expression, and hence, a more relaxed form of scrutiny was applied. Indeed, in *Butler*, the Supreme Court adopted an unusually relaxed standard when assessing the strength of the evidence linking pornography to the harm it was alleged to cause. The Court acknowledged that, in this area, the connection was difficult if not impossible to establish. Rather than hold that this gap in evidence was fatal to the section 1 analysis, Sopinka J stated: "[I]t is reasonable to presume that exposure to images bears a causal relationship to changes in attitude and beliefs."[76] Even with its modern and refined interpretation, the pornography offence is anything but precise. However, the Court frankly admitted that past attempts at a more precise definition had floundered. In this context, the Court was prepared to find that the minimal-impairment test could be satisfied by a law that fell well short of perfection.

The Supreme Court took a similar approach in a case involving a challenge to the *Criminal Code* provisions dealing with child pornography.[77] The law prohibited possession of materials showing a person under the age of eighteen engaged in explicit sexual activity. This definition, if applied casually, posed a serious threat to protected expression. However, rather than strike down the vaguely worded prohibition, the Court found it possible to save it through interpretation. By narrowly interpreting the prohibition, liberally interpreting the defences for mat-

---

75   *Zundel*, above note 18.
76   *Butler*, above note 16 at 502 (SCR).
77   *R v Sharpe*, [2001] 1 SCR 45, 194 DLR (4th) 1.

ters having artistic merit or an educational or scientific purpose, and by reading into the law certain exceptions for purely personal materials that did not involve children in their production, the Court held that its scope was narrowed to a limit on freedom of expression that could be justified under section 1.

In *Little Sisters Book and Art Emporium v Canada (Minister of Justice)*,[78] the Supreme Court once again adopted a deferential approach to Parliament's efforts to deal with the problem of pornography. The Court found that the *Butler* test applied equally to gay and lesbian materials. By seizing and refusing to allow into Canada gay and lesbian books and magazines that did not violate the *Butler* standard, customs officials had violated the freedom of expression of a Vancouver bookstore. However, the majority decision, written by Binnie J, refused to strike down the broad powers of customs officials to intercept obscene materials at the border. Justice Binnie held that although errors would be made in interpretation, Parliament was entitled to assume that the *Butler* definition would be applied properly by public officials. The dissenting opinion, written by Iacobucci J, would have struck down the provision on the ground that there was a long history of misapplication of the law and an absence of safeguards to ensure that *Charter* rights are respected. Justice Iacobucci's approach appears to have been prescient, as customs officials seized further books and magazines sent to the same bookstore shortly after the judgment. The bookstore again launched an action to contest the detention of these materials and sought to have its costs in the litigation funded in advance by the public. The advance costs issue came before the Supreme Court, and a majority refused the request.[79] Justice Binnie in dissent would have granted advance costs, finding the situation to be a "special case."[80]

The *Butler* harm test was further elaborated in *R v Labaye*,[81] a case dealing with an adult-only "swingers" club charged with the offence of keeping a common bawdy house "for the purpose of indecency." The majority held that the *Butler* harm test should be used to determine whether there was sufficient harm to warrant a criminal conviction. Two assessments need to be made. First, the nature of the harm must be

---

78   [2000] 2 SCR 1120. The Court also found that customs officials had violated s 15 of the *Charter* by discriminating on the basis of sexual orientation in targeting the imports of Little Sisters, a gay and lesbian bookstore. See Chapter 15 on equality rights for further discussion.

79   *Little Sisters Book and Art Emporium v Canada (Commissioner of Customs and Revenue)*, [2007] 1 SCR 38, discussed in Chapter 7.

80   *Ibid* at para 137.

81   [2005] 3 SCR 728 [*Labaye*].

one of three different kinds: (1) the loss of autonomy or liberty of those exposed to the material; (2) harm to society by predisposing others to anti-social conduct; and (3) harm to individuals participating in the production of the material. Second, the harm or risk of harm must be of such a degree that it is incompatible with the proper functioning of society. While *Labaye* did not involve freedom of expression, or any other provision of the *Charter*, it is likely that this more elaborate development of the *Butler* test will serve as the new constitutional standard for prohibiting expression deemed to be obscene.

F. JUDICIAL PROCEEDINGS

The Supreme Court has recognized that, in view of the important role played by the courts in our society, "the courts must be open to public scrutiny and to public criticism of their operation by the public . . . . The press must be free to comment upon court proceedings to ensure that courts are, in fact, seen by all to operate openly in the penetrating light of public scrutiny."[82] This principle led the Supreme Court to strike down legislation prohibiting publication of the details of matrimonial proceedings,[83] and it led the Ontario Court of Appeal to give a narrow definition to the offence of contempt of court for intemperate remarks critical of the judicial system.[84]

Yet another area in which freedom of expression collides with other *Charter* rights is the "free press versus fair trial" debate. The right of everyone charged with an offence to a fair trial on the basis of the evidence produced in court is reinforced by the *Charter*, section 11(d). The press is plainly entitled to provide the public with information about cases pending before the courts, but in some circumstances, pre-trial publicity may be thought to affect the right to a fair trial. Before the *Charter*, there is little doubt but that Canadian courts accorded priority to the right to a fair trial. Where pre-trial disclosure of evidence, the identity of the accused, or details of the offence might possibly prejudice potential jurors against the accused or otherwise impair the right of the accused to a fair trial, the courts did not hesitate to impose gag orders delaying publication of such details until after the trial. Such orders plainly limited freedom of expression and freedom of the press,

---

82   *Edmonton Journal v Alberta (AG)*, [1989] 2 SCR 1326 at 1337 and 1339, 64 DLR (4th) 577.

83   *Ibid.*

84   *Kopyto*, above note 2.

but since neither right was expressly guaranteed by the constitution, the courts were entitled to give priority to the statutory right to a fair trial. Some mandatory publication bans have been found to be consistent with the *Charter*. For example, the Court has held that a mandatory publication ban on evidence, representations, and reasons at a bail hearing whenever the accused requests such a ban is a reasonable limit on freedom of expression. The Court stressed not only the accused's right to a fair trial, but also that hearings on whether a discretionary ban could be justified would slow down bail hearings, which were designed to focus on whether the accused could be released. The Court noted that banned material would eventually be released after the criminal proceedings were finished.[85]

In *Dagenais v Canadian Broadcasting Corp*,[86] the Supreme Court was asked to review gag orders in light of the *Charter* and the entrenchment of the rights of freedom of expression and freedom of the press. The Court found that the pre-*Charter* rule inappropriately emphasized the right to a fair trial at the expense of freedom of expression. Under the *Charter*, both freedom of expression and the right to a fair trial enjoy constitutional protection, and "*Charter* principles require a balance to be achieved that fully respects the importance of both sets of rights."[87] This led the Court to conclude that a more stringent test should be applied to publication bans so that the balance between these conflicting rights might be achieved. A ban should be ordered only where it was shown to be necessary to prevent a real and substantial risk to fairness of the trial, and where reasonably available alternative measures, such as adjourning the trial, allowing challenges for cause during jury selection, giving strong instructions to the jury, or changing the venue, would not prevent the risk. To this, the Court added the requirement that it be shown that "the salutary effects of the publication ban outweigh the deleterious impact the ban has on free expression."[88]

The decision represents a significant change in the law with respect to gag orders. The case also provides further insight into the manner in which the Supreme Court responds to measures that limit freedom of expression in the name of protecting another *Charter* right or freedom. As in the cases dealing with hate speech and pornography, the Court has rejected the proposition that one right or freedom should be given priority over another. Rather, the Court has said that the appropriate approach is to reconcile the competing rights through

85 *Toronto Star Newspapers Ltd v Canada*, [2010] 1 SCR 721.
86 [1994] 3 SCR 835, 120 DLR (4th) 12 [*Dagenais*].
87 *Ibid* at 877 (SCR), Lamer CJC.
88 *Ibid* at 878.

the proportionality review of section 1, allowing measures intended to protect one right to limit another but only to the extent necessary and subject to the minimal-impairment test.

In *R v Mentuk*,[89] a publication ban was granted by the trial judge to protect the identity of undercover police officers and police operational methods. Here, the competing interests were the protection of freedom of expression on the one hand and the proper administration of justice on the other. The Supreme Court reformulated the *Dagenais* test in more general terms to accommodate the various competing interests that might arise:

> A publication ban should only be ordered when such an order is necessary to prevent a serious risk to the proper administration of justice, because reasonable alternative measures will not prevent the risk, and when the salutary effects of the publication ban outweigh the deleterious effects on the rights and interests of the parties and the public, including the effects on the right to free expression, the right of the accused to a fair and public trial, and the efficacy of the administration of justice.[90]

Justice Iacobucci stressed that because "the presumption that courts should be open and reporting of their proceedings should be uncensored is so strong and so highly valued in our society," a ban should be ordered only upon "a convincing evidentiary basis."[91]

The Supreme Court found that the public had a right to know about the use and possible abuse of police powers and that the Crown had failed to demonstrate that the ban on publishing details of the operational methods of the police was necessary to protect the proper investigation of crime. However, the Court also found that protecting the identity of undercover police officers for a specifically time-limited period was justified. This ban would protect the personal safety of individual police officers engaged in dangerous operations without impairing the right of the public to know how police powers are exercised.

---

89 [2001] 3 SCR 442 [*Mentuk*].

90 *Ibid* at para 32. See also *Sierra Club v Canada (Minister of Finance)*, [2002] 2 SCR 522, applying this test in a case involving a confidentiality order with respect to documents concerning financial aid for the construction of nuclear reactors in China. In that case, the Court upheld the confidentiality order, holding that the protection of commercial interests was sufficiently important to restrict the open court principle and that the restriction was justified given the narrow scope and the highly technical nature of the information covered by the confidentiality order. See also *Toronto Star Newspapers Ltd v Ontario*, [2005] 2 SCR 188, applying the same test to sealing orders for search warrants.

91 *Mentuk*, above note 89 at para 39.

Although press reporting of judicial proceedings is protected as freedom of expression, this freedom is not absolute either under section 1 of the *Charter* or the balancing of competing rights contemplated under *Dagenais*. In one case in 2011, the Court held that media interviews and filming in a courthouse, and audio broadcasting of judicial proceedings, were protected forms of expression, but that rules of court prohibiting such activities were a reasonable limit under section 1. The rules had been adopted to maintain the fair administration of justice and the serenity of proceedings, and their benefit in allowing vulnerable witnesses and parties not to be interviewed in the courtroom outweighed the harm to freedom of expression. Although audio broadcasting would make media reports more interesting and accurate, broadcasting could undermine the integrity of the judicial process.[92] In a companion case, the Court upheld a judicial order that the media be able to view but not broadcast a statement made by the accused. The Court held that the balance was justified on the particular facts of the case, which included that the accused had been acquitted of assisting a suicide and was vulnerable.[93] Both of these cases suggest that attempts to protect vulnerable people from media reporting of judicial proceedings will be an important and, at times, decisive factor justifying limits on freedom of expression. The Court also affirmed that the burden of justifying limits on freedom of expression under *Dagenais* is not higher than the burden of justifying a limit under section 1 of the *Charter*.[94]

The Supreme Court has reaffirmed the importance of the open court principle, even in the national security context. In *Ruby v Canada (Solicitor General)*,[95] it held that provisions of the *Privacy Act* requiring a reviewing court to hear all cases involving claims of foreign confidences or national security without either the public or the applicant being present constituted an unjustified violation of freedom of expression. The Court acknowledged that the mandatory closed court provisions were rationally connected to the pressing objectives of protecting foreign confidences and national security, but concluded that the statutory requirement that the entire proceedings be held *in camera* were disproportionate. In the result, the Court read down the offending provision so that the Court had the discretion to close proceedings only when and if the release of information would harm foreign confidences and national security.

---

92   *Canadian Broadcasting Corp v Canada (Attorney General)*, 2011 SCC 2, [2011] 1 SCR 19.

93   *Canadian Broadcasting Corp v The Queen*, 2011 SCC 3, [2011] 1 SCR 65.

94   *Canadian Broadcasting Corp v Canada (Attorney General)*, above note 92 at para 56.

95   [2002] 4 SCR 3.

A similar approach was taken in *Re Vancouver Sun*[96] when the Supreme Court held that a rebuttable presumption of an open court applied to the conduct of investigative hearings under the *Anti-Terrorism Act* to obtain information about terrorist activities. The Court overturned a judge's order that the entire investigative hearing would be held *in camera* without notice to the media or the accused in the ongoing Air India trial. The Court affirmed that the stringent tests for justifying restrictions on the open court principle articulated in *Dagenais* and *Mentuk* should be applied to all discretionary judicial decisions that limit freedom of expression. In other words, any publication ban should be ordered only when necessary to prevent a serious risk to the proper administration of justice because reasonably alternative measures would not prevent the risk, and only if the salutary effects of the publication ban outweighed its deleterious effects. Applying these principles of minimal impairment and proportionality, the Court found that, although the application for an investigative hearing and the identity of the person being compelled to reveal information should be kept secret, the existence of the hearing, its subject matter, and the *Charter* challenge to the novel procedure should be open. Two judges dissented on the basis that a presumption of a closed court was justified given the danger of publicity to ongoing terrorism investigations and to those being compelled to reveal information about terrorism.

In total, these cases suggest that the open court principle will be the starting point and that any proposed limitation on it will be subject to stringent standards of justification, including those of minimal impairment and proportionality.

The rulings of administrative tribunals can adversely affect freedom of expression. The courts will not apply a strict *Oakes* test in deciding whether such rulings are reasonable and should survive judicial review, but they will require administrative tribunals to consider the effects of a ruling on freedom of expression and to act reasonably. Applying this test, the Court has upheld a bar tribunal decision that reprimanded a lawyer for writing a letter to a judge to allege that the judge was "fundamentally unjust."[97]

---

96   [2004] 2 SCR 332.
97   *Doré v Barreau du Québec*, 2012 SCC 12, [2012] 1 SCR 395.

G. THE MEDIA: SOURCES AND ACCESS TO INFORMATION

In practical terms, freedom of expression will often depend on the media. A number of cases require the Court to reconcile the media's interests and freedom of expression with other competing values. In *R v National Post*,[98] the Court rejected the idea that freedom of expression required protection for all secret sources of the traditional media or a class privilege for secret sources. It did, however, suggest that a privilege might be established on a case-by-case basis if maintaining a confidential relationship between the press and its sources was more important than the competing interest. In the case, which involved a search warrant that might reveal the identity of a secret source but also might reveal forged documents, the Court determined that the media had "not established that the public interest in the protection of their secret source(s) outweighs the public interest in the production of the physical evidence of the alleged crimes."[99] At the same time, the Court indicated that any warrant should impose conditions such as sealing orders that protected freedom of expression though it rejected a dissenting judgment that the media should presumptively receive notice prior to a search. It is possible that media interests will be preferred in some cases where the state's competing interest is tenuous, but "the bottom line is that no journalist can give a source a total assurance of confidentiality. All such arrangements necessarily carry an element of risk that the source's identity will eventually be revealed."[100]

The media and others may want to argue that freedom of expression requires access to certain public documents. The Supreme Court has, however, been cautious in interpreting freedom of expression to require access to information possessed by the government. It has held that freedom of expression "does not guarantee access to all documents in government hands. Access to documents in government hands is constitutionally protected only where it is shown to be a necessary precondition of meaningful expression, does not encroach on protected privileges, and is compatible with the function of the institution

---

98 2010 SCC 16, [2010] 1 SCR 477. Secret source privilege is also not protected under the Quebec *Charter of Human Rights and Freedoms*, and a similar balancing test is applied. *Globe and Mail v Canada (Attorney General)*, 2010 SCC 41, [2010] 2 SCR 592.

99 *R v National Post*, above note 98 at para 91.

100 *Ibid* at para 69.

concerned."[101] The Court elaborated that, under *Irwin Toy*, to "show that access would further the purposes of s 2(*b*), the claimant must establish that access is necessary for the meaningful exercise of free expression on matters of public or political interest."[102] In this case, the Court concluded that meaningful public discussion of alleged police improprieties in the investigation of an alleged mobster's murder was still possible without access to a 300-page police investigation and legal advice provided by the Crown.[103] This view underlines how the *Irwin Toy* approach can place significant definitional limits on freedom of expression. Even if meaningful public discussion was not possible without access to the requested documents, the state could still claim the benefit of solicitor–client and law enforcement privileges. In addition, freedom of expression would not be engaged if the government could demonstrate that access was incompatible with the functioning of government. Examples given by the Court include access to Cabinet documents and access to pre-judgment memos and research by courts.[104] This approach demonstrates a willingness to impose internal limitations on freedom of expression that do not have to be justified under section 1. In the result, it appears as if legislatures could repeal or curtail statutory entitlements to access to information without violating the guarantees of freedom of expression under the *Charter*.

Access to information legislation also protects personal privacy. The statutory protection of privacy was found to violate freedom of expression in the context of a lawful strike. A union recorded images of individuals to discourage them from crossing a picket line. A privacy adjudicator found that the union had infringed the recorded individuals' privacy interest. That decision was set aside on judicial review as an unjustifiable infringement of the union's right to freedom of expression. The Supreme Court of Canada agreed.[105] Freedom of expression through picketing is fundamentally important. Forbidding the union from recording images of those who cross picket lines restricted the "union's ability to communicate and persuade the public of its cause, impairing its ability to use one of its most effective bargaining strategies in the course of a lawful strike."[106]

---

101 *Ontario (Public Safety and Security) v Criminal Lawyers' Association*, 2010 SCC 23, [2010] 1 SCR 815 at para 5.
102 *Ibid* at para 36.
103 *Ibid* at para 59.
104 *Ibid* at para 40.
105 *United Food and Commercial Workers*, above note 36.
106 *Ibid* at para 37.

H. PROTECTION OF REPUTATION

An individual's reputation enjoys the protection of law. Statements that defame and injure reputation may give rise to a civil right of action for libel or slander, permitting the targeted individual to claim damages for the injury to reputation. The law of libel is notoriously complex and difficult but essentially provides that, where the defendant publishes a statement injurious to the plaintiff's reputation, damages are recoverable. While certain defences are available, including the truth of the statement complained of, it is for the defendant to prove a defence, failing which damages are presumed. In recent years, Canadian juries have been willing to award substantial damages, both compensatory and punitive.

Here again, a laudable and important objective is said to require limiting the rights of freedom of expression and freedom of the press. Canadian law makes no distinction between private and public figures. The press must observe the same strict requirements when describing the activities of political and public figures as apply to ordinary citizens. The presumption of falsity means that any time the press makes a statement that might injure reputation, it must be able to prove the truth of what it has said according to the exacting standards of a court of law. Honest belief in the truth of the statement provides no defence, nor does absence of malice or negligence in the writing of the story. The press must, therefore, be more than cautious in what it says: it must be right. Journalists have to avoid publishing stories, even on matters of immediate public interest and concern, unless they are confident that the truth of statements capable of injuring reputation can be proved.

The Supreme Court of Canada and the courts of England,[107] the United States,[108] Australia[109] and New Zealand[110] have taken distinctive paths in modifying the common law of defamation to accord significantly more weight to freedom of expression.[111] The Supreme Court of Canada was initially reluctant to take this step. In *Hill v Church of Scientology of Toronto*,[112] it was asked to reconsider the common law of

---

107   *Reynolds v Times Newspapers*, [2001] 2 AC 127.

108   *New York Times Co v Sullivan*, 376 US 254 (1964).

109   *Theophanous v Herald and Weekly Times Ltd* (1994), 124 ALR 1 (HCA).

110   *Lange v Atkinson*, [2000] 3 NZLR 385.

111   For a review of these developments from a Canadian perspective, see *Cusson v Quan* (2007), 87 OR (3d) 241 (CA), which adopted the English "responsible journalism" defence. The appeal in the Supreme Court was granted on other grounds, and a new trial ordered: *Quan v Cusson*, [2009] 3 SCR 712.

112   [1995] 2 SCR 1130, 126 DLR (4th) 129.

defamation, particularly the presumptions of falsity and damage, in light of the *Charter* protection of freedom of expression. The plaintiff, a Crown attorney, sued after a lawyer for the Church of Scientology publicly announced that his client intended to take proceedings alleging the Crown attorney had breached an order of the court. These allegations proved to be without foundation, and the jury awarded over one million dollars in damages. As explained in Chapter 6, the *Charter* does not apply directly to the common law in such circumstances. While the Supreme Court did not resist the proposition that the common law must evolve and change in light of *Charter* values, the Court was unwilling to make any significant change in the law.[113] Writing for the Court, Cory J said that defamatory statements are only tenuously connected to the core values protected by freedom of expression, while the right to individual reputation, although not specifically protected by the *Charter*, represents and reflects the innate dignity of the individual, a value that underlies all *Charter* rights. Accordingly, the Court rejected the argument that the law of defamation was in need of significant reformulation and found the balance struck by the existing law in favour of the protection of reputation to be appropriate. Three years later, the Court adopted a similar approach in *R v Lucas*,[114] upholding the *Criminal Code* provisions dealing with defamatory libel. Although finding that the law infringed freedom of expression, the Court reiterated the importance attached to the protection of reputation and held that the law was justifiable under section 1.

The Supreme Court's approach to defamation has changed. The Court has held that defamation actions under Quebec's *Civil Code* strike the correct balance between freedom of expression and protection of reputation. In *Gilles E Néron Communication Marketing Inc v Chambre des notaires du Québec*, the Court stressed the need for proof of fault in terms of actions that violate the standards of a reasonable journalist.[115] In *WIC Radio Ltd v Simpson*,[116] the Court focused on fair comment. The plaintiff was an outspoken opponent of the introduction to schools of materials dealing with homosexuality. When a radio talk-show host criticized the views of the plaintiff on air with comments indicating

---

113 The Court did extend the defence of "qualified privilege" to reports of pleadings and other court documents yet to be filed.
114 *Lucas*, above note 18.
115 *Gilles E Néron Communication Marketing Inc v Chambre des notaires du Québec*, [2004] 3 SCR 3. Justice Binnie dissented on the basis that the award of $673,153 in damages for truthful statements made in the public interest but out of their proper context was a violation of freedom of expression.
116 Above note 4.

that the plaintiff condoned violence against gay people, the plaintiff sued for defamation. The host argued that he was protected by the defence of "fair comment" as he had expressed an opinion based on fact on a matter of public interest. Previous cases had held that the defence was available only where the defendant honestly believed the opinion he had expressed, and the talk-show host did not so swear. The majority held that the *Charter* value of freedom of expression required a change in the common law and that the fair comment defence would be made out if *any person* — not simply a fair-minded person — could honestly express the opinion on the basis of the proved facts. As the Court noted, newspaper editors, who can be liable for comments expressed in their publications, may often not themselves agree with the comments expressed in their publications and if not afforded the more generous defence, public debate on important public issues could be stifled. The *WIC* decision recognizes that "an individual's reputation is not to be treated as regrettable but unavoidable road kill on the highway of public controversy" but also holds that "an overly solicitous regard for personal reputation" should not "be permitted to 'chill' freewheeling debate on matters of public interest."[117]

A year after the *WIC* decision, the Court took a more significant step to rebalance the common law's preference for protection of reputation over freedom of expression by creating a new defence: responsible communication on matters of a public interest. In *Grant v Torstar Corp*,[118] the Court held that the common law of defamation had to be reformulated to better respect freedom of expression. The common law imposed a form of strict liability that made the media liable for statements that could not be proven to be true even though democratic discourse and the seeking of truth could be advanced by the publication of such statements. The Court rejected an American-style defence that would require a publisher of false statements only to establish the absence of malice or subjective fault as not giving enough weight to reputation; however, it also rejected the current law that required the defendant to establish a defence of truth as not giving enough weight to freedom of expression. Instead, the Court created a new defence whereby publishers of defamatory material are allowed to demonstrate that they acted reasonably, responsibly, and proportionately in trying to verify information of public interest before publishing it. The Court

---

117 *Ibid* at para 2.

118 [2009] 3 SCR 640 [*Grant*]. See also *Quan v Cusson*, above note 111 (ordering of a new trial that would give the defendant an opportunity to establish the new defence of responsible communication on matters of public interest).

also defined public interest widely to include more than comments about public figures and about government and politics.[119]

I. LOCATION OF THE EXPRESSION

Individuals who wish to express themselves often seek to do so in a well-travelled public place. For those who lack the resources to place their message in newspapers or broadcast media, expressing oneself in a public place may be essential if the message is to find an audience. An audience may be found at public places such as roads, squares, parks, and airports. Yet each of these places has a public purpose. How should the individual's right to freedom of expression be reconciled with the rights of others to use these places for their intended purpose? Does the state have the right to control access to such places for the purposes of disseminating a message?

In *Committee for the Commonwealth of Canada v Canada*,[120] the Supreme Court of Canada considered this issue in relation to the claim of a group that sought to distribute pamphlets at a major Canadian airport. The Court rejected the contention that the government could preclude the pamphleteers from distributing their materials at the airport. As Lamer CJC noted, government property is held for the benefit of the community at large and ownership does not, by itself, justify refusal of access for expressive purposes. By the same token, however, the right of the individual asserting freedom of expression must be assessed with reference to the public purpose of the place in question. Six of the seven judges sitting on the case found it necessary to write reasons, and hence it is not possible to identify a single rationale for the decision. In the end, however, all the judges agreed that the exercise of the right to freedom of expression did, in the circumstances, include the right to express oneself at the airport.

While the members of the Court found that the pamphleteers' freedom of expression extended to their activities in the airport, they generally accepted that not all types of public property would attract section 2(b) protection. Two different tests were suggested by the Court to determine whether the freedom of expression was protected in a particular public space. The first was based on an analysis of the primary function of the space, and whether that function was compatible with free expression. The second was based on whether protecting

---

119 *Grant*, above note 118 at para 106.
120 [1991] 1 SCR 139, 77 DLR (4th) 385 [*Commonwealth of Canada*].

expression in the space would serve the underlying values of the freedom. Given the split in the Court in this case, neither of these tests was definitively adopted.

A subsequent case[121] dealt with posters and came to a similar conclusion. A musician advertised performances of his band by placing posters on hydro poles. Charged under a municipal bylaw prohibiting the placing of posters on public property, he challenged the bylaw as an infringement of freedom of expression. Justice Iacobucci was conscious of the importance of posters as a form of expression for those with limited resources: "[P]osters have communicated political, cultural and social information for centuries."[122] All members of the Court agreed that the bylaw's complete ban on posters constituted an undue restriction of freedom of expression. The Court found it unnecessary to determine which of the two tests suggested in *Commonwealth of Canada* was preferable.

This issue was addressed again in *Montréal (City) v 2952-1366 Québec Inc.*[123] The respondent operated a strip club in Montréal and set up a loudspeaker in the entranceway to broadcast music and commentary to the street, in order to attract customers. The respondent was charged under a municipal bylaw for emitting sound produced by sound equipment that could be heard outside. The respondent challenged the bylaw, claiming that it was an unjustifiable infringement of his freedom of expression. The Court held that on either of the tests proposed in *Commonwealth of Canada*, the public street was a place in which freedom of expression was protected.

While observing that it was unnecessary to do so, the majority went on to articulate a more definitive test for determining whether section 2(b) protection extends to a particular public space. The Court held that the question to be asked is "whether the place is a public place where one would expect constitutional protection for free expression on the basis that expression in that place does not conflict with the purposes which s 2(*b*) is intended to serve."[124] Two factors were highlighted to be considered in answering this question. First, the historical or actual function of the public place in question, and whether its function or the activities taking place within it are compatible with free expression. Second, whether other aspects of the space indicate that allowing free expression within it would serve to undermine the values underlying the freedom of expression. After determining that the street

121 *Peterborough (City) v Ramsden*, [1993] 2 SCR 1084, 106 DLR (4th) 233.
122 *Ibid* at 245 (DLR).
123 Above note 15.
124 *Ibid* at para 74.

outside the club was amenable to free expression, the majority went on to find that the bylaw was justified under section 1 as a reasonable measure to prevent noise pollution.

In *Greater Vancouver Transportation Authority v Canadian Federation of Students — British Columbia Component*,[125] the Supreme Court held that a public transit authority that sold advertising space on the sides of buses could not refuse to accept political advertisements. The transit authority was held to be an arm of government that afforded access to advertising on its buses but imposed a content-based restriction by refusing messages that had political content. The majority judgment, written by Deschamps J, held the claimants were not advancing a claim that the government was required to provide them with a platform for their expression but rather that they were entitled to use "an existing platform . . . without undue state interference with the content of their expression."[126] Applying the *City of Montréal* test, the Court found that there was both a history and an actual use of the sides of buses as a space for public expression and that as "the space allows for expression by a broad range of speakers to a large public audience" and that allowing expression "could actually further the values underlying section 2(b)," the side of a bus "was a location where expressive activity is protected by section 2(b) of the *Charter*."[127] Refusing political messages could not be justified as a reasonable limit under section 1. Although the Court accepted the sufficiency of the objective of providing a safe, welcoming public transit system and that refusing political messages had a rational connection to that objective, it held that the blanket refusal to accept political advertisements failed the minimal-impairment test and was not proportionate to the claimants' right to express their message.

J. CONCLUSION

The Supreme Court has identified freedom of expression as an important *Charter* guarantee that lies at the heart of a free and democratic society. Nevertheless it has also refused to accord this important freedom anything approaching absolute protection. The Court has given expression an exceptionally wide definition, leaving to the section 1 analysis most of the difficult issues of reconciling this important freedom with other values. Only violence and threats of violence, including

---

125 2009 SCC 31.

126 *Ibid* at para 35.

127 *Ibid* at para 46.

laws against terrorism, seem to be precluded from the breadth of the Court's definition of freedom of expression.

In most cases, freedom of expression cases will be decided under section 1 of the *Charter*, and the results have been mixed. Despite the importance it has attached to freedom of expression, the Court has demonstrated considerable tolerance for laws that limit freedom of expression in the name of protecting minority interests. Laws prohibiting hate speech, pornography, and third party spending during elections have been upheld under relatively relaxed section 1 scrutiny on the ground that significant countervailing equality values are at stake. Although protection of reputation has traditionally prevailed over freedom of expression in the law of defamation, recent cases have consciously sought to liberalize the law of defamation to better accommodate freedom of expression while also valuing reputation. Defamation law is largely a judicial creation and the Court has been reluctant to recognize group defamation for racist speech in comparison to its acceptance of criminal offences enacted by Parliament as a reasonable limit on freedom of expression. The law relating to the reporting of judicial proceedings has been significantly modified under the *Charter* in favour of the media, but the Court has more recently upheld the prohibition of media interviews in courtrooms as well as mandatory publication bans at bail hearings. With respect to commercial speech, an area some observers predicted would not be affected by the *Charter*, the Court has insisted upon a relatively high level of proof that legal restraints are required to achieve state objectives.

It is thought by those who place special value on freedom of expression that this pattern of decisions is inconsistent.[128] While the Supreme Court has never denied the importance of freedom of expression, it has certainly been prepared to see this freedom limited in the name of protecting other important interests. Other observers applaud the judicial refusal to place freedom of expression on a special pedestal and welcome the Court's willingness to grant Parliament and the legislatures a degree of latitude in the protection of equality values.[129] These critics contend that, if anything, the Court has been too solicitous of expression in the area of commercial speech. In the end, as this range of opinion suggests, the Court has proceeded very much on a

---

128 See, for example, A Borovoy, *When Freedoms Collide: The Case for Our Civil Liberties* (Toronto: Lester & Orpen Dennys, 1988) c 2.

129 See, for example, K Mahoney, "The Canadian Constitutional Approach to Freedom of Expression in Hate Propaganda and Pornography" (1992) 55 Law & Contemp Probs 77.

case-by-case basis, avoiding definitive pronouncements on other than the basic structure for analysis of a freedom of expression claim.

FURTHER READINGS

BOROVOY, AA, *When Freedoms Collide: The Case for Our Civil Liberties* (Toronto: Lester & Orpen Dennys, 1988) c 2

CAMERON, J, "A Reflection on Section 2(b)'s Quixotic Journey, 1982–2012" (2012) 58 Sup Ct L Rev (2d) 163

DAWOOD, Y, "Democracy and the Freedom of Speech: Rethinking the Conflict between Liberty and Equality" (2013) 26 Can JL & Jur 293

DYZENHAUS, D, "Regulating Free Speech" (1991) 23 Ottawa L Rev 289

FLOOD, C, "Freedom of Commercial Free Expression: The Most Undervalued *Charter* Right" (2006) 21 NJCL 271

FREIMAN, M, "Hate Speech and the Reasonable Supreme Court of Canada" (2013) 63 Sup Ct L Rev (2d) 295

HUTCHINSON, AC, "Money Talk: Against Constitutionalising (Commercial) Speech" (1990) 17 Can Bus LJ 2

LEE, I, "Can Economics Justify Freedom of Expression?" (2008) 21 Can JL & Jur 355

LEPOFSKY, MD, "The Supreme Court's Approach to Freedom of Expression: *Irwin Toy v Quebec (Attorney General)* and the Illusion of Section 2(b) Liberalism" (1993) 3 NJCL 37

MAHONEY, K, "The Canadian Constitutional Approach to Freedom of Expression in Hate Propaganda and Pornography" (1992) 55 Law & Contemp Probs 77

MOON, R, "The Supreme Court of Canada on the Structure of Freedom of Expression Adjudication" (1995) 45 UTLJ 419

———, *The Constitutional Protection of Freedom of Expression* (Toronto: University of Toronto Press, 2000)

OLIPHANT, B, "Freedom of the Press as a Discrete Constitutional Guarantee" (2013) 59 McGill LJ 283

REID, C, "Freedom of Expression, Commercial Expression and Tobacco in Canada" (2008) 39 VUWLR 343

ROACH, K, & D SCHNEIDERMAN, "Freedom of Expression in Canada" in E Mendes & S Beaulac, eds, *The* Canadian Charter of Rights and Freedoms, 5th ed (Markham, ON: LexisNexis Butterworths, 2013)

SCHNEIDERMAN, D, ed, *Freedom of Expression and the* Charter (Toronto: Carswell, 1991)

SHARPE, RJ, "Commercial Expression and the *Charter*" (1987) 37 UTLJ 229

WEINRIB, L, "Hate Promotion in a Free and Democratic Society: *R v Keegstra*" (1991) 36 McGill LJ 1416

CHAPTER 10

FREEDOM OF ASSOCIATION

Freedom of association, guaranteed by section 2(d) of the *Charter of Rights and Freedoms*, protects the right of individuals to come together to form a wide array of organizations and relationships, including those with political, religious, and social purposes. The difficult threshold issue for the courts has been whether the guarantee not only recognizes the right of individuals to come together in an organization but also confers constitutional protection on the activities essential to ensure the association's meaningful existence.

Nowhere has the issue of the scope of the guarantee of freedom of association been more hotly debated than with respect to the institutions and practices of collective bargaining. Most of the caselaw on section 2(d) deals with labour relations, especially in the public sector. If section 2(d) protects only the right to come together and form an association, its importance is relatively modest. On the other hand, to the extent that it also protects the essential activities of the group, it has enormous impact, particularly in the realm of labour relations. Another important issue for the collective bargaining regime is whether freedom of association includes the right to refuse to be associated with a group or its views and policies. Does section 2(d) include the right to join the trade union of one's choice, or to refuse to join a union or pay it dues?

A. THE RIGHT TO ENGAGE IN COLLECTIVE BARGAINING

The Supreme Court's interpretation of freedom of association and the right to engage in collective bargaining has significantly changed over the life of the *Charter*. The current jurisprudence can be best understood from an historical perspective.

The Supreme Court of Canada first dealt with the claim that section 2(d) protects the right to engage in collective bargaining in 1987 in a trilogy of cases dealing with legislation limiting the right to strike. In the leading case, *Reference Re Public Service Employee Relations Act*,[1] a majority of the Court held that the guarantee of freedom of association did not encompass the right to bargain collectively or the right to strike. The legislation at issue removed the right to strike from public sector workers and, in the absence of agreement, prescribed mandatory arbitration to determine the contents of the collective agreement. Justice LeDain held that the rights to bargain collectively and to strike are not fundamental rights or freedoms. Rather, they are the creatures of legislation that balances a number of competing interests. Clearly, LeDain J felt that the area of labour relations was one requiring specialized expertise. He was influenced by the fact that this area of law had largely been removed from the courts and assigned to the supervision of labour relations tribunals. Justice LeDain limited the protection of section 2(d) to "the freedom to work for the establishment of an association, to belong to an association, to maintain it, and to participate in its lawful activity without penalty or reprisal."[2]

The dissenting judges, Dickson CJC and Wilson J, concluded that the guarantee of freedom of association did include the rights for workers to bargain collectively and to strike. In their view, section 2(d) protected not only the right to join together but also the right of members of the association to pursue together aims that could be lawfully pursued individually. Although there is no individual equivalent to the right to strike, the dissenting judges thought that this activity should be included in section 2(d), given its importance to the protection of the interests of working people. As we shall see, there has been an ongoing debate between these two fundamentally different visions of

---

1   *Reference Re Public Service Employee Relations Act (Alberta)*, [1987] 1 SCR 313, 38 DLR (4th) 161 [*Alberta Reference*]. Justice McIntyre, writing alone and in much greater detail, concluded that s 2(d) did not include a right to strike, although he did not specify whether it included a right to bargain collectively.
2   *Ibid* at 391 (SCR).

section 2(d). The dissenting view in 1987 prevailed and was accepted by a majority of the Court in 2015.[3] In the two companion 1987 cases, a majority of the Court held that limitations on the right to strike and bargain did not violate the right guaranteed by section 2(d). In one case, Saskatchewan legislation banning a strike in the dairy industry was upheld,[4] while the other upheld the federal government's price-and-wage control program, which banned strikes and altered the financial compensation scheme.[5]

Following these decisions, there was still some doubt whether section 2(d) of the *Charter* might include a right to bargain collectively, even if it did not include a right to strike. However, in the *PIPS* case, the majority of the Supreme Court rejected the argument that the right to bargain collectively was included in section 2(d).[6] Writing for the majority, Sopinka J turned to the reasons of McIntyre J in the earlier *Alberta Reference* and summarized his view of the meaning of section 2(d):

> . . . first, that s 2(d) protects the freedom to establish, belong to and maintain an association; second, that s 2(d) does not protect an activity solely on the ground that the activity is a foundational or essential purpose of an association; third, that s 2(d) protects the exercise in association of the constitutional rights and freedoms of individuals; and fourth, that s 2(d) protects the exercise in association of the lawful rights of individuals.[7]

Justice Sopinka concluded that collective bargaining is not protected by section 2(d): "Restrictions on the *activity* of collective bargaining do not normally affect the ability of individuals to form or join unions."[8]

However, in a 2001 decision, *Dunmore v Ontario (Attorney General)*,[9] the Supreme Court began to move away from the exclusion of collective bargaining rights from the protection of section 2(d) and to breathe

---

3   See *Mounted Police Association of Ontario v Canada (Attorney General)*, 2015 SCC 1 [*Mounted Police Association*], and *Saskatchewan Federation of Labour v Saskatchewan*, 2015 SCC 4[*Saskatchewan Federation of Labour*], discussed below.

4   *RWDSU, Locals 544, 496, 635, 955 v Saskatchewan*, [1987] 1 SCR 460, 38 DLR (4th) 277. In this case, Dickson CJC reached the same conclusion as the majority, while Wilson J was alone in dissent.

5   *PSAC v Canada (AG)*, [1987] 1 SCR 424, 38 DLR (4th) 249. Again Dickson CJC and Wilson J dissented.

6   *Professional Institute of the Public Service of Canada v Northwest Territories (Commissioner)*, [1990] 2 SCR 367, 72 DLR (4th) 1 [*PIPS*].

7   *Ibid* at 402 (SCR). See also *Canadian Egg Marketing Agency v Richardson*, [1998] 3 SCR 157, 160 DLR (4th) 1 at 58.

8   *PIPS*, above note 6 at 404 (SCR).

9   [2001] 3 SCR 1016, 207 DLR (4th) 193 [*Dunmore*].

significant life into the reach of freedom of association. For years, agricultural workers had been excluded from Ontario's statutory regime governing collective bargaining. The law was amended by a pro-labour government to afford them certain rights, but then quickly repealed by a newly elected government with a different policy on collective bargaining. Agricultural workers challenged the repealing statute, arguing that they could not hope to form an association to protect their interests without the protective umbrella of labour relations legislation because of their highly vulnerable position. The Supreme Court of Canada agreed and ordered the Ontario government to afford agricultural workers the needed statutory protections.

Writing for the majority, Bastarache J concluded that "the freedom to collectively embody the interests of individual workers"[10] fell squarely within the protection of section 2(d) and that agricultural workers could not enjoy that freedom without protective legislation. Justice Bastarache held that the four-part formulation of the rights protected by section 2(d) adopted in the *Alberta Reference* and *PIPS* should be supplemented:

> [T]here will be occasions where a given activity does not fall within the third and fourth rules but where the state has nevertheless prohibited that activity solely because of its associational nature. These occasions will involve activities which 1) are not protected under any other constitutional freedom, and 2) cannot, for one reason or another, be understood as the lawful activities of individuals.[11]

Particularly noteworthy was Bastarache J's recognition of the collective element in freedom of association, a feature of section 2(d) previously rejected by majority opinions. Reverting to Dickson CJC's dissent in the *Alberta Reference*,[12] Bastarache J wrote that individuals form associations "not simply because there is strength in numbers, but because communities can embody objectives that individuals cannot."[13]

Also notable in *Dunmore* was the remedy ordered by the Supreme Court. Ordinarily, freedom of association is a "negative freedom," one that precludes state interference rather than requires affirmative state assistance. However, *Dunmore* holds that where a group lacks the means to form an association to protect its interests, and the effect of exclusion from a protective statutory regime, designed to facilitate freedom of association "substantially orchestrates, encourages or sustains

---

10   *Ibid* at 224 (DLR).
11   *Ibid* at 213.
12   *Alberta Reference*, above note 1.
13   *Dunmore*, above note 9 at 213 (DLR).

the violation of fundamental freedoms,"[14] the state may be required to act. Consequently, in this and other labour *Charter* cases, the Court employed a suspended declaration of invalidity to give the Ontario legislature an opportunity to enact new legislation which, as will be discussed below, it did do.

Dunmore represented a significant shift by the Supreme Court of Canada. The judgment demonstrated a sensitivity to and concern for the rights of workers and for the importance of collective action. To require a legislature to act affirmatively to enhance the enjoyment of section 2(d) rights is novel.

Dunmore recognized that section 2(d) protects the freedom of workers to organize, but stopped short of constitutionalizing the right to strike or even the right to engage in collective bargaining. However, in *Health Services and Support — Facilities Subsector Bargaining Assn v British Columbia*,[15] the Supreme Court of Canada held that section 2(d) protects the "capacity of members of labour unions to engage, in association, in collective bargaining on fundamental workplace issues."[16] British Columbia had passed legislation giving health-care employers more flexibility to transfer and reassign employees, to contract out certain services, and to lay off employees. The legislation specified that any provision in an existing collective agreement that was inconsistent with these new employer powers was invalid to the extent of the inconsistency. Unions representing the affected employees challenged the legislation, arguing that it violated their rights under section 2(d) because it invalidated portions of their existing collective agreements and rendered any future collective bargaining on the affected topics largely meaningless. The Court accepted the unions' arguments and declared certain provisions of the legislation to be unconstitutional.

In the majority judgment, McLachlin CJC and LeBel J noted that the protection of inherently collective activities recognized in *Dunmore* required a re-examination of both the *Alberta Reference* and *PIPS*. After reviewing the arguments relied on in those cases, McLachlin CJC and LeBel J concluded that "the holdings in the *Alberta Reference* and *PIPS* excluding collective bargaining from the scope of s 2(d) can no longer stand."[17] The Court was careful to note that the right to bargain collectively does not entail a right to any substantive outcome, but is instead

---

14   *Ibid* at 221.
15   [2007] 2 SCR 391 [*Health Services*].
16   *Ibid* at para 19.
17   *Ibid* at para 36.

a right to a "general process of collective bargaining, not to a particular model of labour relations, nor to a specific bargaining method."[18]

As the Court characterized the right to bargain collectively as a right to bargain on "fundamental workplace issues," not every interference with collective bargaining will constitute an infringement of section 2(d). It is only when collective bargaining on matters that are "important to the ability of union members to pursue shared goals in concert"[19] are interfered with that section 2(d) will be violated. Moreover, the Court indicated that it may be possible to alter fundamental workplace issues by legislation or conduct without violating section 2(d), provided that the changes were effected following a process of good faith negotiation.[20]

As *Health Services* dealt with direct government interference with collective bargaining, the case did not necessarily indicate that governments will be obligated to statutorily protect the ability of otherwise vulnerable unions to bargain collectively. However, *Dunmore* has made clear that section 2(d) can impose positive obligations on governments to statutorily protect vulnerable workers. The Supreme Court returned to that issue and to the plight of Ontario's agricultural workers in *Ontario (Attorney General) v Fraser*.[21] Ontario's response to *Dunmore*, the *Agricultural Employees Protection Act, 2002* (AEPA), maintained the exclusion of farm workers from the *Labour Relations Act*, but created a special separate regime that granted farm workers the right to form and join an employees' association and to participate in its activities and make representations to employers on terms and conditions of employment. Employers were bound to listen to and consider those representations. The scheme was challenged by the farm workers on the ground that it failed to extend the full protection of the labour relations regime. The Court of Appeal for Ontario[22] agreed and held that the AEPA did not impose on employers an obligation to bargain in good faith, nor did it provide for the usual dispute resolution mechanisms or for exclusive bargaining rights. The court upheld the agricultural workers' challenge and held that *Health Services* and *Dunmore* required Ontario to enact legislation that provides "sufficient protections to enable agricultural workers to engage in a meaningful process of collective bargaining."[23]

---

18   *Ibid* at para 91.
19   *Ibid* at para 96.
20   *Ibid* at para 109.
21   [2011] 2 SCR 3 [*Fraser*].
22   *Fraser v Ontario (Attorney General)* (2008), 92 OR (3d) 481 (CA).
23   *Ibid* at para 101.

A sharply divided Supreme Court allowed an appeal from that decision and upheld the AEPA in a decision suggesting something of a retreat from the direction taken in *Health Services*. Chief Justice McLachlin and LeBel J, writing for the five-judge majority, held "that bargaining activities protected by s 2(d) in the labour relations context include good faith bargaining on important workplace issues" and that this "is not limited to a mere right to make representations to one's employer, but requires the employer to engage in a process of consideration and discussion to have them considered by the employer."[24] Although the AEPA did not specifically require good faith bargaining, the majority interpreted it to do so. The majority held that the right to a "meaningful process" can be infringed by a ban on employee associations or by setting up "a system that makes it impossible to have meaningful negotiations on workplace matters," but section 2(d) "does not impose a particular process, . . . does not require the parties to conclude an agreement or accept any particular terms and does not guarantee a legislated dispute resolution mechanism in the case of an impasse." The protection of section 2(d) is limited to "the right . . . to a general process of collective bargaining, not to a particular model of labour relations, nor to a specific bargaining method."[25]

Justices Charron and Rothstein, concurring in the result, would have overruled *Health Services* to the extent that it constitutionalized collective bargaining and the right to engage in good faith bargaining on the ground that it departed from the earlier precedents and was unworkable. Justice Deschamps, also concurring in the result, held that *Heath Services* did not go as far as was claimed by the majority and did not accept that it imposed a constitutional obligation to bargain in good faith. Justice Abella, dissenting, would have struck down the AEPA on the ground that it fell short of the minimum level of protection for collective bargaining rights that she considered to be mandated by *Heath Services*.

Despite the apparent retreat in *Fraser*, in a trilogy of cases in 2015 the Court took a significant step to invigorate section 2(d)'s protection of collective bargaining. At issue in *Mounted Police Association of Ontario v Canada (Attorney General)*[26] was a regulation excluding members of the RCMP from forming a union or engaging in collective bargaining. Instead, RCMP members were subject to a non-unionized labour relations scheme that provided for consultation but gave management the

---

24 Above note 21 at para 40.
25 *Ibid* at para 41.
26 *Mounted Police Association*, above note 3.

right to impose conditions of employment. A section 2(d) challenge to similar scheme had been rejected in 1999.[27] The Court overruled that decision and repudiated the 1987 trilogy's narrow view of section 2(d). Freedom of association, said the majority judgment, written by McLachlin CJC and LeBel J, must be interpreted in a purposive and generous fashion consistent with the interpretation of other *Charter* rights. The majority essentially adopted Dickson CJC's dissenting reasons in the 1987 trilogy. Freedom of association "empowers groups whose members' individual voices may be all too easily drowned out"[28] and "helps them work to right imbalances in society."[29] Section 2(d) protects a meaningful process of collective bargaining. The majority rejected the view expressed in earlier cases, including *Fraser*, that collective bargaining is a derivative right and held that collective bargaining must be seen as a necessary precondition of section 2(d)'s guarantee of freedom of association. A "legislative scheme that strips employees of adequate protections in their interactions with management so as to substantially interfere with their ability to meaningfully engage in collective negotiations" will fail to satisfy the demands of section 2(d).[30] While the right guarantees a process rather than an outcome or specific model of collective bargaining, the majority explained the key elements of employee choice and independence that must be protected as follows: "[A] meaningful process of collective bargaining is a process that gives employees meaningful input into the selection of their collective goals, and a degree of independence from management sufficient to allow members to control the activities of the association . . . ."[31] The regulation governing RCMP labour relations failed to meet this test. It imposed a scheme that did not permit members to form their own association and that was dominated by management.

The majority found that the infringement of section 2(d) could not be justified under section 1 as a reasonable limit. While the objective of maintaining an independent police force was sufficiently pressing and substantial, excluding RCMP members from engaging in protected collective bargaining was not rationally connected to achieving that objective. Nor could the scheme satisfy the minimal impairment test as the RCMP was the only police force in Canada excluded from collective bargaining.

---

27 *Delisle v Canada (Deputy Attorney General)*, [1999] 2 SCR 989.
28 *Mounted Police Association*, above note 3 at para 55.
29 *Ibid* at para 58.
30 *Ibid* at para 80.
31 *Ibid* at para 99.

In a strongly worded dissenting judgment, Rothstein J chided the majority for departing from its past decisions, including *Fraser*. In his view, the essential feature required for compliance with section 2(d) is representativeness. Provided employees are able to make their collective demands to the employer and to have those demands considered in good faith, section 2(d) is satisfied. In his view, the majority had essentially entrenched an adversarial *Wagner Act* model of labour relations developed in the United States in the 1930s and unduly curtailed Parliament's capacity to deal with a complex issue of social and economic policy.

In a companion case,[32] the Court rejected the contention that federal wage restraint legislation — enacted in response to the 2008 global financial crisis — that rolled back wage increases for RCMP members violated section 2(d). The wage restraints were time-limited and imposed on all public servants and did not preclude consultation on other compensation issues, past or future.

The expansive view of section 2(d) was taken a step further in *Saskatchewan Federation of Labour v Saskatchewan*.[33] The majority judgment, written by Abella J, held that section 2(d) protects not only the right to engage in collective bargaining, but also the right to strike. At issue was provincial legislation banning public employees who perform essential services from engaging in strike action. Justice Abella wrote that the right to strike "is an indispensable part"[34] of collective bargaining that calls for the constitutional protection of section 2(d).

Justice Abella traced the evolution of labour relations legislation from criminalization of strike activity in the nineteenth century, to the legitimation in modern labour relations legislation as represented by the widespread adoption of the *Wagner Act* model. The right to strike is recognized in the *International Covenant on Economic, Social and Cultural Rights* and "there is an emerging international consensus that, if it is to be meaningful, collective bargaining requires a right to strike."[35] Drawing upon Dickson CJC's dissent in the 1987 trilogy, Abella J wrote that the right to strike may be seen as essential to the recognition of the *Charter* values of dignity, equality, and autonomy of vulnerable workers, allowing them, "through collective action, to refuse to work under imposed terms and conditions."[36]

---

32   *Meredith v Canada (Attorney General)*, 2015 SCC 2.
33   *Saskatchewan Federation of Labour*, above note 3.
34   *Ibid* at para 3.
35   *Ibid* at para 71.
36   *Ibid* at para 54.

The test for determining whether there is a violation of section 2(d) is "whether the legislative interference with the right to strike in a particular case amounts to a substantial interference with collective bargaining."[37] As the Saskatchewan legislation precluded essential employees from engaging in any work stoppage, that test was met.

Turning the question of whether the limitation on the right to strike could be justified under section 1, Abella J recognized that maintaining essential services is a pressing and substantial objective, and that banning strikes was rationally connected to that objective. However, the government failed to show that the means chosen were minimally impairing of the right. The legislation gave the public employer unilateral authority to determine whether and how to maintain essential services and provided no meaningful review or dispute resolution mechanism to resolve bargaining impasses.[38]

In their dissenting reasons, Rothstein and Wagner JJ repeated the caution of earlier cases that striking the right balance between employers and unions is a delicate and essentially political matter best left to legislation. The right to strike is a product of legislation and it was wrong, in their view, to depart from the 1987 trilogy and *Fraser*, and "to intrude into the policy development role of elected legislators by constitutionalizing the right to strike."[39]

Mounted Police Association and *Saskatchewan Federation of Labour* mark a significant development in *Charter* jurisprudence. The issue of whether to accord constitutional protection to collective bargaining and the right to strike has sharply divided the Supreme Court since the early years of the *Charter*. The trajectory of the Court's decisions has been uneven and unsteady. Given the complexity of labour relations, there is bound to be more to come.

B. THE RIGHT NOT TO ASSOCIATE

To this point, the focus has been on the freedom to associate, but sometimes an individual may not want to associate with another. This claim arose in *Lavigne*, where a community college teacher who was not a union member objected to a collective agreement provision forcing him to pay dues to the union. The compelled payment of dues, known as the "Rand formula" (or the agency shop), differs from compelled mem-

---

37 *Ibid* at para 78.
38 *Ibid* at para 81.
39 *Ibid* at para 105.

bership in the union (or a closed shop provision). Even though Lavigne was not compelled to join the union, he disagreed with a number of purposes for which his union dues were being spent, including opposing cruise missile testing and supporting certain causes, such as access to abortion.

The collective agreement was subject to *Charter* scrutiny because the employer, the college's Council of Regents, was closely controlled by government and hence could be considered a Crown agent.[40] Four of seven judges held that the mandatory dues provision did not violate section 2(d), while three members of the Court held that section 2(d) was violated but that the legislation could be saved under section 1.

Justice Wilson and two others concluded that section 2(d) did not include a right not to associate (sometimes called a "negative right"). In her view, however, this did not leave an individual unprotected from the harms that might come from forced association. The section 2(b) guarantee of freedom of expression would be available to an individual who was compelled to be associated with views he or she did not hold.[41] Justice McLachlin concluded that some instances of compelled association might violate section 2(d), but not the requirement to pay union dues. In her view, section 2(d) protected only against "coerced ideological conformity." She did not think that Lavigne's payment of dues associated him with the union's causes.[42]

Justice La Forest, with whom two other judges concurred, found that section 2(d) included a right not to associate, which had been breached in this case. In his view, it is contrary to the *Charter* either to prevent individuals from joining together or to compel them to do so in some circumstances. While certain forced associations are a reality of modern society, La Forest J found that there was a *Charter* violation, since Lavigne was required to contribute to causes beyond the immediate concerns of the bargaining unit. Compelling him to contribute funds to the union for bargaining purposes, including collective agreement administration, served to protect the common good and was consistent with section 2(d), but forced contribution to non-union purposes was not.[43] However, La Forest J concluded that the compelled payment of dues was justified under section 1. He rejected the idea that individual objectors could be given an opportunity to opt out of paying for matters that were not purely "collective bargaining." Permitting

---

40   This point is discussed in greater detail in Chapter 6.

41   *Lavigne v Ontario Public Service Employees Union*, [1991] 2 SCR 211, 81 DLR (4th) 545 at 582–85 [*Lavigne*].

42   *Ibid* at 645 (DLR).

43   *Ibid* at 635.

such opting out would seriously undermine the union's financial security and invite paternalistic scrutiny of union activities by government.

The Supreme Court was again badly split on the question of the right not to associate in *Advance Cutting and Coring v Quebec*.[44] The case involved a challenge to Quebec legislation governing the construction industry that required workers to be members of certain specified unions. This requirement went well beyond the "Rand formula," at issue in *Lavigne*, where workers are required to contribute to the union but free to refuse to become members. Those supporting the law contended that it was necessary to avoid "free riders" who would reap the benefits of union activities, but weaken the union by withholding dues and membership. Four judges held that the law did not infringe freedom of association; four held that it did. The fifth and deciding voice was that of Iacobucci J who held that the law did infringe freedom of association, but that it could be saved by section 1. Justice L'Heureux-Dubé held that freedom of association does not include a negative right. Justice LeBel (with whom Gonthier and Arbour JJ agreed) found that there was a negative element to section 2(d) but that it was not a mirror image of the positive aspect and that it contained certain inner limits necessary to protect the association's "group voice."[45] In the absence of evidence that forced membership in the union would amount to ideological conformity, LeBel J held that forced union membership did not violate section 2(d). Justice Bastarache, in dissent (with McLachlin CJC, Major and Binnie JJ), found that ideological conformity was the inevitable result of forced union membership. The "Rand formula," approved in *Lavigne*, solved the free-rider problem while avoiding coerced association.

C. CONCLUSION

The Supreme Court was initially reluctant to intervene in important aspects of the area of labour relations under the *Charter*. Freedom of association was held not to include the right to strike or the right to engage in collective bargaining, and the Court refused to interfere with mandatory dues and union membership. The Court did not grant unions new protection against legislative action curtailing bargaining and strikes, but neither did it give new tools to those opposed to the majoritarian nature of collective bargaining and intent on overturning agency and closed shop provisions. This cautious approach was de-

---

44   [2001] 3 SCR 209, 205 DLR (4th) 385.
45   *Ibid* at 482 (DLR).

cried by those who had hoped that the *Charter* would expand the scope of collective bargaining.[46] Others saw it as a middle-of-the-road posture, consistent with the Court's tendency in other areas to refuse to recognize economic activity as worthy of *Charter* protection.[47] In the end, however, the narrow interpretation of section 2(d) was found to be inconsistent with the Court's generally liberal approach to *Charter* interpretation and with the concern shown in other areas for the rights and interests of vulnerable groups. The more generous interpretation of section 2(d) in *Dunmore, Health Services, Mounted Police Association,* and *Saskatchewan Federation of Labour* open a new chapter in which collective bargaining rights are accorded significant *Charter* protection.

FURTHER READINGS

ADAMS, R, "Prospects for Labour's Right to Bargain Collectively after *BC Health Services*" (2009) 59 UNBLJ 85

BAKAN, J, *Just Words: Constitutional Rights and Social Wrongs* (Toronto: University of Toronto Press, 1997) c 5

BARRETT, S, "*Dunmore v Ontario (Attorney General)*: Freedom of Association at the Crossroads" (2003) 10 CLEIJ 83

———, & B OLIPHANT, "The Trilogy Strikes Back: Reconsidering Constitutional Protection for the Freedom to Strike" (2013–14) 45 Ottawa L Rev 201

BASU, R, "Revolution and Aftermath: *BC Health Services* and Its Implications" (2008) 42 Sup Ct L Rev (2d) 165

BEATTY, DM, *Putting the* Charter *to Work: Designing a Constitutional Labour Code* (Montréal: McGill-Queen's University Press, 1987)

———, "Labouring outside the *Charter*" (1991) 29 Osgoode Hall LJ 839

CAMERON, J, "Due Process, Collective Bargaining, and s 2(d) of the *Charter*: A Comment on *BC Health Services*" (2006–2007) 13 CLELJ 323

———, "The Labour Trilogy's Last Rites: *BC Health* and a Constitutional Right to Strike" (2009–2010) 15 CLELJ 297

---

46 See, for example, D.M. Beatty, "Labouring outside the *Charter*" (1991) 29 Osgoode Hall LJ 839.

47 See Chapters 3, 4, and 13 for further discussion of this point.

FARADAY, F, J FUDGE, & E TUCKER, eds, *Constitutional Labour Rights in Canada: Farm Workers and the Fraser Case* (Toronto: Irwin Law, 2012)

FUDGE, J, "Labour Is Not a Commodity: The Supreme Court and Freedom of Association" (2004) 67 Sask L Rev 425

———, "Freedom of Association" (2013) 61 Sup Ct L Rev (2d) 527

HUGHES, P, "*Dunmore v Ontario (Attorney General)*: Waiting for the Other Shoe" (2003) 10 CLEIJ 27

LANGILLE, B, "The Freedom of Association Mess: How We Got into It and How We Can Get out of It" (2009) 54 McGill LJ 177

———, "Why Are Canadian Judges Drafting Labour Codes — and Constitutionalizing the *Wagner Act* Model?" (2009–2010), 15 CLELJ 101

———, "The Condescending Constitution (Or, The Purpose of Freedom of Association is Freedom of Association)" (Paper delivered at the Ontario Bar Association, Continuing Professional Development 14th Annual *Charter* conference, Toronto, 2 October 2015)

POTHIER, D, "Twenty Years of Labour Law and the *Charter*" (2002) 40 Osgoode Hall LJ 369

SWINTON, KE, "The *Charter of Rights* and Public Sector Labour Relations" in G Swimmer & M Thompson, eds, *Public Sector Collective Bargaining in Canada: Beginning of the End or End of the Beginning?* (Kingston, ON: IRC Press, 1995)

WEILER, P, "The *Charter* at Work: Reflections on the Constitutionalizing of Labour and Employment Law" (1990) 40 UTLJ 117

CHAPTER 11

DEMOCRATIC RIGHTS

A central argument favouring the entrenchment of rights in a constitution is that checks on the political process are needed to protect certain fundamental values. There is often disagreement about the specific rights that should be entrenched or the degree to which legislatures should be restricted by the constitution and subject to judicial review. Yet one area in which there is widespread consensus on the need for some judicial oversight is that of political activity. Participation in fair elections and vigorous public debate are the cornerstones of democracy.

The *Charter of Rights and Freedoms* contains three guarantees designed to ensure the healthy functioning of Canadian parliamentary democracy. Section 3 provides that every citizen has the right to vote in elections for the House of Commons or a provincial legislature and to be qualified for membership in those houses. Section 4 sets a maximum duration of five years for the life of the House of Commons or a provincial legislature, although that period can be extended in time of war or similar national crisis by a two-thirds vote of the members. Finally, section 5 guarantees a sitting of Parliament and the legislatures at least once in every year. The importance — and the primacy — of these sections is shown by the fact that they cannot be overridden by the exercise of the notwithstanding clause in section 33. The Supreme Court of Canada has indicated that such a status for the democratic rights places them "at the heart of our constitutional democracy."[1]

---

1   *Thomson Newspapers Co v Canada (Attorney General)*, [1998] 1 SCR 877, 159
    DLR (4th) 385. In that case, the Court chose to decide the constitutionality of

Section 4 of the *Charter* is designed to ensure that Canadians have a regular opportunity to elect federal and provincial representatives, while section 5 is designed to ensure that those elected representatives have a regular opportunity to examine and vote upon the actions of the executive branch of government. Sections 4 and 5 are long-standing parts of the Canadian constitution, which derive from our British tradition of parliamentary democracy. Indeed, section 50 of the *Constitution Act, 1867*, also states that the life of the House of Commons is five years, unless an election is called earlier.

Not surprisingly, since sections 4 and 5 of the *Charter* reflect constitutional conventions that have been widely accepted for a long time, they have not generated any litigation. However, section 3, the right to vote, is a much richer and more controversial provision that has given rise to a number of disputes. These include the legitimacy of residency and other qualifications on the right to vote, the drawing of electoral boundaries, and restrictions on third party spending during election campaigns. Section 3 has also often been raised in conjunction with the guarantees of freedom of expression and association, discussed in the two previous chapters, as well as equality rights, which are discussed in Chapter 15 below.

A. VOTER QUALIFICATIONS

Read literally, the right to vote requires that every citizen have the opportunity to cast a ballot in every election. However, election laws have contained a number of qualifications, most commonly restricting the right to vote to those over a certain age, denying the vote to prison inmates and those in psychiatric institutions, to judges, and to citizens not resident in Canada. Historically, the vote was denied to women, Asians, Indians, and others. In addition, many laws require citizens to have been resident within a territory for a specified period, often several months, before they are eligible to vote.

Section 3 of the *Charter* provides a right for citizens to vote in federal and provincial elections only. Lower courts have interpreted section 3

---

the restriction on the publication of polls seventy-two hours before an election under s 2(b) of the *Charter*, which was subject to the override, as opposed to s 3 of the *Charter*, which was immune from the override. Section 2(b) is often the basis for challenges to direct or indirect restrictions on voting or electoral participation. These cases are discussed in Chapter 9.

not to apply to the vote at the municipal or school board level.[2] The Supreme Court has also decided that the right to vote in section 3 of the *Charter* does not apply to referenda. During the 1992 referendum on constitutional amendments known as the Charlottetown Accord, the Court was asked to determine the validity of a residency requirement. Simultaneous referenda were held in all provinces and territories. In Quebec, the referendum was held under provincial legislation, which required six months' residence in the province. In all other parts of Canada, the referenda took place under federal legislation. Graham Haig, having recently moved to Quebec from Ontario, was disqualified under the Quebec legislation because he did not meet the provincial residency requirement. He could not qualify under federal legislation, which required residence in a polling division in the federal referendum area. Haig challenged the failure to include him under the federal election legislation, but his claim was dismissed on the ground that section 3 applied only to federal and provincial elections and did not guarantee the right to vote in a referendum.[3]

Generally, residency requirements have been found to be reasonable limits on voting rights justifiable under section 1 of the *Charter*, in light of the widespread use of territorial representation in the Canadian system of government. As most representatives are elected in a geographically determined riding or constituency, a residency requirement ensures that only individuals with substantial ties to a locality have a right to select its representative. A period of residency also contributes to the voter's knowledge of the issues affecting that community. As well, residency requirements protect the integrity of the election process by preventing individuals from coming into the riding temporarily to disrupt voting patterns.[4] Section 3 has also been invoked in election recount cases. The Court has taken a "substantive approach"

2   The Ontario courts have held that s 3 did not give a right to vote in municipal elections or to run for municipal office in *Jones v Ontario (AG)* (1988), 53 DLR (4th) 273 (Ont HCJ); *Rheaume v Ontario (AG)* (1992), 7 OR (3d) 22 (CA); and *Nunziata v Toronto (City)* (2000), 189 DLR (4th) 627 (Ont CA). Courts have also held that s 3 does not apply to school board elections in *Baker v Burin School Board District #7* (1999), 178 DLR (4th) 155 (Nfld SC); but that s 3 does apply to elections of the legislative assembly of the territories in *Friends of Democracy v Northwest Territories (Attorney General)* (1999), 171 DLR (4th) 551 (NWTSC), leave to appeal to CA refused (1999), 176 DLR (4th) 661 [*Friends of Democracy*].
3   *Haig v Canada (Chief Electoral Officer)*, [1993] 2 SCR 995, 105 DLR (4th) 577 at 602. Justice Iacobucci, with Lamer CJC concurring, dissented on the ground that the denial of the opportunity to vote violated the guarantee of freedom of expression in s 2(b) of the *Charter*.
4   *Reference Re Yukon Election Residency Requirement* (1986), 27 DLR (4th) 146 (YTCA).

to determining whether a new election should be ordered as a result of voting irregularity on the basis that such an approach best reflects the purpose of the right to vote.[5]

Some voter qualifications are linked to the concept of competency. For example, the requirement that a voter be eighteen years of age rests on the assumption that a certain age is a standard for measuring maturity and responsibility. Formerly, judges were disqualified from voting in order to preserve the appearance of judicial neutrality and independence from the political process. A successful *Charter* challenge to this disqualification[6] was followed by a 1993 change to the federal *Elections Act* to allow judges to vote.[7] Until the early 1990s, those who were restrained of the liberty of movement or the management of their property by reason of mental disease were deprived of the federal vote. A successful *Charter* challenge to this disqualification[8] was followed by legislative removal of this restriction in 1993. The 1993 amendments also allowed citizens absent from Canada for less than five years to vote in elections, after a successful *Charter* challenge to provincial restrictions on the ability of citizens who were temporarily absent from the country to vote.[9]

The most litigated voter qualification provision has been the denial of the franchise to prisoners in penal institutions. The traditional reason for denying inmates the vote was to register society's disapproval of those who had broken its laws and thereby were thought to have disqualified themselves from participating in one of the important elements of citizenship. In effect, the denial of the right to vote was a further penalty for the crime. It has also been argued, in some cases, that inmates must be denied the right to vote to preserve prison security. Finally, it has been suggested that, since prison inmates are detached from the community, they cannot participate meaningfully in the public debate necessary to inform themselves as educated voters.

In two 1992 decisions, appellate courts accepted the argument that a prisoner's section 3 right to vote was infringed and this was not a reasonable limit under section 1.[10] In *Belczowski*,[11] Hugessen JA observed that there were some crimes, such as treason, in which the denial of the right to vote was logically linked to the nature of the crime. However,

5   *Opitz v Wrzesnewskyj*, 2012 SCC 55.
6   *Muldoon v Canada*, [1988] 3 FC 628 (TD).
7   *Canada Elections Act*, SC 1993, c 19.
8   *Canadian Disability Rights Council v Canada*, [1988] 3 FC 622 (TD).
9   *Hoogbruin v British Columbia (Attorney General)* (1985), 24 DLR (4th) 718 (BCCA).
10 *Sauvé v Canada (AG)* (1992), 89 DLR (4th) 644 (Ont CA); *Belczowski v Canada* (1992), 90 DLR (4th) 330 (FCA) [*Belczowski*].
11 *Belczowksi, ibid.*

the then existing provision barred an inmate from voting regardless of the nature of the crime committed. Moreover, he held, there was no necessary connection between imprisonment and lack of familiarity with political issues — indeed, many in society would be unfamiliar with important issues, yet they are still allowed to vote. Both decisions were upheld, with very brief reasons, by the Supreme Court of Canada in 1993.[12] The Court held that the blanket prohibition on inmate voting in section 51(e) of the *Canada Elections Act* did not meet the proportionality test under section 1, particularly the minimal-impairment component of the test.

Subsequently, the *Canada Elections Act* was amended in 1993 to limit the prohibition on voting to those sentenced to a term of more than two years. The differentiation between those with less than two-year sentences and those with longer sentences denied the vote only to those who had been convicted of the most serious offences. On the other hand, those who advocate prisoners' right to vote argued that, since no effort was made to tailor the prohibition to the type of offence, the prohibition remained too broad to survive, even in its amended form. The new restriction was challenged under section 3 of the *Charter* in litigation by Richard Sauvé, the same inmate who successfully challenged the earlier voting restriction in the Supreme Court. Sauvé, who was serving a sentence for murder, was still prohibited from voting under the amended Act. The Supreme Court, by a 5:4 majority, struck down the revised law. The government conceded that the *Canada Elections Act* violated the section 3 rights of prisoners, but argued that it was justified under section 1 because it furthered two collective aims of society: to enhance civic responsibility and respect for the rule of law; and to provide additional punishment or enhance the general purposes of criminal sanction. The Court, however, firmly rejected the government's attempts at justification and was highly critical of the "broad, symbolic" or "rhetorical" objectives advanced by the government. Writing for the majority, McLachlin CJC wrote, "The right to vote is fundamental to our democracy and the rule of law and cannot be lightly set aside. Limits on it require not deference, but careful examination."[13] The government's attempt at justification failed each stage of the section 1 analysis. Justice Gonthier, writing for the minority, would have accepted that the government had advanced a "reasonable social or political philosophy"

---

12 *Sauvé v Canada (AG)*, [1993] 2 SCR 438. In *Reynolds v British Columbia (AG)* (1984), 11 DLR (4th) 380, a prohibition on voting by those on probation was found to be unconstitutional by the British Columbia Court of Appeal.

13 *Sauvé v Canada (Chief Electoral Officer)* (1999), 180 DLR (4th) 385 (Fed CA), rev'd [2002] 3 SCR 519 at para 9, McLachlin CJC.

justifying the suspension of voting rights for felons to deliver "a message to both the community and the offenders themselves that serious criminal activity will not be tolerated by the community."[14] Those imprisoned for two years or more had broken the "social contract" requiring them to abide by the rule of law; therefore, it was appropriate to temporarily disenfranchise them, just as it was acceptable to temporarily incarcerate them.

Section 3 of the *Charter* not only gives every citizen the right to vote in federal and provincial elections, but also to be qualified for membership in provincial legislatures and Parliament. The Supreme Court has held that a provincial law that disqualifies a person from sitting as a member of a provincial legislature for five years after a conviction for an elections offence was a reasonable limit on the section 3 right. The limited disqualification applying to specific offences was considered to be a proportionate means to pursue the important objective of protecting the integrity of the electoral system.[15]

B. REGULATING THE ELECTORAL PROCESS

Cases such as *Sauvé v Canada (Chief Electoral Officer)*, discussed in the previous section, involve direct restrictions on the right to vote. The infringement of section 3 in that case was obvious, and the debate between the majority and the minority of the Supreme Court focused on the justification of the infringement under section 1 of the *Charter*. In a democracy, however, the effectiveness of each vote cast depends in large measure on the electoral system created and regulated by the government. The drawing of electoral boundaries, limitations on third party advertising, and restrictions on the availability of funding and other privileges to political parties are all issues that have led to cases that have asked the courts to scrutinize the constitutionality of the electoral process. Because the effect of such regulation on the right to vote or to run for office is indirect, and therefore much harder to gauge than in voter qualification cases, the Supreme Court has been forced to flesh out in greater detail the content of the section 3 right. In three key cases in this area, the Court has defined the section 3 right broadly, finding violations when an individual's right to "effective participation" or the right to play a "meaningful role" in the electoral process has been infringed. At the same time, however, it has endorsed the "egalitarian"

---

14   *Ibid* at para 119 (SCR), Gonthier J.
15   *Harvey v New Brunswick (Attorney General)*, [1996] 2 SCR 876, 137 DLR (4th) 142.

model of elections that permits regulation aimed at ensuring that each individual has an equal opportunity to participate in the electoral process. Unlike the so-called libertarian model, the egalitarian model allows for measures such as spending limits to prevent the wealthy from monopolizing political debate.

1) Electoral Boundaries

The Canadian electoral system is based on territorial representation at both the federal and the provincial levels. Individuals vote for a member to represent their constituency in the provincial legislature or the House of Commons. The government is selected on the basis of having the support of a majority of elected members in the House. The Canadian system is also a first-past-the-post system, with the individual who receives the greatest number of votes winning the seat, even if he or she did not garner a majority of the votes.

Other countries have quite different electoral systems. Some use proportional representation of parties based on the percentage of votes received, with members of the legislature selected from party lists. Members are not necessarily attached to a particular constituency. Other systems also use proportional representation but still provide for the election of members in a particular constituency.

The rationale for proportional representation is to ensure, to the extent possible, that every vote is reflected by the members elected. On the other hand, the rationale for electing members from a geographic constituency is to facilitate legislative representation of interests of the particular geographic riding, while also ensuring that an elected member is available to play a problem-solving role for the citizens he or she represents.

In the Canadian system and others based on territorial representation, difficult issues arise when drawing electoral boundaries for constituencies. Should the goal be an equal number of voters in each constituency? Should there be departures from that goal in order to serve other interests — for example, to recognize the distinctive interests of communities, or to facilitate travel and contact between voters and their representative? Traditionally, rural voters were thought to have different concerns than urban voters, and electoral boundaries were drawn accordingly. With the increasing ethnic diversity in Canadian society, it might be argued that electoral lines should be drawn so as to maximize the opportunity for an ethnic or religious group to vote for a member of its community, rather than dispersing the votes among other ethnic and religious communities where they would have less voting power should the group choose to vote as a block. One might argue that it is justifiable that rural or northern constituencies have smaller numbers of voters than urban ones because of the difficulties of campaigning and maintaining contact in less-populated areas.

Inevitably, the drawing of electoral-boundary lines raises the spectre of "gerrymandering," a term that connotes the exercise of distasteful self-interest on the part of those in control of the process. Not surprisingly, political incumbents have an interest in drawing boundaries in ways that can help them and undermine support for their opponents. Where the process of constituency line drawing is left to politicians, rather than independent electoral-boundary commissions, there may be good reason for the courts to scrutinize the fairness of the outcome. But no matter the process, one cannot avoid difficult and debatable decisions about the size and design of constituencies. The courts have a delicate role in deciding when the electoral system improperly undermines the right to vote, guaranteed under section 3 of the *Charter.*

The most significant decision to date is that of the Supreme Court of Canada in the *Reference Re Provincial Electoral Boundaries (Saskatchewan).*[16] Saskatchewan had established an independent electoral-boundaries commission but had also set a strict quota of urban and rural seats and required that the boundaries of urban ridings coincide with the existing boundaries of municipalities. Aside from two sparsely populated northern ridings, the ridings under consideration were within plus or minus 25 percent of the "provincial quotient," the figure determined by dividing the provincial voting population by the number of ridings.

While the Supreme Court of Canada split 6:3 in upholding the boundaries, all the judges agreed on the general principles underlying the right to vote espoused by the majority judgment of McLachlin J. In reasons supported by four others, she described the meaning of the right to vote as "not equality of voting power *per se*, but the right to 'effective representation.'"[17] The conditions of "effective representation" included not only relative parity of voting power (so that the weight of an individual's vote would not be unduly diluted) but also factors important to "fair" representation of Canada's diversity. In her words,

> Factors like geography, community history, community interests and minority representation may need to be taken into account to ensure

---

16   [1991] 2 SCR 158, 81 DLR (4th) 16 [*Saskatchewan Boundaries*].
17   *Ibid* at 183 (SCR).

that our legislative assemblies effectively represent the diversity of our social mosaic.[18]

Justice McLachlin expressly rejected the American model of "one person, one vote," arguing that it is neither consistent with Canadian history nor a practical alternative in the search for effective representation in a country like Canada:

> Respect for individual dignity and social equality mandate that citizens' votes not be unduly debased or diluted. But the need to recognize cultural and group identity and to enhance the participation of individuals in the electoral process and society requires that other concerns also be accommodated.[19]

Applying these principles, McLachlin J concluded that both the process and the outcome of the Saskatchewan scheme were fair and consistent with section 3 of the *Charter*. In particular, she noted that the division of seats between rural and urban areas approximated the actual population division in the two areas. Moreover, she accepted the argument that rural ridings are more difficult to serve, both because of transportation and communication problems and because rural voters are said to make more demands on their representatives. Finally, discrepancies between ridings were justified on traditional bases such as geography, community interests, and projected population changes.

While accepting these general principles, Cory J, with two other judges, dissented. He found that the underlying process in drawing boundaries in Saskatchewan was contrary to section 3 because the strict rural/urban division interfered with the rights of urban voters and that this was not justifiable under section 1. He was influenced by the fact that Saskatchewan had, in the past, used electoral boundaries that were closer to equal population standards than the impugned boundaries.[20]

---

18   *Ibid* at 184.
19   *Ibid* at 188.
20   Cases in Alberta, Prince Edward Island, and the Northwest Territories have applied the Saskatchewan principles, with the Alberta decision upholding an electoral map that favoured rural over urban ridings (*Reference Re Electoral Boundaries Commission Act (Alberta)* (1991), 120 AR 70 (CA); and the Prince Edward Island and Northwest Territories decisions finding an unjustified violation of s 3 of the *Charter*: *MacKinnon v Prince Edward Island* (1993), 101 DLR (4th) 362 (PEITD); *Friends of Democracy*, above note 2. A subsequent *Charter* challenge to new electoral boundaries in Prince Edward Island was rejected on the basis that variations in voter populations of plus or minus 20 percent and the mixing of some rural and urban districts did not violate the right to effective representation. *Charlottetown (City) v Prince Edward Island* (1998), 168 DLR (4th) 79 (PEICA), leave to appeal to SCC refused (1999), 179 DLR (4th) vi (SCC).

The Saskatchewan case is interesting from several perspectives. We see a distinctive Canadian approach that takes into account concerns about the effectiveness of representation as well as sensitivity to the interests of groups and that can be contrasted with the American courts' insistence on the more individualistic principle of "one person, one vote." The result marks the reluctance of the Supreme Court to give the judiciary a central role in electoral map drawing. By accepting the legislation's allowance for as much as a 25-percent deviation from the provincial quotient for constituency size, the Court gave a great deal of scope for electoral-boundary commissions or legislatures in drawing boundaries. This decision also accords with the Court's approach to equality rights, in which it often defers to legislative attempts to assist the disadvantaged and does not insist on the same treatment for each person. This reading of equality rights is premised on the idea that departures from equal population standards are meant to assist northern (including Aboriginal) and rural residents as disadvantaged groups. Some, however, argue that robust departures from equal population standards under-represent urban populations and with that, visible minorities.[21] As can be seen, the concept of effective representation can be contested. What is clear, however, is that, consistent with the Court's approach to equality rights as opposed to freedom of expression, the *Saskatchewan Boundaries* case is based on the acceptance of significant definitional limits on the right to vote. One consequence of this approach is that the government does not have to justify all departures from equal population standards under section 1 of the *Charter.*

At the federal level, variation in the size of electoral districts is indirectly mandated by the constitution itself. Section 51A of the *Constitution Act, 1867* guarantees that no province will have fewer members in the House of Commons than in the Senate. This section ensures that Prince Edward Island, a province with a population of about 140,000, will always have four members in the House of Commons. Many of the urban ridings in provinces with rising populations, such as Ontario and British Columbia, are substantially larger than those in the island province.[22] Since the House of Commons is unlikely to grow substantially for both political and practical reasons, the result of the "Senate floor" rule is almost certain to create a significant imbalance in con-

---

21 M Pal & S Choudhry, "Is Every Ballot Equal? Visible Minority Vote Dilution in Canada" (2007) 13 Institute for Research on Public Policies Choices.

22 This is discussed further in KE Swinton, "Federalism, Representation and Rights" in J Courtney, P MacKinnon, & D Smith, eds, *Drawing Boundaries: Legislatures, Courts, and Electoral Values* (Saskatoon: Fifth House, 1992) at 17 [*Drawing Boundaries*].

stituency size. To the extent that this imbalance is required by other parts of the constitution, it will likely be immune from *Charter* review because of the Court's prior refusal in the context of denominational school rights found in the *Constitution Act, 1982*, to allow *Charter* challenges to other parts of the constitution.[23]

It has been asked by some whether there is a requirement of "affirmative gerrymandering" to ensure that electoral boundaries are drawn to ensure maximum voting power to racial and ethnic groups.[24] Some argue that "effective representation" for groups traditionally under-represented in Canadian legislatures requires positive action to promote the election of representatives from these communities. This effort could be facilitated within the existing system of geographic representation, if all that is required is to draw lines in a manner alert to ethnic or cultural difference. Even then, courts have held that agreements with Aboriginal peoples and Aboriginal rights do not justify large deviations from equal population standards.[25] Even an equality rights-based approach to electoral districting that tolerates or even requires generous departures from equal population standards to assist disadvantaged groups will not work if a group is not concentrated territorially. For example, to ensure greater representation of women, one would have to argue that section 3 of the *Charter* required a different kind of electoral system — either two-person constituencies with male and female members, or a shift to a proportional representation system in which political parties may have a greater incentive to achieve diversity in the lists of people who will be elected depending on the percentage of the popular vote received by the particular party.

Does the Supreme Court's decision in *Saskatchewan Boundaries* indicate that such challenges would be successful? The Court was clearly sympathetic to a system sensitive to the diversity of interests in Canadian politics that allows for deviation from the principle of "one person, one vote" or "treat all the same." Yet the Court did not go so far as to adopt a "mirror" concept of representation that requires individuals to be represented on the basis of sex or ethnicity. Nor did the Court signal any willingness to alter the "procedural representation" that is at the basis of the Canadian system. That system allows individuals, grouped geographically, to decide, from time to time, whether they see their interests aligning with others on the basis of sex, ethnicity, class,

---

23 *Reference Re Bill 30, An Act to Amend the Education Act (Ontario)*, [1987] 1 SCR 1148; *Adler v Ontario*, [1996] 3 SCR 609, discussed above, Chapter 8, Section D(2).

24 K Roach, "Chartering the Electoral Map into the Future" in *Drawing Boundaries*, above note 22 at 211–14.

25 *Friends of Democracy*, above note 2.

religion, or a combination of these and other characteristics. Although minorities might be better represented in other electoral systems that rely on various forms of proportionate representation and party lists, there is little indication that the courts would invalidate the existing first-past-the-post riding system on *Charter* grounds.

2) Party Benefits

Political parties play a key role in Canada's electoral system. More than ten years after the Supreme Court wrestled with the issue of redistricting in *Saskatchewan Boundaries*, it examined the relationship between section 3 of the *Charter* and the role of political parties in *Figueroa v Canada*.[26] The *Canada Elections Act* provides political parties with a number of significant benefits, including the right to issue tax receipts for donations and the right of candidates to have their party affiliation listed on ballots.

In *Figueroa*, the leader of the Communist Party of Canada challenged a restriction that withheld such benefits to parties who failed to nominate fifty candidates for an election. The government's main justification for the fifty-candidate threshold was that it favoured national parties capable of fielding enough candidates to form a majority in Parliament. Under such a system, a voter has a greater chance of having her vote determine which party forms the government. Parties that do not field enough candidates to form a government do not advance the objective of "effective representation" that the Court had found was embodied by section 3.

The Supreme Court rejected the government's argument and declared the government's fifty-candidate threshold unconstitutional. Writing the majority decision, Iacobucci J expanded on the meaning of "effective representation." He repeated McLachlin J's conclusion (in *Saskatchewan Boundaries*) that effective representation gave each citizen the right to an effective representative in Parliament or a provincial legislative assembly. He added, however, that section 3 also guarantees each citizen the right to play a "meaningful role" in the electoral process. The rights under section 3 are therefore participatory in nature, and the right to participate in an election has an "intrinsic value," regardless of the impact on the actual outcome of the elections. Therefore, the right to vote is infringed if a voter's range of options is limited by making it more difficult for small parties to field candidates and to

---

26   *Figueroa v Canada (Attorney General)*, [2003] 1 SCR 912, rev'g (2000), 50 OR (3d) 728 (CA), rev'g (1999), 43 OR (3d) 728 (Gen Div) [*Figueroa*].

make their candidates' party affiliation known on election day. Finally, Iacobucci J rejected an approach to section 3 that the minority had endorsed, namely, that the individual interest in electoral participation be balanced against other communal aspects of participation. Justice Iacobucci expressly declared that the right of each citizen to play a meaningful role in the electoral process should not be subject to countervailing collective interests.

Justice Iacobucci scrutinized the three goals advanced by the government to justify the fifty-candidate threshold as a reasonable limit under section 1: to improve the electoral process; to protect the integrity of the electoral financing regime; and to ensure that the process is able to deliver a viable outcome in Parliament. While he accepted the pressing and substantial nature of the first two objectives, he found that they failed the proportionality stage of the section 1 analysis under *R v Oakes*.[27] With respect to the third objective, Iacobucci J said it was "extremely problematic"[28] to advance an objective that favoured a certain kind of outcome in Parliament, namely, a majority government, thereby reducing the chances that candidates from regional or marginal parties would be elected. Justice Iacobucci stated that "[l]egislation enacted for the express purpose of decreasing the likelihood that a certain class of candidates will be elected is not only discordant with the principles integral to a free and democratic society, but, rather, is the antithesis of those principles."[29] He went on to consider the proportionality analysis under the *Oakes* test and found that the fifty-candidate threshold could not reasonably be expected to advance the government's stated objective of encouraging majority governments.

An interesting feature of *Figueroa* is the discussion of the first-past-the-post system of election, a matter of current public debate that could conceivably give rise to a *Charter* challenge on the basis that it gives unduly weight to some votes while minimizing others. The dissenting judges stated that the first-past-the-post system is designed to favour "aggregation and cohesiveness"[30] and that such values must be weighed against the value of individual participation when determining whether section 3 has been violated. Justice Iacobucci expressly rejected this suggestion and said "the *Charter* is entirely neutral as to the type of electoral system in which the right to vote or to run for office is to be exercised."[31] While this suggests that the first-past-the-post system is

---

27   [1986] 1 SCR 103, 26 DLR (4th) 200 [*Oakes*].
28   *Figueroa*, above note 26 at para 80.
29   *Ibid*.
30   *Ibid* at para 153, LeBel J.
31   *Ibid* at para 37, Iacobucci J.

not favoured under the *Charter*, Iacobucci J. also cautioned: "this decision does not stand for the proposition that the differential treatment
of political parties will always constitute a violation of s 3. Nor does it
stand for the proposition that an infringement of s 3 arising from the
differential treatment of political parties could never be justified."[32]

3) Third Party Advertising

A year after *Figueroa*, the Supreme Court was faced with another contentious issue in *Harper v Canada (Attorney General)*,[33] a challenge to
election spending limits imposed on third parties by the *Canada Elections Act*. Under the Act, third parties were limited from spending more
than $150,000 nationally or $3,000 per riding during election campaigns, among other restrictions. These provisions were challenged by
Stephen Harper, then leader of the National Citizens Coalition, under
section 2(b) (freedom of expression),[34] section 2(d) (freedom of association), and section 3 (right to vote).

The majority decision by Bastarache J held that the restrictions on
third party spending during election time engaged the "informational
component" of the right to meaningfully participate in the electoral
process. This aspect of the right to vote gives each voter the right to be
"reasonably informed of all the possible choices" before him. Without
spending limits, the affluent might dominate political discourse: "If a
few groups are able to flood the electoral discourse with their message,
it is possible, indeed likely, that the voices of some will be drowned
out." It is the need to prevent the wealthy from monopolizing the public
forum that prevents carefully tailored spending limits from violating
an individual's section 3 rights.[35] As the spending limits still allowed
third parties to undertake modest national campaigns, there was no
violation of section 3.

Justice Bastarache's decision is informed by his acceptance of what
has been called the egalitarian model of elections. This model is premised on the idea that political discourse during elections needs to be
regulated to ensure that the wealthy do not dominate discourse and that
the poor are able to participate. It is contrasted with the libertarian model, under which there would be few, if any, restrictions on election spending. Proponents of the libertarian model view the egalitarian model as
paternalistic, and they argue that voters are best served by receiving as

---

32   *Ibid* at para 91, Iacobucci J.
33   [2004] 1 SCR 827 [*Harper*].
34   See Chapter 9.
35   *Harper*, above note 33 at paras 71–73, Bastarache J.

much information as possible, regardless of the source, and that voters should be credited with sufficient capacity to sort through repeated or unwanted messages and make informed decisions. Justice Bastarache holds that the *Canada Elections Act* regime and cases like *Saskatchewan Boundaries* have both embraced the egalitarian model and its goal of creating a "level playing field" so that "no one voice is overwhelmed by another."[36] Deference to Parliament's judgment as to how to best achieve the egalitarian model informed Bastarache J's analysis of both section 3 and section 1 of the *Charter*:

> Under the egalitarian model of elections, Parliament must balance the rights and privileges of the participants in the electoral process: candidates, political parties, third parties and voters. Advertising expense limits may restrict free expression to ensure that participants are able to meaningfully participate in the electoral process. For candidates, political parties and third parties, meaningful participation means the ability to inform voters of their position. For voters, meaningful participation means the ability to hear and weigh many points of view. The difficulties of striking this balance are evident. Given the right of Parliament to choose Canada's electoral model and the nuances inherent in implementing this model, the Court must approach the justification analysis with deference.[37]

This comment suggests that, even though in *Sauvé* and *Figueroa* the majority of the Supreme Court stressed that potential infringements of section 3 deserve strict scrutiny, the Court will, nonetheless, be less likely to find a *Charter* violation if the government can argue that a challenged law advances the equality of different voters. This trend continued in *R v Bryan*[38] in which a majority of the Court upheld a ban on distributing information on election results while the polls were still open in parts of Canada. The majority accepted that the restriction on expression was a proportionate attempt to ensure informational equality among all Canadian voters. Four judges in dissent, however, found that the goal of informational equality was not important enough to justify limiting political speech.

---

36   *Ibid* at para 62, Bastarache J.
37   *Ibid* at para 87, Bastarache J.
38   [2007] 1 SCR 527.

C. CONCLUSION

The right to vote is one of the most fundamental rights possessed by citizens in a democracy. In the cases that have come before the courts, judges have shown little sympathy for laws that deny the right to vote to particular groups or that discriminate against smaller, more marginal political parties. On the other hand, the courts have respected the historical and representational underpinnings of electoral-boundary design and hesitated to interfere with legislative judgment that is designed to promote the equality of all voters. The courts have also protected the rights of minority political parties to play a meaningful role in elections.

FURTHER READINGS

BREDT, C, & M KREMER, "Section 3 of the *Charter*: Democratic Rights at the Supreme Court of Canada" (2005) 17 NJCL 19

CARTER, M, "Reconsidering the *Charter* and Electoral Boundaries" (1999) 22 Dal LJ 53

CHARNEY, R, & Z GREEN, "It's My Party and I'll Run if I Want To: *Figueroa*, *Harper* and the Animal Alliance Environment Voters Party" (2006–2007) 21 NJCL 257–70

COURTNEY J, P MACKINNON, & D SMITH, eds, *Drawing Boundaries: Legislatures, Courts, and Electoral Values* (Saskatoon: Fifth House, 1992)

COURTNEY, J, *Commissioned Boundaries* (Montréal: McGill-Queen's University Press, 2002)

DAWOOD, Y, "Electoral Fairness and the Law of Democracy: A Structural Rights Approach to Judicial Review" (2012) 62 UTLJ 499

FEASBY, C, "*Libman v Quebec (AG)* and the Administration of the Process of Democracy under the *Charter*: The Emerging Egalitarian Model" (1999) 44 McGill LJ 5

———, "Issue Advocacy and Third Parties in the United Kingdom and Canada" (2003) 48 McGill LJ 11

FRITZ, R, "Challenging Electoral Boundaries under the *Charter*" (1999) 5 Rev Const Stud 1

GEDDIS, A, "Liberté, Egalité, Argent: Third Party Election Spending and the *Charter*" (2004) 42 Alta L Rev 429

KNIGHT, T, "Unconstitutional Democracy? A *Charter* Challenge to Canada's Electoral System" (1999) 57 UT Fac L Rev 1

MANFREDI, C, & M RUSH, *Judging Democracy* (Peterborough: Broadview Press, 2008)

———, "Electoral Jurisprudence in the Canadian and U.S. Supreme Courts: Evolution and Convergence" (2007) 52 McGill LJ 1

MORTON, FL, & R KNOPFF, "Does the *Charter* Mandate 'One Person One Vote'?" (1992) 30 Alta L Rev 669

PAL, M, & S CHOUDHRY, "Is Every Ballot Equal? Visible Minority Vote Dilution in Canada" (2007) 13 Institute for Research on Public Policies Choices

ROACH, K, "One Person, One Vote? Canadian Constitutional Standards for Electoral Distribution and Districting" in D. Small, ed, *Drawing the Map: Equality and Efficacy of the Vote in Canadian Electoral Boundary Reform* (Toronto: Dundurn Press, 1991) vol 11

STUDNIBERG, B, "Politics Masquerading as Principles: Representation by Population in Canada" (2009) 34 Queens LJ 611

MOBILITY RIGHTS

An important element of individual freedom is the right to enter and leave one's country and to move about it freely. In countries with federal systems, such as Canada, it is fundamental to a sense of national citizenship that individuals be able to move to and work in other provinces without prejudice because of their province of origin. The mobility rights protected by section 6 of the *Charter of Rights and Freedoms* are designed to promote and foster these objectives.

Section 6 contains two kinds of mobility rights, one international and the other interprovincial. Section 6(1) guarantees the right of citizens to enter, remain in, and leave Canada, while sections 6(2)(a) and (b) guarantee the right of citizens and permanent residents "to move and take up residence in any province; and to pursue the gaining of a livelihood in any province." The interprovincial guarantee is qualified in two ways. The right is subject to laws of general application in force in a province, provided those laws do not discriminate among individuals primarily on the basis of province of present or previous residence (section 6(3)(a)). Section 6(3)(b) permits reasonable residency requirements for the receipt of publicly provided social services. As well, section 6(4) protects from *Charter* challenge laws and programs aimed at relieving the plight of those who are socially or economically disadvantaged in provinces with rates of unemployment above the national rate. Finally, as with all *Charter* rights, a government may be able to justify laws that violate section 6 under section 1. However, mobility rights are among those rights in the *Charter* that are regarded as so significant that they are not subject to the legislative override in section 33.

A. THE RIGHT TO ENTER AND LEAVE CANADA

Section 6(1) of the *Charter*, the right of citizens to enter and leave Canada, has its origins in the *International Covenant on Civil and Political Rights*. Article 12(2) of that document provides that "[e]veryone shall be free to leave any country, including his own," while Article 12(4) states that "[n]o one shall be arbitrarily deprived of the right to enter his own country." However, the language of section 6(1) of the *Charter* is broader in that it includes a right to "remain in" Canada.

The most obvious uses for this section would be to challenge the denial of a passport, compelled expulsion from the country, or denial of re-entry. Although these scenarios are unlikely in a country with Canada's democratic traditions, national security concerns have given rise to litigation over exclusion of citizens.[1]

Section 6(1) has been invoked most often when Canadian citizens try to resist extradition to another country for trial. Canada has numerous extradition treaties with other countries, which allow a foreign country to seek the surrender of a Canadian citizen who is alleged to have committed an offence according to that country's law. If the individual is found guilty, he or she would ordinarily be required to serve any sentence in the foreign country, although Canada has arrangements with some countries that allow the convicted person to serve the sentence in a Canadian prison.

In *United States of America v Cotroni*,[2] the Supreme Court of Canada concluded that surrender of a citizen pursuant to the *Extradition Act* was a violation of section 6(1) of the *Charter*. Even though the surrender did not amount to an expulsion or banishment, since the individual could return after an acquittal at trial or after serving a sentence, the Court held that the rights in section 6(1) were infringed because the individual was denied the right to remain in Canada.

Although section 6(1) was violated, La Forest J, writing for the majority, concluded that the infringement caused by extradition lay far

---

1 Discussed below. The deportation of a permanent resident under the *Immigration Act* after conviction for a serious offence has been upheld. Section 6(1) is not applicable because it applies only to citizens, and s 7 is not violated (*Chiarelli v Canada (Minister of Employment and Immigration)*, [1992] 1 SCR 711, 90 DLR (4th) 289).

2 [1989] 1 SCR 1469.

from the core values of section 6(1). In his view, the central thrust of
section 6(1) was protection against exile and banishment, "the purpose
of which is the exclusion of membership in the national community."[3]
This opinion led the majority to take a more flexible approach to the
application of section 1 of the *Charter* in the case of extradition. The
Court had no difficulty in finding that there was a pressing and substantial objective underlying the extradition law: it aimed at the suppression of crime through international cooperative efforts. On the issue
of proportionality of means and ends, the Supreme Court divided (5:2).
Cotroni argued that, because he could have been tried in Canada for the
same offence he was charged with in the United States, his extradition
could not be justified as a reasonable limit. While the two dissenting
judges accepted this proposition, the majority disagreed. Cotroni was
alleged to have conspired to possess and distribute heroin. His actions
occurred in Canada, the heroin was to be distributed in the United
States, and most of the witnesses were in that country. Therefore, the
Court held, it was reasonable to allow him to be surrendered to the
United States for trial, and the section 1 test was satisfied.[4] Judicial review on *Charter* grounds of the minister of justice's decision to surrender the claimant for extradition attracts a standard of reasonableness
so that the minister's decision is given deference and will be upheld so
long as it falls within a reasonable range of outcomes.[5]

The Court affirmed the relatively deferential approach to section 6
rights in the extradition context in *Sriskandarajah v United States of
America*,[6] a case involving the extradition of Canadian citizens to face
terrorism-related prosecutions in the United States. The Court affirmed
the *Cotroni* principle that extradition was only a "marginal limitation
of the s 6(1) right to remain in Canada," which was primarily designed
to prevent exile and banishment. Extradition of citizens would generally be a reasonable limit on section 6(1) rights: that is because it might
be required as a way to show international cooperation in the control
of crime. The Court also reaffirmed that the courts would deferentially
review the minister's decisions to surrender a fugitive to another state.
A realistic possibility of prosecuting the citizen for the crime in Canada
was only one of many factors that would guide the minister's reasonable exercise of discretion.

The right of a Canadian citizen to enter Canada was held to be violated in the case of Abousfian Abdelrazik, who had been listed by the

---

3   *Ibid* at 1482.
4   A similar result was reached in *United States of America v Ross*, [1996] 1 SCR 469.
5   *Lake v Canada (Minister of Justice)*, [2008] 1 SCR 761.
6   2012 SCC 70.

United Nations as a person associated with Al-Qaeda and had been denied travel documents by the Canadian government that would allow him to return to Canada from Sudan. Although a process that allows passports to be denied for reasons of national security has been upheld by the Federal Court of Appeal to be a reasonable limit on the section 6(1) right that was proportionate to the objective of preventing terrorism,[7] this process was not used in this case, and the denial of an emergency passport was deemed unreasonable and not justified under section 1 of the *Charter*. In the case of the right to enter and leave Canada, the right entailed positive state obligations with respect to the issuance of a passport.[8] The effective remedy ordered in this case was the issuance of an emergency passport and an escort to ensure that Abdelrazik would be returned to Canada and appear before the judge.[9]

The *Charter*'s mobility right to enter Canada does not give a Canadian citizen, convicted of a serious criminal offence in the United States, the right to serve the sentence in Canada pursuant to the *International Transfer of Offenders Act*.[10] That legislation is the only source of a citizen's right to serve a sentence in Canada, and the right is subject to the discretion of both the foreign state and the Minister to consent to the transfer. Provided that the Minister's refusal to agree to the transfer is reasonable, the citizen has no recourse.[11]

In cases where the accused person would face denial of fundamental rights upon extradition, successful *Charter* challenges have been based on section 7. In *United States of America v Burns*,[12] two individuals were wanted on three counts of aggravated first-degree murder in Washington State, where a finding of guilt would result in either the death penalty or life in prison without parole. The minister of justice ordered the individuals to be extradited without seeking assurances that the death penalty would not be imposed or that, if it were imposed, it would not be carried out. At the Supreme Court of Canada, the individuals argued that extradition without assurances infringed sections 6(1), 7, and 12 of the *Charter*. The Supreme Court held that the real issue was the death penalty and that this issue should be considered under section 7. In the Court's view, "[t]he death penalty is overwhelmingly a justice issue and only marginally a mobility rights issue."[13] As

---

7   *Canada (Attorney General) v Kamel*, 2009 FCA 21.

8   *Abdelrazik v Canada (Attorney General)*, 2009 FC 580 at para 152.

9   *Ibid* at paras 160 and 166–67.

10   SC 2004, c 21.

11   *Divito v Canada (Public Safety and Emergency Preparedness)*, 2013 SCC 47.

12   [2001] 1 SCR 283, 195 DLR (4th) 1.

13   *Ibid* at 317 (SCR).

discussed in Chapter 13, the Court found that to surrender the two individuals without assurances that they would not face the death penalty would violate their section 7 right not to be deprived of life, liberty, and security of the person except in accordance with the principles of fundamental justice.

B. INTERPROVINCIAL MOBILITY

Section 6 of the *Charter* also protects interprovincial mobility. The section was part of a more ambitious set of proposals by the federal government to strengthen the Canadian economic union. Concerned about barriers to the mobility of labour, capital, goods, and services, the federal government proposed to bolster the common market clause in section 121 of the *Constitution Act, 1867*. That section provides that the articles produced or grown in a province shall be "admitted free" into other provinces. It has been narrowly interpreted by the courts as prohibiting customs duties, but it has been ineffective in protecting against rules discriminating against out-of-province labour, property ownership, or access to government contracts.[14] For example, Quebec, for many years, discriminated against workers from out-of-province in the construction industry, while Prince Edward Island restricted land ownership by non-residents.

Despite federal pressure for more ambitious constitutional language in various efforts at constitutional reform, section 6(2) deals only with mobility for citizens and permanent residents. It has been interpreted by the Supreme Court of Canada as guaranteeing a right of interprovincial mobility that ensures a right to move to another province to take up work there, and the right of a non-resident to work in another province without relocating. It is not, however, a free-standing guarantee of the right to work, and for the right to be invoked, there must be some element of interprovincial mobility at issue.[15] While the British Columbia Court of Appeal in *Wilson* interpreted section 7 as including a right of mobility *within* a province,[16] this must be contrasted with the

---

14   See, for example, the discussion of Laskin CJC in *Reference Re Agricultural Products Marketing Act (Canada)*, [1978] 2 SCR 1198 at 1266–68, 84 DLR (3d) 257.

15   *Law Society of Upper Canada v Skapinker*, [1984] 1 SCR 357, 9 DLR (4th) 161 [*Skapinker*].

16   *Wilson v British Columbia (Medical Services Commission)* (1988), 53 DLR (4th) 171 (BCCA).

Supreme Court of Canada's view that section 6(2) is designed to eliminate boundaries between the provinces.[17]

Nor has the section been interpreted as protecting new residents
and non-residents from compliance with the general rules applicable
to existing provincial residents — for example, occupational qualifications and licence requirements that affect everyone.[18] Section 6(3)(a)
makes it clear that residents and non-residents are subject to laws of
"general application" — that is, laws that do not discriminate primarily
on the basis of province of residence.

The leading cases interpreting section 6(2) and section 6(3)(a) of the
Charter are *Black v Law Society of Alberta*[19] and *Canadian Egg Marketing
Agency v Richardson*.[20] In *Black*, the Law Society of Alberta had passed
two rules in an effort to control interprovincial law firms — specifically, a partnership between an Alberta firm and an Ontario firm. The
first rule prohibited partnerships between lawyers resident in Alberta
and non-residents, while the second prohibited partnerships by members in more than one firm. The three-member majority of the Supreme
Court of Canada held that both rules infringed section 6(2)(b), because
their effect was to impair seriously the ability of non-resident lawyers to
carry on a viable business arrangement. These rules did not fall within
section 6(3)(a), because they were not laws of general application. Their
purpose and effect was to discriminate on the basis of residence.

The majority went on to examine the rules in light of section 1 of
the *Charter* and concluded that they were not reasonable limits. Even
though the Law Society had legitimate concerns about the proper governance of the legal profession, including avoiding conflicts of interest
in the practice of law, there were other alternatives that would achieve
their ends without impinging upon the rights secured by section 6(2)(b).

Justice McIntyre, in dissent, argued that the rules about partnership between residents and non-residents or multiple partnerships might
violate the right to freedom of association in section 2(d), but there
was no violation of the mobility guarantee. In his words, "[n]obody is
forbidden entry into Alberta and nobody is prohibited from practising
law or forming a partnership in Alberta."[21] In considering section 1,

---

17   In *Skapinker*, above note 15, Estey J stated at 181 (DLR): "The two rights (in
     paras. (a) and (b)) both relate to movement into another province, either for the
     taking up of residence, or to work without establishing residence."
18   See, for example, *Taylor v Institute of Chartered Accountants of Saskatchewan*
     (1989), 59 DLR (4th) 656 (Sask CA).
19   [1989] 1 SCR 591, 58 DLR (4th) 317 [*Black*].
20   [1998] 3 SCR 157, 166 DLR (4th) 1.
21   *Black*, above note 19 at 636 (SCR).

he concluded that the rule forbidding partnerships between residents and non-residents was not a reasonable limit, although he would have upheld the rule against multiple partnerships.

Black dealt with provisions that were directed at non-residents. However, many provincial laws restrict the practice of an occupation and create barriers to mobility, even though their purpose is not to restrict competition from non-residents or new residents. For example, one province may require higher levels of training for nurses than another. Quebec has rules about proficiency in the French language for those practising professions that create obstacles for non-francophones. Most provincial laws of this kind seem safe from a mobility-rights challenge. Even if they have a disproportionate impact on non-residents, they will likely be characterized as laws of general application within section 6(3)(a) that do not discriminate on the basis of province of residence.

The relationship between section 6(2)(b) and section 6(3)(a) of the *Charter* was considered in *Canadian Egg*. That case concerned the constitutionality of an interlocking federal and provincial egg marketing scheme that prevented the interprovincial marketing and export of eggs produced in the Northwest Territories. Egg producers in the Northwest Territories challenged the scheme under section 6. By a 5:2 majority, the Supreme Court held that there was no violation of section 6. In the view of the majority, section 6(3)(a) is not a "saving" provision like sections 6(3)(b), 6(4), or 1 of the *Charter*. Rather, section 6(2)(b) and section 6(3)(a) must be read together as defining a single right. Section 6 was engaged because the gaining of a livelihood in another province may be pursued by an attempt to create wealth in that province by production, marketing, or performance. However, the egg marketing scheme did not discriminate primarily on the basis of province of residence. The scheme had a valid and non-discriminatory purpose: to ensure the fair and orderly marketing of eggs in Canada by using historical production patterns to distribute quotas. The exclusion of the Northwest Territories was simply an application of the principle of allocating quota on the basis of historical production patterns. The effect of the scheme on the Northwest Territories egg producers had to be compared against its effect on new egg producers in the destination province who have no quota and wish to market their eggs in the destination province. In the majority's view, the Northwest Territories egg producers had failed to establish that their actual prejudice relative to this comparison group displaced the valid purpose of the scheme.

C. CONCLUSION

If section 6 of the *Charter* was meant to have a major impact on the functioning of the Canadian economic union, its supporters have likely been disappointed, for its reach has been limited so far to cases of direct discrimination on the basis of provincial residence in the pursuit of an individual's livelihood or choice of residence. It does not catch many other barriers to the mobility of goods, services, people, and capital, leaving these to be addressed by other institutions and legal rules.[22]

The right to remain in Canada has also not had a major impact on the extradition process. Although courts acknowledge that extradition of a Canadian citizen to face prosecution in another country violates section 6(1) of the *Charter*, they have indicated that extradition will generally be a reasonable limit on that right, justified to maintain international cooperation in the battle against crime. Section 7 of the *Charter* has had much more impact on the extradition process than the section 6 mobility rights of the *Charter*.

FURTHER READINGS

DE MESTRAL, A, & J WINTER, "Mobility Rights in the European Union and the *Charter*" (2001) 46 McGill LJ 979

JACKMAN, M, "Interprovincial Mobility Rights under the *Charter*" (1985) 43 UT Fac L Rev 16

LASKIN, JB, "Mobility Rights under the *Charter*" (1982) 4 Sup Ct L Rev 89

LEE, T, & M TREBILCOCK, "Economic Mobility and Constitutional Reform" (1987) 37 UTLJ 268

MACKLIN, A, "Citizenship Revocation, the Privilege to Have Rights and the Production of the Alien" (2014) 40 Queen's LJ 1

SWINTON, KE, "Courting Our Way to Economic Integration: Judicial Review and the Canadian Economic Union" (1995) 25 Can Bus LJ 280

---

22   See, for example, *Reference Re Prince Edward Island Lands Protection Act* (1987), 40 DLR (4th) 1 (PEICA), where it was found that controls on non-residents' ownership of land did not violate s 6. For further discussion of such barriers and their legal treatment, see KE Swinton, "Courting Our Way to Economic Integration: Judicial Review and the Canadian Economic Union" (1995) 25 Can Bus LJ 280.

LIFE, LIBERTY, AND SECURITY OF THE PERSON AND THE PRINCIPLES OF FUNDAMENTAL JUSTICE

Section 7 of the *Charter of Rights and Freedoms* provides:

> Everyone has the right to life, liberty and security of the person and the right not to be deprived thereof except in accordance with the principles of fundamental justice.

The section is cast in broad language and the scope of the guarantee is potentially significant and far-reaching. In an early decision, the Supreme Court stated that the process of elaborating the meaning of section 7 would necessarily be a gradual and case-by-case exercise.[1] This approach is understandable, for the interpretation of section 7 raises difficult questions. As we shall see, many of these questions involve fundamental moral and social issues, and call for the courts to consider the scope and limits of judicial review under the *Charter*.

Section 7 has had a significant impact in the criminal law context where it has been held to extend important procedural and substantive guarantees to persons accused of crime. That aspect of section 7 is discussed in Chapter 14, though some major cases involving the criminal process must be discussed in this chapter to the extent that they define general principles for section 7. This chapter focuses on the impact of section 7 outside the sphere of guarantees in the criminal process. Here it is significant that section 7 of the *Charter*, unlike the due process protections of the American *Bill of Rights*, does not explicitly protect

---

1   *R v Morgentaler*, [1988] 1 SCR 30 at 51, 44 DLR (4th) 385, Dickson CJC [*Morgentaler*].

property rights. Moreover, unlike some other modern rights protection instruments, section 7 of the *Charter* does not explicitly protect socio-economic rights such as the right to welfare or housing or health care.

As will be seen, however, section 7 still has an important and often controversial role to play outside of the criminal justice context. Should section 7 be narrowly interpreted to protect little more than procedural fairness? Or, does the requirement to respect the "principles of fundamental justice" demand review of the substantive content of legislation to ensure that all laws are just and fair? Does section 7 protect the "liberty" to do as one pleases, or should "liberty" be given a narrower interpretation, embracing only physical freedom? All laws constrain "liberty" in its widest sense. It is a basic tenet of our legal system that one is at liberty to do as one pleases unless constrained by some positive law. Yet ours is also a society governed by law and a society that recognizes that laws, and hence constraints on liberty, are required to preserve order and protect the weak and vulnerable.

Does "security of the person" entail the right to own property or the right to contract for private health insurance? If so, section 7 could help the "haves" in our society by significantly constraining governmental regulatory and redistributive measures. Does "security of the person" guarantee some minimal level of economic entitlement? If so, section 7 could help the "have-nots" by compelling the creation and extension of government welfare schemes. Opponents of abortion have argued that abortion denies the unborn the right to "life," while pro-choice advocates contend that laws preventing abortion infringe a woman's rights to "liberty" and "security of the person."

There is also conflict about the sources of the principles of fundamental justice. Are they found only in the basic or traditional tenets of the justice system? Or, can they be informed by changing standards of domestic and even international justice? Is there a danger of judges reading their own views of good policy into the principles of fundamental justice? How much of a consensus is required before a principle is recognized as a principle of fundamental justice? How do courts distinguish between legal principles and matters of policy that should be left to elected governments? Finally, what is the appropriate relation between section 7 and section 1 of the *Charter*? Is section 7 of the *Charter* such a special right that violations of section 7 rights will rarely if ever be justified under section 1 of the *Charter*? Has the reluctance of courts to hold that violations of section 7 are justified under section 1 affected the content of the section 7 rights both with respect to the definition of the rights to life, liberty, and security of the person and with respect to the definition of the principles of fundamental justice?

In this chapter, we canvass the way the courts have responded to these and other questions. As we shall see, definitive answers have yet to be given in many contentious areas. After three decades of litigation, the task of defining the outer limits of "life, liberty and security of the person" as well as the "principles of fundamental justice" is still very much a work-in-progress.

A. THE REQUIREMENTS OF A SECTION 7 VIOLATION

There are a number of steps in establishing a violation of section 7 of the *Charter*. First, the *Charter* applicant must demonstrate that he or she falls within the reference to "everyone" in section 7. Establishing this will be easy in the context of natural persons, but not in the case of corporations or other artificial entities. Next, the *Charter* applicant must demonstrate a violation of the right to life, liberty, or security of the person. Doing this will be easy in the context of physical deprivations of liberty, but more contentious in the case of other interests. Demonstrating a violation of the right to life, liberty, or security of the person, however, is insufficient to make out a section 7 claim. For example, a person convicted of a criminal offence and sentenced to jail suffers a loss of liberty, but loss of liberty, standing alone, is not contrary to the *Charter* guarantee. The rights claimant must proceed to the final stage of analysis and show that the denial of a right protected by section 7 is contrary to the principles of fundamental justice. The issue under section 7 is not whether the legislation strikes the right balance between individual and social interests, but whether it results in the deprivation of life, liberty, or security of the person in a manner that does not respect fundamental principles of justice. The claimant under section 7 should not bear the burden of demonstrating that the state's action is disproportionate and unjustified: in other words, section 7 does not permit "a freestanding inquiry . . . into whether a particular legislative measure 'strikes the right balance' between individual and societal interests in general."[2]

If all three elements of the section 7 violation have been established, it is still theoretically possible that the section 7 violation could be justified by the government under section 1 of the *Charter*. Nevertheless, the courts have indicated that justifications of section 7 violations will

---

2   *R v Malmo-Levine; R v Caine*, [2003] 3 SCR 571 at para 96 [*Malmo-Levine*]; *Charkaoui v Canada (Citizenship and Immigration)*, [2007] 1 SCR 350 at para 21 [*Charkaoui*].

be rare and, in fact, the majority of the Court has never held that a violation of section 7 of the *Charter* was justified under section 1. The Supreme Court has observed that "a violation of section 7 will be saved by section 1 only in cases arising out of exceptional conditions, such as natural disasters, the outbreak of war, epidemics, and the like."[3] In another case, the Court stated:

> The rights protected by section 7 — life, liberty, and security of the person — are basic to our conception of a free and democratic society, and hence are not easily overridden by competing social interests. It follows that violations of the principles of fundamental justice, specifically the right to a fair hearing, are difficult to justify under section 1. Nevertheless, the task may not be impossible, particularly in extraordinary circumstances where concerns are grave and the challenges complex.[4]

In that case, the Court held that while the protection of intelligence relating to national security "undoubtedly constitutes a pressing and substantial objective,"[5] the government had failed to justify under section 1 the total denial of adversarial challenge to the intelligence that the government provided to the Court to support a non-citizen's detention and possible deportation under a security certificate. In another case, the Court held that the government failed to justify limiting section 7 rights by requiring young offenders convicted of offences of serious violence to rebut a presumption in favour of an adult sentence and the lifting of a publication ban on their identity.[6]

The Court has not ruled out the possibility that some section 7 violation could be justified as a reasonable limit under section 1, but it has also increasingly emphasized general principles of fundamental justice that have analogues under section 1. It is difficult to imagine how a law that violates section 7 because it is arbitrary, overbroad, or grossly disproportionate could then be held under section 1 to be justified, given that, as discussed in Chapter 4, section 1 requires that a law not be arbitrary or overbroad in relation to its objectives and that it must strike an appropriate overall balance. At the same time, the Court has warned that the analysis under section 7 and section 1 are distinct,

---

3   *Suresh v Canada*, [2002] 1 SCR 3, 208 DLR (4th) 1 at para 78 [*Suresh*], citing *Reference Re s 94(2) of the Motor Vehicle Act (BC)*, [1985] 2 SCR 486 at 518, 24 DLR (4th) 536 [*Re BC Motor Vehicle Act*]; and *New Brunswick (Minister of Health and Community Services) v G(J)*, [1999] 3 SCR 46, 177 DLR (4th) 124 at para 9 [*New Brunswick v G(J)*]. See also *R v DB*, [2008] 2 SCR 3 [*DB*].

4   *Charkaoui*, above note 2 at para 66.

5   *Ibid* at para 68.

6   *DB*, above note 3 at paras 91–92.

with only the latter being concerned with the overall social benefits and costs of a law.[7]

1) Everyone

The reference to "everyone" in section 7 of the *Charter* has been interpreted not to include corporations. This view makes sense given that a corporation does not enjoy rights to life, liberty, and security of the person in the same sense as a natural person.[8] However, it does conflict with the interpretation of other sections of the *Charter*, such as freedom of expression and the right against unreasonable search and seizure, under which claims by corporations have been upheld.

The impact of the exclusion of corporations from the ambit of section 7 of the *Charter* is mitigated in a practical sense because the courts have allowed corporations to defend themselves in penal[9] and even civil proceedings[10] by arguing that a law violates the section 7 rights of natural persons and is therefore invalid. A legislature that wanted to insulate a law from section 7 review would thus have to make that law applicable only to corporations, something that is not commonly done.

The word "everyone" is not limited to citizens and includes "every human being who is physically present in Canada and by virtue of such presence amenable to Canadian law."[11] A number of landmark section 7 cases have involved claims made by non-citizens.[12] In one recent case involving the extraterritorial application of the *Charter* to the disclosure of the fruits of interviews that Canadian officials conducted with Omar Khadr at Guantanamo Bay, Cuba, the Supreme Court seemed to base its holding that section 7 of the *Charter* imposes disclosure obligations on the government in part on the fact that Khadr is a Canadian citizen.[13] The effect of the mention of Khadr's citizenship in this context is not clear, and in any event, it related to the extraterritorial application of the *Charter*. It is well established that non-citizens in Canada are protected under section 7's reference to "everyone."

---

7   *Canada (Attorney General) v Bedford*, 2013 SCC 72 at para 121 [*Bedford*].

8   *Irwin Toy Ltd v Quebec*, [1989] 1 SCR 927 at 1004, 58 DLR (4th) 577 [*Irwin Toy*]; *Dywidag Systems International Canada v Zutphen Brothers Construction Ltd*, [1990] 1 SCR 705, 68 DLR (4th) 147; *British Columbia (Securities Commission) v Branch*, [1995] 2 SCR 3, 123 DLR (4th) 462.

9   *R v Wholesale Travel Group Inc*, [1991] 3 SCR 154.

10   *Canadian Egg Marketing Agency v Richardson*, [1998] 3 SCR 157, 166 DLR (4th) 1.

11   *Singh v Canada (Minister of Employment and Immigration)*, [1985] 1 SCR 177 at 202 [*Singh*].

12   *Suresh*, above note 3; *Charkaoui*, above note 2.

13   *Canada (Justice) v Khadr*, [2008] 2 SCR 125 at para 31 [*Khadr*].

There may, however, be other limits on the meaning of "everyone." In holding that a fetus is not protected under Quebec's *Charter of Human Rights and Freedoms*, the Supreme Court has hinted that a fetus is not included in the reference to "everyone" in section 7 of the Canadian *Charter*.[14]

2) Life, Liberty, and Security of the Person

Before it is even possible to determine whether the state has respected the principles of fundamental justice, an applicant under section 7 of the *Charter* must establish that his or her interest "falls within the ambit of section 7: 'if no interest in life, liberty or security of the person is implicated, the section 7 analysis stops there.'"[15] The courts interpret life, liberty, and security of the person as three analytically distinct interests. They have largely taken a case-by-case approach rather than offering a comprehensive definition of what interests are protected by the rights to life, liberty, and security of the person.

a)   The Right to Life
In the assisted dying case of *Carter v Canada (Attorney General)*,[16] the Court stated that "the right to life is engaged where the law or state action imposes death or an increased risk of death on a person, either directly or indirectly. Conversely, concerns about autonomy and quality of life have traditionally been treated as liberty and security rights." In other words, the Court stressed that the right to life was focused on the right not to die, and not on the broader autonomy and dignity interests that would be protected under the rights to liberty and security of the person. Even on this fairly narrow test, the Court still held that the assisted suicide offence violated the right to life by forcing people to end their own lives sooner than they would have otherwise in order to avoid imposing potential criminal liability on those who provided them with assistance in ending their lives.

The lack of potentially life-saving medical treatment can also violate the right to life.[17] In a case dealing with the extradition of fugitives to face the death penalty, the Court concluded that the rights to liberty

---

14   *Daigle v Tremblay*, [1989] 2 SCR 530 [*Daigle*].
15   *Blencoe v British Columbia (Human Rights Commission)*, [2000] 2 SCR 307, 190 DLR (4th) 513 at para 48 [*Blencoe*].
16   [2015] 1 SCR 331 at para 62 [*Carter*].
17   *Chaoulli v Quebec (Attorney General)*, [2005] 1 SCR 791 at paras 191 and 200 [*Chaoulli*]; *Canada (Attorney General) v PHS Community Services Society*, [2011] 3 SCR 134 [*Insite*].

and security of the person were violated and that the lives of the fugitives "are potentially at risk."[18] Similarly, the Court found that section 7 was engaged in a case involving deportation of a refugee applicant to face the substantial risk of torture, by noting that "it is conceded that 'everyone' includes refugees and that deportation to torture may deprive a refugee of liberty, security and perhaps life."[19] Given the interest at stake, a risk to life may itself violate the right to life in section 7 of the *Charter*.

b) The Right to Liberty

The Supreme Court has been divided with respect to the scope of the right to liberty. Some judges, notably Wilson and La Forest JJ, were prepared to interpret the right to include matters involving the right to make fundamental personal decisions without state interference, such as where to live,[20] or whether to permit medical treatment for one's children,[21] and how to educate them.[22] Other judges, most notably Lamer CJC, took a more restrictive approach that emphasized freedom from physical restraint by the state. In a 1995 case, he was prepared to restrict the scope of section 7 to

> the conduct of the state when the state calls on law enforcement officials to enforce and secure obedience to the law, or invoke the law to deprive a person of liberty through judges, magistrates, ministers, board members etc.[23]

A majority of the Supreme Court opted for the more generous approach in *Blencoe v British Columbia (Human Rights Commission)*. Justice Bastarache (McLachlin CJC, L'Heureux-Dubé, Gonthier, and Major JJ concurring) declared that "the liberty interest protected by section 7 of the *Charter* is no longer restricted to mere freedom from physical restraint."[24] This conclusion was qualified by a number of factors. First, Bastarache J indicated that "although an individual has the right to make fundamental personal choices free from state interference, such

---

18 *United States of America v Burns*, [2001] 1 SCR 283, 195 DLR (4th) 1 at para 59 [*Burns*].

19 *Suresh*, above note 3 at para 44.

20 *Godbout v Longueil*, [1997] 3 SCR 844, La Forest J (L'Heureux-Dubé and Gonthier JJ concurring).

21 *B(R) v Children's Aid Society*, [1995] 1 SCR 315, 122 DLR (4th) 1, La Forest J (L'Heureux-Dubé, Gonthier, and McLachlin JJ concurring) [*B(R)*]; *New Brunswick v G(J)*, above note 3, L'Heureux-Dubé J (McLachlin J concurring).

22 *Jones v R*, [1986] 2 SCR 284, 31 DLR (4th) 569, Wilson J.

23 *B(R)*, above note 21 at 340 (SCR).

24 *Blencoe*, above note 15 at para 49.

personal autonomy is not synonymous with unconstrained freedom."[25] Second, on the facts of the case, he found that the rights to both liberty and security of the person were not violated by a thirty-month delay in processing a human rights complaint about sexual harassment. He commented: "[F]reedom from the type of anxiety, stress and stigma suffered by the respondent in this case should not be elevated to the stature of a constitutionally protected section 7 right."[26] Third, the authority of the pronouncement may be qualified by the fact that the four remaining judges did not decide the section 7 issue, holding that the *Charter* applicant was entitled to an independent administrative law remedy.

Moreover, most cases involving fundamental personal choices have arisen from the *Charter* claimant's interaction with the justice system. The extent to which such a claim may arise outside the administration of justice is still unclear. In *Gosselin*, McLachlin J, writing for the majority, agreed with Bastarache J that

> the dominant strand of jurisprudence on s 7 sees its purpose as guarding against certain kinds of deprivation of life, liberty and security of the person, namely, those "that occur as a result of an individual's interaction with the justice system and its administration."

While accepting that "an adjudicative context might be sufficient," McLachlin J found it unnecessary to decide categorically that it was required to ground a section 7 claim.[27]

What "fundamental personal choices" will attract *Charter* protection under section 7? In *Morgentaler*, Wilson J described "the decision of a woman to terminate her pregnancy"[28] as a fundamental personal choice that would attract section 7 protection. A law prohibiting assisted suicide violates the right to liberty and related dignity and autonomy interests by preventing a person with a grievous and irremediable medical condition from making decisions concerning their bodily integrity and medical care.[29]

Privacy has been described as being "at the heart of liberty in a modern state"[30] but the content of the right of privacy outside the criminal justice system remains uncertain. In *R v Clay*, the Supreme Court held that "the liberty right within s 7 is thought to touch the core of

---

25   *Ibid* at para 54.
26   *Ibid* at para 97.
27   *Gosselin v Quebec (Attorney General)*, [2002] 4 SCR 429 at paras 77–79 [*Gosselin*].
28   *Morgentaler*, above note 1 at 171.
29   *Carter*, above note 16 at para 66.
30   *R v Dyment*, [1988] 2 SCR 417 at 427.

what it means to be an autonomous human being blessed with dignity and independence in 'matters that can properly be characterized as fundamentally or inherently personal.'"[31] Applying this test, the Court rejected the proposition that recreational marijuana smoking constitutes an inherently personal activity deserving section 7 protection.

c)   The Right to Security of the Person

The right to security of the person has been interpreted to include serious state-imposed psychological stress. In *New Brunswick v G(J)*,[32] the Supreme Court held that state apprehension of a child from parental custody violated the parent's security of the person. "As an individual's status as a parent is often fundamental to personal identity, the stigma and distress resulting from a loss of parental status is a particularly serious consequence of the state's conduct."[33] The Court hastened to add, however, that "not every state action which interferes with the parent–child relationship will restrict a parent's right to security of the person." For example, a parent's security of the person is not violated when his or her child is sentenced to jail, conscripted into the army, or even negligently shot by the police.

The fact that security of the person is not violated by ordinary stresses and anxiety caused by state action was underlined by the Supreme Court's statement in *Blencoe*[34] that security of the person would be violated only "where the state interferes in profoundly intimate and personal choices" such as "a woman's choice to terminate her pregnancy, an individual's decision to terminate his or her life, the right to raise one's children and the ability of sexual assault victims to seek therapy without fear of their private records being disclosed." As mentioned above, the Court held in that case that a person's security of the person was not violated by a thirty-month delay in processing a human rights complaint of sexual harassment. At the same time, the Court has held that state-imposed delays in access to abortions[35] and delays imposed by waiting lists for medical treatments[36] infringe the security of the person by causing psychological and physical suffering.

Any infringement of the rights to life, liberty, and security of the person must be caused by the state. In *Blencoe*, the Court distinguished

---

31   *R v Clay*, [2003] 3 SCR 735 at paras 31–32.
32   *New Brunswick v G(J)*, above note 3.
33   *Ibid* at para 61.
34   *Blencoe*, above note 15 at paras 83 and 86.
35   *Morgentaler*, above note 1 at 59 (SCR), Dickson CJC; at 105–6 (SCR), Beetz J.
36   *Chaoulli*, above note 17 at para 119, McLachlin CJC and Major J; at paras 205–6, Binnie and LeBel JJ.

between the prejudice caused by the complaint of sexual harassment and the prejudice caused by the state's processing of the complaint. In an early *Charter* case challenging the testing of cruise missiles, the Court held that the causal connection between such actions and threats to life, liberty, or security of the person was too "uncertain, speculative and hypothetical to sustain a cause of action" under section 7 of the *Charter*.[37] In the *Insite* case, the Court held that there was a sufficient connection between drug laws and the risks to public health by the use of contaminated needles to reject the government's argument that the addicts, and not the law, were responsible for any harm to life or security of the person.[38] In *Bedford*,[39] the Court held there was a sufficient connection between laws criminalizing brothels, hiring bodyguards, and public soliciting and the increased risk to the safety of sex workers that the offences infringed upon security of the person, even though the violence that sex workers experienced would come at the hands of third parties. The Court has also found a sufficient causal connection between Canada's decisions to either extradite or deport people and the infliction of the death penalty or torture by a foreign state to find a violation of the rights to life, liberty, and security of the person.[40]

In *R v DB*,[41] a majority of the Court held that section 7 of the *Charter* was violated by a provision that required a young offender to justify the maintenance of a publication ban upon conviction of a violent offence. The majority made reference to the young offender's right to privacy, the stigmatizing effects of publication, and the greater psychological and social stress that would be caused by publication of the offender's name.[42] Four judges in dissent argued that the lifting of the publication ban did not affect the young offender's liberty or security. With respect to the latter, they argued that there was no state action because any harm caused to the young offender would be caused by the media and third parties and not the state.[43] The majority's approach in *DB* may signal a more flexible approach to the requirement of the state-imposed stress in *Blencoe* that will be more generous to *Charter* claimants and more realistic in recognizing the state's role in initiating a process in which both the state and third parties, such as the media, cause harm to a person's security interests.

---

37   *Operation Dismantle v R*, [1985] 1 SCR 441 at 447, 18 DLR (4th) 481.
38   *Insite*, above note 17 at paras 97–106.
39   *Bedford*, above note 7 at paras 58–92.
40   *Burns*, above note 18; *Suresh*, above note 3.
41   *DB*, above note 3.
42   *Ibid* at paras 84–87.
43   *Ibid* at para 178.

3) Principles of Fundamental Justice

Section 7 of the *Charter* does not allow the courts to "engage in a free-standing inquiry under s 7 into whether a particular legislative measure 'strikes the right balance' between individual and societal interests in general."[44] To establish a section 7 violation, the applicant must also show that his or her right to life, liberty, or security of the person has been denied contrary to an identifiable principle of fundamental justice. As we shall see from the following discussion, the definition of the principles of fundamental justice has been a fruitful source of debate and inquiry.

a) Substance, Procedure, and the Basic Tenets of the Justice System

Fair procedure is a matter that falls within the traditional expertise of the judiciary. Judges are experts at the fact-finding processes of the adversarial system and have a keen sense of the procedural values needed to ensure fairness to all who come before the courts. In the common law tradition, judges have also played an important role in monitoring the administrative apparatus of the state to ensure that individuals are dealt with fairly. The common law has evolved "rules of natural justice," which include the right to notice and a hearing if one's rights are affected. There is strong evidence to suggest that, at the time of the *Charter's* adoption, it was widely believed that the phrase "principles of fundamental justice" was restricted to procedural values of this kind.[45] Procedural fairness, the precise meaning of which will depend upon the particular context of the case,[46] is undoubtedly an important element of the principles of fundamental justice.

However, in its first important judgment on section 7, the Supreme Court rejected a narrow interpretation that would have limited the "principles of fundamental justice" to procedural fairness. In *Re BC Motor Vehicle Act*,[47] the Court held that section 7 should be given a more generous meaning, namely, that it allowed the courts to review, from the perspective of substantive as well as procedural justice, laws infringing "life, liberty or security of the person." This means that the courts have the right to strike down laws that do not conform to the judicial view of what is fundamentally just. In *Re BC Motor Vehicle Act*, the Court struck down a law imposing a mandatory jail sentence upon conviction for

---

44   *Malmo-Levine*, above note 2 at para 96.
45   The relevance of the drafters' original intention in *Charter* interpretation is discussed in Chapter 3.
46   See *Ruby v Canada (Solicitor General)*, [2002] 4 SCR 3 at para 39 [*Ruby*].
47   *Re BC Motor Vehicle Act*, above note 3.

driving while under suspension even when the accused was not aware of the suspension. In the Court's view, this was at odds with the fundamental principle that the severe sanction of imprisonment should be imposed only in cases of moral blameworthiness.[48]

Justice Lamer, who wrote the majority opinion, recognized that the case raised "fundamental questions of constitutional theory, including the nature and very legitimacy of constitutional adjudication under the *Charter* as well as the appropriateness of various techniques of constitutional interpretation."[49] While finding that section 7 conferred a mandate on the courts to assess the substantive justice of laws, Lamer J took pains to impose two important qualifications. First, he noted that the very structure of section 7 made it clear that the principles of fundamental justice were not a free-standing guarantee but rather could be invoked only where a law violated the right to "life, liberty or security of the person." Second, Lamer J tied the principles of fundamental justice to what he described as "the basic tenets of our legal system" and to the "domain of the judiciary as guardian of the justice system," distinguishing the latter from what he described as "the realm of general public policy."[50] He made reference, as well, to "the spectre of a judicial 'super-legislature'";[51] to the need to give meaningful content to section 7 while avoiding adjudication of policy matters; and to the necessity for "objective and manageable standards."[52] While this is admittedly imprecise, it does reflect a judicial awareness of the need to limit the power of judicial review to matters for which the courts have some claim to institutional competence and expertise.

The Court has applied a three-part test that principles of fundamental justice must be (1) legal principles, (2) supported by a social consensus, and (3) yielding a manageable standard. This standard has been applied in a manner that has tended to accept principles of fundamental justice that are rooted in the fundamental tenets of the legal system. Hence, the Court has rejected a number of candidates for principles of fundamental justice, including those based on the idea that the criminal law should only respond to harm, that the law should pursue the best interests of children, and that there should be a remedy for a violation of rights. Despite the Court's caution in recognizing new principles of fundamental justice, it has stressed that the principles are not a closed category. As will be seen, the Court, in recent years, has stressed four

---

48   This point is discussed in greater detail in Chapter 14.
49   *Re BC Motor Vehicle Act*, above note 3 at 495 (SCR).
50   *Ibid* at 503.
51   *Ibid* at 498.
52   *Ibid* at 499.

general principles of fundamental justice: namely, that the laws should not be vague, arbitrary, overbroad, or grossly disproportionate.

i)   *Decisions Recognizing Principles of Fundamental Justice*

In *DB*,[53] a majority of the Supreme Court held that the presumption that young people had diminished moral blameworthiness and culpability when they commit offences was a principle of fundamental justice that satisfied the test of being a legal and manageable principle supported by a social consensus. Justice Abella, for the majority, held that this principle was a long-established legal principle recognized in the tradition of separate legislation for young offenders. There was also a domestic and international consensus that age plays a role in the development of judgment and moral sophistication. Finally, the Court stated that the principle could be identified with sufficient precision to provide a manageable standard to determine whether infringements of life, liberty, or security of the person violated the principles of fundamental justice. In the result, the Court held that the presumption that young people convicted of serious violent offences would receive adult sentences violated the principle of diminished responsibility as did the onus on young offenders to justify a publication ban on their names. The Court did not rule out the possibility of young offenders receiving adult sentences or having their names published, but held that the Crown must justify such measures in each individual case.

Four judges dissented. They argued that the lifting of the publication ban did not engage the young person's liberty or security interests because any stigma or labelling would not be caused by state action. They also stressed that the presumption of an adult sentence was rebuttable and concluded that the onus on the young offender reflected a reasonable balance of the competing interests of the offender and society. Although the principle of the diminished responsibility of youth articulated in *DB* could have far-reaching implications, the decision relates to a traditional "basic tenet of the justice system" rather than a broad issue of social or economic policy, namely, the onus Parliament had placed on young offenders to displace presumptions that they would receive adult sentences and have their names published.

The Court has subsequently held that the duty of lawyers to be loyal to their clients was a principle of fundamental justice. It was a legal and manageable principle rooted in the evidentiary rule of solicitor-client privilege and supported by a social consensus. The Court held this section 7 principle was breached by applying duties to collect and

---

53   Above note 3.

disclose information about clients as part of legislation targeting money laundering and terrorism financing.[54] The Court has also held that it is a principle of fundamental justice that prosecutors not act for partisan or other improper purposes.[55] These cases suggest that that Court has been much more comfortable in recognizing principles of fundamental justice tied to the traditional tenets of the criminal justice system.

ii)   Decisions Rejecting Principles of Fundamental Justice
One possible exception to the Court's willingness to accept criminal law principles as principles of fundamental justice was the Court's decision to hold that the fundamental sentencing principle that sentences be proportionate to the crime was not a principle of fundamental justice. However, the Court's decision in this respect was based more on a desire to maintain uniformity with the specific prohibition on cruel and unusual punishment, which is only triggered if a sentence is grossly disproportionate.[56]

The Supreme Court has, affirmed its commitment to the idea that the principles of fundamental justice are found in the basic tenets of the legal system, as opposed to general policy informed by philosophy and social science, which is outside the inherent domain of the judiciary.[57] In *R v Malmo-Levine; R v Caine*,[58] the Court expanded upon Sopinka J's analysis in the *Rodriguez* case where he held that a principle of fundamental justice is a legal principle generally accepted among reasonable people as "vital or fundamental to our societal notion of justice . . . [and] capable of being identified with some precision and applied to situations in a manner which yields an understandable result."[59] In *Malmo-Levine*, the Court refused to strike down the criminalization of simple possession of marijuana, rejecting the argument that it is a principle of fundamental justice "that the *absence* of demonstrated harm to others deprives Parliament of the power to impose criminal liability."[60] The majority ruled that the "harm principle" did not qualify as "a legal principle about which there is significant societal consensus that it is fundamental to the way in which the legal system ought fairly

---

54   *Canada (Attorney General) v Federation of Law Societies of Canada*, 2015 SCC 7.
55   This principle was, however, held not to be violated by giving the Minister of Defence prosecutorial powers in the military justice system: *R v Cawthorne*, 2016 SCC 32.
56   *R v Safarzadeh-Markhali*, 2016 SCC 14 at paras 71–73 [*Safarzadeh-Markhali*].
57   *Suresh*, above note 3 at para 45.
58   *Malmo-Levine*, above note 2.
59   *Rodriguez v R*, [1993] 3 SCR 519 at 590–91, 107 DLR (4th) 342 [*Rodriguez*].
60   *Malmo-Levine*, above note 2 at para 103.

to operate . . . identified with sufficient precision to yield a manageable standard against which to measure deprivations of life, liberty or
security of the person." According to the majority, there is no general
consensus that the criminal law had to be limited to conduct causing
actual harm to others. To the extent that some minimal level of harm
was accepted as a necessary underpinning of a criminal prohibition,
there was no agreement on the nature of harm required and, hence,
the harm principle lacked sufficient precision to serve as a principle of
fundamental justice.

The Supreme Court followed a similar line of reasoning in *Canadian
Foundation for Children, Youth and the Law v Canada (Attorney General)*[61]
when it rejected "the best interests of the child" as a principle of fundamental justice and refused to strike down a *Criminal Code* provision allowing parents and teachers to use reasonable corrective force
to discipline children. Chief Justice McLachlin described the requirements of a principle of fundamental justice:

> First, it must be a legal principle. This serves two purposes. First, it
> "provides meaningful content for the s 7 guarantee"; second, it avoids
> the "adjudication of policy matters" . . . . Second, there must be suf-
> ficient consensus that the alleged principle is "vital or fundamental
> to our societal notion of justice" . . . . The principles of fundamental
> justice are the shared assumptions upon which our system of jus-
> tice is grounded. They find their meaning in the cases and traditions
> that have long detailed the basic norms for how the state deals with
> its citizens. Society views them as essential to the administration of
> justice . . . . [T]he alleged principle must be capable of being identi-
> fied with precision and applied to situations in a manner that yields
> predictable results.[62]

The "best interests of the child" is a legal principle, but the majority
held that as it is only one factor to be considered among others in cases
involving children, it is not a foundational principle vital or fundamental to societal notions of justice, nor is it susceptible to precise and
predictable application.

In *Kazemi Estate v Islamic Republic of Iran*,[63] the Supreme Court rejected the legal maxim that where there is a right, there must be a remedy as a principle of fundamental justice in the course of upholding the
immunity of foreign states from being sued in Canada for torture. The
Chief Justice concluded:

---

61   [2004] 1 SCR 76 [*Canadian Foundation for Children*].
62   *Ibid* at para 8 [case references omitted].
63   2014 SCC 62 [*Kazemi Estate*].

> While rights would be illusory if there was never a way to remedy
> their violation, the reality is that certain rights do exist even though
> remedies for their violation may be limited by procedural bars. Rem-
> edies are by no means automatic or unlimited; there is no societal
> consensus that an effective remedy is always guaranteed to compen-
> sate for every rights violation.[64]

In other words, the Court held that there was not a sufficient consensus
to make this legal maxim a principle of fundamental justice. The need
for remedies, like the best interests of children standard, was so highly
contextual that it did not produce the manageable standard required to
be a principle of fundamental justice.

Provisions in international treaties will only constitute principles
of fundamental justice under section 7 if there is a significant international consensus regarding the treaty's interpretation, and a consensus
that such an interpretation is fundamental to how a just international
law system should operate. Applying this test, the Court in *Kazemi
Estate*[65] held that the immunity of foreign states from civil suits in Canada for torture imposed in a foreign land did not violate section 7. The
Court was prepared to recognize that the prohibition against torture
was a widely accepted conventional international law and "likely"[66] a
principle of fundamental justice, but that the idea that a foreign state
could be sued in Canadian courts for such acts had not attained such
status. Justice Abella dissented on the basis that the peremptory norm
against torture meant that any act of torture could not be an official act
of a state and that the international principle of reparation should allow
the estate of a Canadian killed in Iran to sue the two individuals that it
alleged had engaged in torture.

Despite the caution in articulating new principles of fundamental
justice that are not rooted in fundamental and manageable tenets of the
legal system, the Court has stressed that the principles of fundamental
justice are not a closed category and they will continue to evolve. In
recent years, the Court has emphasized four general principles of fundamental justice that bear some resemblance to the proportionality test
that is used to determine whether a limit on a right is reasonable. As
will be seen, these principles have been used to strike down a growing
list of laws, including those relating to prostitution and assisted suicide.
Decisions under these general principles often hinge on whether laws
violate rights to life, liberty, or security of the person more than is necessary to achieve their objectives.

---

64 *Ibid* at para 159.
65 *Ibid*.
66 *Ibid* at para 52.

The four general principles are prohibitions against unduly vague laws; laws that are arbitrary or bear no rational relation to their legislative objective; laws that are overbroad to their legislative objective; and laws that have a gross disproportionality between their objective and the harms that they impose. The resemblance of these principles to the section 1 proportionality test does not mean that they are identical. The Court has stressed that the applicant has the burden of establishing a section 7 violation whereas the state must justify a law under section 1. Moreover, the section 7 analysis is not concerned with the overall social benefits and costs of a law. It focuses on the qualitative relation between rights infringements and the objective of the law, and not the law's effectiveness or how many people it affects. In other words, a law can violate section 7 because it has arbitrary, overbroad, or grossly disproportionate effects on just one person.[67]

b) Vagueness

A law that is so vague that it fails to provide fair notice to citizens or limit law enforcement discretion violates the principles of fundamental justice. It is a fundamental value of our legal system that citizens are entitled to fair notice of the conduct that is permitted or prohibited so that they can regulate their activities accordingly. A related concept is that the law should set appropriate limits on officials who exercise discretion in applying and enforcing the law. Chief Justice McLachlin has explained the vagueness principle as follows:

> A law must set an intelligible standard both for the citizens it governs and the officials who must enforce it. The two are interconnected. A vague law prevents the citizen from realizing when he or she is entering an area of risk for criminal sanction. It similarly makes it difficult for law enforcement officers and judges to determine whether a crime has been committed. This invokes the further concern of putting too much discretion in the hands of law enforcement officials, and violates the precept that individuals should be governed by the rule of law, not the rule of persons. The doctrine of vagueness is directed generally at the evil of leaving "basic policy matters to policemen, judges, and juries for resolution on an *ad hoc* and subjective basis, with the attendant dangers of arbitrary and discriminatory application": *Grayned v City of Rockford*, 408 U.S. 104 (1972), at p. 109.[68]

---

67   *Bedford*, above note 7 at paras 123–28.
68   *Canadian Foundation for Children*, above note 61 at para 16.

In Chapter 4, we considered these points from the aspect of section 1, the *Charter*'s limitation clause, which requires a certain minimal level of precision in laws that impinge upon protected rights. Where government seeks to uphold a law that infringes a protected right on the ground that the law is justifiable as a reasonable limit, it must show that the limit is "prescribed by law."

The Supreme Court has accepted the argument that the "principles of fundamental justice" include the requirement that laws not be so vague as to fail to respect these values of fair notice and control of discretionary power.[69] On the other hand, the Court has made it clear that there is an inherent element of uncertainty in any legal standard of general application and that it is unrealistic to expect precision and predictability in all cases. While the Court has insisted that the standard supplied must be intelligible and capable of providing a basis for legal debate and rational decision making, it has consistently resisted the argument that a legal norm or standard must provide crystal clear and immediate answers.

In *Irwin Toy*,[70] the 1989 decision challenging a restraint on advertising as an infringement of freedom of expression that we considered in detail in Chapter 9, the majority wrote:

> Absolute precision in the law exists rarely, if at all. The question is whether the legislature has provided an intelligible standard according to which the judiciary must do its work. The task of interpreting how that standard applies in particular instances might always be characterized as having a discretionary element, because the standard can never specify all the instances in which it applies. On the other hand, where there is no intelligible standard and where the legislature has given a plenary discretion to do whatever seems best in a wide set of circumstances, there is no "limit prescribed by law."

The notion of "an intelligible standard" was echoed in the judgment of Lamer J in the *Prostitution Reference* where he speaks of "an ascertainable standard of conduct, a standard that has been given sensible meaning by courts."[71] The theme was taken up again by Gonthier J in *R v Nova Scotia Pharmaceutical Society*.[72] There, the Court had to contend with the offence of conspiracy to lessen undue competition under

---

69   The following discussion is taken from RJ Sharpe, "The Application and Impact of Discretion in Commercial Litigation" (1998) 17:1 Advocates' Soc J 4.

70   *Irwin Toy*, above note 8 at 617 (DLR).

71   *Reference Re ss 193 and 195.1(1)(c) of the Criminal Code (Canada)*, [1990] 1 SCR 1123, 56 CCC (3d) 65 at 91 [*Prostitution Reference*].

72   [1992] 2 SCR 606, 93 DLR (3d) 36.

the *Competition Act*, a measure that was challenged as failing to respect the principles of fundamental justice:

> Legal rules only provide a framework, a guide as to how one may behave, but certainty is only reached in instant cases, where law is actualized by a competent authority . . . .
>
> By setting out the boundaries of permissible and non-permissible conduct, these norms give rise to legal debate. They bear substance, and they allow for discussion as to their actualization. They therefore limit enforcement discretion by introducing boundaries, and they also sufficiently delineate an area of risk to allow for substantive notice to citizens.
>
> Indeed, no higher requirement as to certainty can be imposed on law in our modern state. Semantic arguments, based on a perception of language as an unequivocal medium, are unrealistic. Language is not the exact tool some may think it is. It cannot be argued that an enactment can and must provide enough guidance to predict the legal consequences of any given course of conduct in advance. All it can do is enunciate some boundaries, which create an area of risk. But it is inherent in our legal system that some conduct will fall along the boundaries of the area of risk; no definite prediction can then be made. Guidance, not direction, of conduct is a more realistic objective . . . .
>
> A vague provision does not provide an adequate basis for legal debate, that is for reaching a conclusion as to its meaning by reasoned analysis applying legal criteria . . . . [I]t fails to give sufficient indications that could fuel legal debate.[73]

These statements indicate a judicial recognition that the problem of uncertainty of result in any given case is pervasive and inherent in any standard phrased broadly enough to provide us with guidance in more than one situation.[74] The objective of law is not and cannot be complete predictability of results — that must be left to judgment in each case. At the same time, however, the idea of law does require a minimum "intelligible standard," "an ascertainable standard of conduct," a norm that "give[s] rise to legal debate" or "provide[s] an adequate basis for legal debate" and "give[s] sufficient indication that could fuel legal debate."

Claims that legislation is so vague as to violate the principles of fundamental justice have almost invariably been rejected. Broadly

---

73 *Ibid* at 638–40 (SCR).

74 For another case reiterating the point, see *R v Lucas*, [1998] 1 SCR 439, 157 DLR (4th) 423, dealing with the offence of defamatory libel.

worded statutes have been narrowly interpreted to avoid constitutional infirmity.[75] A statute providing for the release of those found not criminally responsible because of mental disorder if they did not present a "significant threat to the safety of the public" was held not to be excessively vague.[76] The Supreme Court also found that undefined references to "terrorism" and "threats to the security of Canada" in immigration legislation were not unconstitutionally vague. Although such terms require judicial interpretation, the Court held that the meaning of the word "terrorism," for example, was not "so unsettled that it cannot set the proper boundaries of legal adjudication."[77] The Court has continued to reject vagueness challenges and has stressed that a law will only be vague if it fails to give fair notice and limits law enforcement discretion after the courts have discharged their interpretative function.[78]

c) Arbitrariness

For a time, there was no agreement about the precise test for determining that a law violated section 7 on the grounds of arbitrariness. In the 2011 *Insite* case, the Court recognized that three dissenting judges in *Chaoulli*[79] would only find a law to be arbitrary if it bore no relation or was inconsistent with its objectives, while three other judges held that the law prohibiting the purchase of private health insurance was arbitrary and violated section 7 on the basis that it did not satisfy the more demanding standard that it was "necessary" to further the state objective in preserving the medicare system.[80] *Insite* did not settle the differences in approach because it found that the denial of an exemption from drug laws for a supervised injection site was arbitrary under either test because the evidence in the case indicated that denying an exemption would not advance, and was not necessary for, the state's interests in either controlling crime or promoting public health.

The Court subsequently made clear in *Bedford* that laws will only be arbitrary if there is no "rational connection between the . . . measure that causes the s. 7 deprivation, and the limits it imposes on life, liberty, or security of the person . . . . A law that imposes limits on these interests in a way that bears no connection to its objective arbitrarily impinges on those interests."[81] In *Carter*, the Court explained that "an

---

75 *Canadian Foundation for Children*, above note 61.

76 *Winko v British Columbia*, [1999] 2 SCR 625, 175 DLR (4th) 193.

77 *Suresh*, above note 3 at para 96.

78 *R v Levkovic*, [2013] 2 SCR 204 at para 47.

79 *Chaoulli*, above note 17.

80 *Insite*, above note 17 at para 132.

81 *Bedford*, above note 7 at paras 111 and 113.

arbitrary law is one that is not capable of fulfilling its objectives. It exacts a constitutional price in terms of rights, without furthering the public good that is said to be the object of the law."[82] This is a more deferential standard and one that is more consistent with the rational connection test under section 1 than the standard of necessity that was used by the three judges who invalidated the Quebec law restricting private health insurance in *Chaoulli* under section 7. This is demonstrated by the fact that the Court found that none of the prostitution-related offences in *Bedford* were arbitrary or bore no connection to their objectives in preventing nuisances or exploitation, even though they were overbroad and went further than required, and some were grossly disproportionate. Similarly, the Court found that the assisted suicide offence in *Carter* was not arbitrary to its objective in protecting the vulnerable from being coerced into suicide, even though it was overbroad.

In short, laws that rationally advance or are rationally capable of fulfilling their objectives will not violate the principle of fundamental justice against arbitrary laws. This is a demanding test — but not an impossible test — for *Charter* applicants to satisfy. In 2015, the Court found that a law that prohibited medical marijuana except in a dry form that could be smoked was arbitrary because it bore no relation or connection to Parliament's objectives of protecting the health and safety of patients given evidence that the prohibited form of marijuana use was actually less risky to health and safety.[83]

d) Overbreadth

Legislation drafted more broadly than is necessary to attain its objective and thereby impinging unduly upon a protected right or freedom may be struck down under section 7 of the *Charter* on grounds of overbreadth. Overbreadth is related to, but distinct from, both vagueness and arbitrariness. Overbreadth does not depend upon vagueness. The intended effect of a statute may be perfectly clear and not suffer from vagueness, but may be overly broad in its application. On the other hand, vagueness often entails overbreadth. Uncertainty flowing from the vague wording of a statute may have the effect of overly broad application.[84]

An overbroad law can be seen as a law that is arbitrary in some of its (overbroad) applications, even though some of its applications are rationally connected to its objective. As the Court has recognized,

---

82   *Carter*, above note 16 at para 83.
83   *R v Smith*, [2015] 2 SCR 602 [*Smith*].
84   *R v Heywood*, [1994] 3 SCR 761 at 791–92, applying *R v Zundel* (1987), 58 OR (2d) 129 (CA) at 157–58.

"overbreadth allows courts to recognize that the law is rational in some cases, but that it overreaches in its effect in others."[85] Overbreadth is also closely related to the minimal-impairment component of the section 1 proportionality analysis (discussed in Chapter 4), though the focus under section 7 is on overbreadth in relation to individuals whose life, liberty, or security is affected and not the broader social impact.[86] In both cases, care must be taken in defining the precise objective of the law because too broad a definition of the objective will "short-circuit" and foreordain the analysis by making it impossible to conclude that a law is overbroad or grossly disproportionate, while too narrow a definition of the objective may similarly foreordain a finding that the law is overbroad. In some cases, the Court has rejected the objective asserted by both the government and those challenging the law. It is clear that determining a law's objective is a critical and potentially determinative step when determining whether a law is arbitrary or overbroad.[87]

In R v Heywood,[88] the Supreme Court of Canada struck down a Criminal Code provision making it a crime for persons convicted of specified offences to be "found loitering in or near a school ground, playground, public park or bathing area" on the ground that it was overly broad and therefore infringed the liberty interest protected by section 7 of the Charter. The provision was aimed at the protection of children; however, it applied to all parks, not just those frequented by children; it was unlimited in time and offered no process of review; it applied to those convicted of offences not involving children; and it could be enforced without notice to the accused. Justice Cory explained the overbreadth principle in the following way:

> Overbreadth analysis looks at the means chosen by the state in relation to its purpose. In considering whether a legislative provision is overbroad, a court must ask the question: are those means necessary to achieve the State objective? If the State, in pursuing a legitimate objective, uses means which are broader than is necessary to accomplish that objective, the principles of fundamental justice will be violated because the individual's rights will have been limited for no reason. The effect of overbreadth is that in some applications the law is arbitrary or disproportionate.[89]

---

85 Bedford, above note 7 at para 113.
86 Carter, above note 16 at para 85.
87 Ibid at para 77; R v Moriarity, [2015] 3 SCR 485 at paras 24–33 [Moriarity].
88 Above note 84.
89 Ibid at 792–93.

The overbreadth principle was applied again in *R v Demers*, invalidating a *Criminal Code* provision that denied those permanently unfit to stand trial the possibility of an absolute discharge. The Supreme Court held that "the continued subjection of an unfit accused to the criminal process, where there is clear evidence that capacity will never be recovered and there is no evidence of a significant threat to public safety, makes the law overbroad because the means chosen are not the least restrictive of the unfit person's liberty and are not necessary to achieve the state's objective."[90]

The Court has held that a provision allowing nearly every federal offence, by even off-duty members of the military, to be prosecuted in the military justice system is not overbroad because it is rationally connected to the legislative objective of maintaining discipline, efficiency, and morale in the military.[91] This is a case where the breadth of the government's objectives may have saved the law from being declared overbroad.

At the same time, the Court has held that a number of other laws are overbroad. For example, the Court held that an offence of living off the avails of prostitution was constitutionally overbroad because it could apply to those who received money from sex workers in a non-exploitative relationship. The offence of assisted suicide was also overbroad to the legitimate objective of protecting vulnerable people from being coerced into taking their lives because it could apply to competent adults who clearly made a choice to have a physician assist them in ending their lives when they were subject to intolerable and enduring suffering from an irremediable and grievous condition.[92]

Overbreadth has emerged as one of the most powerful principles of fundamental justice. A law that prevented assisting people to enter Canada in violation of immigration laws was overbroad to the extent that it prevented humanitarian aid to undocumented entrants, mutual assistance among asylum-seekers, or assistance to family members.[93] A law was also overbroad to the extent that it prevented those who were eligible for medical marijuana from possessing it in a non-dried form. Finally, a law restricting the deduction of time spent in pre-trial detention was overbroad to the extent that it applied to those previously convicted of an offence but who were not a danger to public safety.[94] In all of these cases, the state understandably was unable to justify an over-

---

90   *R v Demers*, [2004] 2 SCR 489 at para 43.
91   *Moriarity*, above note 87.
92   *Carter*, above note 16 at para 147.
93   *R v Appulonappa*, [2015] 3 SCR 754.
94   *Safarzadeh-Markhali*, above note 56.

broad law that went further than was necessary to advance its legitimate objectives under the section 1 proportionality test for determining reasonable limits. Another interesting feature of these overbreadth cases is that the Court is taking a purposive approach to remedies and increasingly only declaring the impugned law to be invalid and of no force and effect to the extent that it is overbroad and infringes life, liberty, or security of the person more than is necessary to achieve the objective. This feature of these cases will be discussed in Chapter 17 on remedies.

e) Gross Disproportionality

The Supreme Court of Canada has identified "gross disproportionality" as a principle of fundamental justice: "Gross disproportionality describes state actions or legislative responses to a problem that are so extreme as to be disproportionate to any legitimate government interest."[95] The Court has warned that "[t]he rule against gross disproportionality only applies in extreme cases where the seriousness of the deprivation is totally out of sync with the objective of the measure."[96]

Gross disproportionality would seem to parallel the final stage of the *Oakes* test for section 1; namely, comparing the overall benefits that a law achieves in fulfilling its legislative objectives with the overall costs of the law in infringing upon freedoms — though an important difference is that, under section 7, a law may be grossly disproportionate because of its impact on only one person, and section 7 analysis is not concerned with "the beneficial effects of the law for society." In other words, the section 7 principle balances "the negative effect on the individual against the purpose of the law, *not* against societal benefit that might flow from the law."[97] This means that a law that has a grossly disproportionate effect on just one person may violate the section 7 principle against grossly disproportionate laws.[98]

The courts have used the principle of gross disproportionality to strike down laws in highly contentious areas. In the *Insite* case,[99] the issue was a ministerial denial of an exemption under the *Controlled Drug and Substances Act* for a safe injection site in the drug-plagued downtown Eastside of Vancouver. The Act authorized the minister of health to grant medical and scientific exemptions from the prohibition of possession and trafficking in controlled drugs. A previous gov-

---

95   *Insite*, above note 17 at para 133; *Malmo-Levine*, above note 2 at para 143; *Burns*, above note 18 at para 78.

96   *Bedford*, above note 7 at para 120.

97   *Ibid* at para 121 [emphasis in original].

98   *Ibid* at para 122.

99   Above note 17.

ernment had granted an exemption for the supervised injection site, which provided addicts with a location, clean needles, medical care, and social welfare services (but not drugs). A new government and a new minister strongly favoured a crime-based approach to the problem of drug addiction and refused to renew the exemption. That decision provided the basis for a challenge to the entire Act as an infringement of section 7. Extensive evidence was led to show that the safe injection site had reduced drug-related deaths and illness with no increase in drug use or drug-related crime.

The Supreme Court held that the Act as a whole survived, but it was saved only because the exemption was provided as a "safety valve." The minister's refusal to grant an exemption violated section 7 as it posed a risk to life and security of the person, and was both arbitrary and grossly disproportionate to the objectives of the law, namely, public health and safety and punishment to control illicit drug use. The Court held that, on the evidence, the safe injection site had saved lives while not increasing drug use, so the refusal of an exemption would pose a risk to public health, thereby undermining the statutory objectives. The Court rejected the government's argument that the cause of any death and illness from illicit drug use should be attributed to the personal choice of the users, not government policy, on the evidence that addiction was an illness that impaired the capacity to choose.

Although the matter involved the exercise of ministerial discretion, the Court held that the appropriate remedy was to order the minister to grant the exemption as that was the only decision that could be made to comport with the protected *Charter* right. The Court recognized that the issue of drug use and addiction was complex, that it attracted "a variety of social, political, scientific and moral reactions," and that it was for the "relevant governments, not the Court, to make criminal and health policy."[100] However, it insisted that, where the government's policy infringed *Charter* rights, the Court was entitled to act.

In *Bedford*,[101] the Supreme Court struck down *Criminal Code* provisions outlawing bawdy houses and communicating for the purposes of prostitution on the grounds that they were grossly disproportionate. It stressed that the objective behind both laws in preventing public nuisances associated with the sale of sex were grossly disproportionate to their harmful effects in preventing sex workers from taking steps that could decrease the risk to their safety and lives. These steps included screening customers and using indoor premises that would

---

100 *Ibid* at para 105.
101 *Bedford*, above note 7.

otherwise qualify as bawdy houses. With respect to the bawdy house offence, the Court concluded that "Parliament has the power to regulate against nuisances, but not at the cost of the health, safety and lives of prostitutes."[102] The Court recognized that some sex workers might not always be able to screen out dangerous customers, but stressed the qualitative rather than the quantitative nature of section 7 analysis by concluding that "[i]f screening could have prevented one woman from jumping into [serial murderer] Robert Pickton's car, the severity of the harmful effects is established."[103]

The *Charter* challenge in *Bedford* was based upon an extensive evidentiary record dealing with the conditions of sex-trade workers and the impact of the impugned laws upon their safety. The bawdy house prohibition precluded a single prostitute from working discreetly in the safety of her home, thereby exposing her to the risks involved in street prostitution with no gain to the prevention of public nuisance. The "communicating for the purposes of prostitution" offence prevented sex-trade workers from screening potential customers. The Court recognized that the ultimate danger to sex-trade workers came from private parties such as customers and pimps, but held there was sufficient connection between the impugned laws and the increased risk to the sex-trade workers.[104] Despite finding this increased risk, the Court suspended a declaration of invalidity for twelve months in recognition of Parliament's regulatory role. Parliament responded with new legislation that made it a criminal offence to purchase (but not sell) sex and placed restrictions on advertising sexual services. It repealed the part of the bawdy house provisions relating to prostitution and some parts of the "living off the avails of prostitution" offence.[105]

B. INTERESTS PROTECTED BY SECTION 7

Although section 7 of the *Charter* can be broken up into its component parts of "everyone," "rights to life, liberty or security of the person," and the right not to be deprived of these rights "except in accordance with the principles of fundamental justice," it is also helpful to take a more holistic approach to whether a section 7 violation has been established. In the remainder of this chapter, we take such an approach and

---

102 *Ibid* at para 136.
103 *Ibid* at para 158.
104 *Ibid* at paras 86–89.
105 *Criminal Code*, ss 286.1–286.5, 213, 197 as amended by SC 2014, c 25.

examine some important contexts in which laws and state actions have been challenged under section 7.

1) Control of the Body: Abortion, Assisted Suicide, and Access to Health Care

The Supreme Court of Canada has had a number of opportunities to examine the extent to which section 7 protects the individual in making significant decisions about the body. The first was *R v Morgentaler*,[106] in which the Court held that the abortion provisions of the *Criminal Code* violated section 7 of the *Charter*; the second, *Rodriguez v R*,[107] narrowly upheld the prohibition on assisted suicide in the *Criminal Code*. The third was the *Carter*[108] case, where the Court effectively overruled *Rodriguez* and held that the assisted suicide offence violated section 7 because it was overbroad in applying to those who were not vulnerable to being coerced into suicide — namely, competent adults enduring intolerable suffering from a grievous and irremediable condition.

a) Abortion

R v Morgentaler dramatically demonstrated the *Charter's* impact on highly contested matters of public policy. The *Criminal Code* provision at issue prohibited abortions but also provided an exemption if a woman seeking an abortion obtained a certificate from a therapeutic-abortion committee consisting of three physicians. Such a certificate could be issued if the committee concluded that the woman's life or health would be endangered by the continuation of the pregnancy. These committees could operate only in accredited hospitals, and the doctor performing the abortion could not be included on the committee. Evidence was led to show that access to abortion varied significantly across the country. Many hospitals did not provide abortions at all, while others imposed rules more stringent than those set out in the *Criminal Code*, for example, denying abortions to married women.

The Supreme Court struck down the *Criminal Code* prohibition of abortion, but the Court was sharply divided in its reasoning. Justice Beetz, writing for himself and Estey J, found it possible to strike down the law on relatively narrow grounds. He focused on the fact that the law had a direct impact on a woman's health. In his view, the law infringed the woman's right to security of the person by requiring committee

---

106 *Morgentaler*, above note 1.
107 *Rodriguez*, above note 59.
108 *Carter*, above note 16 at para 147.

approval of medical treatment necessary to protect her life or health. He also found that the therapeutic-abortion committee procedure was not in accordance with the principles of fundamental justice, since it was applied in an arbitrary and uneven fashion, often based on factors not reasonably linked to the protection of the life or health of the woman or her fetus.

Justice Wilson adopted a much more expansive interpretation. In her view, there was a violation of both the right to liberty and the right to security of the person. The right to liberty, Wilson J wrote, "guarantees to every individual a degree of personal autonomy over important decisions intimately affecting their private lives."[109] A woman's decision whether to continue a pregnancy is hers and hers alone, and state interference with her personal autonomy in making that decision violates her right to liberty. In addition, Wilson J found, the state violated the woman's right to security of the person by forcing her to continue a pregnancy. The woman's autonomy right was infringed for she was being treated as "a means to an end which she does not desire," in that she was "the passive recipient of a decision made by others as to whether her body is to be used to nurture a new life."[110]

The third set of majority reasons was written by Dickson CJC, with Lamer J concurring. Some of his language echoed that of Wilson J:

> Forcing a woman, by threat of criminal sanction, to carry a fœtus to term unless she meets certain criteria unrelated to her own priorities and aspirations, is a profound interference with a woman's body and thus a violation of security of the person.[111]

However, other passages suggest an approach closer to that of Beetz J, because of the emphasis on the threat to a woman's physical and psychological health created by procedures that prevented, or at least delayed, access to important medical treatment under the threat of criminal sanction.

Justice McIntyre in dissent, with La Forest J concurring, rejected the view that section 7 included a right to an abortion in any circumstances. In his view, neither the language of the *Charter* nor "the history, traditions and underlying philosophies of our society would support the proposition that a right to abortion could be implied in the *Charter*."[112]

---

109   *Morgentaler*, above note 1 at 171 (SCR).
110   *Ibid* at 173.
111   *Ibid* at 56–57.
112   *Ibid* at 143 & 144.

While all the majority judges rejected arguments made under section 1 to save the legislation, they also made it clear that some restrictions on a woman's access to abortion could be justified under section 1 in order to protect the fetus. Justice Beetz, however, rejected the proposition that Parliament could prevent access to an abortion necessary to protect maternal life or health. Justice Wilson suggested that Parliament's case for intervention to protect the fetus would become stronger as the pregnancy progressed. This suggested an approach similar to that of the United States Supreme Court, which, in *Roe v Wade*,[113] had concluded that increasing restrictions on access to abortion were justified in the later stages of pregnancy.

Morgentaler generated much debate about whether Parliament could enact new legislation limiting abortions that would survive judicial scrutiny. The federal government attempted to do so shortly after the decision with the introduction of Bill C-43, which would have required a doctor to certify that a woman's health was endangered by the continuation of the pregnancy. The bill passed in the House of Commons but was defeated as a result of a tie vote in the Senate. The result is that there is currently no prohibition of abortion in Canada's criminal law. Some provinces have attempted to control access to abortion, particularly by restrictions on free-standing abortion clinics, but some of those initiatives have been found to be unconstitutional under the distribution of powers in the federal system. For example, in *Morgentaler 1993*, the Supreme Court of Canada struck down Nova Scotia's regulation as an attempt to legislate in the area of criminal law, which is within exclusive federal jurisdiction.[114]

There have also been attempts to litigate the abortion issue from the perspective of fetal rights. Joseph Borowski, a pro-life activist, brought an action seeking a declaration that the abortion provisions in the *Criminal Code* violated the fetus's right to life under section 7. He was unsuccessful in the lower courts of Manitoba. By the time the case reached the Supreme Court of Canada, the Court had struck down the abortion provisions of the *Criminal Code* in *Morgentaler*, and the Court declined to consider his case on the merits on the basis that the issue was moot — that is, there was no legal issue, given the invalidity of the legislation.[115]

---

113   410 US 113 (1973).

114   *R v Morgentaler*, [1993] 3 SCR 463, 107 DLR (4th) 537 [*Morgentaler 1993*].

115   *Borowski v Canada (Attorney General)*, [1989] 1 SCR 342, 57 DLR (4th) 231. See Chapter 7 for a discussion of mootness.

In *Daigle v Tremblay*,[116] a man sought an injunction to prevent his former partner from obtaining an abortion. The case involved the interpretation of Quebec's *Charter of Human Rights and Freedoms*, specifically, the scope of the fetus's and prospective father's rights. The Supreme Court of Canada determined that a fetus is not a person with rights under the Quebec *Charter*, but it did not address the issue of whether "everyone" in section 7 of the Canadian *Charter* includes a fetus, since no law was being challenged and the Canadian *Charter* did not apply to a proceeding involving private parties.

b) Assisted Suicide

Rodriguez v R[117] raised the issue of the scope of section 7 in relation to another important personal decision, namely, the right to determine the timing of one's death through assisted suicide. Sue Rodriguez was terminally ill, suffering from Lou Gehrig's disease, which had attacked her neurological system. She wanted to be able to end her own life when she felt that the quality of her life made it no longer worth living. Given the nature of her disease, at that point, she might be unable physically to accomplish the necessary acts, and hence she might need some assistance. Attempting suicide is not a crime, but section 241(b) of the *Criminal Code* makes it an offence for anyone to assist another person to commit suicide. Rodriguez argued that the section violated section 7 of the *Charter* by denying her the right to terminate her life when she wished.

The Supreme Court of Canada divided 5:4 on the issue of the constitutionality of the provision. Justice Sopinka, writing for the majority, held that the legislation did violate the right to security of the person. His reasons drew upon those of Wilson J in *Morgentaler*. He concluded:

> ... personal autonomy, at least with respect to the right to make choices concerning one's own body, control over one's physical and psychological integrity, and basic human dignity are encompassed within security of the person, at least to the extent of freedom from criminal prohibitions which interfere with these.[118]

On the facts of the case, Sopinka J held that denying Rodriguez assistance to commit suicide would deprive her of personal autonomy and cause physical pain and psychological distress. However, when Sopinka J went to the next level of analysis, he found that the restriction on

---

116 *Daigle*, above note 14.
117 *Rodriguez*, above note 59.
118 *Ibid* at 588 (SCR).

assisted suicide did not violate principles of fundamental justice. The purpose of the legislation, he found, was to protect those in a vulnerable situation from exploitation. The prohibition of assisted suicide was grounded in the state interest in the sanctity of human life, a fundamental value of Canadian society. Justice Sopinka conceded that there are exceptions to the principle of the sanctity of life in our law. For example, the law allows for the termination of life through the refusal or consented withdrawal of medical treatment. On the other hand, Sopinka J noted, the law has drawn a distinction between passive and active euthanasia. In Sopinka J's opinion, there was no general societal consensus that active euthanasia is acceptable. Absent that consensus and given the value placed on human life, the majority of the Court held that it should not find the assisted-suicide prohibition in violation of the principles of fundamental justice.

Justice McLachlin, who wrote one of the three dissenting opinions, held that the law did not accord with the principles of fundamental justice, because it was arbitrary in its application to individuals such as Rodriguez. In her view, Parliament has not taken a consistent attitude with respect to decisions to terminate life — for example, it does not prohibit passive euthanasia or suicide. Therefore, she found it arbitrary to deny access to suicide to an individual like Rodriguez who was able to make a free and informed decision about the continuation of her life.[119]

In 2015, the Supreme Court found in an unanimous decision that the ban on assisted suicide was contrary to section 7 and could not be justified under section 1. The Court decided that both the evolution of section 7 jurisprudence and new evidence justified its reconsideration of *Rodriguez*.[120] The Court held that the assisted suicide offence affected the rights to life, liberty, and security of the person to the extent that it could force people to take their own lives before they required assistance from others, and to the extent it affected their autonomy and dignity over fundamental choices. It also decided that while the assisted suicide offence was not arbitrary because it did protect some vulnerable people from being coerced into taking their lives, it was overbroad to the extent that it affected competent adults with grievous and irremediable conditions (including disabilities as well as illnesses) who were dealing with enduring and intolerable suffering and clearly consented to the assistance of a physician in ending their lives. Although the objective of the offence in protecting the vulnerable was im-

---

119 Lamer CJC dissented, but relied on the equality right in s 15 of the *Charter*, rather than s 7.
120 *Carter*, above note 16.

portant enough to limit a *Charter* right and the offence was rationally connected to this objective, the overbroad offence failed the minimal impairment part of the section 1 test because it would apply to competent adults who made a free choice to escape intolerable suffering from an irremediable condition. The Court struck down the assisted suicide offence and a provision that no one could consent to their own death to this extent and suspended the declaration of invalidity for a year to provide Parliament with an opportunity to enact new legislation.

The Court extended the declaration of invalidity for another four months in recognition that Parliament did not operate for four months during the 2015 election, and in a 5:4 decision held the individuals eligible under its original decision or a new Quebec end-of-life law could obtain court-ordered exemptions from the assisted suicide offence during the suspended declaration of invalidity.[121] Shortly after this suspension expired, Parliament enacted new legislation that allowed for physician-assisted suicide, but only in cases when adults face enduring and intolerable suffering from an irremediable condition and when their death is reasonably foreseeable.[122] The government has defended this new legislation on the basis that it not only protects the vulnerable but also responds to concerns about suicide and negative views about the quality of life of the ill, elderly, and disabled. The new legislation has already been challenged under the *Charter*. As with much section 7 litigation, quite a bit will depend on how courts characterize the objectives of the new law and whether they determine that the limits on life, liberty, or security of the person are arbitrary or overbroad to those objectives, and whether the law in its pursuit of its objectives is grossly disproportionate to its effects.

c) Access to Health Care

In *Chaoulli v Quebec (Attorney General)*,[123] the Supreme Court held that although there is no free-standing right to health care, where the public health-care system fails to provide timely access, laws restricting access to private health-care services may be subject to *Charter* scrutiny. The Court held that delays in the public health-care system were serious, widespread, and potentially life threatening. Three judges held that a Quebec law prohibiting insurance to provide access to private health-care services should be struck down as an arbitrary interference with the section 7 right to timely access to necessary health-care

---

121 *Carter v Canada (Attorney General)*, 2016 SCC 4, discussed in Chapter 17.
122 *Criminal Code*, s 227 as amended by SC 2016, c 3.
123 *Chaoulli*, above note 17.

services. The three judges (McLachlin CJC and Major and Bastarache JJ concurring) relied on the judgment of Beetz J in *Morgentaler* for the broad proposition "that rules that endanger health arbitrarily do not comply with the principles of fundamental justice."[124] A fourth judge came to a similar conclusion, but on the basis of Quebec's *Charter of Human Rights and Freedoms*, which requires only the deprivation of life and security of the person and not that the deprivation be in violation of principles of fundamental justice. The three dissenting judges (Binnie and LeBel JJ, Fish J concurring) agreed that access to health care fell within the right to life and security of the person protected by section 7 of the Canadian *Charter*, but strongly disagreed that there was a violation of the principles of fundamental justice. They held that the *Morgentaler* case was distinguishable on the basis that abortions were restricted by the criminal sanction, and they were also arbitrarily prohibited because they could not be legally performed in certain parts of the country where there were no accredited abortion committees or hospitals that performed abortions.[125] The majority decision represents a potentially dramatic expansion of the reach of section 7 though, as discussed above, the Court has now opted for the somewhat more deferential standard that a law is only arbitrary if it has no rational connection with its objective, as opposed to the more exacting standard used by the three judges in *Chaoulli* who would have struck the law down on the basis that its effects on the life, liberty, and security of the person were not necessary to achieve the government's objectives.

Another significant health-care decision is that of the Court of Appeal for Ontario in *R v Parker*.[126] The court held that the prohibition of the cultivation and possession of marijuana violates the section 7 right to security of the person of an individual who requires the substance for the treatment of epilepsy. The Supreme Court subsequently held in *Smith* that a law that only allowed the use of dried marijuana for medical purposes was arbitrary and violated section 7 because the evidence suggested that such a restriction bore no relation to the government's objective in protecting health, and indeed might have the opposite effect, given evidence that marijuana use was safer when it was not smoked in its dried form. The Court also held that the denial of an exemption to a safe injection site in Vancouver was arbitrary because the available evidence suggested that the site contributed to public

---

124 *Ibid* at para 133.
125 *Ibid* at paras 259–63.
126 (2000), 49 O.R. (3d) 481.

health by helping to prevent overdoses and the spread of HIV and that it did not increase crime.[127]

2) Privacy, the Family, and Fundamental Personal Choices

In *B(R) v Children's Aid Society of Metropolitan Toronto*,[128] four members of the Supreme Court held that the right to liberty guaranteed by section 7 of the *Charter* must allow an individual "to make decisions that are of fundamental personal importance."[129] In *B(R)*, the parents were Jehovah's Witnesses who, based upon their religious beliefs, refused medical treatment for their child that would likely have involved a blood transfusion. In the words of La Forest J, "the right to nurture a child, to care for its development, and to make decisions for it in fundamental matters such as medical care, are part of the liberty interest of a parent."[130] In this view, any state intervention to protect a child's interests must be justified as conforming with the principles of fundamental justice.

Chief Justice Lamer took issue with this broad reading of section 7 and reiterated the view he had expressed in other cases limiting the protection of the section:

> The liberty in question must therefore be one that may be limited through the operation of some mechanism that involves and actively engages the principles of fundamental justice. Principles of fundamental justice pertain to the justice system. They are designed to govern both the means by which one may be brought before the judicial system and the conduct of judges and other actors once the individual is brought within it.[131]

Chief Justice Lamer would restrict the scope of section 7 to

> the conduct of the state when the state calls on law enforcement officials to enforce and secure obedience to the law, or invokes the law to deprive a person of liberty through judges, magistrates, ministers, board members, etc.[132]

Justice Sopinka found it unnecessary to deal with the point, while the remaining three judges held that the liberty interest in section 7 did not

---

127 *Smith*, above note 83; *Insite*, above note 17.
128 *B(R)*, above note 21.
129 *Ibid* at 368 (SCR).
130 *Ibid* at 370.
131 *Ibid* at 340.
132 *Ibid*.

allow a parent to deny necessary medical treatment to a child. In their view, the child's right to life, also guaranteed by section 7, placed limits on the parents' right to liberty.

All members of the Court agreed in the result, however, namely, that the wardship order depriving the parents of the right to decide for their child should be upheld. For the majority, La Forest J found that the parents' case could not survive the second stage of the section 7 analysis relating to the principles of fundamental justice. He found that the wardship provisions of the provincial child-welfare legislation conformed to the principles of fundamental justice. The parents had received notice of the wardship application, there had been a hearing before a judge, and they had been afforded an opportunity to present their views.

The Court examined a related issue in *AC v Manitoba (Director of Child and Family Services)*.[133] In that case, a medically required blood transfusion was ordered for a fourteen-year-old Jehovah's Witness. The Court upheld the constitutionality of provincial legislation that allowed medical treatment to be ordered for children under sixteen years of age when it was in their best interests while recognizing that those sixteen years or older could refuse treatment. The Court agreed that the ordering of treatment without the fourteen-year-old's consent violated her rights to liberty and security of the person. Nevertheless, the Court held that the legislation did not violate the principles of fundamental justice given that the best interest standard was sufficiently flexible to accommodate the autonomy interests of mature children. In other words, the legislation reflected "a proportionate response to the goal of protecting vulnerable young people from harm, while respecting the individuality and autonomy of those who are sufficiently mature to make a particular treatment decision."[134] The legislation also contemplated that children would be given notice and an opportunity to participate in the decision-making process, though that was not possible in this case of emergency treatment. Justice Binnie dissented in large part because he interpreted the statute as creating an irrebuttable presumption of incapacity. He thus found it violated the principles of fundamental justice because it was an arbitrary measure that could not advance the legitimate purpose of protecting children who were not capable of making decisions about medical treatment and because, in

---

133 2009 SCC 30.
134 *Ibid* at para 115.

his view (but not the majority's), it denied those under sixteen years of age an ability to rebut a presumption of incapacity.[135]

In *New Brunswick (Minister of Health and Community Services) v G(J)*,[136] a mother was denied legal aid when the state sought an order extending its custody of her three children for an additional six months. The Supreme Court found the denial of legal aid to be a violation of section 7 of the *Charter*. Chief Justice Lamer found that the decision affected that mother's security of the person by constituting a serious state interference with her psychological integrity. In a concurring judgment, L'Heureux-Dubé J (with Gonthier and McLachlin JJ concurring) added that the section 7 interests should be assessed with attention to concerns about gender equality and the disproportionate effects of child protection proceedings on single mothers. Consistent with a broader approach to the right to liberty, these judges also saw the case as implicating liberty interests.

Chief Justice Lamer held that "the principles of fundamental justice in child protection proceedings are both substantive and procedural. The state may only relieve a parent of custody when it is necessary to protect the best interests of the child, provided that there is a fair procedure for making this determination."[137] For the hearing to be fair, the parent must be able to participate effectively. Given the seriousness of the interests at stake, the complexity of the proceedings, and the mother's capacities, Lamer CJC concluded that her right to a fair hearing required that she be represented by counsel. This decision was made on the facts of the particular case and the Court warned as follows:

> . . . a parent need not always be represented by counsel in order to ensure a fair custody hearing. The seriousness and complexity of a hearing and the capacities of the parent will vary from case to case. Whether it is necessary for the parent to be represented by counsel is directly proportional to the seriousness and complexity of the proceedings, and inversely proportional to the capacities of the parent.[138]

The Court emphasized the connection between a fair process and the substantive goal of the hearing by concluding that "without the benefit of counsel, the appellant would not have been able to participate effectively at the hearing, creating an unacceptable risk of error in determining the children's best interests and thereby threatening to

---

135 *Ibid* at paras 223–24.
136 *New Brunswick v G(J)*, above note 3.
137 *Ibid* at para 70.
138 *Ibid* at para 86.

violate both the appellant's and her children's section 7 right to security of the person."[139] The Court's recognition in this case of the intimate connection between procedural and substantive justice was consistent with the Court's rejection in the 1985 *Motor Vehicle Act* case of a strict and artificial dichotomy between the two concepts.

In *Winnipeg Child and Family Services v KLW*,[140] the Supreme Court agreed that even the temporary apprehension of a mother's newborn child who is deemed in need of protection violated the mother's security of the person. However, the Court went on to hold that section 7 of the *Charter* was not violated because, in the context of protecting vulnerable children, prior judicial authorization of the state's apprehension of the child was not necessary. Two judges dissented on the basis that prior judicial authorization was necessary because, unlike in *B(R)*, apprehension of the child was not an emergency.[141] Justice L'Heureux-Dubé for the majority, however, stressed the difficulty of distinguishing between emergencies and non-emergencies in the child protection context. The Court did indicate that "the seriousness of the interests at stake demands that the resulting disruption of the parent-child relationship be minimized as much as possible by a fair and prompt post-apprehension hearing." As contemplated in *G(J)*, "in order to be fair, the hearing must involve reasonable notice with particulars to the parents, as well as an opportunity for them to participate meaningfully in the proceedings."[142]

Future cases are likely to raise difficult questions about the scope of the personal autonomy and privacy interests protected by section 7. They may arise, for example, with respect to government regulation of medical procedures, such as access to new reproductive technologies or with respect to parental control of children.

3) Extradition and Deportation to Face Death or Torture and National Security Matters

In *United States v Burns*,[143] the Supreme Court decided that the extradition of any fugitive without assurances from the foreign state that the death penalty would not be applied would, except in "exceptional cases," violate section 7 of the *Charter*. The decision marked a departure from two decisions by the Court a decade earlier in which it

---

139 *Ibid* at para 81.
140 [2000] 2 SCR 519.
141 *Ibid* at para 3, Arbour J (McLachlin CJC concurring).
142 *Ibid* at paras 122–23.
143 *Burns*, above note 18.

held that extradition of fugitives to the United States to face the death penalty was consistent with the *Charter*.[144] Although the principles of fundamental justice were still located in the basic tenets of the legal system, these tenets were informed by developments such as a growing recognition of wrongful convictions and an international trend against the imposition of the death penalty. The Court decided the case on broad principles that would apply to all fugitives. The decision did not, for example, depend on the fact that the fugitives in the particular case were Canadian citizens or young persons.

The Court emphasized that the ultimate issue under section 7 must be to ensure compliance with the principles of fundamental justice when depriving individuals of their rights to life, liberty, or security of the person. The idea that punishment or treatment that "shocks the conscience" would violate section 7 of the *Charter* should not be associated with public opinion polls. The words were not intended to signal an abdication by judges of their constitutional responsibilities in matters involving fundamental principles of justice. The Supreme Court quoted with approval the following passage written by President Arthur Chaskalson of the Constitutional Court of South Africa in declaring unconstitutional the death penalty in that country:

> Public opinion may have some relevance to the enquiry, but, in itself, it is no substitute for the duty vested in the Courts to interpret the Constitution and to uphold its provisions without fear or favour. If public opinion were to be decisive, there would be no need for constitutional adjudication. The protection of rights could then be left to Parliament, which has a mandate from the public, and is answerable to the public for the way its mandate is exercised . . . . The very reason for establishing the new legal order, and for vesting the power of judicial review of all legislation in the courts, was to protect the rights of minorities and others who cannot protect their rights adequately through the democratic process. Those who are entitled to claim this protection include the social outcasts and marginalised people of our society. It is only if there is a willingness to protect the worst and the weakest amongst us that all of us can be secure that our own rights will be protected.[145]

---

144 *Reference Re Ng Extradition (Can)*, [1991] 2 SCR 858, 84 DLR (4th) 498; *Kindler v Canada (Minister of Justice)*, [1991] 2 SCR 779, 84 DLR (4th) 438. For criticisms of the Court for not overruling these decisions, see R Haigh, "A Kinder, Gentler Supreme Court" (2001) 14 Sup Ct L Rev (2d) 139.

145 *Burns*, above note 18 at para 67, citing *S v Makwanyane*, 1995 (3) SA 391 at para 88 [*Makwanyane*].

Although the Supreme Court of Canada played an anti-majoritarian role in enforcing the constitution, it also emphasized that the interpretation of section 7 of the *Charter* required a balance of conflicting interests. It considered the state interests that would be advanced by extradition without assurances that the death penalty would not be applied but concluded that, except in undefined exceptional cases, these interests could be served by extradition with assurances that the death penalty would not be applied. For example, Canada could still honour its international obligations to assist in the return of fugitives to justice and could avoid becoming a "safe haven" for criminals if fugitives were extradited to foreign countries to face long prison sentences as opposed to the death penalty. The Court concluded:

> The arguments in favour of extradition without assurances would be as well served by extradition with assurances. There was no convincing argument that exposure of the respondents to death in prison by execution advances Canada's public interest in a way that the alternative, eventual death in prison by natural causes, would not. The arguments against extradition without assurances have grown stronger since this Court decided *Kindler* and *Ng* in 1991. Canada is now abolitionist for all crimes, even those in the military field. The international trend against the death penalty has become clearer. The death penalty controversies in the requesting State — the United States — are based on pragmatic, hard-headed concerns about wrongful convictions. None of these factors is conclusive, but taken together they tilt the section 7 balance against extradition without assurances.[146]

In *Suresh v Canada*,[147] the Supreme Court decided that the deportation of terrorists to face torture in a foreign country would, except in exceptional cases, violate section 7 of the *Charter*. The Court looked to both Canadian and international law to determine that torture offended the principles of fundamental justice. The Court held that section 7 would be violated even though the ultimate harm of torture, like the ultimate harm of death in *Burns*, would not be imposed by the Canadian government. There was a "sufficient causal connection between our government's participation and the deprivation ultimately effected."[148]

---

146 *Makwanyane, ibid* at paras 130–31.
147 *Suresh*, above note 3.
148 *Ibid* at para 54.

As in *Burns*, the Court emphasized that the interpretation of section 7 required a balance of conflicting interests. In *Suresh* the Court reasoned:

> On the one hand stands the state's genuine interest in combatting terrorism, preventing Canada from becoming a safe haven for terrorists, and protecting public security. On the other hand stands Canada's constitutional commitment to liberty and fair process. This said, Canadian jurisprudence suggests that this balance will usually come down against expelling a person to face torture elsewhere.[149]

The Court, however, refused to articulate an absolute rule against deportation to face torture. It stated:

> We do not exclude the possibility that in exceptional circumstances, deportation to face torture might be justified, either as a consequence of the balancing process mandated by s 7 of the *Charter* or under s 1. We may predict that it will rarely be struck in favour of expulsion where there is a serious risk of torture. However, as the matter is one of balance, precise prediction is elusive. The ambit of an exceptional discretion to deport to torture, if any, must await future cases.[150]

In cases in which there is a substantial risk of torture, section 7 of the *Charter* requires heightened procedural protection for a person who might be deported or extradited.[151] These procedural rights are informed by common law standards of procedural fairness that, the Court recognized, are basic tenets of the justice system. A full oral or judicial hearing is not required, but the applicant should be able to make written submissions, examine the materials considered by the minister, and receive written reasons for the decision whether to deport. In *Ahani v Canada (Minister of Citizenship and Immigration)*, a companion case to *Suresh*, the Court held that the person subject to deportation to Iran had not demonstrated a substantial risk of torture and section 7 of the *Charter* had not been violated.[152] Subsequently, Ahani unsuccessfully argued that he had a right under section 7 of the

---

149 *Ibid* at para 58.
150 *Ibid* at para 78. For an argument that extradition to face torture would violate Canada's international law obligations, see K Roach, "International, Domestic and Remedial Dialogues: The Canadian Experience" (2005) 40 Texas Intl LJ 537.
151 *Application under s 83.28 of the Criminal Code (Re)*, [2004] 2 SCR 248.
152 *Ahani v Canada (Attorney General)*, 2002 SCC 2, 208 DLR (4th) 57.

Charter to remain in Canada until his appeal to the United Nations Human Rights Commission was heard.[153]

A related question is whether section 7 is violated by procedures that allow the government to make submissions to a court without the affected party being present or having access to the information because of concerns about protecting national security and confidences received from foreign governments. In *Chiarelli v Canada (Minister of Employment and Immigration)*,[154] the Supreme Court held that security certificate procedures in immigration law did not violate section 7 of the *Charter*. The Court, however, stressed that the affected party whom the government sought to remove from Canada would have access to a summary of information presented to the judge. In *Ruby v Canada*,[155] the Supreme Court held that provisions in the *Privacy Act* that allow the government to make submissions about matters affecting national security and foreign confidences without the affected party being present did not violate section 7 of the *Charter*. The Court stressed, however, that fairness could be achieved through other procedural safeguards such as subsequent disclosure, judicial review, and rights of appeal.

In *Charkaoui v Canada*,[156] the Court significantly qualified its prior holding in *Chiarelli v Canada (Minister of Employment and Immigration)*.[157] It held that the security certificate process used under immigration law to detain those believed to be threats to national security violated section 7 of the *Charter* because it prevented any adversarial challenge to secret intelligence submitted by the government to the reviewing judge. Chief Justice McLachlin ruled for a unanimous Court that the detainees' rights to liberty and security of the person were violated even if, as non-citizens, they did not have a right not to be deported from Canada.[158] In a subsequent case involving the same detainees, the Court recognized the reality that "the consequences of security certificates are often more severe than those of many criminal charges."[159] This recognition underlines that section 7 applies beyond the criminal context.

---

153 *Ahani v Canada (Minister of CItizenship and Immigration)* (2002), 58 OR (3d) 107 (CA).
154 [1992] 1 SCR 711 [*Chiarelli*].
155 *Ruby*, above note 46.
156 *Charkaoui*, above note 2.
157 *Chiarelli*, above note 154.
158 *Charkaoui*, above note 2 at paras 12–18.
159 *Charkaoui v Canada*, 2008 SCC 38 at para 54. In that case, the Court held that section 7 of the *Charter* supported its interpretation of s 12 of the *Canadian Security Intelligence Service Act*, RSC 1985, c C-23, as requiring that all intelligence collected about the detainee be retained and made available to the ministers and judges who reviewed the security certificate.

The Court in *Charkaoui* recognized that the national security context would affect the content of the principles of fundamental justice but that "they cannot be permitted to erode the essence of section 7. The principles of fundamental justice cannot be reduced to the point where they cease to provide the protection of due process that lies at the heart of section 7 of the *Charter*."[160] In the end, the Court determined that the detainees had been denied their rights to a fair hearing and the right to know and answer the case against them because there was no adversarial challenge to the secret intelligence that the government provided to the judge to support the security certificate.

The Court held that the government had not justified this violation of section 7 of the *Charter* under section 1 because there was a variety of more proportionate alternatives that would allow adversarial challenge to the secret intelligence while protecting the state's interests in preventing harms to national security and persons that would be caused by the disclosure of the information. The Court suspended its declaration of invalidity for twelve months and, during that time, Parliament enacted new provisions that allow security-cleared special advocates, but not the detainee or the detainee's own lawyers, to see and challenge the secret intelligence that the government provides to the reviewing judge to justify the security certificate.[161] In 2014, the Court upheld this new regime from another section 7 challenge on the basis that while not perfect, it struck a reasonable balance between the competing interests in protecting secrets and treating those subject to security certificates fairly. The Court emphasized that those subject to the certificates should receive enough information to be able to defend themselves and that judges could grant and have granted special advocates permission when necessary to consult with detainees even after the special advocate had been given access to the secret material.[162]

---

160 *Charkaoui*, above note 2 at para 27.
161 The detainees brought other *Charter* challenges to the security certificate regime with mixed success. The Court held that a prolonged lack of review of the detention of foreign nationals as opposed to permanent residents violated the rights against arbitrary detention under s 9 of the *Charter* and the right to *habeas corpus* under s 10(c) of the *Charter*. At the same time, the Court held that prolonged detention did not amount to cruel and unusual punishment under s 12 because the detainees would have regular opportunities to review their detention. The Court also held that the lack of appeal rights and automatic detention did not violate unwritten rule of law principles and that the security certificate scheme which applies only to non-citizens did not violate their equality rights.
162 *Canada (Citizenship and Immigration) v Harkat*, [2014] 2 SCR 33.

In *Canada (Justice) v Khadr*,[163] the Supreme Court of Canada held that Canadian officials had violated the *Charter* and international law when they interrogated Omar Khadr, a Canadian citizen, in 2002 and 2003 while he was detained at the American military base at Guantanamo Bay, Cuba. The Court's decision that this case required the extraterritorial application of the *Charter* has been discussed above in Chapter 6. Having determined that the *Charter* applied in this case, the Court found a violation of section 7. What is significant, however, is that the content of the section 7 violation was not based on general principles of disclosure in domestic criminal cases under *R v Stinchcombe*.[164] Rather, the content of the disclosure duty was "defined by the nature of Canada's participation in the process that violated Canada's international human rights obligations."[165] Thus, in the context of this case, Omar Khadr only received disclosure of the records of the interviews that Canadian officials conducted with him at Guantanamo and the information that Canada gave to the United States as a direct consequence of the interviews at Guantanamo — interviews which, the Court held, violated Canada's international human rights obligations and required extraterritorial application of the *Charter*. Omar Khadr thus received far less disclosure than he would have under *Stinchcombe*.[166] Nevertheless, the case raises the interesting question of whether violations of Canada's international human rights obligations will necessarily also constitute violations of the principles of fundamental justice under section 7. If they do, then Canada's international human rights obligations may effectively have been constitutionalized as principles of fundamental justice under section 7, at least in the limited context of efforts to apply the *Charter* to the activities of Canadian officials acting outside Canada. If so, this could be a major step towards moving Canada away from a dualist tradition, in which its international commitments have to be specifically incorporated into domestic law, to one with less of a distinction between Canada's international and domestic constitutional obligations.

A subsequent case involving the same individual raised the issue of whether the prime minister's refusal to request Khadr's repatriation from Guantanamo Bay amounted to a violation of section 7.[167] Khadr

---

163 *Khadr*, above note 13.
164 [1991] 3 SCR 326, as discussed in Chapter 14.
165 *Khadr*, above note 13 at para 3.
166 The government was given an opportunity to make national security confidentiality claims before the material was disclosed. See *Khadr v Canada (Attorney General)*, 2008 FC 807.
167 *Canada (Prime Minister) v Khadr*, [2010] 1 SCR 44.

did not submit that Canada was required to repatriate citizens held abroad in similar circumstances; instead, he argued that the Canadian government's collaboration with the US military authorities violated his rights and that an order requiring the government to make efforts to have him returned to Canada was the appropriate remedy. The Supreme Court found that there was sufficient evidence of active participation by Canada in Khadr's detention in an illegal regime to establish a breach of his right to liberty and security of the person, and that the deprivation was contrary to the principles of fundamental justice:

> Interrogation of a youth, to elicit statements about the most serious criminal charges while detained in these conditions and without access to counsel, and while knowing that the fruits of the interrogations would be shared with the U.S. prosecutors, offends the most basic Canadian standards about the treatment of detained youth suspects.[168]

Nonetheless, the Court refused to grant Khadr the remedy he sought. Although there was a sufficient connection between the *Charter* breach and Khadr's continued detention, the remedy sought involved the Crown's prerogative over foreign affairs. While the courts have the authority to ensure that the constitution is respected even in this sensitive area, the appropriate remedy was to declare that the applicant's section 7 rights had been violated "and to leave it to the government to decide how best to respond to this judgment in light of current information, its responsibility for foreign affairs, and in conformity with the *Charter*."[169] The Court justified this limited remedy on the basis that the applicant was not under Canadian control, the likelihood that the proposed remedy would be effective was unclear, and the impact upon Canada's foreign relations was not a matter that could be properly assessed by the Court.

The government responded to this declaration with a diplomatic note requesting the United States not to use the fruits of Khadr's interrogations by Canadian officials at Guantanamo in his then pending military commission proceedings at Guantanamo. The United States refused to comply with this request, and a trial judge held in subsequent litigation that Khadr had still not obtained an effective remedy for the *Charter* violation.[170] This judgment was stayed pending an appeal, and an appeal has been declared moot given Khadr's subsequent

---

168 *Ibid* at para 25.
169 *Ibid* at para 39.
170 *Khadr v Canada (Prime Minister)*, 2010 FC 715, appeal dismissed as moot 2011 FCA 92.

decision to plead guilty before a military commission and his return to Canada to serve the remainder of his sentence.

4) Economic Rights

The extent to which the *Charter* should protect economic rights has been the subject of debate from its inception. The language of section 7 would seem to offer a basis to argue against restrictions on economic activity, since its guarantee of the right to liberty could arguably include a right to economic liberty. The right to security of the person, similarly, could encompass a right to economic security in the form of basic rights to social assistance or public housing. To be weighed against these claims, however, is the legislative history of the *Charter*, for property rights were expressly excluded from section 7, and subsequent efforts to add property rights have failed.

To date, the courts have, for the most part, been unsympathetic to those seeking to vindicate pure economic rights through the *Charter*. "The ability to generate business revenue by one's chosen means is not a right that is protected under s 7 of the *Charter*."[171] There have, however, been some successes in the lower courts. In *Wilson*, the British Columbia Court of Appeal upheld a challenge by doctors to provincial regulation of the number of doctors practising in the province and the location of their practices.[172] The weight of authority, however, is to the effect that section 7 does not protect a right to engage in a particular type of professional activity.[173]

More generally, as Dickson CJC stated, the right to liberty protected by section 7 "is not synonymous with unconstrained freedom" in the economic sphere and does not extend "to an unconstrained right to transact business whenever one wishes."[174] In a similar vein, Dickson CJC wrote that care must be taken lest the *Charter* "become an instrument of better situated individuals to roll back legislation which has as its object the improvement of the condition of less advantaged persons."[175] The Supreme Court has flatly rejected the possibility "that economic rights as generally encompassed by the term 'property' are not within the perimeters of the s 7 guarantee," and it has held, as well,

---

171 *Siemens v Manitoba (Attorney General)*, [2003] 1 SCR 6 at para 46.
172 *Wilson v British Columbia (Medical Services Commission)* (1988), 30 BCLR (2d) 1 (CA), leave to appeal to SCC refused, [1988] SCCA. No 352. See also *Mia v British Columbia (Medical Services Commission)* (1985), 17 DLR (4th) 385 (BCSC).
173 *Biscotti v Ontario Securities Commission* (1990), 74 OR (2d) 119 (HCJ).
174 *Edwards Books & Art Ltd v R*, [1986] 2 SCR 713 at 785–86, 35 DLR (4th) 1.
175 *Ibid* at 779 (SCR).

that corporations cannot claim the protection of economic rights under section 7.[176]

The question whether section 7 protects a basic minimum of social assistance still has not been conclusively resolved.[177] Social welfare advocates have pressed for constitutional amendments to add a "social charter" with court-enforced economic and social rights. There was a vigorous debate about the merits of such a change in the last major round of constitutional reform, but ultimately it was not included in the 1992 Charlottetown Accord.[178] In an early decision, Wilson J noted that the broad language of section 7 might extend to the provision of basic necessities, referring to the *Universal Declaration of Human Rights*, which includes a guarantee of "the right to a standard of living adequate for ... health and well-being ... including food, clothing, housing and medical care and necessary social services."[179] Interestingly, when rejecting the argument that section 7 includes property rights, the Supreme Court gave the following caveat, suggesting that consideration of this question is not altogether foreclosed:

> This is not to declare, however, that no right with an economic component can fall within "security of the person." Lower courts have found that the rubric of "economic rights" embraces a broad spectrum of interests, ranging from such rights, included in various international covenants, as rights to social security, equal pay for equal work, adequate food, clothing and shelter, to traditional property — contract rights. To exclude all of these at this early moment in the history of *Charter* interpretation seems to us precipitous. We do not, at this moment, choose to pronounce upon whether these economic rights fundamental to human life and survival are to be treated as though they are of the same ilk as corporate-commercial economic rights.[180]

---

176 *Irwin Toy*, above note 8 at 1003 (SCR). It should be noted, however, that s 1(a) of the *Canadian Bill of Rights* does protect the right of property. As discussed in Chapter 1, the *Bill of Rights* applies only to federal laws.

177 For discussion, see M Jackman, "The Protection of Welfare Rights under the *Charter*" (1988) 20 Ottawa L Rev 257; I Johnstone, "Section 7 of the *Charter* and Constitutionally Protected Welfare" (1988) 46 UT Fac L Rev 1.

178 P Macklem & C Scott, "Constitutional Ropes of Sand or Justiciable Guarantees? Social Rights in a New South African Constitution" (1992) 141 U Pa L Rev 1; J Bakan & D Schneiderman, eds, *Social Justice and the Constitution: Perspectives on a Social Union for Canada* (Ottawa: Carleton University Press, 1992).

179 *Singh*, above note 11 at 206–7.

180 *Irwin Toy*, above note 8 at 1003–4 (SCR).

The majority decision in *Gosselin v Quebec (Attorney General)*[181] disappointed those who hoped to gain *Charter* protection for basic welfare rights. For the time being, the Supreme Court refused to take that momentous step, but the decision explicitly leaves open the possibility that an affirmative right to basic subsistence might one day be protected by section 7. This cautious approach coincides with the Court's general reluctance to interpret *Charter* guarantees as including economic rights as well as the Court's tendency to defer to legislatures where complex economic and social-policy choices are at issue[182] and reflects a judicial unwillingness to become embroiled in social welfare policy. Writing for the majority in *Gosselin*, McLachlin CJC disagreed with Bastarache J that section 7 is necessarily limited to situations directly involving the administration of justice. However, McLachlin CJC ruled that the evidence of hardship in the case was insufficient to require the Court to interpret section 7 as having an affirmative element requiring the state to provide the elements necessary to the enjoyment of life, liberty, or security of the person. On the other hand, invoking the living tree metaphor, she explicitly left open the possibility that section 7 might one day evolve to embrace social welfare rights. Justice Arbour, with whom L'Heureux-Dubé J agreed, wrote a strong dissent, urging her colleagues to adopt an expansive definition of section 7 as including a positive component, such as the right to basic needs.

C. CONCLUSION

Section 7 gives rise to some of the most difficult issues arising under the *Charter*. The right to life, liberty, and security of the person invites the courts to engage a wide array of difficult moral and ethical issues. The Supreme Court's insistence that the principles of fundamental justice have substantive and not merely procedural content signalled an activist role for the Court. The Court initially proceeded cautiously in determining the ambit of section 7. However, more recently the Court has struck down a range of laws, including Quebec's laws prohibiting the purchase of private health insurance, various prostitution laws, the assisted suicide offence, and prohibitions on medical marijuana under section 7. Section 7 has emerged as a powerhouse of the *Charter*.

The Court has interpreted the rights to life, liberty, and security of the person in a broad and generous manner. In addition, however, an

---

181   *Gosselin*, above note 27.
182   See especially Chapter 4.

applicant must demonstrate that a principle of fundamental justice has been violated when these rights are infringed. The principles of fundamental justice are not a closed category and they continue to evolve. As will be seen in the next chapter, some principles of fundamental justice reflect principles of criminal justice, especially those relating to fault. The Court has also recognized principles of fundamental justice in relation to the diminished blameworthiness of youth and in relation to the lawyers' duties of loyalty to their client. At the same time, the Court has rejected other principles, such as the idea that the criminal law only should respond to harms, and that the law should always provide a remedy and pursue the best interests of children on the basis that they do not constitute manageable legal principles that are supported by a social consensus.

A number of more generic principles of fundamental justice have been recognized and they increasingly play an important role. The most important of these principles of fundamental justice are the principles that laws affecting life, liberty, or security of the person should not be unduly vague; they should not be arbitrary in the sense of not advancing their objectives; they should not be overbroad by going beyond what is necessary to achieve their objectives; and they should not have a gross disproportionality between their objectives and their harmful effects. These are powerful proportionality-based principles that have brought issues formerly regarded as falling outside the limits of constitutional adjudication within the ambit of section 7. The principle against overbreadth has most frequently been used, but the Court has also recently found that some laws are arbitrary in the sense that they do not rationally advance the government's objectives in relation to matters such as health and grossly disproportionate because they attempt to control nuisance at the price of placing sex workers lives in increased jeopardy. The Court has frequently used suspended declarations of invalidity in these cases in recognition that legislatures may have a legitimate role in regulating issues related to prostitution, assisted dying and the delivery of health care.

It is a virtual certainty that, in the years to come, the courts will continue to be asked to resolve the conflict between the individual's right to control his or her own body and the broader social interest in the protection of the sanctity of life. These issues have arisen in the past in relation to abortion and assisted suicide and are likely to arise in the future in connection with life-choice and health issues generated by the remarkable scientific advances in genetics. It is also likely that both the "haves" and the "have-nots" will continue to press for recognition of economic or social welfare rights. So far, the Court has shied away from interpreting the *Charter* to include economic rights, but equally it has refused unequivocally to preclude the protection of a right to basic rights of social assistance and housing.

FURTHER READINGS

BAKAN, J, & D SCHNEIDERMAN, eds, *Social Justice and the Constitution: Perspectives on a Social Union for Canada* (Ottawa: Carleton University Press, 1992)

BALA, N, "*R v DB*: The Constitutionalization of Adolescence" (2009) 47 Sup Ct L Rev 211

BRYDEN, P, "Section 7 of the *Charter* outside of the Criminal Context" (2005) 38 UBC Law Rev 507

CAMERON, J, "Positive Obligations under the *Charter*" (2003) 20 Sup Ct L Rev (2d) 65

CANADIAN BAR ASSOCIATION, *The Right to Publicly-Funded Legal Representation in Canada* (Ottawa: Canadian Bar Association, 2002)

CARTER, M, "*Carter v. Canada*: 'Societal Interests' under Sections 7 and 1" (2015) 78 Sask L Rev 209

COLVIN, E, "Section 7 of the *Charter of Rights and Freedoms*" (1989) 68 Can Bar Rev 560

DOWNIE, J, *Dying Justice: A Case for Decriminalizing Euthanasia and Assisted Suicide in Canada* (Toronto: University of Toronto Press, 2004) c 12

GARANT, P, "Vie, liberté, sécurité et justice fundamentale" in G Beaudoin & E Mendes, eds, Canadian Charter of Rights and Freedoms, 4th ed (Toronto: LexisNexis, 2005)

HOGG, P, "The Brilliant Career of Section 7 of the *Charter*" (2012) 58 Sup Ct L Rev (2d) 195

JACKMAN, M, "The Protection of Welfare Rights under the *Charter*" (1988) 20 Ottawa L Rev 257

———, "Poor Rights: Using the *Charter* to Support Social Welfare Claims" (1993) 19 Queen's LJ 65

JENKINS, D, "Rethinking *Suresh*: Refoulement to Torture under the *Charter*" (2009) 47 Atla L Rev 125

JOHNSTONE, I, "Section 7 of the *Charter* and Constitutionally Protected Welfare" (1988) 46 UT Fac L Rev 1

KING, J, *Judging Social Rights* (Cambridge: Cambridge University Press, 2012)

MORTON, FL, & R KNOPFF, Charter *Politics* (Scarborough, ON: Nelson, 1992) c 10

NEWMAN, D, "Judicial Method and Three Gaps in the Supreme Court of Canada's Assisted Suicide Judgment in *Carter*" (2015) 78 Sask L Rev 217

ROACH, K, "*Charkaoui* and Bill C-3: Some Implications for Anti-Terrorism Policy and Dialogue between Courts and Legislatures" (2008) 42 Sup Ct L Rev (2d) 281

————, "The *Charter* and National Security" in J Kelly & C Manfredi, eds, *Contested Constitutionalisms* (Vancouver: University of British Columbia Press, 2009)

SINGLETON, T, "The Principles of Fundamental Justice, Societal Interests and Section 1 of the *Charter*" (1995) 74 Can Bar Rev 407

STEWART, H, *Fundamental Justice* (Toronto: Irwin Law, 2012)

————, "*Bedford* and the Structure of Section 7" (2015) 60 McGill LJ 575

————, "The Constitutionality of the New Sex Work Law" (2016) 54 Alta L Rev 69

WISEMAN, D, "The *Charter* and Poverty: Beyond Injusticiability" (2001) 51 UTLJ 425

CHAPTER 14

RIGHTS IN THE CRIMINAL PROCESS

The *Charter of Rights and Freedoms* has had a profound impact in the area of criminal law. *Charter* claims are routinely asserted in criminal proceedings. The courts have decided thousands of cases, making detailed consideration of investigative techniques, pre-trial procedures, and the trial process itself. Here we offer a sampling of some of the most significant issues raised by the *Charter*.

One way to examine the impact of the *Charter* is to use the abstract models of the criminal process first put forward by the American scholar Herbert Packer to assess the influence of the American Bill of Rights on the criminal justice system.[1] The first is the "crime control model" in which the focus of the criminal justice system is to find and punish the guilty through efficient police and prosecutorial work, usually leading to a guilty plea. The second is the "due process" model in which the focus is on controlling the exercise of police powers through an elaborate series of procedural guarantees, violation of which results in the release of the accused regardless of guilt or innocence. The Canadian criminal justice system, in common with the systems of other liberal democracies, has always exhibited features of both models.

Crime control is bound to be a central feature of any system of criminal justice. The fundamental reason for the existence of the criminal

---

1   H. Packer, *The Limits of the Criminal Sanction* (Stanford: Stanford University Press, 1968). See also K. Roach, *Due Process and Victims' Rights: The New Law and Politics of Criminal Justice* (Toronto: University of Toronto Press, 1999).

law is to protect society from those individuals whose behaviour causes serious harm. The severe sanction of deprivation of liberty and imprisonment is justified by the criminal's significant departure from the norms of civil society and by the need to punish such conduct in order to protect society from further transgressions.

Our system of criminal justice has always recognized, however, that crime control is achieved through the assertion of coercive state power, which inevitably involves risks of abuse and oppression. To guard against these risks, the criminal process has evolved a range of procedural protections, designed to ensure that individuals suspected of crime are dealt with fairly and humanely. These guarantees, products of both the common law tradition and statutes enacted by Parliament, include such basic rights as the presumption of innocence, the right to silence, *habeas corpus*, and the right to be tried by a jury of one's peers. These procedural norms, identified as elements of the "due process" model, restrain the exercise of coercive power in a significant way. They are designed to protect the innocent and to avoid the risk of wrongful conviction. But they also benefit the guilty, since they ensure that everyone caught up in the criminal process should be treated fairly. A part of our tradition is the principle that it is better that ten guilty persons should go free than one innocent person be convicted. It is not possible to have a scheme of rights that protects only those who are innocent of wrongdoing. Procedural rights often cause consternation when they assist the guilty. Yet, that is a price to be paid in a free society where rights are enjoyed by all individuals.

The criminal justice system is continually striving to strike an appropriate balance between crime control and the protection of society on the one hand, and fairness to accused persons and the prevention of abuse of police powers on the other. The courts have always played an important role in this exercise. However, by entrenching a number of procedural rights in the constitution, the *Charter of Rights and Freedoms* has increased the courts' responsibility to delineate the line between crime control and due process. In addition, other values, such as the right of privacy and other rights of victims of crime, and the equality rights of groups such as women, children, and minorities who may be disproportionately subject to some crimes, are relevant. While the fundamental purpose of the Canadian criminal justice system remains the protection of society, there can be little question that the result of the courts' efforts has been to move Canada closer towards the due-process end of the spectrum. At the same time, many of the *Charter* decisions examined in this chapter demonstrate the reality of dialogue between courts and legislatures under the *Charter*. Parliament has frequently responded to the Supreme Court's due-process decisions with new legislation that, while accommodating due-process rights also advances society's interests in controlling crime.

A. SECTION 7 AND THE PRINCIPLES OF FUNDAMENTAL JUSTICE

1) The Fault Element

As noted in Chapter 13, a crucial question that was faced in the early years of the *Charter* was whether the very general language of section 7 permitted the courts to review the substance of laws or whether judicial review was restricted to procedural matters. In *Reference Re s 94(2) of the Motor Vehicle Act (BC)*,[2] the Supreme Court held that "the principles of fundamental justice" are not restricted to procedural values but have substantive content as well. The case involved a fundamental issue in the criminal law, namely, the extent to which moral blameworthiness should be a requirement for conviction. Criminal offences typically require proof of two elements: harm and fault. Ordinarily, the fact that harm has resulted from someone's conduct is not enough to support a conviction. To label someone a criminal, we must also be satisfied that the individual charged is morally blameworthy. The behaviour of the individual accused of a crime must be shown to have fallen short of an expected standard by intending, or at least foreseeing, the forbidden harm. However, the fault requirement is often difficult to prove, and the legislature may judge it to be in the public interest to impose a sanction without proof of fault of the accused. *Re Motor Vehicle Act* involved such a law. It imposed a mandatory penalty of imprisonment for driving an automobile while one's licence was under suspension. There were a number of situations that could lead to a licence suspension without the knowledge of the licence holder. An individual might not have even been aware of a licence suspension, and so the result was that a person who had no criminal intent could face a mandatory jail sentence. In the Supreme Court of Canada's view, such a situation violated the principles of fundamental justice:

> A law that has the potential to convict a person who has not really done anything wrong offends the principles of fundamental justice and, if imprisonment is available as a penalty, such a law then violates a person's right to liberty under s 7 of the *Canadian Charter of*

---

2   [1985] 2 SCR 486, 24 DLR (4th) 536 [*Re Motor Vehicle Act*].

Rights and Freedoms . . . . In other words, absolute liability and imprisonment cannot be combined.[3]

The Supreme Court has subsequently indicated that convicting a person of an offence without the proof of any fault would be acceptable under the *Charter*, provided that the person was not sentenced to imprisonment.[4] Even though conviction of the blameless would violate the principles of fundamental justice, it would violate section 7 of the *Charter* only if the conviction resulted in a deprivation of the right to life, liberty, or security of the person.

The Supreme Court has given further consideration to the principles limiting the imposition of no-fault liability in criminal law in a number of situations. It struck down a "statutory rape" offence that made sex with a girl under fourteen years of age a crime punishable by life imprisonment, even if the accused honestly believed that the girl was older and had consented. The Court's concern was that "a person who is mentally innocent of the offence — who has no *mens rea* [or fault] with respect to an essential element of the offence — may be convicted and sent to prison."[5] Parliament responded with new offences to protect children from sexual interference that required the accused to take all reasonable steps to ascertain the age of the child.

The *Criminal Code* "constructive or felony murder" provisions, obviating the need to prove an intent to kill if death is caused in the commission of certain offences and in specified circumstances, were challenged as violating the principles of fundamental justice. While there is no question that an individual who causes death in the commission of an offence is guilty of manslaughter — a serious crime — the issue was whether an accused who did not intend to kill and did not even foresee the possibility that death might result should be convicted of murder. The Supreme Court ruled that, absent proof of moral blameworthiness connected to the death, such an individual could not be found guilty of murder, the most serious offence known to the law. At a minimum, said the majority, there must be proof beyond a reasonable doubt of at least subjective foreseeability that the conduct could result in death:[6]

The punishment for murder is the most severe in our society and the stigma that attaches to a conviction for murder is similarly extreme

---

3 *Ibid* at 492 (SCR), Lamer J.
4 *R v Pontes*, [1995] 3 SCR 44, 100 CCC (3d) 353.
5 *R v Hess*, [1990] 2 SCR 906, 59 CCC (3d) 161 at 168.
6 *R v Vaillancourt*, [1987] 2 SCR 636, 47 DLR (4th) 399 [*Vaillancourt*]; see also *R v Martineau*, [1990] 2 SCR 633, 58 CCC (3d) 353.

.... [T]here must be some special mental element with respect to the death before a culpable homicide can be treated as a murder. That special mental element gives rise to the moral blameworthiness which justifies the stigma and sentence attached to a murder conviction.[7]

The Court's list of the most serious "stigma" based offences that require subjective fault in relation to all aspects of the offence has remained short. It includes murder, attempted murder,[8] and war crimes,[9] but does not include other serious criminal offences such as manslaughter.

Regulatory offences are at the other end of the seriousness spectrum. They are enacted to enforce non-criminal behaviour with regard to matters that are not inherently unlawful but that require standards to protect an important public interest. These offences do not carry the same moral connotation and have long been regarded as different from traditional criminal law offences. In a 1991 decision, the Supreme Court held that the *Charter* does not require the same degree of moral culpability as a prerequisite for conviction of a regulatory offence. Where such offences carry the possibility of imprisonment, section 7 does require a minimal degree of fault, but that is satisfied by a standard of negligence. Requiring the accused to establish on a balance of probabilities that he or she was not negligent was also accepted as a reasonable limit on the presumption of innocence protected under section 11(d) of the *Charter*.[10]

Between these two extremes are criminal offences less serious than murder but more grave than regulatory offences. In this grey area, the Supreme Court has insisted upon a minimal level of culpability as a prerequisite for conviction. The constitutional standard is satisfied by conduct judged blameworthy on an objective standard and fault need not relate to all aspects of the harm being punished. Thus, offences such as unlawfully causing bodily harm,[11] dangerous driving,[12] and manslaughter[13] have been upheld despite the fact that they do not require proof of fault in relation to all aspects of the prohibited act and require proof of fault only on an objective rather than a subjective standard. Negligence is measured on the basis of a reasonable person standard. Constitutional fault standards are less demanding of the state than common law presumptions, such as those against absolute liability and

---

7   *Vaillancourt*, above note 6 at 653–54 (SCR), Lamer J.

8   *R v Logan*, [1990] 2 SCR 731, 58 CCC (3d) 391.

9   *R v Finta*, [1994] 1 SCR 701, 88 CCC (3d) 417.

10   *R v Wholesale Travel Group Inc.*, [1991] 3 SCR 154, 84 DLR (4th) 161.

11   *R v DeSousa*, [1992] 2 SCR 944, 95 DLR (4th) 595.

12   *R v Hundal*, [1993] 1 SCR 867, 79 CCC (3d) 97.

13   *R v Creighton*, [1993] 3 SCR 3, 105 DLR (4th) 632.

those in favour of proof of subjective fault in relation to all aspects of the prohibited act.[14] One reason may be that common law presumptions can be rebutted by clear parliamentary intent whereas section 7 *Charter* violations are difficult, if not impossible, to justify under section 1 of the *Charter*. The Court has, however, stressed that section 7 of the *Charter* requires more than negligence that would produce civil liability: there needs to be proof of a marked departure from the standards of a reasonable person. The Court was concerned that

> if every departure from the civil norm is to be criminalized, regardless of the degree, we risk casting the net too widely and branding as criminals persons who are in reality not morally blameworthy. Such an approach risks violating the principle of fundamental justice that the morally innocent not be deprived of liberty.[15]

The marked departure standard has now emerged as a constitutional minimum whenever negligence is used as a form of criminal liability.

2) Vague, Arbitrary, Overbroad, and Grossly Disproportionate Offences

As discussed in greater depth in Chapter 13, criminal offences can also violate section 7 of the *Charter* if they are excessively vague so as not to give fair notice to people of what is prohibited or to place limits on law enforcement discretion. However, the courts have almost always rejected claims on this basis and held that all Parliament must do is to determine an ascertainable standard of conduct that establishes a risk zone alerting the individual to the peril of conviction and providing a basis for legal debate. For example, an offence of unduly lessening competition and a defence that allows the reasonable use of corrective force have been held not to be unconstitutionally vague. So too has an offence of disposing and concealing of a child that died before birth.[16] In determining whether a criminal law is so vague that it fails to provide fair notice or limit the exercise of law enforcement discretion, the courts will consider their ability to provide clearer meaning to broad legislative provisions through judicial interpretation.

---

14 *R v Sault Ste Marie*, [1978] 2 SCR 1299; *R v Pappajohn*, [1980] 2 SCR 120.

15 *R v Beatty*, [2008] 1 SCR 49 at para 34.

16 *R v Nova Scotia Pharmaceutical Society*, [1992] 2 SCR 606, 93 DLR (4th) 36; *Canadian Foundation for Children, Youth and the Law v Canada (Attorney General)*, [2004] 1 SCR 76 [*Canadian Foundation for Children, Youth and the Law*]; *R v Levkovic*, 2013 SCC 25.

Criminal laws or, indeed, other laws that infringe the right to life, liberty, or security of the person will violate section 7 of the *Charter* if they are arbitrary in the sense of not being rationally connected to their legislative objectives. The Supreme Court has held that a refusal of the minister of health to grant a statutory exemption from drug laws to allow a safe injection site to continue to operate on Vancouver's downtown Eastside would be arbitrary: all the evidence in the case suggested that a continued exemption would further the legislative purposes of protecting health and controlling crime.[17] The Court also held that a drug law was arbitrary because it only allowed the medical use of marijuana in dried form, even though the evidence indicated that other forms of marijuana were safer to use.[18]

Most criminal laws will not be held to be arbitrary in the sense that they have no relation to their legislative purposes. The Supreme Court has found that the assisted suicide offence was not arbitrary to its purpose in protecting the vulnerable from being coerced into ending their lives, even though it was overbroad.[19] Similarly, offences against the keeping of bawdy houses and public solicitation of prostitution were not arbitrary because they had some relation to the objective of preventing nuisances, even though they were overbroad in going beyond what was necessary to fulfill that purpose, and were grossly disproportionate by pursuing the end of preventing nuisance at the expense of increased risk to the lives of sex workers.[20] A relatively deferential approach to arbitrariness in some sense mimics the rational connection of the section 1 test for justifying limits on rights, and, in most cases, it can be expected that criminal laws will rationally advance their legislative objective in a manner that is not arbitrary.

The prostitution case, however, reveals that section 7 may still be violated by criminal laws that are neither vague nor arbitrary because the Court went on to hold that the living off the avails and bawdy house offences violated section 7 because they were overbroad. A law will be overbroad if the means it uses are far more sweeping than necessary to achieve the legislative objective. The Supreme Court has found a law that made it a criminal offence for any sexual offender to loiter in or near a school ground, playground, public park, or bathing area overbroad to the legitimate legislative purpose of preventing sexual offences against children. The law was overbroad because it applied to all sexual offenders and because it applied to loitering in many locations

---

17   *Canada (Attorney General) v PHS Community Services*, 2011 SCC 44 [*Insite*].
18   *R v Smith*, [2015] 2 SCR 602.
19   *Carter v Canada (Attorney General)*, [2015] 1 SCR 331.
20   *Canada (Attorney General) v Bedford*, [2013] 3 SCR 1101 [*Bedford*].

even when children were not present.[21] The new offence, enacted in response, applied to those convicted of sexual offences with children and to places where those under 16 years of age are present or can reasonably be expected to be present: it is an example of a better-tailored law. In this respect, overbreadth plays a role somewhat analogous to the minimal-impairment requirement of the section 1 test for limiting rights, though an important difference is overbreadth analysis under section 7 is not related to the overall social benefits and costs of a law. The Supreme Court has found a law overbroad because it kept those not fit to stand because of mental disorder in the criminal process even if they were not a significant threat to public safety.[22] On the other hand, the Court held that the offence of participating in a terrorist group was not overbroad to the legislative objective of preventing terrorism, especially given the restrictions that a proper interpretation of the Act and fault elements placed on the ambit of the impugned offences.[23]

In *Bedford*, the Supreme Court found that the bawdy house and public solicitation for the purposes of prostitution offences were grossly disproportionate in the sense that they imposed far greater harms to the safety of prostitutes required to conduct sex work in the street and opposed to the benefits achieved by controlling nuisances. The Court stressed that gross disproportionality under section 7 was based in a qualitative comparison of harms. In other words, a law that risked the life of only one sex worker for the much less important objective of preventing nuisances could violate section 7 on that basis. The Court has stressed that gross disproportionality is a high standard for the applicant to satisfy.[24] The Supreme Court has found that the denial of an exemption from drug laws in the *Insite* case was grossly disproportionate when the harms of not facilitating the use of clean needles to inject drugs were compared with the harms avoided by the enforcement of drug laws given the evidence in the case that the existence of the supervised injection site on Vancouver's downtown Eastside had health benefits without increasing crime.[25]

The Supreme Court has recognized that arbitrariness and overbreadth focus on a lack of a fit between the means used in laws and the ends that Parliament pursues, while gross disproportionality is related

---

21 *R v Heywood*, [1994] 3 SCR 761.
22 *R v Demers*, [2004] 2 SCR 489 at para 43 [*Demers*].
23 *R v Khawaja*, 2012 SCC 69 at para 57 [*Khawaja*].
24 *Ibid*.
25 *Insite*, above note 17.

to a comparison of the type of harm caused by the law and the type of harm that the law tries to prevent.[26]

3) Defences

Section 7 of the *Charter* has been interpreted not only to influence fault elements and the definition of criminal offences, but also to influence the substance of a number of defences to crimes. In the controversial *Daviault* case, a majority of the Supreme Court held that the denial of a defence of extreme intoxication to a charge of sexual assault violated section 7 of the *Charter* because it could allow a person who was not at fault at the time of the offence to be convicted of the offence.[27] Parliament quickly responded with new legislation deeming that the act of being so extremely intoxicated so that a person would not be aware that he or she was committing an assault or a sexual assault was a sufficient form of fault to convict that person of assault or sexual assault. Lower courts have been divided about the constitutionality of this provision, and the Supreme Court will eventually have to decide the issue.

Section 7 of the *Charter* has also been interpreted to prevent the conviction of a person who acted in a morally involuntary manner because, for example, he or she was under duress and was responding reasonably to threats. The Supreme Court held that *Criminal Code* requirements that the threats must be of immediate death or bodily harm from a person who is present at the time that the crime was committed were too strict and violated the *Charter*.[28] Like the fault cases discussed above, this case affirms that section 7 is not limited to the procedural requirement of a fair hearing, but also involves the substantive fairness of laws. There are limits to the degree to which the *Charter* will affect the substantive law of defences in criminal law. The Supreme Court has refused to invalidate section 43 of the *Criminal Code*, which authorizes the use of reasonable corrective force against children on the basis that the defence is inconsistent with the best interests of children. As discussed in Chapter 13, the Court concluded that there was not enough consensus to justify enforcing the best interests of the child principle as a principle of fundamental justice under section 7 of the *Charter*.[29] At the same time, the Court placed new limits on this defence as a matter of statutory interpretation.

---

26   *Bedford*, above note 20 at paras 108–9.
27   *R v Daviault*, [1994] 3 SCR 63, 93 CCC (3d) 21 [*Daviault*].
28   *R v Ruzic*, [2001] 1 SCR 687, 153 CCC (3d) 1.
29   *Canadian Foundation for Children, Youth and the Law*, above note 16.

4) Procedural Rights

The general language of section 7 has been found by the Supreme Court of Canada to incorporate and require respect for certain procedural rights that are not specifically guaranteed by sections 8 to 14 of the *Charter*. In a variety of situations, the Court has held that the "principles of fundamental justice" are broader than the specific rights enjoyed at common law or under particular provisions of the *Charter*. This understanding has had significant implications for all stages of the criminal process.

a) Right to Silence

R v Hebert[30] dealt with a statement made by an accused person, detained in custody, to an undercover police officer posing as a fellow prisoner. The accused had received legal advice and indicated that he did not wish to make a statement. The undercover officer engaged the accused in conversation and an incriminating statement was made. The specific right to counsel (section 10(b)) and right against self-incrimination (section 11(c)) conferred by the *Charter* did not apply in these circumstances. The Supreme Court held, however, that the principles of fundamental justice implicitly include a broader right to silence. An accused person has the right to choose whether or not to speak to the authorities. The police are permitted to question an accused person, but they are not entitled to use their superior power to override the accused's decision to assert his legal rights. The Court viewed the use of an undercover agent as a trick, designed to deprive the accused of the choice he had made upon legal advice to remain silent in the face of questioning. It found that the accused's right not to be deprived of life, liberty, or security of the person except in accordance with the principles of fundamental justice had been denied. A later decision[31] applied this principle where a statement was elicited by a prisoner acting as a police informer: in the circumstances, the informer was an agent of the state and, but for his intervention, the statement would not have been given by the accused. A subsequent case, however, held the right to silence was not violated simply by the accused's conversation with an undercover police officer posing as a fellow prisoner.[32]

The Court has held that the right to silence under section 7 of the *Charter* was not violated in a case where the accused was arrested for murder, able to consult with counsel, and repeatedly questioned despite telling the police on numerous occasions that he did not wish to

---

30   [1990] 2 SCR 151, 57 CCC (3d) 1.
31   *R v Broyles*, [1991] 3 SCR 595, 68 CCC (3d) 308.
32   *R v Liew*, [1999] 3 SCR 227, 137 CCC (3d) 353.

talk to them. The majority of the Court held that in the case of police interrogations, the right to silence will not be violated so long as the accused's subsequent statement to the police was voluntary. It rejected a requirement that the police hold off questioning those who assert a right to silence on the basis that such a requirement would not strike the appropriate balance between the state's interest in the investigation of crime and the protection of the accused from the superior resources of the state. Four judges in dissent argued that the persistence of the police in this case violated the accused's rights to silence and counsel. They stressed that police simply ignored the detainee's choice to remain silent. They argued that there was no evidence that respecting the accused's choice whether to speak to the police would have a devastating impact on criminal investigations. In addition, they argued that, under a purposive approach, an accused's right to silence could be violated even though the accused's statement would satisfy common law requirements that statements given to the police be proven to be voluntary.[33]

The right to silence, along with other *Charter* rights, means that the accused may not be required to testify at their trials. Such a right to silence has not, however, been interpreted to mean that judges must instruct the jury about the accused's right to silence. In one case, a majority of the Court held that such an instruction was unnecessary even though counsel for a co-accused asked the jury to infer the guilt of the other accused from that accused's failure to testify. The majority of the Court was confident that the jury would not have used the accused's silence and failure to testify as evidence of guilt. Four judges, however, dissented and argued that a specific instruction to this effect was required.[34]

b) Right against Self-Incrimination

Although there are more specific protections against self-incrimination in sections 11(c) and 13 of the *Charter*, which will be examined below, there is also an important residual right against self-incrimination under section 7 of the *Charter*. The Supreme Court has not interpreted this right to allow a person "to take the Fifth" (as in the United States) by refusing to answer questions. Rather, it has held that the right will be protected if a person is protected from the use and derivative use of compelled statements in subsequent proceedings. For example, business people can be compelled to produce records and be examined on

---

33   *R v Singh*, [2007] 3 SCR 405.
34   *R v Prokofiew*, 2012 SCC 49.

them under a Securities Act, but the fruits of such compelled incrimination or evidence derived from such information cannot be used against them in subsequent proceedings. If the predominant purpose of the state was to obtain evidence to be used against that person, section 7 of the *Charter* would exempt the person from having to testify.[35] Use and derivative use immunity has been applied to motorists who are compelled under a *Motor Vehicle Act* to provide an accident report,[36] but the right against self-incrimination does not apply to fishing logs that must be kept to prevent over-fishing.[37] The Court has thus taken a contextual approach to the right against self-incrimination.

In 2004, the Supreme Court upheld the constitutionality of investigative hearings introduced after the 11 September 2001 terrorist attacks as a means to compel people to disclose information about terrorism. The majority of the Court held that the new procedure was consistent with the right against self-incrimination under section 7 of the *Charter* because no evidence compelled from a person at an investigative hearing or evidence derived from such evidence could be used in subsequent proceedings, with the exception of a perjury prosecution. The Court, however, extended the statutory use and derivative use immunity provisions to apply in subsequent extradition and immigration proceedings, as well as in criminal proceedings.[38] The Court also indicated that an investigative hearing conducted for the predominant purpose of obtaining evidence to be used in a subsequent criminal trial of a suspect would violate the right against self-incrimination in section 7 of the *Charter*. Three judges dissented on the basis that it was an abuse of process to attempt to use an investigative hearing with respect to a reluctant witness in the middle of the ongoing Air India terrorism trial. Two judges dissented on the more general basis that the procedure violated judicial independence by requiring judges to preside over what were essentially police investigations.[39] The majority, however, stressed the important role that the presiding judge and counsel representing the reluctant witness would play at an investigative hearing, as well as the rebuttable presumption that the investigative hearing be held in open

---

35 *British Columbia (Securities Commission) v Branch*, [1995] 2 SCR 3, 97 CCC (3d) 505 [*Branch*].

36 *R v White*, [1999] 2 SCR 417.

37 *R v Fitzpatrick*, [1995] 4 SCR 154.

38 The right against self-incrimination in s 7 of the *Charter* also requires that use and derivative use immunity apply to any breaches of solicitor–client privilege that may be necessary because someone's innocence is at stake: *R v Brown*, [2002] 2 SCR 185.

39 *Application under s 83.28 of the Criminal Code*, [2004] 2 SCR 248.

court.[40] One judge was prepared to hold that the section 7 right against self-incrimination was violated in a "Mr. Big" case (where undercover police officers held out rewards to an accused if he confessed), but the majority warned that section 7 concerns about self-incrimination were not a "freestanding legal rule." They determined that adjustments to the common law rules governing the acceptance of statements and abuse of process were adequate to regulate such operations.[41]

c) Right to Disclosure of the Prosecution's Case

In *R v Stinchcombe*,[42] the Supreme Court interpreted section 7 to impose upon the Crown a duty of disclosure. The Court was clearly influenced by a number of recent Canadian *causes célèbres* where miscarriages of justice had occurred because the Crown had failed to disclose information important to the defence. It held that, while the defence has no obligation to assist the prosecution, the Crown is obliged to use the information it has in the interests of justice. The Crown, said the Court, must disclose prior to trial any evidence it intends to use and also any evidence that might assist the accused, even if the Crown does not intend to adduce such evidence at trial. The position of Crown counsel, representing the public interest in seeing that justice be done, is not that of an ordinary adversary. Crown counsel are expected to act in the interest of justice, and the fruits of a police investigation must be used in a manner that respects the right of the accused to make full answer and defence, "one of the pillars of criminal justice on which we heavily depend to ensure that the innocent are not convicted."[43] This decision has had a profound effect on the behaviour of both police and Crown counsel. Disclosure to the accused has now become a routine step in pre-trial proceedings.

The Supreme Court has stressed the breadth of the Crown's duty to disclose evidence whenever there is a reasonable possibility that it will be useful to the accused in making full answer and defence. The Crown's disclosure obligations include evidence that the Crown does not propose to use in its case.[44] The Court has affirmed this broad right to disclosure, noting that the police, like the Crown, have a duty to disclose all relevant evidence, including information about police misconduct that could affect the case.[45] The Crown should also disclose

40   *Re Vancouver Sun*, [2004] 2 SCR 332.

41   *R v Hart*, 2014 SCC 52 at para 124.

42   [1991] 3 SCR 326, 68 CCC (3d) 1.

43   *Ibid* at 336 (SCR), Sopinka J.

44   *R v Taillefer; R v Duguay*, [2003] 3 SCR 307 [*Taillefer*].

45   *R. v McNeil*, [2009] 1 SCR 66 [*McNeil*].

criminal background checks that it might have the police conduct on potential jurors. A failure to disclose such jury vetting will result in an unfair trial, however, only if the disclosure would have resulted in a different and perhaps partial jury.[46]

d) Right to Make Full Answer and Defence

Section 7 of the *Charter* protects the fair trial rights of accused persons and has had a significant impact upon the trial process. The accused's right to full answer and defence is related to the accused's right to disclosure of the prosecution's case, but the right to full answer and defence will be violated only if there is a reasonable possibility that the failure to disclose affected the outcome of the trial or its overall fairness. The minimum remedy for a violation of this important right will be the order of a new trial.[47]

The right to make full answer and defence has played an important and controversial role in the prosecution of sexual assault cases. In *Seaboyer*, a *Criminal Code* provision limiting the right of an accused charged with sexual assault to cross-examine a complainant as to prior sexual conduct was struck down as being inconsistent with the principles of fundamental justice.[48] While the majority recognized the importance of protecting complainants in sexual assault cases from unjustified and unwarranted inquiry into their personal histories, it concluded that a complete ban on any questions regarding past sexual conduct went too far and might preclude the trial court from hearing a legitimate defence. As McLachlin J explained, eliminating the possibility that the judge and jury might draw unwarranted and inappropriate conclusions based on sexist or stereotypical attitudes carried the risk of convicting the innocent:

> [I]t exacts as a price the real risk that an innocent person may be convicted. The price is too great in relation to the benefit secured, and cannot be tolerated in a society that does not countenance in any form the conviction of the innocent.[49]

The *Seaboyer* decision was decried by feminist groups that had lobbied for the law and saw it as vital in encouraging women to come forward to the police with complaints. The sting of the judgment was, however, softened by the Court. While the law was struck down, the Court did impose strict guidelines defining the specific circumstances

---

46   *R v Yumnu*, 2012 SCC 73.
47   *McNeil*, above note 45.
48   *R v Seaboyer*, [1991] 2 SCR 577, 83 DLR (4th) 193 [*Seaboyer*].
49   *Ibid* at 274 (DLR).

in which such questions would be permitted. The issue was subsequently addressed by legislation, which prohibits the introduction of evidence that the complainant has engaged in sexual activity other than the subject matter of the charge unless a judge determines at a special hearing that the evidence is relevant and that its evidentiary value is not substantially outweighed by the danger of prejudice to the proper administration of justice. The judge is instructed to take into account not only the accused's right to make full answer and defence but also society's interests in encouraging the reporting of sexual assaults, non-discriminatory fact-finding, potential prejudice to the complainant's dignity and privacy, and the right of the complainant to personal security and the full protection and benefit of the law.[50] This legislative reply to *Seaboyer* has subsequently been upheld as being consistent with the *Charter* on the basis that the procedural aspect of the rule does not require the accused to testify and its substantive part excludes only evidence that is not relevant to the charge against the accused.[51]

A similar issue arose over whether the accused in sexual assault cases should have access to private records of the complainant as part of the right to full answer and defence. This issue is difficult because it pits at least two *Charter* rights against one another — the accused's right to full answer and defence and the complainant's right to privacy. In 1995, in *R v O'Connor*, a majority of the Supreme Court held that the appropriate procedure was to have a judge balance or reconcile the accused's right to full answer and defence with the complainant's right to privacy before ordering that the complainant's private records be disclosed to the accused. Four judges dissented and would have imposed more restrictions on both the judge's and the accused's access to the complainant's private documents by requiring consideration of society's interests in encouraging the reporting of sexual assaults and the equality rights of women and children before the judge even examined the private documents.[52] Parliament responded to the ruling with new legislation following the minority judgment. The new legislation required the accused's rights to full answer and defence to be balanced with the complainant's rights to privacy and equality before private records were produced for the trial judge's inspection. This legislation applies only to confidential records in sexual assault cases, and the Court has affirmed that the accused's right to full answer and defence in other cases will generally require that the accused receive information held

---

50 *Criminal Code*, s 276.
51 *R v Darrach*, [2000] 2 SCR 443, 191 DLR (4th) 539.
52 *R v O'Connor*, [1995] 4 SCR 1411, 103 CCC (3d) 1.

by third parties that is truly relevant to the accused's case because it relates to an issue in the trial.[53]

In *R v Mills*,[54] the Supreme Court upheld the new legislation, noting that it was a legitimate response to the Court's earlier decision. It stressed that the accused had no right to evidence that would distort the fact-finding process, and that balancing the respective rights was appropriate, both at the stage of production to the trial judge as well as in deciding upon disclosure to the accused. The Court added:

> Courts do not hold a monopoly on the protection and promotion of rights and freedoms; Parliament also plays a role in this regard and is often able to act as a significant ally for vulnerable groups. This is especially important to recognize in the context of sexual violence. The history of the treatment of sexual assault complainants by our society and our legal system is an unfortunate one. Important change has occurred through legislation aimed at both recognizing the rights and interests of complainants in criminal proceedings, and debunking the stereotypes that have been so damaging to women and children, but the treatment of sexual assault complainants remains an ongoing problem. If constitutional democracy is meant to ensure that due regard is given to the voices of those vulnerable to being overlooked by the majority, then this court has an obligation to consider respectfully Parliament's attempt to respond to such voices.[55]

The *Mills* decision demonstrates that a robust dialogue can occur between Parliament and the Court regarding the appropriate balance of values in the criminal law without resort to section 33 of the *Charter*.

In a 5:4 decision, the Supreme Court decided that the accused's right to full answer and defence is not infringed by section 651(3) of the *Criminal Code*, which requires counsel for the accused to make a closing address to the jury first if witnesses are called and examined by the defence. The majority recognized that, in certain cases, however, it might be necessary to give the accused a right of reply to the prosecutor's closing address.[56]

---

53   *McNeil*, above note 45.
54   [1999] 3 SCR 668, 180 DLR (4th) 1 [*Mills*].
55   *Ibid* at para 58.
56   *R v Rose*, [1998] 3 SCR 262, 129 CCC (3d) 449.

e) Detention of Those Found Not Guilty by Reason of Mental Disorder

Post-trial proceedings have not escaped the reach of section 7 of the *Charter*. In *R v Swain*,[57] the Supreme Court held that the *Criminal Code* provision for the automatic detention of an accused person found not guilty by reason of insanity at "the pleasure of the Lieutenant Governor" violated the principles of fundamental justice. The *Criminal Code* made no provision for a hearing or for any other procedural protection, and to hold someone indefinitely without according such rights was found to be inconsistent with the *Charter*. The Court recognized, however, that striking down the section immediately could result in a number of dangerous people being released and, accordingly, it declared the law to be valid for a stated period to afford Parliament the opportunity to enact legislation conferring the appropriate procedural protections. Parliament's new legislation, which provided for the release of a person found not guilty by reason of insanity unless that person was a significant threat to the safety of the public, was subsequently upheld by the Supreme Court under both sections 7 and 15 of the *Charter*. The Court found that the law did not impose a presumption or a stereotype of dangerousness on those found not criminally responsible by reason of a mental disorder and that the new legislation represented an appropriate balance of individual and social interests.[58] In subsequent cases, the Court has continued to uphold the new legislation while also stressing the need for the least onerous and restrictive disposition that is consistent with public safety.[59] The Court has also held that the indefinite deprival of the liberty of a person found unfit to stand trial because of a mental disorder violates section 7 of the *Charter* in those cases in which a permanently unfit accused does not pose a significant threat to society.[60]

B. UNREASONABLE SEARCH AND SEIZURE

Section 8 of the *Charter* states:

> Everyone has the right to be secure against unreasonable search or seizure.

---

57   [1991] 1 SCR 933, 63 CCC (3d) 481.
58   *Winko v British Columbia (Forensic Institution)*, [1999] 2 SCR 625, 175 DLR (4th) 193.
59   *Penetanguishene Mental Health Centre v Ontario (Attorney General)*, [2004] 1 SCR 498; *Pinet v St. Thomas Psychiatric Hospital*, [2004] 1 SCR 528.
60   *Demers*, above note 22.

The right conferred by section 8 is of ancient origin. The common law tradition has long recognized the need to protect the property and privacy of citizens against unwarranted incursions by state agents.

This section of the *Charter* has produced a significant volume of caselaw. Many, if not most, criminal trials involve the introduction of evidence seized by the police, and the propriety of the investigative methods employed by the police in obtaining evidence now comes under close scrutiny. Before the *Charter*, illegally obtained evidence was admissible. Now, under section 24(2) (discussed in greater detail below), evidence obtained in a manner that violates a *Charter* right "shall be excluded if it is established that, having regard to all the circumstances, the admission of it in the proceedings would bring the administration of justice into disrepute." This development provides accused persons with a powerful incentive to raise *Charter* challenges to the manner in which the incriminating evidence was obtained.[61]

While the protection of an individual's right to privacy can be readily understood, that right has to be reconciled with the competing state interest to conduct searches and seize evidence as part of the law-enforcement process. The right conferred by section 8 is, by its very terms, relative since the individual is protected only against *unreasonable* searches and seizures. To determine when a search or seizure is unreasonable, it is necessary to consider and balance, on the one hand, the right of the individual to be left alone, and on the other, the legitimate public interest in effective law enforcement.

In one of the Supreme Court's first *Charter* decisions, *Hunter v Southam Inc*,[62] the Court set out the basic framework for analysis of these issues. It started by interpreting section 8 generously. The section was found to confer a broad and general right to be secure from unreasonable search and seizure. This right extended beyond the protection of property and encompassed the protection of an individual's reasonable expectation of privacy. From that basic purpose of the right, the Court reasoned that certain procedural elements had to be imposed to reconcile the competing values of privacy and law enforcement. The first was the need for prior judicial authorization. The justification for a search should be assessed before it has been conducted. It would be inconsistent with the notion of an individual right to hold that, if the

---

61 The Court has, however, held that an accused does not have his own privacy in a girlfriend's apartment or standing to argue in his trial that the search violated the rights of his girlfriend: *R v Edwards*, [1996] 1 SCR 128. Passengers have been held not to have a reasonable expectation of privacy in a search of a car: *R v Belnavis*, [1997] 3 SCR 341.

62 [1984] 2 SCR 145, 11 DLR (4th) 641.

police find something, the search was reasonable, for that is to invite searches on a whim. Protecting individuals against unjustified state intrusion requires preventative measures prior to the search, and hence the Court held that there is a presumption of unreasonableness where a search has been undertaken without a warrant issued by a judicial official. The Court added that, to obtain a warrant, the authorities should be required to justify the need for the search by sworn evidence that satisfies an objective standard. The general standard was "probable cause" or reasonable grounds to believe that a crime was committed and that the search would reveal evidence of the crime. The Court recognized that there could be "exigent" circumstances where the police had to act quickly and where circumstances did not allow time to obtain a warrant, but those cases, said the Court, were very much the exception to the general rule that a warrant is required.

A number of subsequent search-and-seizure cases have turned upon what constitutes a "reasonable" expectation of privacy in particular circumstances. At one end of the spectrum, a person has been held not to have a reasonable expectation of privacy with respect to garbage put out for disposal.[63] At the other end of the spectrum, in a number of cases, the Court has stressed that people have reasonable expectations of privacy with respect to bodily samples taken by physicians for medical purposes[64] or non-consensual seizure of bodily substances.[65] The Court has taken a tough line on this issue, holding that the individual's right to bodily integrity must take priority and that the police have no right to require suspects to give such samples. Legislation authorizing the police to obtain a warrant to take bodily substances for DNA testing without the consent of the suspect has been enacted and upheld under the *Charter*.[66] There are, however, cases where it is more difficult to determine whether the accused has a reasonable expectation of privacy necessary for section 8 protection. The Court has held that, while bodily substances are generally private, they are not private when discarded, for example, by throwing a soiled tissue into the garbage can.[67] The home is usually considered private, but the use of heat detection technology does not infringe a reasonable expectation of privacy because the activities producing the heat are not revealed.[68] At the same

---

63   R v *Patrick*, [2009] 1 SCR 579 [*Patrick*].
64   R v *Dersch*, [1993] 3 SCR 768, 85 CCC (3d) 1.
65   R v *Dyment*, [1988] 2 SCR 417, 45 CCC (3d) 244; R v *Pohoretsky*, [1987] 1 SCR 945, 33 CCC (3d) 398; R v *Stillman*, [1997] 1 SCR 607, 144 DLR (4th) 193 [*Stillman*].
66   R v *SAB*, [2003] 2 SCR 678.
67   *Stillman*, above note 65.
68   R v *Tessling*, [2004] 3 SCR 432 [*Tessling*].

time, there is a reasonable expectation of privacy in luggage at a bus station or in a student's backpack when drug-sniffing dogs are used.[69] In R v Spencer,[70] the Court held that there was a reasonable expectation of privacy in so-called metadata that related to identifying information about someone using the Internet to access child pornography. The Court stressed that privacy was related to the value of anonymity. The determination of a reasonable expectation of privacy is a contextual process, but the courts will not hold that the discovery of evidence of a crime means that the person has no reasonable expectation of privacy.

Although the police can generally frisk-search a person being arrested, the Court has held that because of section 8 of the *Charter*, this power does not extend to delayed inventory searches of cars,[71] to routine strip searches,[72] or to the seizure of DNA samples without a judicial warrant.[73] A majority of the Court distinguished that case to hold that a penile swab can be taken from the accused without a warrant and as part of a search incident to arrest over strong dissents that this was an unreasonable invasion of privacy and bodily integrity.[74] In another divided decision, the Court held that the police can search a cell phone as an incident of arrest subject to certain safeguards, but with a minority dissenting on the basis that such searches should be conducted either with a judicial warrant or in exigent circumstances where it is not possible to obtain a warrant.[75] In a different case, however, the Court recognized the privacy interests in computers and held that searches of computers had to be specifically authorized in a judicial warrant.[76] Section 8 of the *Charter* will not be violated by a warrantless search in cases of exigent circumstances where obtaining a warrant is impossible, but it is violated where Parliament provides no accountability measures for how such warrantless powers of electronic surveillance are exercised.[77]

---

69   *R v AM*, 2008 SCC 19 [*AM*]; *R v Kang-Brown*, 2008 SCC 18 [*Kang-Brown*].

70   2014 SCC 43.

71   *R v Caslake*, [1998] 1 SCR 51, 121 CCC (3d) 97.

72   *R v Golden*, [2001] 3 SCR 679, 207 DLR (4th) 18. To conduct a strip search, there must be reasonable and probable grounds to believe that such a strip is necessary to protect the police or prevent the destruction of evidence, and the strip search must be conducted in a reasonable manner.

73   *Stillman*, above note 65.

74   *R v Saeed*, 2016 SCC 24.

75   *R v Fearon*, [2014] 3 SCR 6.

76   *R v Vu*, [2013] 3 SCR 657.

77   *R v Tse*, [2012] 1 SCR 531 [*Tse*].

In *R v Mann*,[78] the Court held that the police can briefly detain people for investigative purposes if there are reasonable grounds to suspect that they are connected with crime. During such periods of detention, the police can, if reasonably necessary to protect their safety, conduct a protective pat-down search of the detainee. The Court, however, held that a more intrusive search of the accused's pocket after a soft and presumably non-dangerous object was detected was unreasonable and a violation of section 8 of the *Charter*. The object turned out to be illegal drugs that were excluded under section 24(2) of the *Charter*. In a subsequent case, the Court held that section 8 was not violated when the police searched two people who they detained when responding to a 911 call that guns were seen in the area. The Court stressed that the searches, which discovered two illegal handguns, were justified because the officers had reasonable grounds to believe that their safety or the safety of others was at risk when responding to a gun call.[79]

In two complicated cases involving the use of sniffer dogs that detected drugs in a bag of a passenger in a bus station and in a backpack at a high school,[80] the Supreme Court held that the use of the dog constituted a search, that the search was unreasonable in the circumstances, and that the drugs should be excluded under section 24(2) of the *Charter*. The Court agreed that the dog sniff was a search and distinguished the use of the dog from the use of technology that can detect excess heat emanating from houses, which the Court had found not to constitute a search.[81] The Court was, however, divided on the appropriate standard that should be applied in subsequent dog sniff cases. Four judges would allow the use of sniffer dogs only when there were reasonable and probable grounds to believe that such searches would discover evidence of crime while four other judges would allow such searches on the less restrictive grounds of reasonable suspicion. The fifth judge held that a reasonable suspicion standard was appropriate, but that suspicion need not even relate to a particular person. In 2013, the Court agreed that "a reasonable suspicion of criminal activity will be discovered" is the appropriate standard to apply to searches conducted by sniffer dogs. This standard depends on all the circumstances of the particular case.[82] Although the Court now agrees that reasonable suspicion is the appropriate standard, it does not always agree on its application, as seen in a 5:4 decision where there was reasonable suspicion to use a sniffer

---

78   [2004] 3 SCR 59 [*Mann*].
79   *R v Clayton*, [2007] 2 SCR 725 [*Clayton*].
80   *AM*, above note 69; *Kang-Brown*, above note 69.
81   *Tessling*, above note 68.
82   *R v Chehil*, [2013] 3 SCR 220.

dog at a vehicle stop on what the dissenting judge characterized as only generalized suspicion that would allow too many innocent people to be subject to a sniffer search.[83]

The validity of the *Criminal Code* provisions authorizing judicial warrants for electronic surveillance has been upheld,[84] as have provisions that allow a warrant to be obtained without notice to convicted offenders to acquire DNA samples.[85] However, the Supreme Court has not hesitated to limit some other police investigative techniques that are not authorized by a warrant. In *R v Duarte*,[86] the Court found that surreptitiously recording a communication the originator expects will not be intercepted by anyone other than the intended recipient violates section 8 of the *Charter* unless authorized by warrant. The police had used the familiar technique of equipping an informer with a body-pack recorder to tape a conversation with a suspect. No warrant had been obtained since it was thought that the procedure was legal where one party, here the informer, consented. The Court decided that a reasonable expectation of privacy demanded that the police obtain a warrant authorizing such procedures. Parliament subsequently applied a new warrant procedure for consent intercepts and also authorized such intercepts without judicial authorization to prevent bodily harm and in urgent or exigent circumstances.[87] Similarly, in *R v Wong*,[88] the Court held that surreptitious video surveillance constitutes a search and seizure requiring prior judicial authorization when conducted in circumstances in which the suspect had a reasonable expectation of privacy. In that case, individuals engaged in illegal gambling in a hotel room were found to have a reasonable expectation of privacy. Parliament again responded with a new general warrant provision that would allow a judge to authorize any investigative technique (other than an invasion of bodily integrity) that might otherwise violate a person's privacy and constitute an unreasonable search and seizure.[89]

In *R v Kokesch*,[90] the Supreme Court found that a warrantless "perimeter search," during which the police trespassed on the accused's

83 *R v MacKenzie*, [2013] 3 SCR 250.
84 *R v Finlay* (1985), 23 DLR (4th) 532 (Ont CA), leave to appeal to SCC refused, [1986] 1 SCR ix; *R v Garofoli*, [1990] 2 SCR 1421, 60 CCC (3d) 161.
85 *R v Rodgers*, [2006] 1 SCR 554.
86 [1990] 1 SCR 30, 65 DLR (4th) 240.
87 *Criminal Code*, ss 184.1–184.6. The warrantless exigent circumstances powers were later held to violate s 8 because of the lack of accountability measures. See *Tse*, above note 77.
88 [1990] 3 SCR 36, 60 CCC (3d) 460.
89 *Criminal Code*, s 487.01.
90 [1990] 3 SCR 3, 61 CCC (3d) 207.

property and peered into his windows to confirm a suspicion that he was cultivating marijuana, constituted a violation of section 8. The Court has also upheld the individual's privacy interest in a dwelling-house by finding that the police violated section 8 by forcible entry to make a warrantless arrest absent circumstances of "hot pursuit" of a fleeing suspect.[91] Parliament again responded with a new warrant procedure and also statutory authorization for warrantless entry into homes to make arrests in exigent circumstances, in which it was impracticable to obtain a warrant and there were reasonable grounds to suspect that entry was necessary to prevent imminent death or bodily harm or reasonable grounds to believe that it was necessary to prevent imminent loss or destruction of evidence.[92]

A distinction has been drawn between personal information, which is protected against unreasonable search and seizure, and routine commercial records, which are not. In *R v Plant*,[93] the police used information regarding electricity consumption, obtained in the course of a drug investigation from the utility commission, to incriminate the accused who was charged with cultivating marijuana. No warrant had been issued to obtain the records, but the seizure was not found to trigger a section 8 violation. Since these commercial records were not personal and confidential and did not reveal intimate details of the accused's lifestyle or personal choices, there was not a reasonable expectation that they would be protected from state surveillance. The Supreme Court subsequently applied this precedent in *R v Tessling*[94] to hold that the warrantless use of heat detection technology from an airplane did not violate section 8 of the *Charter*. The Court concluded that the technology only detected information exposed to the public and did not expose any intimate details or core biographical data of the occupants. The case might have been differently decided if the technology could reveal what activities in the house were producing the excess heat. In *R v Patrick*, the Court held that there was no reasonable expectation of privacy in garbage bags placed in a back lane for pick-up but distinguished this from garbage in a person's garage or near a porch.[95]

The Supreme Court has also drawn a distinction between the requirements of a reasonable search in the regulatory context and in the criminal context. Generally, the Court has indicated that the *Hunter v Southam* standard of prior judicial authorization on the basis of probable cause

91   *R v Feeney*, [1997] 2 SCR 13, 146 DLR (4th) 609.
92   *Criminal Code*, ss 529–529.5.
93   [1993] 3 SCR 281, 84 CCC (3d) 203.
94   *Tessling*, above note 68.
95   *Patrick*, above note 63.

that a crime has been committed "will not usually be the appropriate standard for a determination made in an administrative or regulatory context. The greater the departure from the realm of criminal law, the more flexible will be the approach to the standard of reasonableness."[96] In a complex case investigating alleged anti-competitive behaviour,[97] the Court was deeply split, but in the result the majority found that compelled production of documents pursuant to anti-combines legislation did not constitute a seizure within the meaning of section 8. This result was confirmed in a subsequent case holding that demands for information and documents pursuant to the *Income Tax Act* do not constitute seizures under section 8.[98] In *R v Jarvis*,[99] however, the Court indicated that even in the income tax context, all *Charter* protections used in the criminal context apply when the state is acting with the predominant purpose of determining penal liability. In another case, the Court recognized that criminal sanctions were not being imposed, but indicated that the safeguard of a meaningful review was necessary before a licence was suspended and a fine imposed under provincial legislation when a driver registered a warning on a roadside breathalyzer.[100] The result is that the requirements of section 8 will vary with the context. For example, school officials must conduct searches reasonably, but they do not require a judicial warrant or reasonable and probable grounds to believe that a crime has been committed.[101] At the other end of the scale, the Court has indicated that searches of a lawyer's office require special safeguards such as notification of the privilege holder because of the need to protect solicitor–client confidences and privilege.[102]

C. ARBITRARY DETENTION AND IMPRISONMENT

Section 9 of the *Charter* guarantees:

Everyone has the right not to be arbitrarily detained or imprisoned.

---

96 *Branch*, above note 35 at para 52 (SCR).

97 *Thomson Newspapers Ltd. v Canada (Director of Investigation & Research)*, [1990] 1 SCR 425, 54 CCC (3d) 417.

98 *R v McKinlay Transport Ltd*, [1990] 1 SCR 627, 55 CCC (3d) 530.

99 [2002] 2 SCR 757.

100 *Goodwin v British Columbia (Superintendent of Motor Vehicles)*, [2015] 3 SCR 250 [*Goodwin*].

101 *R v M(MR)*, [1998] 3 SCR 393, 129 CCC (3d) 361.

102 *Lavallee, Rackel and Heintz v Canada*, [2002] 3 SCR 209; *Maranda v Richer*, [2003] 3 SCR 193.

The meaning of "detention," a term crucial to both sections 9 and 10, was first considered in the context of section 10. In *R v Therens*,[103] an impaired-driving case, the issue of the accused's right to retain and instruct counsel depended upon whether he was "detained" within the meaning of section 10 when asked to go to the police station to give a breath sample. Rejecting the notion of detention as limited to instances of physical constraint, the Supreme Court instead defined the term as including any occasion when a police officer, by some form of compulsion or coercion, "assumes control over the movement of a person by a demand or direction which may have significant legal consequence."[104] The Court found that, even where the individual was not subjected to physical force or to a legally enforceable demand, "psychological compulsion, in the form of a reasonable perception of suspension of freedom of choice"[105] could result in detention within the meaning of the *Charter*. The Supreme Court has subsequently indicated that "the constitutional rights recognized by sections 9 and 10 of the *Charter* are not engaged by delays that involve no significant or psychological restraint."[106] The Court has thus avoided the extremes of detention being limited to physical constraint or expanded to include fleeting delays or interferences, and has held that there is detention under sections 9 and 10 whenever there is significant physical or psychological restraint.[107]

By its very terms, the right that section 9 secures is relative. There are clearly situations where the authorities must have the power to detain or imprison individuals, and the *Charter* right is engaged only where denial of freedom is arbitrary. Yet the Supreme Court has interpreted "arbitrarily" in a manner that favours individual liberty. The Court has recognized the danger posed by giving the police unfettered discretion to detain. There must be some objective standard, defined by the law, governing the power. *R v Hufsky*,[108] and *R v Ladouceur*[109] dealt with provincial legislation authorizing random "spot checks" for impaired drivers. The Court found that stopping a motorist amounted to a detention under section 9 and that such a detention was arbitrary. The selection of which cars would be stopped was at the absolute discretion of the individual officer, and when establishing the program, the

---

103 [1985] 1 SCR 613, 18 DLR (4th) 655.
104 *Ibid* at 642 (SCR).
105 *Ibid* at 644.
106 *Mann*, above note 78 at para 19.
107 *R v Grant*, 2009 SCC 32 at paras 24 and 28 [*Grant*].
108 [1988] 1 SCR 621, 40 CCC (3d) 398.
109 [1990] 1 SCR 1257, 56 CCC (3d) 22.

authorities had failed to provide any criteria for the exercise of this discretion, leaving it subject to the whim of each officer. The Court went on to consider whether a random stop of a driver could be justified under section 1. In view of the importance of highway safety and the deterrent function served by these stops, legislation authorizing random spot checks was found to be a reasonable limit on the right conferred by section 9. In a later decision,[110] the Court limited the powers of the police conducting random spot checks under this legislation. In the absence of reasonable and probable grounds for a more intrusive investigation, questioning by the police, when acting under this legislation, is constitutionally restricted to checking the driver's licence and insurance, the driver's sobriety, and the mechanical fitness of the vehicle.

In R v Mann, the Supreme Court recognized a common law power of investigative and warrantless detention that is consistent with both sections 8 and 9 of the Charter. The Court indicated that "police officers may detain an individual for investigative purposes if there are reasonable grounds to suspect in all the circumstances that the individual is connected to a particular crime and that such a detention is necessary."[111] If the officer has reasonable grounds to believe that his or her safety is at risk, a protective pat-down search is allowed if conducted in a reasonable manner. The Court added "that the investigative detention should be brief in duration and does not impose an obligation on the detained person to answer questions for the police."[112] In addition, the person detained should be informed of the reasons for the detention as required by section 10(a) of the Charter. In a subsequent case, a majority of the Court held that section 9 of the Charter was not violated when the police stopped a car and detained its occupants, eventually searching the occupants and discovering illegal handguns. The Court noted that the car and its occupants matched the description of "black guys" in four vehicles openly displaying handguns in the parking lot of the Million Dollar Saloon. The Court stressed the need to balance the seriousness of the risk to public safety against the liberty of the individuals.[113] Three judges reached the same result, but through a different process. They held that the stop was an arbitrary detention contrary to section 9 of the Charter but was justified under section 1 as a reasonable limit on the right that was proportionate to the objective of protecting the public from handguns. The dissenters stressed that section 1 was the proper mechanism for balancing individual and collective interests.

---

110 R v Mellenthin, [1992] 3 SCR 615, 76 CCC (3d) 481 [Mellenthin].
111 Mann, above note 78 at para 45.
112 Ibid.
113 Clayton, above note 79 at para 31, Abella J.

The source of the section 1 justification was not democratically enacted legislation but the Court's own common law rulings.[114]

The exact parameters of the power of investigative detention and its relation to the right against unreasonable search and seizure in section 8 of the *Charter* and of the right to retain and instruct counsel without delay and to be informed of that right under section 10(b) of the *Charter* will undoubtedly continue to be fleshed out in subsequent cases. The lack of clarity and bright lines in the constitutional jurisprudence may, as discussed below, also affect section 24(2) analysis: it becomes difficult to conclude that the police committed a serious violation of their powers when clear limits on those powers are not established. The Court affirmed in *R v Grant*[115] that psychological detention could exist under sections 9 and 10 when a person either has a legal obligation to comply, or when a reasonable person would conclude that he or she had no choice but to comply with a police demand. There was psychological detention in this case because the police went beyond general questioning of a youth on the street and interrogated him in an adversarial fashion while telling him to keep his hands in front of him. The detention was arbitrary because it was unlawful and exceeded a brief investigative stop on the basis of reasonable suspicion. As will be discussed below, however, the Court admitted as evidence a gun that was discovered as a result of the arbitrary detention, and this was despite a failure by the police to provide the right to counsel upon detention, in part because the legal obligations of the police in this situation were not clear and this mitigated the seriousness of the *Charter* violation. A similar pattern of finding a violation but not excluding evidence is found in *R v Aucoin*.[116] In that case, the Court found that section 9 was violated because it was not necessary to detain an accused apprehended on minor traffic matters in the back of the police car. At the same time, however, the Court concluded that the exclusion of evidence obtained in a protective pat-down search before he was placed in the police car would not bring the administration of justice into disrepute.

Detention following a conviction will not be arbitrary, but in *R v Lyons*,[117] it was argued that the dangerous-offender provision, which allows a judge to impose a sentence of indefinite imprisonment where certain stated criteria were met and where the convicted person posed a serious threat to public safety, was arbitrary. The Court rejected this

---

114 *Ibid* at para 105*ff*, Binnie J.
115 Above note 107 at para 44.
116 2012 SCC 66.
117 [1987] 2 SCR 309, 37 CCC (3d) 1 [*Lyons*].

argument, finding that Parliament had adequately defined the class of offenders subject to this sentence and provided for periodic reviews of dangerousness. Similarly, the Court has upheld the *Criminal Code* provisions providing for minimum periods of imprisonment for first-degree murder without eligibility for parole.[118] At the same time, automatic indeterminate detention following a verdict of not guilty by reason of insanity has been held to be arbitrary because of the absence of standards.[119] As mentioned above, new legislation enacted in response to this decision that ties detention to dangerousness has been upheld under the *Charter.*

D. RIGHTS ON DETENTION AND ARREST

Section 10 of the *Charter* confers certain specific rights that apply upon arrest or detention. As noted above, "detention" has been given a broad interpretation so that the rights conferred under this section may be invoked in circumstances well short of incarceration. Section 10 provides as follows:

> Everyone has the right on arrest or detention
> (a) to be informed promptly of the reasons therefor;
> (b) to retain and instruct counsel without delay and to be informed of that right; and
> (c) to have the validity of the detention determined by way of *habeas corpus* and to be released if the detention is not lawful.

1) Right to Be Informed of the Reasons for Arrest or Detention

Under our system of criminal justice, police powers are limited by law, and before the police interfere with the liberty of an individual, they must be able to justify their actions. Arrest and detention represent a serious interference with personal liberty, and it is a basic right of the individual arrested or detained to know the reason. Requiring the authorities to state promptly the reasons for an arrest or detention permits the person arrested or detained to assess the situation and to decide upon an appropriate response, including submitting to the arrest, seeking counsel, and responding to police questions.

---

118 *R v Luxton*, [1990] 2 SCR 711, 58 CCC (3d) 449 [*Luxton*].
119 *R v Swain*, [1991] 1 SCR 933, 63 CCC (3d) 481 [*Swain*].

The right to be advised of the reasons arises upon arrest, but it may arise again if the reason for the arrest changes. For example, in *R v Borden*,[120] the accused was told that he had been arrested for one sexual assault that did not involve intercourse; on this occasion, he agreed to provide a blood sample. He was not told that the police wanted the sample in relation to another sexual assault of which he was also suspected. The Supreme Court held that the accused's section 10(a) right to be informed of the reason for his detention had been violated. Similarly, in *R v Black*,[121] the accused was arrested for attempted murder. The victim died while she was in custody. The accused was told that she was now charged with murder, but she was not told again of her right to counsel under section 10(b). The Court held that sections 10(a) and (b) required that the police fully advise her of rights again when the reason for the arrest changed. On the other hand, in *R v Evans*,[122] the Court held that, although the police did not specifically inform an individual arrested on a drug charge that he was also suspected of two murders, it was clear to the accused from the nature of the questions being asked that he was being held for the murders as well. In *R v Mann*,[123] the Supreme Court indicated that a person subject to investigative detention should be "advised, in clear and simple language, of the reasons for the detention." At the same time, however, the Court expressed concerns that reading a person subject to brief investigative detention his or her rights to retain and instruct counsel under section 10(b) "cannot be transformed into an excuse for prolonging, unduly and artificially" investigative detentions that should be brief.[124] A delay of twenty-two minutes between detention and informing the accused of the reasons for the detention and the right to counsel has been held to be a violation.[125]

2) Right to Retain and Instruct Counsel and to Be Informed of That Right

The courts have been vigilant in upholding the right to counsel. The rationale for this right is the need to ensure that everyone who is detained has

---

120 [1994] 3 SCR 145, 119 DLR (4th) 74. A sample can, however, be used in connection with a subsequent crime if neither the police nor the accused place limits on its use when the sample was obtained. See *R v Arp*, [1998] 3 SCR 339.

121 [1989] 2 SCR 138, 50 CCC (3d) 1.

122 [1991] 1 SCR 869, 63 CCC (3d) 289.

123 *Mann*, above note 78 at para 21.

124 *Ibid* at paras 19 and 22.

125 *R v Mian*, [2014] 2 SCR 689.

the opportunity to learn immediately of his or her rights and obligations under the law. An individual in police custody is in a vulnerable situation and is entitled to the assistance of someone knowledgeable in the law and independent of the state:

> [W]hen an individual is detained by state authorities, he or she is put in a position of disadvantage relative to the state. Not only has this person suffered a deprivation of liberty, but also this person may be at risk of incriminating him- or herself.[126]

The right to counsel is triggered upon arrest or detention. The reference in section 10(b) to the right to retain and instruct counsel without delay requires immediate provision of the right to counsel upon either arrest or detention.[127] At the same time, a person, even one who is being investigated by the police, will not be detained by a brief encounter with the police that does not result in significant physical or psychological restraint in the sense that a reasonable person would conclude that he or she must comply with the police. The Court has held that the accused was not detained, and the right to counsel not triggered, when a police officer said: "Wait a minute. I need to talk to you before you go anywhere."[128] The accused was trying to leave a parking lot after his friend was detained because of the possible fraudulent use of a credit card. The majority of the Court held that the accused was only momentarily delayed and subject to general questioning, as opposed to focused interrogation which could result in detention for *Charter* purposes. The Court warned: "To simply assume that a detention occurs every time a person is delayed from going on his or her way because of the police accosting him or her during the course of an investigation, without considering whether or not the interaction involved a significant deprivation of liberty would overshoot the purpose of the *Charter*."[129]

Section 10(b) of the *Charter* affords not only the right to counsel but also the right to be informed of that right. In *R v Manninen*,[130] it was made clear that this is more than a formal or hollow right. There, the Supreme Court held that the police must provide the accused with a reasonable opportunity to exercise the right to consult counsel, and they must desist from questioning the accused or attempting to elicit information until he or she has had an opportunity to confer with

---

126 *R v Bartle*, [1994] 3 SCR 173 at 191, 92 CCC (3d) 289, Lamer CJC.
127 *R v Suberu*, 2009 SCC 33 at para 42.
128 *Ibid* at para 10.
129 *Ibid* at para 24.
130 [1987] 1 SCR 1233, 34 CCC (3d) 385.

counsel. Another case, *R v Brydges*,[131] dealt with the situation of an accused who could not afford counsel. The Court held that, where it appeared to the police that the accused wished to consult a lawyer but thought that his inability to afford legal counsel would prevent him from exercising the right, it was incumbent upon the police to advise the accused of the availability of legal aid and duty counsel provided under the legal aid scheme.

While *Brydges* required police to inform a detainee of the availability of free legal advice where it is provided, the Court did not go so far as mandating the legislative enactment of such a system. In *R v Matheson*[132] and *R v Prosper*,[133] the Court rejected the suggestion that section 10(b) imposes a positive obligation on governments to provide free preliminary legal advice through a duty-counsel system. The police instead have a twofold duty to inform detainees of legal services available in the jurisdiction and then to "hold off" questioning until a detainee has had a reasonable opportunity to consult counsel. This may require the police officer to facilitate the detainee's access to a telephone.[134] It has also been held that a detained person must be reasonably diligent in seeking the advice of counsel, failing which the police are entitled to proceed with questioning the suspect.[135]

The right to counsel guaranteed under section 10(b) continues to check police conduct after the initial charges have been laid. In *R v Burlingham*,[136] police impropriety in the plea-bargaining process was found to violate the accused's right to counsel. The police belittled the defence counsel with the express purpose of undermining the relationship between the accused and his lawyer, and they then pressured the accused, in the absence of counsel, to accept a plea bargain. Both aspects of their conduct were found to violate the section 10(b) right to counsel.

Limitations on section 10(b) rights can be justified as reasonable limits under section 1 of the *Charter*. The Court has held that the denial of the right to counsel is authorized, prescribed by law, and justified in the case of roadside breathalyzer tests[137] and roadside sobriety tests.[138] In both cases, the Court recognized that the objective of detecting

---

131 [1990] 1 SCR 190, 53 CCC (3d) 330 [*Brydges*].
132 [1994] 3 SCR 328, 118 DLR (4th) 323.
133 [1994] 3 SCR 236, 118 DLR (4th) 154.
134 *R v Taylor*, [2014] 2 SCR 495.
135 *R v Tremblay*, [1987] 2 SCR 435, 37 CCC (3d) 565.
136 [1995] 2 SCR 206, 124 DLR (4th) 7.
137 *R v Thomsen*, [1988] 1 SCR 640.
138 *R v Orbanski; R v Elias*, [2005] 2 SCR 3.

intoxicated drivers was important enough to justify limiting the right to counsel and that the limit on the right to counsel was proportionate and required to allow prompt checks of the sobriety of drivers.

E. RIGHTS OF PERSONS CHARGED WITH AN OFFENCE

Section 11 of the *Charter* deals with the rights of persons charged with an offence. This section applies only to criminal or quasi-criminal proceedings and proceedings that give rise to penal consequences. Accordingly, it does apply to prosecutions for criminal offences proper, as well as to prosecutions under provincial legislation, but not to licence suspensions with associated penalties.[139] Professional and other similar disciplinary proceedings will be caught only where the consequences are truly penal in nature, reflecting an attempt to redress a wrong done to society as a whole.[140] Section 11 reads:

Any person charged with an offence has the right
(a) to be informed without unreasonable delay of the specific offence;
(b) to be tried within a reasonable time;
(c) not to be compelled to be a witness in proceedings against that person in respect of the offence;
(d) to be presumed innocent until proven guilty according to law in a fair and public hearing by an independent and impartial tribunal;
(e) not to be denied reasonable bail without just cause;
(f) except in the case of an offence under military law tried before a military tribunal, to the benefit of trial by jury where the maximum punishment for the offence is imprisonment for five years or a more severe punishment;
(g) not to be found guilty on account of any act or omission unless, at the time of the act or omission, it constituted an offence under Canadian or international law or was criminal according to the general principles of law recognized by the community of nations;

---

139 *Goodwin*, above note 100.
140 *R v Wigglesworth*, [1987] 2 SCR 541, 45 DLR (4th) 235 [*Wigglesworth*]. A person subject to forfeiture procedures under the *Customs Act* is not a person charged with an offence for the purpose of s 11 of the *Charter*. *Martineau v Canada (Minister of National Revenue)*, [2004] 3 SCR 737. A person charged under the *Income Tax Act* is also not a person charged with an offence under s 11: *Guindon v Canada*, [2015] 3 SCR 3.

(h) if finally acquitted of the offence, not to be tried for it again and, if finally found guilty and punished for the offence, not to be tried or punished for it again; and

(i) if found guilty of the offence and if the punishment for the offence has been varied between the time of commission and the time of sentencing, to the benefit of the lesser punishment.

1) Right to Be Informed without Unreasonable Delay of the Specific Offence

An accused person needs to know the precise nature of the charges he or she faces for a number of reasons. Identification of the specific offence will enable the accused to challenge the proceedings if they are unlawful or to prepare a defence if they are not. The right to be informed of the offence without unreasonable delay also defines and narrows the proceedings, thereby limiting the scope of the prosecution and the powers of the police.

2) Right to Be Tried without Unreasonable Delay

It has often been said that "justice delayed is justice denied." Delay in prosecution may result in unfairness to the accused since it may well become more difficult to defend oneself after the passage of time. Quite apart from the unfairness, all parties — victims, accused persons, and society at large — have an obvious interest in speedy justice.

Delay in bringing criminal charges to trial has been the subject of a number of controversial decisions of the courts. The most significant was *R v Askov*,[141] where the Supreme Court considered a case that had taken twenty-four months to come to trial and where the cause of the delay was no more than the product of an overburdened system. The Court ruled that systemic delay could trigger a section 11(b) claim and established presumptive limits of six to eight months in provincial courts and eight to ten months in superior courts for systemic delay. While the Court indicated that it was mindful that the allocation of resources was a matter for political decision, the right to a speedy trial was vital to both the accused and the community at large, and solutions to systemic delay had to be found. The Court found that in the circumstances of the case, which arose in one of the busiest and most congested judicial districts in Canada, a two-year delay between committal and trial was unacceptable and in violation of the *Charter*'s guarantee.

---

141 [1990] 2 SCR 1199, 59 CCC (3d) 449 [*Askov*].

The impact of the decision was enormous. Thousands of criminal charges were either dropped or stayed, and the entire issue of court delay and the allocation of judicial resources came under intense scrutiny. Although the Court softened its approach somewhat in a subsequent case,[142] the effects of *Askov* continue to be felt. A split Court in 2016 returned to the presumptive limits approach because of a concern that the Court's softened case-by-case approach had become too complex and unpredictable. The majority of the Court set higher presumptive ceilings of eighteen months for cases in provincial courts and thirty months for more serious cases in superior courts. Once such limits, minus any time waived or caused by the accused, are reached, then the Crown will have to establish exceptional circumstances outside of its control to escape a conclusion that section 11(b) has been violated and that the minimal remedy of a stay should be entered. In order to avoid another *Askov* crisis, the Court indicated that transitional exceptional circumstances could apply to cases in the system at the time the Court announced its new rules. Exceptional circumstances are open-ended, but can relate to discrete events such as illness or the inherent complexity of the case. The accused can, in some cases, establish a section 11(b) violation when the delay is below the presumptive ceiling, but must demonstrate sustained efforts to expedite the case, and that the case took markedly longer than necessary.

Four judges dissented from the new approach in *R v Jordan* on the basis that Parliament and not the courts should establish such presumptive limits on trial delay. They opposed placing new requirements on the accused to expedite cases and predicted that the new approach could generate extensive litigation over what was an exceptional circumstance, and if applied to existing caseloads, result in thousands of stays of proceedings. They relied on the case-by-case approach that the Court had used after *Askov*. That said, the entire Court was agreed that a forty-four month delay in a drug case was unacceptable.[143] In a companion case, the Court stayed proceedings in a historical sexual assault because there were no exceptional circumstances justifying a thirty-four month delay, four months beyond the presumptive ceiling for more serious cases, with three judges dissenting.[144]

A distinction has been drawn between pre- and post-charge delay. In Canada, there is no statute of limitations for serious criminal offences. In recent years, significant numbers of sexual assault charges have been laid years after the occurrence of the alleged offence. The

142 *R v Morin*, [1992] 1 SCR 771, 71 CCC (3d) 1.
143 *R v Jordan*, 2016 SCC 27.
144 *R v Williamson*, 2016 SCC 28.

Supreme Court has stated that delay in bringing charges will only rarely be relevant to the right to be tried without unreasonable delay.[145] In certain circumstances, unexplained or unjustified delay in initiating proceedings may give rise to a section 7 claim.[146]

3) Right against Self-Incrimination

The right against self-incrimination is protected in a variety of ways under the *Charter*. There is a residual right against self-incrimination under section 7 that, as discussed above, may provide some protections if an otherwise legitimate procedure is used for the primary purpose of compelling persons to incriminate themselves. The right conferred by section 11(c) relates specifically to the trial of the accused and protects the accused from having to testify. Section 13 of the *Charter* protects witnesses who are compelled from having incriminating statements used against them in subsequent proceedings.

Silence of an accused cannot, by statute, be the subject of comment by counsel or by the judge. Yet, while an accused person does not have to testify, to what extent does section 11(c) protect the accused who elects to remain silent from having the judge or jury draw an adverse inference from his or her silence? In a 1994 decision,[147] the Supreme Court suggested that it would be a violation of the right against self-incrimination to draw an adverse inference where the prosecution has failed to make out any case against the accused. But where there is "a case to meet," the accused who fails to answer must risk the possibility that a failure to testify may lead the judge or jury to convict.

The Supreme Court has held that a corporation is not entitled to claim the protection of section 11(c) and that an officer of an accused corporation can be compelled to testify,[148] a decision that corresponds to the Court's general tendency to avoid applying the *Charter* to protect purely commercial or corporate interests.

After a witness (including the accused) has been compelled to testify, section 13 of the *Charter* provides additional, albeit somewhat uncertain, protections against the subsequent use of that testimony. It provides:

---

145 *R v Mills*, [1986] 1 SCR 863, 29 DLR (4th) 161; *R v Carter*, [1986] 1 SCR 981, 26 CCC (3d) 572.

146 *R v Kalanj*, [1989] 1 SCR 1594, 48 CCC (3d) 459.

147 *R v P(MB)*, [1994] 1 SCR 555, 89 CCC (3d) 289.

148 *R v Amway Corp*, [1989] 1 SCR 21, 56 DLR (4th) 309.

A witness who testifies in any proceeding has the right not to have any incriminating evidence so given used to incriminate that witness in any other proceedings, except in a prosecution for perjury or for the giving of contradictory evidence.

In *R v Dubois*,[149] this section 13 protection was extended to an accused who had testified at his trial, was convicted, appealed, and was given a new trial. The Supreme Court of Canada held that the testimony given at the first trial could not be used at the new trial. The guarantee was further extended in *R v Mannion*[150] where, in similar circumstances, the Court held that the previous testimony could not even be used to cross-examine the accused at his retrial. However, in *R v Kuldip*,[151] the Court held that evidence given at a previous trial could be used to cross-examine as to the credibility of the accused as distinct from the use of such evidence to prove guilt.[152]

In *R v Henry*,[153] the Court attempted to reconcile the confusing jurisprudence and return to first principles. It overruled the extension of the protections against self-incrimination in *Mannion* on the basis that the purpose of the right against self-incrimination was not engaged when an accused chooses to testify at his retrial. In such circumstances, the accused is not being compelled to engage in self-incrimination. The Court also partially overruled *Kuldip* by holding that the accused's prior voluntary testimony on the same indictment could be used in the new trial either to impeach the credibility of the accused or as evidence supporting the accused's guilt. Although *Henry* withdraws section 13 protections in cases involving the accused's voluntary testimony in his or her own trial and retrial, it extends protection against self-incrimination by holding that prior testimony that was compelled from the accused as a witness cannot be used in a subsequent trial of that person either as evidence of guilt or to impeach the accused's credibility. The underlying rationale is the difficulty of segregating the use of prior testimony as evidence of guilt or for the purpose of impeaching the accused's credibility. *Henry* is also noteworthy in demonstrating the Court's willingness to overrule and reinterpret prior *Charter* precedents in an attempt to rationalize the law.

---

149 [1985] 2 SCR 350, 22 CCC (3d) 513.
150 [1986] 2 SCR 272, 28 CCC (3d) 544 [*Mannion*].
151 [1990] 3 SCR 618, 61 CCC (3d) 385 [*Kuldip*].
152 See also *R v Noel*, [2002] 3 SCR 433, holding that the Crown had violated the right against self-incrimination by trying to have the accused adopt incriminating parts of his prior testimony.
153 [2005] 3 SCR 609 [*Henry*].

In *R v Nedulcu*,[154] a divided Court appeared to return to the approach taken in *Kuldip* by holding that a prior compelled answer given by an accused in civil proceedings could be used to impeach his credibility when he gave inconsistent testimony at his criminal trial without violating section 13. The majority reasoned that the prior testimony was not incriminatory evidence of guilt because it was relevant only to the accused's credibility as distinct from his guilt. Three judges argued in dissent that the majority was diluting and complicating *Henry* and diminishing section 13's protections against self-incrimination. In the result, section 13 continues to be a complex and difficult section to interpret. Going forward, it seems that its protection against self-incrimination will not apply if the accused voluntarily provides testimony in a prior proceeding or if the testimony cannot be used to establish the guilt of the accused as opposed to undermining the accused's credibility.

4) Presumption of Innocence and Right to a Fair Hearing by an Independent and Impartial Tribunal

a) Presumption of Innocence

The presumption of innocence has long been an important common law principle in Canada. The accused does not have to prove anything. It is for the prosecution to prove the guilt of the accused beyond a reasonable doubt, failing which the accused is entitled to an acquittal. However, before the *Charter*, this principle was subject to legislation overriding the presumption and Parliament frequently enacted reverse-onus provisions. A "reverse-onus" provision alters the usual rule and requires the accused to prove innocence. A significant body of caselaw challenging legislation of this kind has now developed under the *Charter*.

The case of *R v Oakes*,[155] better known for its articulation of the proportionality test under section 1, provides an example. Narcotics legislation provided that where, on a charge of possession for the purposes of trafficking, it was shown that an accused person was in possession of a prohibited drug, the burden shifted to the accused to prove that he or she was not in possession of the drug for the purposes of trafficking. Describing the presumption of innocence as "essential in a society committed to fairness and social justice," the Supreme Court held that the presumption of innocence was violated and that the violation could

---

154 2012 SCC 59.
155 *R v Oakes*, [1986] 1 SCR 103, 26 DLR (4th) 200, also discussed at length in Chapter 4.

not be sustained under section 1. The reverse-onus provision applied even where an accused was in possession of very small quantities of narcotic, and in light of the lack of a rational connection between the proved fact, possession, and the presumed fact, trafficking, the provision was found to create an unjustifiable risk of conviction without proof of guilt and an unwarranted limitation on the presumption of innocence.

However, many reverse-onus provisions have survived as reasonable limits under section 1. For example, the Supreme Court upheld as a reasonable limit the presumption applicable to drinking and driving cases that, where the accused is found behind the wheel of a car, care and control of the vehicle, an essential element of the offence, shall be presumed absent proof to the contrary.[156] Similarly, the Court upheld as a reasonable limit the presumption that an accused lives off the avails of prostitution if the fact is proved that he lives with or is habitually in the company of prostitutes.[157]

In some situations, a reverse-onus provision may be part of a package that benefits the accused and that would not be made available without the reverse-onus provision. Parliament may be willing to establish a defence but requires the accused to prove it. An example is the anti-hate law, which makes truth a defence but which requires the accused to make out the defence of truth. The Supreme Court found this to be justifiable under section 1.[158] In the Court's opinion, Parliament was not required to afford the defence of truth. It had done so as a concession to the value of freedom of expression. As Dickson CJC explained:

> Parliament has used the reverse onus provision to strike a balance between two legitimate concerns. Requiring the accused to prove on the civil standard that his or her statements are true is an integral part of this balance, and any less onerous burden would severely skew the equilibrium.[159]

The effect of striking down such a reverse-onus clause might well be to make matters worse for the accused since Parliament would be entitled to remove the defence altogether.

One of the most significant cases upholding a reverse-onus provision dealt with the mental disorder defence.[160] Information regarding

---

156 *R v Whyte*, [1988] 2 SCR 3, 51 DLR (4th) 481.
157 *R v Downey*, [1992] 2 SCR 10, 90 DLR (4th) 449.
158 *R v Keegstra*, [1990] 3 SCR 697, 61 CCC (3d) 1.
159 *Ibid* at 70–71 (CCC).
160 *R v Chaulk*, [1990] 3 SCR 1303, 62 CCC (3d) 193.

the state of the mental health of the accused is a matter particularly within the control of the accused. Without the cooperation of the accused, the prosecution would have great difficulty in proving sanity. The Supreme Court found that it would be virtually impossible for the Crown to secure convictions if it had to bear the onus of proving sanity. While the Court accepted that there were a variety of measures that might have been enacted to alleviate the problem, in the end, it found that the adoption of the traditional common law presumption of sanity was justifiable. The Court has been similarly tolerant of judge-made common law rules that arguably violate the presumption of innocence. Rules requiring the accused to establish the defences of extreme intoxication and non-mental disorder automatism on a balance of probabilities have been crafted[161] despite authority suggesting that common law limitations on *Charter* rights should receive no deference and be held to the highest form of section 1 justification.[162]

Another important limitation on the presumption of innocence accepted by the Supreme Court under section 1 is that an accused charged with a regulatory offence must generally establish on a balance of probabilities a defence of due diligence or lack of negligence. A majority of the Court has stressed that it is reasonable for those who enter a regulated field to be required to demonstrate that they took reasonable care to avoid harms such as misleading advertising and health and safety violations.[163]

The Supreme Court continues to interpret the presumption of innocence in a broad fashion so that it is infringed whenever a person may be convicted despite the existence of a reasonable doubt as to guilt. In a complex case dealing with restrictions on the right to challenge the accuracy of breathalyzer readings, the Court ruled that both a requirement that an accused raise a reasonable doubt about the accuracy of the breathalyzer machine and a presumption that the breathalyzer reading represented the accused's blood alcohol levels while driving violated section 11(d). At the same time, however, the Court held that both these presumptions were reasonable limits under section 1. They were rationally connected and proportionate to the objective of protecting the integrity of the breathalyzer as a means to combat drunk driving. On the other hand, the Court held that a requirement that the accused demonstrate that the failure of the breathalyzer machine caused the reading of an illegal blood alcohol level was a serious infringement of

---

161   *Daviault*, above note 27; *R v Stone*, [1999] 2 SCR 290, 134 CCC (3d) 353.
162   *Swain*, above note 119.
163   *R v Wholesale Travel Group Inc*, [1991] 3 SCR 154, 67 CCC (3d) 193.

the presumption of innocence, one that could not be justified under section 1.[164] The Court also found that all these new presumptions in the *Criminal Code* would not apply retroactively because they limited the section 11(d) presumption of innocence.[165]

b) Right to a Fair Hearing by an Independent and Impartial Tribunal

Although the right to trial by "an independent and impartial tribunal" is conferred upon an accused person, it indirectly guarantees the independence of the judges who preside in criminal cases. In a 1985 decision,[166] the Supreme Court of Canada identified the three essential attributes of judicial independence. First, independence requires tenure of office and removal of judges only for a cause related to their capacity to perform a judicial function.[167] Second, independence requires financial security so that judges need not fear diminution in their salary or benefits because of judgments that are unpopular or unfavourable to the government.[168] Third, the Court held that institutional independence in relation to the administration of the courts is a necessary element, in particular, the assignment of judges to particular cases and the establishment of court lists.

5) Fair Trial Rights and Competing *Charter* Rights

The accused's right to a fair trial is a fundamental right that has historically trumped competing rights, such as those involving freedom of expression. Before the *Charter*, judges would order broad publication bans on pre-trial proceedings in response to concerns that extensive publicity might harm the accused's right to a fair trial, including

---

164 *R v St-Onge Lamoureux*, 2012 SCC 57.
165 *R v Dineley*, 2012 SCC 58.
166 *Valente v R*, [1985] 2 SCR 673, 24 DLR (4th) 161.
167 The Court has found that the removal of justices of the peace from office did not violate judicial independence when this was done as a rational means to improve their qualifications for office. *Ell v Alberta*, [2003] 1 SCR 857.
168 The Court has found that this facet of judicial independence requires independent commissions to make recommendations about judicial salaries and requires justification by the legislature for departures from such recommendations. *Reference Re Public Sector Pay Reduction Act (PEI), s 10* (1997), 150 DLR (4th) 577 (SCC). Such recommendations must be made within a reasonable time of the creation of new judicial offices but it is not necessary that the new judicial officers have the same salary or pension benefits as previously appointed judges. *Conférence des juges de paix magistrats v Québec (Attorney General)*, 2016 SCC 39.

the right to impartial jurors. In *Dagenais v Canadian Broadcasting Corporation*,[169] the Court indicated that a hierarchical preference for the accused's fair trial rights was not appropriate and that, henceforth, courts should try to reconcile and minimize the conflict between competing *Charter* rights. As elaborated in the subsequent case of *R v Mentuck*,[170] this understanding meant that courts should not order a publication ban unless there was a serious and substantial risk to the accused's fair trial rights. Even if such a risk existed, courts should strive to avoid a conflict between the competing *Charter* rights of fair trial and free expression by relying on reasonable alternative measures, such as challenging jurors on the basis of partiality because of pre-trial publicity, adjourning trials, or changing their venue in order to eliminate the risk to the accused's right to a fair trial. If such alternative measures could not alleviate the risk, then courts would have to, on the facts of the case, determine whether the salutary effects of a publication ban in protecting the accused's right to a fair trial would outweigh the harms of the ban to freedom of expression and other values, such as open justice. This approach is patterned, in part, on proportionality principles used under section 1 and especially on the final stage of assessing the overall balance. It is a process that requires balancing on the evidence of each particular case and rejects absolute rules.

In *R v NS*,[171] the *Dagenais/Mentuck* approach was applied to possible conflicts between the accused's right to a fair trial and freedom of religion in a case where a complainant in a sexual assault trial wanted to testify while wearing a religious face covering, the niqab. Consistent with *Dagenais*, the Court rejected the extreme alternatives of always allowing witnesses to wear the niqab or never allowing them to do so in favour of a more fact-specific approach that tried to avoid conflicts between *Charter* rights and when necessary strike a just and proportionate balance between conflicting rights. The first step is to assess whether competing *Charter* rights are even in play by determining whether wearing the niqab was based on a sincere religious belief and whether it created a serious risk to trial fairness. Although the Court recognized the traditional importance of being able to see a witness's face in a criminal trial as part of the process of determining credibility, it left open the possibility that there may be some cases where not seeing the witness's face would not present a serious risk to a fair trial. In cases of conflict, the Court indicated that a judge "must try

---

169 [1994] 3 SCR 835.
170 [2001] 3 SCR 442.
171 2012 SCC 72, also discussed in Chapter 8.

to resolve the claims in a way that will preserve both rights. *Dagenais* refers to this as the requirement to consider whether 'reasonably available alternative measures' would avoid the conflict altogether. We also call this 'accommodation.' We find a way to go forward that satisfies each right and each party. Both rights are respected, and the conflict is averted."[172] Finally, if conflict cannot be avoided, the judge must balance the salutary effects of requiring the witness to testify while not veiled against the harmful effects. The salutary effects depend on the importance of the witness's evidence, the nature of the proceedings, and the importance of cross-examination and credibility determinations to the case. The harmful effects would depend on the harm to the witness's religious practices as well as broader social harms, such as discouraging women who wear niqabs from reporting offences.

As in the fair trial versus freedom of expression cases, the appropriate balance in such fair trial versus freedom of religion cases will depend on the particular facts of each case. Nevertheless, the Court has clearly rejected inflexible rules that always prefer the accused's fair trial rights to other competing *Charter* rights. At the same time, the Court did suggest that "where the liberty of the accused is at stake, the witness's evidence is central to the case and her credibility vital, the possibility of a wrongful conviction must weigh heavily in the balance, favouring removal of the niqab."[173]

6) Right to Reasonable Bail

The judicial interim-release provisions of the *Criminal Code* strongly favour affording accused persons bail pending their trial, but one element of the *Code*'s package was found wanting in *R v Morales*.[174] In addition to detaining a person to ensure attendance at trial and to pro-

---

172 *Ibid* at para 32.

173 *Ibid* at para 44. Justices LeBel and Rothstein, in their concurring judgment, expressed a preference for the accused's right to a fair trial more forcefully when they stated that they agreed "with the reasons of the Chief Justice that, when the issue involves the credibility of a key witness in respect of the core questions raised by a charge, the rights of the accused must be protected. Since cross-examination is a necessary tool for the exercise of the right to make full answer and defence, the consequences of restrictions on the rights in question weigh more heavily on the accused, and the balancing process works in his favour" (*ibid* at para 68).

174 [1992] 3 SCR 711, 77 CCC (3d) 91. The Crown generally has to establish grounds for detaining the accused, but the Court has upheld a reversal of this onus in the case of those already on bail and those charged with trafficking in narcotics.

tect the public from a substantial likelihood that, if released, the accused will commit a criminal offence, the *Code* provided as a tertiary ground for denying bail that the detention of the accused "is necessary in the public interest." This was held to be unacceptably vague and imprecise. It imposed a "standardless sweep" that was found to infringe section 11(e) of the *Charter* and could not be saved under the section 1 proportionality test. Parliament responded some time later with a new tertiary ground based on "any other just cause" including where detention is necessary to maintain confidence in the administration of justice having regard to factors such as the strength of the prosecution's case, the circumstances of the alleged offence, the gravity of the offence, and the potential of a lengthy term of imprisonment.[175] The Supreme Court subsequently held that the reference to "any other just cause" was excessively vague but that the reference to the need to maintain confidence in the administration of justice was constitutional because it constituted a just cause for the denial of bail. Four judges dissented from the later decision on the basis that public fears about the release of a person charged but not convicted of a crime did not justify pre-trial detention and that the new tertiary ground was in its entirety excessively vague.[176]

7) Right to Trial by Jury

Section 11(f) of the *Charter* provides that everyone charged with an offence who faces five or more years of imprisonment has the right to a trial by jury. The right to trial by jury has been held to be infringed by a judge's action in instructing a jury that an accused, charged with growing marijuana for his own use, had no defence in law and that they must convict. In a jury trial, the jury, not the judge, must decide whether the accused is guilty.[177] The jury must be representative as well as impartial, but this does not require a jury or a pool of prospective jurors that proportionately represents all groups. The Court found no *Charter* violation even though Aboriginal people were underrepresented on juries because the state had made reasonable efforts to include Aboriginal people on juries.[178]

The *Criminal Code* confers the right to a jury trial in virtually all serious offences even though section 11(f) itself limits the *Charter* right to a jury trial to cases where the accused faces five years of imprison-

---

175   *Criminal Code*, s 515(10)(c).
176   *R v Hall*, [2002] 3 SCR 309.
177   *R v Krieger*, [2006] 2 SCR 501.
178   *R v Kokopenace*, [2015] 2 SCR 398.

ment or more. *R v Lee*[179] dealt with an exception. The accused had initially failed to appear for trial, and the *Criminal Code* provided that, as a consequence, he lost his right to be tried by a jury. The Supreme Court found that the provision violated section 11(f) of the *Charter* but could be upheld as a reasonable limit under section 1. Parliament was entitled to protect the integrity of the criminal process from delay, inconvenience, and expense. Denying the right to a jury trial in such circumstances was held to be proportional to this legitimate governmental objective.

An individual is not required to take advantage of his or her constitutional rights, and ordinarily those rights may be waived. In *R v Turpin*,[180] the accused was charged with murder, an offence at the time required by the *Criminal Code* to be tried by jury. The accused argued that the right to a jury trial implicitly carried with it the right to waive trial by jury and be tried by a judge alone. The Supreme Court did not agree and held that there was no inconsistency between the right to be tried by jury and the statutory requirement that certain offences must be tried by jury. The Court has also held that common law and statutory rules protecting the secrecy of the jury's deliberations are consistent with the *Charter*.[181]

8) *Ex Post Facto* Laws

While the section 11(g) requirement that an act or omission constitute an offence at the time it was committed is an important right, it has not been the subject of substantial litigation since attempts to prosecute individuals for offences created after the fact are extremely rare. The issue was raised, however, in the complex case of *R v Finta*,[182] which dealt with war crimes relating to the Nazi occupation of Hungary. The accused, a captain in the Royal Hungarian Gendarmerie during the Second World War, was charged with war crimes and crimes against humanity for allegedly participating in the unlawful confinement, kidnapping, robbery, and in some cases, manslaughter of more than 8,000 people. The Supreme Court rejected the accused's claim under section 11(g). It stated that justice required the retroactive punishment of those who committed acts that were internationally illegal and known to be morally objectionable, regardless of the fact that the acts were not formally criminal under positive law at the time. The accused was

---

179 [1989] 2 SCR 1384, 52 CCC (3d) 289.
180 [1989] 1 SCR 1296, 48 CCC (3d) 8.
181 *R v Pan*, [2001] 2 SCR 244, 200 DLR (4th) 577.
182 [1994] 1 SCR 701, 112 DLR (4th) 513.

acquitted at trial on other grounds, however, and the Crown's appeals were rejected.

9) Double Jeopardy

Though much of the law on double jeopardy is governed by pre-*Charter* jurisprudence, there have been some significant cases under section 11(h). In *R v Wigglesworth*,[183] an RCMP officer, having been convicted under the *Royal Canadian Mounted Police Act* for assaulting a prisoner, was then charged with criminal assault for the same incident. The Supreme Court allowed the second set of proceedings to continue, noting a "double aspect" to the wrongful conduct. That is to say, while the accused had already answered to his profession through the private sanctions of internal discipline, he must still be made to account to society at large for his actions. The word "offence" in section 11(h) was thus defined narrowly so as to include only truly criminal or penal offences. This approach was applied and affirmed in *R v Shubley*,[184] a case involving a charge of criminal assault where the accused had already been subject to prison discipline in relation to the same incident. Applying the two-stage test from *Wigglesworth*, the Court found that, since the prison discipline was neither by its nature criminal nor did it impose true penal consequences, no violation of section 11(h) had occurred.

The Court has extended the right against double jeopardy to also apply to laws that abolished early parole after an offender had been convicted. It stressed that the abolition of early parole effectively extended the minimum period that the offender would stay in jail and did so after the offender's conviction. The retroactive imposition of increased punishment could not be justified compared to the less intrusive alternative of prospective legislation that would delay parole eligibility to future offenders.[185]

10) Benefit of Lesser Punishment

This guarantee in section 11(i) of the *Charter* confirms a pre-*Charter* common law principle similar to the preclusion of conviction for matters that were not an offence at the time the act was committed (section 11(g)). The guarantee rests on a fundamental principle of legality, namely, that an individual's conduct is to be assessed on the basis of the law in

---

183 *Wigglesworth*, above note 140.
184 [1990] 1 SCR 3, 65 DLR (4th) 193.
185 *Canada (Attorney General) v Whaling*, 2014 SCC 20.

force at the time and that it would be unfair to impose penalties not then provided for by law. Section 11(i) was violated by 2012 provisions that allowed judges to impose restrictions on offenders who committed sexual crimes against children before 2012. The Court held that the new provisions constituted punishment because they were imposed for sentencing reasons relating to public safety and had a significant impact on the offender's liberty or security interests. At the same time, the Court held that the retroactive imposition of a ban on using the Internet but not on contacting all persons under sixteen years of age had been justified as a reasonable limit under section 1 of the *Charter*. The Court noted that both new provisions were rationally connected to the important purpose of preventing sexual offending against children and violated the section 11(i) right as little as possible. Nevertheless, the Court held that harmful effects of banning an offender from having any unsupervised contact with a person under sixteen years of age outweighed its speculative benefits in preventing sexual offences while evidence about the use of new social media to lure children justified the retroactive imposition of the ban on using the Internet.[186]

11) Right to an Interpreter

Section 14 of the *Charter* guarantees parties to proceedings, including the accused and witnesses, the right to an interpreter:

> A party or witness in any proceeding who does not understand or speak the language in which the proceedings are conducted or who is deaf has the right to the assistance of an interpreter.

The *Charter* also contains English- and French-language guarantees that apply to criminal proceedings in certain provinces, as discussed in Chapter 16.

The leading case on the section 14 right to an interpreter is *R v Tran*.[187] Convicted of sexual assault, the accused's interpreter at trial failed to translate much of the key testimony in full and instead merely summarized the evidence. Embracing a "liberal interpretation and principled application" of the right to an interpreter, the Supreme Court allowed the accused's appeal and ordered a new trial. Grounded in the basic requirement that a person charged with a criminal offence has the right to hear the case against him or her and to be given a full opportunity to answer it, the Court stated section 14 guarantees

---

186 *R v KRJ*, 2016 SCC 31.
187 [1994] 2 SCR 951, 117 DLR (4th) 7.

that those who need an interpreter must be given assistance that is continuous, precise, impartial, competent, and contemporaneous. Not every deviation from perfection will constitute a violation of section 14, however. The claimant must establish that the lapse in interpretation involved procedure, evidence, or law and not merely some collateral or extrinsic matter.

F. CRUEL AND UNUSUAL PUNISHMENT

Section 12 of the *Charter* provides:

> Everyone has the right not to be subject to any cruel and unusual treatment or punishment.

Laws requiring minimum sentences for specified offences have been the exception rather than the rule in Canadian criminal law, though their use has increased in recent years. In *Smith v R*,[188] the Supreme Court struck down a minimum punishment of seven years' imprisonment for importing narcotics. Too wide a range of activities was caught by the prohibition against importing drugs, from large-scale trafficking of dangerous drugs by organized crime to the importation of a small quantity of marijuana for personal consumption. While the Court did not settle on a precise definition of "cruel and unusual," a majority found that imposing a minimum sentence of such length would, in many instances, be so grossly disproportionate to the gravity of the offence committed by the accused as to outrage standards of decency and thus offend the guarantee under section 12. The Court was not willing to trust the matter to prosecutorial discretion to charge minor offenders with simple possession, since that would amount to an unacceptable delegation of decision-making authority in a situation where a fundamental right was at issue.

Other challenges to mandatory minimum sentences have, however, failed. The Supreme Court has upheld mandatory life imprisonment without eligibility for parole for twenty-five years for first degree murder[189] and without eligibility for parole for ten years for second degree murder.[190] In both cases, the Court has stressed that the penalty was not grossly disproportionate given the seriousness of the offence. The Court has maintained the high standard that only sentences that are

---

188 [1987] 1 SCR 1045, 34 CCC (3d) 97.
189 *Luxton*, above note 118.
190 *R v Latimer*, [2001] 1 SCR 3, 193 DLR (4th) 577.

grossly disproportionate violate the *Charter* and has rejected the idea that the fundamental sentencing principle of proportionality between the crime and the sentence is a principle of fundamental justice protected under section 7 of the *Charter*.[191]

The Court has also upheld a mandatory minimum penalty of seven days' imprisonment for knowingly driving with a suspended licence[192] and a mandatory ten-year firearm prohibition upon a drug conviction. In the latter case, the Court stressed both that the prohibition was related to the legitimate sentencing goal of protecting the public and that the *Criminal Code* allowed the judge to make exceptions when firearms were required for employment or sustenance reasons.[193]

The Court has also upheld mandatory minimum penitentiary terms when firearms are used to commit serious offences. In *R v Morrisey*, it upheld a minimum sentence of four years' imprisonment for criminal negligence causing death with a firearm[194] and in *R v Ferguson*, it upheld a mandatory minimum sentence of four years' imprisonment for manslaughter with a firearm.[195] The Court in *Morrisey* stressed that in determining whether a particular punishment is grossly disproportionate, the Court can consider both the circumstances of the particular offender and of reasonable hypothetical offenders that may be convicted under the offence and subject to the mandatory penalty. The Court in *R v Ferguson* held that the appropriate remedial response to a finding of gross disproportionality is to strike the mandatory sentence down under section 52(1) of the *Constitution Act, 1982* for all offenders as opposed to crafting a constitutional exemption for particular offenders.[196] Such a remedial approach, in the Court's view, respects Parliament's intent in creating mandatory sentences and the remedial structure of the *Charter*. It means that any exemption from mandatory penalties will have to be fashioned by Parliament and not by the courts on a case-by-case basis.

The Court has recently taken a more aggressive approach to the constitutionality of mandatory minimum sentences. It has held that a mandatory minimum sentence of three years for a first offence, and a mandatory minimum sentence of five years for a second offence of possession of a prohibited or restricted firearm with access to ammunition, was cruel and unusual punishment. Although the punishment was

---

191 *R v Safarzadeh-Markhali*, 2016 SCC 14 at paras 71–73.
192 *R v Goltz*, [1991] 3 SCR 485, 67 CCC (3d) 481.
193 *R v Wiles*, [2005] 3 SCR 895.
194 *R v Morrisey*, [2000] 2 SCR 90, 191 DLR (4th) 86 [*Morrisey*].
195 *R v Ferguson*, [2008] 1 SCR 96.
196 *Ibid.*

appropriate as applied to the offenders in the case, it could be grossly disproportionate as applied to reasonable hypothetical offenders. The Court would not rely on the use of prosecutorial discretion to protect such offenders from the mandatory minimum penalty.[197] Similar reasoning was used to hold that a mandatory minimum penalty of one-year imprisonment for a second conviction of possession of illegal drugs for the purpose of trafficking was unconstitutional, with the Court even suggesting that it was inevitable that mandatory sentences for broadly defined offences could be grossly disproportionate when imposed on less blameworthy offenders unless sentencing judges had some ability to justify a departure from a mandatory sentence or Parliament defined the offence narrowly.[198]

G. REMEDIES IN THE CRIMINAL PROCESS

One of the most difficult issues the courts face is determining the appropriate remedy for a *Charter* breach. Typically, *Charter* rights are asserted by accused persons because the police have obtained incriminating evidence as a result of the conduct that forms the basis for the *Charter* claim. A judicial decision that a *Charter* right has been infringed will have a declaratory effect. The authorities may be expected to abide by court rulings and alter their practices and procedures to comply with the dictates of the *Charter* in subsequent cases. But what of the individual who is before the court and whose rights have been infringed? A decision that merely declares that his or her rights have been infringed will ring hollow if no further action is taken. Can a system of justice premised on respect for certain fundamental rights countenance continuation of the proceedings or reliance on evidence obtained in violation of those rights? On the other hand, if the evidence obtained as a result of the *Charter* breach is not admitted by the court, relevant facts are excluded and the search for the truth is inhibited. As a result, a guilty person may go free. Is exclusion of evidence acceptable in these circumstances? Is this an appropriate way to control police behaviour?

Chapter 17 considers remedial issues in general, while the specific issues of remedies in criminal proceedings is dealt with here. Section 24 of the *Charter* provides as follows:

---

197 *R v Nur*, 2015 SCC 15.
198 *R v Lloyd*, 2016 SCC 13 at paras 35–36.

(1) Anyone whose rights or freedoms, as guaranteed by this *Charter*, have been infringed or denied may apply to a court of competent jurisdiction to obtain such remedy as the court considers appropriate and just in the circumstances.

(2) Where, in proceedings under subsection (1), a court concludes that evidence was obtained in a manner that infringed or denied any rights or freedoms guaranteed by this *Charter*, the evidence shall be excluded if it is established that, having regard to all the circumstances, the admission of it in the proceedings would bring the administration of justice into disrepute.

1) Stay of Proceedings

In certain cases, a prosecution may be so tainted by the *Charter* breach that a stay of proceedings is appropriate. A stay of proceedings is an order that forbids the prosecutor from taking any further steps against the accused on the charges before the court. It is obviously a drastic remedy. Before the *Charter*, stays were available in cases where the court found that a prosecution amounted to an abuse of the court's process. Since the *Charter*'s enactment, the common law stay has been assimilated and adapted as a *Charter* remedy. The Supreme Court had made it clear that, given its severity, the remedy of a stay should be granted only

> "in the clearest of cases," where the prejudice to the accused's right to make full answer and defence cannot be remedied or where irreparable prejudice would be caused to the integrity of the judicial system if the prosecution were continued.[199]

A stay of proceedings will be ordered only if the prejudice caused by the abuse will be aggravated by the trial and no other remedy is reasonably capable of removing that prejudice. In cases of uncertainty, the judge will balance the interests in favour of a stay against society's interest in having a final decision on the merits.[200] The minimum remedy for a violation of the accused's right to full answer and defence will be the order of a new trial, and a stay of proceedings will be appropriate and just only in the exceptional circumstances of an irreparable violation of the right.[201] In contrast, the Supreme Court decided in the early years of the *Charter* that a stay of proceedings was the minimum

---

199 *R v O'Connor* (1995), 103 CCC (3d) 1 at 43, L'Heureux-Dubé J.
200 *R v Regan*, [2002] 1 SCR 297, 209 DLR (4th) 41.
201 *Taillefer*, above note 44.

remedy for a violation of the right to a trial in a reasonable time under section 11(b) of the *Charter*, on the basis that a trial after that time would not be fair and would aggravate the prejudice caused by the pre-trial delay.[202] The Court has deferred to the discretion of a trial judge who stayed proceedings in relation to charges against a prison guard after having determined that the prison guard assaulted a handcuffed and chained prisoner.[203]

2) Exclusion of Evidence

The most commonly ordered remedy for a breach of *Charter* rights in the criminal process is exclusion of evidence. Prior to the enactment of the *Charter*, illegally obtained evidence was admissible, even where it was obtained in a manner that violated a right guaranteed by the *Canadian Bill of Rights*.[204] Section 24(2) of the *Charter* alters that rule but stops short of a presumptive exclusionary rule.

The first question is whether the "evidence was obtained in a manner that infringed or denied any rights or freedoms guaranteed by this *Charter*." The issue here is the extent to which it must be shown that there was a causal link between the *Charter* breach and obtaining the evidence. Evidence found following an unreasonable search may well have been uncovered in any event. Was it obtained "in a manner which violated" a *Charter* right? The Supreme Court has interpreted these words of section 24(2) not to require a strict causal connection. In *R v Strachan*,[205] Dickson CJC stated that the inquiry should focus on the "entire chain of events" and that, ordinarily, a temporal link between the *Charter* breach and discovery of the evidence will be sufficient. The case involved a search and arrest at the home of the accused. The police refused to allow the accused to telephone his lawyer and proceeded to find drugs. Despite the tenuous causal connection between the *Charter* breach of denial of counsel and the discovery of the drugs, the Court found that section 24(2) was engaged. In the end, the majority held that the drugs could be admitted into evidence, but the case stands for the proposition that a strict causal relationship between the *Charter* breach and the discovery of the evidence is not required.

If this initial hurdle is satisfied, the Court must turn to a second issue and the central component of section 24(2), namely, whether admission of the evidence "would bring the administration of justice into

---

202 *R v Rahey*, [1987] 1 SCR 588.
203 *R v Bellusci*, 2012 SCC 44.
204 *Hogan v R*, [1975] 2 SCR 574, 48 DLR (3d) 427.
205 [1988] 2 SCR 980, 46 CCC (3d) 479.

disrepute." A significant body of caselaw has developed on the admissibility of evidence where a *Charter* right has been infringed. The basic framework for analysis was set out in the Supreme Court of Canada's 1987 decision in *R v Collins*[206] and confirmed in the 1997 *Stillman* decision.[207] As will be seen, it has now been altered.

In *Collins*, the Supreme Court stated that the purpose of section 24(2) was not to control the conduct of the police but rather to protect the integrity of the judicial system. Justice Lamer identified as relevant the "disrepute that will result from the admission of the evidence that would deprive the accused of a fair hearing, or from judicial condonation of unacceptable conduct by the investigatory and prosecutorial agencies."[208] The Court rejected the suggestion that disrepute should be assessed on the basis of public opinion or shock to the community. That, said Lamer J, would be contrary to the very purpose of the *Charter*, to protect the individual from the majority. The question of bringing the administration of justice into disrepute is, accordingly, to be assessed on a judicial and dispassionate basis. The relevant question is "[W]ould the admission of the evidence bring the administration of justice into disrepute in the eyes of a reasonable man, dispassionate and fully apprised of the circumstances of the case?"[209] Very often, those who assert *Charter* claims and seek to exclude evidence as a result are undeserving of public sympathy, but *Charter* protections apply to all. As Iacobucci J explained:

> [W]e should never lose sight of the fact that even a person accused of the most heinous crimes, and no matter the likelihood that he actually committed those crimes, is entitled to the full protection of the *Charter*. Short-cutting or short-circuiting those rights affects not only the accused, but also the entire reputation of the criminal justice system. It must be emphasized that the goals of preserving the integrity of the criminal justice system, as well as promoting the decency of investigatory techniques, are of fundamental importance in applying s 24(2).[210]

---

206 [1987] 1 SCR 265, 33 CCC (3d) 1 [*Collins*].
207 *Stillman*, above note 65.
208 *Collins*, above note 206 at 16–17 (CCC).
209 *Ibid* at 18.
210 *R v Burlingham*, [1995] 2 SCR 206, 124 DLR (4th) 7 at 31. See also *R v Feeney*, [1997] 2 SCR 13 at para 83, Sopinka J: If the exclusion of this evidence is likely to result in an acquittal of the accused as suggested by L'Heureux-Dubé J in her reasons, then the Crown is deprived of a conviction based on illegally obtained evidence. Any price to society occasioned by the loss of such a conviction is fully justified in a free and democratic society which is governed by the rule of law.

Collins, and subsequently *Stillman*, set out a three-step test for the determination of whether the admission of the evidence would bring the administration of justice into disrepute. The first set of factors to be considered is the way the evidence affects the fairness of the trial. If the court concludes that admission of the evidence would adversely affect the fairness of the trial, the evidence will almost always be excluded. *Stillman* draws a distinction between "conscriptive" and "non-conscriptive" evidence.[211] Conscriptive evidence is obtained when, in violation of *Charter* rights, an accused "is compelled to incriminate himself at the behest of the state by means of a statement, the use of the body, or the production of bodily samples."[212] "Non-conscriptive" evidence is that which is obtained by the state without the accused's participation or which existed independently of any *Charter* breach. Conscriptive evidence will ordinarily be excluded without considering any other factors, unless the prosecutor can show that it would have been discovered by non-conscripted means. The admission of conscriptive evidence would strike at a fundamental tenet of a fair trial, the right against self-incrimination. Statements obtained following denial of the right to counsel have frequently been excluded.[213] The notion of evidence emanating from the accused has been extended to exclude evidence obtained as a result of a police lineup following the denial of the right to counsel since such evidence could be obtained only through the participation of the accused.[214] Similarly, bodily samples obtained as a result of a *Charter* breach have been considered conscriptive evidence.[215]

On the other hand, non-conscriptive evidence — most often, tangible evidence that exists independently of the accused (such as a weapon or drugs) — will ordinarily not render the trial unfair. To determine whether such evidence should be admitted, it is necessary to proceed to consider the next two steps.

The second set of factors is the seriousness of the *Charter* breach and the reasons for it. Technical or minor violations do not attract the same censure as serious ones. A distinction has been drawn between situations where the police have acted in good faith, relying on what is believed to be the existing state of the law, and cases where the police

---

211 *Stillman*, above note 65.
212 *Ibid* at 655 (SCR), Cory J.
213 See, for example, *Clarkson v R*, [1986] 1 SCR 383, 26 DLR (4th) 493; *Brydges*, above note 131.
214 *R v Leclair*, [1989] 1 SCR 3, 46 CCC (3d) 129.
215 *Stillman*, above note 65.

intentionally or carelessly abuse the rights of the accused.[216] In the latter category of cases, evidence has often been excluded, while, in the former, the good faith of the police will be a factor favouring admissibility.

The third set of considerations involves weighing the effect of excluding the evidence against the effect of admitting it. Disrepute to the administration of justice could result if evidence were excluded because of a trivial breach. The seriousness of the charge is also a factor to be considered.

In *R v Grant*,[217] the Supreme Court recognized that while the *Collins/Stillman* tests outlined above had "brought a measure of certainty to the section 24(2) inquiry," the tests had resulted in decisions about the admissibility of evidence that were inconsistent with the language and objectives of section 24(2) in facilitating a balancing of the competing interests in all the circumstances of each case. In particular, the Court was concerned about the nearly automatic exclusion of conscriptive evidence, such as unconstitutionally obtained statements, bodily samples, and evidence derived from such evidence that would not have been inevitably discovered without a *Charter* violation. The Court articulated a new three-part test under section 24(2) in which trial judges

> must assess and balance the effect of admitting the evidence on society's confidence in the justice system having regard to: (1) the seriousness of the *Charter*-infringing state conduct (admission may send the message the justice system condones serious state misconduct), (2) the impact of the breach on the *Charter*-protected interests of the accused (admission may send the message that individual rights count for little), and (3) society's interest in the adjudication of the case on its merits.[218]

This new and more flexible test for applying section 24(2) has much in common with the previous tests. The focus remains on upholding the long-term repute of the justice system as opposed to deterring the police or compensating the accused. The test for measuring the seriousness of the violation has also not changed. As before, deliberate, wilful, flagrant, or reckless violations of the *Charter* may require the court to exclude the unconstitutionally obtained evidence to avoid condoning serious violations. On the other hand, inadvertent, minor, or good faith violations of the *Charter* are less serious and less likely to require exclusion.

---

216 *Collins*, above note 206.
217 2009 SCC 32.
218 *Ibid* at para 71.

The most significant change in the new test is the abandonment of the singular focus on the effects of admitting evidence unconstitutionally conscripted from the accused on the fairness of the trial, in favour of a more general concern about the impact of the *Charter* breach on "the interests protected by the right infringed."[219] Following a purposive approach to rights, these interests will differ with the particular right. For example, the focus will be on the effects of a section 8 search and seizure violation on privacy, bodily integrity and dignity. Similarly, the focus will be on effects of the principle against self-incrimination and the right to silence when statements are unconstitutionally obtained from the accused. The abandonment of the focus on fair trials also means that, in cases of unconstitutionally obtained statements and bodily samples, courts should consider whether the seriousness of the *Charter* violation and society's interests in adjudication of the case on the merits also require exclusion. In particular, the Court has opened the door to admission of statements obtained through minor or technical *Charter* violations of the right to counsel or in circumstances where the statement would have been made notwithstanding the *Charter* breach. Nevertheless, the Court has maintained the presumption that most statements obtained in violation of the *Charter* should be excluded.[220] The Court has also opened the door to admission of unconstitutionally obtained bodily samples, particularly breath samples, in cases where the *Charter* violation is not serious and where the impact of the violation on privacy, bodily integrity, and dignity is not great. The Court has also recognized that the reliability of bodily samples as opposed to statements "may well tip the balance in favour of admission."[221]

Society's interest in adjudicating a case on its merits may require consideration of the reliability of the evidence, its importance to the prosecution's case, and the seriousness of the offence charged. At the same time, the Court indicated that the seriousness of the offence charged can "cut both ways" because "while the public has a heightened interest in seeing a determination on the merits where the offence charged is serious, it also has a vital interest in having a justice system that is above reproach, particularly where the penal stakes for the accused are high."[222]

In *Grant*, the Court held that a handgun unconstitutionally discovered as a result of an arbitrary detention and a violation of the right to

---

219 *Ibid* at para 76.
220 *Ibid* at paras 92 and 96.
221 *Ibid* at para 110.
222 *Ibid* at para 84.

counsel in the course of an investigative stop should be admitted under section 24(2). Although the impact of the *Charter* violations on the accused's *Charter* interests was significant because the police would not have discovered the gun had they not unconstitutionally detained and questioned the accused, the *Charter* violations were not deliberate or in bad faith in part because the applicable law was uncertain at the time. In addition, the admission of the gun as evidence was "essential to a determination on the merits"[223] for various firearm offences. In a companion case,[224] the Court reversed a trial judge's decision to admit evidence of thirty-five kilograms of cocaine that was obtained after an arbitrary detention and an unconstitutional search of a car. The Court stressed that the blatant and flagrant nature of these *Charter* violations was a significant, albeit not egregious, intrusion on *Charter*-protected interests. The Court held that the trial judge had erred by placing too much emphasis on the third factor, namely the effect of exclusion on society's interests in a determination of the criminal case on the merits. The trial judge had erred by stressing that the police misconduct was less serious than the crimes charged. "The fact that a *Charter* breach is less heinous than the offence charged does not advance the inquiry mandated by section 24(2). We expect police to adhere to higher standards than alleged criminals."[225]

The seriousness of the violation has emerged as the most important factor under the *Grant* test. The Court has not hesitated to exclude evidence when convinced that the police violation was serious,[226] but it has been inclined to admit unconstitutionally obtained evidence if the police acted in good faith.[227]

3) Sentence Reductions

The Supreme Court has indicated that a reduction of sentence may be an appropriate remedy for a *Charter* violation and other abuses of state authority.[228] This remedy is, of course, only available in those cases where an accused is found or pleads guilty. The Court has also indicated that judges must reconcile such sentence reductions with the principles and purposes of sentencing. There is some indication in that case that judges might, in appropriate cases, award a reduced sentence

---

223 *Ibid* at para 140.
224 *R v Harrison*, 2009 SCC 34.
225 *Ibid* at para 41.
226 *R v Cole*, 2012 SCC 53.
227 *R v Aucoin*, 2012 SCC 66.
228 *R v Nasogaluak*, [2010] 1 SCR 206.

below a mandatory minimum sentence under section 24(1) of the *Charter* when justified as an appropriate and just remedy,[229] but there is conflicting authority which suggests that such case-specific exemptions under section 24(1) are not an appropriate remedy and that mandatory sentences should only be struck down under section 52(1) when they have cruel and unusual effects on offenders by imposing grossly disproportionate punishment.[230]

4) *Habeas Corpus*

Habeas corpus is a common law remedy against unlawful detention. It is of ancient origin and permits anyone who is detained to require the person having custody to bring the detainee immediately before a court and to provide legal justification for the detention. If the jailer is unable to satisfy the judge that the detention is lawful, the subject has the right to immediate release.

Section 10(c) of the *Charter* provides a right for all detainees to have the validity of their detention determined by way of *habeas corpus*. The Court has consistently interpreted this remedy in a flexible and generous manner that befits its importance at the common law and its constitutional status. The Court held that prisoners in federal institutions can seek *habeas corpus* in the superior courts as an alternative to judicial review in the Federal Court. In *Steele v Mountain Institution (Warden)*,[231] the Court found that the continued detention after thirty-five years of a sexual psychopath's incarceration could no longer be justified in light of the evidence of experts as to his present state. The parole board was charged with responsibility for assessing such cases, but there had been serious procedural and substantive flaws in the parole board's proceedings. The Court held that the detention of the prisoner had become so grossly disproportionate to the circumstances of his case that it constituted cruel and unusual punishment. It ordered that he be released on a *habeas corpus* application. The Court has also emphasized that superior courts should decline to exercise its *habeas corpus* jurisdiction only "in limited circumstances," such as when a court of appeal has statutory jurisdiction to correct errors of a lower court and release the applicant, or if there is "a complete, comprehensive and expert procedure for review of an administrative decision."[232] The Court has stressed that superior courts hearing a *habeas corpus*

---

229 *Ibid* at paras 6 and 64.
230 *R v Ferguson*, [2008] 1 SCR 96.
231 [1990] 2 SCR 1385, 60 CCC (3d) 1.
232 *Ibid* at para 44.

application have an important role that should not be usurped by alternative administrative processes such as the prison grievance procedure, even as subject to judicial review in Federal Court.[233]

The rights secured by this common law remedy are also guaranteed by other *Charter* provisions: the right to be secure from arbitrary arrest and detention, the right to a speedy trial, and the right not to be denied reasonable bail. The effect of section 10(c) is to reinforce the common law remedy and to require that any legislative curtailment of the remedy satisfy the exacting standards of section 1.

The Supreme Court has affirmed that

> *habeas corpus* is a crucial remedy in the pursuit of two fundamental rights protected by the *Canadian Charter of Rights and Freedoms*: (1) the right to liberty of the person and the right not to be deprived thereof except in accordance with the principles of fundamental justice (s. 7 of the *Charter*); and (2) the right not to be arbitrarily detained or imprisoned (s. 9 of the *Charter*).[234]

H. CONCLUSION

Canadian criminal law has been significantly affected by the *Charter of Rights and Freedoms* and judges have assumed an important law-making role. This reflects both the many rights that apply to the criminal process and that most *Charter* litigation is conducted in the criminal process where accused have the greatest incentive to raise *Charter* arguments and the greatest access to legal aid funding. Not surprisingly, *Charter* decisions have provoked debate concerning how the substantive content of fundamental rights affects the use of the criminal law and how *Charter* litigation and remedies affects the imposition of the criminal sanction in particular cases.

There are two core principles to be considered here.

First is the issue of the legitimacy of judicial review, a matter considered more broadly in Chapter 2. Judicial review qualifies majority rule, and it is evident from the cases considered in this chapter that Canadian judges have not hesitated to exercise the power to strike down laws that they consider to violate *Charter* guarantees, even though accused people are often unpopular and have little political power. One point to be noted, however, particularly in the realm of the criminal

---

233 *Mission Institution v Khela*, [2014] 1 SCR 502.
234 *May v Ferndale Institute*, [2005] 3 SCR 809 at para 21.

law, is that more often than not, what is at issue is not the solemn pro-nouncement of Parliament but rather the action of a police officer or prosecutor. The number of cases challenging the constitutionality of police conduct or that of other unelected state officials far exceeds the number of cases challenging the constitutionality of laws enacted by the representatives of the people. Judicial review of the propriety of the conduct of law-enforcement officials is considerably less controversial and very much more in keeping with the common law tradition. Con-trol of the exercise of power by state officials through judicial review is a cornerstone of the rule of law, and subjecting the actions of police and other state officials to judicial scrutiny is one of the hallmarks of a civilized society. The *Charter* bolsters judicial powers in this area and, in so doing, does not conflict with democratic principles. In addition, it is also significant that many of the *Charter* challenges to both legisla-tion and police conduct examined in this chapter have been the subject of a legislative reply by Parliament in the exercise of its jurisdiction over criminal law and procedure. The constitutionality of this reply legislation, most recently in relation to prostitution and assisted dying, has not been considered in all cases, but the Supreme Court has gener-ally determined that the reply legislation was a reasonable balance of the competing interests.

The second tension concerns the competing conceptions of the ap-propriate focus of the criminal law, identified at the beginning of this chapter, crime control and due process. Crime control is a matter of para-mount concern in most modern societies and Canada is no exception. Condemning anti-social behaviour, convicting the guilty, and punish-ing wrongdoers for their transgressions represent central and import-ant purposes of the criminal law. In recent years, concerns about the effects of some crimes on disadvantaged groups such as women and children have also strengthened the state's interest in crime control. At the same time, however, the criminal law involves the assertion of state power over citizens, and the tradition of liberal democracy requires that coercive powers be limited by law and that those who assert power comply with specified standards. Due-process standards are designed to ensure that the state respects the human dignity of all citizens, even those accused of serious wrongdoing. The *Charter of Rights and Free-doms*, as interpreted and applied by our courts, pushes Canada decid-edly in the due-process direction. It has to be recognized, however, that the imposition of limits on the authority of state officials and the ex-tension of procedural protections to persons accused of crime not only benefit the innocent but also make it more difficult to convict the guilty.

FURTHER READINGS

BERGER, B, & J STRIBOPOULOUS, eds, *Unsettled Legacy Thirty Years of Criminal Justice under the* Charter (Markham, ON: LexisNexis, 2012)

CAIRNS WAY, R, "An Opportunity for Equality *Kokopenace* and *Nur* at the Supreme Court of Canada" (2014) 61 Crim LQ 465

CAMERON, J, ed, *The* Charter's *Impact on the Criminal Justice System* (Toronto: Carswell, 1996)

———, & J STRIBOPOULOS, eds, *The* Charter *and Criminal Justice Twenty Five Years Later* (Toronto: LexisNexis, 2008)

COHEN, S, *Privacy, Crime and Terror: Legal Rights and Security in a Time of Peril* (Toronto: LexisNexis, 2005)

COUGHLAN, S, *Criminal Procedure*, 3d ed (Toronto: Irwin Law, 2015)

———, & R CURRIE, "Sections 9, 10 and 11 of the Canadian *Charter*" 62 Sup Ct L Rev (2d) 143

MAYEDA, G, "My Neighbour's Kid Just Bought a Drone . . . New Paradigms for Privacy Law in Canada" (2015) 35 NJCL 59

PACIOCCO, DM, *Getting Away with Murder: The Canadian Criminal Justice System* (Toronto: Irwin Law, 1999)

———, "Competing Constitutional Rights in an Age of Deference: A Bad Time to Be Accused" (2001) 14 Sup Ct L Rev (2d) 111

PENNY, S, V RONDINELLI, & J STRIBOPOULOS, *Criminal Procedure in Canada* (Markham, ON: LexisNexis, 2011)

QUIGLEY, T, *Procedure in Canadian Criminal Law*, 2d ed. (Toronto: Carswell, 1997)

ROACH, K, *Due Process and Victims' Rights: The New Law and Politics of Criminal Justice* (Toronto: University of Toronto Press, 1999)

———, *Criminal Law*, 6th ed (Toronto: Irwin Law, 2015)

STUART, D, Charter *Justice in Canadian Criminal Law*, 6th ed (Toronto: Carswell, 2014)

CHAPTER 15

EQUALITY

The guarantee of equality contained in section 15 of the *Charter of Rights and Freedoms* states:

(1) Every individual is equal before and under the law and has the right to the equal protection and equal benefit of the law without discrimination and, in particular, without discrimination based on race, national or ethnic origin, colour, religion, sex, age or mental or physical disability.

(2) Subsection (1) does not preclude any law, program or activity that has as its object the amelioration of conditions of disadvantaged individuals or groups including those that are disadvantaged because of race, national or ethnic origin, colour, religion, sex, age or mental or physical disability.

The equality rights jurisprudence under the *Charter* is complex, and it defies any attempt at a quick and accurate summary. This is hardly surprising. Equality is a fundamental value in a democratic society, and yet its precise meaning is elusive in political and legal discourse. As a legal concept, it includes the notion that every individual is entitled to dignity and respect and that the law should apply to all in an even-handed manner. Equality thus involves comparisons between individuals or groups, but there is considerable debate about proper comparisons — who should be equal to whom, and what constitutes equal treatment? Should there be absolute equality, with everyone treated identically? How should differences be taken into account? Should advantaged groups be able to enjoy the benefit of equality rights? Are affirmative action measures that favour disadvantaged individuals and groups acceptable? Some theories of equality emphasize equal opportunity; others emphasize equality of outcomes.[1] These are value-laden issues that cannot be simply resolved by the mechanical application of any test.

Equality rights claims are challenging because they frequently present controversial moral, social, or political issues that many argue should not even be before the courts. For example, can equality rights be invoked to protect the rights of children not to be spanked?[2] Does section 15 give same-sex couples the right to marry?[3] Equality rights cases are also contentious when used as a vehicle to extend legislative benefits such as pensions, social assistance, or health-care coverage. Such cases inevitably have significant policy or budgetary implications, making them the kinds of cases with which courts are the least comfortable.

These are complex and difficult issues, and the search for appropriate responses continues. This chapter begins by tracing the pre-*Charter* origins of equal rights protection in Canada. It next discusses the Supreme Court's efforts to come to grips with a general framework of the analysis of equality rights under the *Charter*. Finally, it discusses how the courts have dealt with particular kinds of discrimination under section 15.

A. EQUALITY UNDER THE *CANADIAN BILL OF RIGHTS*

In order to understand the scope of the *Charter*'s equality guarantee, it is useful to consider briefly the Supreme Court of Canada's treatment of equality under section 1(b) of the *Canadian Bill of Rights*, which guaranteed "the right to equality before the law and the protection of the law." As noted in Chapter 1, the Court's performance under the *Bill of Rights* was generally regarded as a disappointment. The most expansive

---

1   For further discussion of the debate about equality, see M Schwarzschild, "Constitutional Law and Equality" in D Patterson, ed, *A Companion to Philosophy of Law and Legal Theory* (Cambridge: Blackwell, 1996) at 156; L Smith, & W Black, "The Equality Rights" in E Mendes & S Beaulac, eds, *The* Canadian Charter of Rights and Freedoms, 5th ed (Markham, ON: LexisNexis Butterworths, 2013) at 952–55.

2   *Canadian Foundation for Children, Youth and the Law v Canada (Attorney General)*, [2004] 1 SCR 76 [*Canadian Foundation for Children*].

3   *Reference Re Same-Sex Marriage*, [2004] 3 SCR 698 [*Same-Sex Marriage Reference*].

interpretation of the equality guarantee was reached in *R v Drybones*,[4] the 1969 decision where the Court found inoperative a section of the *Indian Act* that made it an offence for an Indian to be intoxicated off a reserve. The *Indian Act* provision was held by the Court to deny racial equality because it imposed more onerous constraints on Aboriginal people than did the general liquor ordinance of the Northwest Territories, which merely prohibited drunkenness in a public place.

While *Drybones* was widely applauded as an important affirmation of the equality principle, the Supreme Court quickly retreated. In *Lavell*,[5] the Court upheld a provision of the *Indian Act* depriving of status an Indian woman who married a non-Indian while not imposing a similar disability on Indian men who married non-Indian women. Despite the blatantly discriminatory nature of this law, a majority refused to find that it violated the equality guarantee of the *Bill of Rights*. Similarly, in *Canard*,[6] the Court upheld a provision preventing an Indian from acting as the administrator of the estate of a deceased Indian, leaving that role to a federal official. In the Court's view, this was not a form of racial discrimination. In *Bliss*,[7] the Court upheld limitations on the rights of pregnant women to unemployment-insurance benefits, finding that discrimination on the basis of pregnancy was not sex discrimination and holding that, since the legislation conferred a benefit, it could not be challenged. In these and other cases, the Court used a variety of rationales to uphold legislation — describing the law as designed to meet a valid federal objective, characterizing it as beneficial rather than burdensome, and focusing narrowly on the question of whether the law was equally applied in the courts without regard to its substantive effect.[8]

B. DRAFTING THE *CHARTER'S* EQUALITY GUARANTEE

In the debates about the appropriate wording of the equality provision of the *Canadian Charter of Rights and Freedoms*, there was a significant

---

4   [1970] SCR 282, 9 DLR (3d) 473 [*Drybones*].
5   *Canada (Attorney General) v Lavell*, [1974] SCR 1349, 38 DLR (3d) 481 [*Lavell*].
6   *Canard v Canada (AG)*, [1976] 1 SCR 170, 52 DLR (3d) 548 [*Canard*].
7   *Bliss v Canada (AG)*, [1979] 1 SCR 183, 92 DLR (3d) 417 [*Bliss*]. The benefit lay in the fact that pregnant women, unlike other unemployment-insurance claimants, did not have to prove they were available for work.
8   A good overview is found in WS Tarnopolsky, *The* Canadian Bill of Rights, 2d rev ed (Toronto: McClelland and Stewart, 1975) c 8.

lobbying effort to strengthen the guarantee so as to prevent a repetition of the experience under the *Canadian Bill of Rights*. It is therefore significant that section 15 of the *Charter* provides that "every individual is equal before and under the law and has the right to the equal protection and equal benefit of the law." The insistence in the careful wording of section 15 that the guarantee includes equality *before* and *under* the law, as well as *equal protection* and *equal benefit* of the law, was meant to signal to the courts that section 15 was intended to be a much more powerful instrument of protection than its predecessor. In particular, the reference to "equal protection" echoed the Fourteenth Amendment to the United States' constitution, which had proven to be a powerful tool in the fight against racial discrimination. The reference to "equal benefit" was a signal that the reasoning in *Bliss*, distinguishing benefits and burdens, was no longer acceptable. Similarly, the explicit protection in section 15(2) of programs designed to ameliorate the conditions of disadvantaged individuals and groups is intended to ensure that legislatures will not be discouraged from taking affirmative measures to enhance equality.

C. THE SCOPE OF THE EQUALITY GUARANTEE

While section 15 of the *Charter* was clearly a departure from section 1(b) of the *Bill of Rights*, its precise meaning was far from clear. The early cases had to confront questions about the scope of the guarantee, particularly the issue of who could claim its protection. As well, there was debate (which continues to the present) about the appropriate method of interpreting section 15 and its interrelation with section 1.[9]

Section 15 contains a list of characteristics that should not be the basis for discriminatory treatment. This list incorporates the most common grounds for discrimination found in human rights codes: race, national or ethnic origin, sex, age, religion, and physical or mental disability.[10] These are commonly referred to as the "enumerated grounds" of discrimination. Although the original draft of section 15 treated the list of enumerated grounds as more limited in its coverage, the final

---

9   Section 15 came into effect three years after the rest of the *Charter* (on 17 April 1985), in order to allow governments time to bring their statutes into line with the section.

10   The first draft of the *Charter* was more limited in its coverage, listing only race, national or ethnic origin, colour, religion, age, and sex.

wording that was adopted makes it clear (because it includes the words "in particular") that the list of prohibited grounds of discrimination is not exhaustive and that further grounds may be added by the courts. As a result, the Supreme Court has accepted that other "analogous grounds" can also form the basis of equality claims.

Many early cases dealt with laws challenged on grounds not included in the "enumerated" grounds in section 15. These cases involved challenges to laws setting shorter limitation periods for suing municipalities, regulatory provisions of various kinds, including the ban on actions in tort for work-related accidents covered by workers' compensation legislation, and regulations prohibiting the use of aluminum cans in order to protect the steel industry from competition. The courts were required to consider the purpose underlying section 15 to decide whether to allow these claims. Since all laws make distinctions between individuals and groups, it is almost always possible to say that a law discriminates in that it imposes burdens or confers benefits on some but not others. Was section 15 meant to give the courts a mandate to oversee the general rationality of the legislative process? Did it forbid different treatment of individuals unless there could be shown in a court of law to be a reasonable basis for doing so? Or did the words "without discrimination" signal a narrower purpose, namely, that the section was meant to address the adverse treatment of certain groups only on the basis of characteristics, such as those listed, which have led to prejudice, stereotype, and unjust disadvantage in many societies, including our own?[11]

Initially, some lower courts adopted a broader approach and were prepared to consider reviewing a wide range of laws under section 15. This direction raised concerns, similar to those raised in relation to section 7, that the courts would exceed their institutional role by requiring the government to justify under section 1 the mass of legislative distinctions drawn in the modern statute book. Advocacy groups, in particular, those representing women and the disabled, saw cause for concern. They feared that, if section 15 were to be applied to such a wide range of laws, it might well lead the judiciary to adopt a relaxed interpretation of section 1 in order to avoid frequent second-guessing of legislatures' decisions. There were also concerns that more advantaged groups and individuals would benefit the most from the equality rights that many believed were enacted to protect and provide remedies for disadvantaged groups and individuals. These concerns have largely dissipated because the Supreme Court has said that section 15 may be

---

11   Section 15 guarantees equality to "individuals," which has been interpreted to mean that people, not corporations, can invoke its protection.

invoked only to challenge legislative distinctions based on enumerated or analogous grounds that have an impact on individuals stereotypically or that reinforce existing prejudice and disadvantage.[12]

The concern has also been laid to rest by the Supreme Court's embrace of the ideal of "substantive" equality. This term requires some explanation. One of the tensions arising under section 15 is between so-called "formal equality" and "substantive equality." The term "formal equality" is used to refer to a conception of equality commonly associated with the use of the "similarly situated" test, reminiscent of certain undesirable aspects of American equal protection jurisprudence. This test has venerable roots in the teachings of Aristotle, who stated that "things that are alike should be treated alike." The test is deceptively simple and superficially attractive.[13] For example, in applications for admission to university, one might argue that anyone receiving a certain grade on a standardized test should be admitted and that no other distinctions should be made. But problems quickly emerge from a mechanical application of this concept of equality. What if there was no oral or braille examination available to enable a blind individual to apply? Is it really consistent with a commitment to equality to ignore visual disability and treat that individual in precisely the same way as sighted individuals? May it not be necessary to look beyond the formal legal rule to ask whether there is equality in substance?

The determination of similarity and difference can be made only in relation to some criterion, which is often the purpose behind the rule or the law. As Ryder, Faria, and Lawrence have stated, "The focus of formal equality is on the individual's situation, and on the relevance of the personal characteristic at issue to the objectives of the challenged law or policy."[14] The similarly situated test essentially asks whether the legislative distinction that is being attacked is relevant to the legislation's objectives. Critics of the similarly situated test argue that this makes the test inherently unreliable because determining the purpose is uncertain and subject to manipulation. It also, in and of itself, provides no guidance for determining whether a certain legislative objective is discriminatory. The *Bliss* decision, finding that pregnant women could

---

12 *Andrews v Law Society of British Columbia*, [1989] 1 SCR 143 [*Andrews*]; *R v Kapp*, [2008] 2 SCR 483 at para 17 [*Kapp*]; *Ontario (Attorney General) v Fraser*, [2011] 2 SCR 3 at para 116.

13 This approach is sometimes called "equality of process." See, for example, K Crenshaw, "Race, Reform and Retrenchment: Transformation and Legitimation in Anti-discrimination Law" (1988) 101 Harv L Rev 1331.

14 B Ryder, CC Faria, & E Lawrence, "What's *Law* Good For? An Empirical Overview of *Charter* Equality Rights Decisions" (2004) 24 Sup Ct L Rev (2d) 103 at 106.

be treated differently from other unemployment-insurance claimants since they were not generally available for work, is often cited as an example of the perils of the similarly situated approach. As under section 1, there was a danger that if the purpose of the law was defined too narrowly and uncritically, then the law would almost always be upheld.

It was argued that, if the promise of equality is to be meaningful, the formal similarly situated test had to be rejected and the emphasis placed on a substantive equality approach that emphasizes consideration of the impact of laws on members of groups subject to stereotyping and historic disadvantage.[15] This approach was reflected by the jurisprudence developed in the interpretation of Canadian human rights codes, which seemed concerned about the actual impact of rules on groups. For example, the Supreme Court found rules requiring everyone to work Saturday in a retail store to be discriminatory. While seemingly grounded in a valid business purpose and not obviously treating anyone differently on the basis of religion, such rules do have an adverse impact on those for whom Saturday is a day of worship. Saturday observers are required to sacrifice their religious beliefs or their job.[16] Similarly, the failure to move furniture in an office to give space for a wheelchair to pass, while seemingly inoffensive, might have the effect of denying access to employment to a person with physical disabilities. The human rights jurisprudence had determined that "adverse-effects" discrimination of this sort gave rise to a duty to accommodate the group adversely affected unless such accommodation would produce undue hardship.[17]

D. THE SUPREME COURT SPEAKS: *ANDREWS V LAW SOCIETY OF BRITISH COLUMBIA*

Andrews,[18] the first equality case to reach the Supreme Court of Canada, was of fundamental importance in charting the future direction of section 15 interpretation. A number of intervenors made submissions, including the Women's Legal Education and Action Fund (LEAF) and

---

15 An early example of this type of writing is G Brodsky & S Day, *Canadian* Charter *Equality Rights for Women: One Step Forward or Two Steps Back?* (Ottawa: Canadian Advisory Council on Status of Women, 1989).

16 *Simpsons-Sears v Ontario (Human Rights Commission)*, [1985] 2 SCR 536, 23 DLR (4th) 321; *Central Alberta Dairy Pool v Alberta (Human Rights Commission)*, [1990] 2 SCR 489, 72 DLR (4th) 417.

17 This jurisprudence is discussed in greater detail in KE Swinton, "Accommodating Equality in the Unionized Workplace" (1995) 33 Osgoode Hall LJ 703.

18 *Andrews*, above note 12.

the Coalition of Provincial Organizations of the Handicapped (COPOH). The case involved a challenge to the citizenship requirement for admission to the Law Society of British Columbia. The Court held, in a 4:2 decision, that this violated section 15 and was not justified under section 1 of the *Charter*.

The most significant aspect of the case was the Court's conceptualization of section 15. It soundly rejected exclusive reliance on formal equality and the similarly situated test, which the Court said "cannot be accepted as a fixed rule or formula for the resolution of equality questions arising under the *Charter*."[19] The Court emphasized that the purpose behind section 15 was to protect vulnerable groups from discrimination. In the Court's view, this meant that section 15 could not be used to challenge every differential treatment created by a law. To succeed in a section 15 claim, a litigant would have to show (1) that there had been a denial of one of the four equality provisions in section 15 — equality before or under the law or equal benefit or protection of the law — and (2) that this differential treatment was discriminatory on the basis of a personal characteristic constituting an enumerated or analogous ground within section 15.

The Court also made it clear that there was a threshold requirement for invoking section 15: there must be discrimination on an enumerated or analogous ground. The enumerated grounds were described as "the most common and probably the most socially destructive and historically practised bases of discrimination."[20] No attempt was made to define "analogous grounds" precisely at this point. Justice McIntyre noted that "[t]he enumerated grounds in s 15(1) are not exclusive and the limits, if any on grounds for discrimination which may be established in future cases await definition."[21] The insistence on enumerated or analogous grounds significantly restricted the reach of section 15 and closed the door on attempts to use the equality guarantee to review all legislative distinctions.[22] The Court insisted, however, that the restriction of section 15 to discrimination on enumerated and analogous grounds was needed to ensure that when it did apply, the guarantee could be given a vigorous interpretation and afford effective protection to members of disadvantaged groups.

---

19 *Ibid* at 168.
20 *Ibid* at 175.
21 *Ibid*.
22 See, for example, *Reference Re Workers' Compensation Act, 1983 (Newfoundland)*, [1989] 1 SCR 922, 56 DLR (4th) 765, holding that being denied a right to sue for work-related accidents is not an analogous ground of discrimination.

The other two important developments in *Andrews* were McIntyre J's definition of what constitutes discrimination and his discussion of the respective roles of section 15 and section 1 in the analysis of equality rights claims.

Discrimination was described by McIntyre J in the following manner:

> . . . a distinction, whether intentional or not but based on grounds relating to personal characteristics of the individual or group, which has the effect of imposing burdens, obligations, or disadvantages on such individual or group not imposed upon others, or which withholds or limits access to opportunities, benefits, and advantages available to other members of society. Distinctions based on personal characteristics attributed to an individual solely on the basis of association with a group will rarely escape the charge of discrimination, while those based on an individual's merits and capacities will rarely be so classed.[23]

Thus, in deciding whether discrimination has occurred, the Court indicated that it would look at the legislature's purpose — for example, whether it acted out of prejudice against a group or on the basis of unjustified stereotypes about its members' capacity. But it would go further and consider as well the impact of laws on a group claiming section 15 protection. This willingness to look at both purpose and effects signalled that the Court would take the same approach under section 15 as it had taken in the interpretation of other *Charter* rights and human rights codes.

Finally, the Court remained true to past *Charter* cases in drawing a sharp line between the consideration of whether a right was violated and whether that infringement was justified under section 1. Some of the lower court cases, including the British Columbia Court of Appeal's decision in *Andrews*, had dealt with the justification for differential treatment within section 15 itself. This seemed to put the onus on the rights claimant to show that the differential treatment was not justified — an approach that the Supreme Court rejected in *Andrews*. Justice McIntyre emphasized that the justification for discriminatory treatment under section 1 should be on the government.

In applying this structure to the facts in *Andrews*, all members of the Court agreed that section 15 had been violated. The law drew a distinction between citizens and non-citizens, and citizenship was held to be an analogous ground within section 15. Discrimination resulted from the burden placed on the non-citizen's ability to practise law until

---

23   *Andrews*, above note 12 at 175.

citizenship was acquired. A majority of the Court held that the law was not justified under section 1, because there were other ways to address the Law Society's justifiable concerns about a lawyer's competence and familiarity with Canadian institutions than through a citizenship requirement — for example, by testing or the requirement of a Canadian law degree. Justice Wilson stressed for the majority of the Court that "given that s 15 is designed to protect those groups who suffer social, political and legal disadvantage in our society, the burden resting on government to justify the type of discrimination against such groups is appropriately an onerous one."[24]

E. A DIVIDED COURT: THE 1995 TRILOGY

Despite the unanimity of the Supreme Court in *Andrews* with respect to section 15 claims, three equality decisions, issued at the same time in the spring of 1995, revealed a Court divided on the proper approach to section 15. *Egan*[25] dealt with a challenge to the spousal allowance under the *Old Age Security Act*, which provided a benefit for the spouse of a pensioner who was between sixty and sixty-five when the couple's combined income fell below a certain level. "Spouse" was defined as a person of the opposite sex to whom the pensioner was married or with whom he or she lived in a common-law relationship as husband and wife. Egan was a gay man, whose partner, Norris, applied for the spousal benefit and was turned down because he was not a spouse as defined by the Act. He argued that this amounted to discrimination on the basis of sexual orientation. *Miron*[26] involved a challenge to a provision of the Ontario *Insurance Act*, which gave married spouses involved in accidents against uninsured motorists benefits for loss of income or damages but did not give the same benefit to common law spouses. Miron, injured in a car accident by an uninsured motorist, sought benefits under his common law spouse's insurance policy, arguing that the law was discriminatory on the basis of marital status and not justified under section 1 of the *Charter*. Finally, *Thibaudeau*[27] involved a challenge to a provision of the *Income Tax Act*, which provided that

---

24   *Ibid* at 153. Justice McIntyre was in dissent in holding that the s 15 violation was justified under s 1 of the *Charter* and in indicating that "the standard of 'pressing and substantial' may be too stringent" given "the necessity for the Legislature to make many distinctions between individuals and groups" (*ibid* at 184).

25   *Egan v Canada*, [1995] 2 SCR 513, 124 DLR (4th) 609 [*Egan*].

26   *Miron v Trudel*, [1995] 2 SCR 418, 124 DLR (4th) 693 [*Miron*].

27   *Thibaudeau v Canada*, [1995] 2 SCR 627, 124 DLR (4th) 449 [*Thibaudeau*].

child-support payments are taxable to the recipient and deductible to the payor. It was argued that this scheme disproportionately burdened women, who were much more likely to be the custodial parents while the payors were more likely to be male.

The decisions in these cases reveal three distinct approaches to section 15 of the *Charter*. More particularly, the difference focused on when a legislative distinction would be viewed as discriminatory, that is, the second part of the test from *Andrews*. Four judges (La Forest, Gonthier, and Major JJ, and Lamer CJC) used what can be called an "internal-relevance" approach that builds on earlier cases such as *Conway*[28] and *Hess*.[29] Four others (McLachlin, Cory, Iacobucci, and Sopinka JJ) continued to use the *Andrews* approach, while L'Heureux-Dubé J adopted her own distinctive approach.

The judges adopting the internal-relevance approach stated that there is no discrimination within section 15 if the distinction drawn between two groups by legislation is relevant "to the functional values underlying the legislation,"[30] even though the distinction is made on the basis of an enumerated or analogous ground. Therefore, according to Gonthier J in *Miron*, one must decide whether a distinction is relevant to "some objective physical or biological reality, or fundamental value."[31] Another requirement was that the "functional values" of the legislation could not be discriminatory.[32]

In both *Miron* and *Egan*, the judges adopting the internal-relevance approach held that the legislative scheme was designed to support the institution of marriage, an institution of fundamental and long-standing importance in Canadian society. In *Miron*, Gonthier J concluded that the legislature had no obligation to confer all the benefits of marriage on common-law couples. Indeed, to do so "would interfere directly with the individual's freedom to voluntarily choose whether to enter the institution of marriage by imposing consequences on cohabitation without any regard to the will of the parties."[33] Similarly, in *Egan*, marriage was described by La Forest J as "by nature heterosexual" and, given its societal importance, Parliament should be able to give it special support:

---

28   *Conway v R*, [1993] 2 SCR 872, 105 DLR (4th) 210 [*Conway*]. For a discussion of *Conway*, see Section I(4), below in this chapter.

29   *R v Hess*, [1990] 2 SCR 906, 59 CCC (3d) 161 [*Hess*]. For a discussion of *Hess*, see Section I(4), below in this chapter.

30   *Miron*, above note 26 at 436 (SCR), Gonthier J.

31   *Ibid* at 446.

32   *Ibid* at 436.

33   *Ibid* at 463.

Neither in its purpose or effect does the legislation constitute an in-fringement of the fundamental values sought to be protected by the *Charter.* None of the couples excluded from benefits under the Act are capable of meeting the fundamental social objectives thereby sought to be promoted by Parliament. These couples undoubtedly provide mutual support for one another, and that, no doubt, is of some benefit to society. They may, it is true, occasionally adopt or bring up chil-dren, but this is exceptional and in no way affects the general picture. I fail to see how homosexuals differ from other excluded couples in terms of the fundamental social reasons for which Parliament has sought to favour heterosexuals who live as married couples . . . .[34]

In contrast, another group of four judges, represented by McLachlin J in *Miron* and Cory J in *Egan*, rejected the internal-relevance approach as unjustifiably narrow. As McLachlin J stated in *Miron*:

If the basis of the distinction on an enumerated or analogous ground is clearly irrelevant to the functional values of the legislation, then the distinction will be discriminatory. However, it does not follow from a finding that a group characteristic is relevant to the legislative aim, that the legislator has employed that characteristic in a manner which does not perpetuate limitations, burdens and disadvantages in violation of s 15(1). This can be ascertained only by examining the effect of the distinction in the social and economic context of the legislation and the lives of the individuals it touches.[35]

The purpose of section 15, McLachlin J wrote, is "the avoidance of stereotypical reasoning and the creation of legal distinctions which violate the dignity and freedom of the individual, on the basis of some preconceived perception about the attributed characteristics of a group rather than the true capacity, worth or circumstances of the individual."[36] While past cases indicated that some distinctions on an enumerated or analogous ground might not constitute discrimination within sec-tion 15, that situation would be rare — arising where "the distinction may be found not to engage the purpose of the *Charter* guarantee" or where the effect of the law is not to impose a real disadvantage, given the larger social and political context.

Applying this approach in *Miron*, McLachlin J found the distinction between married and common-law couples was discriminatory on the basis of marital status, a ground analogous to those enumerated

---

34 *Egan*, above note 25 at 538 (SCR).
35 *Miron*, above note 26 at 742 (DLR).
36 *Ibid* at 748.

in section 15. This denial of equality was not justified under section 1. Common-law couples, like married couples, could suffer economic dislocation if one member was injured in an accident, and there was no reason to bar them from benefits.

In *Egan*, Cory J similarly concluded that the distinction drawn between homosexual couples and heterosexual couples living in a common-law relationship was discriminatory. Noting that discrimination is to be determined from the perspective of the individual claiming a *Charter* violation, he said:

> The definition of "spouse" as someone of the opposite sex reinforces the stereotype that homosexuals cannot and do not form lasting, caring, mutually supportive relationships with economic interdependence in the same manner as heterosexual couples. The appellants' relationship vividly demonstrates the error of that approach. The discriminatory impact can hardly be deemed trivial when the legislation reinforces prejudicial attitudes based on such faulty stereotypes. The effect of the impugned provision is clearly contrary to s 15's aim of protecting human dignity . . . .[37]

Justice L'Heureux-Dubé took a distinctive position, critical of what she described as the "categorical" approach of her colleagues, arguing that the inquiry in section 15 cases should turn on the nature of the group adversely affected by a distinction and the nature of the interest adversely affected.

For a time, the Supreme Court dealt with this basic disagreement about section 15 by referring to the two approaches and then justifying the result under both. For example, La Forest J stated in *Eldridge*:

> While this Court has not adopted a uniform approach to s 15(1), there is broad agreement on the general analytic framework; see *Eaton v Brant County Board of Education*, [1997] 1 SCR 241, at para 62, *Miron, supra* and *Egan, supra*. A person claiming a violation of s 15(1) must first establish that, because of a distinction drawn between the claimant and others, the claimant has been denied "equal protection" or "equal benefit" of the law. Secondly, the claimant must show that the denial constitutes discrimination on the basis of one of the enumerated grounds listed in s 15(1) or one analogous thereto. Before concluding that a distinction is discriminatory, some members of this Court have held that it must be shown to be based on an irrelevant personal characteristic; see *Miron, supra* (*per* Gonthier J.), and *Egan, supra* (*per* La Forest J.). Under this view, s 15(1) will not be infringed unless the distinguished personal characteristic is irrelevant to the

---

37 *Egan*, above note 25 at 604 (SCR).

functional values underlying the law, provided that those values are not themselves discriminatory. Others have suggested that relevance is only one factor to be considered in determining whether a distinction based on an enumerated or analogous ground is discriminatory; see *Miron, supra* (*per* McLachlin J.), and *Thibaudeau v Canada,* [1995] 2 SCR 627 (*per* Cory and Iacobucci JJ.).[38]

Again in *Benner,* the Supreme Court openly acknowledged the three approaches to its interpretation of equality rights.[39] In *Eaton,* Sopinka J declared that there was agreement among members of the Court on certain principles, noting that the majority in *Miron* (the McLachlin view) had agreed with the internal-relevance approach to the extent that it was acknowledged that, in rare cases, distinctions on an enumerated or analogous ground might not constitute discrimination.[40]

F. A UNITED COURT: *LAW V CANADA*

The Supreme Court of Canada resolved its differences in the 1999 decision in *Law v Canada*[41] by holding that a section 15 violation of the *Charter* would require proof of discrimination on an enumerated or analogous ground and substantive discrimination that violated human dignity. The case involved a claim of age discrimination by a thirty-year-old widow who would not qualify for *Canada Pension Plan* survivor benefits until she was sixty-five. She would have received the benefits if she had dependent children or was either disabled or forty-five years of age or older. The Court held that, even though the law imposed a formal and unequal distinction on the basis of the enumerated ground of age, it did not violate section 15 of the *Charter* because it did not violate the human dignity of those under forty-five and, accordingly, did not amount to substantive discrimination. Although the law treats younger people differently, the differential treatment

> does not reflect or promote the notion that they are less capable or less deserving of concern, respect, and consideration . . . . Nor does

---

38   *Eldridge v British Columbia,* [1997] 3 SCR 624, 151 DLR (4th) 577 at 614 [*Eldridge*].

39   In *Benner v Canada (Secretary of State),* [1997] 1 SCR 358, 143 DLR (4th) 577 [*Benner*], the Court struck down a provision in the *Citizenship Act* that imposed more onerous requirements for the acquisition of Canadian citizenship for the children of women who married non-Canadians at a given period than of men who married non-citizens.

40   *Eaton v Brant County,* [1997] 1 SCR 241 at 271, 142 DLR (4th) 385 [*Eaton*].

41   [1999] 1 SCR 497 [*Law*].

the differential treatment perpetuate the view that people in this class are less capable or less worthy of recognition or value as human beings or as members of Canadian society . . . . [T]he legislation does not stereotype, exclude or devalue adults under 45. The law functions not by the device of stereotype, but by distinctions corresponding to the actual situation of individuals it affects.[42]

The Court noted that "adults under the age of 45 have not been consistently and routinely subjected to the sorts of discrimination faced by some of Canada's discrete and insular minorities."[43] Moreover, the legislature was entitled to rely on "informed statistical generalizations"[44] rather than stereotypes that younger people could more easily replace their deceased partner's income and that they should not receive the survivor's pension until reaching the age of sixty-five years.

The framework for section 15 claims set out in *Law* draws on *Andrews* by stressing the need for a purposive and contextual approach to equality rights, requiring proof of both differential treatment and substantive discrimination on enumerated or analogous grounds. As in *Andrews*, the Court stressed that equality is a comparative concept and that a comparator group must be selected in order to ground the section 15 analysis. The Court added that "the claimant generally chooses the person, group, or groups with whom he or she wishes to be compared for the purpose of the discrimination inquiry."[45] However, as explained below, where necessary, a court may refine the comparison group with attention to the subject matter of the impugned legislation, its effects, and the context.

The Supreme Court also made several new statements in *Law*. None of these has proved as important as the Court's use of the concept of "essential human dignity" in its analysis. The Court said in unequivocal terms that the purpose of section 15 was to prevent the violation of "essential human dignity" and "to promote a society in which all persons enjoy equal recognition at law as human beings or as members of Canadian society, equally capable and equally deserving of concern, respect and consideration."[46] Moreover, the determination of whether or not substantive discrimination had been established turns on whether the legislative distinction violated the "essential human dignity" of the *Charter* claimant. In turn, whether the claimant's dignity was violated depended on the

---

42   *Ibid* at para 102.
43   *Ibid* at para 95.
44   *Ibid* at para 106.
45   *Ibid* at para 6.
46   *Ibid* at para 88.

analysis of four "contextual factors," to be analyzed from the claimant's perspective. This use of "dignity" as an analytical tool has been difficult to come to grips with and may play less of a role in the future.

Law is generally seen as having established a three-part test for the determination of equality claims:

1) Does the impugned law (a) draw a formal distinction between the claimant and others on the basis of one or more personal characteristics, or (b) fail to take into account the claimant's already disadvantaged position within Canadian society resulting in substantively differential treatment between the claimant and others on the basis of one or more personal characteristics?
2) Is the claimant subject to differential treatment based on one or more enumerated and analogous grounds?
3) Does the differential treatment discriminate by imposing a burden upon, or withholding a benefit from, the claimant in a manner that reflects the stereotypical application of presumed group or personal characteristics, or that otherwise has the effect of perpetuating or promoting the view that the individual is less capable or worthy of recognition or value as a human being or as a member of Canadian society, equally deserving of concern, respect, and consideration?

Law added factors to the section 15 analysis not found in *Andrews*. The most important is the requirement that a section 15 applicant demonstrate not only differential treatment on enumerated or analogous grounds of discrimination, but also that the differential treatment results in a loss of human dignity:

> What is human dignity? . . . Human dignity means that an individual or group feels self-respect and self-worth. It is concerned with physical and psychological integrity and empowerment. Human dignity is harmed by unfair treatment premised upon personal traits or circumstances which do not relate to individual needs, capacities, or merits. It is enhanced by laws which are sensitive to the needs, capacities, and merits of different individuals, taking into account the context underlying their differences. Human dignity is harmed when individuals and groups are marginalized, ignored, or devalued, and is enhanced when laws recognize the full place of all individuals and groups within Canadian society. Human dignity within the meaning of the equality guarantee does not relate to the status or position of an individual in society *per se*, but rather concerns the manner in which a person legitimately feels when confronted with a particular law. Does the law treat him or her unfairly, taking into account all of

the circumstances regarding the individuals affected and excluded by the law?[47]

Harm to human dignity is to be determined by examining four contextual factors:

1) pre-existing disadvantage;
2) correspondence between the grounds and the claimants' actual needs, capacities, and circumstances;
3) ameliorative purposes or effects; and
4) the nature and scope of the interest affected by the impugned law.

Although the Court stated at the time that this list of factors was "open," no new contextual factors have been added to the list since *Law*. The importance of the contextual factors cannot be overstated. In the decade following *Andrews*, most unsuccessful section 15 claims failed because they were not brought under an enumerated or analogous ground. Under *Law*, most section 15 cases fail because an analysis of the contextual factors persuades a court that the claimant's essential human dignity has not been violated by the impugned legislative distinction.[48]

The additional requirement of an affront to human dignity was determinative in Ms. Law's case. She established differential treatment on the enumerated grounds of age, but her claim was rejected because the Court was "at a loss to locate any violation of human dignity. The impugned distinctions do not stigmatize young persons, nor can they be said to perpetuate the view that surviving spouses under age 45 are less deserving of concern, respect or consideration than any others. Nor do they withhold a government benefit on the basis of stereotypical assumptions."[49]

The *Law* test was criticized for its complexity and for placing additional burdens on section 15 applicants to prove a violation of human dignity and contextual factors that should have been reserved for section 1 analysis. There were also concerns that it follows the functional relevance test by placing too much emphasis on the government's purpose in enacting the law. On the other hand, *Law* has been praised for its insistence on a substantive and contextual approach consistent with the purposes of section 15 and the need for attention to context.

---

47   *Ibid* at para 53.
48   See Ryder, Faria, & Lawrence, above note 14 at 116.
49   *Law*, above note 41 at para 108.

G. *R v KAPP: LAW* QUALIFIED AND SIMPLIFIED?

In the 2008 case of *R v Kapp*,[50] the Court, in a joint judgment by McLachlin CJC and Abella J, qualified the *Law* test for equality and signalled its preference for the simpler 1989 *Andrews* test. As discussed above, the *Andrews* test for equality was based on these two questions: (1) Does the law create a distinction based on an enumerated or analogous ground? (2) Does the distinction create a disadvantage by perpetuating prejudice or stereotyping?

The Court in *Kapp* noted that *Law* had succeeded in unifying what had, since *Andrews*, become a divided approach to equality rights and that *Law* "was an important contribution to our understanding of the conceptual underpinnings of substantive equality."[51] Nevertheless, the Court recognized that the focus on human dignity had created an additional burden on equality claimants. Even with the guidance of the four contextual factors outlined in *Law*, the human dignity concept had become "confusing and difficult to apply."[52] The Court warned that the four contextual factors should not be read as rigid requirements but rather "as a way of focusing on the central concern of section 15 identified in *Andrews* — combating discrimination, defined in terms of perpetuating disadvantage and stereotyping."[53] The *Law* contextual factors should be used as a tool to focus on stereotyping in the form of attributed characteristics that affect the degree of correspondence between the differential treatment and the reality of the claimant's group or the perpetuation of pre-existing disadvantage. The ameliorative purpose or effect of the law was most relevant to whether it qualified as an affirmative action program under section 15(2), but the Court stated, without deciding, that it could also be relevant to determining whether the law would perpetuate disadvantage.[54]

The two-part *Andrews–Kapp* test has been confirmed and followed in several subsequent cases, so it would appear that *Kapp* will have a significant impact on the evolution of equality rights jurisprudence. In *Ermineskin Indian Band and Nation v Canada*,[55] the Court applied the two-part test articulated in *Kapp* to reject a section 15 challenge to provisions of the *Indian Act* that prohibited investment of a band's oil and

50 Above note 12.
51 *Ibid* at para 20.
52 *Ibid* at para 22.
53 *Ibid* at para 24.
54 *Ibid* at para 23.
55 [2009] 1 SCR 222 at paras 201–2.

gas royalties. The Court held that, while the Act drew distinctions on prohibited grounds, the distinctions were not discriminatory because they allowed bands some control over the funds and did not draw a distinction that perpetuates disadvantage through prejudice or stereotyping. The unanimous Court made no mention of the *Law* test, including its reference to human dignity and the four contextual factors used to make judgments about the effect of a law on human dignity. The Court again applied the two-part *Andrews–Kapp*-test in *AC v Manitoba (Director of Child and Family Services)*[56] where it upheld a provincial law that allowed medically necessary treatment to be ordered when in the best interests of children under sixteen years of age. Citing *Kapp*, Abella J concluded that because the law allowed children under sixteen "to lead evidence of sufficient maturity to determine their medical choices, their ability to make treatment decisions is ultimately calibrated in accordance with maturity, not age, and no disadvantaging prejudice or stereotype based on age can be said to be engaged. There is therefore no violation of s 15."[57] Chief Justice McLachlin also cited *Kapp* to conclude that the legislative decision was "ameliorative, not invidious."[58] A minimum grade twelve education requirement for election as Chief or Band Council member in a First Nations code does not violate section 15. While facially neutral qualifications may be discriminatory in some cases, there was no evidence to indicate that the requirement had a disparate impact upon an enumerated or analogous group.[59]

In *Withler v Canada (Attorney General)*,[60] McLachlin CJC and Abella J wrote a joint judgment, further cementing the two-part *Andrews–Kapp* test as the proper approach. The case involved a challenge to federal supplementary death benefit legislation that reduced the claimant widows' benefits because of the age of their husbands at the time of death. The claimants argued that this was age discrimination contrary to section 15. The Court rejected the claim as based upon a formalistic "mirror image" approach that failed to meet the test of substantive equality.[61] The Court reiterated the need to focus on distinctions based upon enumerated or analogous grounds that have a discriminatory impact by perpetuating disadvantage by prejudice or stereotyping. The "*Law* factors" may be helpful in identifying substantive inequality, but "they need not be expressly canvassed in every case in order to fully and

56   [2009] 2 SCR 181 [*AC v Manitoba*].
57   *Ibid* at para 111.
58   *Ibid* at para 152.
59   *Kahkewistahaw First Nation v Taypotat*, [2015] 2 SCR 548.
60   [2011] 1 SCR 396 [*Withler*].
61   See Section H(2), below in this chapter, for further discussion of this point.

properly determine whether a particular distinction is discriminatory."[62] Rather, "[t]he focus of the inquiry is on the actual impact of the impugned law, taking account of social, political, economic and historical factors concerning the group."[63]

The two-part *Andrews–Kapp* test appears, on its face, to be simpler to apply and more directly focused on substantive equality than the *Law* test. However, the decision in *Quebec (Attorney General) v A*,[64] dismissing a challenge to the Quebec *Civil Code* support and partition of property provisions in relation to *de facto* spouses, indicates that the *Andrews–Kapp* test still leaves considerable room for debate. At issue was the exclusion of *de facto* spouses from the mandatory protections afforded married and civil union spouses in relation to support and partition of property. All members of the Court agreed that the two-part *Andrews–Kapp* test applied and that the applicant satisfied the first branch of that test, as she had been denied the protection of the *Civil Code* on the basis of spousal status, an analogous ground for discrimination under section 15(1). However the Court was sharply divided on whether she had established that the distinction created a disadvantage by perpetuating prejudice or stereotyping so as to amount to a denial of substantive equality under the second branch of the test.

A majority (Abella J, McLachlin CJC, Deschamps, Cromwell, and Karakatsanis JJ concurring) held that there was a *prima facie* violation of section 15(1). Justice LeBel (Fish, Rothstein, and Moldaver JJ concurring) disagreed and found no violation of section 15(1). However, the challenge failed in the result as McLachlin CJC found that any breach of section 15(1) was justified under section 1, and Deschamps J (Cromwell and Karakatsanis JJ concurring) found that only the exclusion of the partition of property provisions was justified. The issue that divided the Court was the weight to be placed on autonomy and individual choice. Justice Abella did not consider the applicant's *de facto* spousal status to be properly characterized as a freely chosen exercise of autonomy. She downplayed the need to prove prejudice or stereotyping which, she said, were merely indicia that point to violations of substantive equality. Justice Abella insisted that the analysis should focus not on the intention or attitudes motivating the *Civil Code*'s provisions to foster autonomy and choice, but on the reality of dependence or vulnerability that is created by the spousal relationship and the need for an even hand in affording mandatory protection of vulnerable spouses,

---

62   Above note 60 at para 66.
63   *Ibid* at para 39.
64   2013 SCC 5.

be they married spouses, civil union partners or *de facto* spouses, over the values of freedom of choice and contract. Those matters, she wrote, were properly left to section 1 and should not be used to undermine the recognition of spousal status as an analogous ground. With respect to section 1, Abella J found that the minimal-impairment test was not satisfied as the objective of preserving individual autonomy, and choice could be achieved through a scheme that presumptively included *de facto* spouses in the protection of the *Civil Code* while allowing them to opt out.

Justice LeBel found that the applicant had failed to show that exclusion from the *Civil Code*'s protective regime created a disadvantage by expressing or perpetuating prejudice or by stereotyping. Historic discrimination against *de facto* spouses had disappeared, and such relationships were now both common and accepted. The *Civil Code* simply preserved choice by defining the content of a variety of forms of conjugal relationships from which individuals were free to choose. Personal autonomy and self-determination are integral to the values of dignity and freedom that underlie equality. The scheme had been carefully designed and was the subject of extensive and recent public debate.

Despite the majority view that there was a *prima facie* violation of section 15(1), the *Civil Code* provisions survived as being justified under section 1. Although only McLachlin CJC was prepared to find that the support provisions could be justified as a reasonable limit, she had the decisive voice in upholding that aspect of the *Civil Code* regime because four other judges had dissented in finding no violation of section 15. Chief Justice McLachlin agreed with Abella J that the goal of enhancing autonomy and choice were public interest considerations that should be left to section 1, but she disagreed with Abella J on the section 1 analysis. In McLachlin CJC's view, the legislative scheme did satisfy the minimal-impairment test. Presumptively including all spouses in the mandatory scheme would seriously undermine the legislative objective: "The legislature has chosen to avoid mandatory protective provisions that important segments of the population may view as paternalistic, by instead allowing spouses to weigh the consequences of their choices and to make decisions accordingly."[65] In her view, that scheme fell "within a range of reasonable alternatives for maximizing choice and autonomy in the matter of family assets and support."[66]

---

65   *Ibid* at para 444.
66   *Ibid* at para 447.

This strong division of opinion is striking given the unanimous acceptance of the two-step *Andrews–Kapp* test for finding an infringement of section 15(1).

H. IMPORTANT ASPECTS OF THE TEST FOR EQUALITY

1) Analogous Grounds

It has been accepted, at least since *Andrews*, that equality rights claims can be based not only on one of the nine particular grounds of discrimination listed in section 15(1) of the *Charter* but also on grounds of discrimination analogous to those listed. To date, the Supreme Court has accepted that marital status,[67] sexual orientation,[68] citizenship (or non-citizenship),[69] and off-reserve residence for Aboriginal people[70] constitute analogous grounds of discrimination that fall within section 15(1)'s ambit. On the other hand, marijuana users,[71] workers denied the right to sue their employers by workers' compensation schemes,[72] as well as RCMP officers and health-care workers who are treated differently from other employees for the purpose of labour relations, have

---

67   *Miron*, above note 26; *Nova Scotia (Attorney General) v Walsh*, [2002] 4 SCR 325.
68   *Egan*, above note 25; *Vriend v Alberta*, [1998] 1 SCR 493, 156 DLR (4th) 385 [*Vriend*]; *M v H*, [1999] 2 SCR 3.
69   *Andrews*, above note 12; *Lavoie v Canada*, [2002] 1 SCR 769.
70   *Corbiere v Canada (Minister of Indian and Northern Affairs)*, [1999] 2 SCR 203, 173 DLR (4th) 1 [*Corbiere*]. The Court has repeatedly rejected the argument that residence can be an analogous ground for non-Aboriginals: *R v Turpin*, [1989] 1 SCR 1296; *Haig v Canada (Chief Electoral Officer)*, [1993] 2 SCR 995; *Siemens v Manitoba (Attorney General)*, [2003] 1 SCR 6.
71   *R v Malmo-Levine; R v Caine*, [2003] 3 SCR 571 at paras 184–85, in which Gonthier and Binnie JJ for the majority state that [a] taste for marihuana is not a "personal characteristic" in the sense required to trigger s 15 protection . . . . As *Malmo-Levine* argues elsewhere, it is a lifestyle choice. It bears no analogy with the personal characteristics listed in s 15, namely race, national or ethnic origin, colour, religion, sex, age, or mental or physical disability. It would trivialize this list to say that "pot" smoking is analogous to gender or religion as a "deeply personal characteristic that is either unchangeable or changeable only at unacceptable personal costs."
72   See *Reference Re Workers' Compensation Act, 1983 (Newfoundland)*, above note 22 at 924 (SCR), where La Forest J rejected the claim of victims of work-related accidents: "The situation of the workers and dependants here is in no way analogous to those listed in s 15(1), as a majority in *Andrews* stated was required to permit recourse to s 15(1)."

been held not to constitute groups discriminated against on analogous grounds.[73]

How is a court to determine whether or not a ground is similar enough to be included as analogous? The Supreme Court has usually identified unacceptable forms of discrimination as focusing on "personal characteristics," that is, characteristics that are somehow inherently part of an individual's identity. Moreover, the Court seems to require such characteristics to be either "immutable" — in the way that, say, race or ethnic origin cannot be changed — or "constructively immutable." By constructive immutability, the Court is referring to a characteristic that "the government has no legitimate interest in expecting us to change to receive equal treatment under the law."[74]

The Supreme Court engaged in its most comprehensive examination of analogous grounds in *Corbiere v Canada*.[75] The case involved a section 15 claim by Indian band members who were denied the right to vote in their band's elections if they did not reside on their band's reserve. The Court found that "Aboriginality residence" or the off-reserve status of band members was an analogous ground of discrimination. The Court took a contextual approach and stressed that "the ordinary 'residence' decisions faced by the average Canadian should not be confused with the profound decisions Aboriginal band members make to live on or off their reserves, assuming choice is possible. The reality of their situation is unique and complex. Thus no new water is charted, in the sense of finding residence, in the generalized abstract, to be an analogous ground."[76] Discriminating on the basis of residence is an

---

73   *Delisle v RCMP*, [1999] 2 SCR 989, where the status of being an RCMP officer was not an analogous ground of discrimination; *Health Services and Support–Facilities Subsector Bargaining Assn. v British Columbia*, [2007] 2 SCR 391 at para 165, where restrictions on bargaining by health-care workers were found not to amount to discrimination because "the differential and adverse effects of the legislation on some groups of workers relate essentially to the type of work they do, and not to the persons they are. Nor does the evidence disclose that the Act reflects stereotypical application of group or personal characteristics." See also *Rudolf Wolff & Co. v Canada*, [1990] 1 SCR 695 at 702, in which the Court rejected the claim of those seeking relief against the federal Crown and challenging the statutory requirement that they sue in the Federal Court of Canada: [I]t cannot be said that individuals claiming relief against the Federal Crown are . . . a "discrete and insular minority" or a "disadvantaged group in Canadian society within the contemplation of s 15." Rather, they are a disparate group with the sole common interest of seeking to bring a claim against the Crown before a court.

74   *Corbiere*, above note 70 at para 13 (SCR).

75   *Ibid*.

76   *Ibid* at para 15.

analogous ground of discrimination for Aboriginal people but not for non-Aboriginal people.

The majority's discussion of how to identify analogous grounds was as follows:

> What then are the criteria by which we identify a ground of distinction as analogous? The obvious answer is that we look for grounds of distinction that are analogous or like the grounds enumerated in s 15 — race, national or ethnic origin, colour, religion, sex, age, or mental or physical disability. It seems to us that what these grounds have in common is the fact that they often serve as the basis for stereotypical decisions made not on the basis of merit but on the basis of a personal characteristic that is immutable or changeable only at unacceptable cost to personal identity. This suggests that the thrust of identification of analogous grounds at the second stage of the *Law* analysis is to reveal grounds based on characteristics that we cannot change or that the government has no legitimate interest in expecting us to change to receive equal treatment under the law. To put it another way, s 15 targets the denial of equal treatment on grounds that are actually immutable, like race, or constructively immutable, like religion. Other factors identified in the cases as associated with the enumerated and analogous grounds, like the fact that the decision adversely impacts on a discrete and insular minority or a group that has been historically discriminated against, may be seen to flow from the central concept of immutable or constructively immutable personal characteristics, which too often have served as illegitimate and demeaning proxies for merit-based decision making.[77]

The majority in *Corbiere* also stressed that analogous grounds, once identified and accepted by the courts, will always "serve as jurisprudential markers for suspect distinctions associated with stereotypical, discriminatory decision making."[78] This view differs from the approach of L'Heureux-Dubé J, who would have limited the finding of analogous grounds to the case at hand. In *Corbiere* the entire Court agreed that there was substantive discrimination because the denial of the vote to off-reserve band members was based on a stereotype that they were not interested in or affected by the decisions of their band.

---

77 *Ibid* at para 13.
78 *Ibid* at paras 7 and 11.

2) Comparator Groups

Until recently, equality cases put considerable weight on comparator groups to establish discrimination contrary to section 15. In *Hodge v Canada (Minister of Human Resources and Development)*,[79] Binnie J stated that while it was up to the claimant to make the initial choice of the comparator group, the correctness of that choice was a matter of the law for the court to decide on the following principle:

> The appropriate comparator group is the one which mirrors the characteristics of the claimant (or claimant group) relevant to the benefit or advantage sought except that the statutory definition includes a personal characteristic that is offensive to the *Charter* or omits a personal characteristic in a way that is offensive to the *Charter*.[80]

This principle creates a kind of "but for" test. The comparator group is the group entitled to the legal benefit that the claimant is deprived of and resembles the claimant's group in all relevant respects, except that its members do not share the personal characteristic that is the basis for exclusion. The claimants belong to the group that would be entitled to the legal benefit being sought but for possessing the disqualifying personal characteristic; the comparator group gets the legal benefit because it does not share that disqualifying characteristic.

In *Hodge*, the claimant had been in a common law relationship with the deceased for twenty-two years, but left him because of alleged verbal and physical abuse. When he died five months later, she sought but was denied a survivor's pension under the *Canada Pension Plan* because at the time of his death, she was no longer considered to be his "spouse." Had they been married but separated, she would have received the pension. Hodge argued that she belonged to the category of "separated common law spouses," whose treatment under the *CPP* was discriminatory compared to the treatment of "separated married spouses." Justice Binnie disagreed and found that the appropriate comparison was to formerly married spouses who had divorced their husband or wife. Both divorcées and common law spouses who no longer lived with their partners were former spouses, and neither was eligible for a *CPP* survivor's pension. Therefore, while the claimant had identified the right group (separated spouses), she could not meaningfully compare her treatment under the *CPP* to that group, because she was a *former* (that is, not a separated) spouse. *Hodge* establishes that a court does not have to defer to the claimant's choice of comparator group. As

---

79 [2004] 3 SCR 357 at para 18 [*Hodge*].
80 *Ibid* at para 23.

Binnie J put it, "the correctness of the choice is a matter of law for the court to determine."[81]

Auton (Guardian ad litem of) v British Columbia (Attorney General)[82] demonstrates the importance of this approach to comparator groups. The claimants were infants suffering from the developmental disorder autism. They claimed the provincial government discriminated against them by not funding a particular kind of behavioural therapy. They contended that they should be compared either to non-disabled Canadian children or adults with mental illness who received funding for medically necessary treatment, and this argument succeeded both in the British Columbia Supreme Court and the British Columbia Court of Appeal. Chief Justice McLachlin, writing for the majority, rejected these comparators, however. The behavioural therapy that the petitioners sought was only emerging, but the groups that they wanted to be compared to typically received funding only for therapies that were well established.[83] Chief Justice McLachlin concluded:

[T]he appropriate comparator for the petitioners is a non-disabled person or a person suffering a disability other than a mental disability (here autism) seeking or receiving funding for a non-core therapy important for his or her present and future health, which is emergent and only recently becoming recognized as medically required.[84]

Chief Justice McLachlin found that the evidence did not show that the provincial government had responded to requests for new therapies or treatments by non-disabled or otherwise disabled people any differently than it had for autistic children. Even if the government could have acted more quickly to fund the autism treatment, there was no evidence it had been laggard when compared to other new therapies for non-disabled persons or persons with another kind of disability. The claim was therefore dismissed.

However, the Court's restatement of the two-part *Andrews–Kapp* test in *Withler* downplays the use of comparator group analysis, as it tends to favour formal over substantive equality. As McLachlin CJC and Abella J put it, "[t]he central and sustained thrust of the Court's s 15(1) jurisprudence has been the need for a substantive contextual approach and a corresponding repudiation of a formalistic 'treat likes alike' approach,"[85] as well as the need for "a contextual inquiry

---

81 *Ibid* at para 21.
82 [2004] 3 SCR 657 [*Auton*].
83 *Ibid* at para 55.
84 *Ibid*.
85 Above note 60 at para 43.

into whether the impugned law perpetuated disadvantage or negative stereotyping."[86] They held that "a mirror comparator group analysis may fail to capture substantive inequality, may become a search for sameness, may shortcut the second stage of the substantive equality analysis, and may be difficult to apply."[87] While comparator groups figured in the analysis in *Hodge* and *Auton*, the results were attributed to an inquiry into substantive equality. The Court held that "[i]t is unnecessary to pinpoint a particular group that precisely corresponds to the claimant group except for the personal characteristic or characteristics alleged to ground the discrimination."[88]

3) The Perspective of the Claimant

As we have noted, human dignity has taken on a central role in the analysis of section 15 claims. Discrimination will be held to be established if a legislative distinction has the purpose or effect of demeaning an individual's human dignity. From whose perspective is the claimant's human dignity to be measured? On this score, the Supreme Court stated in *Law* that the effect of the legislative distinction must be assessed from the perspective of the reasonable claimant:

> The appropriate perspective is subjective-objective. Equality analysis under the *Charter* is concerned with the perspective of a person in circumstances similar to those of the claimant, who is informed of and rationally takes into account the various contextual factors which determine whether an impugned law infringes human dignity, as that concept is understood for the purpose of s 15(1).[89]

This assessment of whether the human dignity of the reasonable claimant is infringed has, at times, been a source of disagreement. In cases such as *Gosselin v Quebec (Attorney General)*,[90] dealing with social welfare rights, and *Canadian Foundation for Children, Youth and the Law*, the child spanking case, the Supreme Court divided on the factors that would be considered by a reasonable claimant. In *Gosselin*, the majority held that age-based distinctions were commonly used and that conferring different benefits to young welfare recipients with a view to getting them back into the workforce affirmed rather than infringed their human dignity. The minority regarded the age-based distinction as the

---

86 *Ibid* at para 47.
87 *Ibid* at para 60.
88 *Ibid* at para 63.
89 *Law*, above note 41 at paras 59–61.
90 [2002] 4 SCR 429 [*Gosselin*].

product of stereotypical thinking that demeaned and disadvantaged a vulnerable group. In the child spanking case, the majority held that a reasonable person, knowing of the limitations the law imposes on abusive conduct directed towards children and aware of the harms of criminalization, would not conclude that a child's dignity would be violated by use of corrective force. The dissenting judges disagreed and would have held that the denial of the law's protection against physical force was disrespectful of children and treated them as second-class citizens.

4) The Contextual Factors

As noted above, the contextual factors were the crucial element of the *Law* test, though the Court has now warned in *Kapp*[91] that they "should not be read literally as if they were legislative dispositions, but as a way of focusing on the central concern of section 15 identified in *Andrews* — combating discrimination, defined in terms of perpetuating disadvantage and stereotyping." The four factors are as follows:

1) *Pre-existing disadvantage*: This factor requires a court to examine whether or not the claimant belongs to a group that has historically been vulnerable or the subject of stereotyping and prejudice. If a law has the effect of further disadvantaging an already disadvantaged group, then it is more likely to be found to be discriminatory.

2) *Correspondence*: This factor looks at whether the legislative distinction that is being attacked corresponds to the actual needs, capacities, or circumstances of the claimant. If the legislative distinction is the result of a deliberate design, which is not in itself discriminatory and which has sought to take into account the claimant's traits or circumstances, it will be more difficult to establish discrimination. On the other hand, the distinction will be more difficult to justify if it is based on stereotyping in the form of attributed as opposed to actual characteristics.

3) *Ameliorative purpose*: This factor looks at whether or not the impugned law is aimed at improving the situation of a group more disadvantaged than the claimant's group. Thus, if a law is aimed at a greater need than the claimant's, it is less likely to be discriminatory. The Court in *Kapp*[92] cast some doubt on this factor under section 15(1),

---

91   *Kapp*, above note 12 at para 24.
92   *Ibid*. One objection to the relevance of ameliorative purpose under section 15(1) is that it would allow the government to argue that the impugned law did not violate section 15(1) because it was ameliorative after having lost the argument that the law as an ameliorative program was justified under section 15(2).

noting that it was most relevant to section 15(2) and that it "would suggest, without deciding here, that the third *Law* factor might also be relevant to the question under section 15(1) as to whether the effect of the law or program is to perpetuate disadvantage."[93]

4) *The nature and scope of the interest affected*: The more severe and localized the consequences of the legislation on the affected group, the greater the chance that it discriminates. Thus, for example, if a fundamental interest of the claimant is at stake — for instance, his liberty interest or his physical integrity — then the court is more likely to find discrimination.

In *Law*, the Supreme Court suggested that pre-existing disadvantage was "probably the most compelling factor favouring a conclusion that differential treatment imposed by legislation is truly discriminatory."[94] However, in subsequent cases, the second factor — correspondence — has generally proven to be decisive. One study suggests that in fifteen cases released by the Supreme Court since *Law* — up to *Canadian Foundation for Children* in 2004 — the outcome of the Court's analysis of the correspondence factor matched the outcome of the overall inquiry into the existence of discrimination. In contrast, the first, third, and fourth factors have matched the outcome of the discrimination inquiry seven, six, and eight times out of fifteen, respectively.[95] On a purely quantitative level, then, the correspondence factor has dominated in the application of the *Law* test.

This is readily apparent when one reads the cases. Examples of cases where the correspondence factor is discussed at length include *Canadian Foundation for Children*[96] and *Nova Scotia (Workers' Compensation Board) v Martin; Nova Scotia (Workers' Compensation Board) v Laseur*.[97] In his partial dissent in *Canadian Foundation for Children*, Binnie J warns that the correspondence factor may amount to a reversion to the "relevance" requirement rejected in *Law* and also import into the section 15 analysis considerations best left to section 1.[98] The Court in *Kapp*[99] might have had the correspondence factor in mind when it recognized that "criticism has also accrued for the way *Law* has allowed the formalism of some of the Court's post-*Andrews* jurisprudence to resurface in the form of an artificial comparator analysis focussed on

93   *Ibid* at para 23.
94   *Law*, above note 41 at para 63.
95   Ryder, Faria, & Lawrence, above note 14 at 122.
96   *Canadian Foundation for Children*, above note 2.
97   [2003] 2 SCR 504 [*Martin*].
98   *Canadian Foundation for Children*, above note 2 at paras 97–98.
99   *Kapp*, above note 12 at para 22.

treating likes alike." A focus on stereotyping and attributed rather than real characteristics can perhaps save the correspondence factor from descending into an artificial and formalistic exercise that depends on the choice of comparator groups.

5) Section 15(2)

The purpose of section 15(2) is to save ameliorative programs aimed at improving the lot of disadvantaged groups from being challenged under section 15(1) as "reverse discrimination." The provision recognizes that, for practical reasons, including the availability of resources, it may be necessary for governments to establish priorities and to assist some but not all members of a disadvantaged group at the same time.[100]

The Supreme Court first considered the relationship between sections 15(1) and 15(2) of the *Charter* in *Lovelace v Ontario*.[101] It held that section 15(2) should not be considered as a defence or an exemption from section 15(1) but rather as an "interpretative aid" that is "confirmatory and supplementary" to section 15(1) of the *Charter*. Reading sections 15(1) and 15(2) together "ensures the internal coherence of the *Charter* as a working statute."[102] The Court thus held that a casino project targeting Aboriginal bands did not violate the section 15(1) rights of Aboriginal people not organized in bands. The casino was a partnered and ameliorative program, and it responded to the actual circumstances and abilities of the bands. The Court conducted a full section 15 analysis under the *Law* test, and much depended on its conclusion that there was a correspondence between the program and providing benefits to bands and not to other Aboriginal people. This conclusion about correspondence, however, could be debated. It avoided the claimant's arguments that, as Aboriginal people who were not in government-recognized bands, they were equally, if not more, disadvantaged as the bands that were the beneficiary of the casino project. *Lovelace* meant that governments would not know whether a law or program would be accepted as a legitimate affirmative action measure to ameliorate the conditions of a disadvantaged group until a full section 15 analysis was conducted in each case.

In the 2008 decision in *Kapp*,[103] the Court changed course from the idea that section 15(2) was only an interpretative aid to section 15. The

---

100 *Alberta (Aboriginal Affairs and Northern Development) v Cunningham*, [2011] 2 SCR 670 at para 41 [*Cunningham*].
101 [2000] 1 SCR 950, 188 DLR (4th) 193.
102 *Ibid* at paras 105–6.
103 *Kapp*, above note 12.

Court, in *Kapp*, held that, if the government could demonstrate that a law or program satisfies the criteria of section 15(2), it would be unnecessary to determine whether it violated section 15(1). In other words, a law would not violate section 15(1) if the government could demonstrate under section 15(2) that one purpose in enacting the law was to ameliorate the conditions of a disadvantaged group(s). The government will have an ameliorative purpose if it was rational for the state to conclude that the means chosen would contribute to amelioration.[104] The focus is on the government's purposes, not the effects of the programs. The government's sole purpose does not have to be the amelioration of the conditions of disadvantaged groups, and in this case, one purpose of the program was to manage the fishery. It is also unnecessary that every member of the targeted disadvantaged group be disadvantaged.[105] In the result, the Court held that fishing preferences granted to three Aboriginal bands fell under section 15(2) because they rationally addressed long-standing disadvantages suffered by Aboriginal people that continue to this day. The fact that some individual members of the bands did not suffer disadvantage "does not negate the group disadvantage suffered by band members."[106]

The Court elaborated this approach in *Cunningham*[107] in upholding an Alberta statute that permitted the exclusion of Métis who are also status Indians from the benefit of Métis settlements.[108] *Cunningham* posed a more difficult problem than *Kapp* as the challengers were members of a closely related disadvantaged group. Writing for the Court, McLachlin CJC stated that the government must first show that the program is "directed at improving the situation of a group that is in need of ameliorative assistance." The government must then show that the object of the program corresponds "to actual disadvantage suffered by the target group."[109] The Court held that the statute met this test. The Métis had been historically disadvantaged as being excluded from both the Aboriginal and the European communities, and the program aimed to provide them with a land base to preserve their distinctive identity, culture, and self-governance. It was thus appropriate to exclude other Métis who would qualify for different benefits as status Indians.

The *Kapp* test for section 15(2) should prove simpler than the previous test in *Lovelace*, which required a full section 15 analysis in all

---

104 *Ibid* at paras 49–51.
105 *Ibid* at para 55.
106 *Ibid* at para 59.
107 Above note 100.
108 *Metis Settlements Act*, RSA 2000, c M-14.
109 Above note 100 at para 59.

cases. Governments will now know that their section 15(2) analysis will be based largely on the purposes that underlie the impugned law or program and not on the effects that the program may have on others. While *Kapp* was a simpler case than *Lovelace* because the applicants did not claim to be a similarly disadvantaged group saying that an affirmative action program was under-inclusive, *Cunningham* demonstrates that the abandonment of a full section 15 analysis for section 15(2) programs applies, even where the affirmative action program is challenged on the basis that it is unconstitutionally under-inclusive.

I. GROUNDS OF DISCRIMINATION

So far, we have discussed section 15 of the *Charter* in terms of its analytical parts. In what follows, we take a more contextual and holistic approach by examining the reasoning, outcomes, and remedies in section 15 cases in some of the most important contexts of potential discrimination.

1) Discrimination against Gays and Lesbians

In *Egan v Canada*,[110] the Supreme Court unanimously accepted sexual orientation as an analogous ground of discrimination. Justice La Forest stated:

> that whether or not sexual orientation is based on biological or physiological factors, which may be a matter of some controversy, it is a deeply personal characteristic that is either unchangeable or changeable only at unacceptable personal costs, and so falls within the ambit of section 15 protection as being analogous to the enumerated grounds.

Justice Cory stressed the historical disadvantage and prejudice suffered by gays and lesbians and the decisions to include sexual orientation as a prohibited ground of discrimination in most human rights codes. Justice La Forest, with the concurrence of three other judges, however, held that the exclusion of same-sex couples from old-age security benefits did not violate section 15 of the *Charter* because the exclusion of such couples was relevant to the purposes of the legislation. Justice Cory, with the concurrence of three other judges, held that the exclusion of same-sex couples constituted unjustified discrimination. Justice Sopinka provided the decisive fifth vote. He held that the exclusion

---

110 *Egan*, above note 25.

violated section 15 of the *Charter* but was justified under section 1 because the government was entitled to deference in deciding whether to extend benefits to same-sex couples. He noted that this was the Court's first case to recognize sexual orientation as an analogous ground of discrimination and concluded that "given the fact that equating same sex couples with heterosexual spouses, either married or unmarried, is still generally regarded as a novel concept, I am not prepared to say that by its inaction to date the government has disentitled itself to rely on s 1 of the *Charter*."[111]

In *Vriend v Alberta*,[112] the Supreme Court held that the omission of protection against discrimination on the basis of sexual orientation from Alberta's human rights code constituted unjustified discrimination against gays and lesbians. Although the human rights code regulated private conduct and the discrimination was in the form of a legislative omission, the Court held that the *Charter* still applied to the decision of the Alberta legislature to exclude sexual orientation. The omission of sexual orientation imposed burdens on gays and lesbians by making them vulnerable to private discrimination on the basis of sexual orientation in a manner that heterosexuals were not exposed to discrimination. The Court strongly stated: "[T]he exclusion sends a message to all Albertans that it is permissible, and perhaps even acceptable, to discriminate against individuals on the basis of their sexual orientation."[113] With one judge dissenting, the Court decided that the appropriate remedy was to read sexual orientation into Alberta's human rights code as opposed to striking the entire code down subject to a suspended declaration of invalidity.

A year later in *M v H*,[114] the Supreme Court applied the *Law* analysis to hold that the limitation of support provisions in Ontario's family law legislation to opposite-sex partners was an unjustified violation of section 15 of the *Charter*. The Court held that the law imposed a differential burden on same-sex partners who could not avail themselves of court-ordered support payments. Following *Egan* and *Vriend*, this differential treatment was on the analogous ground of sexual orientation. Finally, the differential treatment resulted in substantive discrimination because it was based on stereotypes that same-sex partnerships could not be as lasting or as meaningful as heterosexual partnerships. The majority of the Court rejected the idea that an ameliorative purpose of ensuring the fair treatment of women after the breakup of a

---

111 *Ibid* at 576 (SCR).
112 *Vriend*, above note 68.
113 *Ibid* at para 101 (SCR).
114 *M v H*, above note 68.

common law partnership justified the exclusion of same-sex partners. The Court declared the Ontario law to be invalid subject to a six-month period of suspension during which the Ontario legislature responded by adding the category of "same-sex partners" to much of its legislation conferring spousal benefits and obligations.

In *Little Sisters Book and Art Emporium v Canada (Minister of Justice)*,[115] which came a year after *M v H*, the Court found that customs authorities had violated section 15 and discriminated on the basis of sexual orientation by targeting the imports of a gay and lesbian bookstore when they did not target the imports of "so-called XXX sex shops that specialize in hard core heterosexual material even though, unlike in the case of Little Sisters, little if any of their stock is found routinely on display in the Vancouver Public Library."[116] The Court found that this discrimination on the basis of sexual orientation was the result of the actions of customs officials, and it was not authorized in customs legislation allowing officials to detain obscene material. The majority of the Court determined that the appropriate remedy was a declaration that section 15 rights had been violated. A minority of the Court felt this was not a strong enough remedy given the systemic problems with the administration of the legislation. The minority would have struck down the customs legislation subject to an eighteen-month period of suspension.

The most important development in this area has been debate concerning same-sex marriage. The best-known decisions were those of the Courts of Appeal of British Columbia[117] and Ontario[118] and a trial-level decision in Quebec,[119] all of which struck down the traditional common law opposite-sex definition of marriage. The reasoning of the Court of Appeal for Ontario is illustrative. The court identified an 1866 English decision as the source of opposite-sex definition of marriage at common law. In that early case, Lord Penzance wrote: "I conceive that marriage, as understood in Christendom, may for this purpose be defined as the voluntary union for life of one man and one woman, to the exclusion of all others."[120] The Court of Appeal rejected the argument

---

115 [2000] 2 SCR 1120, 193 DLR (4th) 193 at para 120.

116 *Ibid.*

117 *EGALE Canada Inc. v Canada (Attorney General)* (2003), 225 DLR (4th) 472 (BCCA), rev'g [2001] 11 WWR 685 (BCSC).

118 *Halpern v Canada (Attorney General)* (2003), 65 OR (3d) 161 (CA), var'g (2002), 60 OR (3d) 321 (Div Ct) [*Halpern*].

119 *Hendricks v Quebec (Procureur général)*, [2002] RJQ 2506 (Sup Ct).

120 *Hyde v Hyde and Woodmansee* (1866), LR 1 P&D 130 at 133, a case dealing with the validity of a potentially polygamous marriage.

that the word "marriage," as used in the *Constitution Act, 1867*, constitutionally entrenched the legal definition of marriage that existed at the time of Confederation as contrary to the notion of the constitution as a "living tree" capable of growth and change over time. The court also declined to find that the issue engaged freedom of religion under section 2(a) of the *Charter*, holding that "[t]his case is solely about the legal institute of marriage. It is not about the religious validity or invalidity of various forms of marriage."[121] Turning to section 15(1), the Court of Appeal applied the *Law* test in a straightforward manner. It found that the opposite-sex definition of marriage created a formal distinction between opposite-sex couples and same-sex couples on the basis of their sexual orientation. Finally, it found that an analysis of the contextual factors pointed to the conclusion that the opposite-sex definition of marriage resulted in substantive discrimination. Unlike the Quebec and British Columbia courts, which had delayed their declarations of invalidity, the Ontario Court of Appeal refused to grant a temporary suspension of invalidity and struck down the opposite-sex definition of marriage immediately.

What happened next is interesting from the point of view of legal process. The Liberal government voiced its support for gay marriage and its intention to pass legislation enshrining a neutral definition. Rather than appeal any of the lower court decisions, it directed a reference to the Supreme Court asking about the constitutionality of proposed legislation stating (1) that marriage for civil purposes is the lawful union of two persons to the exclusion of all others and (2) that nothing about that definition would affect the freedom of religious officials to refuse to perform marriages that conflict with their religious beliefs. The Supreme Court held that the first part of this legislation was within the jurisdiction of Parliament under section 91(26) of the *Constitution Act, 1867*, but not the second, since only the provinces are able to legislate exemptions to existing requirements regarding the solemnization of marriage. The Court then held that the proposed definition of marriage was consistent with the *Charter*. The Court found that it did not trench upon the equality rights or the freedom of religion of groups who oppose gay marriage. With respect to equality rights, the Court found that the new definition did not draw any distinctions nor did it withhold any benefits or impose burdens on a differential basis. For that reason, the section 15 challenge to the new definition failed on the first step of *Law*. With respect to freedom of religion, the Court held that no conflict had been shown to exist between the new definition and the section 2(a) rights of those who opposed same-sex marriages.

---

121 *Halpern*, above note 118 at para 53.

The Court also found that freedom of religion would protect religious officials from being compelled by the government to perform same-sex marriages contrary to their religious beliefs.

The Supreme Court, however, declined to answer arguably the most important of the reference questions: whether the opposite-sex requirement for marriage was consistent with the *Charter*. The Court held that it would be "unwise and inappropriate to answer the question"[122] because the government had said it intended to proceed to amend the marriage definition regardless of the answer. It also refused to answer because the parties to the lower court decisions had relied on the findings that the opposite-sex definition of marriage was unconstitutional. Many same-sex couples had since wed. The Court stated that it would be unfair to jeopardize the rights acquired through litigation by answering the reference question in the affirmative, which was one possible outcome. Finally, the Court held that answering the question in the negative would potentially undermine the government's stated goal of achieving uniformity in respect of civil marriage across Canada. The effect of an advisory opinion on the lower court opinions that had held the opposite-sex definition unconstitutional was considered unclear. As the Court said, "[t]he result would be confusion, not uniformity."[123] As a result, the Supreme Court itself has not addressed the constitutionality of the opposite-sex definition of marriage, but in 2005 Parliament passed the *Civil Marriage Act*, making same-sex marriage the law across Canada.[124]

In *Canada (Attorney General) v Hislop*,[125] the Court dealt with a set of complex legislative amendments designed to provide but also limit retroactive benefits that same-sex partners could receive under the self-funded *Canada Pension Plan*. The Court held that two legislative provisions that limited the benefits of same-sex partners violated section 15 of the *Charter*. Both provisions discriminated against same-sex couples as compared to heterosexual couples. The Court rejected the government's arguments that the comparator group should be further defined to include express distinctions in the impugned legislation, or that section 15 should be interpreted in a manner that recognized the evolution in the legal and social recognition of same-sex couples.[126] In both

---

122 *Same-Sex Marriage Reference*, above note 3 at para 64.

123 *Ibid* at para 70.

124 Bill C-38, *An Act Respecting Certain Aspects of Legal Capacity for Marriage for Civil Purposes*, 1st Sess, 38th Parl, 2005 (as passed by the House of Commons, 28 June 2005).

125 [2007] 1 SCR 429.

126 *Ibid* at paras 38 and 41.

cases, the Court held that the government had failed to demonstrate a pressing objective for the different treatment of same-sex couples under section 1 of the *Charter*.[127] These holdings of the Court are consistent with its strong recognition of the equality rights of gays and lesbians in the cases discussed above.

The Court, however, refused to recognize claims that would have given same-sex couples pension benefits retroactive to the coming into force of equality rights on 17 April 1985. The Court refused to invalidate a facially neutral provision which limited all survivors' in-arrears benefits to twelve months before the applications were received. The plaintiffs argued that this provision had adverse effects on same-sex partners who were unable, until remedial legislation was adopted in 2000, to claim survivor benefits. They also argued that they should be entitled to fully retroactive benefits from when the equality rights in section 15 of the *Charter* took effect. The Court held that it need not decide the validity of this adverse effect discrimination claim because even if the claim was valid, it would not be appropriate to award the retroactive remedy that the applicants had requested. The Court's decision on remedy will be more fully examined in Chapter 17, but the Court found that the government had placed reasonable reliance on the law as it existed before *M v H*. The Court also justified its decision not to provide retroactive relief on the basis that the plaintiffs would receive some relief.

2) Age Discrimination

McKinney,[128] the first significant case after *Andrews*, dealt with a constitutional challenge to the mandatory retirement at age sixty-five years of university professors employed at a number of Ontario institutions. Two companion cases, *Harrison* and *Stoffman*, dealt with mandatory retirement in British Columbia universities and hospitals.[129] In each of these cases, there was a preliminary issue of whether the *Charter* applied directly to universities and hospitals so as to allow a *Charter* challenge to their employment policies, as discussed above in Chapter 6. The majority of the Supreme Court of Canada held that the *Charter* did not apply, but nevertheless proceeded to deal with the constitutionality of the mandatory-retirement policies. In *McKinney* and *Harrison*, the provincial human rights codes were also challenged, since both protected

127 *Ibid* at paras 55 and 65.
128 *McKinney v University of Guelph*, [1990] 3 SCR 229, 76 DLR (4th) 545 [*McKinney*].
129 *Harrison v University of British Columbia*, [1990] 3 SCR 451, [1991] 77 DLR (4th) 55 [*Harrison*]; *Stoffman v Vancouver General Hospital*, [1990] 3 SCR 483, 76 DLR (4th) 700 [*Stoffman*].

against discrimination in employment on the basis of age, but then defined age with an upper limit of sixty-five years, thereby precluding complaints by workers faced with mandatory retirement at age sixty-five. If that cap on the definition was impermissible under the *Charter*, mandatory retirement could be challenged through a human rights complaint, and past cases involving mandatory retirement at ages caught by the human rights codes would have succeeded.[130]

Speaking for the majority in *McKinney*, La Forest J noted that age, as a ground of discrimination, differed from other enumerated grounds in section 15, in that "[t]here is a general relationship between advancing age and declining ability." While courts should protect against age-based discrimination resulting from unfounded assumptions or stereotypes about the capacity of older individuals, courts should also be conscious of the justification for granting or withholding certain social benefits on the basis of age. Justice La Forest found that both mandatory retirement and the cap on age in the human rights codes violated section 15 because of the burden imposed on older workers, but he then went on to apply a relaxed test under section 1 of the *Charter*. In so doing, he stressed the complexity of mandatory-retirement schemes, which also protected older workers through deferred-compensation arrangements and by allowing departure from the workplace in dignity without unpleasant merit reviews. As well, mandatory retirement served the need for renewal through hiring younger workers with different skills and qualities. Moreover, with respect to the human rights codes' protection for existing mandatory-retirement schemes, La Forest J noted that their widespread use in the private sector was generally beneficial. This justified the legislative action, which provided a reasonable balance of competing social values. Finally, with respect to the human rights codes, La Forest J noted that a legislature should be permitted to proceed incrementally in enacting legislation addressing the problems of discrimination, provided that there was a reasonable basis for its cut-off point, as there was here.

Both Wilson and L'Heureux-Dubé JJ dissented. In their view, the legislation and the mandatory-retirement policies could not be justified under section 1 since there were other ways to meet the concerns for productivity and employment turnover that would allow a more individualized treatment of older workers.

In a later case, the Supreme Court unanimously concluded that there was age discrimination in the *Unemployment Insurance Act* provision preventing those over sixty-five from receiving insurance benefits

---

130 For example, *Ontario (Human Rights Commission) v Etobicoke (Borough)*, [1982] 1 SCR 202, 132 DLR (3d) 14.

and restricting them to a lump-sum payment equivalent to three weeks' benefits. This restriction could not be justified, said the Court, because it denied access to benefits to those over sixty-five who needed to continue to work because of inadequate pension entitlements.[131] The Court struck down the exclusion of senior citizens, effectively extending the benefits to this group.

However, most distinctions on the basis of age as a criterion for benefit schemes have been found not to violate section 15. As discussed above, *Law*[132] and *Withler*[133] involved age-based restrictions on survivor benefits that affected widows and widowers. Although the challenged laws clearly denied a benefit on the basis of age, the Supreme Court found no substantive discrimination. The age distinctions were not based on stereotypes about the respective needs of younger and older persons. In *Law*, the Court stated that persons under forty-five years of age did not comprise a disadvantaged group and that they would eventually receive survivor benefits upon reaching sixty-five years of age. In *Withler*, the Court held that, when viewed as a whole and over time, reducing survivor benefits on the basis of the age of the deceased did not impose or perpetuate discrimination.

Gosselin v Quebec (Attorney General)[134] involved a challenge to Quebec's social welfare scheme lowering the amount of social assistance payable to those under thirty unless they participated in education or work experience programs. The scheme was challenged under section 15 on the ground of age discrimination, as well as under section 7 of the *Charter*, and section 45 of the Quebec *Charter of Human Rights and Freedoms*, on the ground that it failed to provide an adequate standard of living. The discussion here will focus on section 15. The debate on section 7 is dealt with in Chapter 13.

By a majority, the Supreme Court rejected the section 15 challenge. The legislation distinguished welfare recipients under thirty from those thirty years and older, and thereby created a distinction based on an enumerated ground. However, the majority concluded that the claim should be rejected on the basis of the first two contextual factors from *Law*: historical disadvantage and correspondence. Chief Justice McLachlin found that, "[b]oth as a general matter, and based on the evidence and our understanding of society, young adults as a class simply do not

---

131   *Canada (Employment and Immigration Commission) v Tétreault-Gadoury*, [1991] 2 SCR 22, 81 DLR (4th) 358.
132   *Law*, above note 41.
133   Above note 60.
134   *Gosselin*, above note 90.

seem especially vulnerable and undervalued"[135] and that, "[i]f anything, people under 30 appear to be advantaged over older people in finding employment."[136] With respect to the second factor, she found that the purpose and design of the legislative scheme "far from being stereotypical or arbitrary, corresponded to the actual needs and circumstances of individuals under 30"[137] because the scheme was designed to encourage young adults to further their education and training so that they could become more employable. Moreover, she relied on the finding of the trial judge that Gosselin had failed to show any adverse effects to welfare recipients under the age of thirty. Ultimately, McLachlin CJC found as follows:

> A reasonable welfare recipient under 30 might have concluded that the program was harsh, perhaps even misguided. (As noted, it eventually was repealed.) But she would not reasonably have concluded that it treated younger people as less worthy or less deserving of respect in a way that had the purpose or effect of marginalizing or denigrating younger people in our society. If anything, she would have concluded that the program treated young people as more able than older people to benefit from training and education, more able to get and retain a job, and more able to adapt to their situations and become fully participating and contributing members of society.[138]

The dissenting judges all took exception to McLachlin CJC's analysis to varying degrees. Justice L'Heureux-Dubé wrote that McLachlin CJC's decision threatened to "presumptively exclude youth from s 15 protection."[139] Justice Bastarache argued that McLachlin CJC did not give sufficient weight to the fact that age was enumerated in section 15, and so distinctions based on age are inherently suspect. Moreover, Bastarache J was prepared to recognize that welfare recipients as a class constituted a vulnerable group, something that McLachlin CJC said was irrelevant when considering an age-based distinction between two different groups of welfare recipients.

At issue in *Canadian Foundation for Children*[140] was section 43 of the *Criminal Code*, which allows parents or teachers to use corrective force towards children. As with *Gosselin*, the case also involved a section 7 claim, discussed in Chapter 13.

---

135 *Ibid* at para 33.
136 *Ibid* at para 34.
137 *Ibid* at para 38.
138 *Ibid* at para 69.
139 *Ibid* at para 110.
140 *Canadian Foundation for Children*, above note 2.

Chief Justice McLachlin wrote the majority judgment. She interpreted the reach of the section 43 defence narrowly, holding that despite its broad language, it does not apply when force is used against children under two or over twelve, does not allow for the use of objects or blows or slaps to the head, and that teachers can only apply force to remove a child from the classroom. The section 15 claim had to be measured accordingly. Chief Justice McLachlin ruled that the claim could not be assessed from the perspective of a reasonable preschooler. Rather, she chose to assess the claim from the perspective of "a reasonable person acting on behalf of a child."[141] She held that the first two parts of the *Law* test were met because section 43 makes a distinction on the basis of age. Furthermore, she held that three of the four elements of the *Law* test favoured a finding of discrimination in this case: children are a highly vulnerable group, whose physical integrity was at stake as a result of a statutory provision that was not aimed at ameliorating the situation of an even more disadvantaged group. The key element of McLachlin CJC's section 15 analysis, however, was the correspondence factor from *Law*. Section 43, she held, struck a balance between the need to protect children from abuse and the need to provide them with guidance and discipline.[142]

Both Binnie and Deschamps JJ, in dissent, found violations of section 15, although Binnie J found that section 43 could be justified under section 1 with respect to parents. (Justice Arbour wrote the third dissenting opinion, finding an unjustified infringement of section 7.) Justice Binnie was particularly critical of the Chief Justice's reliance on the correspondence factor, through which he said she had made the scope of section 15 protection too narrow. The Chief Justice, he argued, had imported into the correspondence factor matters best left to section 1 and, moreover, her analysis threatened to revive the idea of relevancy with respect to a statute's functional values that was adopted by some members of the Court during the mid-1990s. Like Binnie J, Deschamps J found a violation of section 15. Her criticism of the majority, however, focused on its narrow interpretation of section 43. Because the provision, properly interpreted, allowed a broader range of "corrective force" than the majority suggested, she found that the provision did not correspond to the actual needs and capacities of children: "It cannot be seriously argued that children need corporal punishment to grow and learn."[143]

---

141 *Ibid* at para 53.
142 *Ibid* at paras 58–59.
143 *Ibid* at para 230.

In *AC v Manitoba (Director of Child and Family Services)*,[144] the Supreme Court held that a provincial law that allowed medically necessary treatment to be ordered when in the best interests of children under sixteen years of age did not violate the equality rights. Justice Abella stressed that the law did not engage any "disadvantaging prejudice or stereotype based on age" because it allowed those under sixteen years of age to argue that they were mature enough to make the decision.[145] Chief Justice McLachlin also concluded that there was no section 15 violation because the age-based distinction "is ameliorative, not invidious. First, it aims at protecting the interests of minors as a vulnerable group. Second, it protects the members of the targeted group — children under sixteen — in a way that gives the individual child a degree of input into the ultimate decision on treatment. In my view, this is sufficient to demonstrate that the distinction drawn by the Act, while based on an enumerated ground, is not discriminatory within the meaning of s 15."[146]

3) Disability

In *Swain*,[147] the Supreme Court upheld a common law rule allowing the Crown to raise the issue of the accused's insanity in a criminal trial, either after conviction or if the accused led evidence that put his capacity for criminal intent in question. Even though this rule drew a distinction on the basis of mental disability, there was no discrimination within section 15 of the *Charter*, said Lamer CJC, because the rule did not impose a burden or disadvantage on those with mental disabilities. In his words, "it is a principle of fundamental justice that the criminal justice system not convict a person who was insane at the time of the offence."[148] This case raised the question whether the determination of burdens and disadvantages should be made from the perspective of the rights claimant or from a more objective standpoint. From Swain's perspective, it might well seem burdensome to allow the Crown to raise the issue of his insanity, if the outcome was an acquittal by reason of insanity that would lead to indeterminate detention because of his mental state. In contrast, and more beneficial from his perspective, a conviction might have resulted in a fixed sentence, perhaps without incarceration.

144 *AC v Manitoba*, above note 56.
145 *Ibid* at para 111.
146 *Ibid* at para 152.
147 *R v Swain*, [1991] 1 SCR 933, 63 CCC (3d) 481 [*Swain*].
148 *Ibid* at 509 (CCC).

In the subsequent case of *Winko v British Columbia*,[149] the Supreme Court held that provisions providing for the possibly indeterminate detention of those found not criminally responsible because of a mental disorder did not violate section 15 of the *Charter*. Although a distinction between accused persons was drawn on the basis of mental disorder, there was no substantive discrimination. The legislation did not presume or stereotype those with mental disorders as dangerous but rather required an individualized demonstration of a significant threat to the public. The appropriate perspective was a reasonable person with the same characteristics as the *Charter* applicant.

The question of perspective was also raised in *Eaton*,[150] a case involving a challenge to the special-education provisions in Ontario under which a child with cerebral palsy had been assigned to a special-education class after three years in an integrated classroom. Her counsel argued that the decision contravened section 15 of the *Charter*, because it discriminated on the basis of physical disability. The Supreme Court of Canada disagreed, concluding that while integrated classes might benefit some with disabilities, it might be a burden to others. A special-education tribunal, after considering extensive evidence about the child's abilities and needs, had concluded that a special classroom was in her best interests. Therefore, said the Court, there was no discrimination in that there was no burden or disadvantage placed on the child, nor was she denied a benefit. Genuine and subjective perceptions by a *Charter* applicant of discrimination are not sufficient. There must also be an objective basis for the finding of discrimination so that a reasonable person with the same characteristics and circumstances of the *Charter* applicant would perceive there to be discrimination and denial of human dignity.

While *Eaton* was a disappointment to many advocates of the rights of those with disabilities, the Supreme Court's subsequent decision in *Eldridge*[151] was greeted with delight. In that case, individuals with hearing disabilities successfully argued that the failure to provide them with sign-language interpreters when they receive medical services violated section 15 of the *Charter* and was not justified under section 1. This was a case of adverse-effects discrimination, said the Court, which essentially adopted the same approach here as has been used in the interpretation of human rights codes. In the words of La Forest J, sign-language interpretation "is the means by which deaf persons may re-

149 [1999] 2 SCR 625, 175 DLR (4th) 193.
150 *Eaton*, above note 40.
151 *Eldridge*, above note 38.

ceive the same quality of medical care as the hearing population."[152]
He then went on to say that the *Charter* includes a duty to make reasonable accommodation, up to the point of undue hardship, for those adversely affected by a rule — a principle that he concluded should be addressed under section 1.[153] Clearly, cost would be a relevant consideration, since governments have to make difficult decisions about the appropriate allocation of limited public resources. The Court issued a declaration with a six-month delay to allow governments to take steps to comply with this judgment.

Although the section 15 claim advanced in *Granovsky v Canada*[154] — the first case following *Law* dealing with disability rights — was dismissed, the Supreme Court did embrace a broad definition of disability for section 15 purposes. The claimant failed to qualify for a *Canada Pension Plan* benefit because a temporary disability had prevented him from working and making pension contributions for the required period. Had the interruption in making contributions resulted from a permanent disability, the claimant would have qualified for the benefit. Justice Binnie, writing for the Court, found that there was no violation of the human dignity requirement. Although there was differential treatment on the basis of the enumerated grounds of disability, the Court held that Parliament was entitled to ameliorate the conditions of the permanently disabled without extending the same benefit to those temporarily disabled and to do so did not stigmatize or deny the dignity of the temporarily disabled.

While the claim was rejected, the Court did embrace a broad definition of disability for the purposes of *Charter* analysis. The government had been dismissive of Granovsky's disability, "suggesting disbelief that a severe backache could rise to the level of a constitutional challenge."[155] Justice Binnie, however, stated that in disability claims, the focus should not be on the nature of the claimant's impairment, but rather on the government response to that impairment. He divided the idea of "disability" into three parts: the actual physical or mental impairment; the functional limitation that arises as a result of that impairment; and the socially constructed handicap, as a result of which the disabled individual may be marginalized:

> Section 15(1) ensures that governments may not, intentionally or through a failure of appropriate accommodation, stigmatize the underlying physical or mental impairment, or attribute functional limitations

152 *Ibid* at 620 (DLR).
153 *Ibid* at 624.
154 [2000] 1 SCR 703 [*Granovsky*].
155 *Ibid* at para 32.

to the individual that the underlying physical or mental impairment does not entail, or fail to recognize the added burdens which persons with disabilities may encounter in achieving self-fulfilment in a world relentlessly oriented to the able-bodied.[156]

The Court's nuanced appreciation of the nature of disability discrimination was further demonstrated in *Nova Scotia (Workers' Compensation Board) v Martin; Nova Scotia (Workers' Compensation Board) v Laseur*.[157] The claimants suffered from chronic pain and were entitled to participate in a four-week "functional restoration program" but were excluded from the broad range of benefits granted to workers suffering from other disabilities by Nova Scotia's workers' compensation scheme. Justice Gonthier, writing for the Court, held that this exclusion violated section 15(1) of the *Charter* on the basis of disability and could not be justified under section 1. In doing so, he elaborated on the complex nature of disability-based equality claims, in two respects. First, he held a claimant with a disability could properly invoke as a comparator another group suffering from a disability of a different type or severity. Thus, in this case, the claimants suffering from chronic back pain could compare themselves to workers with other injuries. Second, when addressing the third step of the *Law* analysis, Gonthier J suggested that, in disability claims, correspondence would usually be the determinative contextual factor. The reason is that disabilities vary widely from person to person, and programs aimed at accommodating them should be tailored to their individual needs insofar as is reasonable:

> [I]t is vital to keep in mind the rationale underlying the prohibition of discrimination based on disability. As I stated above, this rationale is to allow for the recognition of the special needs and actual capacities of persons affected by a broad variety of different disabilities in many different social contexts. In accordance with this rationale, s 15(1) requires a considerable degree of reasonable accommodation and adaptation of state action to the circumstances of particular individuals with disabilities. Of course, classification and standardization are in many cases necessary evils, but they should always be implemented in such a way as to preserve the essential human dignity of individuals.[158]

Justice Gonthier therefore held: "I am unable to agree that the challenged provisions are sufficiently responsive to the needs and circumstances of

---

156 *Ibid* at para 33.
157 *Martin*, above note 97.
158 *Ibid* at para 93.

chronic pain sufferers to satisfy the second contextual factor."[159] Thus, in both *Granovsky* and *Martin*, the Supreme Court has recognized the unique nature of disability claims and stated that the government has an obligation, within reasonable bounds, to accommodate the particular needs associated with particular forms of disabilities. Otherwise, it may be compounding the physical or mental impairment of a person with a disability and aggravating a socially constructed handicap.

In *Auton (Guardian ad litem of) v British Columbia (Attorney General)*,[160] already discussed above, the Supreme Court rejected the claim of children suffering from autism for a specific form of therapy not provided under the province's medicare scheme. No doubt concerned about becoming embroiled in a complex debate about difficult choices regarding medicare funding, the Court held that the benefit claimed was not one provided by law as the legislation "does not promise that any Canadian will receive funding for all medically required treatment" but leaves funding for non-core medical services (a category found by the Court to include the services sought by the claimants) to the discretion of the province.[161]

4) Sex Discrimination

In several cases coming before the Supreme Court, section 15 *Charter* claims have alleged discrimination on the basis of sex, but few have succeeded. In *Hess*,[162] the accused challenged the statutory-rape provisions of the *Criminal Code*, which made it an offence for a male over fourteen years to have sexual intercourse with a female under that age. The accused argued that this was sex discrimination, because only men could be charged with the crime and only females could be the victims. Justice Wilson held that there was no violation of section 15 here, since biological reality determined that only men could commit the offence: "[W]e are therefore dealing with an offence that involves an act that as a matter of biological fact only men over a certain age are capable of committing."[163] Because men and women are different in their ability to commit the offence, she held there to be no discrimination.

But what of the fact that a woman might have intercourse with a young male under fourteen and escape punishment? Does this not demonstrate that the law is non-inclusive on grounds of gender in its

---

159 *Ibid* at para 97.
160 *Auton*, above note 82.
161 *Ibid* at para 38.
162 *Hess*, above note 29.
163 *Ibid* at 930 (SCR).

coverage of sexual offences against the young? It is up to the legislature to decide whether questions of morality and social disapprobation warrant criminalizing such conduct, and there is no discrimination involved in the legislature proceeding part-way, prohibiting only some sexual misconduct. In contrast, McLachlin J, with Gonthier J concurring, would have found a section 15 violation here, both because of the burden that the offence placed on men but not women and because of the protection provided for young females but not for young males. However, she upheld the legislation as justifiable under section 1, since it protected a particularly vulnerable group: young women. In any event, after the "statutory rape" offence was struck down under section 7 of the *Charter*, Parliament enacted new gender-neutral offences that protected both girls and boys from sexual interference and could apply to both male and female accused.

Justice Wilson's approach in *Hess* was troubling to some, because she rejected the claim within section 15 itself. Her holding that the differential treatment was, in effect, justified and non-discriminatory because of the nature of the offence and the biological difference between men and women seemed to import into section 15 the issues of justification, which were usually left to the state to bring forward under section 1.

Despite these concerns, a majority of the Court followed the same approach in *Conway*.[164] This case rejected a challenge to the practice in the prison system whereby male prisoners could be "frisk-searched" and have their cell areas patrolled by female guards, while the practice in the women's penitentiary was to have women guards perform these duties, except in emergency situations. In an unusually short judgment, La Forest J stated that it was "doubtful" that section 15 was violated, "given the historical, biological and sociological differences between men and women." More precisely, because of the history of violence of men against women, cross-gender searching is "different and more threatening for women than for men."[165] Note was also taken of the ameliorative objective of employment equity for women in non-traditional jobs such as prison guards. Thus, the issue of justification seemed to enter into the finding of discrimination. In contrast, earlier cases had suggested that, if the rights claimant felt burdened or disadvantaged by the rule because of sex, the justification would be discussed under section 1 with the government bearing the onus.

---

164 *Conway*, above note 28.
165 *Ibid* at 214 (DLR).

It is likely that the finding of no gender discrimination in both *Hess* and *Conway* would be affirmed under the *Law* test. The *Charter* applicant must demonstrate not only a disadvantage on the basis of the enumerated ground of sex, but also substantive discrimination and an affront to human dignity. At this stage of section 15 analysis, the court will examine contextual factors such as whether there is a history of disadvantage, whether, as indicated in *Conway*, there was an ameliorative purpose behind the legal disadvantage, and whether there is correspondence with actual abilities. It will be recalled, however, that some criticize the *Law* test for incorporating justificatory factors that should be left for the government to establish under section 1.

In *Symes v Canada*,[166] the Supreme Court was asked to determine whether the provisions in the *Income Tax Act* limiting the amount that a taxpayer can deduct for childcare expenses violated section 15 of the *Charter*. This case was difficult because it required the application of an adverse-effects approach to section 15. On its face, there was no indication of sex discrimination in section 63 of the *Income Tax Act*, which allowed a childcare deduction of a fixed amount to taxpayers while requiring that in families with two supporting parents, the deduction be taken by the lower-income earner. However, the claimant, a self-employed female lawyer, argued that the effect of the legislation was discriminatory against women. It limited her deduction to an amount less than the actual cost that she paid for childcare and prevented her from taking childcare as a business deduction elsewhere in the Act. She argued that this was sex discrimination, because women disproportionately bear the cost of childcare. The denial of a full deduction for childcare, while allowing full deductions for other items that disproportionately benefited businessmen, was said to violate section 15 of the *Charter*.

The majority in the Supreme Court, in reasons written by Iacobucci J, concluded that sex discrimination was not established. Even if the evidence showed that women disproportionately bear the burden of childcare in Canadian society, there was no evidence that they disproportionately bear the *cost* of childcare. In fact, the law requires both parents to provide support and care for their children. While Symes and her husband had made an agreement that she would pay for childcare, this did not change the situation: the cost of childcare is borne by families, not just women. Justice Iacobucci went on to discuss the difficulties of proving adverse-effects discrimination. In particular, he noted that there are potential problems when a law has adverse effects

---

166 [1993] 4 SCR 695, 110 DLR (4th) 470.

on both men and women, implying that it will be difficult to conclude that there is sex discrimination where both men and women are burdened and benefited by legislation.

The Supreme Court allowed a section 15 *Charter* claim based on sex discrimination in *Trociuk v British Columbia (Attorney General)*.[167] Trociuk was the estranged father of triplets whose former partner had "unacknowledged" him at the time of their children's birth, as she was permitted to do for any reason under provincial legislation. As a result of this unacknowledgment, she chose the children's last name as her own, and his particulars were not recorded on their birth registrations. Moreover, the legislation provided him with no means of having the birth registrations altered. Writing for the Court, Deschamps J held that the legislation clearly distinguished between mothers and fathers, and therefore resulted in differential treatment on the enumerated ground of sex. Justice Deschamps went on to find that the differential treatment resulted in an impairment of dignity. She noted that "[p]arents have a significant interest in meaningfully participating in the lives of their children," with which the legislation interfered. The fact that fathers were not historically disadvantaged was not determinative. The unequal treatment sent the message that fathers' relationships with their children were less important than those of mothers. In addition, the legislation lumped fathers like Trociuk — who was unacknowledged arbitrarily — with other fathers who were unacknowledged because they had fathered a child through rape or incest: "Such a state of affairs is definitional of discrimination."[168] Finally, Deschamps J found the section 15(1) violation could not be justified under section 1. The legislation sought to ensure that mothers would not hesitate to register their children because of shame or because of the fear of having a confrontation with the father. However, the Court held it would be a simple matter for the legislature to design a non-intrusive application process, under which a father could seek to have his particulars registered or to have a child's surname changed. Justice Deschamps struck down the legislation but delayed the declaration of invalidity for twelve months. She also denied Trociuk's request to have the Court order his children's names changed immediately, but held that he would have to apply for the change under new legislation.

The most recent case on sex discrimination, *Newfoundland (Treasury Board) v NAPE*,[169] is one of the most striking equality rights deci-

---

167   [2003] 1 SCR 835 [*Trociuk*].
168   *Ibid* at para 24.
169   [2004] 3 SCR 381 [*NAPE*].

sions reached by the Supreme Court under the *Charter*, although the result turns not on section 15, but on the Court's determination that a violation of section 15(1) could be justified under section 1 because of the government's need to cut costs in the face of a severe fiscal crisis. For this reason, the case is discussed in greater detail in Chapter 4. The case involved the *Public Sector Restraint Act*, under which the provincial government delayed by three years an agreement it had made to make pay equity increases to female employees in the health-care sector and also extinguished any arrears owing for those three years, leading to a savings of $24 million. The government argued that it had to take this measure, among others, in response to a severe fiscal crisis. Justice Binnie, writing for the Court, had little trouble concluding that the *Public Sector Restraint Act* violated section 15(1). Not only did it affect women unequally, but its effect "was to affirm a policy of gender discrimination which the provincial government had itself denounced three years previously."[170] Nonetheless, Binnie J found the Act could be justified because of the severity of Newfoundland's budgetary problems at the time. Only a year before, the Court had ruled in *Martin* that "[b]udgetary considerations in and of themselves cannot normally be invoked as a free-standing pressing and substantial objective for the purposes of s 1 of the *Charter*."[171] The *NAPE* decision surprised equality advocates who feared that serious violations of section 15 rights might now be more readily justified because of cost.

J. CONCLUSION

The Supreme Court has consistently given section 15 of the *Charter* a restricted meaning, requiring a claimant to show discrimination on a prohibited or analogous ground and substantive discrimination. These decisions seem to preclude wholesale judicial review of all laws that create burdens or confer benefits on some but not others. As in section 7, some may question whether the Court has achieved the appropriate balance between imposing definitional limits on the right and requiring the government to demonstrate under section 1 that limits on the right are reasonable and demonstrably justified. The Court's approach has disappointed those who saw section 15 as a charter of social rights capable of remedying injustice on a more general scale. However, it coincides with the Supreme Court's general inclination under the *Charter*

---

170 *Ibid* at para 34.
171 *Martin*, above note 97 at para 109.

to defer to legislative judgment on questions of distributive justice. It may be seen as consistent with the Court's cautious approach to the interpretation of "life, liberty and security of the person" in section 7 and its refusal to recognize property rights as protected under the *Charter*.

On the other hand, where substantive discrimination has been shown on a prohibited or analogous ground, the Court has adopted a rigorous approach designed to ensure that the promise of equality will be respected. The Court has insisted that the equality guarantee mandates substantive review, avoiding a formalistic approach that would fail to take into account social reality. The Court has rejected the idea that a discriminatory intention must be shown, and it has proved willing to find a denial of equality from the failure to accommodate circumstances of actual disadvantage. It has also interpreted section 15(1) in a manner that, following section 15(2), defers to government's attempts to ameliorate the conditions of the disadvantaged even when doing so requires distinctions on enumerated or analogous grounds of discrimination. More recently, in *Kapp* and in *Withler*, the Court has confirmed its commitment to substantive equality and the prevention of disadvantage through prejudice and stereotyping in section 15(1); it has held that a government can shelter a law from section 15(1) scrutiny by demonstrating that it has, as one of its purposes, the amelioration of the conditions of a disadvantaged group.

Section 15 has yielded significant gains for gays and lesbians, where the decisions of the Supreme Court can be applauded for leading public opinion. The *Hislop* case disappointed many in not awarding retroactive benefits to same-sex couples, but the Court's decision in that case revolved around an unwillingness to award retroactive remedies given that there had been substantial change in the law in this area, and it did not decide whether a facially neutral law limiting retroactive pension benefits would constitute adverse-effects discrimination to same-sex couples who had historically been excluded from the plan. Until recently, the lot of the disabled had not been significantly improved by virtue of section 15, but the Supreme Court has now signalled a willingness to impose significant burdens on governments to ensure access to health services. While women's groups were among the most active in lobbying for a powerful equality guarantee, the gains to women from equality litigation have been modest. On the other hand, there can be little doubt that general public acceptance of and respect for gender equality has been enhanced by the *Charter*.

FURTHER READINGS

BINNIE, I, "Equality Rights in Canada: Judicial Usurpation or Missed Opportunity?" in G Huscroft & P Rishworth, *Litigating Rights* (Oxford: Hart, 2002)

BREDT, C, & A DODEK, "Breaking the Law's Grip on Equality: A New Paradigm for Section 15" (2003) 20 Sup Ct L Rev (2d) 33

FARADAY, F, M DENIKE, & K STEPHENSON, eds, *Making Equality Rights Real; Securing Substantive Equality under the* Charter (Toronto: Irwin Law, 2006)

GIBSON, D, *The Law of the* Charter: *Equality Rights* (Toronto: Carswell, 1990)

GRESCHNER, D, "Does *Law* Advance the Cause of Equality?" (2001) 27 Queen's LJ 299

———, "The Purpose of Canadian Equality Rights" (2002) 6 Rev Const Stud 291

HUGHES, P, "Resiling from Reconciling? Musings on *R v Kapp*" (2009) 47 Sup Ct L Rev (2d) 255

JACKMAN, M, "Constitutional Contact with the Disparities in the World: Poverty as a Prohibited Ground of Discrimination under the Canadian *Charter* and Human Rights Law" (1994) 2 Rev Const Stud 76

———, "Health Care and Equality: Is There a Cure?" (2007) 15 Health LJ 87

KOSHAN, J, & J WATSON HAMILTON, "Meaningless Mantra: Substantive Equality after *Withler*" (2011) 16 Rev Const Stud 31

LEPOFSKY, MD, "A Report Card on the *Charter's* Guarantee of Equality to Persons with Disabilities after 10 Years — What Progress? What Prospects?" (1997) 7 NJCL 263

MARTIN, S, "Balancing Individual Rights to Equality and Social Goals" (2001) 80 Can Bar Rev 299

MCINTYRE, S, & S RODGERS, eds, *Diminishing Returns: Inequality and the* Canadian Charter of Rights and Freedoms (Markham, ON: LexisNexis Butterworths, 2006)

MCLACHLIN, B, "Equality: The Most Difficult Right" (2001) 14 Sup Ct L Rev (2d) 17

MOREAU, S, "*R v Kapp*: New Directions for Section 15" (2008–2009) 40 Ottawa L Rev 283

———, "The Promise of *Law v Canada*" (2007) 57 UTLJ 415

MORRIS, M, & JK CHENG, "*Lovelace* and *Law* Revisited: The Substantive Equality Promise of *Kapp*" (2009) 47 Sup Ct L Rev (2d) 281

O'BRIEN, S, NADIA LAMBEK, & A DALE, "Accounting for Deprivation: The Intersection of Sections 7 and 15 of the *Charter* in the Context of Marginalized Groups" (2016) 35 NJCL 153

REAUME, D, "The Relevance of Relevance to Equality Rights" (2006) 31 Queens LJ 696

RYDER, B, C FARIA, & E LAWRENCE, "What's *Law* Good For? An Empirical Overview of *Charter* Equality Rights Decisions" (2004) 24 Sup Ct L Rev (2d) 103

SHEPPARD, C, "Grounds of Discrimination: Towards an Inclusive and Contextual Approach" (2002) 81 Can Bar Rev 893

SMITH, L, & E BLACK, "Equality Rights" in E Mendes & G Beaulac, eds, *Canadian Charter of Rights and Freedoms*, 5th ed (Markham, ON: LexisNexis Canada, 2013)

TREMBLAY, L, "Promoting Equality and Combating Discrimination through Affirmative Action: The Same Challenge? Questioning the Canadian Substantive Equality Paradigm" (2012) 60 Am J Comp L 181

TRUESDALE, C, "Section 15 and the *Oakes* Test: The Slippery Slope of Contextual Analysis" (2012–2013) 43:3 Ottawa L Rev 511

WATSON HAMILTON, J, & J KOSHAN, "Adverse Impact: The Supreme Court's Approach to Adverse Effects Discrimination under Section 15 of the *Charter*" (2014–15) 19 Rev Const Stud 191

YOUNG, M, "Unequal to the Task: '*Kapp*'ing the Substantive Potential of Section 15" in Sanda Rodgers & Sheila McIntyre, eds, *The Supreme Court of Canada and Social Justice: Commitment, Retrenchment or Retreat* (Markham, ON: LexisNexis, 2010) 183

CHAPTER 16

LANGUAGE RIGHTS

The appropriate status of the French and English languages has been an ongoing source of debate throughout Canadian history, both in the political and in the legal spheres. The Supreme Court has recognized that minority language rights involve both the rights of individuals and the rights of communities and that language rights must be interpreted in the context of Canada's history. The Court has commented:

> First, the members of the minority communities and their families, in every province and territory, must be given the opportunity to achieve their personal aspirations. Second, on the collective level, these language issues are related to the development and existence of the English-speaking minority in Quebec and the French-speaking minorities elsewhere in Canada. They also inevitably have an impact on how Quebec's French-speaking community perceives its future in Canada, since that community, which is in the majority in Quebec, is in the minority in Canada, and even more so in North America as a whole. To this picture must be added the serious difficulties resulting from the rate of assimilation of French-speaking minority groups outside Quebec, whose current language rights were acquired only recently, at considerable expense and with great difficulty. Thus, in interpreting these rights, the courts have a responsibility to reconcile sometimes divergent interests and priorities, and to be sensitive to the future of each language community. Our country's social context, demographics and history will therefore necessarily comprise the

backdrop for the analysis of language rights. Language rights cannot be analysed in the abstract, without regard for the historical context of the recognition thereof or for the concerns that the manner in which they are currently applied is meant to address.[1]

In other words, language rights are both rights for individuals and for collectivities, and they are a crucial element of Canada's complex social contract. Minority language rights have been a part of Canada from the start, and they were reaffirmed and expanded in the *Charter of Rights and Freedoms* for specific remedial purposes.

A. THE NATURE OF LANGUAGE RIGHTS

There is a range of options to protect ethnic communities, including those who share a common language. One possibility is to provide a degree of self-government for an ethnic or language community, giving it the powers to preserve and promote a distinct identity. In a federation, a language group may form the majority in a province while representing a minority in the country as a whole. Another option is to provide specific rights that permit groups to use their language or express their culture. Examples are separate-school rights, access to broadcasting outlets, or guarantees that government services will be provided in a certain language. Yet another device is protection against discrimination on the basis of language or culture, preventing the majority from disadvantaging the minority because of language or cultural practice. As will be seen, all of these options have been resorted to in the Canadian constitution.

The territorial principle, adopted in countries such as Belgium and Switzerland, leaves the determination of language rights to each province or territorial unit. The result is linguistic uniformity in most territorial units. While Canada's federal structure, with a francophone majority in Quebec and anglophone majorities in the other provinces, contains elements of the territorial principle, important features of the Canadian constitution see language as an aspect of the individual's personality, which is to be respected wherever one lives in Canada. Even though francophones are a small minority in most provinces, and anglophones are a minority in Quebec, both groups are given constitutional rights that limit the ability of provinces to impose linguistic uniformity.

---

1   *Solski (Tutor of)* v *Quebec (Attorney General)*, [2005] 1 SCR 201 at para 5 [*Solski*].

Language rights in Canada are distinctive because they are "positive" in nature. They entitle an individual to certain action on the part of government, such as funding for schools, printing of bilingual statutes, and service from government offices in one's chosen official language. They are different from most other rights in the *Charter*, which constrain government from acting but do not require positive action. For example, the guarantee of freedom of expression does not, as a general rule, require the government to ensure equality of access to funds to ensure that one's voice is heard.[2] The positive nature of language rights requires governments to spend funds to respect language rights and to provide facilities for minority language education instruction where numbers warrant. In some cases, judges may play an active role in ensuring adequate remedies for such positive rights.[3]

B. THE *CONSTITUTION ACT, 1867*

The original Confederation bargain in 1867 was shaped very much by Canadian dualism — that is, by the desires and needs of French- and English-speaking communities to express and protect their identities. For the French-speaking population of Quebec, federalism was the primary method to protect its interests. Federalism ensured that the French-speaking majority in that province would have the powers necessary for cultural preservation — notably, education and civil law.

"Language" was not expressly mentioned as a subject of either federal or provincial legislative jurisdiction in sections 91 and 92 of the *Constitution Act, 1867*, the sections that distribute legislative powers between federal and provincial governments. Accordingly, it is treated as an "ancillary" matter — that is, either government can legislate with respect to language when acting within other assigned legislative fields. For example, Parliament has enacted the *Official Languages Act*, which regulates bilingualism in the federal public service.[4] Similarly, Quebec has the authority to require that French be used as the language of business in the province and to regulate the use of English in signs (although these laws are now subject to the *Charter* rights described below).[5]

---

2   *Native Women's Association of Canada v Canada*, [1994] 3 SCR 627, 119 DLR (4th) 224.

3   *Doucet-Boudreau v Nova Scotia*, [2003] 3 SCR 3 [*Doucet-Boudreau*], discussed in Chapter 17.

4   RSC 1985, c O-3. The constitutionality of this Act was determined in *Jones v New Brunswick (Attorney General)*, [1975] 2 SCR 182, 45 DLR (3d) 583 [*Jones*].

5   *Devine v Quebec (Attorney General)*, [1988] 2 SCR 790, 55 DLR (4th) 641.

In addition, the *Constitution Act, 1867* contained limited positive rights protecting the use of the French and English languages in certain federal and Quebec institutions. Section 133 provides as follows:

> Either the English or French Language may be used by any Person in the Debates of the Houses of Parliament of Canada and of the House of the Legislature of Quebec; and both those Languages shall be used in the respective Records and Journals of those Houses; and either of those Languages may be used by any Person in any Pleading or Process issuing from any Court of Canada established under this Act, and in or from all or any of the Courts of Quebec.

This provision was duplicated in section 23 of the *Manitoba Act* upon Manitoba entering Confederation in 1870,[6] while the provinces of Saskatchewan and Alberta were required to comply with similar obligations by section 110 of the *North-West Territories Act.*[7] Those obligations continued after they became provinces in 1905 because of sections 16(1) of their constituent Acts.[8] However, these language rights were not entrenched and could be changed by legislation, and both provinces have since done so.[9]

The Supreme Court has held that these provisions provide a floor of guaranteed rights but that this does not prevent Parliament or the provincial legislatures from expanding on them.[10] Equally, however, prior to the *Charter*, section 133 of the *Constitution Act, 1867* did not prevent provinces from restricting the use of minority languages in areas other than those mentioned in the constitution. For example, the courts upheld the right of Ontario to abolish French-language instruction in Roman Catholic separate schools in 1912,[11] holding that language of instruction was not protected as an aspect of the denominational school rights conferred by section 93 of the *Constitution Act, 1867.*

---

6   *Manitoba Act, 1870*, SC 1870, c 3, s 23.

7   RSC 1886, c 50, s 110, as amended by SC 1891, c 22, s 18.

8   *Saskatchewan Act*, SC 1905, c 42.

9   The state of language rights in these provinces was discussed by the Supreme Court of Canada in *R v Mercure*, [1988] 1 SCR 234, 48 DLR (4th) 1.

10   See *Jones*, above note 4.

11   This was upheld in *Ottawa Roman Catholic Separate School Board v Mackell*, [1917] AC 62, 32 DLR 1 (PC) and *Ottawa Roman Catholic Separate School Board v Ottawa (City)*, [1917] AC 76, 32 DLR 10 (PC).

C. LANGUAGE RIGHTS AND THE *CHARTER*

With the *Charter of Rights and Freedoms* came new protection for language rights. The language provisions in sections 16 to 23 of the *Charter* were a key component of the 1982 constitutional amendments. The government of Prime Minister Pierre Trudeau saw the *Charter* as a whole, and the language rights in particular, as a way to strengthen Canadians' attachment to their country.[12] The language rights expanded on section 133 of the 1867 constitution, affirming in section 16 that French and English are the two official languages of Canada. To emphasize their importance, sections 16 through 23 were not made subject to the legislative override in section 33 of the *Charter*. The clear message was that French and English minority language communities were to be supported and fostered throughout the country.

After declaring that English and French are the official languages of Canada and New Brunswick, section 16(1) goes on to say that these languages have "equality of status and equal rights and privileges as to their use in all institutions of the Parliament and government of Canada," while section 16(2) makes a similar statement with respect to the institutions of the legislature and government of New Brunswick.[13]

Sections 17 to 20 of the *Charter* affirm and expand on the former section 133 of the 1867 constitution. Section 17 guarantees the right to use English or French in debates and other proceedings of Parliament and the New Brunswick legislature, while section 18 guarantees that the statutes, records, and journals of the federal Parliament and the New Brunswick legislature must be in both languages and that both versions are of equal legal authority. Section 19 guarantees the right to use either French or English in pleadings or processes of federally established courts and those of New Brunswick. Finally, section 20 gives a right for the public to communicate in either language with the head or central office of an institution of the Parliament or government of Canada or any office of an institution of New Brunswick's government or legislature. An individual has a right to communicate with other Canadian government offices if there is "significant demand for communications with and services from that office" in French or English, or "due to the nature of the office, it is reasonable that communications with and services from that office" be available in both languages.

---

12 PH Russell, "The Political Purposes of the *Canadian Charter of Rights and Freedoms*" (1983) 61 Can Bar Rev 30.

13 The term "Canada" here refers to the federal level of government.

In addition to these "institutional bilingualism" provisions, there is a right to publicly funded minority language education in section 23 of the *Charter*. This section gives a right to education in the minority language of a province to two groups of children: those of Canadian citizens whose first language learned is that of the French or English minority in the province in which they reside,[14] and children of citizens educated in primary school in Canada in the language of the minority of the province in which they reside. Where some children of a family are receiving education in the minority language because of this section, all children in the family have the same entitlement. This right is qualified by the requirement that the numbers of children warrant receiving public funding for minority language instruction (section 23(3) (a)). Where the number warrants, the right extends to instruction in minority language educational facilities (section 23(3)(a)).

D. FREEDOM OF EXPRESSION AND LANGUAGE

In *Ford*, the Supreme Court of Canada held that the guarantee of freedom of expression in section 2(b) of the *Charter* includes the right to speak in the language of one's choice.[15] Accordingly, section 2(b) provides a check on government action designed to restrict the use of certain languages or to compel expression in a particular language. In effect, this interpretation of section 2(b) protects linguistic minorities against state discrimination and demands tolerance with respect to the use of their languages. Unlike the specific language rights of sections 16 to 23, section 2(b) protects all languages.

Ford, as we have seen, arose out of a challenge to Quebec's language legislation prohibiting the use of any language other than French on commercial signs or firm names. The Court rejected the argument that the constitution's specific language rights were a complete code that belied constitutional protection for any other languages. Instead, the Court quoted from an earlier decision involving the Manitoba language guarantees, where it had stated:

---

14 This clause is not in force in Quebec because of s 59 of the *Constitution Act, 1982*. Section 59 responds to Quebec concerns about immigrants' refusal to assimilate into the francophone community.

15 *Ford v Quebec (Attorney General)*, [1988] 2 SCR 712, 54 DLR (4th) 577 [*Ford*], discussed in greater detail in Chapter 9.

The importance of language rights is grounded in the essential role that language plays in human existence, development and dignity. It is through language that we are able to form concepts; to structure and order the world around us. Language bridges the gap between isolation and community, allowing humans to delineate the rights and duties they hold in respect of one another, and thus to live in society.[16]

The Court went on to say:

Language is so intimately related to the form and content of expression that there cannot be true freedom of expression by means of language if one is prohibited from using the language of one's choice. Language is not merely a means or medium of expression; it colours the content and meaning of expression.[17]

Language is a central way in which a group expresses its cultural identity and individuals express their personal identity. It follows that laws restricting the use of one's language will infringe section 2(b) and have to be justified under section 1.

It was acknowledged that Quebec had a pressing and substantial objective in enacting the legislation, given the vulnerable position of French in Quebec because of declining birth rates among francophones, a tendency for new immigrants to gravitate to the anglophone community in Quebec, and a predominance of English in the more important economic sectors. The Court accepted that the attempt to assure Quebeckers that the *visage linguistique* of Quebec reflected the predominance of French was a serious and legitimate objective. However, the Court was not satisfied that the achievement of this objective required the suppression of all other languages on public signs and in firm names. Rather, the judges concluded that a law requiring the predominance of French on a sign, while still allowing other communities to use their language, would be more consistent with *Charter* rights.

Although the language rights guaranteed by sections 16 to 23 are not subject to the override, the "signs" law was found to violate freedom of expression. As described in Chapter 5, the aftermath was that the Quebec government invoked section 33 of the *Charter* in new legislation limiting the use of English in public signs. This law was then the subject of a successful complaint to the United Nations Human

---

16   *Reference Re Language Rights under s 23 of Manitoba Act, 1870 and s 133 of Constitution Act, 1867,* [1985] 1 SCR 721, (sub nom *Reference Re Manitoba Language Rights*) 19 DLR (4th) 1 at 19 [*Reference Re Manitoba Language Rights*].

17   *Ford,* above note 15 at 604 (DLR).

Rights Committee under the *International Covenant on Civil and Political Rights*. The Committee's reasons echo those of the Supreme Court in *Ford*, stating that the law was an unreasonable limitation on freedom of expression.[18] The Quebec government allowed the override to expire after five years.

E. INTERPRETING LANGUAGE RIGHTS

1) Institutional Bilingualism

The Supreme Court has not been entirely consistent in its approach to the interpretation of language rights. In early cases involving section 133 of the *Constitution Act, 1867*, the Court took an expansive view. In *Blaikie (No 1)*,[19] the Court held that, in deciding which institutions were covered by section 133, the words of the constitution should be given a progressive interpretation, taking into account the changing nature of courts and government since 1867. Although section 133 required that "laws" be in both French and English, the Court found that the guarantee should encompass regulations and delegated legislation, not just statutes, given the proliferation of this type of law making today. In addition, the term "courts" was interpreted to include adjudicative tribunals, like labour relations boards or human rights tribunals, since many legal disputes are now determined by these bodies.

This generous view of language rights was evident again in *Reference Re Manitoba Language Rights*.[20] In an earlier decision, *Manitoba (Attorney General) v Forest*,[21] the Supreme Court had found that legislation enacted by Manitoba in 1890 purporting to repeal the bilingualism requirement in section 23 of the *Manitoba Act, 1870* was unconstitutional. A reference was then launched to determine the effect of almost one hundred years of non-compliance with section 23. The Court held that

---

18   *Ballantyne, Davidson & McIntyre v Canada*, Communications Nos 359/1989 and 385/1989, UN Doc CCPR/C/47/D/359/1989 and 385/1989/Rev 1 (1993). In para 11.4, the Committee stated: "A State may choose one or more official languages, but it may not exclude, outside the spheres of public life, the freedom to express oneself in a language of one's choice."

19   *Quebec (Attorney General) v Blaikie (No 1)*, [1979] 2 SCR 1016, 101 DLR (3d) 394. In *Quebec (Attorney General) v Blaikie (No 2)*, [1981] 1 SCR 312, 123 DLR (3d) 15, the Court expanded on the earlier holding. A more recent application of these cases is found in *Sinclair v Quebec (Attorney General)*, [1992] 1 SCR 579, 89 DLR (4th) 500.

20   *Reference Re Manitoba Language Rights*, above note 16.

21   (1979), 101 DLR (3d) 385 (SCC).

the requirement was mandatory, so that all laws passed only in English were invalid. If the Court had stopped here, a large component of Manitoba law would have been invalid and the legislature would have been improperly elected under an English-only law. Recognizing the need to prevent a "legislative vacuum" and to preserve the rule of law, the Supreme Court suspended the effect of its declaration of invalidity for a period that allowed Manitoba to translate and re-enact its laws — this time, in both official languages.

The Supreme Court was initially unwilling to embrace an expansive view of language rights in relation to court proceedings. In cases decided under both section 133 of the *Constitution Act, 1867* and section 19(2) of the *Charter*, a majority of the Court accepted the argument that the right to use French or English in proceedings of the courts entitles an individual to no more than that — a right to speak in either language. The individual cannot demand that the court proceedings be conducted in the language of his or her choice, nor that the judge understand that language. The right to use French or English in court proceedings extended not only to the litigant but also to the court staff and the judges. In *MacDonald v Montreal (City)*,[22] the use of a unilingual French summons was found to be acceptable, while in *Société des Acadiens*, the Court held that a francophone litigant in New Brunswick could not demand a French-speaking judge.[23] In both cases, Beetz J, writing for the majority, emphasized that language rights were different from most others in the *Charter*. In his view, they were the result of a historic political compromise and should be interpreted more narrowly, with an attitude of judicial restraint.[24] In contrast, legal rights were described as "seminal in nature because they are rooted in principle."[25] It should be noted, however, that in *Société des Acadiens*, Beetz J emphasized that the rules of natural justice or procedural fairness would require that any individual who did not understand proceedings be given access to an interpreter.

In contrast, the dissenting reasons of Dickson CJC and Wilson J emphasized that the right to use one's language included the notion of being understood. Neither stated definitively what this would mean. Chief Justice Dickson stated that this might encompass the use of interpreters or simultaneous translation, although on the facts of the case, it had not been shown that the judges did not understand French.

---

22 [1986] 1 SCR 460 at 483–84, 27 DLR (4th) 321 [*MacDonald*].

23 *Société des Acadiens du Nouveau-Brunswick v Association of Parents for Fairness in Education*, [1986] 1 SCR 549, 27 DLR (4th) 406 [*Société des Acadiens*].

24 *MacDonald*, above note 22 at 496–97 (SCR).

25 *Société des Acadiens*, above note 23 at 578 (SCR).

Justice Wilson felt that section 19(2) of the *Charter* was evolving towards a requirement of a bilingual judiciary.

The Supreme Court has now repudiated the narrow view of language rights that it took in *Société des Acadiens*. In *R v Beaulac*,[26] the Court interpreted the right to be tried in either English or French granted by section 530 of the *Criminal Code*. Although the case did not arise under the *Charter*, the Court explicitly stated that it would no longer be bound by the view that language rights should be interpreted more narrowly than other rights. Writing for the majority, Bastarache J stated:

> Language rights must in all cases be interpreted purposively, in a manner consistent with the preservation and development of official language communities in Canada . . . . To the extent that *Société des Acadiens du Nouveau-Brunswick* stands for a restrictive interpretation of language rights, it is to be rejected.[27]

The Court now takes the position that the language rights in the *Charter* are meant to achieve substantive equality between linguistic groups, rather than formal equality.[28] However, the Court has held that in provinces where *Charter* language rights do not apply, the courts cannot create them using the "*Charter* values" approach.[29]

As an example of this expansive approach to language rights, the Supreme Court found that RCMP officers acting as a provincial police force in New Brunswick were obligated to provide services in both English and French.[30] The decision was based on section 20(2) of the *Charter*, which specifically provides that all services from a governmental body in New Brunswick shall be available in both official languages. The Court found that as the RCMP had contracted with the New Brunswick government to serve as a provincial police force, they were bound by that provision of the *Charter* which applied specifically to services of the New Brunswick government.

Where the *Charter* requires that government services be provided in both official languages, the services provided in each language must be of equal quality.[31] This requirement will not always be satisfied

---

26   [1999] 1 SCR 768, 173 DLR (4th) 193.

27   *Ibid* at para 25.

28   *DesRochers v Canada (Industry)*, [2009] SCR 194 at para 31 [*DesRochers*].

29   *Conseil scolaire francophone de la Colombie-Britannique v British Columbia*, [2013] 2 SCR 774, rejecting the argument that British Columbia could be required to authorize court proceedings in French.

30   *Société des Acadiens et Acadiennes du Nouveau-Brunswick Inc v Canada*, [2008] 1 SCR 383.

31   *DesRochers*, above note 28 at para 3.

simply by ensuring that the services provided in each language are identical to each other. Depending on the nature of the services being provided, it may be necessary to provide services with distinct content in order to achieve substantive equality between the services offered to different linguistic groups.[32] For example, when the content of services is determined through the input and participation of one linguistic group, and the services thus fail to benefit the other linguistic group to the same degree, there may be an onus on the government to consult with the second linguistic group and develop distinct content for the services offered to them.[33]

2) Minority-Language Education Rights

Despite the hesitation to interpret language rights in relation to the courts in a liberal fashion, the Supreme Court of Canada has consistently given minority-language education rights in section 23 of the *Charter* a generous interpretation. The first major section 23 case to come before the Supreme Court was *Mahe* from Alberta, which examined the degree to which minority-language groups could demand management and control of their education system.[34] Chief Justice Dickson, writing for the Court, emphasized that the minority-language education guarantee had two purposes. First, education in one's language provides an important way to preserve and promote the minority group's language and culture. As well, educational institutions can provide a centre for the community, which helps promote the minority culture.[35] Chief Justice Dickson also noted the strong remedial component to section 23: the section was designed to protect the French and English minorities from assimilation and to give recognition and encouragement to the two official language groups in Canada.[36] In sum,

---

32   *Ibid* at para 51.

33   *Ibid* at paras 53–54.

34   *Mahe v Alberta*, [1990] 1 SCR 342, 68 DLR (4th) 69 [*Mahe*]. An earlier case from Quebec, *Quebec (Attorney General) v Quebec Association of Protestant School Boards*, [1984] 2 SCR 66, 10 DLR (4th) 321 had struck down Quebec's attempts to narrow the group who could assert s 23 rights. The Court described this as an attempt to abrogate s 23 that could not be characterized as a "reasonable limitation" on rights under s 1.

35   In a recent case, the Supreme Court recognized that "not only do minority schools provide basic language education, they also act as community centres where the members of the minority can meet to express their culture. Thus, the education rights provided by s 23 form the cornerstone of minority language rights protection." *Solski*, above note 1 at para 3.

36   *Mahe*, above note 34 at 362–63 (SCR).

section 23 represented, for him, the "linchpin in this nation's commitment to the values of bilingualism and biculturalism."[37]

In interpreting the scope of section 23(3), Dickson CJC refused to set out a numerical formula whereby a certain number of students would entitle a group to minority language *instruction* while a larger number would ensure that this instruction then be given in separate educational *facilities*. Rather, he concluded that the section imposed a "sliding scale requirement": "[S]ection 23 guarantees whatever type and level of rights and services is appropriate in order to provide minority language instruction for the particular number of students involved."[38] At the upper end of the sliding scale, minority language students are entitled to the substantive equivalence of the educational experience offered by the neighbouring majority language schools.[39]

With respect to section 23(3)(b) and the guarantee of separate educational facilities, Dickson CJC concluded that this mandated a measure of management and control for the minority group. In some cases, this would require the establishment of an independent minority language school board; in other cases, guaranteed representation and certain exclusive authority within the majority board would be sufficient.[40] In deciding what level of service is required, a province should consider actual and potential numbers of students.

In *Arseneault-Cameron v Prince Edward Island*,[41] the Supreme Court emphasized the importance of the remedial purpose of section 23 of the *Charter*, to redress past injustices and to provide "the official language minority with equal access to high quality education in its own language, in circumstances where community development will be enhanced."[42] The minister of education denied the request of a minority language school board for its own school in favour of a plan to bus the children to a French-language school in another community. The decision was successfully challenged on the ground that the minister had "failed to give proper weight to the promotion and preservation of minority language culture and to the role of the French Language

---

37   *Ibid* at 350.
38   *Ibid* at 366.
39   *Association des parents de l'école Rose-des-vents v British Columbia (Education)*, [2015] 2 SCR 139.
40   *Mahe*, above note 34 at 371–73. Further discussion of s 23 is found in *Reference Re Public Schools Act (Manitoba) s 79(3), (4) and (7)*, [1993] 1 SCR 839, 100 DLR (4th) 723.
41   [2000] 1 SCR 3.
42   *Ibid* at para 27.

Board in balancing the pedagogical and cultural considerations."[43] The Court insisted that provinces have a positive duty to promote minority language educational services. Formal or supposedly objective comparison with the majority community was rejected in favour of a contextual approach that takes into account the unique history and the special needs of minority language communities.

When dealing with minority-language education rights, the courts have to confront the question of how closely involved judges should become in the design and management of school facilities. In *Doucet-Boudreau v Nova Scotia*,[44] the Supreme Court decided 5:4 that a judge who had ordered Nova Scotia to make best efforts to build francophone schools could retain jurisdiction over the case and require the government to report back on its progress. The implications of this case for the remedial powers of courts will be discussed in Chapter 17, but it is significant that such remedial activism arose in the context of the positive right to minority language educational facilities. Justices Iacobucci and Arbour, for the majority of the Court, emphasized the remedial purposes of section 23 of the *Charter* in protecting linguistic minorities from assimilation and the reality that delay in fully implementing section 23 in Nova Scotia was hastening the assimilation of the francophone minority. They rejected an "in all deliberate speed" approach to remedies by observing that

> for every school year that governments do not meet their obligations under s 23, there is an increased likelihood of assimilation which carries the risk that numbers might cease to "warrant." . . . If delay is tolerated, governments could potentially avoid the duties imposed upon them by s 23 through their own failure to implement the rights vigilantly. The affirmative promise contained in s 23 of the *Charter* and the critical need for timely compliance will sometimes require courts to order affirmative remedies to guarantee that language rights are meaningfully, and therefore necessarily promptly, protected.[45]

In *Gosselin (Tutor of) v Quebec (Attorney General)*,[46] the Supreme Court denied a claim by francophone parents in Quebec that they had an equality right to have their children educated in the English language. The parents did not qualify under section 23 of the *Charter* because they did not receive their primary school instruction in Canada in English and their children were being schooled in French

43 *Ibid* at para 30.
44 *Doucet-Boudreau*, above note 3.
45 *Ibid* at para 29.
46 [2005] 1 SCR 238.

in Quebec. The Court concluded that the equality argument of the francophone parents in Quebec would destroy "the carefully crafted compromise contained in s 23 of the Canadian *Charter of Rights and Freedoms*"[47] which allowed Quebec to take steps to protect the minority status of the French language within Canada and allowed anglophone minorities in Quebec, as well as francophone minorities outside Quebec, to manage and control their own minority language schools. The Court also approved of lower court cases that decided that anglophone parents outside of Quebec have no constitutional right to have their children educated in French.[48] Minority language rights are tied to particular minority communities that exist in Canada and they cannot be overridden by more abstract claims of equality rights.

In *Solski (Tutor of) v Quebec (Attorney General)*, the Supreme Court considered the different situation of families whose children had already received part of the primary education in Quebec in English. The right at issue was section 23(2) of the *Charter* which provides for continuity of language instruction by providing that "citizens of Canada of whom any child has received or is receiving primary or secondary school instruction in English or French in Canada, have the right to have all their children receive primary and secondary school instruction in the same language." Quebec had interpreted this right as providing a right to minority language education only where the child had received a mathematical majority of instruction in English. The Supreme Court held that such a quantitative approach was too inflexible and too ungenerous in order to realize the purposes of section 23(2) in providing for continuity of minority language instruction even in cases where the family is not necessarily a part of the particular linguistic minority group. It stated that

> to purposefully assess the requirement for participation in s 23(2), therefore, all the circumstances of the child must be considered including the time spent in each program, at what stage of education the choice of language of instruction was made, what programs are or were available, and whether learning disabilities or other difficulties exist. In this way, it is possible to determine whether a child's overall educational experience is sufficient to meet the requirements of s 23(2).[49]

---

47   *Ibid* at para 2.
48   *Ibid* at para 30, approving of *Abbey v Essex County Board of Education* (1999), 42 OR (3d) 481 at 488–89 (CA) and *Lavoie v Nova Scotia (Attorney General)* (1989), 58 DLR (4th) 293 at 313–15 (NSCA).
49   *Solski*, above note 1 at para 33.

In the result, the Court read down Quebec's requirement that students had spent the majority of their time in minority language education to allow a more qualitative determination of whether students had spent a significant part of their time in such an environment. Although the Court recognized Quebec's need to protect the French language, it still defined the section 23(2) right in a broad and generous fashion. To this end, it suggested that if

> children are in a recognized education program regularly and legally, they will in most instances be able to continue their education in the same language .... Uprooting would not be in the interest of the minority language community or of the child. Nevertheless, a qualitative assessment of the situation to determine whether there is evidence of a genuine commitment to a minority language educational experience is warranted, with each province exercising its discretion in light of its particular circumstances, obligation to respect the objectives of s 23, and educational policies.[50]

Nguyen v Quebec (Education, Recreation and Sports)[51] dealt with Quebec's response to the phenomenon of "bridging schools," unsubsidized, private English language schools used by parents whose children are not eligible for enrolment in publicly funded English schools to qualify their children as having "received primary or secondary instruction in English . . . in Canada" under section 23(2). Amendments to the *Charter of the French Language* provided that periods of attendance in "bridging schools" were not to be taken into account in determining eligibility to attend a publicly funded English school. These provisions were successfully challenged as an infringement of the rights guaranteed by section 23(2). The language of section 23(2) draws no distinction between public and private schools for the purpose of determining eligibility, and *Solski* establishes the obligation to conduct a global qualitative assessment of a child's educational pathway. While Quebec's objective of protecting the promotion of the French language was important enough to justify limiting section 23(2) rights, the means adopted did not satisfy the proportionality test as the law did not permit a proper assessment of the child's educational pathway to the public system. If a school is established primarily for the purpose of enabling transfer to the public English language system, the child's educational pathway would not be genuine. Likewise, a short period of attendance in a private institution would not indicate a sufficiently

---

50   *Ibid* at para 47.
51   [2009] 3 SCR 208.

genuine commitment to confer the status of rights holder. As the challenged law did not permit that type of assessment, however, it failed to meet the section 1 proportionality test.

F. CONCLUSION

Language rights have been a central and controversial feature of the Canadian constitution since Confederation. The recognition and protection of language rights was significantly enhanced under the *Charter of Rights and Freedoms*, and the Supreme Court of Canada has, in recent years, given constitutionally protected language rights a generous interpretation, repudiating an earlier tendency to give them a narrow interpretation.

Minority language rights have at the same time an individual, a collective, and a remedial dimension. Courts will protect the language rights of individuals but also recognize that language rights are related to the collective interests and rights of minority language communities in Canada and are designed to resist the assimilation of such communities.

FURTHER READINGS

BASTARACHE, M, ed, *Language Rights in Canada*, 2d ed (Toronto: Carswell, 2004)

BRAEN, A, P FOUCHER, & Y LE BOUTHHILLER, *Languages, Constitutionalism and Minorities* (Markham: LexisNexis, 2006)

GREEN, LC, & D RÉAUME, "Second-Class Rights? Principle and Compromise in the *Charter*" (1990) 13 Dal LJ 565

MAGNET, JE, *Official Languages of Canada New Essays* (Markham: LexisNexis Canada, 2008, 1995)

NEWMAN, W, "Understanding Language Rights, Equality and the *Charter*" (2004) 15 NJCL 363

POTHIER, D, "Language Rights Remedies in the Supreme Court of Canada: Invisible, Gentle, or Stern Hand?" (2014–2015) 19 Rev Const Stud 147

RÉAUME, D, & LC GREEN, "Education and Linguistic Security in the *Charter*" (1989) 34 McGill LJ 777

——, "Language Rights: Constitutional Misfits or Real Rights" (2006) 31 Sup Ct L Rev (2d) 201

ROULEAU, N, "Section 23 of the *Charter*: Minority-Language Education Rights" (2008) 39 Sup Ct L Rev (2d) 261

SCHNEIDERMAN, D, ed, *Language and the State: The Law and Politics of Identity* (Cowansville, QC: Yvon Blais, 1991)

CHAPTER 17

REMEDIES

The *Charter of Rights and Freedoms* differs from the *Canadian Bill of Rights* in its emphasis on effective remedies. Section 24(1) of the *Charter* provides:

> Anyone whose rights or freedoms, as guaranteed by this *Charter*, have been infringed or denied may apply to a court of competent jurisdiction to obtain such remedy as the court considers appropriate and just in the circumstances.

In addition, section 52(1) of the *Constitution Act, 1982* provides:

> The Constitution of Canada is the supreme law of Canada, and any law that is inconsistent with the provisions of the Constitution is, to the extent of the inconsistency, of no force and effect.

As noted in Chapters 3 and 4, the first stage in any *Charter* case is the consideration of whether a right or freedom has been infringed or denied. If the court finds that there has been a *Charter* violation, it then passes to the second stage to consider whether the violation can be justified as a reasonable limit under section 1. If a violation cannot be justified, the court must then decide what practical measures should be taken in view of the infringement. It has long been a principle of our law that there can be no right without an effective remedy. A remedy is the operative element of a court's order that translates the right into concrete form. There would be little point in claiming rights without effective and meaningful remedies for their violation.

There are a variety of possible remedial options. Section 24(1) of the *Charter* assures the individual whose rights have been violated that he or she will be given "such remedy as the court considers appropriate and just in the circumstances." The remedies of stays of proceeding, sentence reductions, *habeas corpus*, and exclusion of evidence under section 24(2) in criminal cases have been considered in Chapter 14. This chapter will review remedies available under section 24(1) as well as a variety of remedial responses that courts use to enforce the mandate in section 52(1) of the *Constitution Act, 1982* that any law that is inconsistent with the *Charter* is of no force and effect to the extent of the inconsistency. Before the availability of specific remedies is examined, some general considerations about the remedial role of the courts and remedial decision making will be examined.

A. GENERAL CONSIDERATIONS GOVERNING THE EXERCISE OF REMEDIAL DISCRETION

1) The Availability of Remedies under Section 24(1) of the *Charter* and Section 52(1) of the *Constitution Act, 1982*

The Supreme Court has stressed the different roles and purposes of constitutional remedies under section 24(1) of the *Charter* and section 52(1) of the *Constitution Act, 1982*. Chief Justice McLachlin has written in the 2008 case of *R v Ferguson* "that sections 52(1) and 24(1) serve different remedial purposes. Section 52(1) provides a remedy for *laws* that violate *Charter* rights either in purpose or in effect. Section 24(1), by contrast, provides a remedy for *government acts* that violate *Charter* rights."[1] Judges have an explicit grant of remedial discretion under section 24(1) and remedies can be sought under that section only by a person whose own rights have been violated. Section 52(1) is a more general statement of constitutional supremacy and it provides a mandatory rule that legislation that is inconsistent with the constitution is of no force and effect. Remedies under both section 24(1) and 52(1) can only rarely be combined,[2] for example, in cases where a law is declared invalid under section 52(1) but damages are justified under section 24(1) on the basis of governmental fault.[3]

---

1 *R v Ferguson*, [2008] 1 SCR 96 at para 61 [*Ferguson*].
2 *Schachter v Canada*, [1992] 2 SCR 679 [*Schachter*].
3 *Mackin v New Brunswick*, [2002] 1 SCR 405 [*Mackin*].

In *Ferguson*, the Court held that the only remedy for an unconstitutional mandatory minimum sentence enacted by Parliament is to strike down the law in its entirety under section 52(1). The Court was concerned about the uncertainty that would be caused by crafting case-by-case exemptions from the law. At the same time, however, it would be a mistake to assume that striking down a law in its entirety is the only available remedy under section 52(1) to deal with a law that is an unjustified violation of the *Charter*. Although section 52(1) is framed in mandatory terms, judges still have remedial choices when determining remedies under that section. As will be seen, the remedies of reading in, reading down, and severance are alternatives to the complete striking down of a law under section 52(1). Another alternative is a tailored or less than complete declaration of invalidity, as was used when the Court found the assisted suicide offence constitutionally overbroad.[4] In addition, courts sometimes soften the remedy of striking down a law by suspending a declaration of invalidity for six to eighteen months in order to provide the legislature an opportunity to enact new legislation before the declaration of invalidity takes effect. The Court extended the suspended declaration of invalidity in the assisted dying case to sixteen months to account for the time that Parliament was dissolved from the 2015 election campaign, but also provided that individual applicants could obtain court-ordered exemptions from the assisted suicide offence during this extended period.[5]

The jurisdiction of courts and tribunals was discussed in Chapter 7. The provincial superior courts have constant concurrent jurisdiction to award constitutional remedies under both section 24(1) of the *Charter* and declarations of invalidity under section 52(1) of the *Constitution Act, 1982*. The jurisdiction of other courts and tribunals to award constitutional remedies depends on their statutory jurisdiction. In order to award a remedy under section 24(1) of the *Charter*, a court or tribunal must have jurisdiction, independent of section 24(1), over the parties, subject matter, and remedy requested. A tribunal that has jurisdiction to decide questions of law will be presumed to have jurisdiction to apply the *Charter* as the supreme law and to award *Charter* remedies unless the legislature has clearly removed that power from the tribunal.[6]

---

4   *Carter v Canada (Attorney General)*, [2015] 1 SCR 331 [*Carter 2015*].
5   *Carter v Canada (Attorney General)*, 2016 SCC 4 [*Carter 2016*].
6   *Nova Scotia (Workers Compensation Board) v Martin*, [2003] 2 SCR 504 at para 36; *R v Conway*, [2010] 1 SCR 765.

2) Purposes and Constraints in Crafting Remedies

In *Doucet-Boudreau v Nova Scotia*,[7] the Supreme Court outlined some general principles to govern the crafting of appropriate and just remedies under section 24(1) of the *Charter*. Section 24(1) should be given the same generous and purposive interpretation as applies to other parts of the *Charter*. Its purpose is to provide responsive and effective remedies.[8] Section 24(1) can require novel and creative remedies, and "it is difficult to imagine language which could give the court a wider and less fettered discretion."[9] The remedial discretion of the superior courts is not limited by statutes or common law, but only by constitutional principles that require

1) a meaningful remedy that responds to the circumstances of the violation and the claimant;
2) respect for the role of the legislature and the executive;
3) reliance on judicial functions and powers; and
4) fairness to the party against whom the remedy is directed.[10]

This approach stresses the need for remedies to be effective while also setting out constraints on remedies, including the need to respect the roles of courts, legislatures, and the executive, and to be fair to the parties. Effective and meaningful remedies require attention to both the nature of the violation in the past and the need to ensure compliance with the *Charter* in the future. In the result, a majority of the Court upheld a trial judge's decision to retain jurisdiction over a complex minority language school case and to require the government to report back to the court on its progress on implementing rights. Four judges dissented and argued that the remedy was unfair to the government and exceeded the functions of the Court by breaching procedural fairness and the separation of powers. Although the Court was divided on the extent to which constitutional principles restrained the exercise of judicial discretion, they were united in accepting that courts could make mandatory orders against governments under section 24(1) and that the remedial discretion under section 24(1) should be constrained only by constitutional principles.[11]

---

7   [2003] 3 SCR 3 [*Doucet-Boudreau*].
8   *Ibid* at para 25.
9   *Ibid* at para 50, citing *R v Mills*, [1986] 1 SCR 863 at 965.
10 *Doucet-Boudreau*, above note 7 at paras 51–59.
11 *Ibid* at para 105.

In *Vancouver (City) v Ward*,[12] the Court fleshed out in greater detail the purposes of section 24(1) remedies in the course of providing a structure to consider *Charter* damages claims. It indicated that *Charter* damages should serve one of the following three purposes:

1) compensation for the pecuniary and non-pecuniary harms caused by the violation;
2) vindication of the *Charter* right; or
3) deterrence of future violations of the *Charter*.[13]

This formulation of the functional purposes or justifications of section 24(1) damages makes clear that such remedies must seek both to repair past harms and to prevent future violations of the *Charter*. It also recognizes a social need to vindicate *Charter* rights and the danger of *Charter* violations having no effective remedy. At the same time, the Court did not suggest that damages should automatically be awarded in response to every *Charter* violation. Although it upheld a $5,000 damages award for an unconstitutional strip search, it held that damages did not have to be awarded for a short unconstitutional seizure of a car because they were not necessary to provide compensation, vindication of the right, or deterrence of future violations. The Court heeded the constraints placed on the judiciary in crafting remedies and the need to consider competing social interests before awarding remedies.

In a process somewhat analogous to that used to establish rights violations and reasonable limitations under the *Charter*, the Court indicated that, even after a *Charter* applicant had established that damages were necessary to compensate, vindicate, or deter, the government could try to establish that damages would not be an appropriate and just remedy because of an open-ended list of "countervailing factors."[14] These countervailing factors included concerns that damages would adversely affect good governance or that less drastic alternative remedies would be effective. The latter concern suggests that ideas of proportionality, which are central to the justification of limits on *Charter* rights, are also relevant to the crafting of remedies. With respect to concerns about good governance, the Court in *Ward* rejected the argument that section 24(1) damages should be awarded only where governmental fault was established or that they would chill the exercise of governmental functions. Chief Justice McLachlin reasoned as follows: "[I]nsofar as s. 24(1) damages deter *Charter* breaches, they promote

---

12   [2010] 2 SCR 28 [*Ward*].
13   *Ibid* at paras 24–31.
14   *Ibid* at paras 32–45.

good governance. Compliance with *Charter* standards is a foundational principle of good governance."[15]

In addition to the above purposes and constraints, general principles of proportionality, taken from section 1, can also be useful with respect to remedial decision making.[16] Proportionality can be relevant to remedies in at least two ways.

One way that the courts can use proportionality is to determine whether a particular remedy is necessary to achieve specific remedial purposes. For example, in some contexts, damages or an injunction may be necessary to achieve the purposes of compensation or to ensure future compliance with the constitution; in other contexts, however, a declaration alone may suffice. The use of proportionality to inform such questions of remedial choice will also force judges to be clear about the precise purposes of the remedy and the reasons why a less drastic or a more intrusive remedy is required.

The second use of proportionality in remedial decision making is as a means to require the state to justify social interests that limit remedies. The Court, in *Ward*, indicated its acceptance of a broad range of legitimate objectives for limiting the award of damages as a section 24(1) remedy. As under section 1, there should be a rational connection between the government's objective and the proposed limit on any particular remedy. Furthermore, the remedy should be limited as little as possible to serve that governmental objective. In the assisted dying case, the Court extended a suspended declaration of invalidity for four additional months, but this extension was in proportion to the time Parliament was dissolved because of an election.[17] Finally, there should be an appropriate overall balance and reconciliation between the remedy and the limit. An example of this concern about overall balance is in the *Hislop*[18] case, where the Court found that the government had justified not requiring fully retroactive relief because there was a reasonable balance between providing the successful *Charter* applicants with some, albeit not fully retroactive, relief and accommodating the government's interests. The use of proportionality as a guide for justifying limits on remedies can encourage judges to be more explicit and rational about remedial decision making.

---

15 *Ibid* at para 38.
16 G Hoole, "Proportionality as a Remedial Principle: A Framework for Suspended Declarations of Invalidity" (2011) 49 Alta L Rev 107.
17 *Carter* 2016, above note 5.
18 *Canada (Attorney General) v Hislop*, [2007] 1 SCR 429 [*Hislop*].

In *Schachter v Canada*,[19] the Supreme Court outlined some general principles to govern the crafting of remedies under section 52(1) of the *Constitution Act, 1982*. The Court held that courts were not limited to striking down unconstitutional laws in their entirety under that section. Courts could order less drastic remedies in the form of reading down or severance of unconstitutional parts of the legislation or even reading in words in order to cure a constitutional defect. The Court stated that these less drastic remedies may be appropriate in those cases where the law was found to be unconstitutional only because of concerns about the least restrictive means of the section 1 test as opposed to concerns about the importance of the legislative objective or whether the law was rationally connected to that objective. In deciding the appropriate remedy under section 52(1), courts should be concerned with both the purposes of the legislation and the purposes of the *Charter*. One question in determining the purpose of the legislation is whether the legislature would enact the legislation as altered by the court. With respect to the purposes of the *Charter*, courts should consider whether the words they read in or read down were mandated with precision by the interaction of *Charter* analysis and the legislation. The courts should not make *ad hoc* choices best left to the legislature. In the result, the Court held that a reading in remedy that would add biological parents to a leave scheme made available to adoptive parents was not warranted either by the purposes of the legislation or the purposes of the *Charter*. In other cases, however, the Supreme Court has read in and added benefits for smaller groups such as gays and lesbians on the basis that such remedies were consistent with both the purposes of the legislation and the *Charter*.[20] It has also tailored its declaration of invalidity to only strike down laws to the extent that they are inconsistent with the *Charter*.[21]

3) The Norm of Immediate and Retroactive Relief and Justifications for Prospective and Suspended Declarations of Invalidation

Another general consideration that governs remedies under section 52(1) of the *Constitution Act, 1982* is the degree to which constitutional remedies should be immediate or retroactive, as opposed to delayed or

---

19   *Schachter*, above note 2.
20   *Vriend v Alberta*, [1998] 1 SCR 493 [*Vriend*].
21   *Carter* 2015, above note 4; *R v Smith*, [2015] 2 SCR 602 at para 31; *R v Appulo-nappa*, [2015] 3 SCR 754 at para 85 [*Appulonappa*]; *Canada (Attorney General) v Chambre des notaires du Québec*, 2016 SCC 20 at paras 92–93 [*Chambre des notaires*].

prospective. In *Schachter v Canada*,[22] the Supreme Court recognized that courts have an option of suspending or delaying a declaration of invalidation. Building on past cases, the Court stated that such delayed remedies may be appropriate in cases where an immediate declaration of invalidity would cause harm to the social order or rule of law, endanger public safety, or deprive a deserving person of a benefit simply because the benefit scheme was unconstitutionally under-inclusive. As will be discussed in greater detail below,[23] courts have frequently suspended declarations of invalidity for a variety of reasons with some commentators praising their actions for facilitating dialogue with the legislature and avoiding the disruptive effects of an immediate declaration of invalidity. Others have criticized such actions for depriving successful litigants of an immediate remedy and for sanctioning unnecessary delay in complying with the *Charter*.

In *Canada (Attorney General) v Hislop*,[24] the Supreme Court dealt with the related issue of the degree to which departures from retroactive remedies could be justified by competing social interests. The Court recognized that the remedial norm was that courts provide fully retroactive remedies to benefit the successful litigant and to recognize that a legislature never had authority to enact an unconstitutional law. Nevertheless, the Court held that departures from this rule, and the granting of more limited prospective remedies, could be justified in cases where

1) the court made a substantial change in the law;
2) the government reasonably relied in good faith on the law as previously stated;
3) a retroactive remedy would unduly interfere with the role of the governments especially in allocating public resources; and
4) the departure from the retroactive norm would not be unfair to the successful *Charter* applicants.

In the result, the Court held that a fully retroactive repayment of spousal benefits to same-sex partners was not warranted given the substantial change in the law in recognizing same-sex relationships, the reasonable and good faith reliance of the government on previously judicially sanctioned exclusion of same-sex couples, the role of the government, and a conclusion that the successful litigants would still be left with more than a hollow victory even if they did not receive a fully

---

22   *Schachter*, above note 2.
23   See suspended declarations of invalidity in this chapter.
24   Above note 18.

retroactive remedy. In 2014, the Supreme Court, while upholding the immunity of foreign states in Canadian courts, concluded that the legal maxim of "where there is a right, there is a remedy" did not constitute a principle of fundamental justice. It stressed the highly contextual nature of remedial decision-making and a lack of consensus about whether there should always be a remedy.[25]

B. SPECIFIC REMEDIES

1) Declaratory Relief

In some cases, the rights claimant may seek no more than a declaration from the court of the *Charter* right at issue. In the common law tradition, courts tend to avoid making hollow pronouncements of law removed from any concrete order. There is, however, a well-established jurisdiction to award declarations of rights in appropriate cases. In constitutional law, the declaration has proved to be an important remedy because of its flexibility. By declaring the right and going no further, the court defines the respective legal rights and obligations of the parties but leaves to them the task of implementing the demands of the constitution. The Court will make declarations where they can provide practical guidance for resolving disputes, but will not issue declarations that simply reiterate settled law.[26]

From an institutional perspective, it may not be desirable for the court to become too involved in the details of implementation unless absolutely necessary. The alternative to a declaration is often a court order or injunction, which has to be articulated in clear terms because any violation of such an order may be punished as contempt of court. Although "declarations are often preferable to injunctive relief because they are more flexible, require less supervision, and are more deferential to the other branches of governments," they can be inadequate when *Charter* violations are the result of systemic flaws; where "administrators have proven themselves unworthy of trust"; where subsequent litigation is likely; and where there is a need for remedial specificity and ongoing monitoring of compliance.[27]

---

25 *Kazemi Estate v Islamic Republic of Iran*, [2014] 3 SCR 176 at paras 158–67.
26 *Daniels v Canada (Indian Affairs and Northern Development)*, 2016 SCC 12 at paras 53–56.
27 *Little Sisters Book and Art Emporium v Canada (Minister of Justice)*, [2000] 2 SCR 1120 at paras 258–61 [*Little Sisters*], Iacobucci J in dissent, but not on this issue.

Litigation involving minority-language education rights early in the life of the *Charter* serves as an example of the effective use of the remedy of declaration. As seen in Chapter 16, section 23 of the *Charter* guarantees parents the right to have their children educated in English or French in certain circumstances. While the courts are able to determine when section 23 rights arise, it is quite another matter for them to determine the institutional arrangements appropriate to fulfill those rights. The demands of the *Charter* will be one important consideration in the design of a minority-language education facility, but there will be many other matters to be taken into account that have nothing to do with constitutional law. Furthermore, there may be a variety of ways to design a school system that respects the demands of section 23. Courts and judges are not experts in schools or education. Courts do not have the competence to raise resources or allocate public funds among competing claims and demands. In view of this, it may be in the public interest as well as in the interest of the litigants for the court simply to declare the right and leave it to the litigants and the appropriate public authorities to work out the practical arrangements. In *Mahe v Alberta*,[28] the Supreme Court of Canada upheld the section 23 claim of a group of French-speaking parents and granted a declaration of their rights but stopped short of determining the details of school administration. Chief Justice Dickson explained:

> I think it best if the court restricts itself in this appeal to making a declaration in respect of the concrete rights which are due to the minority language parents in Edmonton under s. 23. Such a declaration will ensure that the appellant's rights are realized while, at the same time, leaving the government with the flexibility necessary to fashion a response which is suited to the circumstances . . . . [T]he government should have the widest possible discretion in selecting the institutional means by which its s 23 obligations are to be met; the courts should be loath to interfere and impose what will be necessarily procrustean standards, unless that discretion is not exercised at all, or is exercised in such a way as to deny a constitutional right.[29]

Declarations may be preferred in other contexts. The Supreme Court reversed a mandatory order that Canada make diplomatic representations to the United States for Omar Khadr to be returned to Canada; instead, it issued a declaration that his rights had been violated by Canadian interrogations of him when subject to American military de-

---

28   [1990] 1 SCR 342.
29   *Ibid* at 393.

tention at Guantanamo Bay. The use of a declaration gave the government flexibility in deciding how to respond to the violation in light of its conduct of foreign policy with the United States.[30] The government issued a diplomatic note that requested the United States not to use the results of the Canadian interrogation in military commission proceedings against Khadr.

While declarations provide the government with flexibility to decide what precise steps to take to comply with them, a declaration can, at the same time, result in further litigation if the applicant is not satisfied with the government's response to the declaration. This is what happened in both the *Little Sisters* and *Khadr* cases. Little Sisters bookstore was not satisfied with how customs responded to the declaration that customs had infringed the bookstore's sections 2 and 15 rights; the bookstore commenced further litigation, which was ended when the Supreme Court refused to grant the small bookstore advance costs.[31] In subsequent litigation in the *Khadr* case, a trial judge found that Omar Khadr had not received an effective remedy and that the government should have consulted with him before issuing a diplomatic note in response to the declaration. The trial judge required the government to propose a more effective remedy and said it should have considered Khadr's representations before issuing a remedy, which could have included a mandatory order that Canada request his repatriation.[32] This judgment, however, was stayed pending appeal, with the appeal judge expressing doubts whether courts could require the government to make diplomatic representations on behalf of its citizens. The appeal was subsequently held to be moot after Khadr pled guilty before an American military commission and returned to Canada to serve the remainder of his sentence.[33]

The preference for general declaratory relief, even in the minority-language rights context, is not absolute. For example, when faced with nearly a century of Manitoba's refusal to enact laws in French as well as in English, the Supreme Court did not rely on a declaration in the *Reference Re Manitoba Language Rights*.[34] As will be examined below, the Supreme Court, in its 2003 decision in *Doucet-Boudreau*,[35]

---

30 *Canada (Prime Minister) v Khadr*, [2010] 1 SCR 44.
31 *Little Sisters Book and Art Emporium v Canada (Commissioner of Customs and Revenue)*, [2007] 1 SCR 38.
32 *Khadr v Canada (Prime Minister)*, 2010 FC 715.
33 *Khadr v Canada (Prime Minister)*, 2010 FCA 199 (stay of remedy granted); *Khadr v Canada (Prime Minister)*, 2011 FCA 92 (appeal declared moot).
34 [1985] 1 SCR 721; [1985] 2 SCR 347; [1990] 3 SCR 1417; [1992] 1 SCR 212.
35 Above note 7.

affirmed the availability of injunctive relief and the retention of supervisory jurisdiction in a case where there was delay in implementing
minority-language school rights under section 23 of the *Charter*. In the
Insite case, the Court also found that the use of a declaration would be
inadequate because it might result in delay and further litigation with
respect to the granting of a ministerial exemption from drug laws to allow a safe injection site to operate. The Court issued a mandatory order
that the minister grant the exemption stressing that, on the available
evidence, there was no other constitutional option.[36]

The Supreme Court's preference for declaratory relief rather than
more specific injunctive relief has also been seen in some equality rights
cases. In *Eldridge v British Columbia (Attorney General)*,[37] the Court interpreted section 15 of the *Charter* to require that those who are deaf or
hearing impaired be provided with sign-language interpreters for medically required services. Justice La Forest stated for an unanimous Court
that a

> declaration, as opposed to some kind of injunctive relief, is the ap-
> propriate remedy in this case because there are myriad options avail-
> able to the government that may rectify the unconstitutionality of the
> current system. It is not this Court's role to dictate how this is to be
> accomplished.[38]

A declaration differs from an injunction because it is not enforced
through the court's contempt power. Because of this, declarations can
be more general and vague than injunctions and can give the government more flexibility to decide how to comply with them.

2) Injunctions

An injunction is an order of the court requiring a party to act in a
manner specified by the order. In its usual form, the injunction is a
negative order that forbids a party from doing something that infringes
the rights of another. It is also possible, however, for the court to give
a mandatory injunction that requires the wrongdoer to take positive
steps to respect the rights of the other party. In ordinary civil litigation, injunctions are seen as exceptional remedies, available only where
damages are an inadequate remedy for the wrong. In constitutional
litigation, injunctions and other mandatory orders may be appropri-

---

36 *Canada (Attorney General) v PHS Community Services Society*, [2011] 3 SCR 134
[*Insite*].
37 [1997] 3 SCR 624 [*Eldridge*].
38 *Ibid* at para 96.

ate, especially in cases where declarations or damages would be inadequate. The most difficult issue faced in connection with injunctions as a *Charter* remedy arises where the court is asked to grant an injunction that requires ongoing supervision or judicial involvement. *Charter* litigation often involves the operation of complex public institutions. Granting an injunction requiring that an institution take certain steps implies that the court is willing to enforce its order. If the public institution willingly complies, there is no problem. But what happens if there is resistance to the court's order?

American experience with constitutional injunctions is instructive. In litigation involving desegregation of schools and conditions of prisons, American judges evolved what came to be known as the "structural" or "civil rights" injunction, whereby courts became involved in the detailed management of a scheme required to bring the school system or prison into compliance with the constitution.[39] American judges did not rush into making these orders; they did so only when their directives respecting desegregation and improvement of prison conditions were not obeyed.

As noted in the above discussion of declarations as a *Charter* remedy, Canadian courts have been overtly conscious of the need for judicial restraint when making orders requiring complicated changes to public institutions. In the case of minority-language education rights, the courts' first step was to grant a declaratory order, stating the requirements of the *Charter*, but leaving the task of implementation to the school authorities. While it is to be hoped, and expected, that those authorities will comply, there is every indication that should they fail to do so, the courts will not sit idly by and fail to insist upon respect for the rights protected by the *Charter* as interpreted by the courts. In an Ontario case, a judge granted a mandatory order requiring a local school board "to provide the facilities and funding necessary to achieve . . . the provision of instruction and facilities equivalent to those provided to English language secondary schools."[40] In a subsequent ruling, the court reviewed the plans submitted by the school board to assess their adequacy.[41] Another Ontario judge declared that a long-delayed school construction project for a minority-language facility should be exempted from a ministry moratorium on capital projects on the ground that "the open-ended delay in funding the construction after seven years of temporary and

---

39 See OM Fiss, *The Civil Rights Injunction* (Bloomington: Indiana University Press, 1978).

40 *Marchand v Simcoe County Board of Education* (1986), 29 DLR (4th) 596 (Ont HCJ).

41 *Marchand v Simcoe County Board of Education (No 2)* (1987), 44 DLR (4th) 171 (Ont HCJ).

inadequate facilities does constitute an infringement of the applicant's rights under section 23 of the *Charter*."[42]

In *Little Sisters*,[43] the Supreme Court concluded "with some hesitation, that it is not practicable" to order a "more structured section 24(1) remedy" after finding that the free expression and equality rights of a gay and lesbian bookstore had been denied by unconstitutional targeting of its imports by custom officials on the grounds of obscenity. The Court's reasons for refusing to grant an injunction revolved around the lack of information about what steps customs officials had taken in the six years since trial to comply with the trial judge's finding of a *Charter* violation and the fact that a general injunction requested by the applicant to obey the constitution "would scarcely advance the objectives of either clarity or enforceability."[44] Any injunction issued under section 24(1) of the *Charter* would have to be clear and enforceable. Justice Iacobucci dissented in this case, warning that, while declarations give the government flexibility in deciding what precise steps to take, they could prompt successful *Charter* applicants to commence new litigation if not satisfied with the government's response to a declaration. Indeed, the Little Sisters bookstore did this, ending litigation only after the Supreme Court rejected its application to receive advance costs to finance the new litigation.[45]

In *Doucet-Boudreau v Nova Scotia (Minister of Education)*,[46] the Supreme Court decided in a 5:4 judgment that a trial judge had acted within the bounds of his remedial discretion under section 24(1) of the *Charter* when, after ordering provincial authorities to use their best efforts to provide minority language school facilities, he retained jurisdiction over the case and required the province to report back to the judge on its progress in building French language school facilities in five regions of the province. Justices Iacobucci and Arbour concluded:

> Section 24(1) of the *Charter* requires that courts issue effective, responsive remedies that guarantee full and meaningful protection of *Charter* rights and freedoms. The meaningful protection of *Charter* rights, and in particular the enforcement of s 23 rights, may in some cases require the introduction of novel remedies. A superior court may craft any remedy that it considers appropriate and just in the circum-

---

42 *Conseil des écoles séparées catholiques romaines de Dufferin et Peel v Ontario (Ministre de l'éducation et de la formation)* (1996), 30 OR (3d) 681 at 685 (Div Ct), Hawkins J.

43 *Little Sisters*, above note 31 at para 157.

44 *Ibid* at para 158.

45 *Ibid*.

46 Above note 7.

stances. In doing so, courts should be mindful of their roles as constitutional arbiters and the limits of their institutional capacities.[47]

The two justices stressed the breadth of the trial judge's remedial discretion. They also noted the context of positive rights to minority-language school facilities under section 23 of the *Charter* and a history of delay in implementing those rights in Nova Scotia, combined with assimilation of the francophone minority. The reporting requirements were justified because they could prevent the francophone parents "who had already waited too long and dedicated much energy to the cause of realizing their s 23 rights" from having to start fresh litigation should there not be full and prompt provision of their rights. "Where governments have failed to comply with their well-understood constitutional obligations to take positive action in support of the right in s 23, the assumption underlying a preference for declarations may be undermined."[48] With reference to the traditional powers of courts of equity, the Court also indicated that "constitutional remedies involving some degree of ongoing supervision do not represent a radical break with the past practices of courts."[49]

Four judges dissented on the basis that the trial judge's retention of jurisdiction and order were procedurally unfair because of their vagueness and because the remedy violated the separation of powers between courts and the executive. Justices LeBel and Deschamps concluded that if the trial judge had made further orders after the reporting sessions, he would have violated the separation of powers by entering into the realm of "administrative supervision and decision making." They argued that such a managerial role did not accord with the institutional capabilities of the judiciary or with "the Canadian tradition of mutual respect between the judiciary and the institutions that are the repository of a democratic will."[50] They also suggested that the trial judge risked exerting "political or public pressure on the executive"[51] at the reporting sessions. In the view of the dissenting judges, the only appropriate manner for continued judicial involvement after a court issued an injunction that was consistent with procedural fairness and the separation of powers was to determine whether the government was guilty of contempt of the order.

---

47   *Ibid* at para 87.
48   *Ibid* at paras 61 and 66.
49   *Ibid* at para 73.
50   *Ibid* at para 125.
51   *Ibid* at para 131.

The decision of all the judges in *Doucet-Boudreau* makes clear that courts can order injunctions under section 24(1) against governments when necessary to provide effective remedies for *Charter* violations. The majority's judgment also makes clear that judges can, when necessary, retain jurisdiction and require governments to report back on their progress in complying with the court order. Structural injunctions, as used in the United States, India, South Africa, and elsewhere,[52] are now clearly available in Canada. The extent to which such remedies will be used in Canada, however, will depend on the context and how trial judges exercise their broad remedial discretion to order appropriate and just remedies. The Court has indicated that "structural orders play an important, but limited, role in the enforcement of rights through the courts," and should be treated with special care because of the dangers of insufficient clarity and the burdens of ongoing judicial supervision.[53]

Judges may be confronted with a remedial choice between relying on a declaration and issuing a mandatory remedy. In the *Insite* case, the Supreme Court held that a declaration would be an inadequate remedy and, instead, issued a mandatory order that the minister of health grant the safe injection site an exemption from drug offences so that it could continue to operate. The Court recognized that a declaration that would allow the minister to make a new decision might result in delay and new litigation. It stressed that, on the facts presented in the case, the only constitutional option was for the minister to grant the exemption. It did, however, note that the minister could exercise a discretion to withdraw the exemption if new evidence relating to the effects of the site on health and crime emerged.[54] This case implicitly recognizes the concerns expressed by Iacobucci J in his dissent in *Little Sisters* that declarations may result in delay and further litigation. At the same time, the Court's decision to use a mandatory order rather than a dec-

---

52   After reviewing American, Indian, German, Canadian, and British law, the South African Constitutional Court has concluded: "Where a breach of any right has taken place, including a socio-economic right, a Court is under a duty to ensure that effective relief is granted. The nature of the right infringed and the nature of the infringement will provide guidance as to the appropriate relief in a particular case. Where necessary this may include both the issuing of a *mandamus* and the exercise of supervisory jurisdiction." *Minister of Health v Treatment Action Campaign (No. 2)*, 2002 5 SA 721 at 758. See K Roach & G Budlender, "Mandatory Relief and Supervisory Jurisdiction" (2005) 122 South African LJ 325.

53   *Thibodeau v Air Canada*, [2014] 3 SCR 340 at paras 126–29.

54   *Insite*, above note 36 at paras 141–53.

laration in the *Insite* case was, like other remedial decisions, based on the particular facts of the case.

Another less controversial form of injunction that may be used as a *Charter* remedy is the interlocutory injunction that is awarded pending a full trial on the merits. This remedy, which may also involve the temporary stay or suspension of legislation pending a full trial on its constitutionality, may be of great practical importance. In a series of cases, the Supreme Court has outlined the test for granting pre-trial or interlocutory relief in *Charter* cases.[55] First, the applicant must establish that he is raising a serious question under the *Charter* that is not frivolous or vexatious. There is no presumption that legislation is constitutional, and there will be a serious question in cases in which the applicant demonstrates that the state must justify a violation under section 1 of the *Charter*. Second, the applicant must establish a risk of irreparable harm should the pre-trial relief not be granted. Again, this is not often an onerous requirement given that many *Charter* rights would not be adequately repaired by the award of damages after a full trial. The third and, in most cases, more difficult and crucial requirement is whether the balance of convenience favours granting the relief. Here it is important for the court to consider the public interest. Democratically enacted legislation is presumed to be in the public interest. A suspension of a law for all persons is presumed to be more harmful to the public interest than exempting some subset of the population from the law. The government, however, does not have a monopoly on representing the public interest, and a *Charter* applicant can strengthen a case by establishing that his or her claim is also in the public interest.

3) Damages

In ordinary civil litigation, the most common remedy is damages, a money award designed to compensate the injured party for the wrong suffered. The aim of compensatory damages is, to the extent possible, to put the innocent party in the position he or she would have been in but for the wrong. A commercial case may lend itself readily to monetary assessment of the wrong, but in other cases, damages are a less than perfect remedy. It can be extremely difficult to measure in money terms the amount appropriate to compensate the plaintiff for physical injuries or for damage to reputation, dignity, or privacy or simply for the

---

55 *Manitoba (Attorney General) v Metropolitan Stores (MTS) Ltd*, [1987] 1 SCR 110; *RJR-Macdonald Inc v Canada*, [1994] 1 SCR 311; *143471 Canada Inc v Quebec (Attorney General)*, [1994] 2 SCR 339; *Harper v Canada (Attorney General)*, [2000] 2 SCR 764.

violation of a *Charter* right. Translating into money the extent of the injury amounts to little more than sophisticated guesswork. In many cases, the damage suffered as a result of a *Charter* violation will fall into this intangible category. The rights and freedoms guaranteed by the *Charter* are abstract and intangible, and thus assessment of the extent of the injury in monetary terms will often be difficult. Low awards for the violation of a *Charter* right may trivialize the right while high awards may create an unjustified windfall for the applicant.

In a series of cases, the Supreme Court has indicated that damages under section 24(1) will usually not be appropriate to compensate for harm caused by legislation that is at the same time declared to be of no force and effect under section 52(1) of the *Constitution Act, 1982*. The Court has refused to award damages to those detained under an unconstitutional law providing for imprisonment for failing to pay fines[56] or the unconstitutional revocation of the semi-retired status of a sitting judge.[57] In the latter case, the Court noted that damages were not appropriate in the absence of evidence that the government "acted negligently, in bad faith or by abusing its powers." The reluctance to combine damages under section 24(1) of the *Charter* with a section 52(1) declaration of invalidity under the *Constitution Act, 1982* is based on "a general rule of public law," namely, that "absent conduct that is clearly wrong, in bad faith or an abuse of power, the courts will not award damages for the harm suffered as a result of the mere enactment or application of a law that is subsequently declared to be unconstitutional."[58] The rule creates a qualified or limited immunity from damages for governments that is designed to achieve a balance "between the protection of constitutional rights and the need for effective government."[59] The immunity is not absolute, and the balance could tilt towards rights protection when the government acts in bad faith, abuses its powers, or even negligently enacts legislation that is clearly unconstitutional. In such relatively rare cases, it would be appropriate both to strike the legislation down under section 52(1) and award damages under section 24(1).

Damages may also be an appropriate and just remedy under section 24(1) of the *Charter* when an official violates *Charter* rights without any statutory authorization. As mentioned in Chapter 4, such actions would not be "prescribed by law" and could not be justified under section 1 of the *Charter*. Thus, the *Charter* analysis would move directly

---

56 *Guimond v Quebec (Attorney General)*, [1996] 3 SCR 347.
57 *Mackin*, above note 3 at para 82.
58 *Ibid* at para 77.
59 *Ibid* at para 79.

from rights violation to the determination of the appropriate and just remedy. In *Ward*,[60] the Supreme Court articulated the principles that govern the award of damages against governments under section 24(1) of the *Charter*. After having established a *Charter* violation, the *Charter* applicant will also have to establish a functional justification for the award of damages as an appropriate and just remedy. The Court stressed that

> damages under s 24(1) of the *Charter* are a unique public law remedy, which may serve the objectives of: (1) compensating the claimant for loss and suffering caused by the breach; (2) vindicating the right by emphasizing its importance and the gravity of the breach; and (3) deterring state agents from committing future breaches. Achieving one or more of these objects is the first requirement for "appropriate and just" damages under s 24(1) of the *Charter*.[61]

The Court warned that, while all three purposes will often be present when damages are awarded, only one is required. Specifically, "the fact that the claimant has not suffered personal loss does not preclude damages where the objectives of vindication or deterrence clearly call for an award."[62] This statement recognizes that the *Charter* protects intangible values that cannot readily be reduced to easily calculated financial harms and that there is a public interest in enforcing the *Charter*. Damages are not automatically awarded in response to every *Charter* breach. In *Ward*, the Court upheld a $5,000 award as necessary to compensate, vindicate, and deter an unconstitutional strip search, but it also found that damages were not necessary with respect to a brief unconstitutional seizure of the plaintiff's car.

Even in cases where a *Charter* applicant establishes a functional need for damages to compensate, vindicate, or deter, the government can demonstrate that damages would not be appropriate and just because of an open-ended list of "countervailing factors," the adequacy of alternative remedies and concerns about good governance among them. In *Ward*, the Court held that a declaration that the detention of the plaintiff's car was unconstitutional was adequate, but that a declaration would not adequately compensate, vindicate, or deter the unconstitutional strip search. The Court also rejected arguments that the damages award would harm good governance by chilling governmental action. An important point here is that section 24(1) damages are a

---

60 Above note 12.
61 *Ibid* at para 31.
62 *Ibid* at para 30.

public remedy law awarded against governments and not a private law remedy awarded against individuals.

A final consideration with respect to section 24(1) is the quantum, or amount of damages. This question is guided by the purposes of the remedy so that "to be 'appropriate and just,' an award of damages must represent a meaningful response to the seriousness of the breach and the objectives of compensation, upholding *Charter* values and deterring future breaches."[63] With respect to compensation, damages should repair both pecuniary and non-pecuniary harm to place claimants in the position they would have occupied had the *Charter* violation not occurred. Non-pecuniary damages, such as pain and suffering, should, "absent exceptional circumstances," be "fixed at a fairly modest conventional rate, subject to variation for the degree of suffering in the particular case."[64] In assessing damages in relation to the purposes of vindication and deterrence, the Court warned that the damages should be fair to both the claimant and the state. Specifically, damages "may take into account the public interest in good governance, the danger of deterring governments from undertaking beneficial new policies and programs, and the need to avoid diverting large sums of funds from public programs to private interests."[65] Compensation that vindicates and deters "may assume a punitive aspect," but the Court noted a general reluctance to award purely punitive damages.[66]

The clear test in *Ward* for awarding damages under section 24(1) will not apply in all cases. As discussed above, the Court has given governments a qualified immunity in cases where the damages are caused by the enactment of unconstitutional legislation. The Court indicated in *Henry* that a form of qualified immunity applies to prosecutorial non-disclosure so that an applicant has to establish that a prosecutor intentionally withheld information that the prosecutor knew or ought to have known would be material to the defence and impinge on the accused's right to full answer and defence.[67] Qualified immunities are, however, distinct from absolute immunity, and $7.5 million in damages were subsequently awarded in *Henry* "to serve the vindication and deterrence functions of s. 24(1) of the *Charter*," where full prosecutorial disclosure could have prevented a wrongful conviction.[68] This damage

---

63 *Ibid* at para 54.
64 *Ibid* at para 50.
65 *Ibid* at para 53.
66 *Ibid* at para 56. See also *Augustus v Gosset*, [1996] 3 SCR 268 at para 121, overturning a $4,000 damages award in a fatal police shooting on the basis of no intentional wrongdoing.
67 *Henry v British Columbia (Attorney General)*, [2015] 2 SCR 214 at para 33.
68 *Henry v British Columbia (Attorney General)*, 2016 BCSC 1038 at para 473.

award reflects the twenty-seven years that the applicant spent in jail after a wrongful conviction, but it is also unprecedented in terms of any other *Charter* award.

4) Remedies Affecting Legislation

Remedies affecting unconstitutional legislation are largely dealt with under section 52(1) of the *Constitution Act, 1982*, sometimes known as the "supremacy clause," because it provides as follows:

> The Constitution of Canada is the supreme law of Canada, and any law that is inconsistent with the provisions of the Constitution is, to the extent of the inconsistency, of no force or effect.

The supremacy clause confirms the established doctrine of judicial review in Canadian constitutional law. The constitution is a law unlike all others, and its provisions, including the rights and freedoms guaranteed by the *Charter*, take priority over other laws. Should Parliament, a provincial legislature, or another law-making body enact a law that is inconsistent with the *Charter* that law cannot stand.

The courts have evolved a variety of remedial techniques to carry out the mandate conferred by the supremacy clause and those techniques are considered below. As discussed above, the general principle that governs the choice between remedies is the need to respect the purpose of the *Charter* and the purpose of the legislation. In addition, the presumption in favour of immediate and retroactive remedies can, in some cases, be displaced if the government justifies a departure in favour of more limited prospective relief for reasons such as the need to respect the role of the legislature, the government's good faith reliance on prior law, and other matters of public interest.

a) Striking Down

Before the *Charter*, the most common constitutional remedy for legislation that did not respect the limits of the constitution was for the court to strike down, or nullify, the law in its entirety. When the constitutionality of a statute is challenged on the ground that the enacting body, Parliament or a legislature, has transgressed the limits of its authority under the division of powers between the federal and provincial governments, the emphasis is upon the essential purpose, or the "pith and substance," of the law. While the effects of a law may serve as a measure of the law's purpose, the established constitutional doctrine in federalism review is to concentrate upon purpose rather than effects.

The result is that the courts tend to regard federalism review as an all-or-nothing proposition. As a general rule, the law either falls in its entirety or it is saved in its entirety. If it is upheld, incidental effects it may have in an area of jurisdiction reserved to the other level of government will be tolerated.

By contrast, under the *Charter of Rights and Freedoms*, the focus tends to be upon unconstitutional effects. It is, after all, uncommon for Parliament or a legislature to enact a law that has as its purpose the violation of some fundamental right or freedom.[69] More frequent is a law that, although valid in its purpose, has in its operation an unacceptable impact or effect upon some fundamental freedom. For this reason, the range of constitutional remedies is much more varied and innovative in *Charter* cases than in federalism review. While nullification remains a frequently granted remedy in *Charter* cases, the courts have also developed a range of other remedies.[70] These remedies are designed to lessen the bluntness of an immediate declaration that an entire law is of no force and effect. They are guided by concerns for the purposes of the *Charter*, the purposes of the impugned legislation, and considerations of the proper institutional division of labour between courts and legislatures.

b) Severance and Partial Invalidity

The most common alternative to striking down an entire statute is severance and a declaration of partial invalidity. Doing this results in the nullification of only the unconstitutional portion of the law. This technique is readily employed where the specific provision challenged represents a discrete and identifiable measure that can be excised without altering the overall structure or operation of the law in which it is contained. It had been used frequently, for example, to strike down provisions of the *Criminal Code*. It has never been suggested that the entire *Criminal Code* should be nullified because one of its provisions violates the *Charter*.

At times, however, the remedy of severance may approach judicial drafting of a statute and become more controversial. For example, one

---

69   Perhaps the leading example is the decision of the Supreme Court of Canada striking down the nineteenth-century *Lord's Day Act*, which required Sunday observance. This measure was found to be in violation of the guarantee of freedom of religion and the law was struck down. See *R v Big M Drug Mart Ltd*, [1985] 1 SCR 295, discussed in detail in Chapter 9.

70   The most comprehensive judicial discussion of these remedies is to be found in *Schachter*, above note 2.

case[71] dealt with a provision of the *Criminal Code*, discussed in Chapter 15, making it an offence for a male person to have sexual relations with a female person under the age of fourteen. The offence included the words "whether or not he believes that she is fourteen years of age or more." The Supreme Court found that Parliament was entitled to prohibit this conduct but that, as drafted, the section imposed criminal liability on a no-fault basis contrary to section 7 of the *Charter*. Rather than strike out the entire section and thereby leave unprotected a class of persons deemed by Parliament to be in need of protection, the Court "rewrote" the section by striking out the words "whether or not he believes that she is fourteen years of age or more."[72] The Supreme Court also severed the phrase "or any other just cause" from the tertiary grounds for the denial of bail on the basis that the severed phrase was excessively vague, but the remaining part of the statute referring to the need to maintain confidence in the administration of justice was not vague and constituted a just cause for the denial of bail.[73]

The Court frequently invalidates laws under sections 7 and 1 of the *Charter* because the laws are overbroad in going beyond what is required to fulfill their objectives. In some cases, the Court has issued tailored or limited declarations of invalidity that reflect that the remaining law is constitutionally valid except in specific applications of overreach. This remedy is similar to severance, but may not involve severing part of the law, depending on the way that the law is drafted. The result is a limited or partial declaration of invalidity that may have the same practical effects as a reading down remedy or even a constitutional exemption for a defined group. The most famous example was the Court's remedy in the *Carter* case which held that the offence of assisted suicide was only unconstitutional to the extent it applied to competent adults faced with enduring and intolerable suffering from an irremediable condition.[74] The Court has also issued similarly tailored declarations of partial invalidity in other cases where it found laws to be unconstitutionally overbroad.[75] Such remedies can be justified as informed by the nature of the Court's conclusions about overbreadth and on the basis that they allow impugned laws to continue to operate only insofar as they are consistent with the *Charter*. They allow statutory

---

71   *R v Hess*, [1990] 2 SCR 906.
72   For another example, see *R v Lucas*, [1998] 1 SCR 439, excising certain words from the *Criminal Code*'s defamatory libel section.
73   *R v Hall*, [2002] 3 SCR 309.
74   *Carter* 2015, above note 4 at para 127.
75   *Appulonappa*, above note 21 at para 85; *Chambre des notaires*, above note 21 at paras 92–93.

objectives to be fulfilled but only insofar as the *Charter* allows. At the same time, they create a divergence between the law as written by the legislature and as applied by the courts.

The technique of severance has also been employed in the case of "under-inclusive" laws. An under-inclusive law is one that is valid so far as it goes but constitutionally defective because it does not go far enough. Severance works only where the law is drafted to apply generally but then, in a specific exception provision, improperly excludes certain individuals or groups from the benefit. Where the exclusion of those individuals or class of individuals is contrary to a constitutional provision, the courts have held that the specific exclusion may be severed, thus leaving intact the provision granting the benefit to the larger class. An example is the decision that a provision excluding those over sixty-five years of age from entitlement to unemployment-insurance benefits should be severed and struck down as discriminatory, leaving unqualified the general provision conferring the entitlement to the general class of unemployed workers.[76] Severance in cases of this kind has the effect of extending a benefit and is discussed in greater detail below in Section B(4)(d). In general, these types of remedies should be used only when consistent with both the purposes of the *Charter* and the impugned legislation.

c) Reading Down

An "over-inclusive" law is one that has, at its core, a constitutional purpose and application but that, as drafted, casts too wide a net and infringes constitutional rights in some situations. In such cases, the Canadian courts have frequently resorted to the technique known as "reading down" or giving the law a sufficiently narrow interpretation to bring it into line with the demands of the constitution. A good example is the Supreme Court's decision in a case challenging Canada's obscenity law.[77] This provision of the *Criminal Code* was drafted in extremely broad terms that, if applied literally, would have had an unconstitutional effect upon freedom of expression. While the Court did not explicitly describe its judgment as an exercise of the power to "read down" the law, that was the effect. The Court held that the provision had to be interpreted more narrowly so as to catch only certain forms of pornography. The Court's interpretation of the law reads like a statute, setting out point by point the elements to be established for a

---

76 *Canada (Employment and Immigration Commission) v Tétreault-Gadoury*, [1991] 2 SCR 22.

77 *R v Butler*, [1992] 1 SCR 452, discussed in detail in Chapter 9.

conviction and thereby significantly curtailing the reach of the general words enacted by Parliament. So interpreted, the obscenity law survived *Charter* scrutiny.[78]

The use of reading down in the above case is similar to the process of statutory interpretation in which judges, when faced with an ambiguity in the legislation, select the reading of the legislation that is more consistent with the constitution. In *R v Sharpe*,[79] however, the Supreme Court used a stronger form of the reading down remedy, which reduced the ambit of the offence of possession of child pornography even when it was clear that Parliament had intended the offence to cover such matters. A majority of the Court found that, while most of the new offence when properly interpreted in a manner consistent with the *Charter* was a reasonable limit on freedom of expression, the offence could not be justified as a reasonable limit when applied to material created by the accused for private use or private recordings of lawful sexual activity. The Court read in these exceptions to the legislation on the basis that it was honouring both the purposes of the statute and the *Charter*. Although the remedy may have altered the intent of Parliament, it also preserved as much of the new offence of possession of child pornography as was consistent with the *Charter*. It would have been more drastic for the Court to have struck down the offence of child pornography in its entirety simply because of its overbreadth when applied to a few cases.

Courts will employ reading down both as a device of statutory interpretation and as a stronger and more explicit remedy in order to save those parts of laws to the extent they are consistent with the *Charter*. Strong forms of the reading down remedy may seem to be a judicial assumption of the legislative role because the court reads in new limitations to legislation. As will be seen below, the judicial reading in of words to make legislation constitutional is also a controversial remedy. Nevertheless, both remedies can be justified on the basis that the court is respecting the broader purposes of the legislation insofar as they are consistent with the purposes of the *Charter*. In other words, the court is only invalidating the legislation "to the extent" of its inconsistency

---

78 For other examples, see *Solski (Tutor of) v Quebec (Attorney General)*, 2005 SCC 14, reading down a requirement that students receive a "major part" of their education in English to be entitled to minority-language instruction to require instead a "significant part" as consistent with s 23(2) of the *Charter*; *Canadian Foundation for Children, Youth and the Law v Canada (Attorney General)*, [2004] 1 SCR 76 (the child spanking case discussed in Chapter 13), reading down s 43 of the *Criminal Code*.

79 [2001] 1 SCR 45 at para 122.

with the *Charter*, as contemplated in section 52(1) of the *Constitution Act, 1982.*

d) Reading In and Extension of Benefits

A controversial remedy under the *Charter* is known as "reading in." Here, the problem is that the statute is under-inclusive and fails to extend its reach to those who have a constitutional claim to its protection. In such cases, nullification is unsatisfactory since it would deprive those who are otherwise entitled to the protection of the law, and it would fail to satisfy the constitutional claim of those who ask to be included. On occasion, the courts have decided that the better course is to fill the gap by judicially "reading in" those who have a constitutional claim to the protection of the law, thereby adding to the list of those protected. Perhaps the best example is the decision of the Supreme Court of Canada dealing with Alberta's *Individual's Rights Protection Act*, a general anti-discrimination statute, which prohibits discrimination on certain specific prohibited grounds.[80] Sexual orientation was not a prohibited ground. The Court found that the Act was constitutionally defective in failing to extend the benefit of anti-discrimination protection to gays and lesbians, who were entitled to claim the benefit of the protection of the law pursuant to the *Charter* guarantee of equality. Rather than strike the law down and deprive the other specified groups of its protection, the Court found that the appropriate remedy was to add "sexual orientation" to the list of prohibited grounds.

Reading in is a controversial technique as the Court appears to be exercising a legislative role. However, given the alternative of striking down the law in its entirety, it seems inevitable that reading in should be permitted in certain situations. To strike down an entire statute because it fails to extend its benefit to a group that is relatively small in relation to the overall purpose and application of the statute would seem to constitute an even more serious interference by the judiciary with legislative choice. Another alternative, examined below in Section B(4)(f), is to strike down the under-inclusive benefit, but to suspend the effect of the declaration for six to eighteen months in order to give the legislature an opportunity to decide whether to extend or reduce the benefit or to repeal the benefit altogether.

Probably the most controversial examples of reading in involve statutes that extend monetary benefits. In a Nova Scotia case, a single father

---

80 *Vriend*, above note 20. The Ontario Court of Appeal came to the same conclusion with respect to the *Canadian Human Rights Code* six years earlier: *Haig v Canada* (1992), 94 DLR (4th) 1 (Ont CA).

challenged a welfare statute that granted monetary benefits to single mothers.[81] He argued that failure to extend the same benefits to single fathers amounted to discrimination on grounds of sex contrary to the *Charter's* section 15 guarantee of equal benefit of the law. A trial court in Nova Scotia agreed with his substantive claim but stumbled on the remedy. The court found that it was not possible for a judge to order the legislature to expend the money and hence that the only available remedy was to strike down the entire statute, thereby depriving single mothers as well as single fathers of its benefit. The result was unsatisfactory to all. The single father would plainly be disappointed by the result. He did not get the benefit for himself, and he had no interest in denying the benefit to single mothers. The legislature was clearly entitled to create the benefit scheme provided it acted with an even hand.

In *Schachter*,[82] the Supreme Court of Canada carefully considered, in the context of extending benefits, the remedies of severance and reading in. The Court suggested that the Nova Scotia decision was wrong in that, where the class of persons to be added is relatively small in relation to those already in receipt of the benefit, a court may order that monetary benefits be extended to those not originally contemplated by the legislation.

Chief Justice Lamer outlined the approach courts are to take. The first element to be considered is the extent of the inconsistency with the *Charter*. The courts will not rewrite a law if the constitutional defect is fundamental. In such cases, the law should be struck down. It is only where the law is invalid because it fails to pass the minimal-impairment test that reading in or severance should be considered. Second, severance or reading in will be available only where the legislative objective is obvious, extending the reach of the law would be consistent with that objective, and extension would constitute a lesser interference with that objective than would striking down the law in its entirety. Third, these remedies are appropriate only where the legislature's choice of means is clear and severance or reading in would not intrude into the legislative domain. Particular care must be exercised where the remedy has budgetary effects. Remedies that are so substantial as to alter the legislative scheme are to be avoided. Thus, in the *Schachter* case, the Court would not have extended parental-leave benefits provided for adoptive parents to biological parents. The group that would be added by extension was much larger than the group receiving

81   *Phillips v Nova Scotia (Social Assistance Appeal Board)* (1986), 27 DLR (4th) 156 (NSSCTD), aff'd (*sub nom Attorney General of Nova Scotia v Phillips*) (1986), 34 DLR (4th) 633 (NSCA).

82   *Schachter*, above note 2.

the benefit, and extension would not be consistent with the legislative objective. If a section 15 violation of the rights of biological parents had been established (a matter about which the Court expressed some doubt), the appropriate remedy would have been to strike down the unconstitutionally under-inclusive benefit received by adoptive parents, subject to a temporary delay that would give Parliament an opportunity to enact a new law. Parliament could extend the benefit to all parents, repeal the benefit, or reduce the monetary value of the extended benefit.[83] The Court has subsequently affirmed that reading in should not be used as alternative to a declaration of invalidity if it is not clear that Parliament would not enact the remedy that the court reads in to save the legislation from invalidation.[84] This recognizes the important role of the legislature in making choices about a variety of different ways to comply with the *Charter*.

e) Constitutional Exemptions

Another possible remedy is granting a "constitutional exemption." Here, the law remains valid for all purposes save that a particular individual is exempted from its application. A good example is a decision of the Yukon Territory Court of Appeal in a case dealing with an Aboriginal person convicted of a weapons offence.[85] The *Criminal Code* provided that, upon conviction for the offence, there was a mandatory order prohibiting the convicted party from possessing a weapon for five years. The convicted Aboriginal person established that it was necessary for him to possess a firearm to maintain his traditional lifestyle and to provide for himself and his family. The court found that to deprive him of the right to possess a weapon would, in the circumstances, constitute cruel and unusual treatment, contrary to section 12 of the *Charter*. However, the court also recognized that the law was valid in almost every other conceivable application and that it would therefore be undesirable to strike it down. The court's solution was to hold that the particular litigant before it was to be exempted from the application of the law. Parliament subsequently followed this approach by enacting a

---

83 In response to lower court decisions extending the benefit to all parents, Parliament reduced the benefit from fifteen to ten weeks of leave for all parents. Adoptive parents subsequently challenged this reduction of their benefits as a violation of their s 15 rights without success: *Schafer v Canada (Attorney General)* (1997), 149 DLR (4th) 705 (Ont CA), leave to appeal to SCC refused (1997), 153 DLR (4th) vii (SCC).

84 *Trial Lawyers Association of British Columbia v British Columbia (Attorney General)*, [2014] 3 SCR 31 at para 66.

85 *R v Chief* (1989), 51 CCC (3d) 265 (YTCA).

statute that provided for exemptions from firearm prohibition orders when use of a firearm would be necessary for the offender's sustenance or employment.[86]

The Supreme Court has been reluctant to use constitutional exemptions. The *Seaboyer* case[87] involved an attack on *Criminal Code* provisions precluding an accused charged with sexual assault from cross-examining a complainant on prior sexual behaviour. Writing for the majority, McLachlin J found that exempting those situations where the questioning was necessary to ensure the accused's right to a fair trial would be inappropriate and that the section had to be struck down in its entirety. Granting an exemption would have the effect of giving the trial judge a discretion, the very result Parliament sought to avoid, and would also leave the law in an uncertain state. However, McLachlin J specifically added that she did not foreclose the possibility that an exemption may be appropriate in some other case. Constitutional exemptions were also discussed in a dissenting judgment of the Supreme Court of Canada in *Rodriguez*, the assisted-suicide case mentioned in Chapter 13.[88] There, a minority of the Court, led by Lamer CJC, found that the prohibition against assisted suicide did violate the constitutional rights of the terminally ill plaintiff. However, Lamer CJC hesitated to strike down the entire statute and ruled that the appropriate remedy would be a constitutional exemption permitting this particular individual, or others like her, to have the benefit of an assisted suicide, provided they could bring themselves within a narrowly defined set of criteria laid down in the judgment.

In *Ferguson*,[89] the Supreme Court ruled that constitutional exemptions were an inappropriate remedy for an unconstitutional mandatory minimum sentence. The Court stressed that such a remedy was inconsistent with the intent of mandatory sentences to exclude judicial discretion. The introduction of sentencing discretion that Parliament intended to preclude would, in the Court's view, be an inappropriate intrusion into the legislative sphere.[90] This conclusion can be reconciled with the courts' use of alternatives to striking down laws, such as reading in and severance, on the basis that the latter remedies do not fundamentally change the legislation whereas the introduction of exemptions would fundamentally change the nature of mandatory sentences. The Court also stressed that section 52(1) requires invalidation of

---

86   *Criminal Code*, s 113.
87   *R v Seaboyer*, [1991] 2 SCR 577 [*Seaboyer*].
88   *Rodriguez v R*, [1993] 3 SCR 519 [*Rodriguez*].
89   *Ferguson*, above note 1.
90   *Ibid* at para 56.

unconstitutional laws and that "bad law, fixed on a case-by-case basis by the courts, does not accord with the role and responsibility of Parliament to enact constitutional laws for the people of Canada."[91] The Court has continued to employ declaration of invalidity in other cases where it found mandatory sentences to be unconstitutional.[92]

In the *Carter* assisted-suicide case,[93] the Supreme Court split 5:4 on the issue of whether exemptions could be ordered from an unconstitutional assisted suicide offence during the period of an extended suspension of invalidity. The majority of the Court stressed that not allowing exemptions would cause intolerable suffering. In addition, allowing judges to grant case-by-case exemptions would ensure compliance with the rule of law and provide safeguards for the vulnerable.[94] Four judges dissented and argued that this approach would create uncertainty, offend the rule of law, and usurp Parliament's intent.[95] This fails to recognize that exemptions during a suspended declaration of invalidity will not be a permanent remedy. Either Parliament will enact a new law before the suspended declaration expires or the declaration of invalidity will take effect. The minority's approach would also force judges to make an unnecessary choice between suspending a declaration of invalidity to provide Parliament an opportunity to enact new legislation or immediately declaring laws to be invalid in order to give eligible applicants a meaningful remedy. A number of courts did grant exemptions during the suspended declaration of invalidity and now Parliament has enacted a new law governing access to assisted dying.

f) Temporary Suspension of Invalidity

In certain situations, the Supreme Court of Canada has used the technique of temporary suspension of invalidity. In these cases, the Court has found that, although a challenged law is unconstitutional, the immediate nullification of that law could lead to chaos or a serious threat to public safety. To avoid chaos or serious public harm, the Court has delayed the implementation of its order of invalidity to afford Parliament or the legislature the opportunity to repair the constitutional deficiency.

The leading example is the decision of the Supreme Court of Canada in *Reference Re Manitoba Language Rights*.[96] The Court held that the failure of the legislature of Manitoba to comply with a constitutional

---

91   *Ibid* at para 70.
92   *R v Nur*, [2015] 1 SCR 773; *R v Lloyd*, 2016 SCC 13.
93   *Carter* 2016, above note 5.
94   *Ibid* at para 6.
95   *Ibid* at para 12.
96   [1985] 1 SCR 721.

provision requiring it to enact all the laws of Manitoba in both English and French meant that all Manitoba legislation was invalid. Clearly, however, an immediate nullification of all the laws of Manitoba would lead to a situation of chaos, and the Court held that the overriding principle of the rule of law justified a temporary suspension of invalidity. The Court's order gave the legislature of Manitoba time to have its laws translated and re-enacted in both languages.

Temporary suspension of invalidity has been resorted to in less dramatic circumstances, as well. When the Supreme Court held that provisions of the *Criminal Code* providing for the detention of those found not guilty by reason of insanity were invalid, it held that the immediate release of such individuals, most of whom had escaped convictions for murder because of their mental disorders, would result in a serious threat to public safety. Accordingly, the Court held that the declaration of invalidity should be suspended for a stated period of time to afford Parliament the opportunity to reconsider the matter and to enact a revised law in keeping with the requirements of the constitution.[97] The Supreme Court used a similar suspended declaration of invalidity in a case involving continued restrictions on the liberty of those found permanently unfit to stand trial because of a mental disorder. The Court split over the issue of whether a remedy for affected individuals under section 24(1) of the *Charter* could be ordered during the twelve-month suspension of the declaration of invalidity. The majority ruled that such section 24(1) remedies could be ordered only after the period of suspension while one judge in dissent would have used section 24(1) during the period of the suspended declaration to avoid the mischief of depriving someone of liberty under an unconstitutional law.[98]

In *Schachter*,[99] the Supreme Court indicated another situation where the remedy of temporary suspension of invalidity may be employed. As already noted, there are cases where laws are constitutionally defective because they are under-inclusive. In some cases, that defect can be repaired by having the court add the excluded class by using the techniques of reading in or severance. However, where the case does not permit extending the law to those not included and the law is to be struck down, *Schachter* suggests that the court may temporarily suspend the declaration of invalidity to alleviate the harshness of denying the benefit of the law to deserving persons. This gives the legislature a stated period of time to reconsider the scheme in light of the dictates of

---

97   *R v Swain*, [1991] 1 SCR 933.
98   *R v Demers*, [2004] 2 SCR 489 at paras 56–64 [*Demers*].
99   *Schachter*, above note 2 at 715–17.

the constitution without defeating the operation of the valid portion of the law in the interim.

In *M v H*,[100] the Supreme Court did not read in same-sex couples to a provision providing for support after the breakup of a relationship because of concerns about the far-reaching implications of such a ruling. Instead, it struck down a provision providing for support orders between heterosexual couples as unconstitutionally under-inclusive, subject to a six-month period of delay. In that time, Ontario responded with new comprehensive legislation providing for the new category of "same-sex partners." Other provinces have responded to the ruling in different ways. The suspended declaration of invalidity can be an instrument of remedial dialogue, which invites the legislature to cure constitutional defects in a variety of constitutional ways and recognizes that the legislature can formulate more comprehensive remedies than the court could accomplish on its own. The suspended or delayed declaration of invalidity also allows governments to consult with the affected interests and debate the appropriate remedy in a democratic manner.

Suspended declarations of invalidity have been used in a growing number of cases, but they are not automatic. The Court rejected a government's request for a suspended declaration of invalidity in one case on the basis that it would leave patients entitled to medical marijuana without access to the drug and create additional uncertainty.[101] At the same time, suspended declarations of invalidity have been used in labour relations cases, and also when the Court struck down offences related to prostitution and assisted suicide.[102] In all these cases, the suspension provides the legislature an opportunity to regulate the activities in question. Although the Court suggested in *Schachter* that declarations of invalidity should not be suspended simply because legislatures could enact remedies not open to the court, the ability of legislatures to fashion more comprehensive remedies and to make policy choices about different ways to comply with the *Charter* cannot be denied.

A suspended declaration of invalidity may have the effect of denying a successful *Charter* applicant an immediate remedy. In a few complex cases, the Supreme Court has sanctioned periods of delay of up to eighteen months in order to give the legislature time to consider the

---

100 [1999] 2 SCR 3. For a refusal to suspend a declaration, see *Halpern v Canada* (2003), 65 OR (3d) 161 (CA).

101 *R v Smith*, [2015] 2 SCR 602 at para 32.

102 See, for example, *Mounted Police Association of Ontario v Canada (Attorney General)*, [2015] 1 SCR 3 at paras 154–56; *Saskatchewan Federation of Labour v Saskatchewan*, 2015 SCC 4 at para 103; *Canada (Attorney General) v Bedford*, [2013] 3 SCR 1101 at paras 166–69; *Carter* 2015, above note 4 at paras 126–32.

implications of its ruling and has not exempted the successful *Charter* applicant from the period of delay.[103] Suspended declarations of invalidity have been criticized for preferring dialogue or interaction between courts and legislatures over the court's traditional function in providing successful litigants with immediate remedy. The Court's 2016 5:4 decision in the assisted dying case of *Carter*,[104] however, suggests that it is possible to reconcile giving the legislature an opportunity to act with providing remedies for individuals whose rights are violated. Without an exemption from a suspension, it is possible that even successful litigants in the case will be denied a meaningful remedy. An early case, however, suggested that courts cannot normally use a section 24(1) *Charter* remedy during a suspended declaration of invalidity ordered under section 52(1) of the *Constitution Act, 1982*, and that any section 24(1) remedy for the individual can take effect only after the court-sanctioned delay has expired.[105] The Court could clarify when and why declarations of invalidity will be suspended and whether the litigants in the particular case, and perhaps others similarly situated to them, can be exempted from a suspended declaration of invalidity if necessary to give them an effective and meaningful remedy.

g) Prospective Remedies and Refusals to Grant Retroactive Remedies

A temporary suspension of invalidity can mean that a successful *Charter* applicant will receive no immediate remedy. In some cases, the Court has also fashioned prospective remedies that will apply only at a stated time in the future in order to avoid the disruptive effects of immediate remedies. For example, the Court fashioned a thirty-day transition period in a case in which it declared that the right to counsel under section 10(b) of the *Charter* required detainees to be informed about the availability of legal aid. The Court justified this ruling on the basis that the police needed time to print new caution cards to discharge their new informational burden.[106] In an equality rights case, *Eldridge v British Columbia (Attorney General)*, the Court gave the government of British Columbia six months to devise a system to provide sign language

---

103 *Corbiere v Canada (Minister of Indian and Northern Affairs)*, [1999] 2 SCR 203; *Dunmore v Ontario (Attorney General)*, [2001] 3 SCR 1016.
104 *Carter* 2016, above note 5.
105 *Demers*, above note 98 at paras 56–64.
106 *R v Brydges*, [1990] 1 SCR 190.

interpretation for deaf patients requiring essential medical services.[107] In cases that require the government to take positive action, an immediate remedy may be impossible.

In *Canada (Attorney General) v Hislop*,[108] the Court extended the above precedents and those relating to temporary suspensions of invalidity to hold, in some cases, it may be appropriate to provide no retroactive remedies and to ensure constitutional compliance in the future only. The case involved same-sex couples who argued that they should be entitled to survivor-benefit pension arrears retroactive to 17 April 1985, the day that the equality rights under section 15 of the *Charter* took effect. The Court recognized that this request for retroactive relief was supported by the traditional idea that an unconstitutional law, in this case, a law denying same-sex couples pension benefits, was always invalid. The Court, however, ruled that departures from the traditional approach to retroactive remedies could be justified and were justified in this case in large part because the government had placed reasonable and good faith reliance on law which, until the 1999 *M v H* decision,[109] had excluded same-sex couples from benefits provided to heterosexual couples. The Court was also influenced by its conclusions that the successful *Charter* applicants were not to be left without any remedies.

While the government was required to justify departures from the norm of retroactive remedies, the Court held that the recognition of same-sex partnerships in 1999 constituted a substantial change in the law. It distinguished a 1995 case recognizing common law opposite-sex partnerships as not constituting a substantial change in the law.[110] However, a substantial change in the law by itself will not justify the resort to only prospective remedies. In *Hislop*, the Court also found that the government reasonably relied in good faith on the law that had, until *M v H*, excluded same-sex couples from benefits provided to opposite-sex couples.[111] The Court expressed concerns that, in some cases, a fully retroactive remedy would unduly interfere with the role

---

107   *Eldridge*, above note 37, requiring hospitals to provide sign-language interpreters for deaf patients.

108   *Hislop*, above note 18.

109   *M v H*, above note 100.

110   *Ibid* at 105 discussing *Miron v Trudel*, [1995] 2 SCR 418, and suggesting that a prospective remedy in the case of the exclusion of common law partnerships would not be justified because the government could not place good faith reliance on such an exclusion and because prospective relief would deny the successful applicants any remedy and retroactive relief would not interfere with the role of the legislature.

111   The Court argued that *M v H* was a clear shift from *Egan v Canada*, [1995] 2 SCR 513, in which four judges found no s 15 violation in the exclusion of same-sex

of governments especially in allocating public resources, though some would argue that such concerns should not have been pressing in this case which involved the self-funded *Canada Pension Plan* scheme. Finally, the Court also suggested that courts should consider the fairness of the departure from the norm of retroactive relief to the litigants. In this case, the Court concluded that the recognition of same-sex couples and the granting of some partial retroactive payments meant that the refusal to grant fully retroactive relief would not produce a "hollow victory"[112] for the successful applicants. In this case, the Court found that the government had justified the departure from retroactive relief, making it unnecessary to consider the applicant's challenge to a facially neutral provision that allowed applicants for a survivor's pension to claim only twelve months' pension-benefit arrears.

C. CONCLUSION

Some of the most difficult and controversial *Charter* issues concern remedies. Section 24 confers an express mandate on the courts to ensure that violations of *Charter* rights are remedied in an appropriate fashion. In determining remedial issues, the courts have drawn on existing principles but have also had to find new remedial techniques. As with other *Charter* issues, there is a delicate institutional balance to be struck. Remedial choice is governed in part by the need to ensure that individuals receive an appropriate remedy and in part by consideration of the respective roles of courts and legislatures. In determining remedial measures to right particular wrongs, there is choice ranging from declaratory relief, which entails minimal judicial involvement, to injunctions, which may require ongoing judicial supervision. The *Ward* case clarifies that damages must be justified for purposes relating to compensation, vindication, or deterrence of *Charter* violations. Even if those purposes are present, the government will have an opportunity to demonstrate that the award of damages would harm effective governance.

There is a range of remedial options under section 52(1) of the *Constitution Act, 1982* with respect to the validity of legislation. The courts may strike down all or parts of a law, mandate affirmative changes to the law through reading in, or decide to strike down the law but

---

couples, with a fifth judge holding that there was a violation but that it was justified under s 1 of the *Charter*.

112 *Hislop* above note 18 at para 116.

suspend or delay its declaration of invalidity. In some cases, it may be possible for affected litigants to have exemptions from the period of suspension, but the Court has eschewed using case-by-case exemptions as a permanent remedy to cure unconstitutional laws. There is also the rare option of the courts finding that the government has justified a departure from the norm of retroactive remedies and that only prospective relief is required. As with other areas of *Charter* jurisprudence, the Supreme Court has not hesitated to break new ground, but at the same time, it has tried to proceed in a relatively cautious, incremental manner, conscious of the limits of the judicial function and the need to respect the role and responsibilities of the democratically elected representatives of the people.

FURTHER READINGS

ATTARIN, A, & J Khan, "Solving the 'Khadr Problem': Retention of Jurisdiction — A Comparative Analysis" (2015) 34 NJCL 145

CHARLES, WH, *Understanding* Charter *Damages* (Toronto: Irwin Law, 2016)

CHOUDHRY, S, & K ROACH, "Putting the Past behind Us? Prospective Judicial and Legislative Constitutional Remedies" (2003) 21 Sup Ct L Rev (2d) 205

COOPER-STEPHENSON, KD, Charter *Damage Claims* (Calgary: Carswell, 1990)

FITZGERALD, OE, *Understanding* Charter *Remedies* (Scarborough, ON: Carswell, 1994)

HOOLE, G, "Proportionality as a Remedial Principle: A Framework for Suspended Declarations of Invalidity" (2011) 49 Alta L Rev 107

LECKEY, R, *Common Law Bills of Rights* (Cambridge: Cambridge University Press, 2015)

———, "Enforcing Laws that Infringe Rights" [2016] Public Law 206

PINARD, D, "A Plea for Conceptual Consistency in Constitutional Remedies" (2006) 18 NJCL 105

POTHIER, D, "Language Rights Remedies in the Supreme Court of Canada: Invisible, Gentle, or Stern Hand?" (2014–2015) 19 Rev Const Stud 147

ROACH, K, *Constitutional Remedies in Canada*, 2d ed (Aurora, ON: Canada Law Book, 2013)

————, "Principled Remedial Decision-Making under the *Charter*" (2004) 25 Sup Ct L Rev (2d) 101

————, "A Promising Late Spring for *Charter* Damages: *Ward v Vancouver*" (2011) 29 NJCL 135

ROGERSON, C, "The Judicial Search for Appropriate Remedies under the *Charter*" in RJ Sharpe, ed, Charter *Litigation* (Toronto: Butterworths, 1987)

ROULEAU, P, S BHATTACHARJEE, & N ROULEAU, "Revisiting *Doucet-Boudreau*: Perspectives on Remedies in Section 23 Cases" (2006) 32 Sup Ct L Rev (2d) 301

RYDER, B, "Suspending the *Charter*" (2003) 21 Sup Ct L Rev (2d) 267

SHANDAL, V, "Combining Remedies under Section 24 of the *Charter* and Section 52 of the *Constitution Act, 1982*: A Discretionary Approach" (2002) 61 UT Fac L Rev 175

SHARPE, RJ, "Injunctions and the *Charter*" (1984) 22 Osgoode Hall LJ 474

SUTTON, R, "Dirty Puddles and Safety Valves: The Path from Fact to Remedy in *Canada (A.G.) v. PHS Community Services Society*" (2014) 33 NJCL 39

CONCLUSION

The *Charter of Rights and Freedoms* is a fundamental and defining element of the modern Canadian state. While it draws upon certain aspects of our democratic and parliamentary traditions by entrenching certain rights and freedoms as fundamental and by assigning an important law-making role to the courts, it also marks a break with the past. No longer are Parliament and the legislatures supreme.

We have suggested that this shift of institutional responsibility — subjecting the powers of elected bodies to review by the courts under the *Charter* — is supportive of Canada's traditional democratic values. Experience has shown that majorities, unchecked, may fail to respect the dignity of all individuals, tend to shut out annoying and unpopular views, and ignore or even worsen the plight of vulnerable minorities. The *Charter* protects the values of individual dignity, autonomy, and respect. These attributes of citizenship are essential to a healthy democracy and to free and open democratic debate. The *Charter* also protects the rights of those accused of crime, an otherwise unpopular group. It reflects the view that a healthy democracy cannot be defined in terms of crude majoritarianism. The *Charter* may be seen as Canada's commitment to the principle that the exercise of power by the many is conditional on respect for the rights of the few. The role of the *Charter*, we suggest, is to facilitate, not frustrate, democracy.

It is apparent that the difficult task of ensuring that *Charter* rights and freedoms are respected inevitably embroils the judiciary in difficult and contentious issues of public concern. The courts have been willing to exercise the power of judicial review with a certain vigour in many areas. Religious minorities have succeeded in attacking measures that required them to observe the religion of the majority. In some cases, freedom of expression has been defended against measures that limited open debate and dissemination of information. Freedom of association has strengthened the rights of workers to engage in collective bargaining. The right to "life, liberty and security of the person" has been found to impose significant constraints on the right of the state to criminalize abortion, assisted suicide, and to extradite or deport people to face the death penalty or torture. The *Charter* has had a major impact in the area of criminal justice where judges have not hesitated to subject police powers to close scrutiny. Individual rights of privacy and bodily integrity and the rights to counsel and fair trial have been expanded significantly. The equality guarantee has required legislatures to reassess the manner in which minorities are treated. The Supreme Court has insisted upon close scrutiny of virtually all measures that discriminate on the grounds enumerated in section 15 or on analogous grounds, even where the denial of equality is not intended. The guarantee of minority-language education rights has also been interpreted in a generous fashion to encourage a dialogue between the legislatures and rights claimants about the design of school systems.

On the other hand, there are areas where the courts have demonstrated a marked deference to legislative judgment. To date, the courts have been very unsympathetic to claims of pure economic rights and have refused to become embroiled in most distributional issues. The courts have refused to imply a right of property from the language of section 7 and have similarly rejected overtures to protect contract rights. The refusal to permit the equality guarantee in section 15 to extend beyond substantive discrimination on prohibited or analogous grounds is, we suggest, also consistent with this general pattern of leaving matters of economic and social policy to the legislatures. An open-ended approach to equality would require the courts to review virtually every line drawn by legislation and would divert attention from, and perhaps dilute the protection accorded to, those groups that have been the subjects of particular disadvantage because of specified and analogous personal characteristics.

The Supreme Court's approach to determining acceptable limitations of *Charter* rights and freedoms under section 1 largely coincides with this pattern. The Supreme Court has not taken a uniform approach to section 1, and the level of scrutiny to which challenged legislation is subjected varies. The Court has seen section 1 as a recognition of the institutional role of Parliament and the legislatures to enhance and protect some of the same values that inform judicial review. Legislative initiatives to protect vulnerable groups have often been upheld when such initiatives have been challenged as violating the fundamental freedoms or equality rights of more powerful interests in society. Similarly, the Court has given legislatures considerable latitude where broad questions of social or economic policy are involved.

After over three decades of *Charter* jurisprudence, certain broad outlines have been drawn, but we certainly do not yet have a fully completed picture. During the *Charter*'s comparatively short history, the Court has already revisited a number of its prior precedents concerning matters such as freedom of association, including the right to strike; assisted suicide; prostitution; extradition to face the death penalty; self-incrimination; equality rights and affirmative action; and the exclusion of unconstitutionally obtained evidence. It is often suggested, both by *Charter* "believers" and by *Charter* "skeptics," that the uncertainty of *Charter* jurisprudence reflects an inadequate and uncertain response from the Supreme Court.

We suggest that an element of uncertainty is to be expected. First, a constitution is an expression of a society's most fundamental values. It is an enduring document that must allow our public institutions to address the issues of today but also offer the flexibility to meet the unknown challenges of the future. Definitive judicial pronouncements on every detail of the constitution or rigid adherence to what the words of the constitution may mean in one historical context could produce an institutional straightjacket inconsistent with this broader vision. The courts in the era of the *Charter* have quite appropriately remained faithful to the pre-*Charter* metaphor of the constitution as a "living tree" capable of growth and expansion within its natural limits. Second, there are inherent limits in the judicial process. The most obvious is that *Charter* issues are decided in the context of specific cases. The judicial method is necessarily responsive and incremental, and must be responsive to the evidence presented in the particular case, especially on questions of the effects and necessity of impugned laws. While the Supreme Court has some control of the cases it hears through the leave-to-appeal process, it does not have the capacity to set its own agenda, but rather must deal with the issues that the litigants bring before it.

Much can be accomplished through litigation, but the democratically elected representatives of the people retain primary responsibility for social and economic policy and for resolving most of the ills that beset our society. Even on issues that are the subject of *Charter* litigation, courts have frequently used remedies that provide governments with flexibility in crafting their responses.

While the *Charter* assigns an important role to the courts, it is but one aspect of a constitution that speaks to all who exercise power in our society. We continue to have a strong parliamentary tradition that has always imposed a moral and political duty upon our elected representatives to respect fundamental rights and freedoms. We also have traditions of respect for the rights of minorities, federalism, and constitutionalism and the rule of law, which pre-date the *Charter*. The enhanced power of the courts under the *Charter* should be seen as both a continuation and an enrichment of Canadian constitutional traditions. In this book, we have canvassed the way in which the *Charter* has altered the nature of public debate in Canada. We propose that, on the whole, experience to date suggests that the *Charter* offers the promise of a stronger and more vibrant Canadian democracy.

GLOSSARY

Absolute liability. An offence for which the accused is guilty once it is proven that the prohibited act was committed and regardless of the existence of any fault, including negligence.

Adjudicative facts. Facts relating to the immediate dispute between the parties, "who, what, where, and how" (as distinguished from "legislative facts").

Affirmative action. Positive measures intended to benefit a disadvantaged group.

Agency shop provision. A provision in a collective agreement compelling payment of dues to a union by non-member employees.

Appellate court. The court that hears appeals from judgments of the trial courts. There are provincial appellate courts to hear appeals from the provincial courts and the provincial superior courts, and a Federal Court of Appeal to hear appeals from the Federal Court, Trial Division.

Arbitrariness. A law that infringes a right, but bears an insufficient relationship with the state interest that lies behind the legislation.

Attorney general. The member of Cabinet who is the senior legal adviser to the government and who is ultimately accountable for prosecutions.

Civil law. A legal system in which private law is enacted by the legislature and is predominantly contained in a Civil Code. It is in contradistinction to the common law where the basis of private law is made by a judge. Quebec has a civil law tradition.

Closed shop provision. A provision in a collective agreement compelling membership in a union.

Commercial expression. Expression conveyed for the purpose of earning money, usually in the form of advertising.

Common law. Judge-made law, reflected by precedents established by the decisions of the courts, as distinct from statute-law passed by the legislature. In all provinces other than Quebec, the primary source of private law is the common law.

Constitutional convention. An unwritten rule, rather than formal law, that is enforced through the political process rather than in the courts. The Canadian constitution consists of the written constitutional texts, judicial precedents, and constitutional conventions.

Constitutional exemption. The law remains valid for all purposes, save that the court exempts a particular individual or situation from its application.

Contextual analysis. Assessing *Charter* issues in the light of the specific social, cultural, economic, and political factors that bear upon the right claimed or the basis asserted for limiting the right.

Damages. Monetary award received by the injured party to compensate for the wrong suffered or to vindicate or deter *Charter* violations.

Declaratory proceedings. A suit in which the only relief sought is a statement by the court delineating the ambit of a right, or stating that a statute or practice is contrary to the constitution, with no other concrete remedy provided.

Deference. The view that a court order is not the appropriate solution and that the matter should be left to the legislature.

Delayed declaration of invalidity. *See* **Suspended declaration of invalidity**

Dialogue. The relationship of give-and-take between courts and legislatures resulting from judicial decisions striking down laws and fresh legislation being enacted in response.

Disclosure. The obligation of the Crown to notify the accused prior to trial of any evidence it intends to use and any evidence that might assist the accused, even if the Crown does not intend to adduce such evidence at trial.

Division of powers. The constitutional allocation of authority between the federal and provincial governments to enact legislation.

Dualism. The conception of Canadian Confederation as being a historical compromise between the French- and English-speaking communities. It also refers to the traditional understanding of international and domestic law as distinct, with international law not being enforced in domestic courts unless specifically adopted in domestic legislation.

Due process. Principles of procedural fairness that have evolved through the common law.

Ex parte **injunction.** An injunction issued without notice to the defendant.

Expression. Any activity that conveys or attempts to convey meaning.

Federalism. A governmental structure whereby the power to legislate is divided between various levels of government. In Canada, the division of powers is between the Parliament of Canada and the ten provincial legislatures.

Federalism review. Judicial consideration of whether Parliament or a provincial legislature has the authority under the division of powers to enact legislation.

Freedom. ". . . embraces both the absence of coercion and constraint, and the right to manifest beliefs and practices." (*R v Big M Drug Mart Ltd* (1985), 18 DLR (4th) 321 at 354 (SCC))

Gerrymandering. A term connoting the exercise of self-interest on the part of political incumbents in control of the process of drawing electoral boundary lines.

Gross disproportionality. "[S]tate actions or legislative responses to a problem that are so extreme as to be disproportionate to any legitimate government interest." (*Canada (Attorney General) v. PHS Community Services Society*, [2011] 3 SCR 134 at para 133)

Habeas corpus. A common law remedy permitting anyone who is detained to require the person having custody to bring the detainee immediately before a court and to provide legal justification.

Injunction. An order of the court requiring a party to perform some act or refrain from some conduct so as to respect the rights of another.

Judicial activism. An inclination by the court to be fairly bold about striking down laws and policies that contravene the constitution.

Judicial Committee of the Privy Council. During the British Empire, the Privy Council was the final court of appeal for the colonies. The right of appeal from the Supreme Court of Canada to the Privy Council was abolished in 1949.

Judicial interim release. The release of an accused person pending trial, formerly referred to as bail.

Judicial restraint. An inclination by the court to be more cautious about overturning government laws and policies.

Judicial review. The power of the courts to determine the constitutionality of legislation enacted by the people's elected representatives. It is a consequence of having a written constitution that is the supreme law of the land.

Jurisdiction. The legal authority to decide.

Legislative facts. Facts relating to the causes and effects of the social, cultural, economic, and political issues that legislation addresses (as distinguished from "adjudicative facts").

Legislative override. Section 33 of the *Charter of Rights and Freedoms* permits a legislature to declare, for a period of five years, that a law shall operate "notwithstanding a provision included in section 2 or sections 7 to 15" of the *Charter*.

Minimal impairment. The most important element of the section 1 proportionality test: does the challenged legislation infringe the right or freedom more than is necessary to attain the legislative objective?

Mootness. A case becomes "moot" when the immediate concrete dispute between the parties no longer exists, even though the legal or constitutional issue remains unresolved.

Natural justice. Procedural rights evolved by the common law that apply when a decision affecting one's legal rights is taken, including the right to be heard by an impartial tribunal.

Negative right. A right to be left alone, thereby precluding Parliament or a legislature from interfering.

Notwithstanding clause. *See* **Legislative override**

Oakes **test.** The method described by the Supreme Court of Canada for determining whether a law that violates a fundamental right or freedom should be saved as a reasonable limit under section 1 of the *Charter*.

Overbreadth. Legislation that is drafted more broadly than is necessary or permissible to attain the legislative objective with the result that it impinges unduly upon a protected right or freedom.

Override. *See* **Legislative override**

Parliamentary supremacy. The principle that the elected representatives of the people, assembled in Parliament, have unlimited power to make the law (the one exception being that Parliament cannot bind its successors).

Positive right. A right to be accorded some privilege or benefit, thereby requiring action on the part of Parliament or a legislature.

Presumption of constitutionality. The presumption that evolved under federalism that legislation enacted by Parliament or a legislature does not violate the constitution.

Presumption of innocence. The principle, now protected by section 11(d) of the *Charter*, that everyone accused of a crime is presumed to be innocent until the Crown has proven the accused's guilt beyond a reasonable doubt to the satisfaction of a judge or jury.

Prima facie. A case of sufficient weight presented by the party having the burden of proof to warrant judgment in that party's favour absent a response from the other side.

Private action. Acts by individuals or corporations not subject to the direct control of government.

Proportionality. The central element of the *Oakes* test under section 1 of the *Charter*, weighing the breach of *Charter* rights against the government interest advanced by a challenged law. A law will be a proportionate limit on rights if it is rationally connected to an important objective, violates the rights as little as is reasonably possible to achieve the objective, and if there is an overall balance between the effects of the rights infringement and the advancement of the objective of the legislation.

Prospective relief. A remedy that only applies to future conduct and does not attempt to correct the effects of past *Charter* violations.

Provincial court. A court consisting of judges appointed by a provincial government that deals with criminal cases not tried by jury, cases involving family matters, and small civil claims cases.

Punitive damages. A monetary award given to an injured party, designed in such a way that, rather than merely compensate the injured party, the wrongdoer is punished and others are deterred from following the same course of conduct.

Purposive approach. A method of interpretation based upon delving into the fundamental and underlying reason for a law or constitutional guarantee.

Rational connection. The first element of the section 1 proportionality test: does the challenged legislation further the legislative objective in a rational and non-arbitrary way?

Reading down. Where a court gives an over-inclusive statute a sufficiently narrow interpretation to bring it into line with the demands of the constitution.

Reading in. Where a court adds something to a statute to make it conform to the constitution.

Reference. The government may refer directly to the court questions of law or fact concerning the interpretation of the constitution, or the constitutionality of any legislation. A reference is an exception to the usual two-party, adversarial system.

Regulatory offences. Offences that regulate risky behaviour that may cause harm but do not ordinarily involve truly criminal or morally reprehensible behaviour.

Retroactive relief. A remedy that attempts to repair the effects of past *Charter* violations.

Rule of law. The ideal of the supremacy of law in the social order. There are three aspects to the rule of law: no one can be punished except for breach of a duly enacted law; everyone, from the highest official to the ordinary citizen, is subject to the ordinary law of the land; and the courts have ultimate responsibility for the protection of rights and respect for the legal order.

Search and seizure. A state activity that invades a reasonable expectation of privacy.

Severance. Where a court excises a discreet and identifiable measure of a challenged law without altering the overall structure or operation of the law in which it is contained.

Standing. The requirement that an individual must show a specific legal right or interest before bringing an action to challenge the constitutional validity of a law.

Stare decisis. The principle by which decisions of a higher court are binding on and must be followed by lower courts.

Stay of proceedings. A disposition where a court does not allow a prosecution to proceed because of objectionable police or prosecutorial conduct or a violation of the accused's rights.

Superior court. The highest level of trial court in each province. The judges of the superior courts are appointed by the federal government. The superior courts have exercise over a broad jurisdiction in both civil and criminal cases and have the authority to apply both federal and provincial laws.

Suspended declaration of invalidity. A declaration of invalidity that does not take effect until some set period (usually six, twelve, or eighteen months) after the court has issued its ruling finding legislation to be an unjustified violation of the *Charter.*

Temporary suspension of invalidity. *See* **Suspended declaration of invalidity.**

Torts. Non-contractual civil wrongs recognized at common law.

Under-inclusive law. A law that is found to be constitutionally defective in that it fails to extend its reach to those who have a constitutional claim to its protection.

Vagueness. An unacceptable lack of precision in legislation that leaves its meaning and application so uncertain as to unduly threaten a protected right or freedom.

CONSTITUTION ACT, 1982

SCHEDULE B

CONSTITUTION ACT, 1982

PART I
CANADIAN CHARTER OF RIGHTS AND FREEDOMS

Whereas Canada is founded upon principles that recognize the supremacy of God and the rule of law:

Guarantee of Rights and Freedoms

Rights and freedoms in Canada
1. The *Canadian Charter of Rights and Freedoms* guarantees the rights and freedoms set out in it subject only to such reasonable limits prescribed by law as can be demonstrably justified in a free and democratic society.

Fundamental Freedoms

Fundamental freedoms
2. Everyone has the following fundamental freedoms:
- (*a*) freedom of conscience and religion;
- (*b*) freedom of thought, belief, opinion and expression, including freedom of the press and other media of communication;
- (*c*) freedom of peaceful assembly; and

(*d*) freedom of association.

Democratic Rights

Democratic rights of citizens
3. Every citizen of Canada has the right to vote in an election of members of the House of Commons or of a legislative assembly and to be qualified for membership therein.

Maximum duration of legislative bodies
4. (1) No House of Commons and no legislative assembly shall continue for longer than five years from the date fixed for the return of the writs of a general election of its members.

Continuation in special circumstances
   (2) In time of real or apprehended war, invasion or insurrection, a House of Commons may be continued by Parliament and a legislative assembly may be continued by the legislature beyond five years if such continuation is not opposed by the votes of more than one-third of the members of the House of Commons or the legislative assembly, as the case may be.

Annual sitting of legislative bodies
5. There shall be a sitting of Parliament and of each legislature at least once every twelve months.

Mobility Rights

Mobility of citizens
6. (1) Every citizen of Canada has the right to enter, remain in and leave Canada.

Rights to move and gain livelihood
   (2) Every citizen of Canada and every person who has the status of a permanent resident of Canada has the right
   (*a*) to move to and take up residence in any province; and
   (*b*) to pursue the gaining of a livelihood in any province.

Limitation
   (3) The rights specified in subsection (2) are subject to
   (*a*) any laws or practices of general application in force in a province other than those that discriminate among persons primarily on the basis of province of present or previous residence; and
   (*b*) any laws providing for reasonable residency requirements as a qualification for the receipt of publicly provided social services.

Affirmative action programs
(4) Subsections (2) and (3) do not preclude any law, program or activity that has as its object the amelioration in a province of conditions of individuals in that province who are socially or economically disadvantaged if the rate of employment in that province is below the rate of employment in Canada.

Legal Rights

Life, liberty and security of person
7. Everyone has the right to life, liberty and security of the person and the right not to be deprived thereof except in accordance with the principles of fundamental justice.

Search or seizure
8. Everyone has the right to be secure against unreasonable search or seizure.

Detention or imprisonment
9. Everyone has the right not to be arbitrarily detained or imprisoned.

Arrest or detention
10. Everyone has the right on arrest or detention
    (a) to be informed promptly of the reasons therefor;
    (b) to retain and instruct counsel without delay and to be informed of that right; and
    (c) to have the validity of the detention determined by way of *habeas corpus* and to be released if the detention is not lawful.

Proceedings in criminal and penal matters
11. Any person charged with an offence has the right
    (a) to be informed without unreasonable delay of the specific offence;
    (b) to be tried within a reasonable time;
    (c) not to be compelled to be a witness in proceedings against that person in respect of the offence;
    (d) to be presumed innocent until proven guilty according to law in a fair and public hearing by an independent and impartial tribunal;
    (e) not to be denied reasonable bail without just cause;
    (f) except in the case of an offence under military law tried before a military tribunal, to the benefit of trial by jury where the maximum punishment for the offence is imprisonment for five years or a more severe punishment;

(g) not to be found guilty on account of any act or omission unless, at the time of the act or omission, it constituted an offence
under Canadian or international law or was criminal according
to the general principles of law recognized by the community
of nations;

(h) if finally acquitted of the offence, not to be tried for it again and,
if finally found guilty and punished for the offence, not to be
tried or punished for it again; and

(i) if found guilty of the offence and if the punishment for the offence has been varied between the time of commission and the
time of sentencing, to the benefit of the lesser punishment.

Treatment or punishment
12. Everyone has the right not to be subjected to any cruel and unusual
treatment or punishment.

Self-crimination
13. A witness who testifies in any proceedings has the right not to have
any incriminating evidence so given used to incriminate that witness
in any other proceedings, except in a prosecution for perjury or for the
giving of contradictory evidence.

Interpreter
14. A party or witness in any proceedings who does not understand or
speak the language in which the proceedings are conducted or who is
deaf has the right to the assistance of an interpreter.

Equality Rights

Equality before and under law and equal protection and benefit of law
15. (1) Every individual is equal before and under the law and has the
right to the equal protection and equal benefit of the law without discrimination and, in particular, without discrimination based on race,
national or ethnic origin, colour, religion, sex, age or mental or physical
disability.

Affirmative action programs
(2) Subsection (1) does not preclude any law, program or activity
that has as its object the amelioration of conditions of disadvantaged
individuals or groups including those that are disadvantaged because
of race, national or ethnic origin, colour, religion, sex, age or mental or
physical disability.

Official Languages of Canada

Official languages of Canada
16. (1) English and French are the official languages of Canada and have equality of status and equal rights and privileges as to their use in all institutions of the Parliament and government of Canada.

Official languages of New Brunswick
(2) English and French are the official languages of New Brunswick and have equality of status and equal rights and privileges as to their use in all institutions of the legislature and government of New Brunswick.

Advancement of status and use
(3) Nothing in this Charter limits the authority of Parliament or a legislature to advance the equality of status or use of English and French.

English and French linguistic communities in New Brunswick
16.1 (1) The English linguistic community and the French linguistic community in New Brunswick have equality of status and equal rights and privileges, including the right to distinct educational institutions and such distinct cultural institutions as are necessary for the preservation and promotion of those communities.

Role of the legislature and government of New Brunswick
(2) The role of the legislature and government of New Brunswick to preserve and promote the status, rights and privileges referred to in subsection (1) is affirmed.

Proceedings of Parliament
17. (1) Everyone has the right to use English or French in any debates and other proceedings of Parliament.

Proceedings of New Brunswick legislature
(2) Everyone has the right to use English or French in any debates and other proceedings of the legislature of New Brunswick.

Parliamentary statutes and records
18. (1) The statutes, records and journals of Parliament shall be printed and published in English and French and both language versions are equally authoritative.

New Brunswick statutes and records
(2) The statutes, records and journals of the legislature of New Brunswick shall be printed and published in English and French and both language versions are equally authoritative.

Proceedings in courts established by Parliament
19. (1) Either English or French may be used by any person in, or in any pleading in or process issuing from, any court established by Parliament.

Proceedings in New Brunswick courts
    (2) Either English or French may be used by any person in, or in any pleading in or process issuing from, any court of New Brunswick.

Communications by public with federal institutions
20. (1) Any member of the public in Canada has the right to communicate with, and to receive available services from, any head or central office of an institution of the Parliament or government of Canada in English or French, and has the same right with respect to any other office of any such institution where
    (a) there is a significant demand for communications with and services from that office in such language; or
    (b) due to the nature of the office, it is reasonable that communications with and services from that office be available in both English and French.

Communications by public with New Brunswick institutions
    (2) Any member of the public in New Brunswick has the right to communicate with, and to receive available services from, any office of an institution of the legislature or government of New Brunswick in English or French.

Continuation of existing constitutional provisions
21. Nothing in sections 16 to 20 abrogates or derogates from any right, privilege or obligation with respect to the English and French languages, or either of them, that exists or is continued by virtue of any other provision of the Constitution of Canada.

Rights and privileges preserved
22. Nothing in sections 16 to 20 abrogates or derogates from any legal or customary right or privilege acquired or enjoyed either before or after the coming into force of this Charter with respect to any language that is not English or French.

Minority Language Educational Rights

Language of instruction
23. (1) Citizens of Canada
    (a) whose first language learned and still understood is that of the English or French linguistic minority population of the province in which they reside, or

(*b*) who have received their primary school instruction in Canada in English or French and reside in a province where the language in which they received that instruction is the language of the English or French linguistic minority population of the province,

have the right to have their children receive primary and secondary school instruction in that language in that province.

Continuity of language instruction

(2) Citizens of Canada of whom any child has received or is receiving primary or secondary school instruction in English or French in Canada, have the right to have all their children receive primary and secondary school instruction in the same language.

Application where numbers warrant

(3) The right of citizens of Canada under subsections (1) and (2) to have their children receive primary and secondary school instruction in the language of the English or French linguistic minority population of a province

(*a*) applies wherever in the province the number of children of citizens who have such a right is sufficient to warrant the provision to them out of public funds of minority language instruction; and

(*b*) includes, where the number of those children so warrants, the right to have them receive that instruction in minority language educational facilities provided out of public funds.

Enforcement

Enforcement of guaranteed rights and freedoms

24. (1) Anyone whose rights or freedoms, as guaranteed by this Charter, have been infringed or denied may apply to a court of competent jurisdiction to obtain such remedy as the court considers appropriate and just in the circumstances.

Exclusion of evidence bringing administration of justice into disrepute

(2) Where, in proceedings under subsection (1), a court concludes that evidence was obtained in a manner that infringed or denied any rights or freedoms guaranteed by this Charter, the evidence shall be excluded if it is established that, having regard to all the circumstances, the admission of it in the proceedings would bring the administration of justice into disrepute.

General

Aboriginal rights and freedoms not affected by Charter
25. The guarantee in this Charter of certain rights and freedoms shall not be construed so as to abrogate or derogate from any aboriginal, treaty or other rights or freedoms that pertain to the aboriginal peoples of Canada including

(a) any rights or freedoms that have been recognized by the Royal Proclamation of October 7, 1763; and

(b) any rights or freedoms that now exist by way of land claims agreements or may be so acquired.

Other rights and freedoms not affected by Charter
26. The guarantee in this Charter of certain rights and freedoms shall not be construed as denying the existence of any other rights or freedoms that exist in Canada.

Multicultural heritage
27. This Charter shall be interpreted in a manner consistent with the preservation and enhancement of the multicultural heritage of Canadians.

Rights guaranteed equally to both sexes
28. Notwithstanding anything in this Charter, the rights and freedoms referred to in it are guaranteed equally to male and female persons.

Rights respecting certain schools preserved
29. Nothing in this Charter abrogates or derogates from any rights or privileges guaranteed by or under the Constitution of Canada in respect of denominational, separate or dissentient schools.

Application to territories and territorial authorities
30. A reference in this Charter to a Province or to the legislative assembly or legislature of a province shall be deemed to include a reference to the Yukon Territory and the Northwest Territories, or to the appropriate legislative authority thereof, as the case may be.

Legislative powers not extended
31. Nothing in this Charter extends the legislative powers of any body or authority.

Application of Charter

Application of Charter
32. (1) This Charter applies

(a) to the Parliament and government of Canada in respect of all matters within the authority of Parliament including all matters relating to the Yukon Territory and Northwest Territories; and

(b) to the legislature and government of each province in respect of all matters within the authority of the legislature of each province.

Exception

(2) Notwithstanding subsection (1), section 15 shall not have effect until three years after this section comes into force.

Exception where express declaration

33. (1) Parliament or the legislature of a province may expressly declare in an Act of Parliament or of the legislature, as the case may be, that the Act or a provision thereof shall operate notwithstanding a provision included in section 2 or sections 7 to 15 of this Charter.

Operation of exception

(2) An Act or a provision of an Act in respect of which a declaration made under this section is in effect shall have such operation as it would have but for the provision of this Charter referred to in the declaration.

Five year limitation

(3) A declaration made under subsection (1) shall cease to have effect five years after it comes into force or on such earlier date as may be specified in the declaration.

Re-enactment

(4) Parliament or the legislature of a province may re-enact a declaration made under subsection (1).

Five year limitation

(5) Subsection (3) applies in respect of a re-enactment made under subsection (4).

Citation

Citation

34. This Part may be cited as the *Canadian Charter of Rights and Freedoms.*

TABLE OF CASES

INDEX

ABOUT THE AUTHORS

Robert Sharpe was formerly a professor at the Faculty of Law, University of Toronto, where he wrote and taught in the areas of constitutional law, remedies, civil procedure, and criminal law. From 1990 to 1995 he served as Dean of the Faculty. He has appeared as counsel in a number of *Charter* cases in courts at all levels, including the Supreme Court of Canada. From 1988 to 1990, he served as the Supreme Court's Executive Legal Officer. He was appointed to the Ontario Court of Justice (General Division) in 1995 and to the Ontario Court of Appeal in 1999. Robert Sharpe was elected as a Fellow of the Royal Society of Canada in 1991, presented with the Ontario Bar Association Distinguished Service Award in 2005, and elected as a Senior Fellow of Massey College in 2006. In 2008, he received the Mundell Medal for making a distinguished contribution to law and letters. In 2011, he was appointed as a Visiting Professor, Oxford University, and received honorary doctoral degrees from the Law Society of Upper Canada and the University of Windsor. Justice Sharpe has published many scholarly articles and is the author of several award-winning books on law and legal history, including *The Law of Habeas Corpus*, 3d ed (2011); *The Last Day, the Last Hour: The Currie Libel Trial* (1988); *Injunctions and Specific Performance*, 4th ed (2011); *Brian Dickson: A Judge's Journey* (with Kent Roach) (2003); *The Persons Case: The Origins and Legacy of the Fight for Legal Personhood* (with Patricia McMahon) (2007); and *The Lazier Murder: Prince Edward County, 1884* (2011).

Kent Roach is a professor of law at the University of Toronto, where he holds the Prichard-Wilson Chair in Law and Public Policy. He formerly served as a law clerk to Justice Bertha Wilson of the Supreme Court of Canada. In 2002, he was elected a fellow of the Royal Society of Canada; in 2013, he was awarded a Pierre Trudeau Fellowship; and in 2015, he was appointed a member of the Order of Canada. Professor Roach is the author of thirteen books, including *Constitutional Remedies in Canada* (awarded the 1997 Walter Owen Book Prize) and now in its second edition; *Due Process and Victims' Rights* (shortlisted for the 1999 Donner Prize); *The Supreme Court on Trial: Judicial Activism or Democratic Dialogue* (shortlisted for the 2001 Donner Prize) and now in a revised edition; *Brian Dickson: A Judge's Journey*, co-authored with Robert Sharpe (winner of the 2003 Defoe Prize); *The 9/11 Effect: Comparative Counter-Terrorism* (co-winner of the 2012 Mundell Medal); and *False Security: The Radicalization of Canadian Anti-Terrorism*, co-authored with Craig Forcese (winner of the 2016 Canadian Law and Society book prize). He is also the author of *Criminal Law*, now in its sixth edition, in the Irwin Law Essentials of Canadian Law series. Professor Roach has represented interveners in many *Charter* cases, including *Downtown Eastside Sex Workers* on standing, *Khawaja* on terrorism, *Sauvé* on voting and equality, *Latimer* on mandatory penalties, *Golden* on strip searches, and *Ward* on *Charter* damages.